MODERN CHINA–MYANMAR RELATIONS

NIAS – Nordic Institute of Asian Studies
Monograph Series

NIAS Press is the autonomous publishing arm of NIAS – Nordic Institute of Asian Studies, a research institute located at the University of Copenhagen. NIAS is partially funded by the governments of Denmark, Finland, Iceland, Norway and Sweden via the Nordic Council of Ministers, and works to encourage and support Asian studies in the Nordic countries. In so doing, NIAS has been publishing books since 1969, with more than two hundred titles produced in the past few years.

UNIVERSITY OF COPENHAGEN

 **norden**

Nordic Council of Ministers

MODERN CHINA– MYANMAR RELATIONS

Dilemmas of Mutual Dependence

**DAVID I. STEINBERG
AND HONGWEI FAN**

niasPRESS

Nordic Institute of Asian Studies
Monograph series, no. 121

First published in 2012 by NIAS Press
NIAS – Nordic Institute of Asian Studies
Leifsgade 33, 2300 Copenhagen S, Denmark
Tel: +45 3532 9501 • Fax: +45 3532 9549
E-mail: books@nias.ku.dk • Online: www.niaspress.dk

British Library Cataloguing in Publication Data
Steinberg, David I., 1928-
    Modern China–Myanmar relations : dilemmas of mutual
    dependence.
    1. China–Foreign relations–Burma. 2. Burma–Foreign
    relations–China. 3. Burma–Foreign relations–1948-
    4. China–Foreign relations–1949- 5. China–History–
    1949- 6. Burma–History–1948-
    I. Title II. Fan, Hongwei.
    327.5'1'0591-dc22

ISBN: 978-87-7694-095-9 (hbk)
ISBN: 978-87-7694-096-6 (pbk)

Typesetting by NIAS Press
Printed in Thailand

Cover photograph: Muse border crossing, Myanmar
(photograph David Steinberg).

Contents

Contents

Tables

Figures

Maps

Plates

Acknowledgements

The authors wish to thank and acknowledge the strong support given to them both by Xiamen University and the Georgetown University Fellowship Program, which allowed them to work together at Georgetown University during part of 2008. This relationship was fostered by the Georgetown School of Foreign Service, which provided research and travel support to enable the authors to meet at international conferences and to work together at Xiamen University in June–July 2010. The program was developed in China under the auspices of the China Scholarship Council. Xiamen University's Research School of Southeast Asian Studies also supported the research efforts of Professor Fan, while the School of Foreign Service provided research grants to enable Professor Steinberg to visit Myanmar and pursue his research agenda in and on that country. Professor Fan would like to thank and acknowledge the support of Professor Zhuang Guotu, the Director of the Research School of Southeast Asian Studies, Xiamen University, and Professor Steinberg the assistance of Dean Robert Gallucci of the School of Foreign Service, Georgetown University.

Both authors are indebted to the readers of various drafts and chapters of this volume. They include Professor Robert Sutter of George Washington University; Dr. Andrew Selth of Griffith University, Brisbane; Mr. Bronson Percival of the CNA; Ms. Yun Sun of The Brookings Institution; Mr. Maxwell Harrington of Georgetown; and various anonymous readers.

Several of the maps appearing in the volume were based on initial drafts by Wang Di and Li Feiying of Xiamen University. The Hon. Cheng Ruisheng, former Chinese ambassador to Myanmar (1987–1991) and India (1991–1994), supplied some of the photographs. Our thanks to Gerald Jackson and his team at NIAS Press for their support, not least to Don Wagner for his patience with many changes to the typesetting as the situation rapidly evolved in Myanmar.

The authors would like also to acknowledge the patience of their families throughout the long, arduous process that sometimes involved shirking home responsibilities for more esoteric chores.

Author Notes

"The plural of anecdote is not data."
– Professor Donald Emmerson

About the Data

*D*ata on all aspects of Myanmar should be treated with caution. The statistical base is often flawed, and sometimes inflated to assure the leadership that the country is rapidly progressing. Even such basic statistics as the country's population is subject to question – ranging from about 48 million to the most recent official figure in June 2010 of 59 million. Although the ethnic Burman population is said to be about two-thirds of the total population, there are analysts who believe that this number is overestimated. Muslims consider that their number is perhaps double the official count, and the Chinese population is subject to widely differing calculations, and is even more in doubt because of large-scale illegal immigration. Economic data is also subject to manipulation, and there are extensive discrepancies between Chinese and Burmese bilateral trade statistics between the two states. In addition, there is an extensive underground economy that is beyond calculation, and smuggling and undervalued imports abound. Foreign investment figures must be treated with a degree of caution because approved investment is officially higher than actual investment, although official and informal investment combined is likely to be greater than approved official investment. Smaller investments, especially from the Chinese community, often do not go through the Myanmar Foreign Investment Commission. Even tourist figures vary among Burmese ministries. Macro-economic data such as the money supply have not been publicly released for some years.

Even the data of China's investment in Myanmar are not reliable because they exclude private investment, and many state-owned enterprises have invested in Myanmar without the Chinese government's approval. Such companies have been reluctant to submit applications for foreign investment permission due to red tape or lack of official qualifications to invest abroad.

Incalculable BOT (Build–Operate–Transfer) projects by Chinese corporations are not accounted for in investment figures; these projects are both extensive and expensive. Consequently, the official statistics on China's investment in Myanmar from both sides only reflects major investments and leading cooperative projects authorized by the two central governments.

Less than three percent of the Yunnan border export trade settled in RMB is through China's customs clearance. The majority of export traders choose blackmarket banks to settle accounts because they can provide more convenient and more expeditious services with fewer remittance charges than international banks, in addition to evading customs duties. A considerable disparity exists between the statistics on Yunnan–Myanmar trade between official Kunming customs figures and reality; the amount and number of investments, trade, and economic cooperation projects between China and the cease-fire groups' controlled areas are heavily underestimated.

The reader is thus cautioned to consider all data generally as indicative trends, rather than reflecting actuality. Much of what passes for data in and on Myanmar are instead anecdotal references.

Exchange Rates

The official Kyat–U.S. Dollar exchange rate is approximately K5.8–6.3 to the dollar and is only used for certain government statistics, which skews what data are available. However, the unofficial, widely used rate was approximately K1,000 to the dollar in the summer of 2010, about K850 in the spring of 2011, and about K780 in the fall of 2011.

The Chinese currency exchange rate is approximately RMB6.8 to the dollar.

Burma–Myanmar and Other Name Changes

In 1989, the military junta changed the name of the state from Burma to Myanmar, a centuries-old written form.[1] They have rigidly adopted that name for all uses including the historical period. The United Nations and most countries have accepted that change, but the Burmese opposition has not done so, claiming it was imposed by an illegal government. The United States and

---

1   "The natives call their country *Myanma* in their writings, and in common parlance, *Byamma*, which is spelled *Bram-ma*, of which foreigners make Burmah." The Rev. Howard Malcom, *Travels in Southeastern Asia, Embracing Hindustan, Malaya, Siam, and China with Notices of Numerous Missionary Stations and a Full Account of The Burman Empire.* London: Charles Tilt, 1839, p. 3.

several other countries have kept the Burma designation. This division has become a surrogate indicator of political persuasion.

The military government has also changed the names of various cities and regional divisions to conform to Burmese orthography. Yangon, rather than Rangoon, is the most prominent example. Many city street names were also changed, as have the official names of various ethnic groups.

Older Form	Newer Form
Akyab	Sittwe (City)
Arakan	Rakhine (State)
Chindwin	Chindwinn (River)
Irrawaddy	Ayeyarwady (Division and River)
Karen	Kayin (State, ethnic group)
Magwe	Magway (Division)
Maymyo	Pyin-U-Lwin (City)
Mergui	Myeik (City)
Moulmein	Mawlamyine (City)
Pagan	Bagan (Old Capital)
Pegu	Bago (Division)
Prome	Pyay (City)
Rangoon	Yangon (City)
Salween	Thanlwin (River)
Tenasserim	Tanintharyi (Division)

In this volume, Myanmar has been used for the national designation for the period since 1989, and Burma for previous periods. The term Burmese is used for all citizens of that country (including all ethnic groups), for the official language of the state, and as an adjective. Burman is used as the name of the majority ethnic group in the country. These uses are not intended to have any political connotations.

Personal Names

There are no surnames in Burmese usage (this sometimes is altered when Burmese go abroad). Everyone, including children, has their own name, which is from one to four syllables. The singular exception is Aung San Suu Kyi, whose mother legally incorporated the name of her husband (Aung San) onto her children's names; e.g. Suu Kyi, thus Aung San Suu Kyi. Titles in Burmese evolve from family relations. The honorific for a senior male is "U" (lit. "uncle"), and for a senior female "Daw" (lit. "aunt"). Thus, the name of the former Prime Minister is "Nu," although he is universally known as U Nu.

Chinese names are generally printed in the authorized *pinyin* system of Romanization with the family name first and no hyphen between multiple given names (e.g., Zhou Enlai). An exception here is made for Mao Tsetung, the Romanization thus of which is better known in the West, and for the term Kuomintang (KMT), the name of the Nationalist ruling party in China until 1949.

There is no standard Romanization system used for Burmese names; those employed follow the preferences of the individual concerned or general usage.

Ethnic Names

The Myanmar government claims there are 135 ethnic groups in the country. This is based on obscure colonial estimates that report dialect differences, but neither ethnicity nor language groupings. Thus, there are said to be 53 groups among the Chin minority alone. The Burmese government often uses the term "race" to describe people. The problem is complicated by the use of the Burmese term *lu-myo* (lit., person type). The term has been used for race, ethnicity, nationality (e.g., French *lu-myo*), etc., and does not conform to modern social science terminology.

Abbreviations

ADB	Asian Development Bank
AFPFL	Anti-Fascist People's Freedom League (Burmese coalition government, 1949–1958)
AMFA	Archive of Ministry of Foreign Affairs, People's Republic of China
ARF	ASEAN Regional Forum
ASEAN	Association of Southeast Asian Nations
BCP	Burma Communist Party
BOT	Build–Operate–Transfer
BSPP	Burma Socialist Programme Party (1962–1988)
CCP	Chinese Communist Party
CGGC	China Gezhouba Group Corporation
CNOOC	China National Offshore Oil Corporation
CNPC	China National Petroleum Corporation

CPB	Communist Party of Burma, aka "White Flags"
CPI	China Power Investment Corporation
CPPCC	Chinese People's Political Consulting Congress
FDI	Foreign Direct Investment
GMS	Greater Mekong Subregion
KMT	Kuomintang
MOGE	Myanmar Oil and Gas Enterprises
MoU	Memorandum of Understanding (Myanmar)
NCNA	New China News Agency
NDRC	National Development and Reform Commission (China)
NPC	National People's Congress (China)
PBELP	Prosper the Borders to Enrich Local Peoples (China)
PLA	People's Liberation Army
PPP	Phnom Penh Plan for Development Management
PRC	People's Republic of China
SEZ	Special Economic Zone (Myanmar and China)
SME	Small and Medium Enterprises
SINOMACH	China National Machine Industry Corporation
SLORC	State Law and Order Restoration Council (Myanmar 1988–1997)
SPCC	State Power Corporation of China
SPDC	State Peace and Development Council (Myanmar 1997–2011)
YMEC	Yunnan Machinery and Equipment Import and Export Company

Glossary

Burman	Ethnic majority in Myanmar – some two-thirds of the population
Han	Ethnic Chinese
Sawbwa	Shan hereditary rulers
Tatmadaw	Burmese armed forces

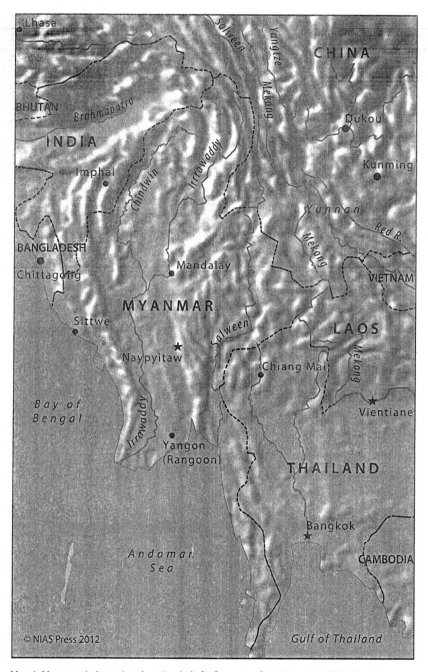

Map 1: Myanmar in its regional setting (relief information from Mountain High Maps®)

Map 2: Myanmar administrative units (based on a map by the Myanmar Information Management Unit, MIMU – see www.burmalibrary.org/docs6/MIMU001_A3_SD%20&%20 Township%20Overview.pdf)

Introduction

Conceptions and Misconceptions

Contemporary internal diplomatic pronouncements and media reporting on Sino-Burmese relations in both countries, in each of which state control of the media has been ubiquitous, weave a positive web of unadulterated support and friendship, while the foreign reporting on this bilateral relationship in official and unofficial circles very often exudes similar conclusions, but with a negative focus. So the China–Myanmar association and the constant travel of high-level delegations back and forth on productive missions are given prominence in their respective media, while the same events prompt concerns that the relationship is detrimental to improved governance or human rights in Myanmar and undercuts Western sanctions. The regional strategic implications of this virtual alliance prompt quiet angst in both informed and popular circles.

The knowledgeable observer is more skeptical. Informed Chinese recognize the latent possibility in Myanmar for popular and ethnic unrest, potentially affecting their southern frontier and their extensive national interests in Myanmar. Burmese unofficially and *soto voce* raise questions about the intensity of Chinese commercial expansion and population in their country, while the government quietly softens dependence on China by buying military aircraft and other hardware from Russia and elsewhere.

This volume is an effort to rectify misconceptions about the history and nature of this important bilateral relationship, and to explore its nuances and the resulting dilemmas for all concerned in the region and beyond, so that policy options might more effectively be explored. Its thesis is that the following, simplistic, common perceptions are erroneous – that:

- Myanmar is a client state of China; that Chinese influence is monolithic;
- China is so dominant that the current and any future Burmese administration will be singularly dependent on its northern neighbor;

- every move by the Chinese is part of a calculated plan to advance their power and interests in Myanmar;
- Burmese democratization is dependent on Chinese attitudes;
- Chinese perceptions of U.S. policy changes under the Obama administration toward Myanmar are attempts to encircle China; and
- the previous U.S. policy of "regime change" in Myanmar did not succeed because of Chinese support to the military junta.

Yet strong security relationships between the two states are evident based both on potential and perceived external threats that each regards as inimical to its national interests, and there are policy and bureaucratic associations that influence internal actions on both sides, as well as informal working relations that affect business and trade.

It was said since independence that Burma was neutral in China's shadow. The influence of China today is obviously important, and, as this volume hopes to demonstrate, pervasive. Into the future, it will continue to loom large in the Myanmar context and indeed in the region. But the nationalism that has been so evident in contemporary Myanmar is likely to mitigate too adhesive an adherence to the Chinese, who have supplied the glue in terms of assistance in military equipment, economic aid, training, and infrastructure development. The Burmese, in response, have sought to diversify their dependence. Following the 2010 elections and the movement into a civilianized administration, Naypyitaw (Myanmar's new capital) may further try to reduce its reliance on Beijing. Meanwhile, if the future political situation evokes continuing dialogue and more changes in the U.S.'s Myanmar policy, Myanmar's autonomy from China will likely grow.

This volume argues that as China has invested and continues to invest heavily in Myanmar, and as China's dependence on external energy sources expand, its need for a compliant Myanmar has increased and will increase. But the fact of these investments, and the types of investments in non-transferable assets and infrastructure, particularly the Sino–Myanmar oil and gas pipelines and a multitude of major hydroelectric projects, as well as mining, give Myanmar a far stronger say in their mutual relationship. And as Chinese penetration of the Burmese economy becomes more apparent to the Burmese, these links become more delicate. China and Myanmar are increasingly dependent on each other, and with that new and growing dependence comes the need for both parties to explore and resolve the multiple dilemmas that exist and are likely to grow at all levels in both states if their perceived national interests are to be met. It becomes essential to states and institutions concerned about the Sino-Burmese relationship, such as the U.S., the E.U., India, Japan, ASEAN, and the U.N., that these nuances and dilemmas are understood in any policy formation toward either country.

Neither Chinese nor Burmese interests are, however, monolithic, a factor often overlooked in the policy discourse. Chinese provincial and lower administrative level and sectoral interests may stress different priorities. There have been apparent antagonisms in issues related to Myanmar between Kunming and Beijing, and even between Kunming and the Yunnan *xian* (counties). Burmese state and assorted minority interests have blatantly diverged, especially in the Sino-Burmese border areas. And as Myanmar enters a new era of local legislatures under the 2008 constitution that came into force in early 2011, even if under military (and thus centralized) control, new and potentially ambiguous interests and relationships are bound to develop that may affect Chinese holdings in those regions.

Both states have external strategic concerns that reinforce the closeness of ties. China has residual worries about Western encirclement, a leftover attitude from the Cold War era, so in the past ensuring a neutral Burma was an element of Chinese foreign policy that has been replaced by its presence in Myanmar. Myanmar fears a U.S. invasion because of a score of years of a U.S. "regime change" policy, and its closeness to China effectively mitigates that concern to some degree.

It also becomes incumbent on foreign states and organizations to reexamine their premises about the multiple relationships between China and Myanmar to determine how best the peoples of Myanmar may be assisted to improve their sorry state – with a poverty level the worst in the region – and how tranquility may be maintained. Each of these states and institutions (the U.S., Thailand, the European Union, ASEAN, India) have national or organizational and strategic concerns that it will attempt to pursue, and the evolution of Sino-Burmese relations may be pivotal in all those cases.

The contemporary period is presaged by a historical set of relationships, the understanding of which is essential in interpreting present attitudes and formulating policies. Mercurial Sino-Burmese relations in the pre-colonial period, the colonial heritage in Burma/Myanmar, the governance of Burma from India until 1937, the Sino-Indian War of 1962, and the humiliation of China in the "semi-colonial" era all influence present attitudes toward each other and thus policies, and help determine strategic parameters. Concepts of power and authority, the personalization of loyalties, and patron-client hierarchical relationships formulate how those policies may be conceived and implemented.

Bilateral and regional history does influence contemporary official and personal prejudices and attitudes. So, some Burmese have not so humorously noted that when massive China spits, small Burma/Myanmar swims. Some Chinese disparagingly comment that Burma is a "beggar with a golden bowl" – a poor country seeking assistance but with vast natural resources. Myanmar plays for more Chinese assistance by claiming that Myanmar was the weakest link in the Clinton/Bush administrations' containment policy against China, but when the Obama administration modified its policy toward Myanmar, then some Chinese circles interpreted this as an effort to limit Chinese influence, and that the U.S. fomented the 2007 "Saffron Revolution" in Myanmar to prevent the construction of Chinese pipelines, as it also was said to have done in the 2009 Kokang incident. Cold War stereotypes, and international confrontational politics continue to influence attitudes.

We take the concept of "dilemmas" in the title as a means to capture the policy dynamic for better analysis of the many relationships that comprise the region and the world beyond. There are, in the views of the authors, no simple solutions to these dilemmas that shift and are transformed over time and in response to changing circumstances. The International Crisis Group, in an excellent study, conceived of the dilemma as both singular and from a Chinese perspective.[1] The writing of this volume and that report proceeded independently, but here the authors have broadened the scope of the inquiry to consider the multiple dilemmas that not only face Beijing, but also the varying administration levels in China, among the Burmans and the minorities, and among the foreign states and institutions that relate to Myanmar and the Chinese association. History does matter, and thus it is to the earlier period we first turn.

Sino-Burmese Pre-Independence Relations: An Overview

In a long-term perspective, one that perhaps Zhou Enlai might have liked as he said it was still too early to evaluate the effects of the French Revolution of 1789, China's ethnic Han population's inexorable drive from the Yellow River valley southward toward the area that has become known as Burma/Myanmar has been a pattern since the Han Dynasty, some two thousand years ago, when it was a link in what became known as the southern "silk route" to India.

---

1   International Crisis Group, *China's Myanmar Dilemma*. Brussels: Asia Report #177, 14 September 2009.

The contemporary and profound influence of China in Myanmar, as we hope to demonstrate in this volume, has its antecedents in earlier history, although its impact is through a more contemporary form of geo-political security interests, and a more modern pattern of influence rather than conquest. Burma in its pre-colonial incarnation had to pay considerable attention to China as the overwhelming hegemon in the region, although the various Burmese dynasties regarded Siam (Thailand) as its most important rival – an attitude that inherently links the past to the present as Thailand is an ally of the U.S. As history has also illustrated, the rulers of what became Burma did not take kindly to Chinese incursions into their domain, even if bilateral relationships were complex. Except for the nineteenth-century pre-colonial and colonial period, when the march was to the north as British imperial interests sought to open the supposedly rich markets of Yunnan Province and compete in securing them against the French in Indochina, China has pushed toward the south, first to consolidate its rule over the southern parts of what is now China proper, later to ensure that the Emperor's rule was gloriously recognized by tributary states and chieftains, and most recently to ensure that Chinese modern strategic, political, and economic interests are supported in that region. This volume will concentrate on Sino-Burmese contemporary relations – those since Burmese independence in 1948 and the formation of the People's Republic of China (PRC) in 1949; the historical context, however, is important in understanding the present.

There is an extensive literature covering the expansion of the ethnic Han to what is now south and southwest China. Yunnan was effectively brought under Chinese administration only under the Yuan Dynasty (1279–1368), and there is a theory that a later ethnic Han migratory advance southward under the Ming (1368–1644) and Qing Dynasties (1644–1911) into what today is Burma/Myanmar was only precluded by a particularly virulent type of malaria to which the Chinese from higher altitudes were vulnerable.[2]

One southern pilgrimage and modest trade route that linked China with the Buddhist sites in what is now India and Nepal went through northern Burma. The early, extensive descriptions of the cities and culture of the pre-Burman Pyu people of central Burma were from Chinese travelers.[3] The Chinese destruction of the Nanchao Kingdom centered at Dali in Yunnan in 832, in some manner yet to be completely researched, probably affected the

2   Gordon Seagrave, known as the "Burma Surgeon." Personal interview, Namkham, 1958.
3   See, for example, Janice Stargardt, *The Ancient Pyu of Burma*, Singapore: PACSEA Cambridge, in association with the Institute of Southeast Asian Studies, 1990.

movement of both the Thai and Burman people southward. The Mongols of the Yuan Dynasty captured the Burmese capital of Pagan in 1287, and during the Ming and Qing Dynasties there were sporadic Chinese attempts to invade the Burmese kingdoms (1765–69), and some four attempts were defeated by the Burmese, as the Chinese were far from their logistic bases. One Burmese king is noted in Burmese lore as "the king who ran away from the Chinese" (*Dayokpyemin*).

Even before the British completed their tripartite conquest of Burma in three wars (1822–1824, 1852, 1885), and the longer pacification of the whole country after the conclusion of the Third Anglo-Burmese War, Chinese influence in Burma was in evidence through trade,[4] immigration, the investiture of local chieftains with the symbols of authority as conferred by the court in Beijing, and through tribute paid by the Burmese court itself to the Chinese, and mutual official delegations. During King Bodawpaya's reign (1781–1819), five Chinese delegations visited his capital at Amarapura, and four Burmese delegations went to Beijing. These residual influences were later reflected in some maps from both the Chinese Nationalist and early Chinese People's Republic, eras in which northern Burma, along with other parts of mainland Southeast Asia, were Chinese territory. The Muslim Panthay rebellion in Yunnan (1856–1873) and its suppression by Qing authorities prompted the emigration of significant numbers of Chinese Muslims, some of whom settled in central Burma at the capital, and in northern Burmese cities such as Lashio and Bhamo.[5] Since the latter town was on the Irrawaddy and navigable to the Bay of Bengal, it was the focal point of much of the early trade by mule caravan to and from Yunnan.[6] The British sent a number of expeditions into China from Burma to ascertain the feasibility of increasing trade with Yunnan.[7] As the British expanded their economic interests in Burma, especially with the investment in rice production in the Irrawaddy Delta, which especially flourished after the opening of the Suez Canal in 1869, Chinese from southeast China (Fujian and Guangdong Provinces) arrived by sea. There is evidence that some of the local *sawbwas*

---

4   In 1827, trade was estimated at £228,000. D. G. E. Hall, *Burma*. London: Hutchinson House, 1950, p. 119.

5   There are many discrepancies in the population estimates of the Panthays. In 1931 in Panglong on the China border there were said to be 5,000, but in all Burma in 1911, according to the census of that year, there were 2,202; in 1921 1,517, and in 1931, 1,106.

6   In 1855, there were said to be some 2,000 Chinese families living near the capital and 500 in Bhamo. John Cady, *A History of Modern Burma*, Ithaca: Cornell University Press, 1958, pp. 45–56.

7   The most famous of such expeditions was that of the Margary. *The Journey of Augustus Ramond Margary from Shanghai to Bhamo and Back to Manwyne*. London, 1876.

(hereditary maharajas) in the area of the Shan State were invested as paying tribute to, and under the protection of, the Chinese Emperor.[8] Some were known as the *tusi*. More importantly, the Burmese court at Ava and later at Mandalay sent tribute in the form of local products to the court at Beijing in ten-year cycles. When the British completed their seizure of the Burmese state, they signed a treaty with the Chinese in 1887 in which the British agreed that the tribute (although the term was not used) would continue but would be delivered by members of the "Burmese race," and not personally by the British themselves.[9] The process was never implemented, however.[10] Britain also signed an agreement with China for rights (the annual rent was 1,000 rupees) to the small parcel of borderland called the Namwan Assigned Tract through which an important road passed linking the Shan and Kachin areas of the country. It was only returned to China as part of the Sino-Burmese border settlement of 1960 (see Chapter 3).

The Sino-Japanese War affected Burma as it became the supply route to the Nationalist forces in China's southwest. Burma played a pivotal role in the supply of war material through the construction of the Burma Road (completed for motor traffic in 1938). It ran from the railhead in Lashio in the Burmese Shan State to the China border and then to Kunming, the capital of Yunnan Province. Lashio was connected by rail to Mandalay and the seaport of Rangoon.[11] Later, in World War II, Japan invaded Burma in its attempt to surround China, to garner its natural resources, and as a prelude to its attempted conquest of India. During World War II, Burma was one of the most fought-over areas in the Pacific theatre. As the Japanese advanced and the British retreated toward India, a scorched earth policy was implemented that destroyed much of the state's infrastructure. Three years later, when the British advanced back into Burma, the Japanese applied much the same policy. The country was devastated.[12]

---

8   See, Intelligence Branch, Army Headquarters, India. *Frontier and Overseas Expeditions from India.* Volume V. Delhi: Mittal Publications. Reprinted 1983. Chapter on the Shans, pp. 357–399.

9   *Ibid.*, Appendix VIII for the text of the treaty, p. 467. "Inasmuch as it has been the practice of Burma to send Decennial Missions to present articles of local produce, England agreed that the highest authority in Burma shall send the customary Decennial Missions; the members of the Missions to be of Burmese race."

10 Personal communication, Michael Carney, SOAS, University of London.

11 There were plans to extend the railroad to the China border in April 1941, but this was blocked by the Japanese invasion. Plans in 2011 call for its extension to meet a Chinese rail link from Kunming.

12 The British historian Hall said "Burma suffered more from the war than any other Asiatic country." See Hall, *Burma*, p. 172.

The economic role of the Chinese in Burma during the colonial period was certainly not as extensive as that of the Indians (all those from the subcontinent), since Burma was governed as a province of India until 1937. Yet it was important, for in the early period most Burmese were not acquainted with a monetized economy, and were thus subject to exploitation in terms of trade and debt. The Chinese, with their own clan and linguistic associations, were able to play important roles in the economy in trading as they had private access to sources of credit through these groups.

The Burmese census of 1983 calculated the number of Chinese as 233,470, of whom 191,699 were Buddhist and 2,897 Sunni Muslim (68 were Shiite).[13] These figures probably exclude an extensive number of Sino-Burmese who identify themselves as Burmese. Many such individuals attained considerable prominence in Burmese affairs, and include General Ne Win, General Khin Nyunt, Brigadier Aung Gyi, General San Yu, Colonel Kyi Maung, General Maung Aye, and others, although all of the above identified themselves as Burman and played by Burman rules. Since the legal opening of the Sino-Burmese border to trade, following the coup of 1988, and the self-destruction of the Burma Communist Party a year later, large-scale illegal Chinese immigration has occurred with extensive, new penetration of the economy, especially in central and northern Myanmar. There are estimates of perhaps two million illegal Chinese in Myanmar.[14]

Since the independence of Burma in 1948 and the founding of the People's Republic of China in 1949, bilateral relations have evolved with strategic implications for both states and for the region. Those relations for the first forty years were in the shadow of the Cold War and the formulation and reformulation of Chinese domestic and foreign policies. Thereafter, in the post-Cold War era, a different set of traditional and non-traditional concerns emerged involving the interplay of both strategic and economic interests. Myanmar as a nexus in Sino-Indian relations assumed a new and vital role.[15] Myanmar's domestic politics from independence ranged from civilian rule to a

---

13 *Burma 1983 Population Census*. Rangoon: Immigration and Manpower Department, Ministry of Home and Religious Affairs. June 1986. Table 11, pp. 2–57/58. A more extensive discussion of the Chinese in Burma/Myanmar follows in Chapter 8.

14 A former Burmese military official cited that figure. Personal interview, Yangon. Foreign embassies have variously estimated the Yunnanese population of Lashio at 50 percent, and that of Mandalay, the seat of Burman culture, at 20 percent.

15 In an attempt to influence the incoming Bush administration to consider strategic issues associated with Myanmar, especially related to India–China relations, this author organized a conference in February 2000 in Washington on Burma/Myanmar as nexus on the Bay of Bengal. Unpublished report. It had no discernable effect.

socialist military junta, a military-dominated socialist single-party mobilization system along an Eastern European model, to an authoritarian military regime and in 2011 a "discipline-flourishing democracy." These varied administrations influenced its foreign policies and especially Sino-Burmese relations. All had vital roles in the interplay between China and Myanmar.

The period since Burmese independence is especially germane to contemporary policy decisions in the current era. This book is devoted to clarifying, or at least exploring, the ramifications of the Sino-Burmese present and future relationships.

Scope of the Study

The importance of Sino-Burmese relations has been evident in policy articles over the past two decades, even if it has not been publicly discussed in official U.S. discourse for much of that period. A wide range of articles and studies have explored aspects of Sino-Burmese bilateral ties, some dating from the early 1950s. These have been mentioned in the bibliography, and cited in the text when appropriate. The authors acknowledge their contribution to the current analysis. Most articles have concentrated on Chinese assistance to the Burmese military regime since 1988, and have castigated China for its perceived role supportive of an authoritarian Burmese military government that has denied many rights to its own diverse peoples. Few of these essays have used Chinese sources and discussed the subject in the context of China's domestic political and economic situation, regional or sub-regional integration, and China's stakeholders at different administrative levels in Myanmar. This book employs declassified official Chinese records that illustrate Chinese attitudes toward the various Burmese governments and personalities, and some of the internal Burmese policies. It is an attempt to fill the gaps in a comprehensive view of the connections, or at least narrow our lack of understanding of them, which, as we will demonstrate, are composed of complex and multiple strands at different administrative levels in both countries, and are constantly changing.

The book is a product of joint authorship. Both Professor Fan Hongwei and David I. Steinberg have written extensively on Myanmar, and both were fortunate to come together in 2008 under Georgetown University–Xiamen University auspices to spend several months in beginning drafting of it. Professor Fan has made extensive use of Chinese sources, but his knowledge of the literature on Myanmar is far more catholic. A large segment of the footnoted sources are from the Chinese, and Professor Fan has provided the necessary translations.

This study is divided into four parts. Part I concerns the Cold War period, which equates to the civilian period in Burma (1948–1962) and the socialist military era (1962–1988). Part II concentrates on the post-Cold War period, and covers the formation in Myanmar of the military State Law and Order Restoration Council (SLORC, 1988–1997), and its successor the State Peace and Development Council (SPDC, 1997–2011). Cold War attitudes did, however, persist in many circles and in many policies. Part III is devoted to the international implications of the bilateral Sino-Burmese relationship, and Part IV concentrates on the dilemmas that the various actors face. Part I and Part II have short preludes placing the bilateral relationship in the context of the internal Burmese political milieu.

This book is neither a paean to nor a critique of either the Burmese or the Chinese political scene. These have been extensively written about in other studies. This is, rather, an attempt to provide a balanced analysis of an important bilateral relationship with profound implications for the region. There is no party or actor on which our criticism has not been levied to some degree. This study has been written in the hope that a bilateral Sino-Burmese relationship will develop that will improve the lives of the peoples of both states while providing the stability necessary for such progress and the international support that may be necessary.

There are no solutions to many of these dilemmas, and actions toward resolving any are likely to have unintended consequences on others. An immediate dilemma may in fact not be the most important over a longer term. The hope, however, is that by articulating the issues, serious study of the relationship between The People's Republic of China and the Union of Myanmar may contribute to their amelioration, if not resolution.

Part I: The Vicissitudes of Sino-Burmese Relations During the Cold War

Prelude: Setting the Stage

Independent, post-colonial Union of Burma was born in fragile unity, a unity that had been lacking in both the pre-colonial and colonial eras, a lack that still persists, perennially haunting the state. Since 4 January 1948, on independence from Britain, Burma has never been able to fashion a multiethnic state in which power and finances were distributed in a manner deemed "fair" to its diverse populations.[1] That ethnic issue has bedeviled every government since that time, and is yet to be resolved.[2] Whether as the "Union of Burma" or, later, "The Socialist Republic of the Union of Burma," and still later (since 1989) "The Union of Myanmar," and since 2011 "The Republic of the Union of Myanmar," that very concept of "Union" has been subject to differing, antagonistic interpretations – from quasi-centralized civilian rule, to authoritarian unitary military control, to minority proposed but rejected federal structures, to blatant secessionist attempts, to an ambiguous relationship following the 2010 elections. The issue presently affects Sino-Burmese ties along their long, shared frontier. Little wonder that the Burmese military's prime goal remains national unity, at almost any cost.

If Burma was a fragile state at its inception, its pregnancy was marred by the assassination in July 1947 of its chief independence negotiator, Aung San, who more than any other single individual had the trust of the diverse populations, trust that rapidly deteriorated with his death. The potential fragmentation of the state began with two communist rebellions, the mutiny of many left-wing paramilitary groups, the Chinese Nationalist Kuomintang incursion into its northern region, the Karen insurrection – in the first

---

1   Aung San famously said that if the Burmans got one *kyat* (Burmese currency), the minorities would get the same. Some interpreted this as an even split between the Burman majority and seven major minorities; others that the Burmans should get one-eighth. Neither has ever become a reality.

2   See David I. Steinberg, "The Problem of Democracy in Myanmar: Neither Nation-State Nor State-Nation?" [University of Hong Kong conference, June 2011]. This is an application to Myanmar of Alfred Stepan, Juan J. Linz, and Yogendra Yadav's article "The Rise of State-Nations," *Journal of Democracy*, Vol. 21, No. 3, July 2010, pp. 50–68.

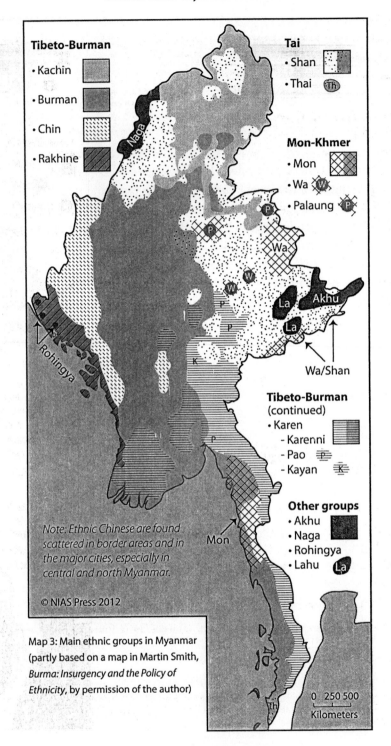

Tibeto-Burman

- Kachin
- Burman
- Chin
- Rakhine

Tai

- Shan
- Thai

Mon-Khmer

- Mon
- Wa
- Palaung

Tibeto-Burman
(continued)
- Karen
  - Karenni
  - Pao
  - Kayan

Other groups
- Akhu
- Naga
- Rohingya
- Lahu

Note: Ethnic Chinese are found scattered in border areas and in the major cities, especially in central and north Myanmar.

© NIAS Press 2012

Map 3: Main ethnic groups in Myanmar (partly based on a map in Martin Smith, *Burma: Insurgency and the Policy of Ethnicity*, by permission of the author)

0 250 500
Kilometers

Plate 1: U Nu, Zhou Enlai and Zhu De, Beijing, 25 October 1956 (photograph courtesy Cheng Ruisheng)

years of independence, one could realistically only speak of a "Rangoon government."

This fragmentation was reflected as well in the personalization of power. Such intense rivalries split the Anti-Fascist People's Freedom League, the ruling civilian coalition since independence. The threat of civil war led to the "constitutional coup" in 1958. The civilian legislature, under Prime Minister U Nu, voted to allow the military to take over government for six months (later extended to 18 months); if the legislature had not approved, the coup would have taken place in any case. After eighteen months of effective military rule,[3] the military supervised an election that brought back into power a civilian government led by U Nu, a government to which the military was antithetical. Its increasingly ineffective rule was ended by the second military coup of 2

---

3   The Burmese military in this period was one of the models Western social scientists used to describe the third-world military as perhaps the best hope for rational, forward-thinking, developmental administrations. This was, of course, in the Cold War period and such military-ruled states were anti-communist. At the close of their "caretaker" administration, the military published its analysis of its rule: *Is Trust Vindicated? A Chronicle of Trust, Striving, and Triumph. Being an Account of the Accomplishment of the Government of the Union of Burma, 1 November 1958–1 February 1960*. Hercules was pictured on the dust cover cleaning the Augean stables.

March 1962, ostensibly to protect the Union and oppose minority secessionist plots. The "Burmese Way to Socialism" was immediately introduced – deemed at the time to be the beginnings of perpetual military control, although eventually in civilianized form.

The bureaucratic failure of the intense, mal-administered socialism of the Burma Socialist Programme Party, which the Chinese viewed with disdain and suspicion, resulted in abject economic collapse and the proliferation of ethnic rebellions. The dire economic and political malaise was compounded by the military-mandated 1974 constitution and elections that established a single-party, authoritarian, unitary, socialist state along an Eastern European model. A portion of every significant ethnic minority group went into rebellion. The country essentially eschewed normal economic ties with much of the world beyond, and economically became dependent on Japanese foreign economic assistance.

Ironically, on independence Burma had been considered by many observers potentially to become the most developed of all Southeast Asian states. But by the 1980s with mismanagement rife, an increasing economic deterioration resulted as export prices fell and prices on necessary imports of raw materials and spare parts increased. By December 1987, Burma was essentially bankrupt with foreign exchange reserves of some US$30 million; the United Nations declared it a "least developed" nation.[4] A major and ill-conceived currency demonetization (the third under military rule) in September 1987 created further economic and social chaos, raising rice prices and the demand for smuggled Chinese consumer and other products, and contributed, along with pent-up political frustration, to the people's revolution in the spring and summer of 1988. It was brutally suppressed by the military resulting in the third coup of 18 September 1988, designed to shore up a collapsed military control. This engendered a new military era, which approximately coincided with the end of the Cold War and the collapse in 1989 of the Burma Communist Party, all of which are the subjects of Part II of this volume.

Burma/Myanmar has always been conscious of existing in China's vast shadow. As a form of self-protection, Burma early formulated a policy that was ostensibly neutralist in the great power struggles following the end of World War II. That was the essential reason why Burma's U Thant, former

---

4 Burma lobbied for that designation, for it lowered interest rates on loans. (personal interview, Rangoon). However, Burma did not really qualify because its literacy rate was too high, but this was ignored. The government never formally announced this to the people (it was buried in an economic document) because it was so embarrassing.

Plate 2: China–Myanmar Memorial for Friendship, Mangshi, Yunnan province (photograph David Steinberg)

Burmese ambassador to the United Nations and U Nu's secretary, was chosen as Secretary General of the United Nations (1961–1971); he was acceptable to both power blocs. Although neutralism was decried by both the People's Republic of China and the U.S. Department of State, for obviously antithetical reasons, it served the Burmese well in those turbulent times. But, as was noted by Pettman in 1973, the proximity of the PRC dominated Burma's foreign political concerns, and its leaders evolved a policy of non-alignment that sought to prevent or at least minimize Chinese intervention in Burmese affairs.[5]

During the Cold War, relations between China and its peripheral countries were critical elements in China's evolving foreign relations. Burma's development was hostage to the triangular relations among China, the Soviet Union, and the U.S. (together with the Colombo Plan). Thus, China–Burma relations were one of highlights in Beijing's peripheral diplomacy in the 1950s and 1960s. Burma was the first non-communist country to recognize the PRC. The Cold War was the defining factor in Sino-Burmese relations both during the Burmese civilian administration (1948–1962), and that of the military-led Burma Socialist Programme Party period (1962–1988). Sino-Burmese ties, after a frosty beginning, became cordial, and were termed *Pauk Phaw* before 1967. The term *Pauk Phaw*, which may be translated as "fraternal" but has a closer Chinese connotation of siblings from the same womb, was used uniquely for

5   Ralph Pettman, *China in Burma's Foreign Policy*. Canberra: Australian National University, Contemporary China Papers No. 7, 1973, p. 1.

Burma. A major memorial to this relationship was built in 1956 in the Yunnan city of Mangshi (see Plate 2) and celebrated by Premier Zhou Enlai and Burmese Prime Minister U Ba Swe. It is still a center of ceremonial bilateral occasions. Chinese President Hu Jintao invoked the *Pauk Phaw* relationship again when Senior General Than Shwe visited Beijing in September 2010.

Prior to 1967, both leaderships maintained frequent exchanges of visits and contacts between the two countries. Because of its neutralism and non-alignment, Burma became an important observation post for both China and the West, and later in Sino-Soviet friction. With the encirclement of China by the West, Burma was the only friendly non-Communist territory through which the Chinese Communists physically could go abroad, and through which delegations and official missions from Africa, Latin America, and the rest of Asia to China could travel with ease.[6] Former Prime Minister Winston Churchill remarked that Burma was a gap in the encirclement campaigns against China.[7]

This warmth only developed during and after satisfactory negotiations on a number of critical bilateral issues that had to be resolved. These included the status of the overseas Chinese in Burma; the presence in northern Burma of Kuomintang (Chinese Nationalist) remnant troops[8] that had fled from the Chinese communists and which were assisted by Taiwan and the U.S.'s CIA; the rebellion of the Burma Communist Party with strong Chinese influences; and the solution to the problem of the Sino-Burmese border, which both the Chinese Nationalists and the PRC had not recognized. China went to considerable lengths not only to assuage Burmese concerns, but also to demonstrate through the example of its benign intentions toward the Southeast Asia region and other states along its periphery. Nevertheless, the Chinese were quietly dubious about the authenticity of Burmese "socialism," and made scathing private remarks about the Burmese leadership.

The closeness of the relationship came to an end, however, when the internal Chinese chaos of the Cultural Revolution spread overseas.[9] By 1970–1971, China and Burma had re-established closer ties, but it took some years before the wound that incident created was healed. Efforts were made to increase Chinese

---

6   William C. Johnstone, *Burma's Foreign Policy: A Study in Neutralism*, Cambridge: Harvard University Press, 1963, p. 199.

7   Record of Chairman Mao Tsetung's Talk with Visiting Burmese Vice Prime Ministers, U Ba Swe and U Kywa Nyein, Archive of Ministry of Foreign Affairs, People's Republic of China (hereafter AFTA), No. 105-00339-01(1).

8   When the Qing Dynasty took over in China, some Ming Dynasty troops from the previous regime in 1644 retreated into what is now Burma, much as the Kuomintang did in 1949–50.

9   For a general discussion of such problems, see Roderick MacFarquhar and Michael Schoenhals, *Mao's Last Revolution*, Cambridge: The Belknap Press, 2006. pp. 222–229.

economic assistance and to project Chinese cultural soft power. Cultural exchanges were an important element of this strategy. Irritants remained, however, such as Chinese support to the Burma Communist Party. At the same time, Burma's status in Chinese foreign relations as a buffer state to counter U.S. containment declined. Rangoon was not as important to Beijing as before due to the important changes in China–Soviet–U.S. triangular relations, particularly the Sino–U.S. rapprochement, and the changes in China's domestic politics and economy in the 1970s and 1980s. China also increasingly de-ideologized foreign policy and no longer perceived the outside through some ideological lens (although its strategic focus was ever-present). China gradually abandoned the ideal of world revolution and focused on economic modernization. As a result, China was losing interest in the isolated and economically backward Burma.

Nevertheless, the relationship underwent a transformation following the Burmese coup of 1988, which approximately coincided with the end of the Cold War, the demise of the Burma Communist Party, and the growing need of imported energy to feed Chinese industrial expansion. The closeness of the relationship between China and Myanmar since the formation of the Burmese military administration following the coup of 18 September 1988 (the SLORC, State Law and Order Restoration Council; SPDC, State Peace and Development Council) belies the turbulence of the earlier period, and is often overlooked. Indeed, Beijing's attitude toward Burma was initially changed by political upheavals: the 8 August 1988 (8-8-88) suppressed popular uprising in Rangoon and the Tiananmen Square massacre in Beijing in 1989. Each resulted in international sanctions against the state, and drove the two states closer together. The forces behind the vicissitudes in the bilateral ties were essentially a product of domestic Chinese programs and relations that reverberated in its foreign policy.

The closeness of the relationship between China and Burma since the formation of a Burmese administration on independence was also strongly affected by the personal ties between the leaders of both countries. During this period, Burma was effectively responding to Chinese actions, but not in an obsequious or demeaning manner. It was able to exert pressure on the Chinese on occasion when the Chinese wanted to use Burma as a positive policy example to other states.

By 1988, the outstanding issues that were divisive in the bilateral relationship had been resolved, except for the continued existence of the Burma Communist Party, and Chinese foreign policy had abandoned its ideological fervor. The relationship underwent a transformation following the Burmese coup of 1988.

1

Sino-Burmese Relations 1949–1953: Suspicions and Equivocations

S ino-Burmese relations were one of the highlights in Beijing's peripheral diplomacy in the early period (1950s–1960s) after the establishment of diplomatic relations. Although overshadowed by Korea, the Taiwan issue, and the Sino-Soviet split, Sino-Burmese relationships were formed within the context of a pervasive Chinese world-view of revolutionary theory, resulting in suspicions that were only gradually allayed. Strong left-wing pressures within Burma for good relations with the PRC were also apparent, not only within the two communist parties in revolt but among the above-ground National Unity Front and other political forces that sought recognition of China and were suspicious of the "imperialist" powers – Britain and the U.S. At this stage in the newly forming relationship, China took the lead.

The Ideological Context of Sino-Burmese Relations

In the history of PRC foreign relations, Burma held several first places. Burma was the first non-communist country to recognize the PRC, the first county to settle a border dispute with China, and the first to sign a treaty of friendship and mutual non-aggression with China. But Beijing did not attach much importance to its southern neighbor in the early period (1949–1953) after the establishment of diplomatic relations; bilateral ties then were cold. It was only in 1954 that Burma engendered some enthusiasm in Beijing.

The Cold War featured periods of relatively calm confrontation and some real wars, sometimes called "proxy wars" between two blocs led by the U.S. and the Soviet Union. The evaluation of the U.S.–USSR relationship during the post-1945 years is configured by two slogans: the Cold War and Yalta. The Cold War symbolized total antagonism. Yalta, to the contrary, symbolized mutual accommodation (or for some a "sell-out" by the U.S. to the USSR).[1]

---

1   Immanuel Wallerstein, "The Global Picture, 1945–90," in Terence K. Hopkins and Immanuel Wallerstein (eds), *The Age of Transition: Trajectory of the World System 1945–2025*,
London: Zed Books, 1996, p. 216.

The Cold War was "cold" in Europe, but it was quite "hot" in Asia. It was "cold" in that neither the U.S. nor the Soviet Union used its military in combat against the other at any time. The Yalta agreement was an agreement that there would be no violence, and that neither side would attempt to change the frontiers, primarily in Europe, that were established in 1945.[2] How did the CCP and Rangoon perceive the Cold War, especially the hot war in Asia? How did the two countries see their places in the world in the early period of Cold War? How did the two new regimes think of each other in the early 1950s? Answers to these questions are important to understand China–Burma relations from 1949 to 1953.

U Nu articulated Burmese attitudes toward the two blocs in the "Leftist Unity Program" in 1948: Burma should "secure political and economic relations with Soviet Russia and the democratic countries of Eastern Europe in the same way as we are now having these relations with Britain and the United States."[3] The program was considered "astonishing" and "most disagreeable" by the British.[4] Although many Burmese also admitted that the British among the three powers – the British, the Americans, and the Russians – were "the closest to us for a variety of reasons," and "our relations with the British are thus absolutely straightforward", they still stressed that "our relations with other countries must be equally straightforward," and "we must make friends with them and our relations with them must be the most cordial."[5]

At the end of 1949, U Nu elucidated in a speech: "Our circumstances demand that we follow an independent course and not ally ourselves with any power bloc ... we must not lay down a Communist programme merely because Chinese Communists are overrunning China and therefore we must adopt a pattern acceptable to them ... The only political programme which we should pursue is the one which we believe to be the most suitable for our Union whatever course the British, the Americans, the Russians and the Chinese Communists might follow."[6] U Nu explained that Burma must "be

---

2   Immanuel Wallerstein, "What Cold War in Asia? An Interpretative Essay", in Zheng Yang-wen, Hong Liu and Michael Szonyi (eds), *The Cold War in Asia: The Battle for Hearts and Minds.* Leiden and Boston: Brill, 2010, pp. 19–20.

3   "U Nu: Leftist Unity Program", [25 May 1948], Roger M. Smith (ed.), *Southeast Asia: Documents of Political Development and Change.* Ithaca and London: Cornell University Press, 1974, pp. 101–102.

4   *British Documents of Foreign Affairs: Reports and Papers from the Foreign Office Confidential Print*, Part IV from 1946 through 1950, Series E Asia 1948, Vol. 7, Bethesda: University Publications of America, 2001, pp. 19 and 37.

5   Thakin Nu, *From Peace to Stability*, The Ministry of Information, Government of the Union of Burma, 1951, pp. 21–22.

6   *Ibid.*, pp. 51–52.

friendly with all foreign countries. Our tiny nation cannot have the effrontery to quarrel with any power".[7] "A small, weak nation like ours, howsoever we strengthen our defences, can never successfully defend ourselves alone ... The explanation is that we are a nation of only 17 million people ... Take a glance at our geographical position – Thailand in the East, China in the North, India in the West, and stretching southward, Malaya, Singapore and so on. We are hemmed in like a tender gourd among the cactus. We cannot move an inch."[8] U Nu vividly illuminated Burmese perceptions of world politics and its position. Following this logic, Rangoon would maintain good relations with China – either a Communist or Kuomintang (KMT) regime.

Chinese relations with Burma 1949–1953 were during the formative period of PRC foreign policy. Before its full formation, PRC foreign policies and principles were established by the leaders of CCP based on Chinese revolutionary theory, experience, and practice, and the obvious antagonisms between the two world camps. The CCP designed its relations with Asian countries and the world from its revolutionary viewpoint, classifying different countries by their ideological leanings. All countries beyond the socialist camp were imperialist or controlled by imperialist or anti-revolutionary forces.[9] This determination was based on the CCP theory of two camps and the "New Democratic Revolution," and its revolutionary experience in the civil war.

At the end of 1947, the CCP believed that "the Chinese people's revolutionary war has now reached a turning point."[10] In May 1948, the CCP professed that there was not "a third road" in China's civil war. "There are only two roads in China now: retain the enemy's arms and privileges, namely the semi-feudal and semi-colonial, dictatorial line followed by the big landlord class and the big bourgeoisie ... or annihilate the enemy's arms and privileges."[11] As the KMT retreated in defeat, the CCP was convinced of an earlier victory in the civil war than it originally estimated. "As we now [1948] see it [the war situation], only another year or so may be needed to overthrow it [the KMT government] completely."[12] The CCP's victory solidified a firm belief in its revolutionary theory and experience. In its eyes, "The law of historical development is that

7   *Ibid.*, p. 53.
8   *Ibid.*, pp. 98–102.
9   Niu Jun, "The Formation of Diplomatic Policy in New China and its Main Characteristics." *Historical Research*, No. 5, 1999.
10   *Selected Works of Mao Tsetung*, Vol. 4, Beijing: People's Press, 1991, p. 1243.
11   Chinese Central Archives (ed.), *Selected Documents of the CCP Central Committee*, 1948, Vol. 17, Beijing: Party School of the Central Committee of the CCP Press, 1992, p. 643.
12   *Selected Works of Mao Tsetung*, Vol. 4, p. 1361.

Plate 3: Mao Tsetung declares the founding of the People's Republic of China, Beijing, 1 October 1949. Despite a warming of Sino-Burmese relations in the 1950s, Mao remained personally cool towards Burma, whose neutralist policies he regarded as implicitly pro-Western.

only by means of revolutionary war can the class be eliminated. The war can be permanently eliminated only when the class is abolished."[13]

Mao determined that if there were to be revolution, there must be a revolutionary party.[14] Under such a revolutionary viewpoint, the CCP could not accept and recognize Burma's independence, the legitimacy of U Nu's government, or its foreign policy. As a result, the CCP thought the nationalism movement of Burma was unsuccessful, regarded Aung San as a "traitor," and U Nu as a "running dog" of imperialism.[15] U Nu's government was a "reactionary regime subject to foreign imperialism" and "British imperialism's puppet."[16] On 25 May 1948, U Nu announced the "Leftist Unity Program, which proposed "To form a league for the propagation of Marxist Doctrine, composed of Socialists, Communists, Pyithu Yebaws and others who lean towards Marxism and to really discuss and propagate the writing of Marx, Engels, Lenin, Stalin, Mao Tsetung, Tito, Dimitrov and other apostles of Marxism."[17] The CCP deemed

13 *Military Works of Mao Tsetung Since the Establishment of the PRC* (January 1959–February 1976), Vol. 3, Beijing: Military Science Press, Central Party Literature Press, 2010, p. 69.
14 *Selected Works of Mao Tsetung*, Vol. 4, p. 1357.
15 "The Leader of BCP Declaimed Against Reactionary Government", *People's Daily*, 3 April 1948.
16 "U Nu's Tricks Go Bankrupt", *People's Daily*, 25 August 1948.
17 "U Nu: Leftist Unity Program", p. 102.

that U Nu's government was using the trick of false Marxism to deceive the Burmese people and save its increasingly dying regime.[18] Only the Burma Communist Party (BCP) was identified as a real revolutionary party. Only the BCP could lead the Burmese people to win the freedom, peace, and independence of Burma.[19] Consequently, Mao still called Burma a semi-independent and almost independent state even after the shift of China–Burma relations in 1954. During the Cold War period, before Beijing de-ideologized its foreign policy and no longer perceived the outside through some ideological lens, its perceptions of Rangoon and the BCP did not change even when the two countries maintained cordial relations. Beijing's Burma policy shift in 1954 was nothing more than opportunistic and pragmatic when facing the increasingly national security pressures caused by the U.S.

In September 1947, the Communist Party Intelligence Agency conceived the world as split into two camps: socialist and imperialist. The CCP soon accepted this theory. In his article, *Internationalism and Nationalism*, Liu Shaoqi in December 1948 emphasized that neutralism was impossible during the period of antagonism between the two opposing camps,[20] and in June 1949 he argued that neutralism was deceptive. Mao Tsetung also stated that there was no "third way" and decried "fence-sitting."[21] Countries pursuing neutralist policies, like Burma, thus were regarded as in the Western camp and were not on the list with which China first needed to establish close relations.

During Liu Shaoqi's visit to the Soviet Union in August 1949, he reported to Stalin that "In East Asian countries like Vietnam, Malaya and Burma, the proletariat has no right to pursue revolution, and the means of revolutionary struggle has been or will be armed guerrilla warfare."[22] In the meeting of labor unions in Asia and Australia in November 1949, Liu declared that, "We should give all kinds of moral and physical aid to the proletariat and to labor needing help in the countries reigned by capitalism and imperialism." China should, thus, shoulder the international responsibility to aid them in all capitalist countries, particularly in Asia.[23] Continuing in this vein, in 1950 Liu stated in a CCP document that, "It is the CCP's and the Chinese people's duty-bound

18 "U Nu's Tricks Go Bankrupt", *People's Daily*, 25 August 1948.
19 Fang Hui, "Which Counties Are People Liberation War Going on?", *People's Daily*, 7 April 1949.
20 Liu Shaoqi, *Internationalism and Nationalism*, Beijing: People's Press, 1951, p. 25.
21 *Selected Works of Mao Tsetung*, Vol. 4, p. 1473.
22 *Works of Liu Shaoqi Since the Establishment of the PRC*, Vol. 1, Beijing: Central Party Literature Press, 2005, pp. 50–51.
23 *Ibid.*, p. 177.

international responsibility, and one of the most important means of consolidating China's revolutionary victory in international circumstances, to use all possible measures to aid the Communist parties and people in the oppressed Asian nations, and to struggle for their liberations."[24]

The Establishment of Diplomatic Relations

Following Burma's independence in January 1948, Rangoon monitored closely the status of China's civil war between the CCP and the KMT. When the People's Liberation Army launched their attacks on the KMT's contravallation along the Yangtze River, Burma began to pay more attention to internal Chinese political and military affairs. The presence of a disbanded Chinese division on the border of Kengtung in 1947 had already caused Burmese unease. Although there were no signs of Chinese infiltration into Northeast Burma on more than the scale of the usual seasonal movement of coolie labour, there was a growing fear that the communist success in China would provide encouragement to the communists in Burma at a moment when their strength seemed to be on the wane.[25] In July 1949, high officials of the Burmese ruling coalition, the Anti-Fascist People's Freedom League (AFPFL), considered the potential international influence of China's revolution. During the Burmese Foreign Minister's visits to the U.K. and the U.S. that same year, he discussed the potential impact on Burma of the CCP's seizure of power.

On 1 October 1949, Mao Tsetung announced in Tiananmen Square that "This government is the only legitimate government to represent the people of the People's Republic of China. It is ready to establish diplomatic relations with all foreign governments that are willing to abide by the principles of equality, mutual benefit, and mutual respect for each other's territory and sovereignty."[26] This announcement was delivered to U Myint Thein, Burmese Ambassador in Nanjing, on the same day. Rangoon thus had to address the question of recognizing the new Beijing government. U Myint Thein was soon recalled to Rangoon to consult on this problem. "With the formation of the PRC, leftists in Burma began a campaign for the AFPFL government to recognize the Peking regime. This pressure was buttressed by some forty Chinese associations in

---

24 *Chronicle of Liu Shaoqi: 1898–1969*, Vol. 2, Beijing: Central Party Literature Press, 1996, p. 245.
25 *British Documents of Foreign Affairs*, Vol. 9, p. 7.
26 Liao Zhengbao (ed.), *Declassified Diplomatic Documents: Archives on Establishment of Diplomatic Relations by the PRC*, Beijing: China Pictorial Press, 2006, p. 9.

Burma, led by the Chinese Chamber of Commerce and the Chinese Trade Association, all favoring recognition."[27]

With internal pressure for recognition steadily mounting, Foreign Minister U E Maung, who was visiting London, declared on December 3 that, "We shall have to recognize the new government of China very soon. Nothing has been decided yet, but it is a question of recognizing facts." Back in Rangoon on December 6, U E Maung told press reporters that Burma would recognize Communist China before Christmas and it would mean the automatic breaking of relations with the Nationalist Chinese government.[28] According to the memoir of the Indian Ambassador to China (1948 to 1952),

> Indian government recognition of the new Government of China should be conveyed to Peking by the end of the year [1949]. For some reason Burma was anxious that it should be the first State outside the Soviet bloc to recognize the New China and we were approached with a request to wait for a few days in order to give Burma the start. In due course, Burma announced its recognition and we followed in a few days.[29]

Actually, that "some reason" was that the Burmese hoped to avert communist Chinese hostility.[30] A declassified document of the British Foreign Ministry reveals that the Burmese overestimated the seriousness of the CCP's threat then. They firmly believed that "the Chinese would not hesitate to attack Burma. They would probably advance 150 miles into Burmese territory and occupy almost the entire Kachin state, a very valuable part of Burma where the Burmese Corporation now operates."[31]

On 16 December, Foreign Minister U E Maung gave a note to Zhou Enlai that Rangoon "decided to recognize the PRC, and hopes to establish diplomatic relations and exchange diplomatic envoys." Two days later, Zhou Enlai replied that Beijing agreed to establish diplomatic relations with Rangoon and exchange diplomatic envoys on the premise of Burma breaking relations with the KMT government.[32]

However, Mao Tsetung, who was visiting Moscow, telegraphed to Liu Shaoqi and Zhou Enlai on 19 December, "Regarding the issue of Burma's

27 Johnstone, *Burma's Foreign Policy*, pp. 55–56.
28 *Ibid.*, p. 56.
29 K. M. Panikkar, *In Two Chinas: Memoirs of a Diplomat*, Westport: Hyperion Press, 1981, p. 68.
30 *British Documents of Foreign Affairs*, Vol. 9, p. 46.
31 *Ibid.*, p. 38.
32 *Documents on PRC Foreign Relations: 1949–1950*, Beijing: World Knowledge Press, Vol. 1, 1957, p. 17.

request to establish diplomatic relations with us, you should ask whether Rangoon is willing to sever relations with the KMT, and at the same time ask Rangoon to appoint a delegate to negotiate the establishment of Sino-Burmese relations. Then you decide whether the two countries relations should be established. Such procedures of negotiating on establishing relations are absolutely necessary, and it should be the same with all capitalist countries."[33]

Consequently, on 21 December, Zhou Enlai replied again that only after the Burmese government had broken off relations with the KMT government, "The PRC central people's government is willing to establish diplomatic relations between the PRC and the Union of Burma on the basis of equality, mutual benefit, mutual respect for sovereignty, and territorial integrity, and hopes the Burma government will dispatch a negotiator to Beijing."[34] Beijing's reply was thought "cold" and "rather unexpected" in Rangoon.[35] As the Indian Ambassador to China explained, "We, as well as other nations including Britain, had assumed that diplomatic relations would automatically follow recognition of the new Government, and that previous Embassies would therefore be automatically revived without discussion or argument. That, however, was not the Chinese point of view. They held that diplomatic relations had to be settled separately by negotiations."[36]

The distinctly ungracious Chinese reply came as a severe disappointment to the many Burmese who expected that by her hurried recognition Burma would acquire special merit with Communist China. As a result, at the end of 1949 the Burmese government had not replied to the Chinese note and was waiting to see how China's relations developed with other countries.[37]

The Chinese mode of negotiations, although different from international norms, was in accordance with new but established Chinese diplomatic guidelines. The *Common Programs*, which had the nature of a provisional constitution and was promulgated in September 1949, stipulated (Article 56) that the Chinese government could negotiate with "any foreign government that broke relations with Kuomintang reactionaries, and is friendly to the PRC." Then China could establish diplomatic relations with them on the basis of equal-

---

33 *Works of Mao Tsetung Since the Establishment of PRC*, Vol. 1, Beijing: Central Party Literature Press, 1987, p. 193.

34 Notes on the Establishment of China–Burma Diplomatic Relations, AMFA, File No. 105-00001-01(1).

35 Panikkar, *In Two Chinas*, p. 69.

36 *Ibid.*, p. 69.

37 *British Documents of Foreign Affairs*, Vol. 11, p. 7.

ity, mutual benefit, mutual respect for sovereignty and territorial integrity.[38] The Burmese reply thus had to meet the requirements of the Article 56 of the *Common Programs* and the instructions given by Mao on 19 December 1949 from Moscow.

On the eve of the PRC's birth, Zhou Enlai stated that "We won't recognize the diplomatic position of all remaining foreign Embassies in China except those of socialist countries. From now on, the establishment of foreign relations should be by means of negotiation. We would recognize the establishment of diplomatic relations if they make it clear to break all diplomatic relations with Taiwan. We establish diplomatic ties on some principles. Negotiation-establishment of diplomatic relations is unprecedented in the international community, and it's a pioneering work which we make according to our country's specific condition."[39] Beijing thus broke normal international conventions due to the CCP foreign policies of "leaning to one side" and "starting anew."[40]

The establishment of diplomatic relations between the PRC and other socialist countries was still determined by international conventions – all ten countries that established diplomatic ties with the PRC were socialist. The policy of "leaning to one side" determined China's identity and role in international politics. Before the CCP adopted its Peaceful Coexistence policy in 1954, Beijing definitively divided the world into two opposing camps. "China identified with the socialist countries camp, and capitalist countries were regarded as a distinct group by China. Obviously, relations between China and the West were [based on] rivalry."[41] Beijing lacked trust for and a sense of identity with non-socialist countries.

The policy of "starting anew" adopted by Beijing aimed to set up a new model of Chinese diplomacy; the mode of negotiation-establishing relations was simply the implementation of that policy. On 8 November 1949, at the foundation ceremony of the new Chinese Foreign Ministry, Zhou Enlai said,

---

38 Chinese Central Archives (ed.), *Selected Documents of the CCP Central Committee*, pp. 595–596.

39 Lan Sou, Li Ding, "Welcoming the birth of New China every day and night", *Materials from CCP History*, No. 5, 1989.

40 To make a clean break with the foreign policy of KMT China, the CCP renounced all the diplomatic relations the Kuomintang Government had established with foreign countries; treated heads of foreign diplomatic missions accredited to Old China as ordinary foreign nationals instead of diplomatic envoys; reviewed all the treaties and agreements Old China had concluded with foreign countries; gradually cleared up the prerogatives and influence the capitalist countries had in China; and established new diplomatic relations with other countries.

41 Liu Zhiyong, "Chinese National Identity and the Choices in China's Diplomatic Strategy", China Foreign Affairs University, Ph.D. dissertation, 2005, pp. 41–45.

"When we pioneer diplomatic space now, it is necessary first to distinguish friend from enemy."[42] After the founding of the PRC, when some socialist countries quickly established diplomatic relations with China, Zhou Enlai explained, "These countries established diplomatic relations with us on the basis of genuine equality, mutual benefit, mutual respect for sovereignty, and territorial integrity. Therefore, we quickly established diplomatic relations with them. As regards capitalist countries, colonial and semi-colonial countries, we have to test whether they accept our principle of establishing diplomatic relations through the procedure of negotiations. We not only listen to their oral positions but observe their actions."[43]

Non-socialist countries, moreover, initially took a wait-and-see attitude toward the new Chinese regime, and some of them still supported the KMT. The CCP tested the non-socialist countries "sincerity" of establishing diplomatic relations, and assessed their attitude toward the KMT regime and the legitimacy of the PRC.

On 18 January 1950, Burmese Foreign Minister, Sao Hkun Hkio, wrote a letter to Zhou Enlai that Burma's government had received Zhou's message of 21 December 1949, and stated that the KMT Embassy in Rangoon had received notice that Burma had cut ties with it, and that Burma recognized the PRC, so the Taiwan Embassy would be soon closed. Additionally, Rangoon appointed the former first secretary and consul general in Kunming to the KMT government as chargé d'affaires ad interim to the PRC to attend the negotiations. The process progressed as Beijing had planned. "The first step of negotiations is that we orally ask whether Burma agrees to establish diplomatic relations. If Burma replies satisfactorily, the first step ends. The second step follows, and both sides begin to negotiate on exchanging diplomatic envoys."[44]

In late April 1950, U Phyo, Burma's negotiator, arrived in Beijing. On 29 April, 5 May, and 12 May 1950, Zhang Hanfu, China's Vice-Foreign Minister, held three meetings with him. During these negotiations, both parties discussed the issues of Burma severing relations with the KMT, and of how Rangoon would dispose of all KMT organizations and their property in Burma. On 12 May, U Phyo orally replied that "The Burmese government never recognized any other Chinese Kuomintang organizations except the former Chinese Embassy to Burma." After Burma recognized the PRC, "The former Chinese

---

42   *Selected Diplomatic Writings of Zhou Enlai*, Beijing: Central Party Literature Press, 1990, p. 3.
43   *Ibid.*, p. 49.
44   Records from four discussions about the establishment of China–Burma relations, AMFA, File No. 105-00001-02(1).

Embassy will immediately not be recognized, and the personnel of the former Chinese Embassy will be regarded as common citizens. Any property and funds of China in Burma will be transferred to the [newly] recognized government."[45]

On 19 May, Vice-Foreign Minister Zhang Hanfu replied that the Chinese government had discussed Burma's reply of 12 May, was satisfied with it, and hoped that both sides immediately would begin to negotiate the exchange of diplomatic envoys. Meanwhile, Beijing determined that China would appoint Yao Zhongming as Ambassador to Burma. China and Burma established diplomatic relations on 8 June 1950, and Burma became the sixteenth country to do so.

Tentative Contacts: 1950–1953

Although Burma was the first non-socialist country to recognize the PRC, this favorable beginning did not quickly develop. On the contrary, China–Burma relations were "noncommittal and very cold."[46] Both sides were politically suspicious and mistrustful of each other. China thought Burma an underling of imperialist countries. Burma worried that China would possibly invade it and threaten its national security, and it carefully balanced relations between the West and China.

China's new Ambassador to Burma arrived in Rangoon on 28 August 1950. Burma's press was lukewarm about his arrival and commented sharply on the attitude of the local Chinese and warned them against divided loyalty as well as against any attempts by the Chinese communists to interfere in Burma's internal affairs. The new Ambassador didn't endear himself to the Burmese by his frank claims on the loyalty of all "overseas Chinese" in Burma.[47]

In 1950, the Chinese Embassy held a reception for China's National Day (1 October), and invited some Burmese officials and overseas Chinese to attend. China intended to use the reception to propagandize the new regime and expand its influence; Burma wanted to understand better Beijing's intentions through the reception. After the reception, the Chinese Embassy in Burma submitted a report to Beijing:

> Concerning our National Day celebrations, the Burmese government was perfunctory and impeded our efforts in fear that we may take this opportunity to greatly expand our political influence. They were reluctant to offer

45 *Ibid.*
46 Abstract of Burmese Prime Minister U Nu's speech in parliament, AMFA, File No. 105-00814-01(1).
47 *British Documents of Foreign Affairs*, Vol. 11, p. 40 and 50.

[us] the list of invitees on the Burmese side and deliberated over it when we conferred with them. Also, they set up a barrier to the place and decoration of the celebration ... They intended to spy on our latest development via this celebration ... Burma's government is basically against our country, but it is double-faced, and is seemingly and purposely anxious about us.[48]

At the same time that Burma was courting China, Burmese leaders were suspicious of China and wanted to balance relations by ensuring ties with the U.S. – an important factor influencing Sino-Burmese relations both in terms of Chinese concerns and Burmese perceived needs. In October 1950, Burma's Foreign Minister met with China's Ambassador Yao Zhongming, and pointed out that Yao's speech at the local overseas Chinese assembly on 1 October used improper anti-U.S. imperialist words. "In order to avoid trouble, you should pay attention [to this] ... I don't agree to a U.S. imperialist invasion, and agree with your opposition. However, you could express general objections to U.S. imperialism or be against it according to a specific event, but don't generally oppose it lest it arouse trouble."[49]

On 13 September 1950, Burma and the U.S. signed an economic coopera-tion agreement. After the defeat of the KMT in China and the Korean War, and fearful of the potential for Chinese subversion through its overseas Chinese community, Washington sent a team to Southeast Asia to determine what might be done to hinder what Washington perceived as Chinese expansionism. This involved the beginnings of U.S. support to Southeast Asian economic de-velopment programs. In accordance with this agreement, Washington provided Rangoon with economic and technological assistance. China was dissatisfied. An editorial in the *People's Daily* on 13 December 1950, noted that "Fully known, the U.S. imperialists have strengthened the invasion of our country's peripher-ies, and attempt to change all our neighboring countries into bases for invading China ... The U.S. has signed military and economic agreements with Thailand and Burma in order to strengthen economic plunder in these countries, and, on the other hand, to change them into its military bases for invasion."[50]

The Burma–U.S. economic agreement caused Burmese leftists much dis-content. Thakin Lwin, the Chairman of the Burma Conference to Defend World

48 Review of the National Day celebration from the Chinese Embassy to Burma, AMFA, File No. 117-00038-02(1).

49 Burmese Foreign Minister Opinion on Chinese Ambassador Remarks at Local Overseas Chinese Gathering and China Response to it, AMFA, File No. 105-00067-02(1).

50 "Comments on Joint Communique of Atlee and Truman", *People's Daily*, 13 December 1950.

Peace (World Peace Congress, Burma), wrote an article and published it in the *Yunnan Daily* of 18 October 1951, that "U.S. imperialism is upgrading and building airfields throughout Burma in the good name of economic aid. The U.S. is using Burma to destroy the pioneer of anti-imperialism, the PRC." One month later, U Mya Tun, the first secretary of Burma's Embassy in Beijing, explained to the Chinese that the construction and upgrading of the Rangoon airfield was supported by the Burmese government, and planned to use the airfield for large international passenger airliners, so it was not true that U.S. imperialism was upgrading and building airfields throughout Burma. Meanwhile, Burma declared that no country was permitted to take destructive action against the PRC or any other country from Burmese territory. "Burma's government is completely complying with the policies of neutralism and good neighborliness."[51] In addition, U Mya Tun asked the Chinese Foreign Ministry to help him publish an article in the *Yunnan Daily* to correct Thakin Lwin's article.[52]

Washington's influence in Burma was soon weakened by another event. At the beginning of 1950, some KMT troops retreated into the northeast Burma. Soon after, these troops united to found the "Yunnan Anti-Communist Salvation Army." In the early 1950s, it launched many attacks and raids on Yunnan Province.

In the first half of 1952 alone, KMT troops attacked Tengchong, Longling, and Zhenkang, three counties neighboring Burma, over sixty times, and killed over one hundred CCP cadres and inhabitants (see Map 4).[53] Furthermore, they attempted to enkindle border conflict, and inflame both countries' military. According to a "top secret" document of the Burma KMT troops captured by Burma's Ministry of Information, "From now on you and your men must make all attempts to attack the weak outposts of the Burmese troops in the disguise that you are Mao's Communist bandits and also must propagate that Mao's Communist bandits have invaded Burma . . . Therefore to make our plans successful we must create trouble between these two governments."[54] The Burmese government viewed the KMT's offensive actions into Yunnan

---

51 First Secretary of Burma's Embassy in China denies the establishment of US military bases in Burma, AMFA, File No. 105-00174-02(1).

52 Burmese Embassy in China requests the Ministry of Foreign Affairs of the PRC to assist them in publishing a clarification in the *Yunnan Daily* with regard to the "incorrect message" in Thakin Lwin's essay, AMFA, File No. 105-00078-01(1).

53 *Development of the Military in Contemporary China*, Beijing: China's Social Science Press, 1989, p. 373.

54 *Kuomintang Aggression against Burma*, Ministry of Information, Government of The Union of Burma, 1953, p. 159.

as an attempt not to destroy Communist China, but rather to destroy Sino-Burmese relations.[55]

The Burmese government wanted to solve the KMT problem by diplomatic approaches through the United Nations, but its attempt failed because of U.S. obstruction. Burma's military power was weak; since it was also attempting to control internal ethnic and other ideological rebels, the KMT problem could not be solved by force. By 1953, the situation became more serious: the number of KMT troops rose to 16,000 from 1,700 in early 1950;[56] their arms were more abundant and sophisticated, and they raided several places in Burma in collaboration with anti-government Karen troops.[57] By March 1953, the Burmese government was forced to concentrate over 80 percent of its defensive forces against these intruders. Most troublesome to the Burmese was the possibility that the Chinese Communists might use the KMT presence as a pretext to invade Burma.[58]

Facing the worsening situation, Prime Minister U Nu worried that if he did not do something, China might invade Burma, or he might find himself forced out of office.[59] "Burma was particularly worried lest the Chinese government would get the impression that Burma was harboring the KMT troops in her country."[60] Rangoon stopped accepting U.S. aid in 1953 and closed its aid program. Beijing praised Burma's action. When Zhou Enlai met with the Burmese Government Labor Delegation in May 1953, he said Burma's action "made many Asian countries excited."[61]

Complicating the situation was the Sino-Burmese undemarcated border issue that had been pending since the end of the nineteenth century. Chinese maps printed by the KMT government after the Second World War included some territory in the north of Burma as Chinese (see Map 5), and this was

55 Kenneth Ray Young, "Nationalist Chinese Troops in Burma – Obstacle in Burma Foreign Relations: 1949–1961", New York University, Ph.D. dissertation, 1970, p. 57.

56 Chen Hurngyu, "Complaint by the Union of Burma Regarding an Aggression against it by the Government of the Republic of China in 1953", *Journal of Overseas Chinese and Southeast Asian Studies*, Vol. 4, No. 3, July 2004.

57 Robert H. Taylor, *Foreign and Domestic Consequences of the KMT Intervention in Burma*, Data Paper: No. 93, Southeast Asia Program Department of Asian Studies, New York: Cornell University, July 1973, p. 16.

58 Chi-shad Liang, *Burma's Foreign Relations: Neutralism in Theory and Practice*, New York: Praeger Publishers, 1990, p. 70.

59 Victor S. Kaufman, "Trouble in the Golden Triangle: The United States, Taiwan and the 93rd Nationalist Division", *The China Quarterly*, No. 166, 2001, p. 447.

60 Kalyani Bandyopadhyaya, *Burma and Indonesia: Comparative Political Economy and Foreign Policy*, New Delhi: South Asian Publishers, 1983, p. 154.

61 Account of Premier Zhou Enlai's meeting with a Burmese governmental labour delegation, AMFA, File No. 105-00110-01(1).

obviously unsatisfactory to Rangoon. But the new 1950 PRC map also included the area north of Bhamo.

An authoritative Chinese Communist atlas published in 1953 showed most of the frontier with Burma as undemarcated and laid claim to everything north of Myitkyina. With reference to the border dispute between China and Burma, the map of Yunnan noted, "These problems await the establishment of a people's Burma and the final victory of the Asian People's revolution; then they can receive a complete and reasonable solution."[62] The area where the KMT was sheltering in Burma was along the disputed borderland between two countries, further increasing Rangoon's fear for its territorial unity.

China–Burma economic and cultural relations were insignificant from 1950 to 1953. Compared with bilateral trade before World War II, trade decreased. From 1950 to 1953, China's yearly average imports and exports were US$3.2825 million and US$0.8725 million from Burma, and were 0.32 percent and 0.12 percent of China's gross imports and exports respectively.[63] The trade structure between two countries was still unchanged, with raw and primary products being the main commodities. Cultural intercourse between Beijing and Rangoon was limited; it was only after the two countries' premiers visited each other in 1954 that the situation improved.[64]

Analysis of Early Sino-Burmese Relations

Under the "New Democratic Revolution" theory, only the Communist Party could lead newly independent peoples to win national and democratic revolutions. Beijing believed, "Whether in economic, military, or political dimensions, Burma's nature has not been changed; it still is a typical colonial country" even after its independence. The President of Burma, Sao Shwe Thaike, was "a big feudal lord," and Prime Minister, U Nu was "an extremely vicious, and a notorious Burmese traitor." Burma's government was "the representative of big landlords and big bourgeoisie," and "the loyal lackey of imperialism – Burma's reactionary circles of big landlords and big compradors."[65] On 3 September 1952, when Zhou Enlai visited Moscow and talked with Stalin, he stated that

---

62 Harold C. Hinton, *China's Relations with Burma and Vietnam: A Brief Survey*, New York: International Secretariat, Institute of Pacific Relations, 1958, p. 40.

63 *Yearbook of China's International Trade and Economy*, Beijing: Foreign Economic and Trade Publishing House of China, 1984, pp. iv–15.

64 Review by Chinese Embassy to Burma of Sino-Burmese cultural ties in the past decade, AMFA, File No. 105-00603-02(1).

65 "Burmese People's Struggle", *People's Daily*, 10 May 1948.

the "Burmese government concealed its real position on China, but it actually pursued the policy of anti-China following the U.K. and U.S. lead."[66]

In this early period of establishing diplomatic ties, distrust and limited contact became the keynote of China's policy toward Burma. The principle of "putting the house in order before inviting guests,"[67] adopted by the CCP at that time, also restricted its relations and communications with Rangoon. Moreover, China's foreign relations focused on aligning with the Soviet Union, and aiding Vietnam against France and North Korea against the U.S. A new small country such as Burma was not on the preferential list and not a priority for developing close relations.

Rangoon gradually established a neutral foreign policy towards China during 1948–1953. Although both sides appointed Ambassadors during this period, Burma was suspicious of "China's intentions."[68] Suspicion, vigilance, and fear were the main characteristics of Burma's policy toward China. The aim of Burma in recognizing China lay in taking precautions against a potential Chinese invasion. In 1988, former President Maung Maung explained that, "The fear of aggression was at the back of the Union Government's mind when it decided to be the first [non-Communist government] to recognize the new Communist regime in China."[69] Burma's Prime Minister U Nu, even compared China and Burma to elephant and lamb, and stated that "We once were very afraid, and suspicious that the PRC could possibly intervene in our country's internal affairs."[70] U Nu also referred to Burma as a tender gourd between two cactuses (China and the West). In this early period, Beijing controlled the initiative in the development of Sino-Burmese relations.

Burmese apprehension of China was evident. In 1954, Sao Shwe Thaike, the head of the upper house of the Burmese parliament, said to Zhou Enlai, the visiting Chinese Premier, "Burma is a small country and has to maintain friendly relations with its neighbors."[71] In December 1957, during the visit of Burmese Vice Prime Minister U Kyaw Nyein and U Ba Swe, they said to Mao Tsetung, "Prior to Prime Minister U Nu's visit to China and his meeting with Chairman Mao, Burma was, indeed, afraid of China, because Burma is a small

66   Minutes of Conversation between I. V. Stalin and Zhou Enlai, APRF, f. 45, op. 1, d. 329, ll. 75–87.
67   See footnote 40 in this chapter.
68   Yunnan Institute of History Studies (ed.), *Documents on the History of China–Burma Friendship*, 1954, Vol. 2, No. 2, p. 58.
69   Maung Maung, *Burma in the Family of Nations*, Amsterdam: Djambatan Ltd, 1956, p. 145.
70   Yunnan Institute (ed.), *Documents on the History of China–Burma Friendship*, p. 13.
71   Responses by Burmese officials and media to Premier Zhou Enlai's visit to Burma, AMFA, File No. 105-00259-03(1).

country while China is a big one."[72] There was a border of over two thousand kilometers between Burma and China. In 1954, Burma's population and size were 3.2 percent and 7 percent respectively of China's. So Burma was very cautious, wanting neither to offend the Western bloc by having close contact with China, nor displeasing China by having too intimate a relationship with the West. Zhou Enlai, when visiting Burma in 1956, publicly expressed his understanding of Rangoon's apprehension, and stated, "It is easy for a newly founded big country to cause suspicion in other countries."[73]

Burmese historical memory intensified Rangoon's distrust and worry about China. China had invaded Burma in times of the Chinese Yuan and Qing dynasties. During Prime Minister U Nu's first trip to China in 1954, he intentionally mentioned this history at the state banquet hosting him. Although he ascribed the Chinese invasions not to the Han (ethnic Chinese) nationality but to the expansion of Mongols and Manchus, the foreign warlords,[74] U Nu used history to express Burma's present anxiety about China. Yet Burma's first Ambassador to the PRC, U Myint Thein, said that "Han, Manchu, Nationalist, Communist, it makes no difference to the Burmese. A Chinese is a Chinese and to be feared." U Nu fully accepted this view.[75] In 1957, while Burma's Vice Prime Minister U Ba Swe visited China, he told the Chinese, "Our fear is very natural because in history big countries always were buckoes. Burma lay among powers."[76] The CCP attitude toward national revolution in other Asian countries was also a concern. In 1957, U Nu spoke in Burma's parliament that "New China's relations with the insurrectional BCP are not clear, but it expressed some fraternal care."[77] The Burmese viewed the Sino-Burmese border issue, KMT troops, the problem of the overseas Chinese, and the CCP relations with the BCP as potential sources of Chinese invasion and subversion.

With the end of the Korean War, the increasing pressure of the U.S. containment policy against China, and China's urgent need for a peaceful environment necessary to recover and develop its economy, Beijing began to pursue a new foreign policy. This policy – "Peace and United Front" – focused on China's national interests. From 1954, it ended the policy of "putting the house

---

72 Record of Chairman Mao Tsetung's talk with visiting Burmese Vice Prime Ministers, U Ba Swe and U Kyaw Nyein, AMFA, File No. 105-00339-01(1).
73 All the manuscripts from Premier Zhou Enlai's talks in Burma (Chinese, English, and Burmese), AMFA, File No. 203-00085-01(1).
74 Prime Minister U Nu's banquet speech, *Xinhua Monthly*, No. 1, 1955.
75 Richard Butwell, *U Nu of Burma*, Stanford: Stanford University Press, 1963, p. 177.
76 Record of Chairman Mao Tsetung's talk, AMFA, File No. 105-00339-01(1).
77 Abstract of Burmese Prime Minister U Nu's speech, AMFA, File No. 105-00814-01(1).

in order before inviting guests." That year also saw the shift in Sino-Burmese relations. However, Burma's fear and distrust of China, reflected in the early period after the establishment of diplomatic relations, did not disappear; it continued throughout the Cold War, although its quality differed at various stages in the two country's relations.

2

China–Burma Ties in 1954: The Beginning of the Pauk Phaw Era

rom 1954, Beijing and Rangoon began to have closer relations and more frequent contacts. Sino-Burmese relations entered the friendly *Pauk Phaw* (fraternal) era until China's Cultural Revolution spilled over into Burmese territory in 1967. The shift in relations in 1954 was due to a complex of bilateral, systemic, and dynamic factors coupled with strong personal influences. China changed its overall foreign policy, but particularly its policy toward Burma. Rangoon actively responded to Beijing's change.

This process was speeded up through the personal rapport that was established by the leaders on both sides, but especially by U Nu and Zhou Enlai. The amelioration of suspicions between the two states may have eventually occurred, but it seems evident that it would have taken considerably longer to do so without this personal empathy; the generic shift in Chinese policy did not resolve the outstanding and consequential issues facing the two states, which were finally settled much later. This chapter focuses on the manifestations, the causes, and the impact of the changed relations. The turn in 1954 basically consisted of two dimensions: diplomatic-political and economic relations.

International Factors

The United States's perennial policy in Asia is characterized by preventing the rise of any hegemonic power in the region. A fear of the Sino-Soviet bloc and its expansion was caused by the Chinese role in Korea, Tibet, and Vietnam, and in the potential of the overseas Chinese communities in Southeast Asia. Communist insurrections had begun in Burma, Malaya, and the Philippines. In the early 1950s, the U.S. responded by establishing military bases in the region, increasing U.S. troop numbers in the countries around China, signing a series of military treaties with China's neighboring countries, and forming what was perceived in China as a military encirclement against that country. These instruments included the Thailand–U.S. Military Assistance Agreement (17 October

1950), the Philippines–U.S. Mutual Defense Treaty (30 August 1951), the Korea–U.S. Mutual Defense Treaty (1 October 1953), the U.S.–Taiwan Mutual Defense Treaty (2 December 1954), the U.S.–Japan Mutual Defense Assistance Agreement (8 March 1954), and the Manila Pact (8 September 1954).

Zhou Enlai delivered the "Report on the Work of the Government at the First Session of the First National People's Congress" on 23 September 1954, in which he stated: "In order to build a prosperous socialist industrialized country, we need a peaceful environment and a peaceful world. Therefore, we should strengthen and develop unity and collaboration with the Soviet Union as well as other socialist countries, and attach importance to the peaceful collaboration and the promotion of economic and cultural ties with all countries, particularly Southeast Asian and other neighboring countries."[1] Beijing therefore made efforts to break out of U.S. encirclement, and sought support from Asian and African countries, particularly those on its periphery. These efforts became the main mission of China's diplomacy after the Korean War ceasefire. To this end, Zhou encouraged the formation and enlargement of the "area of peace," composed of such countries as Burma, Cambodia, Ceylon, India, Indonesia, and Nepal. In contrast to the initial negative communist attitude towards the "neutral forces," Zhou stressed the importance of the "uncommitted countries" and devoted much attention to their growing role in fortifying "the international forces of peace."[2]

China's Policy Toward Burma

When the CCP seized power in 1949, Beijing pursued a foreign policy of "leaning to one side" and insisted that the world was divided into two antagonistic camps, and it was impossible for neutralism to exist between them.[3] All non-socialist nations were classified as "stooges" or "running dogs" of imperialism. However, both domestic needs and the international environment in the early 1950s impelled Beijing to alter its black and white, with us or against us, conception of world politics, and to begin to stress national interests in its foreign policy. "In the development of foreign relations Chinese policy shifted gradually away from attempting to drive Western influence out of Asia by direct confrontation or unequivocal support for revolutionary wars, and toward efforts

---

1   Song Enfan and Li Jiasong (eds), *Chronology of the PRC's Foreign Affairs*, Vol. I, Beijing: World Affairs Press, 1997, p. 159.
2   Kuo-kang Shao, "Chou Enlai's Diplomatic Approach to Non-Aligned States in Asia: 1953–60", *The China Quarterly*, No. 78, June 1979, p. 326.
3   Liu Shaoqi, *Internationalism and Nationalism*, p. 25.

to win Asian neighbors away from alliances with the West through offers of peaceful coexistence."[4]

In 1952, Zhou Enlai spelled out that policy with respect to neutral countries, "We can't be hostile to them and push them into the enemy's camp. We can make friends with them." Policies toward the nationalist countries in Southeast Asia that had established diplomatic relations with Beijing changed. "We will try for their neutral stance at war, and at peace make them keep imperialism at arm's length."[5]

In 1954, China's new foreign policy was formed, focusing on breaking through the U.S.'s containment and encirclement, uniting all countries that wished to maintain peace with China, and creating a peaceful, stable regional environment for its domestic economic development and recovery. The new policy was characterized by building "collective peace and security" and expanding a "peaceful area" in order to form a safe buffer zone between China and the West. "This new course in Peking's foreign policy was apparently directed by three major considerations: first, the enhancement of China's national security; second, the need for diplomatic flexibility; and third, Beijing's quest for major power status."[6] "To achieve these ends Beijing would respect the concept of non-alignment as a legitimate approach to Cold War issues."[7]

On 8 July 1954, Mao Tsetung gave 11 instructions on China's diplomacy which included: "Begin to establish a Southeast Asian peace zone, effect and develop cooperation in the zone, and sign non-aggression pacts or collective peace treaties"; "unite all peaceful forces (including government), isolate and split up U.S. [interests]"; "International Peace and United Front."[8]

In August 1954, Zhou Enlai spoke at the 33rd session of the central government that it was necessary to insist on and carry out the "Peaceful Coexistence Five Principles". "We believe ... to establish more and broader peace zones in Asia so that these areas won't become the hothouse where the U.S. invader

4   Peter Van Ness, *Revolution and Chinese Foreign Policy*, Los Angeles and London: University of California Press, 1970, p. 12.
5   *Selected Diplomatic Writings of Zhou Enlai*, pp. 52–54.
6   Kuo-kong Show, "Communist China's Foreign Policy toward the Non-aligned States with Special Reference to India and Burma, 1949–1962", University of Pennsylvania, Ph.D. dissertation, 1972, p. 37.
7   Kuo-kang Shao, "Zhou Enlai's Diplomatic Approach", p. 324.
8   CCCPC Party Literature Research Office, *Biography of Mao Tsetung: 1949–1976*, Vol. 1, Beijing: Central Party Literature Press, 2003, pp. 562–563.

group wages war and organizes military groups. This central government will strive for Asian collective peace in the light of this guideline."[9]

The shift in China–Burma relations in 1954 was one of the results of this changed foreign policy – a logical approach of seeking a peripheral environment featuring peace and security for Beijing. On 2 December 1954, Zhou Enlai claimed that, together with Burma, China "will struggle to implement the 'Peaceful Coexistence Five Principles', establish and expand a peaceful zone, and maintain Asia and World peace."[10] In addition, the communique released during U Nu's visit to Beijing in 1954 stipulated that "The two countries' premiers expressed deep concern over strengthening and expanding the peaceful area."[11] The Chinese appeal for an "Asia Peace Zone," however, obviously could not be implemented without Rangoon's interaction and support.

Burma's Policy Toward China

By 1954, Burma had gradually formulated a neutralist and non-alignment foreign policy. A clear policy on non-alignment was not evident in the early years after independence; Burma was simply groping in the dark.[12] Rangoon's determination and formation of its policy were affected by multiple factors. At the end of 1950, the People's Liberation Army (PLA) entered both Tibet and the Korean War. The Burmese viewed these violent Chinese actions as potentially dangerous. "The experience of Korea convinced them that they would have to avoid at almost any cost the possibility of becoming a battlefield for the Western Nations – Communist conflict."[13] On 8 March 1951, Prime Minister U Nu reaffirmed his government's determination to adhere to its policy of neutrality. By the beginning of 1951, both Burma and India had definitely perceived the necessity of friendship with China, which had cast its shadow over Asia.[14] Consequently, U Nu explained the reasons for Burmese neutralism: Burma

---

9   Zhou Enlai's Report on Diplomacy at the 33rd Session of Central People's Government Committee (11 August 1954), File No. 206-Y0037, in Bureau of Archives, Ministry of Foreign Affairs, PRC (ed.), *Selected Diplomatic Documents of the PRC: Geneva Conference 1954*, Vol. 1, Beijing: World Knowledge Press, 2006, p. 495.
10 Premier Zhou Enlai's speech at the banquet for Prime Minister U Nu, *Xinhua Monthly*, No. 1, 1955.
11 Communiqué of the premiers of China and Burma, *Xinhua Monthly*, No. 1, 1955.
12 B. Pakem, *India Burma Relations*. New Delhi: Omsons Publications, 1992, p. 29.
13 M. D. Stephens, "The Sino-Burmese Border Agreement", *Asian Review*, Vol. LIX, No. 217, January 1963, p. 49.
14 Uma Shankar Singh, *Burma and India, 1949–1962: A Study in the Foreign Policies of Burma and India and Burma's Policy towards India*, New Delhi, Bombay, Calcutta: Oxford and IBH Publishing Co., 1979, p. 164.

was located in the sphere of influence of two rival camps; Burma's military and economic powers were weak; it needed to defend itself.[15] China was a primary factor in Burmese policy formulation. "Burma's non-alignment is primarily to assure China of non-aggression from Burmese soil and to avoid the destruction of Burma in another war."[16] "Fear of antagonizing China has also been at least partially responsible for Burma's policy of neutralism."[17]

After KMT troops, which had been defeated and driven from the mainland, fled to Burma, Rangoon unsuccessfully attempted to resolve the problem through U.N. channels. Because of U.S. actions, the KMT issue was not only not effectively resolved, but became more serious. By 1953, KMT troops in Burma had became more powerful with the support of Taiwan and the U.S., and its threat to Burma's national security was more dangerous. The Burmese feared Beijing might use the presence of the KMT forces as an excuse to invade Burma. In 1952, the PLA crossed the disputed border, the so-called "1941 Line," into Burma to annihilate the KMT forces. Hence, the Burmese had good reasons to worry.

"The result of this experience in the United Nations was to make most Burmese leaders feel that their original hopes that membership in the United Nations offered a small nation like theirs protection against outside interference were changed . . . It was also quite apparent after Burma's disillusionment with the United Nations, as a protector of the security of small states as shown in the case of the handling of the KMT issue by this body, that the Burmese government began to move towards closer friendly relations with Communist China."[18] At the same time, Beijing also soothed Rangoon's anxieties. China offered assurances that so long as adequate steps were being taken against the KMT troops, the issue would not be a cause of trouble between the two states.[19] China's forbearance on the KMT issue in Burma created a favorable impression in Rangoon; the Burmese saw the possibility of friendly relations with its northern neighbor. "China's attitude on the matter was one designed to indicate that it only harbored peaceful intentions and friendly feelings toward

15 U Nu, "Burma's Neutral Policy", *Burma*, January 1955, Vol. V, No. 2, p. 1.
16 David Wen-wei Chang, "A Comparative Study of Neutralism of India, Burma and Indonesia", University of Illinois, Ph.D. dissertation, 1960, p. 122.
17 John Seabury Thomson, "Burma: A Neutral in China's Shadow", *Review of Politics*, Vol. 19, No. 3, 1957, p. 336. For other similar arguments, see Jerry Rose, "Burma and the Balance of Neutralism." *The Reporter*, XXVIII, No. 1, 3 January 1963, p. 24; Johnstone, *Burma's Foreign Policy*, p. 164; Frank Trager, "Burma and China", *Journal of Southeast Asian History*, Vol. 5, No. 1, March 1964, p. 61.
18 Singh, *Burma and India*, pp. 171–172.
19 Panikkar, *In Two Chinas*, p. 169.

Burma and this undoubtedly had the effect of making the Burmese government more receptive to the 'peace offensive' that was launched in 1954."[20]

Furthermore, India and Burma had established cordial relations, and the two countries' leadership often consulted on world affairs. New Delhi had developed a non-alignment foreign policy and took a friendly attitude toward Beijing. These had important impacts on Burmese diplomacy. Also, internally the communists and the left-wing socialist elements within Burma forced the U Nu government to appear non-aligned.

Rangoon gradually transmitted more gestures of goodwill to Beijing between 1951 and 1953, such as the vote on China in the U.N. during the Korean War, approving private shipments of rubber to China, and supporting the PRC's seat in the U.N.[21] "On the part of Burma, [efforts] to please Communist China had become quite unmistakable by the middle of 1953."[22]

Rangoon's and Delhi's attitudes toward Beijing's actions in the Korean War also pushed China to reorient its policy to win the support of those nationalist governments and employ their neutrality in world politics. Rangoon and Delhi refused to join in branding China as an aggressor in Korea in January 1951. In the same year, Burma, India, and some other Asian–African countries abstained on the U.N. resolution on a strategic war materials embargo against China. Additionally, a Burmese private company exported some rubber to China during the Korean War although its volume was modest.[23] As Burma and India adopted policies different from the West, Beijing re-evaluated the position of neutral countries and now considered them as part of the united front.

As China gradually adjusted its policy toward neutral countries, the Soviet Union's position on those countries further drove changes in Beijing's policy toward Burma. After Stalin's death in March 1953, Moscow began to seek detente with the West and rethink its relationships with Asian neutral countries. Russian leaders emphasized "peaceful coexistence" and peaceful competition between communist and non-communist countries.

Burma responded positively as the CCP devised these new tactics. Thus, a new prospect in Sino-Burmese ties opened in 1954. Although bilateral

---

20 Robert Alexander Holmes, "Chinese Foreign Policy Toward Burma and Cambodia: A Comparative Analysis", Columbia University Ph.D. dissertation, 1969, pp. 15–16.
21 During this period, for detail of how Rangoon pleased Beijing see Shen-Yu Dai, "Peking and Rangoon", *The China Quarterly*, No. 5, January–March 1961, p. 135.
22 *Ibid.*, pp. 134–135.
23 Xu Simin, *An Overseas Chinese Experience: The Memoir of Xu Simin*, Hong Kong: The Mirror Post Cultural Enterprises Co. Ltd, 1981, pp. 100–102.

relations fluctuated in the succeeding twelve years, both resolved the problems of the border dispute, the KMT troops, and the dual nationality of overseas Chinese. Burma became one of the closest partners of China in Asia.

Personalized Political Relations in 1954

The transformation of bilateral relations, or at least its timing, was in large part due to the personal efforts and relationship between Zhou Enlai and U Nu. Mutual suspicion had haunted early relations. The change began symbolically with the exchange of visits between the two premiers, after which China–Burma relations improved. U Nu indicated, "China–Burma amity had not been established until my good friend Premier Zhou Enlai's first trip to Rangoon [in 1954] ... Before Premier Zhou Enlai visited Rangoon, I should admit that there were some misgivings between the two countries peoples. On Burma's side, many had a feeling of fear about whether China would subvert Burma's government."[24] "When China was founded in 1949, our two countries' relations were not friendly. Because China's Premier visited Burma and I visited China, understanding between us increased. Based on this new understanding, we issued a statement supporting the famous 'Five Principles'. We signed economic and trade agreements, and cultural delegations visited each other. "[25]

In 1954, both sides consulted and exchanged views on the issues disturbing Sino-Burmese relations, and jointly advocated the "Peaceful Coexistence Five Principles," and took them as the "rudder of China–Burma relations."[26] Zhou's trip to Rangoon ended with a joint statement. U Nu said that "Your visit and our joint statement greatly promoted more understanding between [our] two countries."[27] "In the beginning, notwithstanding, we were still suspicious of China's intentions." However, Premier Zhou's visit and the announcement of the 'Five Principles' "assuaged the tension."[28] Zhou agreed with U Nu, and said, "When two neighboring and newly founded countries with different political systems begin contact, it is natural that both fear and misunderstand each other ... These apprehensions, nevertheless, were gradually allayed" because of the two premiers' exchange visits and the establishment of the "Five Principles".[29]

24 Premier Zhou Enlai hosts Prime Minister U Nu in Kunming, *Xinhua Semi-Monthly*, No. 9, 1957, p. 56.
25 Abstract of Burmese statesman U Nu's Speech (10 a.m., 13 October 1955), AMFA, File No. 105-00446-04.
26 Joint statement of the premiers of China and Burma, *Xinhua Monthly*, No. 7, 1954.
27 Burmese Prime Minister U Nu's letter to Premier Zhou Enlai on the distorted coverage by Burma's press of the China–Burma joint statement, AMFA, File No. 105-00037-01(1).
28 Prime Minister U Nu's banquet speech, *Xinhua Monthly*, No. 1, 1955.
29 Premier Zhou Enlai's speech at farewell banquet, *Xinhua Monthly*, No. 1, 1955.

More importantly, both parties worked on how to implement these "Five Principles", and reached a three-point consensus on issues of common interest. First, contact between the two countries' leaders increased understanding and confidence in developing bilateral relations. When the CCP and the AFPFL came into power for the first time, both lacked diplomatic experience, and both were prejudiced against each other. Before 1954, the CCP thought the Burmese leaders were the proletariat's enemy.[30] Burma feared the CCP's leaders were like Hitler,[31] and was afraid that Zhou Enlai was a cocky, irascible, and tricky statesman.[32] U Nu articulated his psychological status before and after his trip to Beijing in 1954. "When I reached Beijing just now, I had some apprehensions ... [However] Our apprehensions disappeared after the visit of eleven days."[33] U Nu's discourse may have sounded simply like diplomatic parlance, but it was direct and candid on a range of issues.

In December 1954, Mao Tsetung met U Nu when he visited Beijing, and praised his visit to China. Mao said that China wanted to establish diplomatic ties with Thailand. Nevertheless, "Thailand said it was afraid that China could invade it, but Burma also feared such an invasion. However, Burma uses the means of developing friendly relations with us, and comes here to find out whether we will invade it. And yet, Thailand is even reluctant to come to China to have a look. If you have suspicion and dissatisfaction, you can speak out."[34] During the same meeting, U Nu also admitted that, "In the past, we dared not say what we wanted to say, fearing that you would mistake us as the U.K.'s and U.S.'s lackey, and that our opposition parties in Burma would report such conditions to you. However, after we met each other now, and discussed issues and understood each other, we won't be afraid to speak straightforwardly any longer. This is the most significant achievement of my trip to China."[35]

Moreover, Zhou Enlai's distinct personal charm impressed the Burmese who feared China, and increased the Burmese leadership's favorable impressions. For example, after Zhou's trip to Rangoon, some Burmese felt that "Premier Zhou is young and graceful," respected Burmese traditional customs, and "is adept at

30 "Burmese People's Struggle", *People's Daily*, 10 May 1948.
31 *Works of Mao Tsetung*, Vol. 6, p. 382.
32 Yunnan Institute (ed.), *Documents on the History of China–Burma Friendship*, p. 5.
33 Prime Minister U Nu's speech at farewell banquet, *Xinhua Monthly*, No. 1, 1955.
34 *Works of Mao Tsetung*, Vol. 6, pp. 377–379.
35 *Ibid.*, p. 379. There was, however, significant differences between U Nu and the Burmese military, which had determined that China was Burma's only potential enemy. See David Steinberg, "Burma and Lessons from the Hungarian Revolution", *Irrawaddy*, October 2006.

diplomacy and is a statesman."[36] "His behavior shows that he is a Premier not of a power but of a fraternal country. Premier Zhou's attitude removed our wrong guesses in half an hour. Since then, we completely believe: if a Premier treats a small country so modestly and hospitably, the country and people which he governs will be even more generous and hospitable."[37] In regard to the effect of Zhou's visit to Burma, U Nu wrote to Zhou that "For you as an individual, for the whole of China, you have made a wide circle of friends here."[38]

Second, Burma made promises on the issues about which China was worried, allaying Beijing's suspicions. Beijing had entered the Korean and Indochina wars, and the U.S. and its allies in Asia had countered by trying to contain China. China's security situation on its periphery had increasingly worsened. Consequently, if Burma joined the West, China believed its southwest security would be endangered. The economic agreement signed by Burma and U.S. in 1950 had caused Beijing to worry. During U Nu's first visit to Beijing in 1954, he especially mentioned the issue. "Although Burma has no ability to interfere in China's internal affairs by itself, it is able to damage China if it allows itself to be an underling of China's enemies ... We could provide some vital locations which could be used as navy and air force strategic bases to launch attacks on the PRC. We could also facilitate China's enemies' espionage and subversion in China."[39] U Nu gave Beijing his promises regarding those possibilities that "Through fair and foul, we by no means will become the underling of any country ... We in no case will do anything to jeopardize peace.[Burma] at no time will accept unilateral aid which [might] lead to suspicion between the two countries, and in fact never had thoughts of accepting such aid. We won't adopt any demarche causing China's apprehension at the instigation of other some country."[40]

Third, China partly assuaged Rangoon's fear and suspicion. Before Zhou Enlai visited Burma, Rangoon was worried that Beijing was exporting revolution and subverting the Burmese regime largely because of the CCP's attitude toward the BCP and Burma's civil war. In 1954, however, Zhou Enlai claimed in Rangoon that "Revolution cannot be exported. If tried, there is no chance of success. Communist parties of various countries win out only by themselves."[41]

---

36 Responses by Burmese officials and media to Premier Zhou Enlai's visit to Burma, AMFA, File No. 105-00259-03(1).
37 Prime Minister U Nu's banquet speech, *Xinhua Monthly*, No. 1, 1955.
38 Burmese Prime Minister U Nu's letter to Premier Zhou on the distorted coverage, AMFA, File No. 105-00037-01(1).
39 Prime Minister U Nu's speech at farewell banquet, *Xinhua Monthly*, No. 1, 1955.
40 *Ibid.*
41 *Chronicle of Zhou Enlai: 1949–1976*, Vol. 1, Beijing: Central Party Literature Press, 1997, p. 393.

Zhou's Rangoon speech on the Communist Party's "Export of Revolution" had special significance for the Burmese. Furthermore, the ad hoc joint statement issued by the two countries' premiers during Zhou's visit to Burma stressed that "The two premiers restated: every country's people have the right of choosing its state system and lifestyle, and other countries should not interfere in the choice. Revolution cannot be exported. Also, the common volition of the people in one country should not suffer foreign interference."[42]

Burma's turbulent situation after independence, various insurrections, and the possibility of external interference concerned China, but Mao Tsetung told U Nu in Beijing in December,

> We wish for peace in Burma. Concerning how you acquire that peace, you need to deal with it yourself... Each country solves its problem by itself... Each country has several kinds of parties. With respect to these parties, we can't allege to oppose or support any party. The counterpart with which we negotiate must be each country's government. We won't invade Burma as the U.S. interfered in the Guatemalan revolution. We won't move fighting forces into Burma, and our Ambassador, Yao Zhongming, meanwhile, will not act undercover in Burma. Yao will in no case do this. If he does, we will by all means immediately dismiss him from his post.[43]

During the Cold War, the populous overseas Chinese in Southeast Asia were regarded as a potential "fifth column." Although the population of the overseas Chinese in Burma was not large compared with those in some other Southeast Asian states, Rangoon still worried about the issue of the Chinese and their indoctrination through the Chinese school system. Burmese fear focused on their potential political role and "dual nationality." Therefore, Mao pledged that "We won't establish Communist parties in the overseas Chinese communities, and its branches have been closed. We have done so in Indonesia and Singapore. We have enjoined the overseas Chinese not to undertake political activities in Burma. They can only participate in activities permitted by Burma's government, such as celebrations ... There are some radicals in the Burmese overseas Chinese community, and we have persuaded them not to interfere in Burma's internal affairs. We have instructed them to abide by Burma's law, and we don't have contacts with Burmese opposition parties fighting againsrt Burma's government."[44]

---

42 Joint statement of the premiers of China and Burma, *Xinhua Monthly*, No. 7, 1954.
43 *Works of Mao Tsetung*, Vol. 6, pp. 374–376.
44 *Ibid.*, pp. 376–377.

Mao's promise on overseas Chinese issues was affirmed by the China–Burma communique in December 1954. It stated that overseas Chinese should "respect the laws and social customs in Burma, and should not participate in local political activities ... Concerning the issue of [the former] colony's nationality, the two countries' governments will negotiate it through normal diplomatic channels as soon as possible."[45]

When U Nu visited China, the two premiers, after consultations, thought it was necessary to establish consulate-generals in each other's major cities. In fact, this suggestion was also a step in assuaging Burmese apprehension about China. Mao explained that, "In the past, Burma thought Yunnan dark, and didn't know how many troops Beijing had stationed there, or what Chinese trick was being aimed at Burma. Burma fears us very much. So we have suggested that Burma establish a consulate general in Yunnan to watch us."[46]

Economic Relations in 1954

Like Sino-Burmese political relations, economic ties also shifted in 1954. On 22 Apri 1954, China and Burma signed the first economic trade agreement (valid for three years). According to the agreement, China would export coal, silk, silk fabrics, cotton fabrics, paper, agricultural implements, light industry products, handicrafts, porcelain enamel, porcelain, canned food, tea, and cigarettes to Burma. Burma would export rice, rice products, pulse seedcake, minerals, timber, rubber, and cotton to China.[47] On 3 November 1954, both signed a goods exchange protocol on Burmese rice and Chinese commodities, and a contract in which China bought 150,000 long tons of Burmese rice.

In addition, U Nu's first trip to Beijing promoted bilateral economic relations. After negotiations, "Both premiers think that it is necessary to open China–Burma airline [traffic], resume road traffic, and conclude postal agreements. In order to develop the trade between the two countries, the two premiers agree that China will annually import 150,000–200,000 long tons of rice from Burma from 1955 to 1957; during the same period, Burma will import industrial equipment and daily necessities from China."[48]

Although the amount, value, and categories involved in the 1954 trade agreement and contract were not significant in the two countries' total foreign trade, it symbolized a change of attitude. The 1954 shift in the China–Burma

45   "Joint Communique of China and Burma's Premiers", *People's Daily*, 13 December 1954.
46   Record of Chairman Mao Tsetung's talk, AMFA, File No. 105-00339-01(1).
47   "China and Burma Sign Trade Agreement Valid for Three Years", *People's Daily*, 23 April 1954.
48   "Joint Communique of China and Burma's Premiers", *People's Daily*, 13 December 1954.

economic nexus was further strengthened in subsequent years. The trade value between the two countries in 1955 increased by 30 times over 1954, and 44 percent in 1956.

The 1954 change in China–Burma economic ties was attributable not only to the promotion of political relations, but also to trade as a political lever. At that time, the quality of both countries' economy and industrialization was backward, but China still had some comparative advantages over Burma. Consequently, in respect of China–Burma bilateral trade, "The needs of Burma's production and life can easily be met by our country's exports while Burma's export commodities are inconsistent with China's import requirements."[49]

In October 1954, when Zhou Enlai met Burma's foreign trade delegation in Beijing, he remarked that "Henceforth, we are prepared to meet Burma's import needs, and hope that Burma can list the needed goods … In the following two years, if China–Burma trade cannot balance, we are willing to trade using cash with special funds. This method is special in our foreign trade because we ordinarily swap [barter]."[50] Zhou's promise clearly showed that China was taking advantage of trade to promote political relations. The case in point was the rice trade between the two countries.

Rice was vital to Burma's economy. However, "Rice is also one of China's staple export goods; it is impossible to buy a great deal of Burma's rice with foreign exchange. Only when Burma urgently asks us to buy its rice, can we consider buying some rice in order to do a favor and help Burma out of difficulty."[51] China's Vice Minister of Foreign Affairs, Zhang Wentian, stressed the significance of promoting economic relations with Asian countries at the session of China's Ambassadors to Asian countries in 1956. "Because we are a power, at times we don't need some goods such as Burma's rice, but we still buy a bit."[52]

In December 1954, the memorandum that U Nu gave to China's counterpart mentioned that "The contract of ordering 200,000 tons of 1953 Burma rice was signed by two countries' government on 3 November 1954. About the rice produced in 1953, we are also not sure whether it is edible. So China needs to dispatch investigators to Rangoon to 'very carefully inspect' it."[53]

---

49 Review by Chinese Embassy to Burma of Sino-Burmese economic ties in the past decade, AMFA, File No. 105-00603-01.

50 Account of Premier Zhou Enlai's meeting with a Burmese delegation, AMFA, File No. 105-00130-01(1).

51 Review of Sino-Burmese economic ties, AMFA, File No. 105-00603-01.

52 *Chronicle of Zhang Wentian: 1942–1976*, Vol. 2, Beijing: CCP History Press, 2000, p. 1021.

53 Burmese Prime Minister U Nu's letter to Premier Zhou Enlai about the China–Burma rice trade, AMFA, File No. 105-00036-01(1).

Beijing's intention of promoting bilateral ties through the rice trade was self-evident.

Rangoon applauded Beijing's goodwill on the rice trade, and U Nu publicly praised it many times. On 2 December 1954, U Nu stated in Beijing that "There is a great deal of surplus rice. Without buyers, we will be caught in a dilemma. Meanwhile, due to war destruction, my country's economy is backward. If the rice can't be sold, it will undermine Burma's economic base." Concerning China's purchase of Burmese rice, "We think the generous action is a friendly illustration."[54]

In the same year, U Nu remarked at the ceremony of Burma's National Day that China was buying Burma's rice in order to help Burma. "Actually, the New China has surplus rice to export, but considering Burma's rice market, China has taken these exciting steps. And the profit that Burma has got from China has exceeded Rangoon's original hopes."[55] This was significant for Burma, because Burmese economic planning had been premised on the high export price for rice because of the Korean War, but Burma's implementation of its economic planning staggered when the price declined.

---

54 Yunnan Institute (ed.), *Documents on the History of China–Burma Friendship*, p. 7.
55 "Premier U Nu's Report at the National Day Meeting", (Rangoon) *China's Daily*, 22 November 1954.

3

The Honeymoon Period: 1955–1966

For Friends in Burma

I live by the river's head.	*You live by its tail.*
Limitlessly, we love each other.	*We drink the same river's water.*
I drink from the upper flows.	*You drink from below.*
Endlessly the river flows.	*We share everlasting happiness.*
We are neighbors.	*Our friendship lasts.*
Like the ageless evergreen.	*The waters flow forever.*
Our lands are connected.	*At the mountain's foot, beside the same river*
Anti-imperialism begets freedom.	*We are peacefully united.*
We are paukphaw.	*Our languages are connected.*
We are united and help each other.	*Peace is powerful*
Living by the rivers, we praise their breadth	*Climbing the mountains, we sing of their majesty.*
The mountains face north.	*The river flows south.*

Chen Yi , 1956

A decade-long honeymoon followed the shift from suspicion to friendship in the China–Burma nexus in 1954. Chinese media and scholars usually described the close relations by quoting Chen Yi's poem *For Friends in Burma*. Beijing's honeymoon with Rangoon until 1966, however, also verified a Chinese proverb: things always reverse themselves after reaching a climax. After Sino-Burmese relations reached their peak in 1960–61, subsequent important changes in the domestic political situation and foreign policy in the two countries signaled that this honeymoon period would end. Strains in China's relations with Burma increased after 1962 under the new military regime in Rangoon.

World events after 1954 played their part in the improvement in Sino-Burmese relations. The emergence of the non-aligned movement and the Bandung Conference, in which both China and Burma played important

Plate 4: Border near Namkham, China. Statuary illustrating poem 'For Friends in Burma' (photograph David Steinberg)

roles; the Hungarian Revolution of 1956; the Chinese invasion of Tibet; the Indo-Pakistan War; the Sino-Indian War of 1962; and the development of the Sino-Soviet split, including these two powers vying for influence in Burma – all contributed to both sides' realization that the sore points of contact needed to be resolved.

The U Nu Period

One of Beijing's fundamental foreign policy objectives toward its periphery, prior to China's foreign policy shift to radicalism in the mid-1960s Cultural Revolution, was to construct "collective peace and security," expand "peaceful regions" in Asia, and recruit Burma into its united front as a buffer in its confrontation with the West – and even as a means of limiting the American containment and isolation of China.

After the establishment of diplomatic relations in 1950, however, Sino-Burmese relations faced four major problems: (1) the overseas Chinese issue, (2) the Burma–China boundary dispute, (3) the KMT troops in Burma, and (4) the BCP issue. The settlement of these four issues had a direct bearing on whether Beijing could realize its fundamental objectives in Burma.

The Overseas Chinese Issue

The first Chinese Nationality Law was promulgated in 1909. It operated on the basis of *jus sanguinis* – all Chinese anywhere were regarded as citizens of China alone.[1] Tsai noted that toward the end of the Qing Dynasty Chinese opposition to "*jus soli* alone affords ample material for conflicts between states."[2] China did not recognize dual citizenship until Beijing and Jakarta signed the Sino–Indonesian Dual Nationality Treaty in 1955.

During the Cold War, the overseas Chinese in Southeast Asian countries were regarded by the West with suspicion – potentially to be used by China for subversion and expansion. The issue of Chinese nationality and treatment created tensions between China and some Southeast Asian states, and their resolution had been an issue after World War II.[3] Although the population of the overseas Chinese in Burma was relatively small, the Burmese government still regarded the Chinese with vigilance in varying degrees at different times and on different issues. The Burmese were especially concerned about their political activities. The Chinese, in addition, had important commercial roles in Burma throughout the country, so they could not be ignored.

In the early 1950s, there were said to be some 350,000 overseas Chinese in Burma, according to the Chinese Embassy in Rangoon.[4] In light of the Nationality Law and the provisions of the two countries, they included: (1) about 140,000 Sino-Burmese of "mixed blood," or 39 percent,[5] who, according to Burmese provisions, should have had Burmese citizenship; (2) about 120,000 Chinese, or 33 percent, born in Burma. Two-thirds of the locally-born Chinese were second or earlier generation and could have had Burmese citizenship as it was supposedly automatic. Those of the first generation might apply for citizenship;[6] 260,000 of them might have dual nationality, accounting for 74 percent of the total.

1   "Law on the Acquisition and Loss of Chinese Nationality," *The American Journal of International Law*, Vol 4, No. 2, Supplement: Official Documents, 1910, pp. 160–166.

2   Tsai Chutung, "The Chinese Nationality Law, 1909", *The American Journal of International Law*, Vol. 4, No. 2, 1910, pp. 408–409.

3   George Pukung Jan, "Nationality and Treatment of Overseas Chinese in Southeast Asia," New York University, Ph.D. Dissertation, 1960, p. 215.

4   *Reference Material of Overseas Chinese Population*, Research Association of Overseas Chinese, 1956, p. 75.

5   During British rule, marriage between Chinese and Burmese, particularly between Chinese men and Burmese women, was the most common form of intermarriage. (See, Ikeya Chie, "The Modern Burmese Woman and the Politics of Fashion in Colonial Burma," *The Journal of Asian Studies*, 67:4, 2008, p. 1299.) "When a Chinese marries a Burmese wife, the daughters usually receive Burmese names and wear Burmese dresses and are regarded as Burmese, while the sons are regarded as Chinese." (see M. B. Hooker, "The 'Chinese Confucian' and 'Chinese Buddhist' in British Burma, 1881–1947", *Journal of Southeast Asian Studies*, 17 September 1990, Vol. XXI, No. 2, p. 395. So the actual number of Sino-Burmese is vastly underestimated but unknown.

6   *Introduction on [the] Overseas Chinese Condition*, Office of Overseas Chinese Affairs Commission, 1963, p. 25. The law was changed in Burma in 1982, giving Chinese and other foreigners "associate citizenship," with less rights.

During U Nu's first visit to China in December 1954, he expressed Burmese concerns over the Chinese nationality question, and wished that it could be solved as soon as possible.[7] On 13 October 1955, U Hla Maung, Burmese Ambassador to China, inquired whether China would approve of the renunciation of Chinese nationality by the overseas Chinese who had attained Burmese citizenship. Burma, however, was ready to negotiate with China on dual nationality.[8] In response to Burma's request, China drafted a joint communique and was ready to accept dual nationality.[9] China, however, later changed its mind, holding that the Burmese government was really intending to reach only a partial agreement on the overseas Chinese question, either by continuing negotiations or dragging them on.[10] Therefore, China did not respond to Burma's request and no negotiations took place. In spite of this, China was positively disposed toward the overseas Chinese attaining Burmese nationality: "Given that the acquiring of Burmese nationality was beneficial to our country both politically and economically, a policy should be adopted to encourage a large number of overseas Chinese to acquire Burmese nationality."[11]

When meeting with the Burmese Ambassador to China on 22 June 1956, Zhou Enlai said, "China endorses [the concept] that the overseas Chinese who were born in their host countries and are willing to stay there could acquire the nationality of their residence countries."[12] Zhou's posture meant that China accepted the Burmese government's plan to give citizenship to eligible overseas Chinese. At the welcoming meeting hosted by local overseas Chinese on 18 December 1956, Zhou Enlai explicitly stated to the overseas Chinese and Burmese that it was good that some overseas Chinese who had long stayed in Burma should become Burmese citizens as long as they made the choice voluntarily, and they no longer held Chinese citizenship.[13]

That the overseas Chinese did not become an obstacle to Sino-Burmese friendship was due to their relatively small population, a high level of assimilation, and good ethnic relations, unlike their counterparts in Indonesia, Malaysia, and some

7   "Joint Communiqué of China's and Burma's Premier", *People's Daily*, 13 December 1954.
8   Speech notes for Foreign Minister Zhang Hanfu and Burmese Ambassador to China U Hla Maung (10:30 a.m. on 13 October 1955), AMFA, File No. 105-00175-03(1).
9   Instructions and additional comments on the nationality problems facing Overseas Chinese in Burma, AMFA, File No. 105-00510-03(1).
10 Files on dual nationality of Overseas Chinese in Burma compiled by the Asian Affairs Department of the Ministry of Foreign Affairs, AMFA, File No. 105-00510-10(1).
11 *Ibid.*
12 Summary of discussion between Premier Zhou Enlai and Burmese Ambassador to China U Hla Maung (22 June 1956), AMFA, File No. 105-00307-02(1).
13 Speech of Premier Zhou Enlai at the welcoming ceremony by Overseas Chinese in Rangoon, Burma, AMFA, File No. 105-00510-08(1).

other Southeast Asian countries, where religious differences were a factor in their lack of assimilation. In the early 1950s, there were some 140,000 Sino-Burmese, and a second generation of about 80,000 of their descendents. According to Burma's Citizenship Act, the government could naturally grant Burmese nationality to these 220,000 Chinese, and China also approved of this approach.

Since the first high-level mutual visits in 1954, China had made clear its position on the overseas Chinese political role: China would not use the overseas Chinese to interfere in Burmese internal affairs and subvert Burmese state power.[14] In the early 1950s, China disbanded the Democratic League of China and China's Communist Party in Burma. At the welcoming meeting held by the Rangoon Chinese community on 18 December 1956, Zhou Enlai further articulated that: "The overseas Chinese should be law-abiding and exemplary residents in Burma. Those who have obtained Burmese nationality should politically distinguish themselves from those who haven't. The former are not to be admitted into the overseas Chinese organizations and the latter are not to engage in Burmese political activities. The Chinese are not allowed to join Burmese parties, or take part in elections and all other political activities. They should stay away from these ... In addition, we would not establish any organization of the communist party and other Chinese democratic parties in the Chinese community."[15] During the visit, Zhou Enlai explicitly told the Burmese Prime Minister, "Politically, we hold that those who have attained suffrage in Burma should be regarded as Burmese citizens and will no longer possess Chinese nationality; therefore they will not be allowed to join the overseas Chinese organizations and their activities. Similarly, if some Chinese still maintain their Chinese citizenship, they should be excluded from Burmese political activities."[16] In addition to Zhou's vow in Rangoon in 1956, he made similar statements during his other eight visits to Burma that "The overseas Chinese should not get involved in local political activities."[17] Although the Chinese government and leadership made promises about proscribing any Chinese political role in Burma, disturbing political events still occurred because some pro-Beijing Chinese were found to be involved in Burmese political activities.

In August 1956, U Hla Maung told Zhou Enlai that some Chinese and China's Embassy in Rangoon supported some parties in Burmese domestic

---

14   *Works of Mao Tsetung*, Vol. 6, pp. 376–377.
15   Speech of Premier Zhou Enlai, AMFA, File No. 105-00510-08(1).
16   *Chronicle of Zhou Enlai*, Vol. 2, p. 647.
17   Interview Ye Keqing, 8 December 2005, Yangon, Myanmar.

election campaigns.[18] When meeting with Zhou Enlai in 1960, former Burmese Prime Minister, U Ba Swe, told Zhou Enlai again, "Before the general election of this year, the overseas Chinese endowed the 'Clean' faction of AFPFL [i.e., U Ba Swe's opponents] and they spent money like water. We hope Your Excellency could do something to prevent this. The leaders of the 'Clean' faction of AFPFL raised money from Chinese businessmen in their own names and the businessmen did not hesitate to give to them."[19] U Ba Swe also admitted that "China had instructed the overseas Chinese to alienate themselves from Burmese politics. However, the overseas Chinese actually funded the 'Clean' faction regardless of their oral promises."[20] The Bank of China in Rangoon was accused of sponsoring U Nu, of the "Clean" faction, to run for Prime Minister.[21] The leader of the overseas Chinese Communist Party in Burma recalled that it was only realistic for the overseas Chinese to support local politics: "Although the Chinese government prohibited them from participating in Burmese politics, they were generally reluctant to offend the Burmese, especially those who were influential and to whom they owed their survival and development. As a result, they had to make donations to the local parties in power. The BCP at times [also] collected donations from them. The two sides in fact had a tacit understanding in this respect."[22]

In general, the issues concerning the overseas Chinese political role in Burma had not been major obstacles in bilateral relations, mainly due to Beijing's restraint, the weak power of the resident Chinese, the internal strife between the CCP and KMT in the Chinese community, and more threatening and overshadowing border and KMT army issues.

The Burmese Kuomintang Army Issue

On 29 November 1949, Zhou Enlai warned southern bordering countries not to shelter the KMT army that had retreated into that area.[23] One month later,

---

18   Summary of discussion between Premier Zhou Enlai and Burmese Ambassador to China U Hla Maung (25 August 1956), AMFA, File No. 105-00307-03(1).

19   Account of discussion between Premier Zhou Enlai and former Burmese Prime Minister U Ba Swe, AMFA, File No. 203-00036-04(1).

20   *Ibid.*

21   Brief account of talks and meetings during Premier Zhou Enlai's visit to Burma, AMFA, File No. 203-00036-07(1).

22   "Memoirs of LWZ, Part III: Assignment on Overseas Chinese after the Dissolution of the Burmese Overseas Chinese Communist Party". Unpublished manuscript, 1993. Initials are used to protect the identity of sources.

23   *Works of Zhou Enlai since the Establishment of PRC*, Vol. 1, Beijing: Central Party Literature Press, 2008, p. 593.

Mao Tsetung cabled Liu Shaoqi: "The PLA should not pursue and attack the armies of Li Mi and Yu Chengwan [both KMT generals] in haste lest they withdraw to Vietnam and Burma ahead of our besiegement."[24] Although the CCP had anticipated that the KMT troops would withdraw to Vietnam and Burma, it did not predict their later threat to the security of southwest China, and their significance in Sino-Burmese relations.

In early 1950, more than 1,700 KMT troops crossed the border into Kengtung, preyed upon the countryside, and caused great hardship to local inhabitants by their demands for food and forced labor. Units of the Burmese army made contact with these troops and demanded that they should either leave Burmese territory forthwith or submit to disarmament and internment in accordance with international law. On the refusal of the KMT troops to comply with either of these alternatives, units of the Burmese army took offensive action to enforce compliance. After several engagements in the latter half of 1950, the KMT troops were dislodged from Kengtung; they withdrew westward and established a new headquarters at Mong Hsat near the Burma–Thailand frontier, where they constructed a regular airfield to facilitate the receipt of supplies from sources outside Burma. "New recruits had been obtained from the Burma–Yunnan border area. The number of the troops was then estimated at about 12,000. General Li Mi had been moving between Mong Hsat and Taiwan and there was other evidence of a direct link with the Kuomintang Government. At the end of 1952, the troops which had so far been operating in areas east of the Salween River had extended their activities to areas west of the river in conjunction with elements in active rebellion against the Government of Burma."[25]

Although the CCP seized provincial power in Yunnan peacefully in 1950, it did not wholly and effectively control Yunnan. Some local warlords, rebellious KMT army units that previously had surrendered to the PLA, and minority armed forces jointly launched armed insurrections and riots around the province.[26] Beijing believed that the threats of the KMT army in Burma probably resulted from the U.S. making use of the Burmese KMT army to open a second front during the Korean War, and also that the KMT was colluding with anti-communist forces in China to assault and subvert the Yunnan government.

---

24 *Works of Mao Tsetung since the Establishment of the PRC*, Vol. 1, p. 198.
25 *Yearbook of the United Nations 1953*, New York: Department of Public Information, United Nations, 1954, p. 162.
26 *Campaign to Eliminate Banditry in the Southwest Region*, Beijing: PLA's Publishing House, 2001, p. 625.

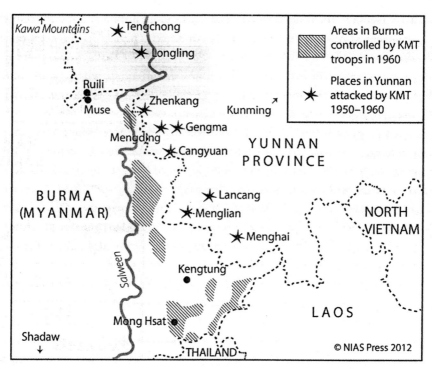

Map 4: Kuomintang troops in Burma, 1950–1961 (based on a map by Wang Di and Li Feiying, in part sourced from material in the PRC Foreign Ministry archives)

In the first half of 1952 alone, some small groups of KMT troops launched more than 60 attacks against border areas in three counties of Yunnan: Tengchong, Longling, and Zhenkang. Over 100 officials and local residents were killed.[27] Between May and June 1951, Li Mi dispatched 6,000 soldiers and launched cross-border attacks one after another along four routes in Yunnan; parts of Gengma county, Menglian county, Menghai county and Zhenkang county were occupied. In July, KMT troops were divided into two columns to re-enter into Yunnan, and occupied Cangyuan, Menglian, and Lancang counties. But their attacks and seizures were short-lived, and under the PLA's counterattacks they finally retreated back into Burma.

The increasing strength of the KMT army in Burma with the military assistance of Taiwan and the U.S. increased Beijing's anxiety. The KMT constructed an airfield, updated and renewed armaments, and recruited new soldiers. Most of the new recruits consisted of anti-communists from border areas of Yunnan and Chinese deserters in Burma. For example, when KMT troops attacked

27 *Development of the Military in Contemporary China*, Vol. 1, p. 373.

Yunnan and retreated back to Burma under the PLA's offensive in the summer of 1951, during which they had occupied Mengding and eight other counties in Yunnan for several months, some anti-communists followed them and together they withdrew to Burma. Thus, their armed force rose to 12,000.[28] Since the CCP had came to power in mainland China, various internal and disruptive political campaigns were mounted at intervals, such as those against landlords. During each political movement, some Chinese fled from Yunnan and other provinces to Burma to dodge political persecution; the KMT in Burma also encouraged them to escape. Some of them became the supporters of and participants in the KMT armies.

In addition, the KMT army in Burma attempted to create border conflicts between China and Burma in order to sour Sino-Burmese relations. According to a KMT document of 1952 that was captured by Burmese intelligence units, they were ordered to come between the two countries' armies when the Burmese army attacked them. "You and your affiliated troops should disguise yourselves as PLA to attack Burmese army barracks and subsequently make announcements that China should invade Burma."[29] On 16 September 1959, the Kunming Military Region reported to Beijing that "Some KMT soldiers disguised as PLA have slipped into the northern section of the unsettled border three times since the early July . . . They intended to attack the Burmese army or PLA in disguise in order to provoke and destroy Sino-Burmese relations."[30]

To Rangoon, the KMT army above all meant that Burmese sovereignty and territorial integrity were jeopardized. As a result, the AFPFL was under internal nationalistic political pressure in addition to other, previously mentioned, international issues. In addition, the alliance of the KMT army and ethnic insurgents further aggravated the issue. On 22 January 1953, the Burmese Ministry of Defense stated that some evidence revealed military cooperation between the KMT army and Karen insurgents, who received arms aid from the former. The KMT armies also obtained support from the Padaung ethnic group when they were expelled from Shadaw by the Burmese army on 25 February 1953.[31] China's declassified archives also indicate that KMT troops colluded with

---

28 Command paper of the 12th session of the Legislature, Archives of Academia Historica (Taiwan), Cat. No. 069, Roll No. 150, File No. 11-4-3, 22 December 1953, pp. 44–48.

29 *Kuomintang Aggression against Burma*, p. 159.

30 Operations by remnants of Chiang Kai-shek's troops in Burma–China border areas and the negotiations with Burma, AMFA, File No. 105-00604-02(1).

31 *Keesing's Contemporary Archives*, London: Keesing's Publications Limited, March 28-4 April 1953, p. 12838.

the Sawbwa of Kengtung, and supported their separatist movement. "They [KMT] actively encouraged the anti-government armed forces in the Shan State to attack the Burmese army east of the Salween River, and discouraged a Sawbwa of the Shan State from handing over power to Rangoon."[32]

Beijing, however, adopted a restrained attitude toward the problem of the KMT, which the Burmese appreciated. In 1957, U Nu spoke out in parliament: "I have to appreciate the PRC's attitude and sincerity. When KMT troops allegedly attacked Yunnan, China could have made trouble for us if it had wanted to do so. On the contrary, China took a sincere and patient attitude towards us, so I give my thanks to the PRC."[33] In 1960, Zhou Enlai told Ne Win that "Regarding the KMT troops in Burma, we know that it is hard for you to annihilate them because they have arms, and notably strong support from a foreign power [i.e., the U.S.]. We adopt an attitude of understanding, and await the Burma's government exterminating them stage by stage."[34] Beijing even attempted to resort to force to solve directly the KMT problem in Burma. In the early 1950s, China proposed to deploy the PLA to help Burma annihilate them, but Burma refused. In fact, for a long period China was very dissatisfied with the Burmese failure effectively to cope with the KMT issue. Declassified documents from Taiwan indicate that Beijing made use of leftists in the Burmese government to promote it attacking the KMT. Meanwhile, Beijing ordered the PLA to disguise themselves as KMT troops to project KMT's image as the aggressor to the Burmese.[35]

Facing the aggravating KMT crisis, Burma stopped American aid and submitted the KMT issue to the United Nations.[36] Between November 1953 and May 1954, Taiwan withdrew 6,986 troops from Burma in 3 batches, handed over 1,323 pieces of weapons, and 822 personnel were evacuated to Taiwan. There were still 6,000 KMT affiliated people staying in Burma and most weapons were still in their hands and those of some minority rebels.[37]

After the first troop withdrawal to Taiwan in 1954, Rangoon's attitude to this issue relaxed because the threat caused by the KMT and their power

---

32 Situation of Chiang Kai-shek's troops fleeing to Burma and Burmese attitude, AMFA, File No. 105-00605-02.
33 Abstract of Burmese Prime Minister U Nu's speech, AMFA, File No. 105-00814-01(1).
34 Account of the discussion between Premier Zhou Enlai and Ne Win, Chief of the General Staff of Burma, AMFA, File No. 203-00036-01(1).
35 "Return of the Yunnan Anticommunist National Salvation Army to Taiwan", Archive of Political and History Department, Defense Ministry (Taiwan), File No: 542.5/1073, June 1953–February 1954.
36 Bandyopadhyaya, *Burma and Indonesia*, p. 154.
37 *Yearbook of the United Nations 1953*, pp. 53–54.

declined. The Burmese government then concentrated on the BCP and ethnic rebels. The KMT troops were no longer able to pose a dire threat to Rangoon's sovereignty. The KMT affair, however, had an important impact on the Burmese military, which took over the administration of part of the Shan State as a result, and perhaps this experience contributed to their confidence in administering the whole country later.[38]

On 17 December 1954, when meeting the Burmese Ambassador to China, Zhou Enlai pointed out that China hoped the Burmese government would take powerful action to wipe out or disarm the KMT army and remove an obstacle in Sino-Burmese relations.[39] In August 1956, Zhou Enlai told U Hla Maung that "Concerning the KMT troops in Burma, we have for seven years kept silent on it in the newspapers and never deliberately made it difficult for Burma. However, the KMT army would be a considerable threat to China with the support of America."[40]

In December 1957, Military Intelligence of the PLA General Staff Department analyzed the attitude of the Burmese government toward the Burmese KMT army:

> The Burmese government has centered on civil war in recent years and the KMT troop issue plays second fiddle to it. Although Burma's government is disgusted that the U.S. and Taiwan support them, Rangoon attempts to take advantage of this situation to blockade the China–Burma border. Consequently, they have maintained the confrontation with the KMT troops, and don't launch aggressive attacks on them. However, when they [the KMT] expand their sphere of influence, the Burmese army undertakes military operations to counterattack. Early this year, the 9th Infantry Brigade of Burma asked the Headquarters of the Burmese Army General Staff for permission to attack, but failed to get the permission. Afterwards, the Burmese army didn't carry out any large-scale military operation from January to October. Burma's government deployed one brigade and four and a half battalions (about 4,000 men) to cope with the KMT troops, and revoked the command post at Po-Ren Meng. During July, the Burmese army made a concession without fighting back when KMT troops occupied Mill Mountains, which Burmese local armed forces occupied.[41]

38 See Mary P. Callahan, *Making Enemies: War and State Building in Burma*, Ithaca: Cornell University Press, 2003.

39 *Chronicle of Zhou Enlai's Diplomatic Events: 1949–1975*, Beijing: World Knowledge Publishing House, 1993, p. 96.

40 Main points of two conversations between Premier Zhou Enlai and Burmese Ambassador to China U Hla Maung, AMFA, File No. 105-00752-02(1).

41 Situation of Chiang Kai-shek's troops fleeing to Burma, AMFA, File No. 105-00605-02.

In early March 1959, the Burmese army launched its "Spring Campaign" to attack the KMT. The PLA Intelligence Department predicted, according to its analysis of Burmese military offensive performance and the deployment of forces, that the purpose of the Burmese military operation was to limit the KMT sphere of influence, and to crack down on KMT arrogance in order to reap political capital for the Burmese military caretaker government. Therefore, the Burmese military operation was on a limited scale, and intermittent war continued.[42]

China was dissatisfied with the Burmese attitude and repeatedly urged Rangoon to solve the problem, but Rangoon seemed deliberately to play down its seriousness. In March 1956, U Hla Maung told Zhou Enlai that the Burmese KMT army was not large. They could not take possession of any base area and hid in the jungle so they had to move around and harass travelers. Many in the KMT army had sent letters to express their willingness to surrender. "The Burmese KMT army, including dependants, amount to around 3,000; they are distributed along the Thai–Burma, Laos–Burma, and China–Burma border areas."[43] When U Hla Maung met Zhou Enlai three months later, he stressed again that the KMT troops were only 2,000–3,000 (families included). They operated in the area of Kengtung and marauded passengers and villages. They did not exist as a whole unit, but moved around in a dispersed manner.[44]

When Burmese Vice Prime Ministers U Ba Swe and U Kyaw Nyein visited China on 14 December 1957, Mao Tsetung asked again about the number of Burmese KMT troops. U Ba Swe responded that it was estimated to be 1,000–1,500 but that they were not political but rather bandits looting everywhere they went. At most, they once were 12,000–16,000 strong.[45] On 17 April 1958, Zhou Enlai once more inquired from U Hla Maung about the size of the KMT army in Burma. U Hla Maung's answer was less than 2,000 including their families. "They have been reduced to banditti and are found in the border areas of Burma–Thailand–Laos. The Burmese government is trying to resolve this problem."[46]

Beijing had continuously questioned the Burmese since 1954 about the number and military strength of the KMT troops, and the Burmese answer was

---

42 *Ibid.*

43 Summary of discussion between Premier Zhou Enlai and Burmese Ambassador to China U Hla Maung (7 March 1956), AMFA, File No. 105-00307-01(1).

44 Summary of discussion between Premier Zhou Enlai and U Hla Maung (22 June 1956), AMFA, File No. 105-00307-02(1).

45 Record of Chairman Mao Tsetung's talk, AMFA, File No. 105-00339-01(1).

46 Abstract of talks between Premier Zhou Enlai and Burmese Ambassador to China U Hla Maung on Burmese domestic situation, AMFA, File No. 105-00858-01.

quite different from that of Chinese intelligence sources: from December 1957 to October 1958, the KMT army commanded by Liu Yuanlin had carried out the *Anzai Plan* in northern Burma; it was to train troops to assault the southwest region of China.[47] Information from Military Intelligence of the PLA General Staff Department in December 1957 also revealed that KMT troops in Burma had 4 armies, 10 divisions, 7 independent regiments, 1 artillery group, and 1 guard group, amounting to 4,500, and were dispersed along the Sino-Burmese border area in northeast Burma and the triangle area of Burma, Laos, and Thailand.[48] Up to 12 December 1958, according to preliminary estimates at that time, 114,510 Yunnanese escaped to neighboring countries because of the Great Leap Forward and 80 percent of them fled to Burma.[49] On 24 October 1958, a report submitted by the Chinese Embassy in Burma to the Foreign Ministry depicted the situation: after the outflow of Chinese residents from the Yunnan border areas, KMT troops in Burma seized the opportunity to "despise the socialist system, slander our party's policy, smear the Great Leap Forward for its 'slave labor,' and the outflow due to 'governmental persecution,' and to counteract the influence of socialism." "A large number of escapees were enlisted with the KMT troops in Burma, which had expanded (it was reported that their troops had increased by more than 2,000 in one year)."[50]

PLA intelligence also pointed out that "Since the second half of 1958, KMT troops have energetically beguiled Chinese escapees to enlist, and they expand their sphere of influence northward in Burma. It is learnt that they have increased to approximately 8,000 from 5,300, and have established the 'Ximeng Military Region' in the Kawa Mountains, the southern section of the sparsely settled China–Burma border."[51] In 1959, Yunnan anti-communists took advantage of the occasion of Tibet's rebellion to incite armed insurgence by more than 2,400 in the Ximeng frontier area, and instigated the escape of a large number of border residents. The KMT seized this chance to expand their forces once again. Up to November, they totaled more than 9,400, comprising 5 armies, 15 divisions, 6 columns, 6 independent regiments, 3 independent detachments, and 1 military region. Taiwan supported their expansion. Beginning in March 1959, Taiwan airdropped arms to them. In July 1960, Taiwan shipped a special

---

47 *Memoirs of Liu Yuanlin at the Age of 88*, Taipei: History and Political Bureau of Compilation and Translation of National Defense, 1996, p. 106.

48 Situation of Chiang Kai-shek's troops fleeing to Burma, AMFA, File No. 105-00605-02.

49 Reports on the flight of inhabitants in Sino-Burmese border areas, AMFA, File No. 105-00604-01.

50 *Ibid.*

51 Situation of Chiang Kai-shek's troops fleeing to Burma, AMFA, File No. 105-00605-02.

operation force of 400 members to northern Burma as well as airdropped a large number of weapons and equipment. In September, Maung Pai Airstrip was built, and Taiwan was planning to deploy troops in northeast Burma, using it as an outpost to reconquer Mainland China.

The number of KMT troops reported to China by Burma's government, 1,000–3,000 including their families, could not convince the former. This seemed not to be an intelligence error, but a Burmese maneuver to deliberately undervalue this issue. China did not believe the Burmese version that the KMT army had become dispersed bandits. Beijing began increasingly to worry about the expansion of the KMT army in Burma.

In October 1960, both sides signed an agreement to settle the border dispute, and they agreed to "continue to carry out necessary surveys of the boundary line between the two countries, to set up new boundary markers, and to examine, repair, and remould old boundary markers."[52] China declared that it was necessary to attack the KMT in order to ensure the security of the border survey and avoid any disturbance of the demarcation. On 4 December, China and Burma signed an agreement in Kunming on guard duty for erecting boundary markers. The two countries agreed on 22 December 1960 to launch a joint military operation to eliminate the KMT troops. Between 22 December 1960 and 9 February 1961, the PLA entered Burma twice and engaged in battle.[53] It took the PLA and the Burmese army three months to defeat them and destroy their general headquarters in Burma. Most of the KMT army moved to the frontier area of Burma–Laos–Thailand, and 4,349 of Liu Yuanlin's troops were withdrawn to Taiwan.[54]

The remaining KMT had lost their main strength and could not conduct threatening attacks on Yunnan, although Taiwan went on supporting them after 1962 and ordered them to continue trying to attack the mainland. From March 1963 to September 1966 there were 8 invasions by the KMT forces in the frontier areas of Yunnan; these were defeated by the PLA. Thereafter, KMT troops retreated to the Burma–Thailand border area and gradually stopped aggressive attacks on the Yunnan border region.

---

52 Boundary Treaty Between the Union of Burma and the People's Republic of China, United Nations Treaty Series, Vol. 1010, No. 1–14847, p. 142.

53 According to Chen Yixiang, acting as the translator of the China–Burma joint border survey team, the PLA entered Burma to assault KMT troops in the border area of China–Burma–Laos in the second half of 1961. See Chen Yixiang, "Memories of the Sino-Burmese joint boundary survey", *At Home and Overseas*, 2003, No. 12.

54 *Memoirs of Liu Yuanlin*, p. 275.

Rangoon's consent for the PLA to enter Burma to destroy the KMT troops played a significant role in finally solving the KMT army problem. But the Burmese continuously had great suspicions concerning the PLA's presence in Burma. For instance, in the second half of 1961, when China proposed to send troops to exterminate the remaining KMT army in Burma for reasons of the security of the boundary settlement, "Burma hesitated to reply and worried that the PLA would not be evacuated from Burma but would help the BCP expand its military forces. China promised again and again that the combat would be conducted in the name of Sino-Burmese joint operations; the Burmese could watch the combat at some commanding height when the battle started. After the battle, all the trophies like firearms and ammunition would belong to Burma; the communique would be released in the name of Sino-Burmese joint operations; and the PLA guaranteed to entirely retreat from Burma."[55] At last, Burma agreed and the PLA entered Burma. This reflected the increasing trust between China and Burma, which was based on the peaceful settlement of Sino-Burmese boundary dispute. The solution of the border dispute itself promoted bilateral ties. The settlement of the KMT problem was one of the byproducts of overcoming the border dispute.

The Burma–China Boundary Settlement

When the CCP seized power in China in 1949, the Sino-Burmese border dispute became a difficult challenge for Beijing in the context of the regime change in China, the decolonization of Asian countries, and the rise of the Cold War. The undemarcated boundary was one of the most significant and controversial issues of Sino-Burmese relations in the 1950s.

~ The Divergence of Interests in the Border Dispute

China claimed that there were three sections of the undemarcated borderline to be resolved: the southern section of the Akha mountain area; the middle section's Meng–Mao Triangle area at the confluence of the Nmai Hka and Ruili rivers; and in the northern section, the northern part of the High Conical Peak. Initially, Beijing maintained that the "1941 Line" was void, and that the Meng–Mao Triangle area and the northern lost areas including Hpimaw, Gawlum, and Kangfang should be returned to China. The Burmese bargained for the status quo, as they had inherited from the British the "1941 Line" and the traditional borders. They continued to dominate the Meng–Mao Triangle area but thought

---

55   Chen Yixiang, "Memories of the Sino-Burmese joint boundary survey".

that a 50-square-mile territory – including Hpimaw, Gawlum, and Kangfang could be returned to the Chinese. As a result, Burma claimed that only the northern part was the unsettled boundary. China attributed the Sino-Burmese border issue to "a product of imperialist policies of aggression" and attempted to change the result while Burma stressed its "inheritance from history"? The process of resolving the China–Burma border issue was not smooth sailing.

~ Burma–China Strains in 1956

China originally was not anxious to resolve the boundary dispute with Burma. The PLA had crossed the "1941 Line" and entered the debated ground in Burma to pursue KMT troops in 1952, and had stationed troops there. But Sino-Burmese conversations on the border problem began in 1954. In December 1954, when U Nu visited China, the joint communique referred to the "incomplete delimitation of the boundary line," and acknowledged the necessity "to settle this question in a friendly spirit at an appropriate time through normal diplomatic channels."[56] The two parties agreed to keep the boundary status quo for the time being. Soon after, however, an armed conflict between the two countries erupted at Yellow Orchard in the Wa State in 1955. "The border problem having thus assumed urgency and importance, negotiations for an early and final settlement were started in earnest at the highest levels of the two governments."[57]

On 20 December 1955, a skirmish between the Burmese army and PLA occurred at Yellow Orchard to the west of "1941 Line", causing several casualties in the two armies.[58] Burmese domestic media and the Western press continually reported the story and accused China of invading Burma. The U.S. then supported the Manila Pact countries in carrying out a military exercise to show their disapproval of the Chinese incursion. Beijing felt the pressure caused by the conflict, which caused the border dispute to be placed on China's agenda of the day. When Zhou Enlai presented a report on the China–Burma border problem to the National People's Congress in 1957, he purposely mentioned the conflict. "Although the event was resolved through a joint effort by the two sides, in the meantime it also gave the two governments an opportunity to understand the urgency and necessity of resolving

---

56　"Joint Communique of China's and Burma's Premiers", *People's Daily*, 13 December 1954.
57　Maung Maung, "The Burma–China Boundary Settlement", *Asian Survey*, Vol. 1, No. 1, March 1961, p. 40.
58　Burmese note to China relating to talks on the shooting incident in Sino-Burmese border areas, AMFA, File No. 105-00745-01(1).

the boundary problem."[59] Negotiations were conducted over several years beginning in early 1956.

Soon after the Yellow Orchard event, Burma presented a note to China stating that the two parties should respect the "1941 Line" to avoid a recurrence of similar incidents. Burma made suggestions that two parties should withdraw their respective troops from the controversial area and that a Joint Boundary Commission should hold meetings as soon as possible.[60] The Chinese Embassy in Burma, analyzing the Burmese suggestions, concluded that Burma was attempting to shirk responsibility for the event, and noted that "[Burma] asked China to recognize the '1941 Line', which would validate their [the Burmese] position and unilaterally incorporate the location of the conflict into Burma, as well as urging us [China] to withdraw our army to the east of the '1941 Line'. Burmese claims violated the consensus of maintaining the temporary boundary status quo reached by U Nu and Zhou Enlai in Beijing." As a result, the Chinese Embassy in Burma proposed not to withdraw to the "1941 Line".[61]

On 31 July 1956, *The Nation*, a leading Rangoon English daily, reported that hundreds of Chinese troops had invaded Burma and occupied 500 square miles of Burmese territory, and were moving south. This report brought the situation to the attention of the two leaders and international public opinion. Prime Minister U Ba Swe convened the Cabinet and other leadership to discuss the serious situation. On the day that the report was released, the Burmese government partly denied it, but admitted that the Chinese army had invaded Burma, disclosed that the PLA had set up an outpost in Wa State near the Burma–China border, but stated that the situation was not as severe as reported in *The Nation*.[62] "Although Rangoon's public statement inclined to play down the degree and extent of Chinese infiltration, U Kyaw Nyein recognized that the coverage was indeed true and conflicts and casualties had occurred (in November last year)."[63] In response to the Burmese official statement, Zhou Enlai wrote a letter to U Nu on 4 August saying that although the Burmese Foreign Ministry denied the truth of the coverage, it nevertheless proclaimed that "the PLA had entered the Wa State and posted sentinels." Zhou criticized Burma, stating that it should not censure the Chinese border

---

59 "Reports of Sino-Burmese Boundary Problem", *People's Daily*, 10 July 1957.
60 Burmese note to China, AMFA, File No. 105-00745-01(1).
61 *Ibid.*
62 "Declaration Announced by Government of Union of Burma", *PLA Daily*, 4 August 1956; "Burmese Government Issued Statement", *People's Daily*, 4 August 1956.
63 Shen Zhihua and Yang Kuisong (ed.), *The Declassified Record of U.S. Intelligence on China: 1948–1976*, Vol. V and VI, Beijing: Oriental Press, 2009, p. 312.

crossing before negotiations and consensus building. The Burmese *modus operandi*, he believed, only offered agitators a chance to alienate China–Burma ties, and work against the boundary settlement.[64] The Bureau of Intelligence and Research of the U.S. Department of State, in analyzing the event, deemed that the Burmese government had made use of the coverage in *The Nation* to reveal the information that it was reluctant to release itself. It seemed that the Burmese government had enticed the newspapers into publicizing the news because it wanted to attract world attention to the Chinese invasion of Burma and charge Beijing with aggression through unofficial channels.[65] Also, Beijing believed that Burmese public opinion's condemnation of China was officially instigated and supported by Rangoon. Hence China explicitly told the Burmese that "The reports had definitely something to do with your government."[66] The Chinese government hoped that the Burmese government would not increase political tension in order to oppress China.[67]

In general, Rangoon won an overwhelming victory in the boundary dispute in 1956. Burma denied China's invasion publicly but recognized a Chinese presence and infiltration to the west of the "1941 Line." Thus, Burmese tactics not only affirmed the legitimacy of the traditional borderline but also caused international public opinion pressure on China. In the same year, incidents in Poland and Hungary heavily impaired the international image of socialist countries and powers, and also produced a chilling effect on China–Burma relations. Burma was discontented with, as well as afraid of, the Soviet interventions in Poland and Hungary. Therefore, Rangoon was suspicious of the truth of Chinese sincerity about the "Five Principles of Peaceful Coexistence," and was afraid that China would perform a Southeast Asian version of the events in Poland and Hungary. The Burmese felt that the Chinese presence in the undemarcated areas was similar to the Hungarian situation, so Burma should learn a lesson from the incidents in Hungary.[68] Consequently, Burma–China relations were strained, and Burma after July 1956 was inclined to follow the Western

---

64 "Premier Zhou Enlai's Reply to Former Burmese Premier U Nu on Visiting Burma and Sino-Burmese Boundary Issue", in Zhuo Renzheng (ed.), *Cordial "Pauk Phaw": A Grand Gathering of Chinese and Burmese Residents in Border Areas between China and Burma in 1956*, Beijing: Central Party Literature Press, 2003, p. 7.

65 Shen Zhihua and Yang Kuisong (eds), *The Declassified Record*, p. 312.

66 Main points of two conversations between Premier Zhou Enlai and U Hla Maung, AMFA, File No. 105-00752-02(1).

67 Summary of discussion between Premier Zhou Enlai and U Hla Maung, AMFA, File No. 105-00307-03(1).

68 "Burma Nationalist Alliance Salutes Hungarian Struggle: 'Burma Should Take Lesson'", *The Nation*, 17 November 1956.

countries in international affairs. China came under considerable pressure from the Burmese media's and international public opinion's condemnation of the Chinese incursion into Burma, the West's sowing dissension about the border dispute, and the blow-back from the Poland and Hungary incidents.

~ Beijing's Response

Beijing took some measures to reverse the tide. First, contrary to the silence of the Chinese media prior to the 1955 Yellow Orchard event, they published some editorials and reports on the boundary issue in order to refute accusations and reports prejudicial to China.[69] Second, China tried to relieve tensions by employing Burmese leftists and pro-China forces. On 8 August, the Burma–China Friendship Association issued an appeal for a peaceful boundary settlement on the basis of the "Five Principles of Peaceful Coexistence" and criticizing the intrigue against Sino-Burmese friendship.[70] Burmese leftist newspapers carried editorials and reports to deny the domestic accusations of China invading Burma. Third, a major rally of residents living in the border areas in Burma and China was speeded up. During 15–17 December 1956, the rally was staged in Mangshi, Yunnan, with about 350 official representatives and 15,000 border residents of the two countries. "The function nominally was a festival of border residents, but actually it was essentially a mass rally and diplomatic event which both officials and ethnic glitteratis attended."[71]

Finally, both sides began to negotiate the Burma–China boundary dispute. From 22 October to 8 November 1956, U Nu, the President of AFPFL, was invited to Beijing to negotiate the boundary settlement, but before his departure for Beijing, Rangoon had already received Beijing's promise of a settlement. On October 2, Vice Prime Minister U Ba Swe told the newsmen at his monthly press conference that "The Chinese Government has accepted the '1941 Line' as a basis for the negotiations."[72] In Beijing, "The Burmese Prime Minister suggested that the two states accept the boundaries in effect at the time of Burmese independence [1948]. The Communist regime, after a brief period, countered with the suggestion that: (a) the 'traditional line' including the portion of the McMahon line in the north be accepted; (b) the Namwan

69 "Alert to Conspiracies of Damaging Sino-Burmese Relations", *People's Daily*, 4 August 1956.
70 "Burma–China Friendship Association Appeals to Prevent Conspiracies of Damaging Sino-Burmese Relations", *People's Daily*, 10 August 1956.
71 Yunnan Province's final report on Chinese and Burmese inhabitants gathering in the border areas, AMFA, File No. 105-00512-04(1).
72 "China Has Accepted '1941 Line' as Basis For Negotiations", *The Nation*, 3 October 1956.

lease be abrogated; (c) the 1941 line be validated; and (d) Hpimaw, Gawlam, and Kangfang villages be returned to China."[73] China registered its policy principles on the border settlement and suggested a package solution to the problem. Although China did not publicly accept that Beijing would recognize the validity of "1941 Line", the press communique intimated it would. In the 1956 communique, both sides agreed that China would withdraw to the east of "1941 Line" and that Burma would evacuate Hpimaw, Gawlum, and Kangfang before the end of 1956.[74] This demonstrated that China actually accepted the "1941 Line," though Beijing demanded that the Burmese army should not enter the area before the border settlement (an area from which the PLA were to retire). More importantly, China at the same time agreed that "Burmese government employees could step into the area."[75] On 5 November 1956, Beijing's plan was passed by the 50th meeting of the Standing Committee of the National People's Congress of China. When a joint communique was issued on 10 November, U Nu gave a detailed broadcast talk on the border problem in Rangoon. He stated that China was prepared to accept the frontier that Burma had inherited on achieving independence except for the three Kachin villages that were to be returned to China, and that the Namwan Assigned Tract was to be abrogated.[76]

Over 10–20 December 1956, Zhou Enlai visited Burma. "The timing, selection, and effect of this visit were crucial, given that Burma–China relations were strained. U Nu's trip to China partly restored Burmese confidence in peaceful coexistence with us, but the imperialists took advantage of the border dispute in Hpimaw and the Hungary event to sow discord in Burma ... Premier Zhou opposed other countries', as well as China's, chauvinism. The Premier's position further allayed Burmese suspicion of China and promoted its trust in us ... The other side understood our true attitude towards the border dispute through the negotiations." Zhou's visit alleviated the adverse impact of the Hungarian Uprising and enlisted the amity of both U Nu's and U Ba Swe's cliques.[77]

~ *China's Concessions*

In essence, Chinese concessions on the border issue turned Sino-Burmese ties in 1956 from pessimism to optimism. After U Nu returned to Rangoon from

---

73 Burma–China Boundary, International Boundary Study, No. 42, 30 November 1964, Bureau of Intelligence and Research, U.S. Department of State, p. 7.

74 "Joint Press Communique of Burma and China", *People's Daily*, 10 November 1956.

75 "Reports of Sino-Burmese Boundary Problem", *People's Daily*, 10 July 1957.

76 Richard J. Kozicki, "The Sino-Burmese Frontier Problem", *Far Eastern Survey*, Vol. 26, No. 3, March 1957, p. 35.

77 Popular reactions to Premier Zhou Enlai's visit to Burma, AMFA, File No. 105-00512-08(1).

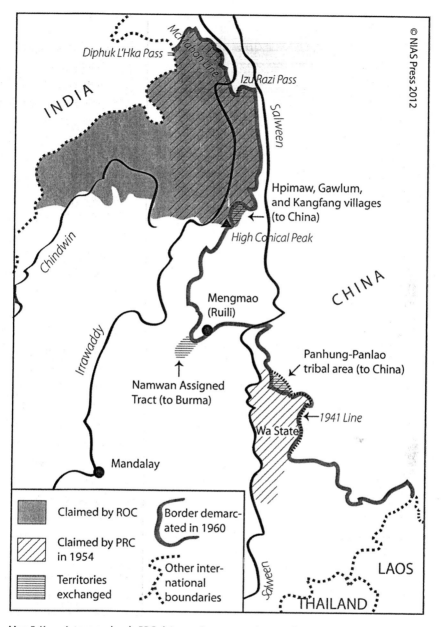

Map 5: Kuomintang and early PRC claims to Burmese territory, with Sino-Burmese border settlement, 1960 (based on a map by Wang Di and Li Feiying)

Beijing, he announced at a news conference that Zhou Enlai had accepted the 200 mile "McMahon Line" from Diphuk L'Hka Pass to Izu Razi and the "1941 Line" in the Wa State. Thus, the Chinese government stated that it recognized and respected the status quo of the China–Burma boundary, and gave up its previous territorial claims but asked the return of Hpimaw, Gawlum, and Kangfang and the Namwan Assigned Tract near Namhkam (see Map 5).[78]

Beijing's relinquishing the previous claim of unsettled territory prompted opposition from the Chinese Embassy in Burma, from Yunnan province, and from the military. For example, the ethnic elite of the Wa State claimed to be independent of Burma and China when they learned that most areas controlled by them were to be allocated to Burma. "Our cadres and soldiers have stayed there [west of the "1941 Line"] for several years, and established cordial relations with local residents. In the past, we propagandized that the 'Akha Hills Belongs to China', 'No Division of Akha Hills', and 'No Land for Peace'. We feel puzzled and will fail to persuade local residents to accept the area west of the '1941 Line' is being ceded to Burma."[79] In October 1956, the Burmese media reported that Chinese soldiers had crossed the border to Hpimaw, and were levying taxes on local villagers and asserting that Hpimaw actually belonged to China and would be returned to China sooner or later.[80]

The Yunnan provincial government enjoined local officials and populace to move to the east of the "1941 Line". The central government instructed, "Do not emphasize that it is traitorous that the KMT government signed the 1941 Pact. And do not refer to the 1941 Pact as a quisling agreement, or you will not only fail to clarify the reasons [for the agreement] but also lead to more puzzleheadedness among the populace." You should "try to persuade and induce the headmen and the common people around the '1941 Line' on both sides."[81]

Beijing gave these instructions to Yunnan because China's concessions on the border dispute with Burma in 1956 were not rooted in public opinion but rather in the CCP's central control and arbitrary decisions. When Zhou Enlai visited Rangoon in 1956, he told Prime Minister U Ba Swe that Beijing's difficulties were caused by China's concessions to Burma. These included: "(1) Explaining the reasons to the Chinese people. (2) Persuading Tibet's

---

78 "U Nu In Favour of 'Package Deal' Giving up Hpimaw and Two Villages in Return For the Namwan Tract", *The Nation*, 11 November 1956.

79 Zhuo Renzheng, "A promising beginning to resolving the Burma–China boundary problem: PLA withdrawal to the west of '1941 Line'", *Hundred Year Tide*, no. 9, 2003, p. 25.

80 "Red Chinese Soldiers Claim H'maw Area for Their Own", *The Nation*, 6 October 1956.

81 Zhuo Renzheng, "A promising beginning", pp. 25–26.

Dalai Lama *et al.* to accept the McMahon Line. (3) Explaining the KMT's condemnation of our 'quislingism.' However, we have to concede to you [Burma] in order to solve, once and for all, all China's border disputes with neighboring countries. We will make every effort to overcome the difficulties to fulfill the scheme."[82] On 13 March 1957, Zhou Enlai told the Burmese Ambassador to China that "Some committee members of the People's Congress and the National Committee of Chinese People's Political Consultative Conference (CPPCC) had some complaints about the Chinese concessions and the joint communique. As a result, it will take us some time to persuade them and explain the reasons."[83]

Accordingly, the CCP made efforts to reach domestic consensus in 1957 and explain the necessity of compromise with Burma. In March 1957, Zhou Enlai made speeches on the Burma–China boundary problem successively in the Third Plenary Session of the Second National Committee of the CPPCC, and in a conference attended by all circles and ethnic minorities convened by the Yunnan Committee of the CPPCC. A heated debate occurred in the two meetings, and the government " ... reached a consensus of all concerned on the Burma–China boundary settlement."[84] Particularly at the latter conference in Yunnan, Zhou Enlai patiently tried to persuade the delegates and alleviate Yunnanese discontent with Beijing's concessions. "Zhou made a series of speeches and reports in Kunming, which made us gradually agree to the demarcation policy of the central government."[85] On 9 July 1957, Zhou Enlai presented a subject report, *Report on the Burma–China Boundary Problem*, at the fourth Plenary Session of the first National Peoples' Congress. Zhou once again expatiated on China's proposals for and guidelines on the Burma–China boundary settlement.[86] The Congress approved Zhou's report and agreed that the government could thereby negotiate the border problem with Burma.[87]

The border settlement, however, could not be successfully concluded in 1958 largely because the AFPFL split into two factions. The political infighting culminated in a military caretaker government under General Ne Win (1958–1960). Ne Win was not only bound up in the border settlement, but had

82 Main points of talks between Premier Zhou Enlai and leading figures in Burma, AMFA, File No. 203-00019-02(1).

83 Song Fengying, "Zhou Enlai and Burma–China boundary negotiations", *Overview of CCP History*, no. 11, 2005, p. 7.

84 "Reports of Sino-Burmese Boundary Problem", *People's Daily*, 10 July 1957.

85 Song Fengying, "Zhou Enlai and Burma–China boundary negotiations", p. 8.

86 "Reports of Sino-Burmese Boundary Problem", *People's Daily*, 10 July 1957.

87 "Resolution on the Report of Sino-Burmese Boundary Problem Presented by Premier and Foreign Minister Zhou Enlai", *People's Daily*, 16 July 1957.

Plate 5: Mao greeting U Nu (left) and Ne Win (right), Beijing, 29 September 1960 (photograph courtesy Cheng Ruisheng)

won the cooperation of the Kachin and Shan leaders in working for a final settlement.[88] Both signed the *Friendly Agreement on the Question of the Burma–China Boundary* and *The Boundary Treaty between the People's Republic of China and the Union of Burma* in 1960, representing the settlement of the Burma–China boundary disputes (see Map 5).

In 1960 and 1961, the boundary settlement pushed China–Burma ties to their acme. After the conclusion of the Friendly Agreement and the Boundary Treaty, Rangoon organized a series of massive celebrations in the border areas neighboring China, including Bang Kam, Putao, Lwejel, Bhamo, and Myitkyina, which from 3,000 to 30,000 people attended. Burmese frontier guards also invited the Chinese army to participate in their celebrations. In response to Burmese celebrations and gatherings, the Chinese government held celebrations in Mangshi, Ruili, Zhangfeng, and Nansan, whose scales ranged from 1,000 to 20,000.[89] In October 1960, Prime Minister U Nu led a delegation of 350 members to attend China's National Day's celebration and signed the boundary treaty in Beijing. China organized three million people to welcome the Burmese delegates when they arrived. On 2 October, Beijing city held a mass rally of 100,000 to celebrate the signature of the boundary treaty. Burma presented one million Chinese residing on China's side of the border with 2,000 tons of rice and 1,000 tons of salt.[90] 1961 was styled Burma–China Friendship Year. In January, Zhou Enlai visited Burma with nine groups of 400

88   Maung Maung, "The Burma–China Boundary Settlement", p. 41.
89   China holds celebrations for signing of the friendship treaty and settlement of the boundary agreement for border areas, AMFA, File No. 105-00681-01(1).
90   Burmese gifts of rice and salt to Chinese border inhabitants and reciprocal gifts, AMFA, File No. 105-00680-01(1).

Plate 6: U Nu, Zhou Enlai and Ne Win, Rangoon, 2 January 1961 (photograph courtesy Cheng Ruisheng)

delegates to take part in the celebration of Burma Independence Day and exchanged the ratification papers of the Boundary Treaty. China gave 1.2 million residents living along Burma's side of the border 2.4 million meters of printed cloth and 600,000 pieces of porcelain plates as reciprocal gifts "in order to avoid and eliminate the detrimental political effect on China's border area caused by Burmese gifts as well as to meet Burmese border residents' needs, improve friendship, and increase our political influence."[91]

The explanation for the Burma–China boundary settlement involves several interrelated issues. China gave up the strong policies and territorial demands it held prior to 1956, and this change of attitude in 1956 related to the CCP's changing perception of the world and the international situation.

China introduced its foreign policy based on the "Five Principles of Peaceful Coexistence" in 1954, which was aimed at creating a peaceful international environment for its domestic economic development and at counter-attacking

91   *Ibid.*

the West's containment policy. The new policy was attributed to Beijing's clear self-appraisal of its national power and its objective judgment of the world situation. In the 1950s, China optimistically believed in the future of world development, that the world's tense situation could be relieved, and that world peace possibly could be achieved. China had to gain national and international support and permanent world peace to bring about socialist industrialization.[92]

In the 1950s, the boundary dispute was a potential source of conflict between China and its bordering countries, and in order to isolate and demonize China the West was using the problem to accuse Beijing's foreign policy of hypocrisy, namely: real aggression but ostensible peace. In 1956, China's compromise on the border dispute with Burma was based on the premise of a "package deal." Beijing's concessions and the agreement of a "package deal" displayed China's sense of crisis and urgency concerning the border dispute, which directly stemmed from the strained bilateral relations in 1956 and international pressures. Meanwhile, her neighboring countries distrusted China's vow of peace. Therefore, Chinese policy objectives of boundary settlement with Burma were to "try to relieve the tension of the world situation, and peacefully coexist with the countries of the world, notably our adjacent countries. This policy advances our socialist construction, and also accords with the people's interest of the world."[93] In conclusion, China's approach to the border dispute with Burma was "land for peace."

China also planned to hold the Sino-Burmese boundary settlement up as a "brilliant model" for all to see.[94] As Daphne E. Whittam pointed out, behind the Chinese approach to the China–Burma boundary dispute, Beijing's considerations were: "First, the security of China's frontiers; second, the preservation of China's historical image as a great Asian power in relation to her neighbours; third, the preservation of China's ideological image as the champion of Peaceful Co-existence among Asian nations. The Sino-Burmese Boundary Treaty, hailed by the two governments as a model of how Asian nations should settle historical disputes and maintain peace among themselves, enabled the Chinese authorities to satisfy all these three considerations."[95] Now that Burma

---

92 "Resolution on Political Reports of the 8th National Congress of CCP", *People's Daily*, 28 September 1956.

93 "Reports of Sino-Burmese Boundary Problem", *People's Daily*, 10 July 1957.

94 "Minutes of Talks between of Zhou Enlai and U Nu, 3 December 1956", quoted in CCCPC Party Literature Research Office, *Biography of Zhou Enlai*, Vol. 2, Beijing: Central Party Literature Press, 2008, p. 1177.

95 Daphne E. Whittam, "The Sino-Burmese Boundary Treaty", *Pacific Affairs*, Vol. 34, No. 2, Summer, 1961, p. 183.

was selected to be a "brilliant model" of a boundary settlement, Beijing could not implement a tough policy toward Burma, and fail to solve the dispute. Accordingly, China had reluctantly to accept the Burmese bargain in order to completely solve the border dispute.[96] Indeed, China also used the Burma case to prove the authenticity of its peaceful foreign policy. In the 1950s, the non-socialist countries mistrusted China and worried about its communist military and political expansion. Therefore, China tried to win their trust. As Zhou Enlai said in 1957, "We, the socialist country, will certainly not invade, but other countries disbelieve us. As a result, we will gradually make them believe us in a practical way and strive for peaceful coexistence. We will do our best to settle boundary disputes with all bordering countries starting with Burma. Then, they will trust us after the solution of Burma's case."[97] When Beijing and Rangoon solved the border dispute, China stated that "It proves that China unhesitatingly implements a peaceful foreign policy and is willing to coexist and cooperate with the countries with different social systems on the basis of the 'Five Principles of Peaceful Coexistence' ... It's no use distorting and defaming China's foreign policy."[98]

Why did China select Burma to be a "brilliant model" of a boundary settlement? China's first Ambassador to Burma explained the reason: "Zhou Enlai told me, 'We have no experience in solving border disputes so we need to select a country to conduct an experiment. Burma maintains good ties with China, and was an initiator of the 'Five Principles of Peaceful Coexistence', which are the political foundation of our negotiations. The Burmese stance on the border dispute with China is typical of that of some small countries. If we amicably solve the border problem with Burma, it will be beneficial in dispelling Burmese fears of China and pacifying the peripheral countries. More important, Burma's case will help the border solutions between China and other countries."[99]

Strategically and politically, Burma was no threat to China and the Chinese Communists had no strategic interest in the disputed area. This important factor led to the boundary settlement for mutual benefit of Burma and China.[100]

---

96 Main points of talks between Premier Zhou Enlai and leading figures in Burma, AMFA, File No. 203-00019-02(1).
97 CCCPC Party Literature Research Office, *Biography of Zhou Enlai*, Vol. 2, p. 1179.
98 "Zhou Enlai's Speech at the Farewell Banquet Held by Premier U Nu", *People's Daily*, 14 October 1961.
99 "Interview Yao Zhongming", quoted in *Biography of Zhou Enlai*, Vol. 2, p. 1178.
100 Luke T. Chang, *China's Boundary Treaties and Frontier Disputes*, London, Rome, and New York: Oceana Publications, Inc, 1982, p. 50.

In addition, also playing a part was the Ne Win factor. In 1958, the border negotiations were brought to a halt by the political crisis in Burma that followed the AFPFL split. "But the crisis brought to office General Ne Win, who tackled the boundary problem with determination." He emphatically told the Chinese that "he had been able to make these proposals only by virtue of his position as a non-partisan Prime Minister and that the Chinese should therefore regard his proposals as the maximum offer that any Burmese government could make. He suggested that, instead of further negotiations, the Chinese should take the small remaining step needed to reach an agreement and offered to go to Peking immediately to sign it."[101] "Towards the end of 1959, as his departure from political office drew near, General Ne Win made forthright and soldierly proposals to Mr. Zhou, not failing to point out that, as leader of the interim government, he commanded the support of all the major parties in Burma as an elected party government might not be able to do."[102] Personally, Ne Win wanted to solve in a friendly manner the dispute with China to increase his political capital in the Burmese political arena. After the two sides had signed the Boundary Treaty and the Friendly Agreement in 1960, the Ne Win government held massive celebrations in border areas to improve Ne Win's personal reputation as well as the legitimacy of the interim government,[103] to show the two factions of the AFPFL that Ne Win had won the support of the Shan state, the Kachin state, and the people on the border problem.[104] When either Ne Win visited China or China's leaders visited Burma in 1960 and 1961, he unequivocally told China about the political cleavages and his dissatisfactions with U Nu, the U.S. and India.[105] Also, China's *Bulletin of Foreign Affairs* in 1960 indicated that Ne Win was the most friendly to China among the various Burmese factions.[106]

The Burma Communist Party Issue

The relations between the CCP and the BCP were a bilateral sensitive issue during the Cold War. Some claim that Sino-Burmese relations in the period

---

101 Whittam, "The Sino-Burmese Boundary Treaty", pp. 179–180.
102 Maung Maung, "The Burma–China Boundary Settlement", p. 41.
103 Burmese government holds celebrations for signing of the friendship treaty and settlement of the boundary agreement for border areas, AMFA, File No. 105-00681-02(1).
104 China holds celebrations for signing of the friendship treaty and boundary agreement, AMFA, File No. 105-00681-01(1).
105 Debriefing after visit to Burma by Zhou Enlai, AMFA, File No. 203-00047-05; Bulletin regarding the conditions of Premier Zhou Enlai's discussions in Burma, AMFA, File No. 203-00036-08(1); Reception to state guests (some of U Nu's responses), AMFA, File No. 204-00119-17(1).
106 Bulletin regarding the conditions of Premier Zhou Enlai's discussions in Burma, AMFA, File No. 203-00036-08(1).

1948–1988 were largely defined by the BCP issue. "Characterized by a form of delicate friendship, they remained the norm until the remarkable transformation of the post-September 1988 period."[107] In general, there is some truth in such a conclusion, but more specifically, the BCP played different roles at different stages. The BCP was not a hurdle in Sino-Burmese relations between 1949 and 1966 because the CCP gave limited support to the BCP and the party-to-party ties were subject to state-to-state relations.

Before the birth of the PRC in 1949, the CCP had publicly and morally supported the BCP's armed combat. After the CCP seized power in China, it maintained secret ties with the latter. Some high-ranking officials of BCP had lived in Beijing since early 1950 and received CCP training. According to the leader of the overseas Chinese Communist Party in Burma, "The secretary of Working Committee of the Overseas Chinese Communist Party, KPX, led two members of the BCP Central Committee to Beijing from Burma soon after the foundation of the PRC. At the end of October 1950, I returned to Beijing to report on our work on behalf of the Working Committee of the overseas Chinese Communist Party in Burma. It was arranged that I lived with three leaders of the BCP, two of whom were led by KPX to Beijing. Several times, LLY introduced the experience of China's land reform and united front work to its fraternal party members."[108]

Some pointed out that the BCP had secretly received moral, material, financial, organizational, and ideological support from the CCP as well as the government before the 1967 "6.26" [June 26] incident (see Chapter 4).[109] Nevertheless, other evidence proves the contrary: the BCP rebels were lacking ammunition and supplies although they were accomplished in bushfighting, and they obviously had not received massive aid from the CCP, according to the CIA's report.[110] China's material support to the BCP rebellions was not significant before the rift in Burma–China relations in 1967.[111] FG, Vice Chairman of the BCP, also verified that massive material support from the CCP started after the break of relations in 1967.[112]

---

107 Chi-shad Liang, "Burma's Relations with the People's Republic of China: from Delicate Friendship to Genuine Co-operation", Peter Carey (ed.), *Burma: The Challenge of Change in a Divided Society*, London: Macmillan Media Ltd, 1997, p. 71.

108 "Memoirs of LWZ, Part II: The Dissolution of the Burmese Overseas Chinese Communist Party". Unpublished manuscript, 1991.

109 Tin Muang Maung Than, "Myanmar and China: A Special Relationship?", *Southeast Asian Affairs*, Singapore, Institute of Southeast Asian Studies, 2003, p. 192; Wayne Bert, "Chinese Relations with Burma and Indonesia", *Asian Survey*, Vol. XI, No. 6, June 1975, p. 475.

110 Shen Zhihua and Yang Kuisong (ed.), *The Declassified Record*, p. 299.

111 *Ibid.*, p. 529.

112 Interview, Vice Chairman of BCP, FG, 17 February 2005, Xiamen.

Beijing also pursued a prudent news policy to avoid irritating Rangoon. There were only 20 pieces of coverage and articles on the BCP in the *People's Daily* from 1947 to July 1949. Only 11 reports appeared in the newspaper from October 1949 to 25 June 1967 and none of them mentioned the overthrow of the Burmese government. However, two reports drew attention. First, the BCP sent a letter of congratulations to the CCP for its 1956 Eighth Session and the letter was published in the *People's Daily*. Although the letter did not touch upon anti-Burmese government sentiment, it was the first time that China publicly released a BCP Central Committee letter in the *People's Daily*.[113] Second, the BCP sent a congratulatory telegram to Beijing on the tenth anniversary of its national celebration in 1959. The letter was carried in the *People's Daily* and half of the congratulations focused on accusations concerning Burma's domestic politics and foreign policy. The BCP criticized the Burmese government for accepting U.S. military aid, constructing the Rangoon–Mandalay strategic highway with U.S. aid, and suppressing domestic unions and the opposition parties.[114] The publication of this letter to some extent indicated that the CCP had begun to loosen its news policy on the BCP. However, China still kept a delicate balance between party-to-party relations and state-to-state relations during U Nu period. In addition, Beijing suggested several times that Rangoon hold peaceful negotiations with the BCP, but this was rejected by Rangoon. For instance, Zhou Enlai visited Burma in 1956 and proposed that U Ba Swe hold peaceful negotiations with the BCP but "they [the Burmese] don't listen yet."[115]

The Ne Win Period (1962–1967)

On 2 March 1962, Ne Win launched a military coup to seize power. The *coup d'etat* raised the curtain on the age of military rule in Burma. Although Ne Win promulgated a new constitution in 1974, it only institutionalized the power of the Burma Socialist Programme Party (BSPP) under military domination. Political upheavals occurred in both China and Burma during 1962–1967. Given the anti-Chinese riot in Rangoon in 1967, this period of 1962–1966 was, in hindsight, on the eve of a great change in bilateral ties.

---

113 "BCP Central Committee's Letter of Congratulations for the 8th National Congress of CCP", *People's Daily*, 21 September 1956.
114 "Telegram of Congratulations from the Central Committee of BCP", *People's Daily*, 30 September 1959.
115 Main points of talks between Premier Zhou Enlai and leading figures in Burma, AMFA, File No. 203-00019-02(1).

Beijing's Posture Toward Ne Win's Military Coup

In the evening of 1 March 1962, Ne Win and his family saw a performance presented in Rangoon by the China Ballet, and this concealed his imminent covert action. At 1:00 a.m. of 2 March, Ne Win took action to wrest power. On the same day, the Chinese Embassy in Rangoon reported the breaking news to Beijing and stressed that the Burmese coup was allied to Nasser's Egyptian coup. "As of now, the Burmese side has not informed foreign embassies that the new government is established... The military government has presently been in complete control of the situation, and the regime won't be changing hands, and will be consolidated. Given this fact, we suggest that our government should recognize it as soon as possible once we receive the served [official] notice about the establishment of the new government."[116]

On 3 March, the Chinese Embassy asked for instructions from their Ministry of Foreign Affairs about whether Ye Jizhuang, the Minister of Foreign Trade visiting Burma, should ask to see Ne Win, and whether they should ask to see the new Foreign Minister, and present congratulations to the new Burmese leadership. Beijing replied, "Now, we should not publicly pronounce on the new regime in a hurry... You pay close attention to other countries' responses and behaviors towards the new government... Give every man the ear, but few the voice... You can congratulate the Ministers for their new appointments on your own behalf."[117]

Beijing took a wait-and-see attitude in the following days. However, at 14:00 p.m. of 6 March, the Embassy sent a telegram to Beijing saying, "Today, the Indian government has instructed its Ambassador to Burma to visit the new Burmese Foreign Minister and deliver a note recognizing the new government. The Foreign Minister of Burma received him this afternoon... The Burmese side dropped our Embassy a hint that the Chinese Ambassador would not be received by the Foreign Minister unless we present the note of recognition. The Embassies of U.K., Thailand, and Indonesia in Rangoon have not received instructions so our recognition should not be postponed. Please send the note of recognition endorsed by Zhou Enlai in the name of Chinese government as soon as possible." At 22:00 p.m., the Chinese Embassy reported back to Beijing that the Burmese government had released a news bulletin that India and the U.K. had submitted notes to recognize the new Burmese government that

---

116 Recognition of the Burmese military regime (Chinese and English version), AMFA, File No. 105-01780-01.
117 Telegrams between Beijing and the Chinese embassy to Burma regarding Chinese recognition of the Burmese military government, AMFA, File No. 117-01344-04.

evening.[118] At 24:00 p.m. Beijing telegraphed the Ambassador, Li Yimang, to "submit the note of recognition endorsed by Chen Yi, the Foreign Minister and the congratulatory telegram to General Ne Win signed by Zhou Enlai ... We will publish the news at home in the evening of 7 March."[119] On the afternoon of 7 March Ambassador Li Yimang submitted the note of recognition and the congratulatory telegram to the Burmese Foreign Minister and Ne Win, respectively. China became the fourth country to recognize the Ne Win military junta.

In fact, Ne Win had disclosed that he wanted to seize power during his trip to China in 1961.[120] Thereafter, the Chinese Embassy to Burma had analyzed the Burmese political situation and predicted a military regime or a military coalition government through a coup possibly occurring in Burma in 1962. The new Burmese government would continue to carry out a peaceful neutralist policy and come to terms with imperialists and feudalists.[121] China's Foreign Ministry responded to the prediction by stating that China should maintain good relations with the military junta considering the overall international situation. But China still should pay attention to the military regime's attitude towards China.[122] As a result, China had mental preparation for Ne Win's coup. It was not a problem for Beijing whether Rangoon's new military regime would be recognized; Beijing only need determine when and in what manner. Put another way, China's hesitation showed that Beijing was uncertain about how to start their new bilateral ties. While detailed information of the coup and the new military regime was unavailable, other countries' reactions were crucial for Beijing to make a decision because they were an important "reference index." Consequently, Beijing stressed the importance of "watching other countries' reactions"[123] in the matter of when China would recognize the Ne Win government and whether Zhou Enlai would send a congratulatory telegram to Ne Win.

China wanted to maintain friendly relations with Burma so it wanted to take the lead in recognizing the Ne Win government and win the new Burmese leadership's favor. Yet the instability of a military junta was influential in

---

118 Responses of other countries to recognition of the Burmese military coup as well as their official acceptance of the new military government, AMFA, File No. 105-01077-04.
119 Recognition of the Burmese military regime, AMFA, File No. 105-01780-01.
120 Course of the Burmese military coup in March 1962, AMFA, File No. 105-01077-01.
121 1961 work review and 1962 work program of the Chinese Embassy to Burma and the official reply of the responsible department, AMFA, File No. 105-01079-01.
122 *Ibid.*
123 Chinese Embassy reply to note from the Burmese Foreign Ministry about the Burmese foreign policy statement, AMFA, File No. 105-01780-02.

Beijing's decision. Although Rangoon declared on the day of the coup that it would still adopt a neutralist foreign policy, Beijing was suspicious of the Burmese position. When China observed the international responses toward the Burma's coup, the reaction of the neighboring countries exerted a crucial influence on Beijing's decision. The first recognition by the United Arab Emirates on 4 March did not change the Chinese policy of wait-and-see. But as soon as India, the important geopolitical rival to China, recognized Rangoon, China immediately followed. In Chinese calculations, China was eager to counter India's influence in Burma. Later, China adopted a different policy than that of India toward Burmese economic nationalization.

The Burma Communist Party Issue

In April 1963, Liu Shaoqi's visit to Burma played a crucial part in the peaceful negotiations between the BCP and the government.[124] There are two versions of Liu Shaoqi's mediation. The first: according to Wang Guangmei's memoir, Liu's wife accompanied him on the trip to Burma, and Ne Win arranged a talk on the BCP issue with Liu Shaoqi at Ngapali seaside resort in order to avoid wiretapping. Ne Win told Liu that "He would like to discuss national problems with the BCP and he expected China to serve as a bridge."[125] The second version: according to Cheng Ruisheng's memory, the accompanying translator of Liu Shaoqi, Liu Shaoqi suggested to Ne Win on the way to Mingaladon airport when he concluded his visit on 26 April that he could negotiate with Thakin Ba Thein Tin in Beijing. Ne Win replied that he needed to talk further with his colleagues about the problem. This conversation directly helped to bring about negotiations between the Ne Win government and the BCP that year.[126] A declassified document of China's Foreign Ministry has proven the second version to be correct, because the conversation records of Liu and Ne Win coincide with Cheng Ruisheng's memory.[127]

On 11 June 1963, the Burmese government issued the negotiation statement. Thakin Than Tun, the Chairman of the BCP Central Committee, wrote to Ne Win welcoming the statement and negotiations. Meanwhile, Thakin

---

124 Foreign Ministry's reply to the Chinese Embassy to Burma on the 1963 Burmese politics summary and the 1964 work program, AMFA, File No. 105-01864-01.

125 Huang Zheng, *Interview with Wang Guangmei*, Beijing: Central Party Literature Press, 2006, p. 317.

126 Cheng Ruisheng, "Records of Sino-Burmese Friendship", in Li Tongcheng and Yu Mingsheng (eds), *Chinese Diplomats in Asia*, Shanghai People's Publishing House, 2005, p. 173.

127 Record of talks between Liu Shaoqi and Burmese leaders, checked and approved by Liu Shaoqi, AMFA, File No. 203-00576-01.

Plate 7: Liu Shaoqi and Ne Win, Rangoon, 20 April 1963 (photograph courtesy Cheng Ruisheng)

Ba Thein Tin, the Vice Chairman of the BCP living in Beijing, asked China to help contact Kyaw Win, the Burmese Ambassador to China, and arrange their meeting and negotiations instead of Than Tun. On 28 June, the two parties met in the CPPCC Auditorium and held talks for one and a half hours. Ba Thein Tin forwarded three points to Ne Win: that two BCP Central Committee members abroad should be sent back to consult with the BCP Central Committee on peace negotiations; that the military operations of the government should be stopped; and that the BCP did not agree to the "Bill of Oblivion" (a general amnesty), which was useless to national peace. On 29 June Ne Win consented to the return of the two committee members. Ba Thein Tin immediately sent two telegrams to the Central Committee of the Communist Party of the Soviet Union and the Central Committee of the Communist Party of Vietnam, and asked them to notify Than Myiang, on vacation in the Soviet Union, the member of the Political Bureau of the Central Committee of the BCP, and Sai Yal in Laos, the alternate member of the BCP Central Committee, to return to Beijing.[128]

128 Contact between the Foreign Ministry and Burmese Embassy to China for return of BCP leaders to Burma, AMFA, File No. 105-01818-01.

From 11 July to 29 September, the leaders of the BCP returned to Burma in three batches including one Vice Chairman, three members of Central Committee and 25 high-ranking cadres. Between 2 September and 31 October, both sides held eight formal negotiations and some informal talks. On 14 November, the peace talks broke down. On 15 November, the Burmese government released a statement from the Revolutionary Council, the National Democratic United Front (NDUF), and the BCP on the failure of negotiations. According to the statement, the Ne Win government took the negotiators to their bases in Burma and Ba Thein Tin was permitted to return to China.[129]

Although the peace talks in 1963 were mediated by Liu Shaoqi and some leaders of the BCP lived in China, the result of talks indicated that the CCP's controlling influence over the BCP did not seem to be predominant. The two parties had different judgments of Ne Win's regime. The CCP only played the role of intermediary and did not participate in the talks. For example, Aung Gyi, the member of the BCP Central Committee, asked China to give some suggestions about peace talks: "How will we negotiate with the government? What should we talk about? What requirements should we raise? How should we cope with Ne Win's policy? We have not deliberated on these problems and wish the CCP to give us some proposals."[130]

Moreover, Aung Gyi articulated the BCP's perceptions on the Ne Win government's differences with the CCP. "He personally thought that the divergences among the CCP, the BCP, and the Soviet Communist Party (SCP) toward Ne Win would affect their respective postures on the talks. The SCP regards Ne Win as a petty bourgeoisie who possibly takes Castro's route so it [wants to] persuade the BCP into laying down arms to cooperate with Ne Win. In the CCP's eyes, Ne Win belongs to national bourgeoisie and will follow Sukarno's political line. The BCP takes Ne Win as a big bourgeoisie and an object to be overthrown."[131] Ba Thein Tin agreed with Aung Gyi and stated that "It's a political offensive against the BCP. Ne Win accedes to peace talks with us because he comes across difficulties now and seeks to get through difficult situations. The nature of the Ne Win government is big bourgeois and it has resolutely opposed the Communist Party all along, so we should not cherish illusions about the Ne Win government."[132] Also, he criticized the SCP's opinion that Ne Win belonged to the petty bourgeoisie and would become a Castro, and

---

129 Peace talks between the BCP and Burmese government, AMFA, File No. 203-00515-02.
130 Contact between the Foreign Ministry and Burmese Embassy for return of BCP leaders, AMFA, File No. 105-01818-01.
131 *Ibid.*
132 *Ibid.*

its suggestion that the BCP should cooperate with Ne Win. "We are against any similar Soviet proposal of cooperation between the BCP and Ne Win, whoever will present it."[133]

The reasons for this failure of negotiations involve many factors. To the BCP, especially its leadership living in China, the result of the talks was inevitably unsuccessful because they believed that it was necessary to topple Ne Win rather than cooperate with him. The BCP acceded to peace talks with the government due to the CCP's influence as well as its own political considerations. Since the CCP praised the BCP for their peace talks with Ne Win, "They [the BCP] gained the political initiative, sounded out Ne Win's intention of peace, and took advantage of the opportunity to contact widely all sides and expand their political influence whether the talks were successful or not."[134] In July 1964, Ne Win told Zhou Enlai that "At that time, the Revolutionary Council really hoped to achieve an agreement with the BCP, and anticipated that the BCP had changed their analyses of the Revolutionary Council. In the past, the BCP argued that we [the Burmese government] had advocated the socialism system not in deeds but in words, and that we were the agents of capitalists and military capitalists, and took the capitalist road to protect the interests of the bourgeoisie. The slogan of socialism advocated by us was a trick and didn't stand for the people's welfare. During the peace talks, the BCP expanded their base areas, drummed up support of the masses, and imposed taxes on the people. They considered that it would be very good if the peace talks were successful; if not, they would still benefit from the negotiations because they had made use of the talks to expand their base areas."[135]

The CCP promoted the negotiations out of several considerations. First, the BCP's military strength was too weak alone to overturn Ne Win in the short run. Second, in order to maintain friendly relations with Burma, China wanted to remove or alleviate Rangoon's apprehensions and suspicions that Beijing was making use of the BCP to subvert the government. Third, China took the chance of the talks to promote cooperation between Ne Win and Burmese leftists to weaken pro-U.S. factions. Finally, the Soviet Union supported Ne Win's Burmese Way to Socialism and suggested that the BCP cooperate with the government instead of engaging in armed combat. More importantly, the Soviets used the BCP problem to harm Sino-Burmese relations.[136] As a result,

---

133 *Ibid.*
134 *Ibid.*
135 Summary of discussion between Premier Zhou Enlai and Chairman Ne Win, AMFA, File No. 203-00583-05.
136 Trends in the Burmese political situation, AMFA, File No. 105-01227-01.

Beijing's aim was to counterattack the Soviet Union's intention of alienating Burma from China.

In June 1963, Chairman Mao instructed that a Vice Foreign Minister should replace the Chinese Ambassador to Burma, "in order to enhance friendly relations and support the current peace talks in Burma."[137] Thus, Geng Biao, Vice Foreign Minister, was appointed the new Ambassador; he had rich experience of military affairs and peace talks.[138] As Vice Foreign Minister, Geng was in charge of foreign affairs with Burma. In 1946, he had worked as the CCP's negotiator in the Beijing Executive Headquarters supervising the cease-fire negotiations between the CCP and the KMT. The replacement of China's Ambassador to Burma reflected Beijing's painstaking care in regard to the peace talks.

"Before China's new Ambassadors to foreign countries went to their posts, at that time they generally were collectively or individually received by one or two central leaders. However, Geng's treatment before he left for Burma was very unusual, which indicated that his mission and responsibility was of high importance."[139] According to Geng Biao, Mao Tsetung, Liu Shaoqi, Zhou Enlai and Chen Yi met him respectively, and gave instructions to him. All of their instructions emphasized boosting bilateral friendship and cooperation.[140]

On 23 November 1963, Ne Win asked Vice Premier Marshal He Long, who was visiting Indonesia by way of Rangoon, to send words to Chinese leaders that "The failure of peace talks is a Burmese internal affair and by no means impacts on Burma–China friendly relations."[141] "This event did cause our two countries a dilemma but we understand each other."[142] Although Ne Win repeatedly asserted that the broken peace talks wouldn't impair bilateral relations, "He is very dissatisfied and apprehensive that we support not his Burmese Way to Socialism, but the BCP."[143] "Thanks to the shattered peace talks, Burma knows that we fail to provide the desired supports to them and so they will contain our influence in Burma and take more precautions against

---

137 Geng Biao, Memoir of Geng Biao: 1949–1992, Nanjing: Jiangsu People's Press, 1998, p. 168.
138 Cheng Ruisheng, Forty Years of Good-neighborly Diplomacy, Chengdu: Sichuan People's Press, 2006, p. 66.
139 Cheng Ruisheng, "Account of Geng Biao's service as an envoy to Burma", Hunan Tide, No. 8, 2009.
140 Geng, Memoir of Geng Biao, pp. 171–172.
141 Burmese domestic situation and foreign relations, and Sino-Burmese relations, AMFA, File No. 203-00515-03.
142 Vice Premier He Long Met Chairman Ne Win via Burma to Indonesia, AMFA, File No. 105-01819-01.
143 Materials for investigation and research on Burmese domestic politics and foreign affairs conducted by the First Asian Department of the Foreign Ministry, AMFA, File No. 105-01314-02.

China."[144] In July 1964, Zhou Enlai visited Burma and suggested once again that Rangoon and the BCP resume peace talks. Ne Win rejected the suggestion, stating that the trust between the two sides had been destroyed.[145]

At the time of the fifteenth anniversary of China's National Day, the BCP sent a letter of congratulations to Beijing. Beijing broadcast the letter in English and Burmese, and published it in the *People's Daily* of 3 October. In the letter, the BCP attributed the failure of the peace talks in 1963 to the sabotage of the imperialists, domestic reactionaries, and revisionists.[146] Although China had published the BCP's congratulatory letter in 1958, the 1963 publication seemed more sensitive and meaningful due to its publication soon after the failed peace talks. Also, China foresaw that Burma would remain unsatisfied. Hence, on October 10, 1964, the Ministry of Foreign Affairs and the International Department of the Central Committee of the CCP gave instructions to the Chinese Embassy in Rangoon on the potential Burmese response to the BCP's congratulatory letter problem: "If Burma refers to the problem, you reply that the letter of congratulations was sent by the Central Committee of the BCP to the Central Committee of the CCP. The CCP will publish and broadcast all letters and telegrams of congratulations in full sent by fraternal parties no matter whether they are legal or not in their own countries. It was not the first time to publish the BCP's letter of congratulations, which related to party-to-party relations rather than state-to-state relations. Burma–China relations are friendly."[147] On 7 October, the official Burmese newspaper *The Guardian* carried an editorial criticizing the letter of congratulations from the BCP and expressed discontent with China. "The BCP is not loyal to the Burmese revolutionary road but to foreign countries ... China adopts a janus-faced policy towards Burma."[148]

China made efforts to keep a balance between party relations and state relations, but in reality its dual track approach was impossible. Over 1962–1966, the BCP problem between Beijing and Rangoon was more evident and serious than during the U Nu period. Although the CCP had not publicly supported the BCP, the aborted peace talks and the congratulatory letter problem damaged bilateral relations, which became two important causal factors why Ne Win was annoyed with Beijing. After the failure of negotiations, the Burmese grudge

---

144 Burmese domestic situation and foreign relations, AMFA, File No. 203-00515-03.
145 Summary of discussion between Zhou Enlai and Ne Win, AMFA, File No. 203-00583-05.
146 "Letter of Congratulations of the BCP Central Committee", *People's Daily*, 3 October 1964.
147 The problem caused by the publication of BCP congratulatory letter, AMFA, File No. 105-01600-04.
148 *Ibid.*

against China was repeatedly mentioned in the documents of China's Foreign Ministry and the reports of the Chinese Embassy to Burma.[149]

Beijing's Attitude toward The Burmese Way to Socialism

Soon after Ne Win came to power, he advocated the Burmese Way to Socialism. The CCP's perception of the Burmese Way to Socialism and how Beijing viewed the nature of Ne Win's regime are important in exploring the essence of Burma–China relations during this period.

China did not comment following the announcement of the Burmese Way to Socialism. Soon after Ne Win's military coup in 1962, the Chinese Embassy to Rangoon requested instructions from the Foreign Ministry how tactically to respond to the military government because they "are endeavoring to collect our perspectives on the Burmese Way to Socialism through various channels."[150] The Ne Win government paid special attention to the reactions from all countries to its new ideology. China's press did not report it at all, while the Soviet Union, Romania, Czechoslovakia, Poland, and Hungary expressed support. Accordingly, "The Burmese military government was disgruntled at our silence toward its political platform."[151] In reply, Beijing instructed that although the Burmese junta advocated the Burmese Way to Socialism, they actually practiced the policies of an anti-communist and anti-people party, an economic monopoly, and a military dictatorship. "We certainly can not support such 'socialism'. However, because Burma has implemented a peaceful and neutral foreign policy and a friendly policy toward China, it is our object to unite and compete for [influence]. Tactically, we still will properly clarify our position on different occasions."[152]

China did not directly comment on the Burmese political platform and the Burmese Way to Socialism whether in public or in personal contacts. China only expressed general support for Rangoon's neutral and peaceful foreign policy, Burmese national independence, and its friendly attitude towards China.[153]

---

149 Assessment by the Chinese Embassy to Burma of the Burmese political situation, AMFA, File No. 105-01225-01; More efforts to pull Burma into China's orbit, AMFA, File No. 105-01865-01; Negotiations of Premier Zhou Enlai's visit to Burma, AMFA, File No. 203-00582-04.
150 The problem of clarifying our position on the Burmese Way to Socialism, AMFA, File No. 105-01816-01.
151 Burmese materials: Introduction and general situation of Burma, the problems of Sino-Burmese ties, and Sino-Burmese chronicles of events, AMFA, File No. 203-00473-02.
152 The problem of clarifying our position on the Burmese Way to Socialism, AMFA, File No. 105-01816-01.
153 *Ibid.*

The quieter China kept its attitude toward the Burmese Way to Socialism, the more eager Rangoon was to know Beijing's attitude.[154] In April 1964, Liu Shaoqi visited Burma and voiced Chinese opinions on the Burmese Way to Socialism in political and diplomatic parlance. "The Socialist Road is at an experimental stage. The socialism of China as well as the Soviet's is on a road that will continue long before it ends ... Burma has chosen to try the Socialist Road. If Burmese socialism is successful and has positive results, China also may learn from Burma ... The socialism pursued by each country is permitted to vary and be a trial effort by which we can learn from each other. Burma may carry out an experiment on Burmese socialism as long as Burma does not label Burmese socialism as the correct international socialism route."[155] Liu's comments were tactful, which revealed two points: on the one hand, China did not object diplomatically to the Burmese Way to Socialism; on the other hand, Beijing ideologically disfavored Burmese Socialism.

Ne Win told Liu that although Burmese socialism was different from those of other countries, the objective of both China's and Burma's socialism was the same. "In the end, we will still carry out Marxism–Leninism. We are gradually realizing the goal. If we advocate Marxism–Leninism now, the people will fear that we are the same as a communist party. We must educate the people and enlist their support ... Burmese socialism is different from the socialism of the right-wing Socialist Parties of Europe so we hope that you do not identify us with right-wing Socialist Parties ... We don't follow Western countries and take the capitalist road, but we politically and economically construct socialism."[156]

Ne Win's statement demonstrated that he wanted to convince Beijing of the same objective and nature of the two countries' socialism, and sought to win China's support and recognition. According to the translator of the Ne Win – Liu Shaoqi talks in 1964, Cheng Ruisheng, "Ne Win was very pleased and grateful when he heard Liu Shaoqi's opinions."[157] Later, the Embassy's report to Beijing also proved that Ne Win had appreciated Liu Shaoqi's comments on the Burmese Way to Socialism, which had greatly removed his suspicion of China because Beijing had reserved its judgment on it prior to 1964.[158] But

---

154 Recommendations from the Chinese Embassy to Burma to the Ministry of Foreign Affairs, AMFA, File No. 105-01816-02.
155 Record of talks between Liu Shaoqi and Burmese leaders, AMFA, File No. 203-00576-01.
156 Record of talks between Liu Shaoqi and Burmese leaders, AMFA, File No. 203-00576-01. A dissident colonel in Yangon, when asked whether Ne Win was a socialist, replied, "Ne Win will be a socialist when Mao Tsetung learns to play golf!" Personal interview.
157 Cheng Ruisheng, *Forty Years of Good-neighborly Diplomacy*, p. 64.
158 Burmese foreign relations, AMFA, File No. 105-01157-03.

Liu's statement was only a Chinese tactic; Beijing had not changed its opinion of Burmese socialism.

In 1964, a report from the Chinese Embassy to Burma to the Foreign Ministry analyzed Burmese socialism, and drew the conclusion that it was not true and scientific socialism but bureaucratic capitalism with the outward appearances of socialism. The report listed nine reasons to prove that conclusion.[159] In 1965, the First Asian Department of the Foreign Ministry also concluded that Ne Win "fancies to pursue 'socialism' not under the leadership of the Communist Party in Burma, . . . [this] is state capitalism in effect, and [the Burmese] have taken the capitalist road of military dictatorship."[160]

After Liu's trip to Burma, China still remained silent on Burmese socialism, so Ne Win's pleasure brought about by Liu's statements proved to be temporary; Rangoon remained discontent that China did not recognize Burmese socialism.[161] In contrast, the Soviet and eastern European states favored it in high profile and propagandized it. In early 1965, the Chinese Embassy in Rangoon reminded Beijing that "It is worth noting that the propaganda of the Soviet Union caters for Ne Win junta's needs and that Soviet influence is expanding [in Burma] . . . In less than half a year, the Soviet Union has published at great length nearly 20 articles to boost the Burmese Way to Socialism, prettify the Ne Win junta, and give enormous publicity to Ne Win's 'achievements'." The three documents, *Program of Burmese Way to Socialism, Philosophy of Burmese Program Part,* and *Special Characteristics of Burmese Socialist Programme Party* would lead Burma on the socialist road.[162] "Recently, there are signs that Ne Win cherishes more illusions about the new leadership of the Soviet revisionist government, and Burma is building closer relations with the Soviet Union."[163]

China's non-recognition of Burmese Way to Socialism also meant that Beijing's judgment about the nature of Ne Win's military government was inevitably negative. When Rangoon released the *Special Characteristics of the Burma Socialist Programme Party* on 4 September 1964, China's Embassy commented on the document: "It [the government] acts like the bourgeoisie, and is the

---

159 Assessment by the Chinese Embassy to Burma of the Burmese political situation, AMFA, File No. 105-01225-01.

160 Materials for investigation and research on Burmese domestic politics and foreign affairs, AMFA, File No. 105-01314-02.

161 Purchasing of 100,000 tons of Burmese rice in 1965, AMFA, File No. 105-01604-01.

162 Materials for investigation and research on Burmese domestic politics and foreign affairs, AMFA, File No. 105-01314-02.

163 Materials for investigation and research on Burmese domestic politics and foreign affairs conducted by the Chinese Embassy to Burma, AMFA, File No. 105-00314-01.

dictatorship of military junta and a military party."[164] This analysis was adopted by Beijing because, as another later report of the First Asian Department of the Foreign Ministry expatiated on the nature of the Ne Win government, "The Ne Win military clique is a special group deriving from the Burmese bourgeoisie. It belongs to a centrist [group] of bourgeoisie according to its political positions ... The Ne Win military government takes on domestic policies of an anti-communist party and anti-people rather than depending on the masses. Although the government opposes U.S. imperialist's subversion and safeguards national independence, it doesn't dare to offend U.S. imperialism, cherishes illusions about the Soviet revisionism, and is wary of China."[165]

China's Backing of Ne Win

Although China ideologically was skeptical about the Burmese Way to Socialism and regarded the Ne Win military government as a bourgeois regime, Beijing carried out a realistic foreign policy to maintain good relations with Rangoon. China still subordinated party-to-party relations to state-to-state relations. Of course, Ne Win's China policy weighed heavily in Beijing's decision-making. Because Ne Win continued to implement a neutralist foreign policy, China sought to win over Ne Win's regime.[166]

After Ne Win came into power, the government carried out a program of economic nationalization in order to achieve the Burmese Way to Socialism. This catastrophic and absurd program caused political and economic turbulence, social turmoil, and popular discontent in Burma. China seized the opportunity to expand Chinese influence in Burma.

On 19 March 1964, Ne Win nationalized the economy and pursued a policy of autarky. More than 10,000 private stores were nationalized, of which 6,700 were owned by the Chinese and their funds were estimated to hold more than Kyat 0.2 billion.[167] On 17 May, the government issued a decree that 50 and 100 kyat notes would cease to be legal tender, so that the Chinese community's economy suffered heavy losses. Although limited compensation was offered, countless Chinese savings were wiped out overnight. All the schools and newspapers operated by the overseas Chinese were nationalized or banned.

---

164 Assessment of the Burmese political situation, File No. 105-01225-01.
165 Materials for investigation and research on Burmese domestic politics and foreign affairs, AMFA, File No. 105-01314-02.
166 The problem of clarifying our position on the Burmese Way to Socialism, AMFA, File No. 105-01816-01.
167 Current situation and problems of Burmese Overseas Chinese, AMFA, File No. 105-01662-05.

Two Beijing banks, the Bank of Communications and the Bank of China, were nationalized. Ne Win's nationalization cut off the channels and eradicated the main source of China's influence over the Chinese community in Burma. "This situation presented the Chinese Communists with a dilemma: either they could make known their dissatisfaction with this action and it would result in a reduction of Peking's influence in Burma, or they could remain silent because Western influence was also being reduced."[168] Beijing not only kept quiet but supported Ne Win. "Facing these situations, China's government takes a supportive attitude towards Burmese fundamental domestic and foreign policies, and actively promotes its improvement of the conditions according to the established foreign policy."[169]

China withdrew the assets from the two nationalized banks, Kyat 5 million, and presented them as a gift to the military government. "India issued a written protest against Burma and claimed compensation. China's action formed a sharp contrast to Indian attitude, which was of great political benefit."[170] On 1 April 1965, 129 private middle schools including 16 Chinese schools were announced to be nationalized. In the afternoon of 1 April, the Chinese Embassy made an appointment to meet U Tun Tin, the chief of the 3rd Politics Department of the Burmese Foreign Ministry, where he stated that "China's government always instructs the overseas Chinese to abide by the laws and decrees of their country of residence. China's Embassy completely supports that Burmese government takeover of the Chinese schools, and we are ready to give our cooperation to you if you need our help during the take-over."[171]

During this demonstration of Burmese nationalisation, aliens transferred their property and funds. According to a report of the Chinese Embassy, by 1964, several hundreds of millions Kyat funds fled Burma and over 20,000 Indians were forced from the country (200,000 followed later). "Widespread panic occurred in the Chinese community. Some leaders of Overseas Chinese associations shipped their property to the Embassy for safekeeping, and some Chinese escaped to Yunnan with gold requesting that the Chinese government transfer the capital to China. In a word, the

---

168 Robert A. Holmes, "Burmese Domestic Policy: The Politics of Burmanization", *Asian Survey*, Vol. 7, No. 3, March 1967, p. 193.
169 Situation report by Chinese Embassy to Burma on Ne Win's economic nationalization, AMFA, File No. 118-01251-03.
170 Nationalization of Burmese banks and China abandons the assets of China Bank and Bank of Communications (Chinese and English Version), AMFA, File No. 105-01822-01.
171 Reduction of Burmese rice production, and fiscal and economic measures, AMFA, File No. 105-01303-04.

overseas Chinese universally demanded official help in transferring their property and funds."[172]

India reacted against Burmese nationalization. On 21 April, nearly 1,000 Indians demonstrated in front of the Indian Embassy, a demonstration said to be hatched by the Embassy itself. On May 6, the Indian Foreign Ministry stated that the Indian government had passed on Burmese Indian concerns to the Burmese government and asked Rangoon to reconsider their plight. An Indian diplomat was dispatched to Rangoon to negotiate the problem. On 20 May, the Indian Embassy issued a special press communique and notified the Indians in Burma to hand their gold and jewelry to the Embassy. The Burmese government commented, "This is a disgraceful act."[173]

Although the Ambassador Geng Biao on 22 May expressed China's concerns about the overseas Chinese unfavorable situation and asked Burma to protect their legitimate rights and interests, Beijing was reluctant to displease Ne Win for the sake of overseas Chinese interests. Compared with India, China's banks in the Yunnan border area were ordered to stop transacting Kyat deposits[174] and large overseas remittances in Kyat[175] in order to keep friendly relations with Rangoon.

Beijing's apathy triggered overseas Chinese anger and discontent. They complained that China's government disregarded their interests, and that "the motherland sacrificed overseas Chinese interests."[176] Although the Embassy did endeavor to propitiate the Chinese community again and again, it served no purpose because China failed to help them solve their practical difficulties.[177] Conversely, Beijing stressed: "At this moment of upheaval, it is necessary to enhance the ideological work aimed at the overseas Chinese. This ideological work on the overseas Chinese bourgeoisie is based on patriotism and mainly includes improving their consciousness of anti-imperialism and anti-colonialism, pushing them to further Burma–China friendship, demanding that [the government] carry out our policies for the overseas Chinese, [urging them] to comply with Burmese laws and decrees, and to drop out of Burmese political activities

---

172 Information of the Department of Consular Affairs: Overseas Chinese in the situation of Ne Win's nationalization, AMFA, File No. 118-01328-01.
173 Trends in the Burmese political situation, AMFA, File No. 105-01227-01.
174 Situation report on Ne Win's economic nationalization, AMFA, File No. 118-01251-03.
175 Notice, queries and replies to the General Bank as well as to branch banks with regard to overseas remittances, Documentation in the Archives of Fujian Province, Roll No. 230, Cat No. 3, File No. 806, 1963.
176 Situation report on Ne Win's economic nationalization, AMFA, File No. 118-01251-03.
177 Current situation and problems of Burmese Overseas Chinese, AMFA, File No. 105-01662-05.

... The overseas Chinese proletariat should be educated in both patriotism and internationalism. They should be instructed to love the motherland as well as the Burmese people, to correctly understand the Burmese situation, and China's Burma policy."[178] "Regarding the education of China–Burma friendship among the overseas Chinese, first inculcate the idea in the leaders and cadremen of the Chinese community, and then make popular the overseas Chinese understanding of the significance of our friendly policy toward Ne Win."[179]

Obviously, China was not content with Burmese nationalization but it was still in favor of Ne Win's scheme. Beijing instructed that overseas Chinese interests should be subordinate to Beijing's interests and the friendship of the two countries. When Zhou visited Rangoon in July 1964, he asserted in Rangoon that "China favors the Ne Win government gradually taking back the enterprises operated by foreigners, including overseas Chinese."[180] "The overseas Chinese should abide by Burmese laws and orders and you need not give lenient treatment to the overseas Chinese breaking the law."[181] On the way to the airport when Zhou was concluding his visit, he specially told Ne Win again that he had ordered the Chinese Embassy to convene the leaders of the Chinese community and had urged them to abide by Burmese laws and decrees. "There are sure to be some profiteers among overseas Chinese capitalists, and some have connections with Hong Kong and Taiwan."[182] Moreover, the relationship between economic independence to political independence were underlined by the China–Burma joint communiqués issued during Zhou Enlai's and Liu Shaoqi's trips in February 1964 and April 1966, respectively, and Ne Win's visit to China in July 1965.

While Ne Win was taking firm steps to implement the Burmese Way to Socialism program, some opposition was brewing to overthrow his regime. On 5 June 1964, the Chinese Embassy reported to Beijing that according to its intelligence, Sein Win, the commander of the Burmese Middle Military Region, was planning to launch a military coup in the following two weeks after 30 May.[183]

After the policy debate, Beijing concluded on 9 June that "Although the current bilateral relations are not warm, overall ties are normal. Presently Ne

178 Situation report on Ne Win's economic nationalization, AMFA, File No. 118-01251-03.
179 Reports of the Chinese Embassy to Burma on Burmese assistance for the return to China of Overseas Chinese, as well as replies from the Central Committee of the Overseas Chinese and the Foreign Ministry, AMFA, File No. 118-01322-01.
180 Diplomatic bulletin of Premier Zhou Enlai's visit to Burma, AMFA, File No. 203-00583-04.
181 Summary of discussion between Zhou Enlai and Ne Win, AMFA, File No. 203-00583-05.
182 *Ibid.*
183 More efforts to pull Burma into China's orbit, AMFA, File No. 105-01865-01.

Win has politically isolated himself in the extreme, faces a sea of economic troubles, and is facing the danger of being subverted and even murdered by imperialists and the domestic right-wing factions. Although Ne Win is reactionary and passive, he has sharp friction with American imperialism and his ties with Soviet revisionists are not solid. By and large, Ne Win's attitude toward China is friendly. Under the current situation in Burma, whoever comes into power will be more reactionary than Ne Win, and the U.S., the U.K. and Japan will definitely penetrate Burma. This scenario is detrimental to China and the Burmese people."[184] Therefore, Zhou Enlai instructed the Foreign Ministry to telegraph to Ambassador Geng Biao, and "Ask him to inform Ne Win of three points face to face: 1. the intelligence of a military coup against him; 2. ask him what aids Burma urgently needs now; 3 say that Zhou Enlai or Chen Yi is willing to go to Rangoon to exchange views with Ne Win if he feels it necessary."[185] Over 10–11 July 1964, Zhou Enlai secretly visited Burma. Zhou Enlai and Ne Win held three talks for total 11 hours in the two days. Zhou Enlai suggested that Ne Win should not take drastic measures in the economic sphere and that his policy should focus on annihilating speculators and the colonialist economic power in Burma and uniting medium- and small-sized traders.[186]

Beijing's energetic support of Ne Win arose from its judgement that "If Ne Win falls from power, a more reactionary government will ensue, and the U.S. and U.K.'s influence will spread in Burma. The upshot would be disadvantageous to the Burmese people, the whole struggle of anti-U.S. imperialism in Southeast Asia, as well as to us. As a result, we should firmly support Ne Win."[187] In addition, Beijing believed that the BCP and other revolutionary forces were too weak to seize power. If Ne Win were overturned, the "reactionary" factions would be stronger. If Ne Win's reign continued, the Burmese revolution would have more time to build up its strength.[188]

The political relations of Burma–China between 1955 and 1966 can be interpreted from three Chinese perspectives: global, regional and bilateral relations. Globally, Burma–China political relations were guided by Beijing's peaceful foreign policy and its strategic objective of establishing an international anti-American united front. China made an attempt to present Burma–China rela-

184 *Ibid.*
185 *Ibid.*
186 Vice Premier Chen Yi informed Burmese Ambassador to China of Premier Zhou Enlai's trip to Burma, AMFA, File No. 106-01144-02.
187 Diplomatic bulletin of Zhou Enlai's visit to Burma, AMFA, File No. 203-00583-04.
188 Schedule for Premier Zhou Enlai's visit to Burma, AMFA, File No. 203-00582-01.

tions as a "brilliant model" of peaceful coexistence with non-socialist countries. At a regional level, political relations served in countering the U.S. containment policy, defending Chinese national security, and creating peaceful zones around China. Bilaterally, Beijing adopted flexible and realistic policies towards Burma so that the barriers between the two countries, such as the border dispute, KMT troops, the overseas Chinese problem, and the export of revolution, did not damage their relations.

Economic Relations 1955–1966

Since the shift in Burma–China relations in 1954, their scale of trade had expanded. While China's exports to Burma increased by 32 times, from US$0.37 million in 1954 to US$10.68 million in 1955, its imports from Burma expanded by 28 times, from US$0.52million in 1954 to US$17.29 million in 1955. During 1955–1966, the annual average import and export volumes reached US$14.5 million and US$18.26 million, respectively.[189]

In March 1955, the purchasing group of the Burmese government visited China and signed three contracts worth £1.9 million, to purchase 36 kinds of merchandise like steel, cotton yarn, and plastic. On 21 February 1958, a new trade agreement was signed by the two parties valid for one year. In October 1960, a Burmese government trade delegation visited China and a consensus was reached on expanding bilateral trade and reopening the Burma–Yunnan road. On 15 October 1960, China's trade delegation arrived in Rangoon to further develop and expand bilateral trade. An agreement that China would purchase Burmese rice was signed on 24 October. At the end of January 1961, Burma and China signed a trade agreement in Beijing valid for five years. In 1966, *Exchange of Notes on Extension Burma–China Trade and Payment Protocol* was signed and both sides agreed to continue adopting the bilateral trade and payment protocol signed in 1961 before the signature of a new trade protocol. In the same year, Beijing promised to buy 10 long tons of Burmese rice produced in 1966 and 8 long tons of rice produced in 1967.

In Beijing's calculation of foreign policy, economic and technological cooperation between China and the developing countries "Played important political and economic roles in uniting them and winning their support."[190] Sino-Burmese economic and technological cooperation dated from the mid-1950s. On 17 July 1956, China provided all machinery and equipment, engineering design, and technical experts to expand a Burmese spinning mill. Moreover,

189 *Yearbook of China's International Trade and Economy*, pp. iv–15.
190 *Chronicle of Zhang Wentian*, Vol. 2, p. 1021.

another spinning mill, a rubber plant, and a soap factory were built with the support of Chinese equipment and technology. According to the economic and technological cooperation protocol signed in January 1961, China gave a loan of £30 million to Burma. Up to mid-1960, 300 experts and technicians in the paper industry, hydroelectricity, bridges, botany, geology, chemical engineering and light industry sectors were dispatched to Burma, assisting in the construction of 12 projects with Chinese loans.

China held that "It is necessary to economically conduct proper as well as active propaganda towards Burma, and introduce our economic experience to them ... In order to unite Burma and impair imperialist influence in the country, and to boost the friendly relations and bilateral economic and trade ties." It was also useful to hold exhibitions on China's economic achievements in Burma and initiate reciprocal visits in the economic sphere.[191] There were dozens of official economic and commercial missions between China and Burma between 1954 and 1966.

The profile of Burma–China economic relations of this period was shaped by the correlation between economic factors and political considerations; political warmth drove the trade and economic ties, and the economic nexus served political relations. On the whole, the development of Sino-Burmese economic ties was not motivated by economic considerations but by China's political and security interests in Burma. Beijing even stated that China's economic and trade deals with Burma should meet the demands of Sino-Burmese political relations, and cater to China's diplomacy towards Burma.[192] For instance, although the two countries were economically backward, the level of China's industrialization was higher compared with Burma. Accordingly, "Our exports to Burma can meet Burmese needs but their available export commodities are not demanded by China,"[193] especially rice.

Burma was once the world's largest exporter of rice. After its independence, rice was the most important agricultural commodity of Burma, whose export accounted for 70–80 percent of gross export values. However, just as Zhou said, "Rice is also the major item of export in China. As a result, it is impossible for China to expend foreign exchange on importing rice in large quantities from Burma. Only when Burma woos us to purchase its rice, do we take into consideration the circumstances to buy some rice in order to help them out

191 Review by Chinese Embassy to Burma of Sino-Burmese economic ties in the past decade, AMFA, File No. 105-00603-01.
192 *Ibid.*
193 *Ibid.*

of difficulties."[194] China played the "rice card" to please Burma on occasion. In 1957, Zhou Enlai told U Kyaw Nyein, Vice Prime Minister of Burma that "China's grain yield is increasing but Burma does not need to worry about it and we won't impact the market share of Burmese rice."[195] Beijing's rice offensive did win Burmese appreciation and a favorable impression of China in the 1950s. U Nu even publicly expressed thanks to China for the rice deals on several occasions.[196]

Although trade developed, economics were not crucial to the two party's foreign relationships. This mainly resulted from the low level of bilateral economic development, the low degree of industrialization, and weak complementarities in the two economies. Politics promoted the development of the bilateral trade represented by the rice trade, and economic grants and co-operation. The economic relations between Burma and China in 1955–1966 were, however, a crucial component of bilateral political relations. Politics and diplomatic policies played significant roles in promoting bilateral economics and trade.

Cultural Relations 1955–1966

From 1950 to 1966, dozens of cultural delegations exchanged visits between Rangoon and Beijing, which chiefly included sports, religion, arts, medicine, media and movies. There were 39 cultural interchanges during 1949–1959, with Chinese delegations to Burma amounting to 17 visits with 453 members, and Burmese delegations to China reaching 22 and 244 visitors.[197]

Cultural relations at this stage were the indication as well of political relations. As China's Embassy in Rangoon generalized, "As a rule, cultural intercourse is premised with politics because politics needs concerted actions in the cultural domain. If bilateral relations are amicable, the cultural missions are easy to be undertaken. If cold, they are impossible to be carried out." Therefore, China–Burma "cultural intercourse is intensive sometimes and infrequent once in a while."[198] For example, when they solved the border dispute over 1960–1961, a climax of cultural exchanges occurred. In 1960, China's Cultural Delegation, the National Ensemble of Ethnic Minorities Songs and Dances,

---

194 *Ibid.*
195 Record of talks between Premier Zhou Enlai and Vice Prime Minister U Kyaw Nyein, AMFA, File No. 105-00339-02(1).
196 Review of Sino-Burmese economic ties, AMFA, File No. 105-00603-01.
197 Review by Chinese Embassy to Burma of Sino-Burmese cultural ties in the past decade, AMFA, File No. 105-00603-02(1).
198 *Ibid.*

and the Basketball Team of Chengdu visited Burma, while the Burmese Cultural and Amity Troupe, a strong government mission of 370 members led by U Nu, visited China, and included cultural, sports, news, trade, and military delegations. In 1961, Premier Zhou Enlai headed a strong mission of 430 delegates to visit Burma, and it consisted of delegations of government, military, culture and art personnel, as well as those from Yunnan province, Buddhists, movies, sports, news and boundary supervisors. Among them, the cultural and arts delegation alone comprised 300 delegates and performed 24 times for 270,000 throughout Burma.

Beijing regarded cultural communications as an instrument to push political ties. "Play the role of cultural intercourse in promoting bilateral relations as far as possible," in order to "draw Burma over to our side, impair imperialist influence, further expand our country's influence in Burma, and encourage Burma into defending its national independence and countering colonialism."[199]

Buddhism in Burma is predominantly of the Theravada tradition, and is practiced by an overwhelming majority of the country's population. It plays an important part in Burmese politics, society, and economy. In the mid 1950s, various rumors about China's Buddhism were prevalent in Burma. Rumor had it that "Buddhism has been banned in China." Chinese monks "were expelled and killed."[200] To counter such charges, religious exchanges were placed on Beijing's preferred cultural agenda. Especially important was the Buddha Tooth Relic, which was delivered in October 1955 from China to Burma to be worshipped; it "played great role of boosting bilateral amity."[201] When the Buddha Tooth Relic arrived in Rangoon, the President, Prime Minister, two House Speakers, the leading figures in the government and military, honor guards of the army and foreign envoys welcomed it at the airport, and a grand welcome ceremony was held at the same time. Rangoon city turned out to welcome it and the citizens worshipped it along the road from the airport to downtown. The pilgrimage of the Buddha Tooth Relic "had extensive as well as a profound influence on Burmese."[202] According to the escort of Buddha Tooth Relic, "Burma's government and the Buddhist community adopted warmer and more cordial attitudes to us when our Buddhism delegation visited Burma six months ago." "During the pilgrimage of the Buddha Tooth Relic, some

---

199 *Ibid.*
200 Zhao Puchu, "Independence, Peace and Friendship", *People's Daily*, 28 May 1955.
201 Review of Sino-Burmese cultural ties, AMFA, File No. 105-00603-02(1).
202 Report of the Chinese Buddhist Association on transport of the Buddha's tooth relic, AMFA, File No. 105-00182-10(1).

leading figures in the Buddhist community established closer relations with us. Some attitudes were changed by this activity."[203]

In early 1955 and 1956, skirmishes broke out in China–Burma border areas, which resulted in the tension and estrangement between the two countries. For this reason, leaders conducted mutual visits in the second half of 1956 to negotiate the border dispute. Under this circumstance, Beijing dispatched artistic delegations to visit Burma several times in order to "mitigate the tension between two countries caused by boundary problems, create a friendly atmosphere and political impact when Zhou Enlai, Marshal Ye Jianying and the Governor of Yunnan province were to visit Burma."[204]

From the end of the 1950s and in the early 1960s, Beijing gradually changed its realist foreign policy largely based on national security and interests to a radical revolutionary policy highlighting the dominant role of ideology in policymaking. By the mid 1960s, China had established a radical revolutionary foreign policy characterized by countering imperialism, revisionism, and all reactionaries of various countries, and supporting and aiding the revolutionary movements in Asia, Africa, and Latin America. The shock of Beijing's radical revolutionary position to Burma was not immediately obvious. Nevertheless, after the eruption of the "Cultural Revolution," Burma could not escape the export of revolution. On 4 January 1967, Vice-Premier Chen Yi declared at the reception of the nineteenth anniversary of Burmese Independence held by Burmese Embassy in Beijing that "An eternal socialist China will more effectively struggle against imperialism, modern revisionism, and reactionaries of foreign countries, more forcefully patronize people's struggle for world peace, national independence, people's democracy and socialism in Asia, Africa, and Latin America, and the world, and more successfully fulfill our international responsibility."[205] From January to 26 June 1967, namely before the anti-Chinese riots in that year, articles and reports about the propaganda of Mao Tsetung thought, anti-Soviet articles, support to the Chinese Cultural Revolution, and the personality cult around Mao in Burma were continually published in the *People's Daily*.[206] In these reports, Beijing used the title of "Burmese Friends"

---

203 *Ibid.*
204 Review of Sino-Burmese cultural ties, AMFA, File No. 105-00603-02(1).
205 "Eternal Socialist China Will Fulfill International Responsibility", *People's Daily*, 5 January 1967.
206 For Example, "Burmese Friends Eager to Learn *Quotations from Chairman Mao*", *People's Daily*, 19 January 1967; "Cheer of Burmese Friends for Revolutionary Action in Shanxi Revolutionary Rebels in Shanghai", *People's Daily*, 31 January 1967; "Burmese Workers Active Learning *Quotations from Chairman Mao*", *People's Daily*, 4 March 1967; "Burmese

to refer to the Burmese supporters of the "Cultural Revolution." Although the supporters of Beijing's "Cultural Revolution" in Burma were not mentioned, the reports in the CCP's organ newspaper indicated that China's turmoil had spread to Burma. The Ne Win government had no patience with Chinese revolutionary penetration because the military regime since 1962 had adopted a policy of eliminating all foreign influence in Burma. It meant that a conflict between Beijing's revolutionary diplomacy and Ne Win's political platform and foreign policy could not be avoided.

Friends' Compliment for Mao Tsetung Thought Becoming the Strongest Weapon of World Revolutionary People", *People's Daily*, 14 April 1967.

4

The Anti-Chinese Riots of 1967: The Rupture of the Pauk Phaw Ties

C hinese academic studies on Sino-Burmese relations have long been unbalanced. Research is generally done under the intellectual framework and rubric of friendship and harmony – more diplomatic than analytical.[1] To some degree, academic research is also subject to political propaganda. The conflict and frustration between the two countries have often been "omitted" or "neglected" in Chinese books and papers devoted to this topic. A case in point is the study of Burma's anti-Chinese riots in 1967. This was the most important anti-Chinese event in modern Burmese history. Rich in significance, it has been too little understood. Few Chinese scholars have dealt in depth with these riots, which had an important impact on Sino-Burmese relations during the Cold War. A few western scholars have analyzed this subject, but most of the research was conducted in the 1970s and 1980s, and lacked Chinese sources, especially local materials from the overseas Chinese community in Burma. This chapter focuses on the causes, reasons, and impacts of these anti-Chinese riots against the spread of the Chinese cultural revolution to Burma.

The "6.26" (26 June) Anti-Chinese Riots

The BSPP's efforts to nationalize the entire economy following the coup of 1962 included private educational institutions. After the military government promulgated the "Nationalization of Private Schools Law" in April 1965, all Chinese schools in Burma were nationalized, and all teachers were dismissed, except those with Burmese citizenship. According to the education law, however, private schools with less than twenty students were still allowed to function.

---

1   These include such Chinese books as *The History of Sino-Burmese Relations, Study of Friendship between China and Burma, Two Thousands Years Friendship of China and Burma, Pauk Phaw Friendship: Residents' Get-together Between China and Burma in 1956,* and *Documents on China-Burma Friendship History.*

Thus, overseas Chinese intellectuals throughout Burma founded a number of smaller Chinese schools, using local Chinese houses and business sites.

When the Cultural Revolution broke out in China in 1966, it gradually affected the Chinese community in Burma. Some Chinese students and teachers wore Chairman Mao badges and recited quotations from Mao Tsetung. The local authorities in the northern city of Bhamo early in June 1967 prohibited Chinese students from entering school wearing Mao badges. When they got the news, the Chinese Chamber of Commerce, the Chinese Association of Beneficence, and the Chinese Teacher's League in Rangoon dispatched several representatives to negotiate with the Bhamo authorities. The local authorities felt pressure from the overseas Chinese, so they asked for instructions from the capital. "At the same time, Rangoon was being plagued by overseas Chinese students who followed the Red Guard in China and wore Mao badges. In order to control the situation, the Burmese Ministry of Education enacted a law that all students were forbidden to wear any badge in school other than the Burmese national emblem and the Aung San badge. However, the Chinese did not abide by this rule. Overseas Chinese students not only continued to go to school with Mao badges, but their number increased."[2]

When the students of Rangoon No. 3 National Elementary School (formerly the Chinese Women's Middle School) went to school with Mao badges on 22 June 1967, some teachers tore off the badges and threw them into the sewer. The students who had broken the rule were locked in one room. After they learned what had happened, some students' parents came to the No. 3 School and argued with some teachers. Finally, the teachers confessed that they had acted improperly, and thus the dispute died down. The neighboring Zhong Zheng Middle School, however, closed its gate while its students were inside, thus preventing some 80 students from going home for lunch. They then protested against the school administrators. At about four p.m., the police arrived and ended the dispute. The closed gate was reopened and the students inside left school.

The military government took steps to control the situation on 24 June. Rangoon No. 3 National Elementary School and the Zhong Zheng Middle School were closed, while military officers were appointed as heads of the Overseas Chinese Middle School and the Nan Yang Middle School. They issued regulations against Mao badges that all Chinese students were ordered

---

2   Lin Zhu, "Recalling a painful experience: the origin of the 1967 anti-Chinese riots in Burma", in *Collection of Overseas Chinese history*, Vol. IV, Fuzhou: Fujian Society for Overseas Chinese History, 1987, p. 246.

to sign and obey, on pain of being denied entrance to the school. On 25 June, crowds began to assault the Overseas Chinese Middle School, but the attack was not massive.

Anti-Chinese riots, however, began to escalate from 26 June. With sword and cudgel, Burmese attackers first gathered at the square behind the Shwedagon Pagoda, at the train station, and near the Rangoon No. 4 department store. The crowds proceeded along three routes. The first group mainly attacked the Overseas Chinese Middle School. The second confronted the Chinese community, besieging the Chinese Teachers' League, the Irrawaddy River Glee Club, and the Chinese Clerks' Association. The third headed for the Chinese Embassy.

In the Overseas Chinese Middle School, many Chinese students still wore Mao badges on 26 June. They were asked to sign a pledge to obey the ban against badges in school, but they declined. Both sides refused to budge. The school closed its gate when some students' parents heard the news and went to inquire. The students gathered together and shouted slogans, reciting quotations of Chairman Mao. Shortly thereafter, the Chinese Embassy sent someone to encourage the students. Before long, the attackers along the first route reached the Overseas Chinese Middle School and stood facing students inside the campus. They "assaulted" the students' parents and those Chinese wearing Mao badges near the gate. One died, and over twenty were injured. Police, meanwhile, were attacking Nan Yang Middle School. Five students were arrested and more were injured.[3] During the afternoon, "mobs" continued to attack Chinese near the Overseas Chinese Middle School. Some Chinese wearing trousers were killed or beaten and others wearing trousers were attacked indiscriminately because Burmese always wear longyis and it was assumed that anyone not wearing a longyi was not Burmese. "Mobs" even blocked buses to check the passengers, and then killed ones wearing trousers.[4] The military regime on 27 June finally gave orders that nine schools, in which most students were Chinese, were to be closed indefinitely.

At 1:00 p.m. on 26 June, a crowd of over one thousand surrounded the Chinese Embassy in Rangoon and threw stones and tiles at it. Two groups assaulted the Embassy successively at about 8:00 p.m. and made off with the Chinese national emblem, while the Burmese police responsible for guarding

---

3   "Burmese authority violently counters China and excludes overseas Chinese for the pur-
     poses of its internal policy and external diplomacy", *People's Daily*, 29 June 1967.
4   Zeng Guanying and Chen Zunfa, "Witnessing two anti-Chinese riots in Burma". Unpub-
     lished manuscript.

the Embassy either stood by or left. "Mobs" made six attacks, one after the other, on the offices of The New China News Agency (NCNA), China's Civil Aviation Administration, and the office of the Economic and Commercial Counselor of the Chinese Embassy, and burned their properties on 27 June.[5] A crowd of two thousand started the third attack, and finally invaded the Chinese Embassy on 27 June and killed Liu Yi, an aid technician, and injured several Chinese diplomats. On the afternoon of 28 June, the military government announced martial law from 29 June in the Chinese Embassy area and Rangoon's Chinatown. The personnel of the Chinese Embassy were not allowed to go out.

The attacks on the Chinese community had two foci. The first on 26 June was besieging and destroying the Chinese Teachers' League, the Irrawaddy River Glee Club, and the Chinese Clerks' Association. This attack resulted in thirty-one Chinese dead, twenty-seven victims in Chinese Teachers' League, three in the Irrawaddy River Glee Club, and one in the Chinese Clerks' Association. In addition, dozens of other Chinese associations were burned or destroyed, and some members of these associations were arrested or injured.

Second, Chinese shops, houses, and properties in Chinatown and other blocks were sacked, burned, and destroyed. "Mobs" struck anyone whom they met wearing trousers or Chairman Mao badges. "Almost all Chinese shops and dwelling houses were completely destroyed. Rangoon looked like a city damaged by bombs. Burnt-out Chinese-owned cars and scorched properties lay topsy-turvy in the street and were piled on the roadsides. Footpaths were covered by broken glass and smashed pots and pans. Several hundred Burmese in batches took part in the affray and street attacks in Rangoon, and destroyed and looted Chinese shops, restaurants, cinemas, beauty parlors, and photoshops."[6]

The riots began on 26 June and ended on 28 June. The military government imposed a curfew in Rangoon and effectively kept the riots within limits. Although Rangoon was the only site of Chinese deaths, the riot's influence spread over Burma. Chinese in other parts of the country suffered in differing degrees. Anti-Chinese protests in Magway on 29 June consisted of over two thousand Burmese, and over twenty Chinese shops and houses were destroyed. On the same day, an anti-Chinese protest occurred at Yenangyaung and over one hundred Burmese destroyed one Chinese shop selling tea. One day later, approximately one thousand Burmese paraded to protest against Chinese in

5   For China's first coverage on the anti-Chinese riot in Rangoon see "Burmese reactionary government undisguisedly plotted anti-Chinese riot", *People's Daily*, 29 June 1967. These assaults took place at 0:40 p.m., 0:55 p.m., 1:10 p.m., 2:00 p.m., 13:40 p.m., and 14:10 p.m.

6   "Burmese reactionary government went its own way to continue anti-Chinese riot", *People's Daily*, 2 July 1967.

Mandalay. Parades and demonstrations against Chinese, moreover, occurred in two hundred and eighty-one cities and towns, such as Pyinmana, Taunggyi, Pye, Mawlamyine, Dawei, Myingyan, Pathein, and others.

Wrestling between Beijing and Rangoon

Beijing's Response

After the anti-Chinese rioting started in Rangoon, Beijing's first official response was on 28 June, when Han Nianlong, the Vice Foreign Minister, called in Burma's Ambassador to China and presented a note of protest. In it, China charged that the military regime connived at instigating riots, and lodged the strongest and most urgent protest against Burma. In addition, China demanded that the Burmese government take immediate emergency measures to prohibit anti-Chinese rioting from worsening, assure the safety of China's Embassy and other Chinese organs as well as Chinese citizens, return the pillaged Chinese national emblem, and chastise the murderers.[7] This note appeared on the front page of the *People's Daily* on 29 June. On the same day, the chargé d'affaires of the Chinese Embassy in Rangoon, Hsiao Ming, put forward a five-point demand to the Burmese government: (1) severely chastise the murderers; (2) comfort and compensate the bereaved families; (3) apologize publicly; (4) assure the safety of China's Embassy, other Chinese organs, and Chinese citizens; (5) stop at once the fascist violence against the overseas Chinese.[8]

On 30 June, Beijing issued a statement that the military regime was instigating and engineering the Rangoon riots catering to U.S. imperialism and Soviet revisionism, and was using them to deflect the strong dissatisfaction of the Burmese people with Ne Win's government. Beijing delivered the strongest and most urgent protest against Burma again and decided that the Chinese Ambassador, who had gone back to Beijing before the Rangoon rioting, would not be sent back to his post. The Chinese government repeated the five demands of 29 June, and declared it would take other steps according to the state of affairs in Rangoon.[9] Subsequently, more official notes and protests were delivered to Burma, after all Beijing's demands were rejected by Rangoon. In the three months from August to November of 1967, "The Peking leaders have sent to the Burmese government more than 20 notes and statements of a

---

7   "Burmese government consecutively goaded mobs to attack China's Embassy, kill Chinese the aid technician and persecute Overseas Chinese", *People's Daily*, 29 June 1967.

8   "Central Committee of BCP issued statement on anti-Chinese riot contrived by reactionary Burmese government", *People's Daily*, 2 July 1967.

9   "PRC government issues a statement in the strongest and most urgent protest against anti-Chinese fascist violence of Burmese government", *People's Daily*, 30 June 1967.

threatening nature. They assert, taking a position of great-power chauvinism, that 'the Burmese government of Ne Win will definitely be severely punished by the Chinese people and their National Liberation Army.'"[10]

The Chinese media also attacked Burma and Ne Win after the Rangoon incident. From 29 June through December in 1967, there were 153 reports and articles attacking Burma in the *People's Daily* alone. These attacks against Burma reached a climax in July and August, with 75 reports and 33 articles in the *People's Daily*. This media offensive diminished gradually thereafter.

On 29 June, demonstrating outside Burma's Embassy in Beijing, 200,000 people protested against the Burmese anti-Chinese riots and supported Beijing's 28 June note of protest. From 30 June to 3 July a total of over one million Chinese sequentially joined rallies and demonstrations in front of the Burmese Embassy in Beijing. The demonstrators declared: "Overthrow Burmese reactionists and Ne Win." "It was their sacred right that overseas Chinese and Burmese people studied, propagandized, and defended Mao's thought." "The Burmese government must confess in public and apologize to Beijing, the Chinese people, and the overseas Chinese in Burma." Among the demonstrations noted above, the march and rally of 3 July went out of control. Red Guards broke into the Burmese Embassy and tore up the Burmese national flag and smashed the Burmese national emblem, which became one of four notorious incidents in China during the Cultural Revolution, along with invading the Indian and Indonesian Embassies, and burning the British office of the chargé d'affaires. During the same period, massive demonstrations and rallies continuously occurred in Shanghai and Kunming.

China submitted a memorandum on 1 July to Burma wherein Beijing refused Rangoon's demand that the Chinese government stop massive demonstrations. In addition, it demanded that the Burmese government stop the siege of the Chinese Embassy and Chinatown in Rangoon, and fulfill the Chinese demands.

Apparently, Beijing used the BCP as a lever or countermeasure against the anti-China activities in Burma in addition to their verbal and media attacks, and massive demonstrations in Beijing, Shanghai and Kunming. The BCP Central Committee issued a statement on 28 June on the anti-Chinese riots in Rangoon, stating: "We absolutely support the overseas Chinese revolutionary brave and just action." They called on all Burmese people to try their best to support their Chinese brethren in Burma and oppose the anti-Chinese riots.

10 A. Shchetinkin, "Peking's Crude Interference", *The Current Digest of the Post-Soviet Press*, No. 41, Vol. 19, 1 November 1967, p. 25.

"All Burmese people strive for the complete overthrow of the Ne Win military government and the establishment of a people's democratic and united front government."[11]

A memorial rally for Liu Yi was staged on 5 July, attended by Political Bureau of the CCP Central Committee member, Vice Premier Li Xiannian. At the memorial rally, Thakin Ba Thein Tin, first Vice Chairman of the Central Committee of the BCP, gave a speech titled "The Military Government of Ne Win, the Chiang Kaishek of Burma, is bound to fail; the people are bound to win." In the address, he enumerated the malfeasances of the Ne Win regime and called upon the Burmese people to overthrow it. On behalf of the BCP, he affirmed that "The overseas Chinese struggle in Burma was absolutely just and right-on. We, the BCP, heartily support the overseas Chinese correct struggle and strongly protest against the fascist killing of the overseas Chinese by the military government."[12] This address was fully published, not only in the *People's Daily*, but in the CCP organ, *Red Flag*.

The BCP not only expressed its stance in its statement and speech about the Rangoon incident, but also took action against the anti-Chinese rioting in Burma. The BCP staged rallies to protest against anti-Chinese activities within its base area at Bago, Pathein, Tharrawaddy, as well as other places, and distributed leaflets and pasted notifications in Rangoon, Myaung Mya, and Taikkyi, warning the military government, "Don't persecute the overseas Chinese." In July 1967, the BCP executed a Burmese who had taken the lead in demonstrating and protesting against China.[13]

Rangoon's Reaction

In the face of Beijing's vehement response to the anti-Chinese rioting in Rangoon, the Burmese reacted quickly and strongly. When 200,000 Chinese gathered and demonstrated in front of the Burmese Embassy in Beijing on 29 June, Rangoon presented a memorandum to Beijing, which waved aside the Chinese five demands and asked Beijing to stop the massive demonstrations.[14] In addition, Rangoon repudiated Hsiao Ming's denouncement and stated that

11 "BCP issues a statement about the anti-Chinese riot instigated by the reactionary Burma government", *People's Daily*, 2 July 1967.
12 "The Military Government of Ne Win, the Chiang Kaishek of Burma, is bound to fail; the people are bound to win", *People's Daily*, 6 July 1967.
13 "Revolutionary people staged massive rally within BCP base area," *People's Daily*, 11 August 1967; "Firmly reject and oppose Ne Win reactionaries' anti-Chinese activities", *People's Daily*, 4 November 1967.
14 "China submitted a memorandum to Burma refusing the absurd demands of the Burmese reactionary government", *People's Daily*, 2 July 1967.

the anti-Chinese riot was not plotted by the Burmese government and that the Chinese Embassy had no right to interfere in Burmese internal affairs.

Rangoon's uncompromising attitude prompted Beijing's even stronger response. It should be noted that the *People's Daily* first editorial about the Rangoon riot appeared on 30 June, and the BCP statement of 28 June about the riot was not published in the *People's Daily* until 2 July. This suggests that Beijing at first took a wait-and-see attitude toward Rangoon's reaction. Consequently, Chinese policy became more radical as Rangoon refused to provide a satisfactory reply. In particular, Burma ignored the Chinese five demands, which irritated Beijing. China broadcast and published the BCP statement to "overthrow the Ne Win military regime, and establish a people's democratic and united front government."[15] Compared with previous Chinese policy toward Burma, this change was unprecedented. "The Maoist leadership finally supported the BCP not because of any new finding of strength in the Burmese Communist movement, but because the situation in Burma had developed to the point where Beijing had to choose between backing down (by retracing or shelving its demands) or supporting its officials and overseas Chinese, some of whom had lost their lives."[16]

The Burmese media countered Beijing's verbal attacks, publishing articles and reports that were anti-Chinese and anti-communist. Rangoon broadcast that Chinese students were metaphorically sowing dragon's teeth, had been trained for over one year in Beijing, and their actions had been plotted by China. In order to refute Beijing's blame that the military regime was creating a white terror in Burma, the Burmese press reported that some Chinese had joined the anti-Beijing protest and parade in Burma, and called on local Chinese to oppose all "evil" forces and defend their interests.[17]

The crude interference by Beijing in the internal affairs of Burma elicited a protest on the part of the Burmese public. "A wave of rallies and demonstrations spread throughout the country, and their participants sternly denounced the provocative actions of the local *hung weiping* (red enemies) and their Peking sponsors. Waving over the heads of the demonstrators were banners bearing the slogans: "We Burmese are the masters here! We do not want Mao's ideas!"[18]

---

15 "BCP issued a statement about anti-Chinese riot instigated by reactionary Burma's government", *People's Daily*, 2 July 1967.
16 Melvin Gurtov, *China and Southeast Asia: The Politics of Survival*, Baltimore and London: The Johns Hopkins University Press, 1975, p. 118.
17 Ralph Pettman, *China in Burma's Foreign Policy*, pp. 36–37.
18 A. Shchetinkin, "Peking's Crude Interference", p. 25.

After the anti-Chinese riots, the military authorities placed pro-Beijing leaders and activists in the Chinese community under surveillance and arrested some Chinese, which led to a new series of Beijing protests and warnings. Nevertheless, Rangoon insisted on trying those who were accused of "stirring up Chinese students to demonstrate" or "starting something." In addition, the government took the opportunity to crack down on pro-Beijing leftist leaders and silence propaganda outlets. At least 100 officials of well-known Communist front organizations, like the Burma–China Friendship Association and the Afro–Asian Solidarity Committee in Rangoon, were arrested.[19]

The Burmese government also took some measures to weaken Beijing's influence on both the Chinese community and the political situation in Burma; it restricted contacts between the Chinese Embassy and the Chinese community in Rangoon. The areas of Chinatown and the Chinese Embassy were under military administration from 28 June, which again prompted Beijing's protest. In July, Beijing informed Rangoon that China would deliver some vegetables, fruit, and drugs to the Chinese Embassy, but Burma refused this demand and subsequently detained all relief supplies when China persisted in sending them to Rangoon. At the same time, Ne Win prevented the Chinese government from sending a plane to ship seriously injured Chinese back for treatment. In August, China re-attempted to airlift some relief supplies to its Embassy in Rangoon, but failed.

At the beginning of September, China's Central Committee of Overseas Chinese Affairs wanted to dispatch a delegation to convey their sympathy to the Chinese in Burma, but the Burmese government disapproved. In the same month, Rangoon recalled its Ambassador to Beijing. Burma terminated the Chinese economic assistance program, and presented a note to China, in which China was asked to withdraw all its Chinese aid personnel in October. A total of 412 Chinese aid experts and technicians returned to China prior to 4 November 1967.

Four NCNA correspondents in Rangoon, Yu Minsheng, Teng Wenqi, Li Chengyi and Liu Dejin, were expelled from the country in July 1967 and January 1968. On 19 March 1968, the Burmese police detained some leaders of Chinese associations and pro-Maoist Chinese activists throughout Burma on the pretext of inspecting their ID cards. Over the following two days, more Chinese were detained in Mandalay, Moulmein, Bassein, Myitkyina, Bamo, Lashio, and Taunggyi. In addition, some pro-Beijing Chinese were deported.

---

19   Gurtov, *China and Southeast Asia*, p. 117.

In the course of this wrestling between the two sides, some pro-Taiwan Chinese joined the anti-Beijing protests and parades and delivered speeches against the CCP and mainland China. This was criticized by Beijing, which charged that Rangoon had used pro-Taiwan Chinese to counter the CCP.[20] The anti-communist Chinese set up an "Overseas Chinese Freedom Association in Burma" in Rangoon in September 1968. The Chinese Embassy submitted a memorandum to the Burmese government on 24 October 1968 and requested the latter to take immediate steps to prohibit pro-Taiwan Chinese from anti-Beijing activities.

The Impact of the Anti-Chinese Riots

Disappointed and Dazed Overseas Chinese

The overseas Chinese in Burma were the direct victims of the anti-Chinese riots; their lives and properties were under attack and their living environment deteriorated. Hence, a large number of Chinese in Burma emigrated. "Tens of thousands of overseas Chinese returned to China, thirty to forty thousand to Hong Kong and Macao," and some to Europe, America. and Australia.[21] In addition to the direct impact of the anti-Chinese riots, they had more profound and long-term effects.

One female overseas Chinese described her mood after the rioting: "Then, we were scared as well as angry."[22] This was not a particularly pro-Beijing mood; it was ubiquitous in the Burma Chinese community. Many pro-Taiwan and neutral Chinese felt the same. One pro-Taiwan Chinese, touching on the situation in Burma after the riot, said that the terror atmosphere caused by the anti-China incidents continued to about 1980. After the riots, half of the Cantonese[23] left Burma for the U.S., Taiwan, Hong Kong, Malaysia, and Singapore.[24] During the riots, even the Japanese in Rangoon also panicked because of their similar appearance to the Chinese. Some Japanese cars were stoned.[25]

In order to escape being attacked again, many Chinese gradually assimilated. Some Chinese began to conceal their personal identity and Chineseness.

---

20 "Reactionary Ne Win authority colludes with Chiang Kaishek junta to the teeth. Extends anti-China riot to towns and countries throughout Burma", *People's Daily*, 13 July 1967.

21 Wen Xing, "Ne Win's autarchy and 1967 anti-Chinese accident", *Overseas Chinese Monthly*, No. 11, 1988, p. 15.

22 Interview Cun Shoubin, Mandalay, 7 December 2005.

23 Historically, the percentage of Cantonese supporting the Kuomintang was higher than Fujianese.

24 Interview LFH , Yangon, 18 November 2005.

25 Sakuma Hirayoshi, *Living in Burma: the People and Their Lives in the Isolated Country*, Tokyo: Keiso Shobo, 1994, p. 56.

Offspring born in the 1970s and the 1980s were not given Chinese names. They claimed not to be Chinese, but from Shan and other Burmese minorities.[26] This phenomenon of the Chinese concealing their identity was more noticeable in Rangoon. There, after the anti-Chinese riots most overseas Chinese usually did not speak Chinese even at home.[27] Thus, today Chinese who are under forty-five years old and who lived in the former capital during that time generally cannot speak Chinese.

Many overseas Chinese were unwilling to appear in public and participate in social activities lest their Chinese identity should be exposed and bring trouble to them if new anti-Chinese riots emerged. Overseas Chinese associations decreased their programs. Their associations kept low profiles even when they held some activities.[28] This condition did not change until the 1980s. Before the "6.26" event, skirts and trousers were popular costumes in the Chinese community, but the Chinese changed to dress in the Burmese fashion – longyis and slippers – after 1967.[29]

Beijing openly supported the BCP while the BCP supported the overseas Chinese, and some overseas Chinese joined the BCP; the serial interlinkages made those overseas Chinese speak and act more cautiously, even these who had no relation with the BCP.

It was the experience and lessons from the "6.26" anti-Chinese riots that prompted many overseas Chinese in Burma to become indifferent to politics, and to orient themselves as just simple businessmen. The riots made them more careful and they learned to how to protect themselves more effectively. The "6.26" event played the role of accelerating the process of Chinese assimilation.

The Drop in Beijing's Influence in Burma

During and after the anti-Chinese riots, the most affected were the Maoists; those killed and arrested were the elite and hard-core Maoists in the Chinese community. Other Chinese Maoists were monitored by the authorities. As a result, the CCP greatly lost influence in the Chinese community. "Many overseas Chinese were jailed; some had to flee abroad; some joined the BCP; some were killed. It could be said that Maoists in the Chinese community in Burma lost seventy to eighty percent of their group."[30]

---

26   Interview Cun Shoubin, Mandalay, 7 December 2005.
27   Interview Luo Xilong, Yangon, 11 November 2005.
28   Interview Wang Qinliang, Yangon, 20 November 2005.
29   Interview Li Jiamei, Mandalay, 7 December 2005.
30   Interview HHZ, Kunming, 7 December 2003.

In fact, the Chinese Maoists' "angry" mood after the rioting meant that Beijing had no effective measures to help them escape from the dilemma brought on by the CCP's export of revolution. So the overseas Chinese, especially Maoists, were in trouble. Some became unbalanced mentally, some "complained that Beijing was inept and could not handle the trouble and crises."[31] Some Chinese complained that "Our shops and factories were nationalized, and we lost all our properties. Also, Chinese schools were nationalized and our offspring couldn't be educated in Chinese. How sad we are. You [the Beijing authorities] did not say any word about the situation then, but on the contrary you persuaded us to put up with the facts. Nevertheless, just for a badge we now have to face the tragic results. We tread on eggs in the current situation."[32] Even some Chinese asserted that "Mao's thought harms us and we are scapegoats."[33]

Beijing's leftist foreign policy, and the harm and loss that the Chinese suffered during the riots made some overseas Chinese change to support the Kuomintang or alienate themselves from the CCP. This was especially true in Upper Burma, where the Kuomintang had had more influence. Beijing's influence had increased to some degree through its efforts in the 1950s, but it decreased again after the 1967 riots. Meanwhile, some Chinese had fled to Burma to escape the CCP's political persecution, and Taiwan made more effort to secure overseas Chinese support and favor.

The Shock to China–Burma Ties

On 29 June 1967, Beijing declared that the Chinese Ambassador to Burma would not return to his post. Burma recalled its Ambassador to Beijing two months later; China–Burma diplomatic relations were kept at the chargé d'affaires level until 1970.

Indeed, the anti-Chinese riots caused China's policy toward Burma to change. Before the riots, China had emphasized the preservation of state-to-state relations between the two countries. National interest played a critical role in Chinese policy toward Burma. Consequently, although Beijing supported the BCP before the riots, it was cautious and covert. However, after the riots, China changed its policy toward Burma and strongly and openly supported the BCP.

31 Interview Cun Shoubin, Mandalay, 7 December 2005.
32 Lin Zhu, "Recalling a Painful Experience", p. 249.
33 Interview Zhao Hua, Kunming, 7 December 2003.

The CCP's Central Committee sent a telegram to the BCP's Central Committee in August 1967, congratulating them on the 28th anniversary of the founding of the BCP. It declared that "The CCP and the Chinese people firmly support the people's revolutionary armed struggle led by the BCP. We regard such support as our bounden proletarian international duty . . . It is our firm conviction that the BCP headed by comrade Thakin Than Tun, which persists in the revolutionary line of 'winning the war and seizing political power', will assuredly unite all Party comrades and Burmese people of all ethnic groups to overthrow the reactionary Ne Win government and win complete victory in the revolutionary war in Burma."[34]

Moreover, the Chinese media published articles written by the BCP's leaders and cadres, and broadcast their speeches, which urged the Burmese people to support its armed struggle and overthrow the Ne Win regime.[35] According to the index of the *People's Daily*, before the riots Beijing's official newspaper only occasionally published the BCP's activities and news. The number of related reports on the BCP in the *People's Daily* did not exceed fifteen, and their contents did not deal with the BCP's anti-government stance. Beijing was careful when dealing with relations between the Burmese government and the BCP.

After the "6.26" event, however, China began to support the BCP openly and provided it with weapons, training, advisors, logistics, etc.[36] On 1 January 1968, troops of the BCP in China led a military offensive across the Burmese frontier along three routes. Each route included one PLA detachment (company), which consisted of China's southwest minority soldiers from various Chinese military areas.[37] These PLA minority soldiers were trans-frontier minorities, such as the Shan and Kachin, and thus had the same origin as some Burmese minorities. Some Chinese Maoists in Burma were directed to join the BCP after the anti-Chinese riots, and it had some voluntary members from the local Chinese communities. In addition, a large number of educated Chinese youths came to Burma and joined the BCP. Chinese BCP cadres significantly increased.

---

34 "Central Committee of CCP ardently congratulates the 28th anniversary of BCP", *People's Daily*, 15 August 1967.

35 For instance, some of their articles were: *Overthrow Chiang Kaishek of Burma – Ne Win; Statement of BCP's Central Committee on Chairman of BCP's being murdered; The most powerful weapon, the most important aid; Burmese people's armed struggle is bound to win; The sharpest weapon of Burmese armed revolution; Dare to make sacrifice, dare to struggle, dare to win victory.*

36 Interview FG, former Vice Chairman of BCP Central Committee, Xiamen, 17 February 2005.

37 Interview ZZT, Taunggyi, 16 December 2005.

Table 1: China's trade with Burma, 1966–1972 (US$ million)

Year	1966	1967	1968	1969	1970	1971	1972
Imports	15.92	8.12	–	–	77	872	1392
Exports	7.99	12.97	1.41	(negligible)	371	908	1152
Balance	–7.93	4.85	1.41	(negligible)	294	36	–240

Source: Ministry of Foreign Economics and Trade, PRC, *The Comprehensive Foreign Trade Statistical Data*: 1950–1989, 1990, p. 51.

The rift between the two countries resulted in a sharp decline in bilateral trade after 1967. The bilateral trading value in 1969 was only four thousand dollars, a decrease of ninety-three percent compared with 1967, which set the low record in the history of the two nation's trading. This trade stagnation did not change until diplomatic normalization in 1971 (see Table 1).

Causes of the Anti-Chinese Riots

The Beijing Dimension

China's policy toward Burma after 1962 was focused on minimizing Soviet and U.S. influence in Burma. On the other hand, China enlisted Burmese support on the Sino-Indian border dispute, Vietnam, Laos, and other international issues. Zhou Enlai visited Burma in February 1964, and he repeated his trip again in July that year, just after Vice Prime Minister of the Soviet Union, Mikoyan, had visited Rangoon just one week earlier. Zhou's second visit to Burma began to balance and minimize Soviet influence in Burma and the military ties between Burma and the West.

In addition to Zhou's visit in February 1964, Ne Win went to Beijing in July 1965, and Liu Shaoqi visited Rangoon in April 1966. All three issued communiques during their visits stressing that economic independence was significant for political independence. Their purpose was focused on the economic deterioration and disturbances in Burma due to Ne Win's drastic Burmese socialist policy. Beijing was worried that the U.S. and the U.S.S.R. would "fish in troubled waters" and entice Rangoon to abandon its neutralist foreign policy in pursuit of aid with attached political and economic strings. Hence, the Chinese intent was to remind Rangoon to watch out for any other major power's subversion.

During Ne Win's trip to Beijing in 1965 and Liu Shaoqi's visit to Rangoon in 1966, the Chinese leaders both emphasized the Vietnam issue at state banquets in the two countries' capital. Obviously, China wished Burma to support her struggle against the U.S., but Ne Win was reluctant to do so and did not come out against the U.S. He also avoided the question of Vietnam in Beijing and Rangoon. Both China–Burma joint communiques in 1965 and 1966 just took a general stance against imperialism and colonialism and did not mention the U.S.

China not only failed to make Burma change her neutralist policy, but faced more troubles. The BCP sent a message of greetings to Beijing on the fifteenth anniversary of the PRC in 1964. Beijing broadcast the congratulations in English and Burmese and published it in the *People's Daily*.[38] Burma responded strongly to it and closed the Chinese consulates in Mandalay and Lashio.

Since the late 1950s and early 1960s, China had begun gradually to give up its previous realist foreign policy in pursuit of national security interests, and had introduced instead a hardline and irrational foreign policy which gave prominence to ideology, especially "proletariat internationalism," as its guiding principle. It neglected or denied the decisive role of national interest in the process of decision making. By the middle of the 1960s, China had formed a radical revolutionary foreign policy characterized by its declared struggle against imperialism, revisionism, and all reactionaries of various countries, while helping and aiding revolutionary movements in Asia, Africa and Latin America.

Leftist factions gradually took control of foreign affairs after the Cultural Revolution broke out in China. The Minister as well as other Vice Ministers of the Foreign Ministry, including Chen Yi, were savaged. The political bureau of the Foreign Ministry was stoned and the offices of the Vice-Ministers of the Foreign Ministry were closed by rebels. Consequently, the Central Committee of the CCP lost control of foreign affairs for a time. During 1966–1967, diplomatic disputes broke out between China and nearly thirty countries, while China had diplomatic and semi-diplomatic relations with only forty countries.[39] Furthermore, after September 1966, Beijing recalled all its ambassadors to foreign countries except Egypt. They were ordered to return to join the Cultural Revolution. The Embassies abroad could not function effectively. The Chinese Ambassador to Burma, Geng Biao, and his 21 colleagues were recalled to Beijing in March 1967. When Geng Biao arrived at the Beijing airport, he lost his freedom and was taken to the Foreign Ministry and was questioned about whether Liu Shaoqi and Chen Yi had some problems during their trips to Burma.[40] Some

---

38 See "Central Committee of BCP's Congratulatory letter", *People's Daily*, 3 October 1964.
39 *Contemporary Chinese Diplomacy*, Beijing: China's Social Science Press, 1987, p. 209.
40 Geng, *Memoir of Geng Biao*, p. 221.

leftists came to Rangoon later and soon controlled the Embassy. They actively promoted the Cultural Revolution in the Chinese community and ignited the fuse of the anti-Chinese riots in Rangoon.

That in 1967 all students were forbidden to wear any badge in school except the Burmese national emblem and Aung San badges made some officials of the Chinese Embassy very dissatisfied; they deemed that "wearing Mao's badge was the principle of supporting Beijing and could not be banned."[41] Some Chinese students continually defied the government with the support of the Chinese Embassy. Although the conflict between Chinese students and the Rangoon Chinese Womens'Middle School administration had been resolved on 22 June 1967, some Chinese associations convoked their students' parents and encouraged their children to go on wearing Mao badges in school. Some Chinese students on the evening of 22 June were organized to see the film *Red Lantern*, and encouraged to fight.[42] One ethnic Chinese, a teacher at the Rangoon Overseas Chinese Night School recalled, "We convened the students [encouraging them] to wear Mao badges, and the students' parents were worried about this. On 25 June, the Burmese radio broadcast that no students could wear badges to school the next day. Some parents asked us if their children would still wear badges. I then asked the Chinese Teachers' Association for instructions and they told us to go on fighting."[43] Thus, the conflict between the Chinese community and the military regime was unavoidable.

Most observers believed that the major cause of the riots was the Cultural Revolution and China's attempt to export it.[44] China's Red Guard diplomacy was the inherent continuation of internal chaos in China.[45] The "6.26" event was essentially a by-product of the Cultural Revolution[46] and the direct result of Beijing's revolutionary foreign policy.

On the other hand, some argued that "China's frustration over its failure to get Burma to identify with and support Chinese foreign policy may be one of the factors that precipitated the Sino-Burmese rift in 1967."[47] Burma acted

---

41 Zeng Guanying and Chen Zunfa, "Witnessing two anti-Chinese riots".
42 *Ibid.*
43 Interview WXX, Yangon, 23 December 2005.
44 Robert A. Holmes, "Burma's Foreign Policy Toward China Since 1962", *Pacific Affairs*, Vol. 45, No. 2, Summer, 1972, p. 245.
45 *Ibid.*; John H. Badgley, Burma's China Crisis: The Choices Ahead," *Asian Survey*, Vol. VII, No. 11, November 1967, p. 758; Martin Smith, *Burma: Insurgency and the Politics of Ethnicity*, Dhaka: The University Press, 1999, p. 225.
46 "Peking and the Burmese Communists: the Perils and Profits of Insurgency", CIA Intelligence Report, RSS No. 0052/71, July 1971, p. 46. For the Executive Summary, see Appendix 6.
47 Holmes, "Burma's Foreign Policy", p. 245.

quite independently on some major international problems against the wishes of China. Burma's independent actions on major world issues ultimately led to the Sino-Burmese rift in 1967.[48] Ne Win visited Washington in 1966 and supported the U.S. presence in Vietnam and elsewhere in Southeast Asia. The CCP thought Burma had abandoned its neutralist foreign policy and support of China's stand. This was also said by some to be the cause of the Rangoon event.[49] Moreover, some thought that Ne Win's "socialistic" policy cut the channel of Beijing's influence over the Chinese community and Burmese internal politics. Ne Win nationalized two Beijing-owned banks, all Chinese schools, and closed down all Chinese newspapers in Burma. This irritated Beijing and encouraged it to export the Cultural Revolution to Burma.[50]

These arguments place effects before cause. The exported Cultural Revolution fundamentally arose not from any external situation, but because of Chinese domestic political developments. Consequently, "Burma's shift to a more isolated stance after 1963 cannot be construed as contributing to the Chinese antagonism of the Cultural Revolution period. The hostile policy toward Burma was similar to that toward other Asian countries."[51] More importantly, when Ne Win visited Beijing and held talks with Zhou Enlai in 1971, Zhou explained, "The cause of the Rangoon riot has little relation to the border issue. As regards your visit to the U.S., it caused some attention and remarks, but it didn't worry me."[52] Also, Zhou admitted that "We disapprove of the actions of some Burmese overseas Chinese schools in 1967, too ... Overseas Chinese should obey the law of local countries and should not disobey it. They should work and live there according to local custom."[53]

The Rangoon Dimension

The Ne Win regime defended its national security in the "6.26" incident, which strengthened his political legitimation. After Ne Win came in office by coup d'etat in 1962, he promulgated the Burmese Way to Socialism in domestic policy, and adhered to a neutralist policy in foreign affairs. Rangoon minimized as much as possible all foreign influences in Burma. Comparatively speaking,

---

48 Bandyopadhyaya, *Burma and Indonesia*, p. 170.
49 Frank N. Trager, "Sino-Burmese Relations: The End of the Pauk Phaw Era", *Orbis*, Vol. XI, Winter, 1968, No. 4, p. 1053. Holmes, "Burma's Foreign Policy", p. 245; Bandyopadhyaya, *Burma and Indonesia*, pp. 170–171.
50 Bandyopadhyaya, *Burma and Indonesia*, pp. 170–171.
51 Wayne Bert, "Chinese Policy Toward Burma and Indonesia", *Asian Survey*, Vol. XXV, No. 9, September 1985, p. 965.
52 *Selected Diplomatic Writings of Zhou Enlai*, p. 481.
53 *Chronicle of Zhou Enlai*, Vol. 2, p. 473.

"Ne Win sought more vigorously than U Nu to balance the influence of major states within Burma, often by eliminating such influence altogether, or as much as possible."[54] "Independence, however delimited, has been a real touchstone in Burmese foreign policy, and Ne Win took this to its logical extreme by closing down the avenues through which outside states, and particularly China, pursued their political objectives in Burma at Burma's expense."[55] Among foreign observers, Burmese foreign policy was considered inward-looking, xenophobic, and immature in its weltanschauung.[56]

The Burmese media covered the anarchy in China after the Cultural Revolution burst out in 1966. Rangoon was afraid that the Cultural Revolution possibly could affect it. In November 1966, Ne Win made a speech at the Burmese Socialist Programme Party (BSPP) assembly and reprimanded the overseas Chinese for their "illegal revolutionary action." Whereafter, Rangoon heightened security measures to control the China–Burma border and clamped down on illegal Chinese migration.[57] When worry became reality, "Ne Win was far from compliant, and this episode gave a most marked autonomous tinge to an otherwise acquiescent relationship." For the Ne Win military junta, characterized by "self-isolation," it was vigilant against its giant northern neighbor and had strong nationalist sentiments. It was unacceptable that the Chinese continuously violated Burmese law. "It is conceivable that after the long series of chauvinist exercises in the Chinese community the authorities wished to teach the Chinese a lesson and that cadres of the Burmese Socialist Programme Party (BSPP) were encouraged to stir up popular feeling."[58] The "6.26" incident was Burmese counteraction in pursuit of defending its national security and interests. The counteraction developed into a bloody and violent conflict and was closely connected with Burma's domestic political situation and the political legitimacy crisis of the Ne Win military government.

Two factors contributed to the extraordinary violence of the reaction in Burma: the 1967 rice crisis and the increasingly xenophobic atmosphere that enveloped the country after Ne Win's seizure of power.[59] After Ne Win's *coup d'etat*, the military government was facing a crisis of political legitimacy.

54 Pettman, *China in Burma's Foreign Policy*, p. 27.
55 *Ibid.*, p. 45.
56 Maung Maung Gyi, "Foreign Policy of Burma Since 1962: Negative Neutralism for Group Survival", in F. K. Lehman (ed.), *Military Rule in Burma Since 1962*, Singapore: Maruzen Asia, 1981, p. 10.
57 Sakuma Hirayoshi, *Modern Political History of Burma*, Tokyo: Keiso Shobo, 1993, p. 218.
58 Jay Taylor, *China and Southeast Asia: Peking's Relations with Revolution Movements*, New York: Praeger Publishers, 1976, p. 211.
59 Martin Smith, *Burma*, p. 225.

"Resentment against the repressive military–socialist regime grew and festered, periodically bursting out in the open in the form of urban uprisings (1962, 1963, 1964, 1965, 1966, 1967, 1970, 1974, 1975, 1976, and so on)."[60] "Rice riots broke out in Rangoon during the summer [1967] and the rising black market price, which according to official statistics was 700 per cent of the controlled price in Rangoon, drew more of the production into illegal trade channels."[61] "In 1967, Burma probably came closer to civil war than at any time during this period. There was a total breakdown in the distribution of cooking oil, rice and other basic necessities."[62] As a result, the rice crisis was a crucial contributing factor. Two overseas Chinese witnessing the anti-Chinese riots remembered that "The serious rice crisis even compelled civil servants to be absent and go to the villages to buy rice. Then there was a rumor that dock workers in Rangoon had been prepared to breach the barn and snatch rice."[63] Another witness also mentioned this detail in his memoir: "The leader of the Burmese Labour and Peasant Party disclosed that the Ne Win regime was in a political quandary because of rice deficiency and students' and citizens' petitions as well as demonstrations. The generals were plotting to connect the rice shortage crisis with the event of badgewearing and instigated the anti-Chinese riot so that they could distract domestic dissatisfaction and retrieve a tumbledown reign."[64] In 1967, Ne Win said that Burma, once the largest exporter of rice, could not feed itself.

Some scholars shared similar opinions. Silverstein considered that "In fact Ne Win was able to transform an internal problem into an international one which drew the nation to his side and made the Chinese become the target of Burmese wrath, and gave the military a breathing spell that led to gradual reversals of many of the socialist and other policies the military had adopted."[65] "As Beijing accused, Ne Win actually used secret police and recruits to engage in anti-Chinese activities for the sake of stirring up Burmese nationalism." The Burmese riotous response to the export of the Chinese Cultural Revolution was possibly organized and abetted by the Ne Win government itself. The Burmese elite deliberately manipulated the anti-Chinese riot as an external

60 Yawnghwe, Chao-taang, "Burma: The Depoliticization of the Political" in Muthiah A Lagappa (ed.), *Political Legitimacy in Southeast Asia – The Quest for Moral Authority*, Stanford: Standford University Press, 1995, p. 188.

61 Laurence D. Stifel, "Burmese Socialism: Economic Problems of the First Decade," *Pacific Affairs*, Vol. 45, No. 1, 1972, p. 67.

62 Josef Silverstein, "A New Vehicle on Burma's Road to Socialism", *Asia*, Spring, No. 29, 1973, pp. 64–65.

63 Zeng Guanying and Chen Zunfa, "Witnessing two anti-Chinese riots".

64 Lin Zhu, "Recalling a Painful Experience", pp. 246–247.

65 Silverstein, "A New Vehicle", p. 66.

stimulus for internal ends so that it could reduce the considerable discontent at home caused by drastic nationalization policies and a bad harvest season.[66] The incident of Chinese badgewearing was used by Ne Win to defuse economic and political crisis, and divert domestic discontent.[67] The overseas Chinese became the scapegoat of Rangoon and the object of Burmese exclusionism.[68] A CIA declassified document shows that "US Embassy observers on the scene were impressed that the police and army, although visible on the streets, made no attempt to prevent the destruction of Chinese property or the killing of Chinese citizens. In effect, the Chinese government began a chain of events which the Burmese government allowed to accelerate."[69]

The anti-Chinese riots were one of the military regime's steps to strengthen its power. This argument can be further substantiated by some oral history material, including Japanese observers. Sakuma Hirayoshi, a Japanese diplomat in Rangoon, verified that Burmese soldiers and police had let the mob attacks go unchecked at the beginning of the riot until the situation deteriorated. He argued that the Burmese government took advantage of the riot, due to the public discontent with rice shortage, to preserve its tottering regime.[70] Ono Toru, a foreign language teacher in Rangoon, recalled that the 1967 crisis faced by the Ne Win regime was at first provoked by the food shortage and the Chinese Cultural Revolution. The Rangoon incident helped deflect popular dissatisfaction from Burma's government to China.[71]

One returned overseas Chinese recalled that on 26 June, her relative saw many military trucks carrying Burmese soldiers into a prison beside her house. They changed out of their military uniforms into longyis and rushed out to attack the Chinese. Although the soldiers wore longyis, their uniform short-sleeved shirts were not taken off, so they still could be easily recognized.[72]

Mr. Chen Zunfa, a former reporter of the *People's Daily*, a Chinese newspaper in Rangoon, escaped from the Burmese killing because of his fluent, accentless Burmese and his local costume. He got the message from his relative who was a member of the BSPP ten days before the anti-Chinese riot that the BSPP had

66   Ralph Pettman, *China in Burma's Foreign Policy*, pp. 41–42.
67   Imakawa Eichi , *Burma under the Ne Win Military Regime*, Kyoto: Review Press, 1971, p. 187.
68   Tsuchifu Nagao, *New Colonialism and Nationalism Revolution*, Kyoto: Newsletter Press, 1973, p. 205.
69   "Peking and the Burmese Communists", p. 52.
70   Sakuma Hirayoshi, *Living in Burma*, pp. 56–57.
71   Ono Toru, "The Current Situation of Burma", *Southeast Asian Studies*, Vol. 5, No. 2, 1967, p. 190.
72   Interview Guo Huilan, Xiamen, October 21, 2003.

held a meeting and had decided to organize a "mob" of five thousand to loot and make trouble in Chinese areas.[73] Another reporter on a Chinese newspaper in Rangoon also got similar news and reported it to the Chinese Embassy, but it was ignored.[74]

The popular Burmese reaction to what they perceived was Chinese-instigated violence, involving Embassy support, was to invade and sack the Chinese business quarter of Rangoon.[75] Undeniably, some Burmese nationalists participated in the riot, but it is generally believed that most of killers were soldiers and rent-a-crowd people. However, there is another side to the coin. Many Chinese were rescued, protected, and helped by Burmese. "When the mobs searched for Chinese along streets during the riot, some Burmese told the attackers on their own initiative that there were no Chinese dwellings on the street. For example, the boss of a Burmese restaurant under my house told mobs that the upstairs residents were Burmese, and saved my family," said a returned overseas Chinese.[76] Another pro-Maoist leader of the Overseas Chinese Association was protected by his Burmese landlord. The monk of the temple behind his house also was willing to provide shelter for him.[77] We still often hear such stories in the Chinese community in Burma now. Relations between the overseas Chinese and Burmese became one of the more harmonious models of Chinese-indigenous relations in Southeast Asia, but the situation is undergoing change as Chinese influence has grown since 2000. The phenomenon has been widely recognized in academic circles.[78]

The Chinese Community Dimension

The anti-Chinese riot was also attributable to some political Chinese and their misjudgment of the political situation of the day.

---

73   Interview Chen Zunfa, Xiamen, 31 August 2003.
74   Interview Lai Baoluo, Yangon, 23 November 2005.
75   John F. Cady, *The United States and Burma*, Cambridge and London: Harvard University Press, 1976, p. 258.
76   Interview Zeng Wenmian, Xiamen, 19 August 2003.
77   Interview Zeng Wenmian, Xiamen, 5 September 2003.
78   For related discussions see Victor Purcell, *The Chinese in Southeast Asia*, London: Oxford University Press, 1965, p. 69; John Leroy Christian, *Burma and the Japanese invader*, Bombay: Thacker and Company , Limited, 1945, p. 279; Victor Purcell, "The influence of racial minorities", in Philip W. Thayer (ed.), *Nationalism and Progress in Free Asia*, Baltimore: The Johns Hopkins Press, 1956, p. 244; G. E. Harvey, *British Rule in Burma 1824–1942*, London: Faber and Faber, 1946, p. 70. Records of Burma Overseas Chinese, Taipei: Committee to Compile records of Overseas Chinese, 1967, p. 121; Wang Zhongmin, *Yearbook of Overseas Chinese in Burma*, Shanghai: Shanghai Commercial Press, 1936, p. 15.

With increasingly close Sino-Burmese relations since the mid-1950s, numerous Chinese leaders and various delegations frequently visited Burma. Beijing constantly influenced and tried to unite the Chinese community in Burma through political, cultural, educational, and economic means. Beijing's force and influence in the Chinese community continuously increased. Before Chinese schools were nationalized by the government, there were over 250, with nearly 40,000 students. Among these schools, the pro-Beijing percent was higher than those pro-Taiwan; some Maoists or pro-Maoist activists were being produced. They told the author that although they were born in Burma they grew up singing quotations from Mao.[79]After the Cultural Revolution broke out, many overseas Chinese supported the movement, virtually worshiped Mao as well as loved Mao's quotations and badges, which were the continuity of their political identity. In this context, pro-Maoist's allegiance was difficult to control.

A Burmese overseas Chinese wrote an article, published in the *People's Daily* in June 1967, which reflects the pro-Beijing Chinese judgement and attitude to the Cultural Revolution:

> The Cultural Revolution brings immense inspiration and profound instruction. Overseas Chinese patriotic fervor grows as never before. Everybody is deeply concerned about the great revolutionary movement in history and writes to Chairman Mao and the central committee of the CCP and show their firmest support, which involves the future of the motherland, of the world, and of their offspring's happiness.

> Today, reading Chairman Mao's works is the first demand in the lives of patriotic Chinese. We try our best to get the *Little Red Book*. Some have asked for it from their relatives in China; some borrowed it from their friends; some shared one book; some extracted Mao's quotations from newspapers and compiled them; some listened to Beijing Radio and wrote down Mao's quotations. Now many can recite some apothegms or complete sections of the *Three Old Works of Chairman Mao*.

> Today, the portrait of Chairman Mao can be seen in both overseas Chinese associations and their houses throughout various towns and cities in Burma. More and more overseas Chinese associations hang the red brand of Chairman Mao's quotations. During festivals, the overseas Chinese present Mao's badges to each other as the most precious gift. Studying Mao's

79 Interview Huang Renmei, Hong Kong, 14 September 2007; Interview Zeng Xiuying, Hong Kong, 14 September 2007.

quotations before any gathering has been in fashion. *The East is Red, Sailing the Seas depends on the Helmsman,* and other Songs of the Quotations from Chairman Mao are favorite songs in the Chinese community. Overseas Chinese wearing Mao's badge can be found everywhere in Burma. Everybody regards it as the symbol of glory and happiness.

Chairman Mao is our Greatest Leader, and anyone who opposes Chairman Mao is our absolutely irreconcilable enemy.

If the song doesn't pay a tribute to Mao thought, we don't sing it; if the drama doesn't propagandize Mao thought, we don't perform it; if the action doesn't accord with Chairman Mao's instruction, we don't take it. Patriotic overseas Chinese in Burma are loyal to Chairman Mao and socialist China, which is unchanging for ever.[80]

In terms of Burma's Chinese community as a whole, the writer's description is exaggerated, but pro-Beijing Chinese in Burma indeed were prevalent, especially among Chinese students, teachers, and cadres of Chinese associations.

Some pro-CCP Chinese with loyalty to Beijing actively supported and responded to the Cultural Revolution. Therefore, they "forgot their status as foreign subjects and the motherland's former instruction of abiding by local law and dropping out of local political activities, but were guided and instructed by Beijing's leftist policy and thoughts of the 'red world,' and had a blindfold superiority complex that a powerful homeland was backing them."[81] "It's the legitimate right of overseas Chinese to wear Mao badges. No one can deprive us of that right. We fight against anyone who dares to oppose our badge-wearing."[82] Many pro-Beijing Chinese then had such opinions.

The overseas Chinese underestimated and mistakenly judged the government's reaction when they antagonized the Rangoon authorities. A pro-Mao Chinese teacher in Rangoon said that "Our couples prepared clothes for the worst – imprisonment. We thought that since China had a population of 700 million, the Burmese government dare not take action against us because Burma was so weak and small. Our estimate was far from exact. [But] if we could keep calm, the incident would not happen."[83] Not only Chinese teachers but also their students had the same opinion then. "I prepared my clothes and shoes

---

80   "Burma patriotic Overseas Chinese stay loyal to Chairman Mao for ever", *People's Daily*, 30 June 1967.
81   Lin Zhu, "Recalling a painful experience", p. 250.
82   Interview Wu Xizhi, Yangon, 23 November 2005.
83   *Ibid.*

for being imprisoned at any moment," said a pro-Beijing Chinese student in Mandalay.[84] A survivor of anti-Chinese riots, Ms. Guo Huilan, perhaps is more persuasive. "We didn't anticipate violent action taken by the government and at first thought that we were similar to the Indonesian overseas Chinese, who were injured and repatriated to China. We all were willing to return to China. Our worst estimate was that we would not be killed but just be bruised."[85] Of course, Beijing was primarily responsible for the overseas Chinese underestimating the result of defying the Ne Win regime. "The PRC was primarily responsible for starting the chain of events that led to the riots."[86]

The International Community Dimension

It is noteworthy that the provocations in Rangoon were not an isolated phenomenon. Similar disturbances also occurred in India, Singapore, Malaysia, and several other countries of Asia. It seems that the Mao Tsetung's group was at pains to create the impression that the "Cultural Revolution" was finding support in other countries.[87] The anti-Chinese wave around the world in the late 1960s was a model for the anti-Chinese riots in Burma. Following the deterioration of Sino-Indian relations in the early 1960s and the border war, anti-Chinese activities emerged in India. After an anti-Chinese movement in Indonesia in 1957, massive counter-Chinese violence happened again in 1966, when Chinese consulates were time after time besieged and destroyed.[88] These anti-Chinese riots and the split between China and some other countries resulted from Beijing's radical "World Revolution" foreign policy. When Beijing tried to export the Cultural Revolution to Burma, Rangoon realized that China had followed the same old disastrous road.

The anti-Chinese movements in India, Indonesia, Hong Kong and so forth, and Beijing's reaction to these activities abroad before the "6.26" incident, strengthened Ne Win's confidence and determination to confront China. During anti-Chinese movements in other countries, whether a Chinese Embassy, a

---

84   Interview He Lihua, Mandalay, 7 December 2005.
85   Interview Guo Huilan, Xiamen, 21 October 2003.
86   "Peking and the Burmese Communists", p. 50.
87   G. Zafesov, "Chinese Provocations in Burma," *The Current Digest of the Post-Soviet Press*, No. 26, Vol. 19, 19 July 1967, p. 27.
88   Even the Chinese consul-general in Indonesia was held under duress and overseas Chinese were killed, attacked and looted. In February 1966, Ghana severed diplomatic relations with China; Cuba issued an anti-Chinese statement on the same month; the senate of Kenya approved an anti-China proposal in March; anti-China turbulence bursted out in Hong Kong in May 1967. At the same time, Chinese diplomats and reporters of the NCNA were injured, detained, and overseas Chinese were persecuted in Mongolia.

consulate or diplomats were attacked or local overseas Chinese were persecuted, Beijing's policy basically was: protest, protest again and again . . . finally evacuating some overseas Chinese refugees from some countries such as in India, Indonesia, and Vietnam. On the whole, Beijing had no effective instrument to protect the overseas Chinese in trouble and settle disputes caused by its irrational foreign policy. Instead, it organized massive domestic protests and parades, and lodged protests. A case in point was Indonesia. The enforced passivity of Chinese foreign policy during this phase was graphically illustrated by Beijing's inability to deal effectively with the challenge to Chinese state interests made by Indonesia. Anti-Chinese Indonesian violence peaked in early and mid-1966 with attacks, raids, forced searches, the sacking of the Chinese Embassy and several consulates, and expulsion of Chinese diplomatic personnel. But China could still do little except protest, withdraw official persons and students, and cut off economic assistance.[89]

The policymakers of Burma noticed the weakness of Beijing and balanced the cost and risk of antagonizing China. Thus they dared to counter the PRC, from which Burma was always afraid of invasion and subversion. Facing anti-Chinese riots in Rangoon, Beijing first lodged protests. Second, it organized massive protests in China.[90] Third, Chinese aid experts were withdrawn and Chinese loans to Burma terminated. Last, some overseas Chinese were evacuated.

The 6.26 incident in Rangoon in 1967 was one of the most obviously adverse consequences of the CCP's "Revolutionary Diplomacy." It symbolized the end of *Pauk Phaw* relations between the two countries, which had been in place since the mid 1950s. The anti-Chinese riots in Rangoon involved some complicated factors. Although it was the immediate result of China's revolutionary foreign policy, the matter also included Burmese domestic issues, the international situation, and Sino-Burmese political identity and judgment.

Sino-Burmese antagonism was relatively short-lived. After early 1968, Chinese verbal hostility to and attacks on Burma declined. "The Chinese paid

---

89 Thomas Robinson, "China confronts the Soviet Union: warfare and diplomacy on China's Inner Asian frontiers," in Roderick MacFarquhar and John K. Fairbank, *The Cambridge History of China*, Vol. 15, The People's Republic, Part 2: Revolutions within the Chinese Revolution, 1966–1982, Cambridge: Cambridge University Press, 1991, pp. 235–236.

90 About the massive Chinese protest and demonstration against Burma, see "200,000 people protest outside Burmese Embassy in Beijing", *People's Daily*, 30 June 1967; "Savage Anti-China Burmese government will inevitably be hoisted by its own petard", *People's Daily*, 2 July 1967.

increasingly less attention to the Burmese government over time and, beginning in January–June 1968, China began to stress almost exclusively the activities of the BCP and Burmese guerrillas waging war against the government, virtually ceasing direct verbal criticisms of the latter."[91] Burma also tried to relax the two countries' relations. China–Burma ties were renormalized over 1970–1971. However, Beijing's policy of openly supporting the BCP did not change because of the diplomatic normalization. The CCP did not give up its policy of open support to the BCP until 1978. The BCP continued to be a sensitive and core issue in bilateral relations.

The BCP issue had additional significance. The change of Beijing's policy toward the BCP reflected Beijing's balance between national interests and ideology, Sino-Soviet rivalry in Southeast Asia, party relations and state relations, and the China–Burma interest game in the Cold War. The BCP issue made Burma much more aware of the role of the geographic factor in its foreign policy, although it had anticipated the threat from the north.

---

91 Daniel Tretiak, "Changes in Chinese Attention to Southeast Asia, 1967–1969: Their Relevance of The Future of The Area", *Current Scene*, No. 21, November 1969, p. 5.

5

From Rift to Renormalization of Relations: 1967–1971

*A*lthough Burma was touted as a "model" of China's foreign relations, the Rangoon events in 1967 led to a break in Sino-Burmese relations, which was in neither country's national interests. This rift, however, did not widen further in 1968. The renormalization of Sino-Burmese relations after the high tide of the Cultural Revolution of 1966–1967 and the re-establishment of relations between the two countries is not only a case study for such issues, it provides an avenue to review changes in Chinese foreign policy, and Chinese interests in global, regional, and bilateral relationships.

The Renormalization of Sino-Burmese Relations

During the 1968, the two countries reduced their hostility, and relations gradually thawed. Although the Chinese media continued to condemn and attack Rangoon, the number and frequency of verbal attacks decreased sharply, and the phraseology was less acrimonious compared with Beijing's response in 1967. There were 154 articles about Burma in the *People's Daily* from June to December in 1967, but only 29 articles in 1968, and words like "reactionary" and "fascist" were hardly used again. China donated US$4,000 to Burma for hurricane relief.

Burma reciprocated. From the summer of 1968, Burma refrained from openly accusing China of training and providing sanctuary for insurgents, and started to depict the rebellion of the BCP as more of a local event.[1] The focus of Burmese criticism was shifted from the Chinese government to the BCP and its insurgent allies. "Demonstrations began to take the form of 'work protests', and free labor donated by workers in a carefully orchestrated but more constructive use of anti-Chinese feelings; Burmese accusations once again became indirect."[2]

---

1 Bert, "Chinese Relations with Burma and Indonesia", p. 476; Robert A. Holmes, "China–Burma Relations since the Rift", *Asian Survey*, Vol. 12, No. 8, August 1972, p. 694.
2 Pettman, *China in Burma's Foreign Policy*, p. 37.

In January 1969, when Ne Win visited Pakistan, he discussed there with Chinese officials the possibility of resuming relations.[3] In 1969, Rangoon decided to stop border patrols along the Sino-Burmese border in order to avoid further conflict with the Chinese army. At a conference of the BSPP in November, Ne Win asserted "With regard to China, we would like to restore the cordial and friendly relations that previously existed. This will require efforts by both sides. For our part, regarding the clashes at the borders and the present situation, we shall do whatever we can to restore the old friendship and keep the situation from getting worse. We regard the 1967 incident as an unfortunate one. We would like to heal its wounds and forget the ugly incident."[4]

Both sides began to be invited to attend some diplomatic functions held by the other party. On 19 July 1968, the Chinese chargé d'affaires in Burma attended the commemoration on Burma's Martyr's Day, and placed a wreath on the tomb of Burma's "National Father," Aung San. In October 1968 and August 1969, some Burmese officials, public figures, and military officers were invited to attend the National Day and Army's Day receptions sponsored by Chinese Embassy in Rangoon. During the same period, Chinese officials were present at receptions given by the Burmese chargé d'affaires in Beijing. Both Chinese and Burmese attenders at various national celebrations and commemorations, however, were low-ranking government officials and military officers. Thus, the reconciliation progress was slow. The first sign of a real thaw was on 3 January 1970, when the Chinese Vice Minister of Foreign Affairs, Xu Yixin, appeared at the celebration of Burmese Independence held by the Burmese Embassy in Beijing, and the Xinhua News Agency briefly reported it. By mid 1970, however, reconciliation gestures had become very bold.

Chairman Mao Tsetung directly expressed the wish to improve relations with Burma. On the evening of 1 May 1970, Mao met diplomatic envoys of 35 countries attending the May Day celebrations on the Tiananmen Square rostrum; he expressed his wish to improve and thaw the relationship between China and their countries, and shook hands with each of the envoys. When Mao greeted the chargé d'affaires of Burma, he asked him to give his regards to Ne Win. Mao's posture on May Day was critical to a Beijing–Rangoon rapprochement. In August 1971, Zhou Enlai mentioned this detail to Ne Win, who was visiting Beijing, saying that "On May 1st

---

3   *Far Eastern Economic Review*, 20 February 1969, p. 311.
4   Holmes, "China–Burma Relations since the Rift", p. 695.

last year, Chairman Mao asked your chargé d'affairs to convey his regards to you, Sir. You also made active responses at this time. In this way, the situation took a favorable turn."[5]

The rank and number of those attending national celebrations sponsored by each side also rose.[6] The two countries returned their Ambassadors to their posts. In October 1970, Rangoon appointed U Thein Maung as the new Ambassador to China, and he arrived in Beijing on 16 November. In March 1971, the new Chinese Ambassador, Chen Zhaoyuan, reached Rangoon. Thus, seemingly, the broken bilateral relationship due to the 1967 anti-Chinese incident in Rangoon was healed.

Finally, Ne Win's trip to China in 1971 symbolized the real renormalization of China–Burma ties. Between 6–12 August 1971, Ne Win visited Beijing on invitation. At the welcoming banquet on 6 August, Zhou Enlai praised Ne Win for his great contribution in boosting good bilateral relations and solving the Sino-Burmese border issue. Zhou also hoped that Ne Win's visit could further improve relations. Ne Win reaffirmed the *Pauk Phaw* friendship of the two countries, and stated that bilateral cooperation on national peaceful development and world peace would "constantly promote the interests of both sides."[7] Mao Tsetung also met Ne Win.

The subjects of China–Burma relations and the overseas Chinese in Burma were discussed at five talks between Zhou Enlai and Ne Win. Ne Win expressed "deep regret" over the "6.26" event in 1967, agreed to make up to the Chinese victims of the Rangoon event, and asked for Zhou Enlai's advice on appropriate compensation. Zhou said "We also disapproved of some actions of the Chinese schools in 1967 . . . At that time, ultra-leftism permeated our Ministry of Foreign Affairs. But our government still controlled the situation, especially the relations with Burma . . . We declared that the overseas Chinese should not violate local

---

5 *Selected Diplomatic Writings of Zhou Enlai*, p. 483.

6 On 1 October 1970, the Burmese acting Foreign Minister, Vice Foreign Minister, the commander-in-chief of Rangoon Military Region and other high-ranking officials attended the reception for National Day held by the Chinese embassy. On the same day, Ne Win sent a congratulatory telegram to Zhou Enlai for Chinese National Day. On 4 January 1971, the Vice Chairman of the Standing Committee of the People's Congress, Guo Morou, and the Vice Foreign Minister, Han Nianlong, attended the reception for Burmese Independence Day. On 1 August the Director of the Military Intelligence Department of the Burma Defense Ministry, the Secretary of the Defense Ministry, and the commander-in-chief of the Rangoon Military Region attended the reception in the Chinese Embassy celebrating the founding of the PLA.

7 "Chairman Ne Win and First Lady Reach Beijing, Premier Chou Hosts Burmese Visitors", *People's Daily*, 7 August 1971.

law but abide by the law of the host countries, living and working according to the local lifestyle . . . We oppose dual nationality."[8]

During Ne Win's visit to China, China restated its policy to adhere to a friendly and peaceful policy toward Burma while Rangoon promised to insist on a peaceful and neutral policy toward China. Soon after Ne Win visited China, at the request of Burma China restarted its aid program, which had been suspended by the 1967 riots. On 22 November 1970, Burma voted for the proposal brought forward by eighteen countries concerning the PRC's seat in the U.N. and depriving Taiwan of its membership. On 9 October 1971, Burma and 20 other countries proposed to the U.N. that the PRC's seat in the U.N. and Permanent Membership on the U.N. Security Council be approved; Burma had changed from simply being a voter to a proposer. Zhou Enlai's secretary, Tong Xiaopeng, recalled that U Thant, the Burmese Secretary-General of the United Nations (1961–1971), had supported the PRC's admission to the U.N. His attitude could be attributed to friendly China–Burma relations.[9]

Causes of the Renormalization of Sino-Burmese Relations

Only four years separated the rift from the renormalization of bilateral ties. Although largely an immediate result of both sides' active interaction, there were broader causes: changes in the international situation and in Beijing–Washington–Moscow triangular relations.

Burma's Reconciliation Dynamics

From the viewpoint of the Burmese, the need for and the process of the renormalization of Sino-Burmese relations were dependent not only on understanding the causes of the anti-Chinese riots, Burmese judgments about China's internal upheaval, and the effects of China's reaction to the Rangoon events, but also on the essence and purpose of Burmese foreign policy.

The direct cause of the Rangoon riots was Beijing's leftist foreign policy, but the Burma junta also used the event to transfer domestic dissatisfaction onto foreigners, and seek internal political legitimacy. Although Rangoon orchestrated its nationalistic response to counterattack the Chinese provocation, it intentionally controlled the riot situation because Ne Win did not want to make a complete break with Beijing. After the riots, Burma recalled its Ambassador from Beijing, but did not sever diplomatic relations. Compared

---

8   *Selected Diplomatic Writings of Zhou Enlai*, p. 484.
9   Tong Xiaopeng, *Memoir of Tong Xiaopeng*, Fuzhou: Fujian People's Press, 2000, pp. 469–470.

with some anti-Chinese riots in other Southeast Asian countries, the scale and degree of the Rangoon riots were relatively moderate. The anti-Chinese riots in Rangoon caused heavy losses to Chinese life and property, but other incidents occurring outside Rangoon were generally limited to protests and demonstrations.

Burma's restrained attitude concerning the anti-Chinese riots and the domestic situation was related to Rangoon's judgment and perception of the turmoil of the Cultural Revolution. When Ne Win visited China in 1971, he discussed the Burmese process of decision-making about the riot. "I remember that your Ministry of Foreign Affairs had suffered two strikes, so I felt that your government could not completely control the situation at that time … Whatever they said to us, we thought that this was not the Chinese leadership's opinions. For a period of time, even I was under pressure to break off foreign relations with China, but I rejected this … We understood when Premier Zhou expressed his attitude on Sino-Burmese relations to the foreign media: 'What China does depends on what Burma does. Where China goes relies on where Burma goes' … We figured that Premier Zhou wished to maintain diplomatic relations with us. This was also what we wished. We didn't want to cut diplomatic ties with China, because it is easy to break off relations, but it is hard to resume them."[10] During the anti-Chinese riots and the succeeding antagonisms between Beijing and Rangoon, Burma had refrained from more violent or controversial responses. It did not attempt to draw support from the U.S. and the Soviet Union. These were all important preconditions on which to renormalize Sino-Burmese relations.

The Rangoon riots didn't signify that Burma's fundamental foreign policy had changed – Burma did not choose to fall back on U.S. or Soviet support, and it still pursued its neutral and non-aligned policy. In March 1968, Ne Win remarked, "We should not depend on other countries but on ourselves. Although the Rangoon event was deplorable, we shall not give up our neutral policy."[11] Burma's stance was an important precondition for rapprochement. Although there seems an apparent contradiction between the anti-Chinese riots in Rangoon and Burma's neutral policy, the distinction should be made between a tactical need and a broader purpose.

---

10   Chen Yangyong, *Zhou Enlai in 1967*, Chongqing: Chongqing Press, 2005, p. 287.
11   Rangoon Domestic Service, 1 March 1968, quoted from Zhang Guozhong, "Burma and Communist China, 1950–1990", Taiwan National Chengchi University, M.A. thesis, 1995, p. 55.

Burma formulated its neutral foreign policy soon after its independence, and claimed not to ally with any country, and declared that it would not be involved in any dispute, and would maintain friendly international relations. China was a major factor behind Burma's neutralism and non-alignment. Some said that the making of Burma's foreign policy was based on the fact that China, with a 700 million population, was to its north.[12] "Burmese non-alignment policy is primarily to assure China of non-aggression from Burmese soil and to avoid the destruction of Burma in another war."[13] The British historian D. G. E. Hall argued that "Independence is a word that has a very special meaning to them; it represents the supreme end of their policy, domestic as well as foreign."[14] In the midst of the Cold War, Burma was more cautious and prudent in maintaining its independence and national security compared with many other countries.

China's reaction after the Rangoon events further strengthened the Burmese conviction of the need for amicability with China. In addition to organizing massive domestic protests and parades, after the 1967 Rangoon incident Beijing openly supported the BCP's efforts to overthrow the military regime. This last measure of Beijing's counterattack against Rangoon did endanger the Ne Win government.

At the Opening Session of the Fourth Party Seminar on 6 November 1969, Ne Win stated that "The list of insurgencies that I have given is far from complete. The most serious situation prevails in the regions which share the border with China ... Let it suffice to say that from January 1 to the end of August this year, there were eight major engagements in that area, and ten which might be classed as minor or medium. It is not our way of doing things to raise a hue and cry every time something serious happens".[15] "We in Burma are therefore pledged to peace; and more, we shall undertake never to allow any piece of our territory to be used by any force, indigenous, or coming from abroad, as a base or foothold from which aggression may be committed or any trouble may be made against any of our neighbors. Even though our relations with a neighbor are at [this] juncture embarrassed, we should not restore the short-sighted policy of looking elsewhere for aid in the solving

12 Rose, "Burma and the Balance of Neutralism", p. 24.
13 David Wen-wei Chang, "A comparative study of neutralism", p. 122.
14 D. G. E. Hall, "Review of *Burma's Foreign Policy: A Study in Neutralism*", *Pacific Affairs*, Vol. XXXVII, No. 2, Summer 1964, p. 231.
15 "Address delivered by General Ne Win, Chairman of the Burma Socialist Programme Party, at the Openning Session of the Fourth Party Seminar on 6th November 1969", Burma Socialist Programme Party, 1969, p. 33.

of our problem."[16] Facing this serious challenge, Ne Win asserted, "We have no strength to retaliate . . . Therefore, I appeal to the people of the country to remain calm, and not be provoked into anger and harsh words or drastic action by the clashes on the borders."[17]

Meanwhile, former Prime Minister U Nu declared that he would change Burmese neutral policy and seek arms aid from all quarters, including the U.S., China, and the Soviet Union; his goal was to recapture power and thereby reestablish democratic socialism. Over 1969–1970, there were reports that he had made an alliance with the Karen and Mon insurgents to overthrow the Ne Win regime.[18] These factors also pushed Ne Win to reconcile with China. In 1970, Burma stopped the U.S. military aid program that had started from 1958, and the American personnel carrying out the program left the country at the end of June 1971. At the same time, Burma declined to join the Asian collective security system initiated by the Soviet Union and to sign a security accord with Moscow. This demonstrated that Burma did not want to further irritate China.

Explanations from China

From the viewpoint of China, the reconciliation between Beijing and Rangoon had different dimensions: the internal Chinese factors that caused the anti-Chinese riots in Burma, the changing internal domestic situation, the impact of the China–Burma rift on China, and the reorientation of China's foreign policy.

As earlier discussed, the extension of China's Cultural Revolution directly caused the anti-Chinese riots in Rangoon. Two factors connected the Rangoon incident with the Cultural Revolution. First, Beijing had propagandized Mao Tsetung thought internationally and intrusively. The "Propaganda Outline of the Cultural Revolution" put forward in June 1966 emphasized that "the Cultural Revolution is of vital significance, bearing on the destiny and future of our Party and state as well as World Revolution."[19] In October 1966, The Publicity Department of CCP Central Committee approved distributing the *Little Red Book* all over the world.[20] The CCP Central Committee decreed that the main mission of China's Embassies abroad was to propagandize Mao

---

16   *Ibid.*, pp. 33–37.
17   *Ibid.*, p. 35.
18   Bandyopadhyaya, *Burma and Indonesia*, p. 172.
19   "Instruction outline for disseminating information related to the Cultural Revolution", *Xinhua Monthly*, No. 6, 1966, p. 29. Or see *People's Daily* and *PLA Daily* of 6 June 1966.
20   Ma Jisen, *The Cultural Revolution in the Foreign Ministry of China*, Hong Kong: Chinese University of Hong Kong Press, 2003, p. 134.

Tsetung thought and the Cultural Revolution overseas.[21] Consequently, the Chinese Embassy in Rangoon disregarded the objections of the Burmese government and took its own course and launched the Burmese version of the Cultural Revolution.

Second, radicals had seized diplomatic power. "These events-in Hong Kong, Phnom Penh, Rangoon, and to a lesser extent elsewhere-had multiple causes. But they would probably not have occurred had the Chinese Foreign Ministry not suffered radicalization during this mid-1967 period, had Foreign Minister Chen Yi not been subject to personal attack, and had the physical destruction of some ministry records not taken place."[22] Mao Tsetung confirmed to Edgar Snow that the Ministry of Foreign Affairs was in a mess, and that "It was out of control for one and a half months and its power was seized by counter-revolutionaries."[23] Since early 1967, Chen Yi had not functioned as minister and had lost power in August when Wang Li took over the Foreign Ministry. On 24 October 1967, Zhou Enlai asked the visiting President of Mauritania to pass on messages to Kim Il-sung, Norodom Sihanouk, and Gamal Abdel Nasser: "We always instruct overseas Chinese that they should abide by the local laws; but we can't control their actions; we don't conceal that our embassies abroad made some mistakes but we can correct them at any moment."[24]

It was because Mao himself had opened the Pandora's Box of internationalizing the Cultural Revolution in the summer of 1967 that the revolutionary rebels were able to take power in the Foreign Ministry. On 9 September 1966, Mao Tsetung wrote in a report that "All China's diplomatic establishments abroad should be revolutionized."[25] And he also decided to call back all China's Ambassadors (except the Ambassador to Egypt) and most of the top embassy staff members to join the Cultural Revolution.[26] "This action obviously severely impaired Peking's ability to perceive and analyze events abroad. But an equally important consequence was that it radicalized both the embassies, once the staff returned to them, and the Foreign Ministry departments at home."[27] "The recall of ambassadors was to have important consequences several months

21 Zhu Liang, "Selfless and fearless truth-seeker, Wang Jiaxiang", *Yan-Huang Historical Review*, No. 8, 2006, p. 6.
22 Robinson, "China confronts the Soviet Union", p. 244.
23 *Works of Mao Tsetung Since the Establishment of the PRC*, Vol. 13, Beijing: Central Party Literature Press, 1998, p. 163.
24 *Chronicle of Zhou Enlai*, Vol. 2, p. 196.
25 *Works of Mao Tsetung Since the Establishment of the PRC*, Vol. 12, Beijing: Central Party Literature Press, 1998, pp. 128–129.
26 Du Yi, *Chen Yi in the Cultural Revolution*, Beijing: World Knowledge Press, 1997, p. 95.
27 Robinson, "China Confronts the Soviet Union", p. 246.

later, for it probably facilitated the manipulation of several embassies by fanatical followers of Mao."[28] In the same way, the Chinese embassy in Burma was completely entangled in the domestic political turmoil. In March 1967, China's Ambassador to Burma, Geng Biao, and 21 colleagues were recalled. Some radicals subsequently came to Rangoon and seized power in the embassy. They actively pushed the Cultural Revolution in Burma, and ignited the fuse of the anti-Chinese riots.

The seizure of power in the Foreign Ministry by radicals was influential in the anti-Chinese riots as well as in the subsequent rift in bilateral ties. In 1971, Zhou told the visiting Ne Win that "China's government tried its best to confine the Rangoon event to the negotiations between the two governments."[29] But the state of affairs could not be controlled by Zhou, and the actions by the radicals in the Foreign Ministry and in the Chinese embassy in Burma continuously aggravated tensions. Zhou explained, "At that time, our embassies directly sent notes to foreign countries on some vital political issues. It was unprecedented that our embassy in Rangoon presented notes of protest to your Foreign Ministry without the permission of China's Foreign Ministry. Up to now, we have not ascertained how many notes were delivered to your Foreign Ministry without the approval of our Foreign Ministry."[30]

In August 1967, supported by Mao Tsetung, Zhou seized diplomatic power again and began to restore the order in foreign relations that had been affected by the chaos of the Cultural Revolution. Zhou's regaining power in the Foreign Ministry was the turning point in mending the break with Rangoon. In 1971, when Zhou retrospectively considered the rapprochement between the two countries with Ne Win, he stressed, "With regard to China–Burma relations, we always took measures to control the state of affairs, and later you, Sir, did so too, so bilateral ties didn't worsen further. It was good and favorable for our two countries to improve and resume diplomatic relations."[31]

Nevertheless, the renormalization of Sino-Burmese ties was not simply the result of the changing political situation in China. The fundamental explanation was that Beijing gradually reoriented its foreign policy and strategy. China was isolated from the rest of the world during the height of the Cultural Revolution in 1966–1967. When the upheavals subsided, Beijing began to take a more practical foreign policy line in 1968 and attempted to regain the initiative.

28 Melvin Gurtov, "The Foreign Ministry and Foreign Affairs during the Cultural Revolution", *The China Quarterly*, No. 40, October-December 1969, p. 72.
29 *Selected Diplomatic Writings of Zhou Enlai*, p. 481.
30 *Ibid.*, p. 482.
31 *Ibid.*, p. 484.

In May 1968, Mao Tsetung objected that the appellation "The center of the world revolution-Beijing" was wrong and self-centered, and instructed that China's external propaganda should not be intrusive. "Don't propagandize that revolutionary movements in foreign countries are affected by China."[32] In early 1970, the Central Committee of the CCP dispatched "military representatives" to the Foreign Ministry, and a "revolution committee" was established in June. As a result, China gradually stabilized its external relations.

China also made conciliatory gestures to the outside world. On the evening of 1 May 1969, Mao and Zhou received eight new Ambassadors to China on the Tiananmen Square Rostrum, and said that China wished to improve and develop relations with countries all over the world. A group photo was taken with each of the eight Ambassadors in sequence, and all the eight pictures were published in the *People's Daily* the next day. Soon, China's missions returned their posts and Beijing began taking some measures to restore the external ties impaired during the height of the Cultural Revolution.

Additionally, the significance and consequences of the split in China–Burma relations for China could not be ignored. Prior to 1967, China had set Burma up as a model of its adherence to the Five Principles of Peaceful Coexistence, and had peacefully solved the border dispute. China's revolutionary foreign policy heavily tarnished its international image. An aggressive self-righteous China caused widespread apprehension and fear in peripheral countries, particularly in small ones. Therefore, the renormalization of China–Burma relations, which had been the previous good model of China's external relations, enhanced other countries' trust in China's foreign policy and the sincerity of Beijing's reconciliation, as well as expedited and promoted the return of normalcy in China's foreign relations.

Moreover, the change in the international environment during this period, especially in China's circumjacent regions, was another important factor pushing a return to the pre-Cultural Revolution policy and renormalizing China's foreign relations.

The Context of China–U.S.–Soviet Triangular Relations

In the late 1960s and early 1970s, a variety of political forces had formed new international relations out of those that had been structured and integrated for more than 20 years after World War II. In the contention for hegemony between the U.S. and the Soviet Union, the former was less dominant at that

---

32 *Works of Mao Tsetung Since the Establishment of the PRC*, Vol. 12, pp. 274–276.

stage. The Sino-Soviet split and the fearsome military threat from Moscow pushed the two weaker countries (the U.S. and China) into an alliance to balance the strongest within the great power triangle.

In August 1968, the Soviet Union occupied Czechoslovakia. Following the Soviet's signing a 1964 military pact with Mongolia, by 1969 about one million Soviet troops were stationed on the Sino-Mongolian and the Sino-Soviet borders. In March 1969, the Sino-Soviet border conflict over Zhenbao Island (Damansky Island) broke out, and further border clashes along the western section of the Sino-Soviet border in Xinjiang occurred in August 1969. The Chinese suffered casualties in this engagement. Heightened tensions raised the prospect of a nuclear war between China and the Soviet Union. Also, Moscow proposed an Asian collective security system to seek "to organize an anti-China united front in Asia to encircle or contain the PRC just as it was beginning to emerge from the turmoil and isolation of the Great Proletarian Cultural Revolution."[33] India, Pakistan, Afghanistan, Burma, Cambodia, and Singapore were among the Asian states specially sought after in this security system framework.[34]

Thus Moscow became Beijing's biggest threat instead of Washington. Some regard the nature of the Cultural Revolution and the events after the autumn of 1967, as indicating no real revolution in foreign policy. "The Cultural Revolution has been an internal phenomenon, and its seepage abroad to become a factor in China's relations with other countries seems to have been an uncalculated though perhaps an inevitable by-product. As such, those instances in which the Revolution had deleterious consequences for China's foreign relations might be characterized as aberrant episodes rather than as reflections of a persistent or prominent new strand in China's foreign policy line."[35] Yet this seems questionable given the official Chinese admonition to spread the Cultural Revolution abroad, at least for a period.

The Soviet menace and China's self-isolation caused Beijing gradually to return to a practical foreign policy after the summer of 1967. Meanwhile, Sino-American rapprochement after 1969 required Beijing to change its self-centered perceptions and arrogance in the policy debate: a shift in China's foreign policy from fanaticism to realism.

---

33 Arnold L. Horelick, "The Soviet Union's Asian Collective Security Proposal: A Club in Search of Members", *Pacific Affairs*, Vol. 47, No. 3, Autumn 1974, p. 269.
34 *Ibid.*, pp. 271–272.
35 Gurtov, "The Foreign Ministry and Foreign Affairs", p. 102.

Rangoon sought detente with Beijing primarily in its own national interests, and the chain reaction of Sino-U.S. rapprochement through the world also further allayed Burmese hesitation on reconciliation with China and dimmed Burmese suspicions of Chinese intentions. (From 1970 to 1972, 33 countries established diplomatic relations with China and six countries resumed relations with China.) For Beijing, the change in China–U.S.–Soviet triangular relations in the late 1960s and early 1970s meant new security challenges and opportunities of balance created by the great powers game. This was partly responsible for the Sino-Burmese rapprochement. After the Rangoon incident, the Soviet Union, the U.S., and other countries in the two camps supported Burma against China, and provided economic and technical aid to Burma. Rangoon and Washington signed a military training pact. These countries used the Sino-Burmese rift to minimize and counter China's influence in Burma, so China, in its security dilemma, subsequently had to try regaining its power in Burma.

In summary, between 1954 and 1966 China gradually shifted its foreign policy from the pragmatic to the irrational; ideological considerations, especially "proletariat internationalism," overwhelmed national security and realistic interests in the process of decision-making. China's foreign relations thus moved from a united front to self-isolation. The split between China–Burma in 1967 was a conspicuous example of this course.

The deleterious consequences for China's foreign relations caused by the Cultural Revolution were amplified by the Beijing–Moscow split and confrontation. However, the Sino-U.S. détente was undoubtedly the force to push Beijing to return to pragmatism in foreign relations. The Ne Win military regime had faced a legitimacy crisis since it seized power in the 1962 *coup d'etat*. Although the anti-Chinese riot provided Ne Win with an opportunity to divert domestic discontent by orchestrating nationalism against a foreign target, he had to defuse the strain caused by the rift with China. China's support for the BCP had severely threatened the Rangoon regime. Consequently, Rangoon needed to restore relations with Beijing more urgently than China did with Rangoon.

6

Sino-Burmese Ties: The Cicatrized Sino-Burmese Relationship 1972–1988

*T*he turn from confrontation to negotiation between China and the U.S. became apparent during the 1970s and 1980s. China's domestic political situation and foreign relations underwent drastic changes. The period 1972–1988 was a thaw in bilateral relations between China and Burma. It was an attempt to erase the scars of the earlier Cultural Revolution. In the light of the changes in the geopolitics in Southeast Asia and of the triangular relations of China, the Soviet Union and the U.S., however, Beijing now attached less importance to Rangoon compared to its policy orientation before 1966.

Political Relations

The Beijing–Rangoon Thaw

Although the broken relations between China and Burma due to the anti-Chinese riots in 1967 were renormalized in 1971, both states could not get over their shadows in such a short period. By the end of the 1970s, China had not yet put an end to the domestic chaos of the Cultural Revolution and readopted the peaceful foreign policy of the 1950s. This factor, coupled with Burmese distrust of Beijing's shifting policy, led to continued suspicion between the two countries. In the early and mid 1970s, Sino-Burmese ties faced the conundrum of how to heal the rupture. China attempted to assuage Burmese apprehension of China's export of revolution, while Burma wanted to reassure China about its neutral role in the game of power politics.

In August 1975, U Hla Phone, the Foreign Minister of Burma, visited China. This visit was regarded as the preparation for, and a prelude to, Ne Win's visit three months later. During talks with U Hla Phone, Vice Premier Deng Xiaoping complimented him that "Burma did not participate in the agreements initiated by United States in Asia and evinced no interest in the

Soviet Union's Asian Collective Security Proposal."[1] Over 11–15 November, Ne Win as President of Burma visited China by invitation. This was the most crucial diplomatic contact since the breakup of bilateral relations in 1967. Chinese newspapers extolled Ne Win's visit with elevated wording. Two articles were published in The *People's Daily*, on 11 and 12 December 1975, "Warm Welcome to the Burmese Distinguished Guests" and "Burmese Government Sticking to Independent and Nonalignment Policy and China–Burmese '*Pauk Phaw*' Friendship Ongoing", stressing the traditional *Pauk Phaw* ties and amity, and Chinese contentment with Rangoon's sustained policy of neutralism. On 13 November, Mao Tsetung, although seriously ill, persisted in meeting Ne Win, which served to show that Beijing made much of his visit.[2]

Ne Win's trip to China in 1971 focused on the Rangoon incident of 1967, and this time Zhou Enlai and Ne Win reaffirmed their commitment to the Five Peaceful Principles of 1954. On 11 November at the welcoming banquet, Ne Win claimed that "Burma never allows any country to maintain military bases on Burmese soil to antagonize other countries, especially our neighbors. We won't do so in the future."[3] When Prime Minister U Nu paid his first visit to Beijing in 1954, Burma made China similar promises in order to cast aside Beijing's doubts that Burma was siding with the U.S. Ne Win's reemphasis on the "base" problem on November 11 largely resulted from the Asian Collective Security proposal initiated by the Soviet Union at that time. Such a promise was a guiding principle of Burma's China policy and the prerequisite to winning Beijing's favor. Ne Win stated that "The problems [discord in bilateral ties] are not unlikely to be solved in the long run as long as we both, tolerantly and patiently, cope with them for the sake of friendship."[4] By all appearances, the problems mentioned by Ne Win were China's support of the BCP. At the end of the visit, a Joint Communique was issued, which stressed the significance of the Five Principles of Peaceful Coexistence for bilateral ties, and the unanimous agreement on the proposition of building up a peaceful, neutral, and liberal zone in Southeast Asia.[5]

1   *Chronicle of Deng Xiaoping, 1975–1997* Vol. I, Beijing: Central Party Literature Press, 2004, p. 80.
2   In 1974, Mao was suffering from a terminal illness so he told Wang Hongwen that he would not meet any foreign guest even if they requested to see him. Mao's health further deteriorated. See *Biography of Mao Tsetung*, Vol. 2, pp. 1715–1740.
3   "Speech of President Ne Win", press release, Xinhua News Agency, 12 November 1975. The Burmese constitution of 2008 stipulates that there will be no foreign bases in Myanmar.
4   *Ibid.*
5   "Joint Communique of PRC and the Socialist Republic of the Union of the Burma", *People's Daily*, 16 November 1975.

By 1975 the cool Burma–China relations had become somewhat better, but both sides had not made substantive progress in improving relations because Beijing had failed to fulfill its promise on the Five Peaceful Principles. Deng Xiaoping tried to appease Ne Win's fear with high-sounding rhetoric that "We strictly and consistently observe the Five Principles of Peaceful Coexistence ... China will never be a superpower to invade and bully other countries."[6] "We believe the revolution of any country should depend on its national strength ... China would never intervene in the affairs of other countries."[7] In reality, China was still implementing a "dual track" foreign policy and maintaining support for the BCP. In the meantime, Burma was reluctant to stand by the Chinese and publicly counter the Soviets and the U.S. Accordingly, although the joint communique stressed anti-hegemonism, phrases denouncing U.S. and Soviet imperialism were not used.

Over 5–11 February 1977, Deng Yingchao, the Vice Chairman of the People's National Congress, visited Burma.[8] She was the first Chinese state leader to visit Burma since the rift of Burma–China relations in 1967 and the end of the Cultural Revolution. A number of factors can account for Deng's visit: to demonstrate the end of China's political upheaval and the elimination of the Gang of Four political force; to prevent Rangoon from deviating from its neutral policy and to counter-attack Moscow's encirclement of China;[9] to exploit her special status as Zhou Enlai's widow to boost bilateral ties because he played such important roles in Burma–China relations[10] as well as having a good personal friendship with Ne Win;[11] and to signal and stress that its Burma policy had returned to the Zhou era.[12]

Burma thought highly of Deng Yingchao's visit. The enthusiastic reception Ne Win gave to Deng- usually only reserved for heads of state- was a clear sign of the junta's attempt to re-establish the cordial relations of Zhou's era and to enlist Beijing's support in the BCP problem. (BCP leaders had visited Beijing two months before Deng's trip to Burma, and were received and hosted by Hua Guofeng, the successor to Mao Tsetung).

6 "Speech of Vice Premier Deng Xiaoping", press release, Xinhua News Agency, 12 November 1975.
7 *Chronicle of Deng Xiaoping*, Vol. I, p. 129
8 In November 1975, Mao Tsetung made suggestions to Ne Win that he invite Chinese leaders to visit Burma when he met Ne Win in Beijing. Ne Win accepted Mao's suggestion.
9 "The Editorial of Hong Kong South China Morning Post, Zhou Enlai's Wife Visited Burma", *Reference News*, 13 February 1977.
10 Interview Chinese Former Ambassador to Burma, Cheng Ruisheng, 12 July 2009, Beijing.
11 Interview Chinese Former Ambassador to Burma, Chen Baoliu, 14 July 2009, Beijing.
12 Bert, "Chinese Policy Toward Burma and Indonesia", p. 966.

On 27 April 1977, after nearly one and a half years' interval, Ne Win led a high-level delegation to visit Beijing at the invitation of China. The interval between this visit and Deng's trip to Burma amounted to less than three months, which drew outside attention. The main intention of Ne Win's visit was to bargain with Beijing about the BCP problem. At the welcoming banquet, Ne Win stated that "If there are some unfavorable problems in bilateral relations caused by some unavoidable circumstances, the two parties should be honest and patient in dealing with them. If the problems aren't solved by this means for a while, we should not escalate them lest our existing friendship be impaired."[13] Although neither of the two sides released the outcome of the negotiations, Ne Win told the press that "During the talks, both of us adopted frank and mutual understanding attitudes."[14]

The mutual visits of Deng Yingchao and Ne Win in the first half of 1977 did not end the visits between both leaderships. In early September, the Foreign Minister of Burma, U Hla Phone, made a detour to Beijing to inform China of his visit to Cambodia the moment he wrapped it up. On 18 September, Ne Win dropped in during his visit to Korea by way of Beijing. Hua Guofeng met Ne Win and Vice Premier Deng Xiaoping discussed with him China's domestic situation and foreign relations with the U.S., Japan and Yugoslavia. Ne Win, very familiar with Chinese politics,[15] was convinced of Deng Xiaoping's crucial future role in China's political arena. As a result, Ne Win invited Deng Xiaoping to visit Burma.

Over 26–31 January 1978, Vice Premier Deng Xiaoping visited Burma and received high-level, red-carpet treatment. He was given a 19 gun salute and a guard of honor accompanied by Ne Win. President Ne Win and the leading high officials received Deng Xiaoping at the airport; 100,000 civilians were arranged to welcome him along the route between the airport and the State Guest House. Deng Xiaoping's photo was published in the Burmese newspapers on arrival day. Both governments set their propaganda machines in motion and gave Deng's visit a tremendous build-up.

In terms of timing, Deng's trip was the first visit after the Cultural Revolution of the most important Chinese state leader since the end of 1960, not only to Burma but to foreign countries. From the beginning of the Cultural Revolution to Deng Xiaoping's foreign tour in 1978, Chinese leaders hardly visited foreign countries, while foreign leaders unilaterally visited China. Deng

---

13   "President Ne Win's Speech at the Welcoming Banquet Held by State Council", *People's Daily*, 28 April 1977.
14   "President Ne Win's Toasts at the Welcome Banquet for Chinese Leaders", *People's Daily*, 2 May 1977.
15   Interview, Cheng Ruisheng, 12 July 2009, Beijing.

Plate 8: Deng Xiaoping and Ne Win, Rangoon, 26 January 1978 (photograph courtesy Cheng Ruisheng)

Xiaoping's visit to Burma indicated that China had restored internal order and stability. The occasion of the visit marked Beijing's concern with countering Vietnam's influence in Burma. In January 1978, border disputes between Vietnam and Cambodia had intensified. Deng Yingchao subsequently visited Cambodia. At the same time, Foreign Minister of Vietnam, Nguyen Duy Lo, visited some countries of Southeast Asia. On Deng Yingchao's heels, Deng Xiaoping's visit to Rangoon was an important step in countering Vietnamese influence in Southeast Asia.

Deng Xiaoping was not only the Vice Premier, but also the Vice Chairman of the Central Committee of the CCP, the Vice Chairman of the Military Commission of the CCP Central Committee, and the Chief of the PLA. Deng Xiaoping's 1978 foreign tour in eight countries, including Burma, symbolized that he had come to power for the third time and that his era was underway, which meant that the pragmatists and moderates began to control the country's political situation.

Deng's first and second legs of his overseas trip in 1978 were Burma and Nepal, which was no accident. Among the third world countries, both Burma and Nepal carried out non-aligned and friendly policies towards China, so Beijing selected them as the first two legs of Deng's tour to demonstrate that the new Chinese leadership would carry on Zhou Enlai's good-neighbor diplomacy. The purpose of the visit was also to establish a united front against the Soviets in order to contend against Soviet and Vietnamese expansion in Southeast Asia.[16] The Soviet Union had sent some parliamentary, cultural, and sports delegations to Burma before Deng's visit, but Ne Win was averse to the increasing any Soviet influence. Beijing was likely to seize the opportunity to enhance bilateral political relations.[17]

Beijing's Dual-Track Diplomacy

After the anti-Chinese riots in Rangoon in 1967, the CCP politically, economically, and militarily started publicly to support the BCP. On 1 January 1968, BCP troops, heavily armed and well equipped by China, crossed the border into Burma and seized place after place with Chinese support. Some overseas Chinese in Burma were ordered or volunteered to join the BCP after the riots, and many Chinese-educated youths crossed the border to enlist in the BCP during the Cultural Revolution. Thus, a considerable proportion of middle- and upper-cadres and officers of the BCP were Chinese. In spite of the renormalization of Burma–China relations in 1971, the CCP still publicly remained supportive of the BCP.

The *People's Daily*, the mouthpiece of the CCP and the most authoritative newspaper in China, was a weathervane illustrating Beijing's dual-track diplomacy, whose editorials and coverage reflected CCP and BCP relations.

During 1971–1978, some Chinese leaders passed away, and the BCP sent telegrams of condolence to the CCP.[18] The *People's Daily* published from 1971

---

16 Cheng Ruisheng, "Records of Sino-Burmese Friendship", p. 174.
17 "Deng Xiaoping's Visit to Rangoon Will Influence Asia", *Reference News*, 23 December 1977.
18 Telegrams of condolences on the deaths of Chen Yi, Xie Fuzhi, Li Fuchun (Vice Premier and member of the CCCP), Dong Biwu (senior statesman of the CCCP), Kang Sheng (the Vice Chairman of CCCP), Premier Zhou Enlai, Zhu De (Chairman of the Standing Committee of the National People's Congress and member of the standing committee of the Political Bureau of the CCP), Mao Tsetung, Guo Morou (Vice Chairman of the Standing Committee of the National People's Congress and Member of Central Committee of the CCP) and Luo Ruiqing, were published in full in the *People's Daily*. Meanwhile, the BCP'S congratulatory letters also appeared in the *People's Daily*, including those for the 10th National Congress of the CCP, the 25th anniversary of National Day, the 4th session of China's National Congress, the 55th anniversary of the founding of the CCP, Hua Guofeng's election as both the Chairman of the Central Committee of the CCP and the Chairman of the Military Commission of the CCP Central Committee, the third Plenary Session of the eleventh Central Committee, and the opening of the 11th China's National Congress, and Deng Xiaoping's election as the President of the Chinese People's Political Consultative Conference.

Table 2: Reports on the BCP in the *People's Daily,* 1971–1988

Year	Nature	Format	Number
1975	BCP Statement	Fully Published	1
1975	CCP to BCP: Telegram of Condolence	Fully Published	1
1976	News	Photo	2
1971–1978	BCP to CCP: Telegram of Condolence	Fully Published	10
1971–1978	BCP to CCP: Telegram of Condolences	Fully Published	8
1971–1978	News	Brief mention	13
1979–1988	BCP to CCP: Letter of Congratulation	Partly Published	1
1979–1988	BCP to CCP: Letter of Congratulation	Brief mention	3

Source: *The People's Daily,* 1972–1988

to 1978 eight telegrams and letters of congratulation, 10 telegrams of condolence and consolation sent by the BCP, and 13 coverages on the BCP leaders' presence in Chinese celebrations and mournings.

The *People's Daily* on 21 May 1975 released the full text of the CCP's telegram of condolence on the deaths of the Chairman of the BCP Central Committee, Thakin Zin, and the Secretary of BCP Central Committee, Thakin Chit. This telegram recognized the leading role and contribution of the BCP in the Burmese struggle against class enemies at home and abroad, and deemed that the BCP "will undoubtedly win outright victory in the revolutionary war."[19] On the same day, the Central Committee of the BCP issued a statement on the deaths of the two leaders, stating that the party would proceed with armed combat and carry the struggle to the end under the guidance of Marxism and Mao Tsetung thought.[20]

On 25 January 1976, the member of the Standing Committee of the Political Bureau of the CCP Central Committee, Zhang Chunqiao, met and banqueted Thakin Ba Thein Tin, the Chairman of the BCP. On 18 November 1976, Hua Guofeng, the Chairman of the CCP Central Committee, received and gave a welcome dinner for Thakin Ba Thein Tin and the Vice Chairman of

19 "CCP Telegrammed BCP on the death of Chairman Thain Zin and Secretary Thain Chit", *People's Daily,* 21 May 1975.
20 "Carrying out the Revolution till Victory: BCP Central Committee's Announcement on the Death of Chairman Thain Zin and Secretary Thain Chi", *People's Daily,* 21 May 1975.

the BCP, Thakin Pe Tint. The two meetings between the two parties in 1976 were covered by the *People's Daily*, accompanied by photographs. The second meeting appeared on the front page of the daily, which indicated that Hua Guofeng succeeded Mao as the leader of world revolution and was continuing to carry out Mao's policy to support the communist movements in Southeast Asia as well as reassuring pro-Beijing communist parties in Asia of the change of Chinese leaders.

In March 1971, the Voice of the People of Burma (VOPB) started its transmission from the Chinese side of the border and the radio signal covered all Burma. The VOPB broadcast in five languages: Burmese, Kachin, Karen, Shan, and Chinese, every morning at 7:00–8:00 a.m. and in the evening at 18:30–19:30 p.m. According to CIA's declassified document, "The [assistance] the Chinese are providing the insurgents – as of April 1971 – includes, in addition to the weapons mentioned above, ammunition, explosives, tools, clothing and uniforms, medicines, food grains, printed propaganda (including Mao badges) and extra funds (in Burmese currency). During the past two years, Chinese support of Naw Seng has grown significantly. Not only has the supply of weapons increased but the type has improved: as of May 1971, the Chinese were supplying B-40 rocket launchers, mortars, light machine guns, and a few heavy machine guns, in addition to the semi-automatic weapons and submachine guns which they had been providing since late 1967."[21] Beijing permitted the BCP to recruit Chinese ethnic minority peoples living on the Chinese side of the border to serve with the insurgents in Burma. "In some cases, however, local Chinese officials have been actively involved in the recruiting. The pressure that government authorities exerted on Chinese non-Han citizens living near the border to join the Burmese insurgents is reported to have considerably increased in 1969 and 1970."[22] On 9 April 1975, the VOPB broadcasted that during 1968–1975, the BCP fought 1,300 battles with Ne Win's troops, and killed and captured 16,000 soldiers of the government army. By 1975, their bases had expanded to 34,000 square kilometers, in which there were 3,000 villages and 575,000 people.[23]

Beijing's dual-track diplomacy naturally caused Burmese discontent and hindered the comeback of the friendly relations of the Zhou Enlai era. At the same time, Burma had to put up with its giant and aggressive neighbor.

21 "Peking and the Burmese Communists", p. 78.
22 *Ibid.*, p. 79.
23 *Chronology of Burma* (2 March 1962–9 April 1975), Historical Research Institute of Yunnan, 1975, p. 164.

Rangoon actively kept close contact with Beijing to seek to find a solution to the BCP problem, while carrying out an equidistant diplomacy in the great powers game, and particularly maintaining their moderate relations with the Soviet Union and Vietnam. Rangoon attempted not only not to provoke Beijing, but also to use China's opponents to counterbalance the Chinese.

On 27 April 1977, Ne Win was invited to visit China and negotiate the BCP problem with Beijing. It seemed that China had to make some concessions to appease Burmese anger during this visit. It was sensible to gain Burmese support especially when the Soviet Union had increasingly expanded its influence in Vietnam and in the region of the Indian Ocean. Meanwhile, the pragmatist faction of Deng Xiaoping's entourage had regained power and had initiated a shift in the dual-track diplomacy. After 1978, the *People's Daily* never published in full the BCP's telegrams of condolence, letters of congratulation, or the BCP leaders' presence at China's official functions. During 1979–1988, the BCP's congratulatory letters and telegrams appeared only four times in that daily, one only in part and the other three only mentioned by name (see Table 2).

Over 20–23 October 1980, Ne Win paid his 11th visit to China and met the top leaders in Beijing such as Hua Guofeng, Ye Jianying, Zhao Ziyang, Deng Xiaoping, and Li Xiannian. Before his trip to China, Ne Win declared a general pardon for any disarmed anti-government forces, but the BCP refused to receive the pardon. Therefore, Ne Win still needed to win the support of Beijing to stamp out its domestic rebellions. By the mid 1980s, the BCP problem had ceased to matter in bilateral relations. When Ne Win (who had retired as President but still remained Chairman of the BSPP) visited China on 4 May 1985, Deng Xiaoping stated that "There is no great problem to be solved between China and Burma." Ne Win agreed with Deng.[24] In May 1987, Burmese President U San Yu met China's Vice Premier Qiao Shi in Rangoon and stated that Chinese and Burmese relations were continually amicable and "there is no problem between the two countries."[25]

Regional Security

To a large extent, the Cold War found expression in regional security and conflict in Asia. Regional security issues dominated relations between China

---

24 Chai Shikuan and Zhu Minzhi, "Compliments on Sino-Burmese Friendship and an Example of Implementing the Five Principles when Deng Xiaoping Met Ne Win", *People's Daily*, 5 May 1985.

25 Lu Jimin, "Burmese President U San Yu Met Vice Premier Qiao Shi", *People's Daily*, 26 May 1987.

and its peripheral countries. After the Beijing–Moscow split in the 1960s and the Sino–U.S. détente in the 1970s, the confrontation between China and the Soviets entangled China's relations with adjacent countries and regions. Deng Xiaoping pointed out three major impediments to the renormalization of Sino-Soviet relations: "First, one million Soviet garrison troops along the Sino-Soviet border, including the Soviet garrison in Mongolia; second, Vietnam's invasion of Cambodia; third, the Soviet invasion of Afghanistan." Both Vietnam and Afghanistan shared a land border with China (as did Mongolia), so the problems of Vietnam and Afghanistan were perceived as threats to China.[26]

Since the renormalization of Sino-Burmese relations, regional security was an unavoidable topic in their bilateral relations. Beijing tried to draw Burma into the international united anti-Soviet front, to weaken Soviet influence in Burma, and to push the Burmese into standing by the Chinese on the problems of Vietnam and Afghanistan. China stressed the common status of both as third world or developing countries and thus asserted during the high-level exchanges of visits in the 1970s that the two countries should undertake the "common tasks" of anti-imperialism and anti-hegemonism. These visits were Ne Win's trips to China in December 1975 and April 1977, Deng Yingchao's trip to Burma in 1977, and Burmese Prime Minister U Maung Maung Kha's visit to Beijing in 1979.

In spite of Chinese appeals and initiatives against the Soviets, the two countries did not issue unanimous statements opposing imperialism and hegemony, except for the joint communique in 1975 that both countries "are against any country or country bloc that conspires to establish hegemony over other nations and spheres of influence in any region of the world."[27] The Burmese remained silent about Chinese verbal attacks and comments on the imperialism and hegemony of the Soviets and Vietnam. Although Burma objected to Vietnam's invasion of Cambodia and the Soviet invasion of Afghanistan, the Burmese media did not publish any editorials or comments on them, but only quoted the relevant reports of foreign newspapers and foreign wire services in accordance with its neutralist and non-alignment foreign policy. In 1977, U San Yu, the General Secretary of the BSPP reiterated at the third Congress of the BSPP that "According to [our] independent foreign policy, Burma will

---

26 *Chronicle of Deng Xiaoping*, Vol. I, p. 851.
27 "Joint Communique of the P.R.C. and the Socialist Republic of the Union of the Burma", *People's Daily*, 16 November 1975.

keep its word to maintain good relations, mutual understanding, and mutual help with all countries."[28]

The general objective of Burma's China policy was to foster good-neighbor relations to ensure national security. Although Burma's policy objective was not unique, it had exceptional meaning. Burma possessed sensitive and important geopolitical significance, lying wedged between China and India with a long, exposed border both with them as well as with Thailand. "The Burmese see their security in recognizing the geographical realities of their situation and providing their larger neighbors with no pretext for invasion. Even in the face of China's aiding the Burma Communist Party in its war against the government, the Burmese limit themselves to protests to China and warfare against their local communists."[29] In addition, Rangoon deemed that "An overview of the international situation shows that there are two blocs, capitalism and socialism. Two blocs are scrambling for a balance of power by hook or by crook. Moreover, they are extending and expanding their sphere of influence in order to enhance their political systems."[30] In this context, Burma prudently conducted balanced diplomacy between the Soviet Union, Vietnam, the United States, and China.

For instance, when Deng Xiaoping ended his visit to Burma in January 1978, Ne Win promptly invited Vietnam Prime Minister Pham Van Dong to visit Rangoon. In 1979, Burma announced its withdrawal from the Non-Aligned Movement, which was to meet in Cuba, mainly because of its Soviet domination. Burma was worried that the anti-Soviet countries, notable China, would be suspicious of its neutral and non-alignment policy if it continued to hold its membership.

Burma still followed a conservative and cautious policy to protect its interests without offending any parties even in the face of regional security problems in Indochina. After the eruption of the Sino-Vietnamese War in February 1979, President Ne Win visited Thailand in March to conduct emergency consultations on the Indochina situation. Both parties voiced concern about the armed conflict and its danger of escalation, supported international organizations, and urged the parties concerned to seek a peaceful settlement of the conflict.[31]

---

28 "General U San Yu, the Secretary of the Burma Socialist Program Party, Addressed the Political Report of the BSPP Central Committee at the 3rd Party Congress", *Information of Southeast Asia*, No. 46, 1980.

29 Josef Silverstein, "The Military and Foreign Policy in Burma and Indonesia", *Asian Survey*, Vol. 22, No. 3, March 1982, p. 287.

30 "General U San Yu Addressed the Political Report of the BSPP", *Information of Southeast Asia*, No. 46, 1980.

31 "Joint Press Communique of Burma and Thailand on Peaceful Settlement of Conflicts in Indochina", *People's Daily*, 7 March 1979.

However, Burma did not make known its position on the China–Vietnam conflict. When Ne Win received Japanese Foreign Minister Ito Masayoshi in August 1980, he denounced foreign troops' invasions of Cambodia and Afghanistan, and said Burma would follow ASEAN's lead at the forthcoming United Nations session on the seating of a Kampuchean delegation. However, "The Burmese representative was absent during the vote on the seating of a Kampuchean representative. Thus Burma avoided giving public support for the ASEAN and China position and at the same time did not back the stance of Vietnam and the Soviet Union."[32]

In the 1980s, although China tried to get Burmese support on regional security issues to contain Russian expansion in Asia, the intensity of China's diplomatic ideology was gradually fading. The speeches of the Chinese leadership revealed that Beijing highlighted not their common status as third world countries, but rather their common historical experience and the "common tasks" of both – "the maintenance of independence and peace and economic development." Discussion of anti-imperialism and anti-hegemonism was avoided as each tried to express its stance in a more tactful and more moderate manner. "Our two countries' opinions about the international situation are similar."[33] "Both have similar or analogous judgments on the major international problems."[34] "[Our] two countries share unanimous views on the current great international problems."[35] These speeches during the visits of China's Premier Zhao Ziyang and President Li Xiannian visits to Rangoon in 1981 and in 1985 respectively, Burma's President U San Yu's trip to China in October 1984, and that of Burma's Prime Minister U Maung Maung Kha in 1986.

The Overseas Chinese Issue

The overseas Chinese issue wasn't a problem in Burma–China relations during this period. China continued the policy (obeying local laws and customs) on overseas Chinese affairs that had obtained before the Cultural Revolution and sought to retain the loyalty, support, and favor of the overseas Chinese in Burma after the reconciliation.

Deng Yingchao received more than 150 representatives of the Chinese community throughout Burma in Rangoon in February 1977. She reiterated that

32 Josef Silverstein, "Burma in 1980: An Uncertain Balance Sheet", *Asian Survey*, Vol. 21, No. 2, A Survey of Asia in 1980: Part 2, February 1981, p. 222.
33 "Political Talks of Zhao Ziyang and U San Yu", *People's Daily*, 31 October 1984.
34 "U Maung Maung Kha Held Return Banquet", *People's Daily*, 14 April 1986.
35 "Wu Xueqian Met Burmese Foreign Minister", *People's Daily*, 6 May 1988.

China was implementing the overseas Chinese policy from before the Cultural Revolution, as constructed by Zhou Enlai, and explained the causal relation between the "Gang of Four" in power and irrational China's diplomacy as well as China–Burmese rift. In January 1978, Deng Xiaoping further expounded the reasons for the overseas Chinese policy change to Chinese representatives in Rangoon, and stated that China was resuming the overseas Chinese policy formulated by Mao Tsetung and Zhou Enlai before 1966. China "encourages the overseas Chinese in voluntarily acquiring the citizenship of their countries of residence and protects their legitimate rights."[36]

China's President Li Xiannian reaffirmed the main principles of the 1956 Zhou Enlai speech in Rangoon in the same city in March 1985. "The overseas Chinese who hold Burmese nationality are Burmese citizens, should be loyal to Burma and take the responsibility of Burmese citizens." The Chinese without local citizenship "should abide by laws enacted by the Burmese government, respect Burmese habits and customs, and live in harmony and get along with them."[37] For the first time, Li Xiannian, during his visit to Burma, recognized China's fault in the 1967 Rangoon riot. "China–Burma relations were disturbed by China's domestic problems on one occasion but our Burmese friends adopted a forward-looking policy. As a result of which we are greatly touched."[38] The above-mentioned speeches of Chinese leaders reveal that Beijing intended to dispel Burmese suspicion of the overseas Chinese and the shadow of the Rangoon incident, to promote bilateral political relations.

On the whole, Sino-Burmese relations were immune from the overseas Chinese problem between 1972 and 1988. First, most overseas Chinese had obtained Burmese citizenship. By the downfall of Ne Win in 1988, the Chinese in Burma amounted to about 0.8 million according to official Burmese statistics, among whom only 73,272 were Chinese citizens.[39] Under Ne Win's rule, the military regime distrusted and discriminated against foreign immigrants and non-indigenous peoples. Under the 1974 Burmese Constitution and the Burma Citizenship Law promulgated in 1982, Chinese were only recognized as second and third class citizens in Burma–namely Associate Citizens and

---

36 *Chronicle of Deng Xiaoping*, Vol. I, pp. 260–261.
37 Zhao Xinkao and Wang Mianlan, "President Li Xiannian Received the Representatives of Burmese Chinese Community", *People's Daily*, 7 March 1985.
38 "President Li Xiannian's Speech at the Welcoming Banquet of President U San Yu", *People's Daily*, 6 March 1985.
39 Burmese Central Bureau of Statistics, *Statistical Yearbook of Ministry of Finance of Union of Burma, 1979–1989*, Kunming: Institute of International Studies, Yunnan, 1991, p. 15.

Naturalized Citizens-and had no right to be elected.[40] Beijing kept silent regarding this discrimination against the Chinese. China was reluctant to impair bilateral ties because of the issue, which it largely regarded as Burma's internal affairs.

Second, by Beijing's calculations, the overseas Chinese should be subject to China's overall foreign policy. When China decided to abandon the dual nationality principle and encourage overseas Chinese to become citizens of local countries in the mid-1950s, it was a maneuver to build up a brand-new reputation for China among its neighbors, and to demonstrate the Chinese implementation of the Five Principles of Peaceful Coexistence.[41] As Deng Xiaoping said in Rangoon in 1978, considering the large number of overseas Chinese in Asia, notably in Southeast Asia, it's advantageous to China and local countries to encourage them to become naturalized in their resident countries.[42]

Third, China's influence sharply declined in the overseas Chinese community because of its revolutionary foreign policy. Most overseas Chinese relatives in China suffered political persecution, and their legitimate interests were infringed upon, during the Cultural Revolution. Consequently, the overseas Chinese were widely disgusted with the CCP regime. The revolutionary diplomacy badly marred China's international image and caused discontent among the overseas Chinese. After the "6.26" event, Chinese losses in the riots and Beijing's paralysis in improving their miserable plight alienated the overseas Chinese from Beijing and politics. The reduction of Beijing's influence in the Burmese overseas Chinese community objectively weakened the seriousness of the overseas Chinese issue in Burma.

Economic Relations

Between 1972 and 1988, Burma–China economic relations did not occupy an important position in the two countries' foreign relations. Macroscopically, China's economic relations with Burma still served Beijing's political intention of balancing the Soviet Union's and the United States's influence in Burma, and stabilizing Rangoon on its side. Microscopically, economic factors gradually became the major momentum in economic bilateral ties after the mid-1980s.

40 Paisal Sricharatchanya, "Some are More Equal", *Far Eastern Economic Review*, 8 October 1982, Vol. 118, No. 41, p. 27.

41 Cheng Xi, *The relationship between Overseas Chinese and foreign relations: Review and reflection on China's abandonment of dual nationality*, Beijing: The Overseas Chinese Publishing House of China, 2005, p. 130.

42 *Chronicle of Deng Xiaoping*, Vol. I, pp. 260–261.

Table 3: China's trade with Burma, 1976–1988 (US$ million)

	Total	Exports	Imports	Imbalance
1967	21.09	12.97	8.12	4.85
1968	1.41	1.41	–	1.41
1969	(negligible)	(negligible)	–	(negligible)
1970	4.48	3.71	0.77	2.94
1971	17.80	9.08	8.72	0.36
1972	25.44	11.52	13.92	−2.40
1973	22.66	16.82	5.84	10.98
1974	55.54	17.38	38.16	−20.78
1975	31.23	14.65	16.58	−1.93
1976	26.95	6.78	20.17	−13.39
1977	29.34	9.35	19.99	−10.64
1978	42.29	13.40	28.89	−15.49
1979	31.13	12.80	18.33	−5.53
1980	51.43	17.09	34.34	−17.25
1981	48.48	18.07	30.41	−12.34
1982	49.01	19.92	29.09	−9.17
1983	36.08	18.47	17.61	0.86
1984	32.64	19.00	13.64	5.36
1985	70.24	30.67	39.57	−8.90
1986	76.71	30.66	46.05	−15.39
1987	150.65	64.42	86.23	−21.81
1988	255.62	140.83	114.79	26.04

Source: *Statistics of Foreign Trade, 1950–1989*, 1990, p. 51.

With the thaw in China–Burma ties in 1971, economic cooperation and trade between the two countries were renewed. Compared with 1966, bilateral trade volume in 1971 increased by 3 times. From 1973 to 1984, trade volume between Burma and China fluctuated between US$30 million and US$50 million and the annual average volume of trade amounted to around US$35 million (see Table 3).

Although trade skyrocketed in 1971 due to the improvement in Burma–China relations, it only had modest growth before the mid-1980s. There was a steep rise after 1984 and trade in 1985 amounted to US$70.24 million dollars, up over 100 percent. 1987 and 1988 also witnessed sharp rises. Over 1985–1987, the increases in trade resulted from the growth of border trade. Border petty trade in Yunnan reached RMB124.07 million, up 182 percent, largely boosted by overall China–Burmese trade (see Table 4).

Table 4: Yunnan's cross-border petty trade, 1980–1988 (RMB million)

	Total	Up	Exports	Imports
1980	28.13	–	16.88	11.25
1981	49.94	77.53%	32.09	17.85
1982	33.60	–32.80%	16.80	16.80
1983	32.24	–4.05%	15.73	16.51
1984	44.04	36.60%	21.15	22.89
1985	124.07	181.72%	57.30	66.77
1986	198.09	59.66%	93.10	104.99
1987	462.32	166.39%	226.04	236.28
1988	860.81	86.19%	485.98	374.83

Source: Jiang Yongren, *Research and Guide of Burma Investment and Trade*, Mangshi: Dehong Ethnic Press, 2000, p. 369.

Border trade in Yunnan was at a standstill during the Cultural Revolution.[43] In 1985, Yunnan Province authorized border trade zones in 27 counties and cities, reduced policy restrictions on border trade, and stimulated it by tariff reductions and exemptions. In May 1985, the Secretary General of the CCP Central Committee made a suggestion to Ne Win in Beijing that both legalize border trade. Three months later, China's Ambassador to Burma once again asked Burma's President to legalize it. At the end of the same year, Burma agreed to conduct border trade with China's Foreign Trade Ministry.

Two months after Ne Win visited China in 1971, China renewed its program to supply economic and technological assistance to Burma. In accordance with Burmese needs, Beijing agreed to prolong the repayment terms of China's 1961 loan, and to postpone the expiry date of the agreement on China–Burmese economic and technological cooperation. China's assistance projects, suspended by Rangoon after the anti-Chinese riots in 1967, restarted and Chinese aid technicians and experts returned to Burma. In November 1971, Burma's Foreign Trade Minister, Maung Lwin, led a government trade delegation to China and signed a trade pact and a loan agreement. The two parties agreed to give the most-favored nation treatment in trade to each other's customs, tariffs, tallage expenses, and custom clearance.[44]

On 12 July 1979, a new Agreement on Economic and Technological Cooperation was signed by the two countries. Under the agreement, China

---

43 Zi Gui, "Trade Between Yunnan and Burma", *Explore Asia*, No. 15, 1984, p. 5.
44 Ministry of Foreign Affairs, PRC (ed.), *Collection of Treaties of the People's Republic of China*, 1971, Vol. 18, Beijing: People's Press, 1973, pp. 92–93.

would provide Burma with a RMB0.1 billion interest-free loan for 7 years from 1980 to 1986.[45] On 3 July 1980, both signed a Protocol on Economic and Technological Cooperation that China should help Burma construct 8 projects according to the first clause of the 1979 agreement: 1) Thanlyin Bridge; 2) a spinning factory with 40,000 spindles; 3–5) 3 rice mills with daily capacity of 150 tons; 6) a water supply project in Moulmein city; 7) 1 lock factory; and 8) supply equipment items worth RMB3 million. On June 21, 1984, an Agreement on Economic and Technological Cooperation was signed and another in 1987. In 1987, Beijing promised to supply an interest-free loan to Rangoon.

When the two summit leaders held talks during this period, particularly in the 1980s, they began to pay more and more attention to economic issues. China's economic reform, "open door," and rapid development drew Burmese attention and interest. Three of Burma's key leaders visited Shenzhen, the first special economic zone in China, as well as other cities in east-coast China. Additionally, there were frequent exchanges of economic and trade delegations between the two countries.[46]

The Decline of Burmese Status in Chinese Diplomacy

In 1975, an American scholar predicted that "The Chinese have not, and perhaps will not succeed in re-establishing the warm relationship they had with Burma in the pre-Cultural Revolution period."[47] Facts proved the accuracy of his speculation, but only until 1988. Compared with the relations before 1967, Sino-Burmese ties in this period were characterized by the decline of Burma's status in Chinese foreign relations; Beijing paid less attention to Rangoon. The differences in the reporting on Burma in the *People's Daily* before and after 1972 reveal this.

---

45 Ministry of Foreign Affairs, PRC (ed.), *Collection of Treaties of the People's Republic of China*, Vol. 26, p. 62.

46 The economic trade delegations of China visiting Burma during 1971–1987 included: Chinese Trade Delegation (December 1972), Chinese Trade Delegation (August 1982), Chinese Delegation of the Textile Industry (November 1982), Chinese Delegation of the Textile Industry (November 1985), and Chinese Government Economic Delegation (November 1987). Meantime, the economic trade delegations of Burma visiting China: a Burmese Government Trade Delegation (November 1971), Burmese Government Economic Delegation (May 1972), Burmese Agriculture Delegation (June 1973), Burmese Trade Delegation (October 1974), Burmese Industry Delegation (October 1975), Burmese Trade Delegation (September 1977), Burmese Government Trade Delegation (April 1980), Burmese Industry Delegation (June 1980), Burmese Industry Delegation (May 1984), Burmese Government Delegation (July 1986), and Burmese Government Trade Delegation (April 1987).

47 Bert, "Chinese Relations with Burma and Indonesia", p. 479.

When China–Burma relations were cold over 1949–1953, there were only 188 reports about Burma in the *People's Daily*, with an annual average of 37.6. Both established warm relations in 1954 and maintained the amicability until the split of 1967. The reports increased to 62 in 1954, and 1,278 over 1955–1966, which averaged 106.5 annually. There were 592 reports in 1972–1988, and the average annual number reached 34.82. Thus, 266 reports were published between 1980–1988. This partly resulted from the decrease of bilateral intercourse compared with that before 1967, and partly stemmed from the Burmese lowered status and importance in Beijing's calculation of foreign relations.

Although from 1972 to 1988, Burmese and Chinese leaders paid many visits to each other's countries,[48] the disparity in the quantity of bilateral visits before and after 1972 indicated that Beijing's interest in Burma was cooling off.

Disappearance of Rangoon Corridor

During the 1950s and 1960s, China considered itself strategically encircled by the West. Although China and the Soviet Union launched an air service between Beijing and Irkutsk in 1955, the Beijing–Moscow course flight plan failed because of the lack of airline capacity in China. The launch of the Beijing–Kunming–Rangoon route in 1956 partly improved the situation. In the 1950s, "China communicated with the outside largely through the two routes of Beijing–Irkutsk and Kunming–Rangoon."[49] China "found a new outlet to the world and a potential position of strength for activity elsewhere in Asia. Burma is the only friendly non-Communist territory through which the Chinese Communists can come and go, and through which delegations and official missions from Africa, Latin America and the rest of Asia can come and go with ease."[50] Behind the frequent Chinese frequent visits to Rangoon between 1954 and 1966, lay both the fact of warm bilateral ties, and the fact that the function

---

48 These visits to China included 5 visits of the top leader Ne Win, 5 visits of the President, 4 visits of the Foreign Minister, 4 visits of the Prime Minister and Vice Prime Minister, and one visit of the Chairman of the ruling party. Chinese leaders conducted 7 visits to Burma including one visit of the Foreign Minister, 4 visits of the Premier and Vice Premier, one visit of the President, and one visit of the Vice Chairman of the Standing Committee of the National People's Congress. During 1950 and 1966, Zhou Enlai visited Burma 9 times, the President 2 times, the Vice Premier 16 times (Vice Premier and Foreign Minister Chen Yi 13 times), Vice Chairman of the Standing Committee of the National People's Congress twice. The Burmese Prime Minister and Vice Prime Minister visited China 9 times (including the Chairman of the Revolutionary Council), the Chief of General Staff of the *Tatmadaw* 4 times. U Nu visited China 6 times (5 times as Prime Minister and one time as the Chairman of AFPFL) and Ne Win 6 times.

49 Yao Jun, *Aviation History of China*, Zhengzhou: Elephant Press, 1998, p. 324.

50 Johnstone, *Burma's Foreign Policy*, p. 199.

of the Rangoon Corridor was to facilitate Chinese leaders' additional arrivals in Burma. For example, Burma invited Chinese leaders to drop in on Rangoon when they visited other countries. The 1972 U.S.–China rapprochement caused great changes in Asian geopolitics. The U.S. stopped the encirclement of China and in succession American Asian allies established relations with China. Thus, the radical changes in the international situation and in Asian geopolitics deprived the Rangoon route of any special significance for China.

The Loss of Buffer State Status

Before Beijing adopted its revolutionary foreign policy in the mid-1960s, countering U.S. containment and establishing a buffer zone against the U.S. was the core of China's policy goals for its periphery. China succeeded in solving both the Burma border dispute, and the issue of the KMT troops in Burma, and mitigated the overseas Chinese problem with Burma, and so both maintained good ties before 1967. Burma, implementing its neutral and non-alignment policy, became an important buffer state between China and the West and the later the Soviet Union.

Although the Cold War still burned hotly across the world, Nixon reached China and drank toasts with the Chinese leaders in February 1972. Soon after, the United States dropped its opposition to Chinese entry into the United Nations and the groundwork was laid for the eventual establishment of diplomatic relations. This dramatic change not only enhanced China's international and strategic status,[51] but also had a ripple effect on China's periphery. Over 1972–1975, one after another, Japan, Malaysia, the Philippines, and Thailand established diplomatic relations with China.

Compared with the 1950s and 1960s, the security environment of China's southern and eastern borders was greatly improved and Burma's strategic value as a buffer state for China was thereby lessened. Although it was impossible for China to ignore Burma in this period because of Soviet and Vietnamese expansion in Indochina, the threat caused by this expansion was less serious than that of the Western camp. Therefore, the strategic significance of Burma to China was accordingly reduced with the changes in the international situation.

The Reorientation of Chinese Foreign Policy

During the Cold War, Burma could not occupy a central position in Chinese diplomacy without two preconditions: (1) the confrontation between China

---

51   Chen Jian, *Mao's China and The Cold War*, Chapel Hill and London: University of North Carolina Press, 2001, p. 239.

and the West, led by the United States, and the U.S's policy of containment, threatening China's security; (2) Burma's neutralist and non-alignment policy, which had geopolitical significance for China. The first precondition disappeared after the normalization of Sino–U.S. relations and the value of Burma therefore declined.

China's adjusted foreign policy and the structure of its foreign relations heavily influenced the decline in Burmese importance. Starting from the late 1960s and early 1970s, Beijing gradually changed its radical foreign policy and returned to a realist policy, although China had not completely jettisoned its belief in world revolution. The reorientation of China's foreign policy and Sino–U.S. rapprochement greatly decreased Beijing's isolation. Between 1970 and 1972 alone, China renormalized or improved diplomatic relations with Korea, Yugoslavia, Kenya, Tunisia, Burundi, Ceylon, and Ghana, and established diplomatic relations with 23 countries. In 1975, China formally recognized ASEAN as a regional organization and favored the ASEAN-proposed establishment of the Zone of Peace, Freedom and Neutrality (ZOPFAN) in Southeast Asia. China "progressively disassociated itself from the communist-led insurgencies in Southeast Asia because of a perceived need to secure ASEAN support on the Indochina question, thus alleviating the suspicion and apprehension of Southeast Asian countries caused by Chinese ties with insurgent communist parties. Beijing hoped to reassure these countries that China had no covert expansionist ambitions towards them and that its intentions with respect to Kampuchea are similarly benign."[52]

After the third Plenary Session of the Eleventh Central Committee of the CCP in 1978, China changed its perception that an imminent world war was unavoidable, and began to take an optimistic view of the international situation. Beijing defined "peace" and "development" as the two major themes of the contemporary world, which were the foundation-stone for China's domestic and foreign policies.[53] China also abandoned the ideal of world revolution and focused on economic modernization. "Of major importance now are China's economic needs and the political changes that will ensure order and security in the world, overcome the backwardness of the country, and fulfill its plans for modernization. The necessity to create favorable external conditions in order to realize its program of economic growth made the Chinese leadership change

---

52   William R. Heaton, "China and Southeast Asian Communist Movements: The Decline of Dual Track Diplomacy", *Asian Survey*, Vol. 22, No. 8, August 1982, p. 781.

53   Lev Deliusin, "The Influence of China's Domestic Policy on Its Foreign Policy", *Proceedings of the Academy of Political Science*, Vol. 38, No. 2, 1991, pp. 58–59.

its view of Soviet–American relations."[54] China abandoned its policy of an international united front against the Soviets, framed in the 1970s, and pursued non-alignment with all the great powers. The 12th CCP National Congress attempted to outline a new policy agenda for the 1980s. In September 1982, Deng Xiaoping proposed at the opening ceremony of the Congress that China faced three major tasks in the 1980s: national reunification, anti-hegemonism, and maintenance of world peace. "Economic construction is at the core of the three tasks as it is the basis for a solution of China's external and domestic problems."[55] This core task determined that China's foreign affairs centered on raising foreign resources to suit the needs of modernization, and China's diplomacy towards developed countries accepted that China hungered for greater capital and advanced technologies. Isolated and economically backward Burma, which had adopted a closed door policy, was not important to China.

In the 1980s, China increasingly de-ideologized its foreign policy. The global situation was no longer depicted in black-and-white terms but was seen as multicolored. By contrast, Burma was still pursuing a policy of autarky – economic isolation from the world. The catastrophic Burmese Way to Socialism had turned Burma into one of the world's most impoverished countries. The 1988 nation-wide uprising against the Ne Win regime, the military coup, and the Chinese Tiananmen Square massacre in 1989 caused upheavals to domestic politics and foreign relations in the two countries. Both also suffered attendant international sanctions. These important events lifted the curtain on new China–Myanmar relations in the post-Cold War.

---

54 *Ibid.*, pp. 58–59.
55 *Selected Works of Deng Xiaoping*, Vol. III, Beijing: People's Press, 1993, p. 3.

Part II: The Challenges of China–Myanmar Relations in the Post-Cold War Era

Prelude

The confluence of a series of closely timed, if not related, events prompt consideration of the changes in Sino-Burmese relations beginning approximately in 1988. These events were both international and internal to Myanmar.

Internal to Burma, a variety of factors strongly influenced, both directly and indirectly, Sino-Burmese relations from that period. These included: the incredibly obtuse Burmese complete demonetization of 7 September 1987 of two-thirds of the currency (*kyat*) in circulation, ending whatever residual confidence existed in the *kyat* and in the governance of the Burma Socialist Programme Party, with the resultant deluge of Chinese imports; the end of socialism and the official but ineffectual encouragement of the private sector and Chinese investment; the failed people's revolution against the BSPP government; the military coup of 18 September 1988; the opening to foreign investment; extensive gas exploration and exploitation; the unrecognized elections of 1990; cease-fires with some 17 minority insurgencies, some along the Chinese frontier; and all finally followed by the internal collapse of the Burma Communist Party (BCP) in 1989.

Internationally, new factors affected bilateral ties as well. These were the end of the Cold War; Tiananmen; India's policy shift in light of extensive Chinese penetration of Myanmar; and later Myanmar's joining of ASEAN in July 1997. Chinese influence increased because of expanding Chinese strategic concerns (both in Beijing and in Yunnan Province), and because of non-traditional security issues (narcotics, health, etc.), especially China's vastly expanding reliance on imported energy and minerals for its continued economic growth and employment – the latter a critical political issue.

The formation of SLORC/SPDC military rule since 18 September 1988, continued the domination of the state by the Burma armed forces (the *Tatmadaw*), a pattern of direct rule by edict that has ended following the elections for a new government on 7 November 2010 based on a constitution that was approved by a clearly manipulated referendum in May 2008. Under the

Plate 9: Than Shwe, chairman of the State Peace and Development Council (SPDC), 1992–2011 (photograph from 2010, courtesy Government of Thailand). Than Shwe built a military career during the rule of Ne Win but only really came to prominence after the events of 1988.

new government that emerged from the elections in the spring of 2011, the military will, however, continue its hold on to essential power and governance under that constitution. The role of Senior General Than Shwe, former head of state, remains ambiguous; how much he will continue to influence Myanmar events and if so, of what nature and to what degree, remains unclear. He holds no constitutional office.

If Sino-Burmese relations in the period from independence to 1988 were characterized as essentially determined by internal Chinese policy shifts that were expressed in international affairs and to which the Burmese responded, the era in Sino-Burmese relations since 1988 has been driven by Chinese requirements at national and local levels for strategic and economic access to Myanmar and its resources to help fuel China's growth; and by internal Burmese needs for both economic support and a strategic partner against what the Burmese junta perceived as external threats, especially from the United States and through its ally, Thailand.

The relationship has been expressed largely through economic and military associations, and thus Part II of this volume focuses on the economic relations that have, and will continue to have, strategic impacts. The Burmese government was on the cusp of change in 2011, and it is the thesis of this volume that this new era, essentially because of the growing need for close cooperation between Myanmar and China, will result in a mutuality of a series of dependencies at various levels that may change bilateral relations for the foreseeable future. This evolution will have a profound effect on other state and regional actors, including India, ASEAN and its component states, the United States, the European Union, and Japan. This evolving, dynamic bilateral relationship is little understood outside the region and needs explication.

The growing concerns about and even antipathy toward Myanmar first by the Western states, and later by some of the ASEAN countries, was a result of a series of military actions and policies that have defied established international norms. They have resulted in a country with growing economic capacity if not competence, and in spite of considerable present and future resources a seeming unwillingness, at least until the spring of 2011, to improve the lot of its diverse populations.[1]

To the West, these deficiencies have prompted both disapproval and a refusal to provide a mantle of international legitimacy to the junta, and to the government that has followed. The SLORC/SPDC junta, however, has in its view vastly increased infrastructure throughout the country and negotiated a series of fragile cease-fires that, if they did not resolve the continuing problems of the multi-cultural state, at least stopped most of the killings in the seeming myriad of insurrections since independence that have cost about a million lives, according to General Saw Maung, former head of state (1988–1992). The junta has increased the foreign exchange reserves from some US$30 million to about US$5 billion (with much more to come when the Chinese pipelines are operational), and built a new capital at Naypyitaw. The lot of the people, however, has languished, with the lowest per capita income in the region (some US$350–450 in 2010).

The Western regard of Myanmar as a pariah state is based on a persistent pattern of human rights violations that indicate that the junta has had as little regard for international opinion as it has for the well-being of its peoples. This pattern has been continuous until the formation of the new administration in

---

1   In his inaugural speech, President Thein Sein on 31 March 2011 indicated that the government planned to take measures to improve health, education, and other diverse social needs.

2011, and expressed through a series of actions that have prompted international concern. First, the violent suppression of the people's revolution in 1988, followed by the brutal repression of opposition to the coup within the country (estimates are that some 6,000 people were killed in both events); the failure of the Burmese government to recognize the results of the May 1990 elections, which it had sponsored and then ignored; and the house arrest and ill treatment of the Nobel Laureate Aung San Suu Kyi, who has become a personalized avatar of democracy to much of the Western world. The outrage of the May 2003 Depayin incident in central Myanmar, in which a large number of opposition supporters were killed and Aung San Suu Kyi roughed up exacerbated this antipathy. This concern was increased by the brutality of the repression of the monks' demonstrations in what has been called the "Saffron Revolution" in the fall of 2007, and the slowness of the junta's response to disastrous cyclone Nargis in May 2008 (especially as contrasted with the rapid response of the Chinese leadership to the Sichuan earthquake of the same month). The decision to go on with the constitutional referendum in spite of the resulting chaos contributed to the perception of malaise in Burmese governance. Quiet Chinese suggestions for reform in Myanmar indicate Chinese concerns over future stability in that state – stability that is tied to Chinese interests.

The international impressions of Myanmar are exemplified by the listing of Myanmar (Burma in the documents) on the "failed state index."[2] Of the 177 countries listed, Myanmar rates 16th from the bottom. Somalia is the most "failed state," followed by Chad and the Sudan. Myanmar is listed as slightly better than Yemen and worse than Ethiopia. The rating is based on 12 "social, economic, political, and military" indicators, but the primary criteria are "loss of physical control or a monopoly on the legitimate use of force," and the erosion of legitimate authority. Although the social indicators measuring the well-being of the Burmese population by all international institutions and standards are exceedingly low, the degree of control by the *Tatmadaw* in that society is very high. International legitimacy in the West is low, but this attitude is not necessarily reflected in many other, non-Western states. The used of the term "failed state," or others – "pariah," "rogue," and other pejorative terms – simply reinforces policy predilections and exacerbates the differences between the West (especially the U.S.) and China, India, and other states, and negatively affects efforts to initiate policies that might improve the lives of the diverse populations of that country.

2   The Fund for Peace, and *Foreign Policy*. The calculations are from 2008. Others listed as worse than Myanmar were Pakistan, Iraq, and Afghanistan.

The strained relations with the United States have been exacerbated by U.S. calls for regime change in Myanmar/Burma, and sanctions that have been serially imposed, and to which the E.U. has responded with their own, although less onerous, system of sanctions as well.[3] The purpose of such sanctions was regime change and recognition of the legitimacy of the political opposition after the 1990 elections. This was an unattainable expectation. The unrealistic but nevertheless existential fears of the *Tatmadaw* of a U.S. invasion, as well as the military's own conceptual role as the savior of Myanmar's national unity and as a unique social force, has resulted in a massive build up of the military from some 198,000 in 1988 to approximately 406,000 in 2010 (although the latter figures are imprecise – the target was said to be 500,000).[4] To this end, Chinese support for the military since 1988 is estimated at some US$3.0 billion (but supporting data are lacking). To this must be added extensive Chinese economic assistance and most prominently, investment in infrastructure that will change the nature of the Sino-Burmese relationship. The increases in Chinese trade, investment, and illegal immigration all continue to dominate the Burmese scene, prompting criticisms from the West that these activities undercut the effectiveness of the sanctions policies.

Myanmar is one of several countries in which Chinese and U.S. interests are in opposition. Burmese concerns, as reflected in *Tatmadaw* policies, may have prompted the close ties with China as a means of political and strategic security against what many in the Naypyitaw leadership regard as potential U.S. threats. Although often portrayed in the West as a means for lucrative rent-seeking and corruption, it may be more a matter of security needs (however unrealistic) as interpreted by the leadership. Chinese strategic and security interests, especially the provision of much-needed energy and access to the Bay of Bengal, have prompted Chinese support for the military government. Such support is both positive from a Chinese viewpoint and thus far has denied other states having as considerable an influence as China. Potential Chinese rivalries with India also result in calculations by both governments of supportive policies for Myanmar, which has become a nexus of Sino-Indian relationships. These policies affect the ASEAN states, ASEAN as an institution, the United Nations, and Japan as well.

---

3   The E.U. modestly modified its sanction regimen in April 2011, allowing more travel by Burmese officials.
4   National Bureau for Asian Research, *Asia's Rising Power. Strategic Asia 2010–2011*, Executive Brief, p. 48. Vietnam has 455,000 troops, and Thailand 306,000.

Beyond statistics and agreements, however, are the attitudes of the military leadership that affect Myanmar's relations with the external world. Although much of what emanates from Yangon or Naypyitaw may be considered either diplomatic niceties or propagandistic cant, it would be a grievous policy error to ignore the core set of beliefs that influence Myanmar's external relations, even with a close ally like China, and even if those beliefs may not be grounded in reality as seen from afar.

Myanmar's leadership has exhibited very strong nationalistic sentiments that should not be discounted. They view their role as maintaining the sovereignty and national unity of the state, and believe that civilian politicians and minority groups are bent to subvert those goals. This is not simply whimsy. It affects their calculations of how power should be distributed in their society, and the unique role that the *Tatmadaw* believe they have had, and will continue to have, in safeguarding the Union. The motto above the portals of the Defense Services Academy is "The Triumphant Elite of the Future." This may well portray the role the *Tatmadaw* has envisioned for itself. Although international relations have now changed, the previous, demonstrated experience since independence has been that all Burma/Myanmar's neighbors, together with the U.K. and the U.S., have supported insurrections or dissidents, and that both Muslims and Christians have had international associations that are seen to subvert state-sponsored goals. This history is not forgotten. It increases the sense of nationalistic fervor and vulnerability, prompting over-reactions to purported threats, insults, or demands. These attitudes are unlikely to materially shift over the near term, and thus will influence the relationship with China and the role of the Chinese within Myanmar.

In some sense, issues of the internal and external legitimacy of the new government that came into power at the start of the Burmese fiscal year (April 1) in 2011 have been exacerbated. Western states denounce the constitution as undemocratic, the May 2008 referendum on it as both importune and rigged, the November 2010 national elections as deeply flawed, and the resultant government as essentially a continuation of military rule through other means. Conversely, the government claims that its road-map to "discipline-flourishing democracy" has been achieved with a multi-party political system operating even at local levels for the first time in Burmese history. China has praised this progress as ardently as other states have opposed it.

Reforms have been promised. In the most remarkable public speech by an official in a half-century, President Thein Sein has called for widespread social changes, an end to corruption, economic reforms, better minority relations, an attack on widespread poverty, and even in a later edict the return of those self-exiled motivated by political or economic causes. In a stunning statement, with important but as yet unclear implications, he has also bowed to popular opinion, as he himself has stated, and called for the suspension during his tenure of office (until 2015) of Chinese construction of the both physically massive and unpopular Myitsone Dam on the Irrawaddy River. This could have important effects on Sino–Myanmar relations. These calls for widespread reforms are still fragile, with significant, high-level elements of the *Tatmadaw* opposed to them. One issue for foreign actors is whether to call for increased pressure on the government through additional sanctions and/or a U.N. Commission of Inquiry into human rights abuses, perhaps strengthening those opposed to positive change, or support to the planned changes. Too strong a position on support or rejection of either wing could negatively affect the well-being of the Burmese peoples.

As this volume will demonstrate, the latest era in Sino-Burmese relations, reflecting not only the closeness of the ties but also the changing nature of the relationship, creates a set of dilemmas for both states and for other interested state and institutional actors. These issues have received less consideration than they have deserved for effective policy formulation. Part II of this volume and the sections that follow are essentially dedicated to examining the changes in economic, strategic and security ties.

7

China–Myanmar Strategic and Security Relations

*B*urma/Myanmar remains the site where the dominant cultures of South, Southeast, and East Asia meet and compete for influence. At critical times, Burma has been a cockpit for rivalry between the colonial powers in the 19th century. In the 20th century, the superpowers contested there for influence. In the fluid strategic environment of the early 21st century with the rise of China and India, together with the re-engagement of the U.S. in the region, its important position is once again attracting attention from analysts and officials.[1]

What have been and are the strategic and security implications of Burma/ Myanmar for China? The answers vary by era and environment. The histories of World War II and the Cold War in East and Southeast Asia have shown that Burma played a significant role in China's pursuit of national security. If the strategic importance of Myanmar to China diminished as Chinese international relations normalized, as the Cold War ended, and as Burma was no longer the physical avenue to the region beyond, it began to have a new and enhanced relevance to Beijing, and especially to Yunnan Province. This new emphasis was based on non-traditional strategic interests as well as longer-range traditional concerns over China's regional potential.

These new concerns related to two types of potential strategic blockages: blockages that could interfere with Chinese economic development planning and its expansion of trade and exports, both of which were dependent on greater access to energy. Important as well was the potential of physical blockages (transport, access, etc.) to the import of such energy resources. China's enhanced world economic role and internal stability (and thus employment at home for a more mobile and vast un- and under-employed labor force) height-

---

1   Andrew Selth, "Burma: A Strategic Perspective", Asia Foundation Working Paper #13, May 2001, p. 5.

ened demands for alternative energy sources that had to be imported and in which Myanmar could play a significant role.

These strategic issues (some of which are also discussed in Chapter 10) relate as well to the provision of military support to the vastly expanded *Tatmadaw*, which during this period doubled in size; Chinese assistance greatly increased the sophistication and amount of its weaponry, as well as its logistical capacity.

Energy Issues: Gas, Oil, and Hydroelectric Power

China's Energy Security and Myanmar

Energy security, according to the International Energy Agency, can be described as "uninterrupted physical availability at a price which is affordable, while respecting environment concerns". It consists of two aspects: "Long-term energy security is mainly linked to timely investments to supply energy in line with economic developments and environmental needs. Short-term energy security, on the other hand, is the ability of the energy system to react promptly to sudden changes in supply and demand."[2] China's energy security problem includes these two aspects.

China now continuously relies heavily on imported energy to satisfy the increasing demand of its rapid, sustained economic growth. From a largely self-sufficient energy economy as China began its rush to industrialize, it has become the world's second-largest and fastest growing energy consumer. China's energy imports have risen sharply, raising internal concerns about its energy security, particularly its oil supply. In 1993, China became a net importer of oil. According to International Energy Agency estimates, China's oil consumption will increase from 6.7 mb/d (million barrels a day) in 2005, to 11.1 mb/d in 2015, and 16.5 mb/d in 2030-an average growth of 3.7 percent per year. The country's oil-import dependence will increase sharply, with imports growing from 3.1 mb/d in 2005 to 13.1 mb/d in 2030. It will import as much as all 27 E.U. member states combined in 2030.[3] Oil security has become the core issue of energy security in China, and one of the critical aspects of national security.

It was these threats that pushed Chinese leaders and the government to change their concepts of security. On 5 March 2001, at the 4th Session of the 9th National People's Congress (NPC), Premier Zhu Rongji elucidated,

2   "Energy Security", www.iea.org/subjectqueries/keyresult.asp?KEYWORD_ID=4103.
3   *World Energy Outlook 2007: China and India Insights*, International Energy Agency, p. 288.

"The energy issue, particularly the oil issue, is an important issue of resources strategy. Domestic oil exploration and production can't meet the needs of economic and social development. The contradiction between supply and demand of energy increasingly sharpens. We must leave no stone unturned to economize and alternate [other fuels with] oil, quicken the exploration and production of oil and gas, make full use of overseas resources, and build oil and other strategic resources stocks as soon as possible."[4]

In November 2003, at China's Central Economic Work Conference, President Hu Jintao put forward the concept of finance and oil security for the first time, and the necessity of establishing a new oil development strategy. In December 2005, Vice-Premier Zeng Peiyan reported on the current Chinese energy situation and energy security issues at the 19th Session of the 10th NPC Standing Committee, and while outlining Chinese security needs, noted: "Now and henceforth, China's energy security is facing and will face a very complicated environment."[5]

China's oil security must now address these challenges: the sources of oil imports are concentrated; the pattern of oil imports is unilateral; and a market oil trading system has not been established.[6] Chinese analysts consider oil price volatility and physical supply disruptions, particularly a deliberate interruption by the United States, to be the main threats to energy security.[7] In order to ensure energy security, Beijing has adopted policies to meet current and future challenges. China's Medium and Long Term Energy Development Plan Outline 2004–2020, which was approved at an executive meeting of the State Council in 2005, exhorts: "Take full advantage of domestic and overseas resources and markets ... Take an active part in the exploration and development of world energy and resources ... Diversify the sources of energy imports."[8]

4   Zhu Rongji, "Report on the Outline of The Tenth Five-Year Plan for National Economic and Social Development: Delivered at The Fourth Session of The Ninth National People's Congress on 5 March 2001", *People's Daily*, 17 March 2001.

5   "The Current Situations of Energy and Energy Security Issues in China – Report by Vice Premier Zeng Peiyan at the 19th Session of the 10th NPC Standing Committee", *China Petroleum and Chemical Standard and Quality*, No. 4, 2006.

6   Wang Guiying, "China's Oil Environment and Oil Security Strategy", China University of International Business and Economics, Ph.D. thesis, 2003, pp. 49–54.

7   Erica S. Downs, "The Chinese Energy Security Debate", *The China Quarterly*, No. 177, March 2004, p. 31.

8   The executive meeting of the State Council approves China Medium and Long Term Energy Development Plan Draft, news.xinhuanet.com/zhengfu/2004–07/01/content_1559228.htm.

China indicated that it was necessary to expand cooperation on oil and gas exploration abroad to solve China's energy problem.[9] On 27 January 2010, China's State Council announced the establishment of a National Energy Commission. Premier Wen Jiabao and Vice Premier Li Keqiang lead it as Chairman and Deputy Chairman, respectively. The Commission is tasked to devise China's energy development strategy, review issues of energy security and development, and coordinate domestic energy exploration and international energy cooperation.[10] The establishment of such a super-ministry reflects the Chinese leadership's strong concern for energy efficiency, energy security, and environmental protection.[11]

In response to growing concerns about energy security with particular emphasis on oil security, Beijing has initiated some key measures including the construction of a strategic petroleum reserve system, investment in overseas oil fields, the construction of transnational pipelines, and oil diplomacy.[12]

Beijing is engaged in active world energy diplomacy. All Beijing's diplomatic activities are aimed at mitigating the adverse effects of the increase in oil-import dependence, diversifying the sources and routes of imported oil, and preparing for supply disruptions.

Chinese Enterprises in the Myanmar Oil and Gas Sector

In recent years, Myanmar has been included in the worldwide energy map that China has drawn. In 2004, 2005, and 2007, the Chinese Ministry of Commerce and Ministry of Foreign Affairs promulgated the "Countries and Industries for Overseas Investment Guidance Catalogue I, II, III," respectively. The Catalogue is a major reference for departments in charge of foreign economic cooperation at all levels; it offers guidance for and verification of overseas investment by Chinese enterprises.[13] Myanmar was on the first reference list

---

9   *The Eleventh Five-Year Plan for National Economic and Social Development of The People's Republic of China*, Beijing: People Press, 2006, p. 146.

10   Out of 27 Ministers, 12 are included in the newly established National Energy Commission. Most notably, the Ministers of Foreign Affairs, State Security, Finance, Environmental Protection, Commerce, Land and Resources, and Water Resources are among its 21 members.

11   Bo Zhiyue, "China's New National Energy Commission: Policy Implications", *EAI Background Brief No. 504*, 5 February 2010.

12   Downs, "The Chinese Energy Security Debate", p. 32.

13   Any enterprises complying with the Catalogue and verified to hold the overseas investment approval certificate shall have the priority right to enjoy state preferential policies in such areas as funds, foreign exchange, tax collection, customs, and exit and entry (Item Three).

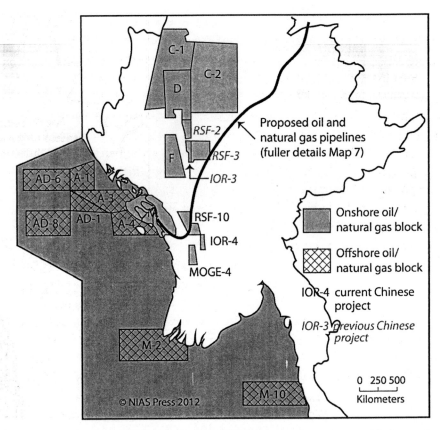

Map 6: Oil and natural gas projects in Myanmar with Chinese involvement – completed, current and planned (based on a map in Earthrights International, *China in Burma: The Increasing Investment of Chinese Multinational Corporations in Burma's Hydropower, Oil and Natural Gas, and Mining Sectors*, 2008, by permission)

released in 2004. Chinese enterprise was encouraged to invest in areas of oil, gas, forestry, agricultural machinery manufacturing, and construction.

Myanmar is rich in oil and has Southeast Asia's largest, and the world's tenth largest, natural gas reserves. According to official estimates, Myanmar has oil reserves of 3.2 billion barrels, total estimated gas reserves of 2.54 trillion cubic meters, and proven reserves of 0.51 trillion cubic meters.[14] The gas and oil sectors have attracted the most FDI since Myanmar passed its foreign investment legislation in 1988. Myanmar authorities intensified the opening of off-shore and on-shore blocks to foreign companies since the end of 2004.[15]

14 An Indian company is exploring an onshore gas block in Myanmar, mandalay.mofcom. gov.cn/aarticle/jmxw/200802/20080205405219.html.

15 The first onshore oil exploration contracts since independence were issued shortly after the 1988 coup to ten foreign firms.

Up to the end of 2007, there were US$3.24 billion FDI in the Myanmar oil and gas sector. Naypyitaw has deals with a total of thirteen countries' oil firms, including Russia, China, India, South Korea, France, and the U.S.

In 2001, Chinese enterprises began to be involved in Myanmar oil and gas explorations. Since 2005, cooperation in the oil and gas sectors between the two countries has increasingly expanded. In September 2004, the China Petroleum & Chemical Corporation (SINOPEC), the Dian–Qian–Gui Petroleum Exploration Bureau of China, and the Myanmar Oil & Gas Enterprise (MOGE) reached a production-sharing contract on cooperation in petroleum exploration. Under this contract, petroleum exploration was carried out at Block D, an onshore block in Myanmar's western Rakhine state. Both sides invested US$30 million for exploration. If the Block D had rich gas and oil reserves, the contract would extend the performance time. Then, Block D would be developed as an oil field with oil output of 1 million tons per year.

One month later, a consortium led by China National Offshore Oil Corporation's (CNOOC) Myanmar unit, China Huanqiu Contracting and Engineering Corp., and Golden Aaron Pte. Ltd. of Singapore signed a production-sharing contract with Myanmar at onshore Block M (Rakhine State) covering a total area of 3007 square miles. On 14 December 2004, the consortium agreed on two production-sharing contracts at offshore Block A-4 (offshore Rakhine State) and Block M-10 (offshore Mottama), with areas of 2,889 square miles and 5,320 square miles respectively. On 25 January 2005, the same consortium signed three deals at onshore Block C-1 (Indaw–Yenan area), Block C-2 (Shwebo–Monywa area), and offshore Block M-2 (offshore Mottama, see Map 6).

Within three months, from October 2004 to January 2005, the consortium led by CNOOC's Myanmar unit entered into production-sharing contracts three times. The six onshore and offshore Blocks cover a total area of over 80,000 square kilometers and their overall exploitation area has surpassed that of the Bohai Sea oil field. The Chinese had built its presence in Myanmar's oil and gas sector.

On 15 January 2007, the China National Petroleum Corporation (CNPC) and the MOGE made three production-sharing contracts. Under the contracts, oil and gas exploration will be carried out at blocks AD-1, AD-6, and AD-8, which cover a total area of 10,000 square-kilometers off the Rakhine coast (see Map 6).[16] Two months later, Myanmar decided to sell the gas from A-1 and A-3 blocks to China through a pipeline. The A-1 and A-3 fields off the Rakhine

16 "CNPC got three contracts of offshore gas exploration in Myanmar", *Shanghai Securities*, 18 January 2007.

coast have proven reserves of 5.7 trillion to 10 trillion cubic feet with up to 8.6 tcf of that volume being recoverable.

On 20 June 2008, CNPC, South Korea's Daewoo International, and the Myanmar government signed a memorandum on the sale and transport of natural gas from the A1 and A3 fields. This signified that China–Myanmar cooperation in oil and gas sector had deepened and expanded.

All three major Chinese oil corporations – CNPC, SINOPEC, and CNOOC – have gained footholds in Myanmar. In addition, massive Chinese investment in Myanmar oil and gas fields has led other Chinese enterprises to Myanmar. They are involved in geological prospecting, petroleum machinery and spare parts, and oil and gas drilling. Generally, when those major Chinese oil firms have contracts with Myanmar, they subcontract some projects to other Chinese companies for technical services, test drilling, equipment supply, and so on. Thus, Chinese expansion in energy is not only in direct production, but also in peripheral industries.

Sino-Myanmar Oil and Gas Pipelines

In addition to undiversified energy supply sources, Chinese energy security is also facing a transportation challenge. China imports most of its oil by marine shipping, except a minor portion by railway from Russia. Chinese energy transportation security has two facets: transportation capabilities and transportation routes. China does not have enough sea-going oil tankers, so it is heavily dependent on foreign oil tankers.[17] Four-fifths of Chinese imported oil must traverse the Straits of Malacca, as does 45 percent of the world's oil supplies. The PLA does not possess the military capability to secure this sea-lane of communication, through which the majority of its oil imports transits, and must rely on the United States to guarantee safe passage. Consequently, Beijing worries that the Straits of Malacca might be closed either by a terrorist attack or a blockade caused by a crisis over Taiwan between China and the U.S. This has become known as China's "Malacca dilemma."

As a heavy user of the Malacca Straits, China has a vested interest in the elimination of transnational threats in the sea lane. "Yet Beijing remains uneasy at the prospect of a greater role for external powers in securing the straits. Chinese security analysts have accused the U.S. and Japan of using the threat of

---

17　About the tanker factor in China's energy security, see Andrew Erickson and Gabe Collins, "Beijing's Energy Security Strategy: The Significance of a Chinese State-Owned Tanker Fleet", *Orbis*, Fall 2007, pp. 665–684.

terrorism as a pretext to expand their naval presence in and around the straits."[18] On 29 November 2003, at China's Central Economic Work Conference, President Hu Jintao pointed out that some powers always had "a finger in the pie" and controlled the Straits of Malacca marine lane; therefore, China had to formulate a new strategy for oil energy, and take active measures to secure national energy security. Besides increasing production opportunities, a second aspect of China's energy strategy involves ensuring reliable delivery networks, reducing its over-dependence on energy transportation through the Straits of Malacca, and escaping the Western-controlled energy marine lanes by building ports and pipelines.

In recent years, China has designed some alternative routes for China's crude imports: the China–Russia oil pipeline, the China–Kazakhstan oil pipeline, the China–Russia gas pipeline, the China–Turkmenistan gas pipeline, the China–Myanmar oil and gas pipeline, and the China–Pakistan gas pipeline. All these designed pipelines, except the China–Kazakhstan oil pipeline, are not yet operational. China expects that such initiatives will reduce China's vulnerability to American dominance of the sea lanes, to its strong Middle East connections, and to the security risks associated with long supply lines by tanker from the Persian Gulf via the Straits of Malacca. "Compared to risks along this 'sea lane,' pipelines from neighboring countries seem favorable for China's energy security. Myanmar is located in a unique position since it can provide natural gas directly to southern China by pipeline."[19]

Over ten years ago, the Chinese Academy of Social Sciences proposed an initiative to build a Sino–Myanmar oil pipeline, but it was not adopted at the time. In 2001, President Jiang Zemin visited Myanmar during which, according to Jiang's suggestions, both sides agreed to make agriculture, human resources, natural resources tapping, and infrastructure construction the key fields of bilateral cooperation.[20] Thus, when Beijing and Yangon signed the Joint Statement of the People's Republic of China and the Union of Myanmar on the Framework of Future Bilateral Relations and Cooperation in Beijing on 6 June 2000 (See Appendix I), the joint statement did not mention cooperation between the two countries in the energy sector. After Jiang's trip to Myanmar, however, both sides began to discuss the oil and gas pipeline project.

---

18 Ian Storey, "China's 'Malacca Dilemma'", *China Brief*, Vol. 6, Issue 8, 12 April 2006.
19 Nobuyuki Higashi, "Natural Gas in China Market Evolution and Strategy", International Energy Agency Working Paper, June 2009, p. 34.
20 Ma Xiaoning, "President Jiang Held Talk with Senior General Than Shwe", *People's Daily*, 13 December 2001.

In August 2004, several scholars of Yunnan University made a proposal to the government, "*Suggestions on Building Oil Pipeline from Sittwe to Kunming.*" The oil for the pipeline would be mainly imported from the Middle East and Africa. In the same year, the Yunnan Government submitted a report to the State Council suggesting building Sino–Myanmar oil and gas pipelines. Beijing, however, did not appraise the proposed project and did not reply.

In 2006, however, the Sino-Burmese oil pipeline initiative was finally considered by Beijing policymakers. In the "Overview of China's Petroleum Industry in 2005" publicized by the National Development and Reform Commission (NDRC) in February 2006, it stated for the first time that China should "expand transportation capabilities ... four major imported oil transportation passages, namely the Sino–Kazakhstan and Sino–Russia crude oil import land corridors, and the Strait of Malacca and Sino–Myanmar oil import marine lanes."[21]

In March 2006, "Yunnan Delegation's Suggestion on Building a Sino-Myanmar Oil Pipeline and Constructing an Oil Refining Industry Base in Yunnan," report was issued.[22] It suggested that all crude oil imported through the Sino–Myanmar oil pipeline phase 1 project be refined in Yunnan, that Yunnan be developed as a new national oil refining base, and that Yunnan's proposal be put into the National Eleventh Five-Year Plan as well as in the National Medium and Long Term Energy Development Plan. Also, Yunnan elucidated, "At the present time, it is the most favorable opportunity to decide to build the Sino–Myanmar oil pipeline, so we request that the NDRC approve and initiate the pipeline project, decide the construction's owner as soon as possible, and push this strategic and important project by building early in order to safeguard national oil transportation security."[23] Beijing and Naypyitaw reached an agreement over the cooperation in the Sino–Myanmar oil & gas pipeline project on 29 October 2006.

A Daewoo-led consortium signed a memorandum of understanding with CNPC about the sale and transportation of natural gas from A-1 and A-3 Blocks off Myanmar on 20 June 2008. In the meantime, six Myanmar, Chinese, South Korean, and Indian companies signed an agreement on the pipeline

---

21 NDRC publicized Overview of China's Petroleum Industry in 2005, www.oilnews.com. cn/gb/misc/2006–02/14/content_654325.htm.
22 Signed jointly by 91 Yunnan delegates who attended the National People's Congress (NPC) and the National Committee of the Chinese People's Political Consultative Conference (CPPCC); was submitted to the Beijing leadership.
23 "Yunnan tries to engage in Sino-Myanmar Oil Pipeline", *Wenhui Daily* (Hong Kong), 19 March 2006 or "The point of fall of Sino-Myanmar Oil Pipeline Challenges Yunnan", *Yunnan Economic Daily*, 12 July 2007.

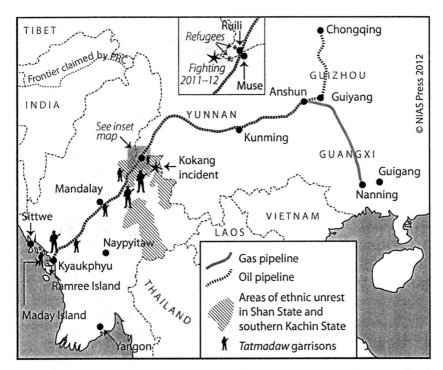

Map 7: Myanmar–China oil and gas pipelines (based on a map by Wang Di and augmented with details from an unpublished map courtesy Earthrights International)

feasibility study. China plans to build a gas reserve base and a wharf for oil tankers on an island near Kyaukpyu in Rakhine State. CNPC will provide 50.9 percent investment for pipeline construction and enterprise operations in Myanmar. The oil pipeline and gas pipeline will cost US$1.5 billion and US$1.04935 billion, respectively, and will reach Kunming via Mandalay and Muse.[24] A major road will be built along the pipelines by the Chinese on the basis of a BOT (Build–Operate–Transfer) arrangement.

China and Myanmar signed an agreement for the joint construction of crude oil and gas pipelines on 26 March 2009. The agreement came during the visit of Li Changchun, a member of the Standing Committee of the Political Bureau of the CCP Central Committee. During Maung Aye's visit to China on 16 June 2009, a MoU relating to the development, operation, and management of the Myanmar–China crude oil pipeline project was signed by The CNPC and Myanmar's Ministry of Energy in Beijing. According to the agreement, the pipeline is designed for an annual capacity of 22 million tons, or 442,000

---

24   Mikawa Masahisa, "China got approval for its bid to operate Myanmar oil pipeline", *Japan Economy News*, 18 November 2008.

barrels. CNPC will be responsible for the line design, construction, operation, and management. The project includes a large-scale crude oil unloading port and a terminal at Maday Island not far from Sittwe in western Myanmar, as well as nearby oil storage and transportation facilities in addition to the pipeline.[25] On 31 October 2009, CNPC began constructing a port at Maday island as part of the Myanmar–China crude pipeline project. On 20 December 2009, CNPC signed an agreement with Myanmar's Energy Ministry to receive exclusive rights to build and operate the pipeline. The deal has granted the operating concession of the pipeline to the CNPC-controlled South-East Asia Crude Oil Pipeline Ltd. The pipeline company will also enjoy tax concessions and customs clearance rights. The agreement stipulates that Myanmar government will guarantee the company's ownership and exclusive operating rights, as well as the safety of the pipeline.[26]

Premier Wen Jiabo visited Myanmar over 2–3 June 2010, to participate in celebrations to mark the 60th anniversary of the establishment of diplomatic relations between the two countries. During the two-day visit, the two Premiers formally launched the construction of the Myanmar–China oil and gas pipeline project. China's official *People's Daily* on 5 June reported that "There are 793 kilometers of gas pipeline in Myanmar, and also a 771-kilometer-long crude oil pipeline. An oil port in Kyaukpyu as a facility is to be built for the planned China–Myanmar oil pipeline project" (see Map 7).

Throughout the stages of proposing, programming, canvassing and first-phase preparations for the oil pipeline, Yunnan province (from scholars to government) played a crucial role. Yunnan is the most important and staunchest supporter of, and lobbyist for, the oil pipeline. Before the oil pipeline was decided, the Yunnan government had made many preliminary preparations on related infrastructure. The Sino–Myanmar oil and gas pipeline and refinery was taken from one of the twenty 2007 and 2008 Yunnan key construction projects to be promoted and developed. In response to the key project, the Yunnan government established a functional office dealing with the project.[27]

At the end of 2009, an oil depot began to be built in Kunming with storage capacity of 85,000 cubic meters in the first phase and 150,000 cubic meters in the second phase; this is a supporting project of the Sino–Myanmar

25 "MoU of China–Myanmar Oil Pipeline Signed", *China Petroleum Daily*, 19 June 2009.

26 "An Agreement of Concession and Duty of China–Myanmar Oil Pipeline Signed", *China Petroleum Daily*, 21 December 2009.

27 Wang Yonggang and Xu Xiaomei, "The Executive Meeting of Yunnan Province Government decided to establish Key Construction Project Responsibility System in Yunnan", *Yunnan Daily*, 2 June 2007.

oil pipeline and the Kunming oil refinery. The China–Myanmar oil and gas pipeline will bring Yunnan about RMB80 billion in investment. In addition, Chongqing city and Guizhou and Guangxi provinces finally get a slice of the action. The oil pipeline will extend to Chongqing via Guiyang and the terminal of the gas pipeline will not be at Kunming, as originally designated, but at Nanning in Guangxi province (see Map 7). The trunk oil and gas pipelines in China's territory stretches 1,631 kilometers and 1,727 kilometers, respectively. The construction of pipelines in China's section began in September 2010 and it is estimated that they will be put into use in 2013.[28]

The Implications and Significance of China–Myanmar Energy Cooperation: The Political Dimension

Myanmar is one of the various baskets into which Beijing places its energy security eggs. Importing oil and gas from Myanmar and building the oil and gas pipelines between the two countries is only one part of Beijing's energy security strategy designed to minimize its oil supply vulnerability. Given Sino–Myanmar close ties, Western powers will have little possibility of control, especially in an international or regional conflict involving China. Myanmar, however, will not replace the important position of the Middle East in Chinese energy security. On the other hand, the imported gas and the gas pipeline will ease the negotiations about importing gas between China and Russia.

Although the Sino–Myanmar oil and gas pipelines may ease China's worries about its over-dependence on energy transportation through the Straits of Malacca, it still cannot take the place of that route. Some in China exaggerated the role of the Sino–Myanmar oil pipeline and Myanmar in China's energy security, and argued that the pipeline could completely solve the "Malacca dilemma".[29] According to the design of the oil pipeline, its annual transportation capacity is 20 million tons, still only 10 percent of the Malacca sea-lanes transmission capacity.

The imported oil and gas from Myanmar and the Sino–Myanmar pipeline still constitute an essential component of China's energy diplomacy and strategy. Further, from the perspective of Beijing's comprehensive strategy in Myanmar, China–Myanmar energy cooperation is only one part of Beijing's "Two Ocean Strategy." China is making great efforts to gain access via Myanmar to the

---

28   "The Construction of China–Myanmar Oil and Gas Pipelines Has Begun", *China Petroleum Daily*, 13 September 2010.

29   John Walsh, "Myanmar Solves Malacca Dilemma: Burma Is Now China's Main Ally in Southeast Asia", 8 August 2007, john-walsh.suite101.com/myanmar-solves-malacca-dilemma-a28005.

Indian Ocean as a passage for Chinese commodities, traffic, and energy. China–Myanmar energy cooperation is characterized first by its immediacy, and second as instrumental in solving the oil security dilemma and promoting Chinese economic development. It has also become a diplomatic and tactical tool for "China's Rising."[30] This phenomenon is reflected in China–Myanmar–India triangular relations.

From the start of the Cold War, Beijing has regarded Burma/Myanmar as a geo-strategic buffer zone, whether in its confrontations with the West, its rivalries with the Soviet Union and Vietnam, or its "Peaceful Rise" strategy in the post-Cold War era. In the light of China maintaining and strengthening its influence in Myanmar after 1988, New Delhi has become Beijing's biggest competitor in Myanmar. After changing its Burmese policy from idealism to realism in 1993, India is steadily developing its relations with Myanmar. The two countries' cooperation in recent years in the energy sector is especially important. China is a critical factor behind this change of New Delhi's policy. Fearing a Chinese threat to its east, India has reviewed its Burmese policy and is attempting to balance China's growing economic and military influence there.[31] India's Burmese policy is aimed at China–Myanmar strategic relations.[32] India sees China as its principal competitor in the global quest for energy. Indian officials are loath to admit publicly the existence of such competition, to avoid possible political friction with their behemoth northern neighbor.[33] Accordingly, when China first developed relations with Myanmar, Beijing could keep a low profile to assuage Indian perceptions. "But now India has been aggressive and publicly clamoring to curb China. China has to throw away its scruples, and do what it should do."[34]

China is increasingly wary of India's naval capabilities in the Indian Ocean and of its ability to interdict tanker traffic headed for China. This has been heightened recently by India's improving naval cooperation with the Southeast Asian states, including Myanmar, and the United States. India in its turn is

30 Yu Yohuei, "Hu Jintao's Oil Diplomacy and Challenges", *Mainland China Studies*, Vol. 48, No. 3, 2005, p. 37.
31 Helen James, "Myanmar's International Relations Strategy: The Search for Security", *Contemporary Southeast Asia*, Vol. 26, No. 3, 2004, p. 536.
32 Andrew Selth, "Burma and the Strategic Competition Between China and India", *The Journal of Strategic Studies*, Vol. 19, No. 2, June 1996, p. 213. But see Chapter 10 on the importance of development of India's Northeast as another motivating factor.
33 "Energy Trends In China and India: Implications for the United States". Hearing Before the Committee On Foreign Relations: United States Senate, 109th Congress, First Session, 26 July 2005, p. 50.
34 "Sino–Myanmar Oil and Gas Pipeline Project total investment amounts to several billions U.S. Dollars", *China Petrochem*, 1 March 2007.

increasingly concerned about China's growing efforts to acquire port access along the Indian Ocean coast, with new port-access arrangements in Pakistan, Bangladesh, Sri Lanka, and Myanmar. The zero-sum approaches to energy security increase the risk of spillover into competition over maritime energy transport routes in the Indian Ocean and the Straits of Malacca.[35]

Therefore, the construction of the Sino–Myanmar oil and gas pipelines could counter India and limit its influence in Myanmar, and such efforts could also set up a valuable geo-strategic buffer zone.[36] If China maintains its close ties with Myanmar, this will have a profound impact on the strategic balance in South Asia and change the rules of the game in the Indian Ocean.[37]

In Sino–Myanmar relations, energy cooperation is a bond. More interests between the two sides will be interwoven. Petrodollars are the Myanmar regime's prime source of foreign exchange. China, as one of its important gas buyers, will further increase its influence in Myanmar, which remains under various sanctions of much of the international community. The building of the gas and oil pipelines will boost massive infrastructure construction in Myanmar. The highway, railway, and port which China will build for the pipelines will make Myanmar increasingly reliant on China. But Myanmar always plays its rich gas resources as a trump card in its diplomacy. The oil and gas pipelines and Myanmar's role in China's energy security improves Myanmar's position in neighboring countries and its geo-strategic value. An article published in *Myanmar Times* (23 February 2007) stated that the Sino–Myanmar oil and gas pipelines will cause Myanmar to hold an important position in Beijng's energy strategy.[38] Interestingly, China took notice of this article. Three days later, the Consulate General of China in Mandalay translated the article into Chinese, and pasted it on its website.

Oil and gas are the stabilizers of close China–Myanmar relations, the catalyst of deepening relations between the two countries. To ensure its energy interests, Beijing will have to increase its reliance on Myanmar. Politically, an energy-importing state may slip into a weak bargaining position with respect to the exporting states and overland transit states. "Ships can be diverted but pipelines are immovable. The exporting and transit states on a pipeline have some political leverage over the importing state and this can be used to disrupt

---

35   "Energy Trends In China and India: Implications for The United States", p. 37.
36   Li Chenyang, Qu Jianwen and Wu Lei, "The strategic initiative of China's solving the 'Malacca Dilemma'", *The Reference News*, 5 August 2004.
37   "The Sino–Myanmar Oil and Gas Pipeline Project", *China Petrochem*, 1 March 2007.
38   The Sino–Myanmar Oil and Gas Pipeline through Myanmar will make China–Myanmar ties closer, mandalay.mofcom.gov.cn/aarticle/jmxw/200702/20070204401154.html.

flows in the short term in order to increase the exporting or transit country's bargaining power in some political or economic negotiation with one or more of the other states involved."[39]

"For transit oil and gas pipelines, it is important to consider that the transit country can disrupt the pipeline during its operation simply because it can."[40] This possibility is based on two assumptions. First, it assumes that the Naypyitaw could disrupt or restrict the oil transmission and gas supply to bargain over a higher payoff. The past performance of transit pipelines in some other countries has indicated that, "When oil and gas prices were high, producers and transit countries tended to want to increase volumes to earn greater returns, placing greater stress to renegotiate contracts to take advantage of high prices and inducing more spills and accidents. When prices were low, the operators tended to cut back on maintenance expense, causing corrosion and damage so that they could use the degraded pipeline infrastructure to create negotiating leverage for higher transit prices."[41] China could face the risk of "obsolescent bargaining"[42] in a cross-border pipeline project. Generally, cross-border pipeline projects depend on the committed participation of multiple parties over a long period. In a cross-border pipeline project, some risks may be amplified because the interests of several sovereign states are at stake.

Second, it assumes that the pipelines would be vulnerable to attack by anti-government groups and forces in Myanmar. "Transit oil and gas pipelines face the problem of potential disruption from a number of sources, notably post-construction behavior of the transit country once the pipeline is built and in

---

39 Philip Andrews-Speed, Xuanli Liao and Roland Dannreuther, "The Strategic Implications of China's Energy Needs", Adelphi Paper, No. 346, The International Institute for Strategic Studies, 2002, p. 15.

40 Ekpen J. Omonbude, "The transit oil and gas pipeline and the role of bargaining: A non-technical discussion", *Energy Policy*, Vol.35, No.12, December 2007, p. 6193.

41 The lesson is simple: Russia, for example, limited natural gas supply to Turkmenistan in 1997 to coerce higher prices after a dispute over contracts. "Russia, again, used control of their natural gas pipelines in 2005 to manipulate the market to their advantage and gain concessions on gas prices from Ukraine, even at the risk of blackouts in Eastern Europe and international outrage. Russia has used the same tactic at least five times since in natural gas disputes with Belarus, Georgia, Moldova, and Ukraine suppliers and transporters frequently manipulate dependency to their advantage." Benjamin K Sovacool, "Reassessing Energy Security and the Trans-ASEAN Natural Gas Pipeline Network", *Pacific Affairs*, Vol. 82, No. 3, Fall 2009, p. 476.

42 *Obsolescent bargaining* refers to a situation where the original agreement between the parties becomes obsolete as one or more parties – often sovereign states or state companies – seek to improve their position once the pipeline is built. See "Developing China's Natural Gas Market: The Energy Policy Challenges", OECD/IEA, 2002, p. 232.

operation. The cost and security of supply implications of disruptions to transit pipelines are huge."[43] The grenade attacks on the Thaukyegat hydropower project and the Myitsone dam project launched by anti-government forces in April 2010 demonstrate that assumption. By contrast, pipelines that are over 700 kilometers in length and require many pump stations are easier to be attacked. "Pump stations, critical to moving oil through the pipeline, are highly vulnerable to air assault or sabotage that could result in the pipeline being shut down. The destruction of one or more pump stations will reduce, if not stop, the flow of oil through the line, making pipelines as susceptible to closure as sea-lanes. The replacement of large pumps and drivers can take up to a year. Pipeline operators rarely stock spare pumps of this size because they are expensive, usually costing millions of dollars.[44]

The recent developments in Myanmar's domestic politics since the Kokang event in 2009 have cast a shadow of doubt over the project. "The proposed route of the pipelines passes close to areas controlled by ethnic militias. The prospect of renewed conflict between Naypyitaw and these groups, following government demands that they disarm or be integrated into Myanmar's armed forces, has made Beijing nervous."[45] The security risk to the pipeline is serious. "The pipeline route passes through areas partly controlled by ethnic cease-fire groups, including the Shan State Army – North (SSA–N), the Kachin Defence Army (KDA) and the Myanmar National Democratic Alliance Army (MNDAA)."[46] Due to a dispute over the transformation of "Border Guard Forces," armed conflict broke out in Kokang between both sides in 2009. It led to 37,000 civilians fleeing to China. China faces the challenge and the conundrum of how to keep its balance and avert internal ethnic conflict along the Sino–Myanmar border while still claiming non-interference in the internal affairs of other countries. The dual-pipeline projects provide an incentive to China to further strengthen ties with Myanmar. The Chinese government surely hopes that the pipeline will help to foster political stability along the two countries' border.

In addition, the uncertain political scene in the medium and long-term in Myanmar could also be a potential source of conflict over the pipelines, although it's believed that the *Tatmadaw* will continue to control the government.

---

43   Ekpen J. Omonbude, "The transit oil and gas pipeline", p. 6192.
44   Downs, "The Chinese Energy Security Debate", p. 36.
45   Ian J. Storey, "China a major player in S-E Asia pipeline politics", *The Straits Times*, 23 September 2009.
46   "Corridor of Power: China's Trans-Burma Oil and Gas Pipelines", Shwe Gas Movement, 2009, p. 20.

"There is a widespread view that conflicts over pipelines, including those due to incompatible legal and regulatory regimes, arise because of politics. Some conflicts undeniably have been political, including those that have grown out of a legacy of political divisions."[47]

Although the future of the Sino–Myanmar gas and oil pipelines is difficult to predict, particularly whether Naypyitaw might use it as a bargaining counter in its relations with Beijing and whether a Russia-like incident might occur in Myanmar, it is safe to say that China must in future continue to woo Myanmar with economic projects or military sales. According to the 2009 report of Shwe Gas Movement, the oil and gas pipelines will pass through 22 townships along a 980 kilometers course (according to China's official release, the length of the pipelines is 771–793 kilometers) across Myanmar. "Currently forty-four infantry and light infantry battalions are positioned along the pipeline corridor. Each battalion is thought to have 250–300 soldiers, which means that at this time there are up to 13,200 soldiers positioned along the route. A naval base that includes nine sub-battalions in place on the eastern side of Ramree Island will monitor the deep sea port and oil terminal."[48] Obviously, the safety of the dual pipelines needs to be protected by the *Tatmadaw*. The case of the Yadana gas pipeline from Myanmar's Andaman Sea to Thailand has shown that the Myanmar government had militarized the pipeline region and "The military has been steadily building up its presence to protect the natural gas development activities in the region."[49] As a result, there is every reason to believe that the China–Myanmar military relation will remain close and Myanmar will have incentives to request China's military aid and cooperation.

The Security and Economic Dimension

The main motivation of the China–Myanmar oil and gas pipelines project is to resolve the "Malacca dilemma." "China tends to view its oil security through the prism of American–Japanese containment of China."[50] Beijing believes the U.S. is the primary threat to China's energy security. "China's energy security

---

47   "Cross-Border Oil and Gas Pipelines: Problems and Prospects", Joint UNDP/World Bank Energy Sector Management Assistance Programme, June 2003, p. 9.
48   "Corridor of Power", pp. 7 and 20.
49   Earthrights International and Southeast Asian Information Network: *Total Denial: A Report on the Yadana Pipeline Project in Burma*, 10 July 1996, p. 13.
50   Pak K. Lee, "China's quest for oil security: oil (wars) in the pipeline?" *The Pacific Review*, Vol. 18 No. 2 June 2005, p. 289.

activities reflect this concern; they are largely defensive and are designed to minimize the vulnerability of China's oil supply to American power."[51]

There are two main schools of thought about the necessity of land routes for China's imported oil transportation. The first school contends that "Like all its Asian neighbors, China worries about the security of transport corridors, chiefly the Malacca Strait, through which all Middle Eastern oil reaches its Asian customers. This concern is legitimate."[52] "Apparently, China does not have the capacity to prevent the U.S. from disrupting its sea-lanes. Developing land routes for oil transport appears to be China's best option."[53] The Chinese government and many Chinese scholars also think so.[54]

The second school argues that China exaggerates the threats to navigation in the Straits of Malacca, notably the U.S. factor. Erica S. Downs holds that China need not worry that the U.S. and its allies could disrupt the flow of oil to China during a Sino–American conflict by blocking the Straits of Malacca because "The United States certainly has the military capabilities to destroy any transnational pipelines the Chinese are interested in constructing. Pumping stations could easily be damaged with cruise missiles launched from long-range bombers."[55] Some scholars claim that the abovementioned U.S. blockade against China's energy supply is unlikely: "As China's economy becomes more deeply integrated into the regional production chain, the associated costs of launching such a blockade are increasing as well. Economic interdependence again serves as perhaps the single most powerful deterrent against an embargo or blockade by China's neighbors in terms of traditional military-related risks; the possibility of a risk turning into a threat to China's energy security is getting

---

51 Erica Strecker Downs, "China's Quest for Energy Security", RAND, 2000, p. 53.
52 "China's Worldwide Quest for Energy Security", The International Energy Agency, 2000, p. 64. For other arguments of this school, see Mokhzani Zubir, Mohd Nizam Basiron, "The Straits of Malacca: the Rise of China, America's Intentions and the Dilemma of the Littoral States", Maritime Institute of Malaysia, April 2005; You Ji, "Dealing with the Malacca Dilemma: China's Effort to Protect its Energy Supply", *Strategic Analysis*, Vol. 31, No. 3, May 2007; Robert E. Ebel, "Energy and Geopolitics in China Mixing Oil and Politics: A Report of the CSIS Energy and National Security Program", CSIS, November 2009, p. 52;
53 Hongyi Harry Lai, "China's oil diplomacy: is it a global security threat?" *Third World Quarterly*, Vol. 28, No. 3, 2007, p. 534.
54 See Zhang Jie, "The Malacca Factor of China's Energy Security", *Studies of International Politics*, No. 3, 2005; Li Jinming, "Malacca Straits and the security of Sea-lanes in the South China Sea", *Southeast Asian Affairs*, No. 3, 2006; Ma Xiaoyu, Zhang Ziyang and Hu Liming, "Safety analysis on China's oil transportation at Malacca strait", *China Water Transport*, Vol. 7, No. 1, 2007.
55 Downs, "The Chinese Energy Security Debate", pp. 36–37.

lower, thanks to the forces of economic globalization."[56] In contrast to Beijing's fear that the U.S. may someday try to interdict China's foreign energy supplies, "The actual situation is less dramatic."[57]

We argue that the annual transmission capacity of the China–Myanmar oil pipeline demonstrates that it will not solve the "Malacca dilemma" and will only help mitigate its reliance on the Straits of Malacca marine lanes. The impact of China–Myanmar pipeline projects on China's overall energy picture is small, particularly given China's projected oil import demand. "The Myanmar line will be able to transport 10% of China's 2009 volume of imports, but only 3% of projected demand in 2030, and this oil will still have to come from overseas."[58]

We admit the security advantage that the China–Myanmar oil overland pipeline may have over tanker imports, but one advantage, which Chinese sources do not mention, is political. In order for the United States to disable a pipeline supplying China, it would have to attack Chinese territory or a third country. A blockade, however, could in theory be enforced without having to attack a sovereign state.[59] The pipeline is effectively meaningless in China's energy security because United States has the military capability to destroy and paralyze the pipeline in both Myanmar and Chinese territory. The significance of China–Myanmar oil and gas pipelines is largely embodied in its economic impact on China's Southwest regions and in its strategic effect on ongoing China–Myanmar relations.

Although the future of the Sino–Myanmar gas and oil pipelines is difficult to predict, and whether Myanmar could use the pipelines as bargaining chips, it is safe to say that China must continue to woo Myanmar with economic projects or military sales.

Chinese investment in oil and gas exploration is intended to provide a stable oil supply in price and quantity for China's economic development. The Sino–Myanmar oil pipeline would reduce by over 1,820 sea miles the present journey to Guangzhou from the Middle East. The economic significance of the oil pipeline, however, to an even greater extent will support China's southwestern development.

56 Zha Daojiong, "China's Energy Security and Its International Relations", *The China and Eurasia Forum Quarterly*, Volume 3, No. 3 November 2005, p. 44.
57 Daniel Yergin, "Ensuring Energy Security", *Foreign Affairs*, March/April 2006, Vol. 85, Issue 2, p. 77.
58 John Seaman, "Energy Security, Transnational Pipelines and China's Role in Asia", IFRI Asie Visions 27, April 2010, p. 38.
59 Downs, "The Chinese Energy Security Debate", p. 37.

At present, the oil of the southwest province is supplied by the refineries in South and Northwest China; the transportation distance is far and the cost is high. In particular, Yunnan is located at the end of China's product oil supply network. Insufficient oil has become an obstacle to economic development in the southwest. Consequently, the pipeline firstly can solve the problem of oil shortages in southwest China. Secondly, the tobacco sector is a pillar industry of the Yunnan economy, and residual oil products such as fertilizer could help boost tobacco production. Yunnan wishes to use the opportunity offered by the oil pipeline to construct an oil refining industry base in Kunming. In 2006 it submitted such a proposal to Beijing. According to the plan, after the completion of the Sino–Myanmar oil and gas project, the southwest province will increase its oil refining capacity to 20 million tons per year. It will produce 12.77 million tons of oil, including 3.1 million tons of gasoline, 8.4 million tons of diesel oil, and 1.27 million tons of kerosene. The related products from the pipeline are planned to yield 1 million tons of ethane, 1.53 million tons of synthetic resin, and 1.77 million tons of basic organic material per year.

On 2 December 2007, the Yunnan government and the CNPC concluded a strategic cooperation framework agreement in Beijing. Both sides agreed to push the construction of the Yunnan oil refining industry. Under the agreement, the Yunnan government will give the CNPC approval to set up a product oil pipeline network, and a sales network and distribution center for ethanol gasoline. Furthermore, Yunnan will first build the Kunming–Dali product oil pipeline, and in time, the Kunming–Mengzi, Kunming–Puer, and Kunming–Qujing product oil pipelines. The Yunnan oil refining industry base will greatly reduce the distance and cost of crude oil transportation, and its refined oil can radiate throughout Sichuan, Chonqing, Guizhou, Guangxi, and Southeast Asian countries.

In addition, Chongqing has requested extending the Sino–Myanmar oil and gas pipelines to it. Chongqing hopes to become the other oil refining center. It wants to use this favorable occasion to solve its oil and gas shortage, and apply to build a national emergency petroleum reserve, which could get policy support and funding from the central government. As the traffic hinge on the upper Yangtze River, Chongqing could carry products or crude oil to various ports along the Yangtze River, and become a distributing center of oil products.

In early 2007, Huang Qifan, Vice Mayor of Chongqing, said the CNPC had chosen Chongqing as the destination for the pipelines, noting that the city would build a 10-million-ton capacity refinery to process imported crude, which was due to come on stream in three years. Chongqing plans to invest RMB200 billion in an oil and chemical industry cluster with an annual production value of RMB100 billion.[60] The Chongqing government treated the preparation for the construction of a 10-million-ton refinery as one of its ten key projects in 2008.[61]

At present, natural gas remains a marginal fuel in the Chinese energy system. Pipeline construction and downstream facilities lag behind upstream progress. Nevertheless, "Faced with mounting environmental problems and starkly rising oil imports China could well decide to accelerate building up both its domestic gas delivery system and its gas imports, in a grand national switch toward clean-burning fuels."[62] Since 2002, China has initiated the West–East Natural Gas Transmission Project and the Sichuan–East Natural Gas Transmission Project, and is constructing a nationwide gas pipeline network. The China–Myanmar gas pipeline is not only conjoined with the national strategy, but also will partly promote the readjustment of both the industrial structure and energy consumption. Also, the projects will be a strong response to China's "Western Development" strategy. "As the eastern, coastal provinces have experienced dramatic increases in wealth, much of the interior has been left far behind. Southwestern China is vastly underserved by internal gas and oil distribution networks in particular, but the Myanmar pipeline project could help remedy the situation."[63]

The pipelines will generate a significant windfall for the Myanmar regime over the next 30 years. The annual transit fee of the gas pipeline alone will hit US$150 million.[64] However, the prospects that the government will make full use of gas and oil revenues for the development of the country's economy and social well-being are hardly optimistic. Additionally, natural gas and oil pipelines are capital-and technology-intensive projects, and they will not produce many local employment opportunities. But the pipelines project will generate the boom of infrastructure, particularly roads. The two countries, for example, signed on 18 May 2010 a MoU on the development of cooperation on the China–Myanmar Corridor Project to link Ruili and Kyaukpyu.

The Sino–Myanmar oil and gas pipelines are significant for Yunnan's, Chongqing's and Southwest China's economic development, and an important thrust

60 "Chongqing makes Sino–Myanmar Oil Pipeline Certain?" *Phoenix Weekly*, 2007, No. 11.
61 Wang Huongju, "Report on the Work of Chonqing Government 2008", *Gazette of Chong-qing Municipal People's Government*, No. 3, 2008, p. 10.
62 "China's Worldwide Quest", IEA, p. 73.
63 Seaman, "Energy Security", IFRI Asie Visions 27, p. 30.
64 "Corridor of Power", Shwe Gas Movement, 2009, p. 5.

for the future local economy. This will also lead to the strategic distribution of domestic energy.

The Implications and Characteristics of China's Energy Diplomacy in Myanmar
Chinese investment in Myanmar's oil and gas fields and the Sino–Myanmar pipelines demonstrate several aspects of the new face of China's oil diplomacy: [1] the trend of voluntarily taking risks in securing overseas energy supply sources; [2] the opportunism and pragmatism of Beijing's oil diplomacy; and [3] securing its energy interests even at the cost of challenging the international political order. China's energy security activities reflect its resolution to ensure that national oil security and energy become crucial ingredients in Chinese diplomatic strategies. Chinese investment in the oil fields of Sudan, Iran, Myanmar, and other "pariah states" shows a similar characteristic of its oil diplomacy. These oil dealings are criticized as counter to international norms. "Failure to address these matters could encourage other parties seeking scarce energy supplies to similarly compromise on human rights as they court questionable oil regimes at the expense of local populations, a development that would be detrimental to international peace and security."[65] "Yet China's energy security strategy, for all its success and sophistication, contains an inherent contradiction, and that is Beijing's pursuit of 'pariah' states. In increasing its closeness with regimes that the rest of the world, but particularly the U.S., would prefer to see marginalized, Beijing is undermining its own objective of appearing to be a more responsible global citizen."[66]

Since the end of the Cold War and the failed 1988 people's revolution, Myanmar's international image has been constantly negative. Called one of the "outpost of tyranny" countries by the Bush administration's Secretary of State Designate, Myanmar has been sanctioned and isolated by much of the international community. China uses its position and influence in international fora to lobby for Naypyitaw's interests, or at least to provide public damage control (e.g., in the Security Council). Beijing's role in the United Nations Security Council and also its position in U.N. bodies dealing with sanctions were of exceptional importance to progress in its energy relations with Myanmar. China's oil diplomacy with Myanmar makes Beijing and Naypyitaw both clients and allies. This is a new phenomenon in post-Cold War China's foreign policy;

---

65 Matthew E. Chen, "Chinese National Oil Companies and Human Rights", *Orbis*, Vol. 51, No. 1, Winter 2007, p. 41.

66 Cherie Canning, "Pursuit of the Pariah: Iran, Sudan and Myanmar in China's Energy Security Strategy", *Security Challenges*, Vol. 3 No. 1, February 2007, p. 50.

it deserves attention. Beijing has proven that it has benefited from refusing to support the U.S. sanction policies toward "rogue" or "pariah" states.

In March 2007, for example, Myanmar withdrew India's status as preferential buyer on block A1 and A3 gas fields, and instead sold them to China for a 30-year term, and agreed to a new 800 km pipeline, even through India had conducted furious lobbying and had been an important shareholder of the A1 and A3 gas fields.[67] Many believe that China became the first customer for the A1 and A3 gas fields because in January 2007 China had vetoed a U.S. move to debate Myanmar at the U.N. Security Council as a threat to regional peace and security. The U.S. had argued for "regime change" in the country two days before the contract was signed. The Myanmar official TV news reported this at unprecedented speed and thanked China for supporting Myanmar and blocking the U.S. move in the U.N. Security Council. In 2005, China and Russia also challenged U.S. Burma policies, using the threat of a veto on recommendations on Burma.

Seeking a controlled oil source, China's diplomatic offensive is comprehensive as well as strategic and speculative. It has an impact on the interaction between China and the great powers.[68] It is not just in this single case of Myanmar that China has used its position in the U.N. to provide oil-producing countries with political support and thus to receive economic and energy interests. In its quest for energy, China has also curried favor with Iran and Sudan, oil-rich nations that have difficult relations with the West. It has threatened to use its veto in the United Nations to prevent international sanctions to punish Iran for its nuclear program or Sudan for its alleged genocide. "I see them as becoming less and less conciliatory on issues they consider to be vital interests,"[69] U.S. Deputy Secretary of State Robert B. Zoellick cautioned on 6 September 2005, adding that, "If China continues to seek energy agreement with such countries as Iran, more conflicts will arise between China and the U.S." If Chinese companies continue to seek energy supply from troublemakers such as Iran, Myanmar, Zimbabwe, and to want to lock up energy sources for themselves, China will have difficulty in safeguarding its energy supply, and must make a choice.[70] It

---

67 Daewoo has a 51 percent stake in the A1 and A3 natural gas fields, where it is partnered by India's Oil and Natural Gas Corporation with 17 percent, the Gas Authority of India Ltd with 8.5 percent, Korea Gas of South Korea with 8.5 percent, and Myanmar Oil and Gas Enterprise with 15 percent.

68 Chung-lian Jiang, "China's Oil Strategy and Its Implications for Africa", *Issues and Studies*, Vol. 42, No. 4, 2003, p. 123.

69 Joseph Kahn, "The Two Faces of Rising China", *The New York Times*, 13 March 2005.

70 Tian Hui, "China Has No Intention to Control Oil Sources", *Oriental Morning Post*, 9 September 2005.

seems that China has little choice but to become increasingly reliant on global energy markets. "Beijing's access to foreign resources is necessary both for continued economic growth and, because growth is the cornerstone of China's social stability, for the survival of the Chinese Communist Party (CCP)."[71]

China generally has a "hands off" policy on the internal affairs of its trading partners, eschewing political conditionality. China argues that development requires the correct sequencing of priorities, with economic reforms first and political liberalization a distant second (if it is mentioned at all). Beijing uses this assessment to justify an approach that also happens to coincide with China's own trade priorities and political preferences.[72]

In the U.N. Security Council, China often opposes sanctions based on human rights concerns not only because it fears that such sanctions might be wielded someday against itself, but also because, as a latecomer to the international energy scene, China believes it does not have the luxury of scrutinizing the human rights practices of underdeveloped energy-rich countries.[73]

Chinese oil and gas companies lack the capacity to deal with the legal and financial aspects of international trade, so they rarely win in bids competing with major international oil and gas exploration in resource-rich fields. Tactically, as a latecomer to the international energy market, which has been controlled and segmented by western oil giants, China continuously establishes and promotes energy cooperation with the states that the U.S. and other western countries dislike and sanction. Thus, for Chinese companies, the possibilities for success here are high because of the meager competition from western companies. An IEA report argued that for other major energy importing countries, two messages had been clear. "First, China's manner of entry into the global energy markets carries no surprises. Its strategies bear strong similarities to others' and they are equally aggressive. Therefore, and second, it has become clear that China requires a strong place in the system. Other players must make room for it. China is not a marginal player but a powerful new force in the international energy markets."[74]

Beijing is not impervious to the impact of its realistic oil diplomacy on international politics and the regional geo-political order. Beijing has been

---

71 David Zweig and Bi Jianhai, "China's Global Hunt for Energy", *Foreign Affairs*, Sep/Oct 2005, Vol. 84, Issue 5, pp. 25–26.
72 Elizabeth Economy and Karen Monaghan, "The Perils of Beijing's Africa Strategy", *International Herald Tribune*, 2 November 2006.
73 "U.S.–China Relations: An Affirmative Agenda, A Responsible Course", Report of an Independent Task Force, The Council on Foreign Relations, 2007, p. 32.
74 "China's Worldwide Quest", IEA, 2000, p. 74.

keeping a low profile in its oil diplomacy toward Myanmar. China is obviously aware of the negative influence when it has close and strategic cooperation with a notorious military regime. China still does not have enough power to disregard the attitude and response of India, Thailand, Singapore, and other neighboring countries to China–Myanmar strategic cooperation.

The 2007 "Saffron Revolution," Naypyitaw's slow reaction to Cyclone Nargis in 2008, and some pressures for an Olympic boycott over China's Myanmar policy made China face unprecedented pressures from the international community. Nevertheless, the crises occurring in Myanmar in these two years demonstrate that the military junta has been able to control society and the political situation. Beijing will bet that the military regime will hold power over a long period. If Beijing wants to recover its costs and investments in the Myanmar energy sector and ensure its strategic interest in a future Sino–Myanmar energy pipeline, it will inevitably try to prevent any "saffron" or other "color revolution" from happening in Myanmar. Even if democratization develops in Myanmar, whoever obtains power, the bottom line of China's Burmese policy is that its core interests should be protected because of geopolitics realities. The CCP–BCP relations during the Cold War demonstrated this argument. Beijing used the BCP as lever to contain Rangoon when Burma publicly antagonized China in 1967.

At a micro-level, China's oil diplomacy in Myanmar shows the impact on Beijing's policy-making by Chinese local government and sectoral interest groups. From the initial proposal of the Sino–Myanmar pipeline, Yunnan, Chongqing, Sinopec, and CNPC played very important roles, and were crucial promoters, canvassers, and supporters of the policy. For central and local government, the significance of the Sino–Myanmar oil and gas pipelines, and Myanmar's position in China's energy strategy, are different. Local governments and sectoral interest groups are the direct promoters and beneficiaries of this project. Traditionally, with the Yangtze River as the division line, CNPC is active mainly in north and west China, and Sinopec in south China. The two national heavyweights compete for the domestic energy market. So Yunnan in company with CNPC, and Chonqing with Sinopec, pushed the Sino–Myanmar energy pipeline together with Yunnan's and Chongqing's oil refining industry bases.

If an effective international energy security cooperation mechanism that includes China is not established, China will not hesitate to continue its pragmatic energy diplomacy. From China's perspective, its national interest would be much better served by working with the U.S. to shape the future international system.[75] The bottom line for China is that its government has to generate upwards of 500 million new jobs in the coming two decades, as people flow out of the countryside into the expanding urban areas and capital-intensive investment in manufacturing reduces the number of new jobs created in that sector.[76] Beijing's investments and its clearly established aim of "rising" and pursuing development will not allow it to turn around, although "Chinese mercantilism, particularly when it comes to energy, constitutes a source of tension with the United States."[77]

China's "no strings attached" investment and aid posture undercuts international efforts to condition aid to improved governance. It also impedes international efforts to punish governments like Sudan's for gross misconduct. China probably will continue to exploit the economic and political opportunities that arise in spite of internationally imposed sanctions, even at the risk of antagonizing Washington, unless the leaders in Beijing determine that their conduct fundamentally jeopardizes PRC interests, including China's relationship with the United States and its international image.[78]

China and Myanmar's Energy Security

Concerns over energy issues between China and Myanmar are not limited to oil and gas. Beijing is also having an impressive impact on Myanmar's power sector.

Myanmar has ample amounts of fresh water due to the huge rivers running through its territory. Now, the Myanmar government has targeted these extensive river systems to produce large-scale electricity by implementing its 30-year Hydroelectric Power Strategic Plan. Many dams are being constructed on main rivers and their tributaries throughout the country with both large and small hydropower plants considered as priority national development tasks. China is the leading country to invest in and construct Myanmar's hydropower projects (see Map 8).

---

75 Robert B. Zoellick, "Whither China: From Membership to Responsibility?" Speech delivered to the National Committee on US–China Relations, New York, 21 September 2005, www.state.gov/s/d/former/zoellick/rem/53682.htm.

76 Peter Cornelius and Jonathan Story, "China and Global Energy Markets", *Orbis*, Vol. 51, No.1, Winter 2007, p. 19.

77 Major Lawrence Spinetta, "'The Malacca dilemma' – Countering China's 'string of pearls' with land-based airpower", a thesis presented to the Faculty of the School of Advanced Air and Space Studies for completion of graduation requirements, School of Advanced Air and Space Studies, Air University, Maxwell Air Force Base, Alabama, June 2006, p. 28.

78 "U.S.–China Relations", The Council on Foreign Relations, 2007, p. 32.

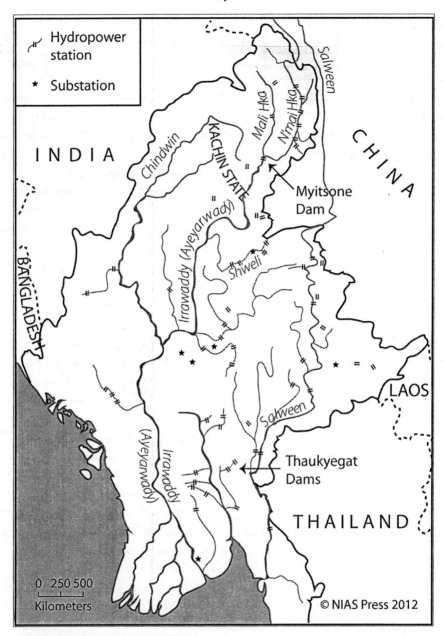

Map 8: Hydropower projects in Myanmar with Chinese involvement – completed, current and planned (based on a map in Earthrights International, *China in Burma: The Increasing Investment of Chinese Multinational Corporations in Burma's Hydropower, Oil and Natural Gas, and Mining Sectors*, 2008, by permission)

In recent years, Myanmar has been facing serious and chronic power shortages, with many parts of the country suffering frequent outages as electricity supply has been unable to keep pace with rising demand, causing the populace to lose confidence in the reliability of electricity supply systems. Although Myanmar has and is constructing some power plants, it remains relatively dark. A common Chinese pun on Myanmar's name plays with its Chinese transcription, *Miandian*, replacing it with a homophone that means "no power". The electricity shortages have become serious economic and political issues. In the cold season,[79] when hydropower plants cannot generate much electricity because of a lack of rain, even the former capital Yangon and Mandalay and other big cities have had no power or have to cut off power in different blocks and at different periods every day. In the rural areas, electricity is hardly available. Myanmar cities are often immersed in the noise produced by numerous power generators because many enterprises, shops, and rich families have personally bought them. Power shortages are hindering the economy and are choke points for its development. Furthermore, Myanmar's dissatisfied populace has satirized its dark condition without power as the "dark reign" of the military junta. Naypyitaw wants to solve this problem and increase its political legitimacy. Under this circumstance, China's enterprises have been extensively involved in the Myanmar power sector since the early 1990s.

China's Involvement in Myanmar Hydropower Plants and Dams

China's dam-building has attracted attention as a result of the current Chinese involvement in at least 93 major dam projects abroad. These projects are particularly concentrated in Southeast Asia and Africa, where China has fostered strategic regional and bilateral ties. China's dam exports are also active in Latin America, South Asia, and Eastern Europe.[80] On the map of China's global dam expansion, Myanmar is an important host country, although the Burmese hydropower sector was not included in the July 2004 list of "Countries and Industries for Overseas Investment Guidance Catalogue (I)" issued by the Ministry of Commerce and the Ministry of Foreign Affairs, and "Countries and Industries for Overseas Contract Project Guidance Catalogue (I & II)" issued by the Department of Outward Investment and Economics

---

79   There are three seasons in Myanmar: rainy season, cold season, and hot season.
80   Kristen McDonald, Peter Bosshard, Nicole Brewer, "Exporting dams: China's hydropower industry goes global", *Journal of Environmental Management*, Vol. 90, Supplement 3, July 2009, p. S294.

of the Commerce Ministry, in 2008 and 2009.[81] The political economics of dams are an important aspect of China–Myanmar relations. China sees the new bilateral role played by China's dam industry as a "win-win" situation for China and Myanmar.

The expansion of China's dam industry in Myanmar adds further weight to the influence of China in Myanmar because Chinese dam construction is not limited simply to the construction of a large number, but also because China has offered or is implementing "package engineering"; that is, peripheral equipment and material – the delivery of dam and hydro components that have become major factors in the increase of imports from China.

Chinese companies have been involved in the construction of 25 massive dams on the Irrawaddy, Salween, and Sittang Rivers and their tributaries. The dams will produce an estimated capacity of 30,000 megawatts and cost a total of more than US$30 billion to construct.[82] During the course of Chinese companies' involvement in the construction of Myanmar power plants, some state-owned enterprises are the first in line.

The Yunnan Machinery & Equipment Import & Export Co., Ltd. (YMEC) is a very active participator in the building of power plants in Myanmar. Since 1990, YMEC has established strong partnerships with Myanmar. As of 2001, YMEC had exported 16 complete sets of facilities as well as electric transmission and transformation equipment, and is one of the largest Chinese exporters to Myanmar of hydro-electricity equipment.[83] From 1990 to 2002, YMEC was involved in 20 hydropower stations in Myanmar.

On 1 December 2005, YMEC signed a memorandum of understanding with the Ministry of Electric Power No. 1 on the joint development of the Ruili River and the Nmai Hka River, and it will gradually build three cascade hydro-power stations on the model of Build–Operate–Transfer (BOT) on the Ruili River (said to be RMB3 billion). Meanwhile, YMEC got the priority rights for constructing a hydropower plant on the Nmai Hka River. On 29 December 2007, YMEC signed three contracts with Myanmar – the reconstruction of the Zawgyi–I hydropower plant, and the construction of the Datawchaing and Wetwun hydropower plants.

81 For the list, see hzs.mofcom.gov.cn/static/column/zcfb/a.html/1; www.china.com.cn/chinese/PI-c/626171.htm.
82 Violet Cho, "Ban the Dam, Say Activists", 14 March 2008, www.irrawaddy.org/article.php?art_id=10888.
83 The Largest Hydropower Plant jointly built by China and Myanmar is shaping up, www.hwcc.com.cn/newsdisplay/newsdisplay.asp?Id=25480.

China's Gezhouba Group Corporation (CGGC) is another important contractor for Myanmar hydropower stations. It has wholly or partially contracted and constructed over 100 large hydroelectric projects in China and has taken on over 30 contracts in hydroelectric projects, highways, as well as water supply in the Middle-East, South Asia, Southeast Asia, and Africa. Up to now in Myanmar CGGC has partially built the Yeya Hydropower project and Tasang Dam. Also, it supplies complete equipment for hydro-electricity generation to Papun, Shwe Gin, and Tasang Hydropower projects, with a contract value US$14.8546 million, €20 million, and US$6 billion respectively.

China has been involved in 7 hydropower plants with the total capacity of 16,500MW in Kachin State; they will be completed by, and include two hydropower plants constructed by the China Power Investment Corporation (CPI), which are expected to generate 6,900 megawatts of electricity. On 28 December 2006, CPI signed a memorandum of understanding with the Myanmar Ministry of Electric Power No. 1 on the development of the Nmai Hka River and Malikha River basins and the Myitsone hydropower station on the Ayeyawady River, construction of which was recently suspended (see Chapter 11). In 2007, CPI got the development rights for seven cascade hydropower stations with a total capacity of 13,360 MW at the confluence of the Nmai Hka River, the Malikha River, and the Ayeyawady River. On 27 February 2008, CPI signed a contract with the Ministry of Electric Power No. 1, for building a hydropower plant in a tributary of the Nmai Hka River. This dam is being built as the electrical source and power supply for the future construction of seven hydropower plants in the Nmai Hka, Malikha, and Ayeyarwady Rivers.

From 2004 to 2005, the China National Heavy Machinery Corporation signed three contracts with Myanmar, for providing complete sets of equipment for generating electricity as well as the design, manufacture, installation, debugging, and technical services for the Kun and Kabaung Hydropower Plants, and are building 300 kilometres of double-circuit and 45 kilometres of single-circuit transmission line, as well as a 230KV substation for the Yeya Hydropower Project.

On 5 April 2007, a memorandum of understanding was signed between the Myanmar Ministry of Electric Power No. 1 and the China Hanergy Holdings Group Company Ltd. According to the MoU, both sides will jointly build a 2,400MW hydropower station in the upper Salween River. They agreed to invest RMB20 billion and finish it within 10 years. In the same month, the Farsighted Group and the China Gold Water Resources Co. signed an agreement with the Myanmar Junta Company for this project.

In the past 20 years, more and more Chinese companies have become involved in the construction of and investment in many dams and power plants in Myanmar. However, these Chinese involvements in Burmese hydropower plants have been only partly funded. Although the above-mentioned leading Chinese enterprises that have played crucial roles in the construction of massive Myanmar hydropower plants are in the limelight as the main investors or contractors, in fact behind each power plant contracted or invested by Chinese companies there are many and various subsidiary Chinese enterprises involved in these projects.

For example, during the construction of the Dapein Hydropower Plant, SINOHYDRO Corporation is the constructor, and the China Datang Corporation and the Central China Power Group Int'l Economic & Trade Co. Ltd are the investors. The Jiangxi Provincial Water Conservancy Planning and Designing Institute are in charge of the design and reconnaissance survey of this project.

The metal structures and complete equipment for the hydro-electricity generation of the Kabaung Hydropower Plant were supplied by the China National Electric Equipment Corporation and the China National Heavy Machinery Corporation, respectively. The Hebei Province No. 2 Electric Power Construction Company provides installation, debugging and technical services for this project.

Another case in point is the Yeywa Hydropower Plant. The Export–Import Bank of China gave US$0.2 billion of preferential buyer's credits for this project. It is built by the China Gezhouba Group Corporation, but the China Hydraulic and Hydroelectric Construction Group Corporation & China Citic Technology Co., Ltd. is supplying and installing complete equipment for hydro-electricity generation and metal structures. The China National Heavy Machinery Corporation constructs transmission lines and substations for this project. Besides these large enterprises and transnational corporations, many domestic small-medium enterprises(SMEs) have also been in involved in the Yeywa Hydropower Plant. The leading contractors sub-contract with Chinese SMEs, which are needed to provide various specific designs, consultation, reconnaissance surveys, technical services, spare parts, and equipment. Other auxiliaries are also involved, such as Zhejiang Orient Holdings Co., Ltd, Shandong Electric Power Engineering Consulting Institute., Ltd, Anhui Province Energy Group Company, Ltd, Chengdu Shuangliu Tianhe Machinery Co. Ltd., Hubei China Gezhouba Project Management Co., Ltd.

In addition to the remarkable number of Chinese enterprises involved in the construction of dams and hydropower plants in Myanmar, major Chinese corporations have begun to ally and collaborate. In order to increase their competitive power in Myanmar, on 8 August 2006, YMEC, Yunnan Huaneng Lancang River Hydropower Co., and Yunnan Power Grid Co. formed a coalition as The Yunnan Joint Power Development Company. To avoid damaging competition among Chinese enterprises in Myanmar, in April 2008 China Southern Power Grid Co., Ltd, China Three Gorges Project Corporation, and SINOHYDRO signed a strategic cooperation framework agreement for the Salween River in Myanmar.

Besides the fundamental factor of close bilateral political relations, the reason why China can play an important role in the Myanmar power sector also lies in the economic needs of both sides.

Except for the new capital at Naypyitaw, Myanmar cities have had to face blackouts. So Myanmar generals sought Beijing's support and help and visited Chinese projects in China.[84]

When the Myanmar delegation, led by the Minister of Agriculture and Irrigation with 18 members, attended the Northeast Asia Investment and Trade Expo in Changchun, the capital of Jilin Province in September 2007, they asked China's side to arrange a visit to the Datang Changchun No. 2 Co-generation Power Co., Ltd. On 24 May 2007, Maj-Gen. Khin Maung Myint, the Minister of Myanmar Electric Power No. 2 made an appointment with the Chinese Ambassador to Myanmar, Guan Mu. "Myanmar wishes China to help it in the construction of transmission and substations," Khin Maung Myint said.[85]

In the fiscal year 2006–2007, all foreign investment totaling US$0.28 billion in the Myanmar power sector was from China.[86] Massive Chinese involvement in Myanmar hydropower projects is also implementing the "Go Global" strat-

---

84 Myanmar Prime Minister Khin Nyunt in July 2004 went to Hubei Province to visit the Three Gorges Hydropower Station under construction, which is the biggest dam in the world. On 30 November 2005, a delegation headed by the Myanmar Electric Power Minister visited Yunnan's Power Grid Corporation. In October 2006, Soe Win went to Hubei Province again and visited the Central China Power Grid Company., Ltd. He called for more hydropower projects and transmission lines and substations, and stated that the funding and technical support were especially urgent needs. In May 2007, a Myanmar power delegation led by the Minister of Myanmar's Ministry of Electric Power No. 1 visited Yunnan. One month later, General Thein Sein, Secretary (1) of the SPDC (now President) led the Attorney-General and 7 Ministers of Ministry of Electric Power No. 1 and No. 2, Energy, Commerce, Mines, and Transport on a visit to Yunnan. They visited the Yunnan Power Grid Corporation and called on Chinese enterprises to invest in and develop hydropower stations in Myanmar.

85 Myanmar plans to expand cooperation with China on electric transmission and substation, mm.mofcom.gov.cn/aarticle/todayheader/200705/20070504709457.html.

86 All foreign investment in Myanmar power sector is from China, www.chinapower.com.cn/newsarticle/1057/new1057505.asp.

egy formulated by Beijing. This expands Chinese companies and enterprises, and increases export and foreign exchange revenue. As noted above, China has not only built many dams but also supplied much of the equipment for Burmese hydropower plants. This equipment included complete hydroelectric generators and all kinds of auxiliaries. The maintenance of this equipment, imported from China, and the supply of spare parts and technical services will continue to be dependent on China. China therefore has, and will have, great influence upon the Myanmar power sector.

Since 1995, Yunnan has exported power to the neighboring border cities in Myanmar. From 1995 to 2004, the export of power to Myanmar was increasing at an annual rate of 40 percent.[87] In 2004, Yunnan stopped the power supply to the Shan State Special Region 4 in order to force it to close the casinos in Myanmar. Without the power supply, the casinos suffered heavy losses and layoffs. (Because a great many Chinese swarmed into the Myanmar casinos, many billions of yuan flowed to Myanmar.)

The Dynamics of China's Dam Expansion in Myanmar

Chinese dam builders have accumulated a vast knowledge base, having constructed almost half of the world's 45,000 large dams within China's borders. Further, Chinese companies can often build dams less expensively than companies from other parts of the world. In recent years, as Chinese dam building capacity has increased, reforms in the power sector have simultaneously created a more pluralized, flexible industry which can act more opportunistically both inside and outside of China.[88] The "corporatization" of China's power sector has been followed by a surge in domestic and overseas dam building, as power companies move quickly to secure existing assets and to begin to develop new ones. These factors facilitate China's increased involvement in overseas dam building.[89]

Meanwhile, the expansion of China's dam industry also has been prompted by favorable policies – a package of initiatives known as the "Go Global" strategy. A clear illustration of the success of the strategy in Myanmar is that, among the eleven power corporations that were carved from the former State Power Corporation of China, four power generator companies, (two power

---

87 The Export of Power to Vietnam and Myanmar has become an important merchandise to earn foreign exchange, www.chinapower.com.cn/newsarticle/1023/new1023750.asp.

88 McDonald et al., "Exporting dams", p. 297.

89 *Ibid.*, pp. 294–297.

grid corporations as well as Sinohydro Corporation and Gezhouba Group Corporation), have been involved in Myanmar's power sector.

China is involved at present in the construction and development of hydropower projects with the model of BOT on the Ruili and Nmai Hka Rivers, and the Malikha River basin, as well as the Ayeyarwady River. In Kachin State, seven dams along the Ayeyarwady, N'Mai Hka, and Mali Hka Rivers, with a combined installed capacity of 13,360 MW, are planned. The CPI signed in 2007 an agreement with the Burmese authorities to finance all seven dams. After the preparatory projects of seven dams began in April 2007, CPIC set about solving the problem of power transmission from Myanmar to China. On 21 May 2007, CPI and China Southern Power Grid Co. Ltd signed a strategic cooperation framework agreement for jointly developing the Nmai Hka, Malikha, and Ayeyarwady river electricity. According to the agreement, China Southern Power Grid Co. Ltd. will construct the power transmission networks by which Myanmar power is transmitted to China.

China is in the process of radically reforming its economy. The country is attempting to change its pattern of economic growth at the cost of the over-consumption of resources, heavy-pollution, and wide environmental degradation that have occurred in the course of development. Approximately 78 percent of China's electricity demand is met by burning coal, which has taken a serious toll on the environment.[90] According to China's plan, the proportion of electricity produced from coal should have been reduced to 68 percent by 2010, and further to 60 percent by 2020.[91] Large-scale hydropower is almost universally considered renewable and sustainable in China. The current leadership's emphasis on sustainable and scientific development, along with its renewable energy targets for the coming decades, stand to more than double the existing installed hydropower generating capacity by 2020.[92] China is exporting its concepts of sustainable development to neighboring areas such as mainland Southeast Asia. In response, Myanmar, with its rich hydroelectric power resources but plagued by power shortages, seems to have no other

---

90   Philip H. Brown, Darrin Magee, and Yilin Xu, "Socioeconomic vulnerability in China's hydropower development", *China Economic Review*, Vol. 19, Issue 4, December 2008, p. 614.
91   "China Expected to Suffer Another Power Shortage in Two Years", *SinoCast China Business Daily News*, London (UK), 28 February 2006.
92   Amy McNally, Darrin Magee, and Aaron T. Wolf, "Hydropower and Sustainability: Resilience and Vulnerability in China's Powersheds", *Journal of Environmental Management*, Vol. 90, Supplement 3, July 2009, p. 292.

choice than to open the door for significant foreign involvement in projects on the main streams of its leading rivers.

The Problems Facing China's Dams in Myanmar

Chinese outward investment that is intended to secure natural resources often occurs in geographically sensitive and/or politically controversial locations because many of the easily accessible and non-controversial locations in which these resources occur are already controlled by predominantly Western multinational companies.[93] As a result, "Countries and Industries for Overseas Contract Project Guidance Catalogue (I & II)" reminds Chinese companies that China's overseas contract projects are increasingly facing security problems due to the factors of politics, ethnic conflict, and terrorism in the host countries.[94]

An official investment guide for Myanmar stresses that "When China's companies contract projects in pursuit of economic interests, they should actively work with the local society, participate in social welfare, and build some small projects benefiting the Myanmar people, in order to get support from the places where the construction project is located and to ensure China's investments' and projects' steady and sustained development."[95]

The complexity of the political situation in Myanmar affects China's dam building projects. Opposition groups and human rights activists charge that the military government cannot represent the Myanmar people, and has criticized the ruling junta for selling out national interests by selling off its natural resources through agreements with energy-hungry China and India. In addition, the dams inevitably affect the environment and society in Myanmar. The Worldwide Fund for Nature (WWF) released its list of the world's top ten rivers at risk in 2007, Salween-Nu river was one of those listed due to the threat of dams.[96]

In December 2007, the Burma Rivers Network as well as 122 Myanmar and international organizations wrote an open letter to Hu Jintao on the influx

---

93 WWF, "Rethink China's Outward Investment Flows", April 2007, p. 6.

94 "Countries and Industries for Overseas Contract Project Guidance Catalogue (I and II)", Department of Outward Investment and Economic, China's Commerce Ministry, December 2008. hzs.mofcom.gov.cn/static/column/zcfb/a.html/1.

95 Chinese Academy of International Trade and Economic Cooperation of Ministry of Commerce, PRC, Investment Promotion Agency of Ministry of Commerce, PRC, Economic and Commercial Counsellor's Office of the Embassy of the People's Republic of China, *Guidelines for Overseas Investment and Cooperation in Other Countries and Regions (Myanmar)*, 2009, pp. 59–60.

96 Worldwide Fund for Nature (WWF), "World's Top 10 Rivers at Risk", WWF International, Gland, Switzerland, March 2007, p. 4.

of Chinese dam building companies to Myanmar. In this letter, they stated, "Burning and looting of villages, forced relocation, systematic sexual violence, and extra-judicial killing by the regime's troops are commonplace. Any dam construction will therefore compound the suffering of ethnic people living in both ceasefire and non-ceasefire areas, many of whom have already become internally displaced people or refugees."[97]

The human rights abuses and forced labor that have occurred in the construction of dams are not confined to Chinese projects. "It's no secret that development and securing future energy reserves take precedence over protecting the environment in most of the world, but what of human rights? And what of the proposed, or lack thereof, benefits for Burma and its people?"[98] But "Chinese dam builders have yet to adopt internationally accepted social and environmental standards for large infrastructure development that can assure these costs are adequately taken into account. The Chinese government, however, is becoming increasingly aware of the challenge and the necessity of promoting environmentally and socially sound investments overseas."[99] In Myanmar:

> The entire decision-making process for the planning and implementation of the hydropower development projects has been conducted in secrecy, with the barest minimum of information revealed. There has been a total absence of public participation among the dam-affected communities in Burma. So far there has been no evidence that any social impact assessments (SIA) or adequate and timely environmental impact assessments (EIA) have been carried out for the dams, despite agreements having been concluded and in some cases construction having already begun. The vast majority of the communities who will bear the negative impacts of dam construction will get no benefit or compensation."[100]

Consequently, some Myanmar people and organizations requested that the Chinese government monitor and regulate Chinese corporations operating and financing hydropower development and other natural resource extraction projects abroad. Businesses should be made to comply with relevant Chinese

97 "Open Letter to the People's Republic of China on the Influx of Chinese Dam Building Companies to Burma/Myanmar", Burma Rivers Network, 3 December 2007.
98 Don Talenywun, "The politics of dam construction along the Salween", *Mizzima*, 15 August 2009.
99 McDonald et al., "Exporting dams", p. 294.
100 "Open Letter to on the Influx of Chinese Dam Building Companies".

domestic and international standards ensuring people's informed participation in decision-making and accountability.[101]

According to the survey of the corporate social responsibility and sustainability of Chinese companies conducted by WWF in 2009, "Regarding sustainable development and corporate social responsibility, the main activities of the companies are philanthropic donations, staff engagement and legal compliance. This shows that the corporate social responsibility of Chinese companies is still at the initial stage ... Few of the companies expressed concern with the environmental impacts of proposed investments. The importance of environmental impact assessment to corporate social responsibility and avoiding possible negative consequences in the future is not yet apparent to the majority of Chinese companies."[102] Obviously, China has to face the challenge of how to deal with international norms. The details of the construction of dams on various rivers are not readily accessible, and the status of these dams is made more uncertain due to the lack of public information about the extent to which they are under reconsideration even in China. This fact reflects a Chinese view that it has no obligation to make public statements about developments within its own territory or other territories until a time of its own choosing. It is evident that Naypyitaw holds a similar stance and attitude.

According to some Chinese contractors, they have paid compensation for the Burmese affected by relocation because of their projects, but that such compensation was paid to the Burmese government, which did not pay those dislocated. They have also claimed that they have not forcibly evicted people from dam sites, but that Burmese companies have done so.

For most Myanmar people, their dissatisfaction and anger lie in the current power shortage in the country while many dams have been built in the past ten years. This means the Myanmar people still have not benefited from the dams. Some ascribe this to Chinese exploitation because they think that most power generated by the hydropower stations is transmitted back to China.[103] In terms of the local communities around the location of the projects, whether they benefit from them, and to what extent their interests can be considered, have an immediate impact on the security of China's investments and major projects in Myanmar.

---

101 *Ibid.*
102 WWF, "Chinese Companies in the 21st Century (II): A Survey on the Social Responsibility and Sustainability of Chinese Companies", April 2010, pp. 11–14.
103 Interview MLM, Myanmar–Chinese, Beijing, 10 July 2010.

Although the country has known violence in the past, the bomb blasts at the Myitsone dam project, built by CPI in April 2010, were aimed at China. Alarm bells have been ringing about the security of the dams contracted by China. Many people resent deals that are cut between Chinese firms and Myanmar's central government without any perceived local benefit. "When you're in a situation where you can't retaliate against your own government, you can perhaps retaliate against investment by outsiders."[104] The grenade attacks on the Thaukyegat hydropower project in Bago division on 27 April 2010, launched by the Karen National Liberation Army (KNLA), also indicate that all large-scale projects backed by the central government are vulnerable to such attacks.

Myanmar and Mineral Resources Security in China

China's investment and involvement in Myanmar's mining sector are not so arresting as its expansion into the sectors of oil, gas, and hydropower plants. "China's involvement in Burma's mining sector is difficult to assess, as many mining projects are small scale – therefore less visible, attracting less publicity – and they are often located in remote areas where access is restricted by the military or obstructed by difficult terrain."[105] Moreover, the opacity is attributable to some other factors. The news media in the two countries pay little attention to small and medium mining projects, and China's enterprises and investors barely release relevant news. In contrast, China's involvements in Myanmar's oil, gas, and hydropower sectors are easier to assess because of relevant information, news, and updates available in the public domain. Some Chinese investment and contracting go beyond the ken of the two countries' central governments. Their mining interests are not known outside the ceasefire areas controlled by ethnic minorities, where warlords illegally issue local exploration or mining licenses.

It was after 2000 that China's large enterprises began to set foot in the mining sector of Myanmar. China's presence in the sector has a connection with the following background.

---

104 "China risks backlash with Myanmar investments – NGO", Reuters, 9 July 2010.
105 EarthRights International, *China in Burma: The Increasing Investment of Chinese Multinational Corporations in Burma's Hydropower, Oil and Natural Gas, and Mining Sectors*, 2008, p. 8.

China's Mineral Resources Security Outlook

As of early 2007, there were 171 minerals with identified resources and reserves in China, including 10 energy minerals, 54 metallic minerals, and 92 nonmetallic minerals.[106] For many centuries, China has valued its vast territory and abundant resources but such a traditional conception is now being reversed. China's import volume of main mineral commodities increased considerably with its rapid industrialization from the 1990s. China became the world's biggest consumer of nonferrous metal in 1995 and of copper and aluminum in 2003. "By 2010, the external dependency of China on iron ore, copper, and aluminum will reach 57 percent, 70 percent and 80 percent, respectively. The gap between the supply of and the demand for mineral resources is growing, and it will have a far-reaching impact on China's development and on the global market of nonmetallic minerals." The strategic significance of China's growing dependence on raw material imports for its minerals has aroused universal attention from all concerned stakeholders.[107] This condition has caused anxiety in Beijing about mineral resources security, which has been reflected in various reports and documents issued by China's State Council.

In 2001, the "National Program on Mineral Resources" was promulgated by China's Ministry of Land and Resources in the "11th Five-year Plan for Land and Resources (2006–2010)." On 31 December 2008, the Chinese Ministry of Land and Resources released the "2008–2015 National Plan for Mineral Resources," which is mainly about policies on reserves of minerals. This plan emphasized that China's response capacity to cope with the impacts of market perturbation in mineral resources in general was weak. It stated that China will have a strong demand for minerals in the process of rapid industrialization and urbanization during the implementation of plan-schemes, and that China's absolute demand for minerals cannot be reduced in the short run. The demand–supply imbalance of mineral resources is growing. Therefore, if the model of geological resource and economic development is not changed, China's security in mineral resources supply will face greater challenges.[108]

---

106 Communique on Land and Resources of China 2007, www.gov.cn/gzdt/2008–04/17/ content_947023.htm.

107 Zhang Jian, "The prospects for cooperation between China and countries with rich deposits of nonferrous metals", *World Nonferrous Metals*, No. 8, 2005.

108 2008–2015 National Plan for Mineral Resources, www.mlr.gov.cn/xwdt/zytz/200901/ t20090107_113776.htm.

China's Countermeasures against the Mineral Resources Dilemma

To narrow the demand-supply gap in mineral resources and enhance the response capacity to deal with the international mineral market's risks and emergencies, China plans to set up a system of mineral reserves and mechanisms for tackling the mineral shortage. The "11th Five-year Plan for Land and Resources (2006–2010)" proposes to carry out geological investigations and mineral resources surveys in peripheral countries; to establish important mineral reserves bases focusing on scarce minerals inside and outside China, with a priority on the periphery; to strengthen the collecting of information about geological resources and the investment environment in other countries' mining sectors; and work out guidelines for investing in overseas mines to support China's enterprises.[109]

In recent years, China's global investment in mining has been in the limelight. And China's surging demand for mineral resources also fuels international concerns. For example, China's expansion into the energy and mining sector in Africa is called a "new colonialism" in the continent.[110] The Chinese thirst and hunt for mineral resources in the world is believed to make China a risk to the planet, the "China Threat" to resources.

Although Chinese involvement in Myanmar mining has not aroused wide international concern like other similar projects in Australia, Africa, and South America, there are the same intentions, driving forces, and policy behind them. The Policy Guidance for Overseas Investment, jointly issued by China's eight ministries and bureau on 5 July 2006, categorizes overseas investment into priority, permission, and prohibition. Investment which can acquire scarce and imperative raw materials and resources for the state is listed as the first prioritized item for domestic enterprise.[111] Meanwhile, the Catalogue for the Guidance of Overseas Investment Industries lists the specific items to be obtained through overseas investment in energy and mining: the exploration for and exploitation of oil and gas; the prospecting for, exploitation of and mine-selecting of e.g. copper, bauxite, nickel, vanadium, tin, lead, and diamonds. The investment in energy and mining industries overseas has become the

---

109 Sketch of "The 11th Five-year Plan for Land and Resources (2006–2010)", www.cgs.gov.cn/YWguanli/ZLyanjiu/ZHyanjiu/334_637.htm.

110 "China faces charges of colonialism in Africa", *The New York Times*, 18 January 2007; Alec Russell, "The new colonialists", *Financial Times*, Nov 17, 2007; Yaroslav Trofimov, "New Management: In Africa, China's Expansion Begins to Stir Resentment; Investment Boom Fuels 'Colonialism' Charges: A Tragedy in Zambia", *Wall Street Journal* (Eastern edition), p. A.1, 2 February 2007.

111 The Policy Guidance for Overseas Investment, policy.tech110.net/html/article_382215_1.html.

most important investment made by domestic Chinese enterprises. The 11th Five-year Plan for Overseas Investment states that the main point of China's overseas investment is to strengthen the exploitation of resources abroad and assure domestic economic security.[112]

In order to promote and implement the strategy of "Go Global," the National Development and Reform Commission (NDRC) and the Export–Import Bank of China on 27 October 2004 set up an operational mechanism to give credit support to the key overseas investment projects encouraged by the state. The first item of key overseas investment entitled to preferential credit support is the project which can ease the supply shortage of mineral resources in China.[113] Also, China's Ministry of Commerce has formulated policies to stimulate China's enterprises to secure overseas mineral resources; financial subsidies from the central government are available.

China's Investment in Myanmar's Mining Sector

China's growing presence in Myanmar's mining sector started in 2001, and intensified when China's Vice Premier Wu Yi visited Myanmar in 2004. This is because the Myanmar mining sector had not opened to foreign investment until the middle-1990s.

In July 2001, China's Ministry of Land and Resources and Myanmar's mining authorities signed a memorandum of understanding regarding cooperation in the promotion of investment in the exploration, mining, and utilization of mineral resources. The memorandum stipulated that the two countries' cooperation included but was not limited to assessment, layout, exploration, and exploitation of mineral resources; establishing a mixed committee about mineral resources' cooperation; and encouraging the two countries' enterprises and research institutes to cooperate.[114]

In March 2004, China's Vice Premier Wu Yi led a strong governmental entrepreneur delegation to visit Myanmar. Zhang Jian, the general manager of the China Nonferrous Metal Mining Group Co., Ltd (CNMC), was recommended to join the delegation by China's Ministry of Commerce. During Wu Yi's trip to Myanmar, CNMC won the Tagaung Taung nickel project.

---

112 The 11th Five-year Plan for Overseas Investment, www.investzj.com.cn/sanji.asp?id_fo-rum=010488.
113 Notice on Providing Credit Supports to the Key Overseas Investment Projects Encouraged by the State, zfxxgk.ndrc.gov.cn/PublicItemView.aspx?ItemID={e7006c85–45ec-4061–8110-b267c59b673c}.
114 Duan Tingchang, "China and Myanmar signed a memorandum of understanding regarding the cooperation of Geology and Mineral Resources", *China Gold News*, 20 July 2001.

During Myanmar Prime Minister Khin Nyunt's visit to China in July 2004, CNMC and Myanmar's Mining Enterprise No. 3 (ME3) signed an agreement for preliminary surveys, mineral exploration, and a feasibility study for the Tagaung Taung nickel project on July 12. On the following day, Myanmar's Mines Minister granted a mining license to CNMC. The Myanmar Ministry of Mining approved a completed feasibility study of the project in June 2007. The production-sharing contract between No. 3 Mining Enterprise and CNMC for the Tagaung Taung nickel project was signed in Naypyitaw on 28 July 2008, which consisted of mining and smelting facilities, and was designed to produce 85,000 tons of ferronickel and 22,000 tons of nickel per annum. The project was scheduled to start operation in 2011, and was granted a 20-year service period by the Myanmar government.[115] On 17 April 2009, President Luo Tao, and the Secretary of the Party Committee of CNMC, Zhang Keli, went to China's Hainan province to visit Myanmar's Prime Minister Thein Sein, who was attending the Boao Forum for Asia (BFA). They negotiated the Tagaung Taung nickel project and Thein Sein expressed interest in promoting the project further. On 17 May 2009, the ceremonial ground-breaking took place to formally begin the construction of the project.

The project is located in the northern Thabeikkyin Township, Mandalay Division, 120 km from the southeastern border town of Liangjiang in China's Yunnan Province and a few kilometers from the Ayeyarwady River. The Tagaung Taung site hosts one of the two identified nickel deposits in Myanmar. With an investment volume of more than US$800 million, the Tagaung Taung Nickel Project is the first and largest project in China–Myanmar cooperation in mining industries, which is also listed as a key project of overseas Chinese investment during the 11th Five-Year Plan.[116] After completion, it will have an annual production capacity of 85,000 tons of nickel iron. CNMC will invest US$500 million in nickel mining operations in a 40-km² section of the nickel project. Part of the investment will be for the construction of an onsite 30,000-ton/year nickel production plant. Preliminary studies revealed potential reserves of 800,000 tons with an average nickel content of 2 percent.[117] This

---

115 China Nonferrous Metal Mining Group Co., Ltd signed the contract of Tagaung Taung nickel project in Myanmar, www.chinamining.com.cn/news/listnews.asp?classid=159&siteid=153059.

116 "Retrospection of the 25th Anniversary of the Founding of China Nonferrous Metal Mining Group Co., Ltd", *China Nonferrous Metal News*, 27 November 2008.

117 Liu Jianjun, "China Nonferrous Metal Mining Group Co., Ltd Arrived at an Agreement with No. 3 Mining Company of Myanmar Mining Ministry", *China Nonferrous Metal News*, 20 July 2004.

project will become Myanmar's first nickel production facility. Another project, Letpadaung copper, is being developed by CNMC, with an annual production capacity of 125,000 tons of Grade A copper.

An agreement was signed between the China Hainan Jiayi Machine Import & Export Co Ltd (CHJMIE) and the Exploration Bureau of the Myanmar Ministry of Mines on 26 July 2004. According to the agreement, CHJMIE received permission to explore copper and other minerals in Monywa with the area of 1,400 sq km, Sagaing Division, and in Sinbo–Nankesan, 700 sq km, Kachin State. This project needs about US$1 billion from exploration to production,[118] and is also the second largest project of Sino–Myanmar cooperation in the mining sector after Vice Premier Wu Yi's trip to Myanmar in 2004.

In March 2005, the Shandong Geology and Minerals Bureau won the gold exploration rights in 8 blocks (50 acre/per block) in Myanmar. Eight lodes were found in 3 blocks. The maximum mining content of a core sample was 120g/t, and its average content was 20–30g/t. In the upper 90-meter layer, there were total reserves of about 5 tons, and the lode still extended in the lower 90-meter layer. On 12 August 2005, China Kingbao Mining Ltd signed a contract for a feasibility survey on the Mwetaung nickel mine with No. 3 Mining Company of the Myanmar Mining Ministry.[119] It is for the exploration of 55 sq km in Tetain and Kalay in Chin State that contains proven nickel reserves in excess of 10 million tons.[120]

Between 19 and 23 November 2006, the Assistant Foreign Minister, Chen Jian, headed a Chinese official economic and trade delegation visit to Myanmar. The two parties held the 2nd high level consultation meeting on forestry and mining cooperation between Myanmar and China, and signed a compendium of the second round of consultations on Sino–Myanmar forestry and mining cooperation. China's Chongqing International Economic & Technical Cooperation Corporation won the mining rights for an iron ore project in 2007, and planned

---

118 Zhang Yunfei, "China and Myanmar Signed the Agreement of Exploring the Copper Deposit", *China Mining News*, 29 July 2004.

119 Kingbao (Jinbao) Mining Co. is a joint subsidiary of Gold Mountain (Hong Kong) International Mining Co. and Wanbao Mining Co., both of which control 50% of the company. Gold Mountain (Hong Kong) International Mining Co. is itself a wholly-owned subsidiary of Zijing Mining Co., while Wanbao Mining Co. is a wholly-owned subsidiary of China North Industries (NORINCO). See EarthRights International, *China in Burma*, 2008, p. 8.

120 China Kingbao Mining Ltd Signed a Cooperation Agreement with Myanmar side for the Mwetaung nickel mine, mm.mofcom.gov.cn/aarticle/jmxw/200508/20050800263296.html.

to invest RMB5 million in iron mining operations in five years. The area of this iron deposit was 8 sq km, and its iron content amounted to 63 percent.[121]

Research by ERI reveals that ten Chinese multinational corporations are involved in six mining deals with the regime. Their number, however, is more than ten. Some other Chinese multinational corporations such as China Minmetals Corporation, the Aluminum Corporation of China (CHINALCO), China Hainan Jiayi Machine Import & Export Co., Ltd, China Mining Association, Beijing Intercontinental Mineral Development Co., Ltd, and Jiangsu Pengfei Group, Co., Ltd are also concerned with Myanmar mining. According to the Myanmar Investment Commission, up to 30 April 2006, foreign countries invested in 58 projects in Myanmar's mining sector with a contracted value of US$534.89 million, including 9 Chinese projects totaling US$670 million.[122] Till the end of 2008, China's contracted investments in Myanmar mining reached US$866 million.[123] The Myanmar official statistics do not present the full picture of China's involvement in mining.

A number of Chinese enterprises and investors have become involved in the field of mining beyond Beijing and Naypitaw's supervision. Particularly in the areas controlled by cease-fired ethnic groups, most Chinese investment and production there are unknown to the outside. For example, in the area ruled by The National Democratic Alliance Army, Chinese businessmen have exploited manganese. "An estimated 1,000 mine workers, all from China, are now living near the mine field." "An estimated 34,000 tons of rock per year were transported from the mine field to the Standing Company Limited of China in both 2004 and 2005."[124] The Kachin Development Networking Group and the Lahu National Development Organization have recently published on-the-ground research indicating that the Chinese companies, Northern Star, Sea Sun Star, and the Standing Company Limited, are involved in numerous smaller-scale mining projects in Kachin and Shan States. In May 2001, the Baoshan Bureau of Geology and Minerals Exploration signed an agreement with Kachin State Special Region No. 1. The Yunnan side would carry out the geologic and mineral exploration in the region under the agreement so that

---

121 "A Chongqing State Enterprise Wins the Exploration Rights of a Iron Ore in Myanmar for Five Years at the Cost of RMB5 Million", *Chongqing Economic Times*, 26 April 2007.

122 China's Investment Ranking 11th on Myanmar FDI List, mm.mofcom.gov.cn/aarticle/jmxw/200607/20060702606645.html.

123 Data of China–Myanmar Economic and Trade Cooperation in 2008, mm.mofcom.gov.cn/aarticle/zxhz/tjsj/200902/20090206038342.html.

124 "Unhindered Prospects", *Undercurrents*, July 2006, Issue 2, pp. 2–3.

the Kachin local government could exploit and open those untapped mineral resources.[125]

Yunnan is an important stakeholder and very active in the process of China's involvement in Myanmar's mining sector. The Yunnan Tin Company Group Limited (YTC) signed an agreement of mine resources exploration and business strategic cooperation with the Myanmar Royal Hi-tech Group Co., Ltd on 1 March 2007. On 5 June of the same year, over 100 Yunnan enterprises held a symposium of cooperation with more than 70 Myanmar entrepreneurs, and five mining cooperation agreements were signed.[126]

The Yunnan Nonferrous Metal Geological Bureau, cooperating with a Myanmar company, won six gold-mining rights in 2008.[127] The Yunnan Geology & Mineral Resources Exploration Engineering Group invested RMB13.0512 million to explore a lead-zinc-copper polymetallic deposit in Lashio. This project was approved by the Yunnan Development and Reform Commission in December 2007.[128]

The Chinese presence in Myanmar's mining sector in recent years is only a component of Beijing's global strategy for seeking mineral resources. Besides Myanmar, China is employing itself in mining activities in e.g. Iran, Zambia, Congo, Laos, Vietnam, Mongolia and North Korea. Inevitably, when China chooses Myanmar as a country from which to obtain mineral resources, it pays the cost of a negative international image, being criticized for pursuing a pragmatic policy in seeking and acquiring overseas mineral resources at the expense of human rights.[129]

Currently, China obtains overseas mineral resources through four channels: trade, preliminary exploration, mine investment, and international merger and acquisition. Until now, only Myanmar manganese ore has occupied an important place in China's import of mineral resources. Among China's staple import of scarce mineral resources in 2008, it imported 757 million tons of manganese from 37 countries, and the import from Myanmar held 4.7 percent,

125 *Yearbook of Baoshan*, Luxi: Dehong Ethnic Press, 2002, p. 125.
126 Zhang Min, "Yunnan Enterprises Signed Five Contracts", *Spring City Evening*, 12 June 2007.
127 Wang Zhengduan, "Yunnan 'Go Global': Making Great Progress in Exploring Overseas Mines", *China Land and Resources News*, 17 July 2008.
128 Yunnan Geology and Mineral Resources Exploration Engineering Group was approved to explore the lead-zinc-copper polymetallic deposit in Lashio, wzs.ndrc.gov.cn/jwtz/jwtzgk/t20080131_188863.htm.
129 "The real China threat", *The Boston Globe*, 7 March 2007.

ranking fifth.[130] China's exploration and investment in Myanmar mining is now also focusing on nickel and cooper. Other Myanmar mines have not assumed much importance for China's mineral resources and economic security.

---

130 Bulletin of China Land and Resources (2008), 202.123.110.5/gzdt/2009–04/01/content_ 1274266.htm.

8

China–Myanmar Economic and Trade Relations

*D*uring the Cold War, economic and trade dimensions counted for little in the China–Burma nexus; these dimensions were principally motivated by political calculations and served as a tool for political relations. Since 1988, however, economic interests have become a prime consideration of Beijing's policy towards Myanmar and have become interlinked with Beijing's longer-term security interests. The two countries' economic ties have also been politicized in the context of Western states' sanctions on Myanmar.

China–Myanmar Trade

The trade between China and Myanmar consists of conventional trade, border trade,[1] and smuggling. On the whole, the volume and value of the trade has greatly increased since 1988 (see Table 5).

Sino-Myanmar bilateral trade grew steadily between 1988 and 1995 at an average annual rate of 25 percent. By 1995, trade had reached a total value of US$767.4 million – a record high in the 1990s. Thereafter, the trade volume declined for four years in a row because of China's and Myanmar's policy changes on border trade. First, in 1996 Beijing abolished the preferential policy on import duties on border trade and tightened regulations.[2] Second, Myanmar was badly affected by the Asian financial crisis, which prompted a sharp drop in the exchange rate of the Myanmar currency (Kyat) against the U.S. dollar. In the crisis, Myanmar's lack of foreign exchange and unfavorable

---

1   China's border trade comprises barter trade between border residents, petty trade in the border areas, and foreign economic and technical cooperation in the border areas.
2   See "Circular of the State Council on Issues Covering Border Trade", tfs.mofcom.gov.cn/ aarticle/date/i/k/z/200301/20030100061518.html.

Table 5: China's imports from and exports to Myanmar, 1988–2009 (US$ million)

		Myanmar		
	Total	Exports	Imports	Balance
1988	255.62	140.83	114.79	26.04
1989	287.40	184.27	103.13	81.14
1990	327.62	223.54	104.09	119.45
1991	392.09	286.17	109.52	180.25
1992	390.44	259.17	131.27	127.90
1993	489.49	324.66	164.83	159.83
1994	512.40	369.11	143.28	225.83
1995	767.40	617.85	149.55	468.30
1996	658.53	521.12	137.41	383.71
1997	643.50	570.09	73.41	496.68
1998	580.90	518.86	62.04	456.82
1999	508.03	406.55	101.48	203.59
2000	621.26	496.44	124.82	371.62
2001	631.54	497.35	134.19	363.16
2002	861.71	724.82	136.89	587.93
2003	1077.24	907.71	169.53	738.18
2004	1145.49	938.59	206.90	731.69
2005	1209.25	938.45	274.40	664.05
2006	1460.07	1,207.42	252.65	954.77
2007	2062.04	1,690.98	371.06	1,319.92
2008	2626.01	1,978.46	647.54	1,330.92
2009	2907.36	2,261.24	6461.2	1,615.12

Source: *Yearbook of China's Foreign Economic Relations and Trade, 1991–2003;*
China Commerce Yearbook, 2004–2010.

balance of trade were severe,[3] and thus the government resorted to strict import controls, particularly on luxury and non-essential goods. At the end of 1997, Myanmar suspended border trade with China, Thailand, and India.

3   Toshihiro Kudo attributed the inflow stagnation of Chinese exports to Myanmar in the second half of 1990s to the fact that "the Myanmar government became annoyed with the country's expanding trade deficits by the mid-1990s and resorted to stricter import controls, particularly on luxury and non-essential goods. Accordingly, the influx of Chinese consumer goods and durables declined." See, Toshihiro Kudo, "Myanmar's Economic Relations with China: Who Benefits and Who Pays?", in Monique Skidmore and Trevor Wilson (eds), *Dictatorship, Disorder and Decline in Myanmar*, Canberra: ANU Press, 2008, pp. 93–94. Only part of the explanation for the decline was the trade deficit, and he neglected Beijing's policy change in 1996 and the factor of the Asian financial crisis.

The dwindling Sino-Myanmar trade scraped bottom in 1999 and has consistently risen since 2000. Compared to the period between 1988 and 1995, from 2000 to 2008 the higher average growth rate per annum was 35.85 percent. Table 5 indicates that Myanmar consistently has suffered from trade deficits with China since 1988.[4] In 2007 and 2008, China's favorable balance of trade vis-à-vis Myanmar surpassed US$1.3 billion. However, when the China–Myanmar oil & gas pipeline project is completed, "Myanmar will have another big source of foreign earnings from gas exports to China in the near future. China will be critically important for Myanmar not only as a supplier of goods and commodities, but also as an export market."[5] Then the trade deficit will narrow.

Myanmar is relatively insignificant in China's external trade. Although Sino–Myanmar trade volume occupied only 1.2 percent of the China–ASEAN trade volume from 2000 to 2008, Myanmar has been and is critically important for Yunnan province. Yunnan–Myanmar trade makes up over 50 percent of China–Myanmar trade. To Myanmar, China has become its second largest trading partner. In the 1990s, China became a major supplier of Myanmar's general merchandise. The dominant position of Chinese consumer products in Myanmar is attributed to the following factors: Myanmar's manufacturing sector lagged behind demand, and its import substitution strategy remained ineffective; sanctions pushed Yangon to rely heavily on China's merchandise; India, ASEAN, and Japan's marginal engagement policies toward Myanmar retarded the entry of their commodities into its market; and China had emerged as the "world's factory" by virtue of its rapid industrialization, and could meet any of the needs of Myanmar's market. In particular, in a poor country with limited purchasing power such as Myanmar, the low price and reasonable quality of China's products were attractive. Accordingly, when Yangon opened its door and legalized border trade with China in 1988–1989, and because of the demonetization of much of Myanmar's currency in September 1987, China's commodities poured into the emerging consumer goods markets in Myanmar through legal and illegal channels. During the same period, China began to export machinery, product lines, spare parts, vessels, trains, and automobiles to Myanmar.

---

4   For the reason for the Myanmar trade deficit with China, see Poon Kim Shee, "The Political Economy of China–Myanmar Relations: Strategic and Economic Dimensions", *Ritsumeikan Annual Review of International Studies*, 2002, pp. 45–47.

5   Toshihiro Kudo, "China and Japan's Economic Relations with Myanmar: Strengthened vs. Estranged", in Kagami Mitsuhiro (ed.), *A China–Japan Comparison of Economic Relationships with the Mekong River Basin Countries*, BRC Research Report No. 1, 2009, p. 280.

After the end of the 1990s and the beginning of the 21st century, the market share of China's consumer goods in Myanmar began to decline. According to the Yunnan Provincial Office of State Administration of Taxation statistics, "Yunnan products' market share in Myanmar gradually dropped in the early 1990s and has fallen to No. 3 after Thailand and South Korea. In Mandalay, for instance, the 50 percent market share held by China has currently decreased over 30 percent."[6] In this period, more commodities and goods from Japan, Hong Kong, India, ASEAN (notably Thailand), and South Korea entered Myanmar. Thailand's commodities have some competitive advantages because of the short transportation distance, low costs, and good quality, as well as meeting Burmese consumption habits.

China lost the market share in the country because of its fake or inferior commodities and the excessive competition among China's enterprises and merchants. For example, before the 2008 "Chinese Milk Scandal",[7] China dominated the milk powder market in Myanmar, and just two companies – Hope Springs of Yunnan and Deng Chuan Butterfly Dairy Co., Ltd. – achieved 70 percent of the total milk market share in 2007.[8] After the "Milk Scandal", not only did Naypyitaw stop the import of China's milk powder, but also the sales volume and price of all China's food products dropped in Myanmar.[9] Another similar event was the fake eggs from China in 2009, which also injured its reputation. In response, Myanmar took measures to curb illegally imported food items from China. Originally, the products of Fujian Mindong Electric Manufacturing Co., Ltd. found a ready market in Myanmar, but Myanmar's consumers lost confidence to them because of fake products. In 2003, 21 motor exporters in Chongqing made an alliance and promised to abide by minimum price-fixing for fear of their companies' predatory price-cutting in Myanmar.[10]

Entering the new millennium, China is massively exporting assemblies, product lines, and bulk equipment to Myanmar. This is largely responsible for the great increase of Sino–Myanmar trade volume and balance after 2000. According to China's former ambassador to Myanmar in 2004, "Myanmar has

---

6 "Probe into the Circulation of RMB30 Billion in Border Trade", *China Business Journal*, 22 February 2004.
7 About the sandal, see en.wikipedia.org/wiki/2008_Chinese_milk_scandal.
8 "Yunnan Hope Group Occupies 70 Percent of Myanmar Milk Powder Market Share", *China Business News*, 15 August 2007.
9 The Market Share of China's Foodstuff Declining in Myanmar, The Economic and Commercial Section of the Consulate General of PRC in Mandalay, mandalay.mofcom.gov.cn/aarticle/ztdy/200812/20081205949989.html.
10 "21 Motorcycle Exporters in Chongqing Allied", *Consumption Daily*, 14 August 2003.

become a major host country of Chinese overseas project contracting. The projects contracted by China in Myanmar mostly include bridges, wharves, plants, manufacturing plants (such as a sugar plant, a shipyard and a caustic soda factory). For Chinese enterprises, the biggest benefit is the export of complete machinery and electronic products, which are boosted by China's contracted projects in Myanmar. The figures from the Chinese customs department show that Chinese machinery and electronic products have accounted for 45–50 percent of total Chinese exports to Myanmar in the recent five or six years."[11]

China–Myanmar Border Trade

The rapid expansion of China–Myanmar trade was caused both by the domestic demands of the two respective countries and by western sanctions against Myanmar. Border trade is an important momentum of this expanding bilateral trade. There is little documentation or comprehensive data relating to the border trade, however, because its activities include informal trade and smuggling, as well as underpricing, all of which are not recorded in official statistics. Thus, real trade volume can only be estimated. Accordingly, Chinese official statistics and data on China–Myanmar border trade just reflect a part of the actual situation. In addition, the different definitions of China–Myanmar border trade also mean that the subject has been and will be understood differently.

Mya Than argues that China–Myanmar cross-border trade includes five types: Formal or official border trade; informal border trade; illegal border trade (smuggling); transit trade; and barter trade.[12] For Winston Set Aung,

---

11 Li Jinjun, "Myanmar Economic Overview and Prospects for China–Myanmar Cooperation", *Overseas Investment and Export Credit*, No. 2, 2004. The most apparent ripple effect between China's contracted projects and export lies in the hydropower stations and dams in Myanmar. The Yeywa Hydropower project had contracts with some China's enterprises. On 2 September 2005, China Hydraulic and Hydroelectric Construction Group Corporation and China Citic Technology Co., Ltd. supplied and installed the whole set of equipment for hydro-electricity generating and metal structures for the Yeywa project with a contract value of US$126 million. On 16 June 2005, China National Electric Equipment Corporation and Zhejiang Orient Holdings Co., Ltd won the bid for the Keng Tawng hydropower plant with contract value of US$15 million, and the China side was responsible for the design of the plant, as well as the supply, installment and adjustment of electronic, mechanical equipment and metal structures. The metal structures and whole set equipment (US$8.92 million) for hydro-electricity generating of the Kabaung Hydropower Plant were supplied by the China National Electric Equipment Corporation and the China National Heavy Machinery Corporation. China's Gezhouba Group Corporation received the supply contract for the Shwe Gin Hydropower Project on 7 September 2007, whose value amounted to EUD 20 million.

12 Mya Than, "Myanmar's Cross-Border Economic Relations and Cooperation with the People's Republic of China and Thailand in the Greater Mekong Subregion", *Journal of GMS Development Studies*, Vol. 2 No. 1, October 2005, pp. 39–40.

"Border trade is trade with neighboring countries through border points by road (or by coastal sea in the case of exports from Myeik to Thailand)." Border trade between Myanmar and its neighboring countries includes formal and informal (documented and undocumented) trade.[13] On 13 August 1994, China and Myanmar signed the "Memorandum of Understanding on Border Trade", which provided the definition of border trade as "It includes bilateral landborne trade and exchanging goods by border residents between Yunnan and Myanmar."[14]

In 1996, the State Council of China classified border trade: 1. exchanging goods by border residents, with the goods value not more than the set amount or quantity at the open-up points or markets designated by the government within the border areas 20 kilometers from the boundary line; 2. border trade in small amounts, referring to trade activity between the Chinese enterprises which are granted operation rights of border trade of small amounts in the border areas, and the enterprises or other trade organizations in the border areas of the neighboring countries.[15]

Besides the above-mentioned two types, Sino–Myanmar border trade includes informal trade and smuggling. On both China and Myanmar soil, there are numerous brokers, who constitute a type of social networking for the underground economy.

On 3 October 1988, Yangon legitimized and formalized the border trade with China, and set up border trade offices in Lashio, Muse, Namhkam, and Kunlong.[16] Myanmar started the implementation of the border trade system in 1991 with China and India. Up to 2009, Myanmar had opened four border trading points with China, namely Muse (opened on 21 January 1998), Lwejel (23 August 1998), Chinshwehaw (19 October 2003), and Kambaiti (reopened 1 August 2009).[17] In 1998, Muse was opened as a border trade point with China and a one-stop service was introduced. On 4 November 2006, the Muse 105 Mile Trade Zone (i.e., at the 105th mile road marker) was established, which covers an area of 370.83 acres linking China's Ruili in Yunnan Province. Also,

---

13　Winston Set Aung, "The Role of Informal Cross-border Trade in Myanmar", Institute for Security and Development Policy Asia Paper, September 2009, p. 9, 30–31.

14　Memorandum of Understanding on Border Trade of China and Myanmar, xxgk.yn.gov. cn/newsview.aspx?id=123341.

15　Circular of the State Council Regarding Relevant Issues on Border Trade, tfs.mofcom.gov. cn/aarticle/date/i/k/z/200301/20030100061518.html.

16　For the process of legalization of China–Myanmar border trade, see Maung Aung Myoe, "Sino–Myanmar Economic Relations Since 1988", Asia Research Institute, National University of Singapore, Working Paper, No. 86, 2007, p. 9.

17　The Kambaiti and Laiza trading points were temporarily closed in June 2006.

Table 6: China's land ports with Myanmar

Name	Level*	Date opened**	Opposite Myanmar points and region
Ruili	National	1978	Muse, Muse township
Wanding	National	1952	Kyukok, Kyukok township
Houqiao	National	August 1991	Kambaiti, Kachin State Special Region No. 1
Qingshuihe (Mengding)	National	August 1991	Chinshwehaw Shan State Special Region No. 1
Daluo	National	August 1991	Mong La, Shan State Special Region No. 4
Menglian	Provincial	August 1991	Bangkang, Shan State Special Region No. 2
Nansan	Provincial	August 1991	Kokang Laukkai, Shan State Special Region No. 1
Cangyuan	Provincial	September 1996	Nandeng, Shan State Special Region No. 2
Yingjiang	Provincial	August 1991	Laza, Kachin State Special Region No. 1
Zhangfeng	Provincial	August 1991	Lwejel, Lwejel township
Pianma	Provincial	August 1991	Datianba, Kachin State Special Region 1.

Source: Ports Office, Department of Commerce, Yunnan Province.

*China's ports are classified as national ports (approved by the central government) or provincial ports (approved by provincial governments). The national land ports are open to both Chinese and foreign vehicles transporting passengers and goods into or out of China by land, whereas the provincial land ports are only for petty trade in the border areas and restricted to the exit or entry of the local residents in these areas.

**Except Ruili and Wanding, the date refers to when the ports were approved to become provincial ones.

Myanmar has been working to transform border trade with China into normal trade to enhance the bilateral trade between the two countries. Myanmar will soon add one more border trade zone in the Kokang region built in Yan Lone Chai Township to facilitate trading between that region and Yunnan. From Myanmar's perspective, its border trade with China has experienced ups and downs, reflecting not only market situations but also political, security, and macroeconomic conditions.[18]

China's policies on border trading have also experienced adjustment and reorientation. In 1988, the Yunnan government formulated the policy of making full use of its geographical and resources advantages to develop Southeast Asian markets. The State Council promulgated rules and preferential policies on taxes, duties, exchange rates, and export drawbacks to boost border trade in 1991 and 1992. In 1992, Yunnan established the Administration of Border Economy and Trade, and Beijing approved Wanding and Ruili as open cities along the Chinese border. In the same year, two state-level border economic cooperation zones, Ruili Border Economic Cooperation Zone (Ruili BECZ) and Wanding Border Economic Cooperation Zone (Wanding BECZ), were founded with the approval of the State Council to promote the border trade between China and Myanmar. Now, Yunnan is lobbying Beijing to establish a China–Myanmar Cross-border Economic and Cooperation Zone in the province.

In accordance with China's border trade regulations of 1996, goods imported as exchanging goods by the border residents in amounts less than RMB1,000 per person per day shall be exempt from tariffs and import duties. In case the amount exceeds RMB1,000, the excessive amount shall be levied on tariffs and import duties in compliance with stipulated tax rates. With the quick progress of border trade, the free-duty and tariff quota was raised to RMB3,000 in 1998 and RMB8,000 in 2008.

The Measures for the Administration of Foreign Exchange in Border Trade, promulgated by the State Administration of Foreign Exchange in September 2003, granted that Chinese traders and enterprises could conduct settlements using RMB in the border trade. With a view to promoting the development of border trade between China and its surrounding countries, Beijing approved a program as of 1 January 2004, that taxes on the export of goods under small-

---

18 Toshihiro Kudo, "Myanmar's Economic Relations with China: Can China Support the Myanmar Economy?" Institute of Developing Economies, JETRO Discussion Paper No. 66, 2006, p. 11. For Myanmar's policy changes on border trade with China, see the same paper, pp. 10–12.

scale border trade in Yunnan settled in Renminbi by means of banking transfers and cash could be refunded 70 percent and 40 percent, respectively. The export tax rebate (exemption) policies shall apply to export transactions settled only in foreign exchange before this new provision. Because the refundable rate of 70 percent was not attractive for the traders and the policy was not effective, "Upon the approval of the State Council, as of October 1, 2004, the rate of the refundable amount of taxes has been adjusted from the present 70 percent to 100 percent if the export of goods under small-scale border trade in Yunnan is settled in Renminbi by means of banking transfers."[19]

At the end of 2008, China signed settlement agreements with eight neigh-boring countries including Myanmar, with a voluntary choice of settlement currency. In a bid to facilitate transactions in border trade in September 2009, the China Construction Bank and the Agricultural Bank of China signed agreements opening RMB settlement accounts with the Myanmar Economic Bank to establish direct banking relations between the two countries in a bid to facilitate transactions in border trade. Commercial banks from Myanmar will link with their counterparts from Ruili and Jiegao in China starting in 2010.

Up to 2009, China had opened 11 land ports with Myanmar (see Table 6), though there are four official trade posts on the Myanmar side of the border with Yunnan. Apart from Muse, Lwejel, and Kyukok, the other trade points are located in ceasefire group-controlled areas.

Among 20 Yunnan ports, the ports to Myanmar are the most important and busiest in terms of trade volume, freight volume, the number of entry-exit vehicle, and personnel. For Myanmar and China, Muse and Ruili have played the most important roles in bilateral border trade. Muse (mile 105) is the most lucrative and the busiest trading point in the country; its trade volume with China accounts for 50 percent of Myanmar landborne trade and 75 percent of border trade.[20] According to Kunming Customs, when Yunnan small-scale border trade volume in 2007 amounted to US$1.01 billion and Sino–Myanmar border trade hit US$0.7m, the Ruili export figure was US$0.3 billion and held 52.6 percent of the border trade export volume in the province.[21] From 2000 to 2008, according to statistics, Ruili border trade volume made up 64 percent of Yunnan–Myanmar trade and 26 percent of China–Myanmar trade. Ruili port

19 "Trial Implementation of Tax Refund (Exemption) for Export of Goods under Small-scale Border Trade Settled in Renminbi", *Finance and Accounting for International Commerce*, No. 1, 2005, p. 13.

20 Study on Ruili–Muse Cross-border Economic and Cooperation Zone, www.dehong.gov. cn/dehong/yearbook/2009/0523/overview-8208.html.

21 "Yunnan Border Trade Hit US$ 1 Billion", *Spring City Evening*, 23 January 2008.

Table 7: Myanmar's border trade with China (1991–2008) (US$ million)

Fiscal Year	Exports	Imports	Total value	Trade balance	Total border trade	% of border trade
1991–92	52.52	54.47	106.99	−1.95	139.27	76.82
1992–93	58.50	131.24	189.74	−72.74	257.93	73.56
1993–94	27.04	90.23	117.27	−63.19	248.04	47.28
1994–95	29.96	65.08	95.04	−35.12	231.87	40.99
1995–96	22.03	229.31	251.34	−207.28	335.95	74.81
1996–97	29.82	158.68	188.50	−128.86	357.13	52.78
1997–98	86.44	59.37	145.81	−27.07	257.06	56.72
1998–99	94.88	99.41	194.29	−4.53	300.27	64.71
1999–00	96.39	94.90	191.29	+1.49	344.39	55.54
2000–01	124.38	100.11	224.48	+24.28	411.74	54.52
2001–02	133.12	115.85	248.96	+17.27	505.83	49.22
2002–03	158.17	132.57	290.74	+25.60	460.57	63.13
2003–04	177.26	163.84	341.10	+83.42	531.80	64.14
2004–05	246.46	176.37	422.83	+70.09	687.88	61.47
2005–06	285.88	195.48	481.36	+90.4	716.73	67.16
2006–07	453.12	296.64	749.76	+156.48	1092.61	68.62
2007–08	555.48	421.95	977.43	+133.53	1329.53	73.52

Source: Maung Aung Myoe, "Sino–Myanmar Economic Relations Since 1988," Asia Research Institute, National University of Singapore, Working Paper No. 86, April 2007, p. 10; Department of Border Trade, Myanmar Ministry of Commerce.

has become the largest border trade port not only in Yunnan province but also among inland provinces and regions in China; 50 to 60 percent of the goods and commodities for border trade in the province passed through Ruili port, where the average vehicle flow per day amounted to over 1,500.[22]

China is the biggest border trading partner of Myanmar. "The Myanmar government also promoted all border trade not only with China but also with Thailand, India, and Bangladesh to compensate for the economic sanctions imposed by the West, and the Chinese border recorded a most meaningful success. Thus, Myanmar's border trade with China has become a main artery of its economy."[23] Table 7 indicates that the lion's share of Myanmar's border trade is with China. The value of China–Myanmar border trade accounted for an average of 61.47 percent of Myanmar's total border trade from 1991/92 to 2007/08.

22 "China–Myanmar Border Trade Routeway: Ruili, the Golden Port", *Spring City Evening*, 10 April 2009.
23 Toshihiro Kudo, "Myanmar's Economic Relations with China", 2008, p. 97.

Myanmar's documented cross-border exports through Muse, Myawaddy, and Kawthaung account for 41 percent, 19 percent, and 12 percent, respectively, of the total value of documented cross-border exports from Myanmar.[24] The data in Table 7 also shows that Myanmar has had a positive border trade balance with China since 1999/2000. In the Myanmar–China border trade, the most frequently exported items are agricultural products, aquatic products, and rubber and its products, while the main items that Myanmar imports from China are electric goods and machinery, textiles, chemicals, steel, daily-used products, and pharmaceuticals. However, as Maung Aung Myoe notes:

> Chinese data can by no means be considered fully accurate in terms of Sino–Myanmar trade, but the figures are generally more reliabie than those of Myanmar. Myanmar data show a different picture on Sino–Myanmar trade. It is generally agreed among Myanmar scholars that the Myanmar trade statistics are notoriously unreliable and that the figures are often completely distorted. Generally, Myanmar trade data are undervalued. This is due not only due to different methods of calculation, but also more importantly to widespread corruption in trade and customs offices as well as among border security authorities. Myanmar data show smaller deficits and even surpluses for Myanmar.[25]

According to Chinese official statistics, the value of Sino–Myanmar trade accounted for only 1.2 percent of China–ASEAN total trade value from 2000 to 2008. Myanmar is also not important for China's overall border trade, and it has not been on the list of China's major border trading partners. In 2008, China's three largest border trade partners were Russia, Kazakhstan, and Kyrgyzstan. However, the border trade between the two countries is critical for Yunnan as indicated in Table 8. Over 50 percent of China–Myanmar trade value is Yunnan–Myanmar trade, while the border trade constituted 76 percent of Yunnan–Myanmar trade volume from 2000 to 2009.

Although Chinese official statistics show that the border trade was a large percentage of Yunnan–Myanmar total trade, the actual value of border trade should be much higher due to the underground trade. In accordance with Myanmar's regulations, the private sector is prohibited from exporting through border areas some agricultural products, minerals, metals, animals, animal products, arms and ammunition, antiques and teak, and importing beer,

---

24 Winston Set Aung, "The Role of Informal Cross-border Trade in Myanmar", p. 24.
25 Maung Aung Myoe, "Sino–Myanmar Economic Relations Since 1988", p. 7.

Table 8: Yunnan's trade with Myanmar, 2000–2009 (US$ million)

Year	Total			Exports		Imports	
	Value	Share of China–Myan-mar trade	Border trade share of Yunnan–Myanmar trade	Value	Share of China–Myanmar trade	Value	Share of China–Myanmar trade
2000	362.99	58.5%	79.1%	293.06	59.1%	69.93	55.9%
2001	348.73	55.2%	73.4%	251.51	50.6%	97.22	72.6%
2002	406.78	47.2%	68.8%	296.08	40.8%	110.70	80.8%
2003	492.79	45.8%	64.9%	356.85	39.3%	135.94	80 %
2004	551.32	48.2%	72.8%	386.61	41.2%	164.71	79.6%
2005	631.62	52.2%	84.2%	410.63	43.9%	220.99	80.7%
2006	692.08	47.4%	81.2%	521.13	43.2%	170.95	67.6%
2007	873.57	42.4%	80.3%	640.68	37.9%	232.89	62.9%
2008	1192.79	45.4%	78.6%	727.69	36.8%	465.10	71.8%
2009	1227.33	42.2%	79.7%	775.06	34.3%	452.27	70.0%

Source: Department of Commerce of Yunnan Province; *Yunnan Yearbook*; Statistics of Kunming Customs.

cigarettes, liquors, plastic household goods affecting the domestic industries.[26] Additionally, "There are still various constraints such as an export-first policy, the licensing system, and high taxes related to exports in conducting formal trade. This has led to a situation where informal practices have expanded drastically, especially in border areas."[27] In 1989, Bertil Lintner wrote that the value of China–Myanmar border trade (including illegal trade) was about US$1.5 billion after Myanmar legalized the border trade.[28] On both China and Myanmar soil, numerous brokers constituted a net working for the underground economy. Now, there are still over 40 underground banks in Ruili, although the government has been fighting illegal banking since 2004.[29]

As a rule, the RMB is chosen as the settlement currency in the Yunnan border trade. Less than 3 percent of the total passes through China's customs clearance using RMB for settlement payments. The majority of export traders

26   For the rule, see www.commerce.gov.mm/eng/dobt/procedures.html.
27   Winston Set Aung, "The Role of Informal Cross-border Trade", p. 6.
28   Bertil Lintner, "The Busy Border: Burma's contraband trade with China is booming", *Far Eastern Economic Review*, 8 June 1989, p. 104.
29   Liu Lang, "Yunnan: Over 95 Percent of the Settlement of Border Trade Using RMB", *China Business News*, 6 January 2009.

choose the blackmarket banks to settle accounts. In addition to evasion of duty, they can provide more convenient and more expeditious settlement with less remittance charges than international banks.[30] Thus, a considerable disparity occurs in the statistics on Yunnan–Myanmar trade between those of the Kunming Customs and reality.

Chinese Development Assistance, and Economic and Technical Cooperation

In the context of sanctions and the nonengagement policy of most Western countries, the development assistance provided by Beijing and the economic and technical cooperation between the two countries have been regarded as one proof that China is that isolated country's leading backer. It is difficult to probe the subject because reliable data on assistance and cooperation are by no means easy to find and both sides seldom release the details of cooperation. The specific number of assistance and cooperation agreements and protocols signed by both sides are not available. According to the Yunnan Commerce Department, from the mid-1980s to 2005, China and Myanmar signed fifteen agreements of economic and technical cooperation.[31] Myanmar released a statement that "The progress of economic cooperation between Myanmar and China can be witnessed as over 30 economic agreements were signed" between 2004 and 2006.[32] It is estimated that up to 2010, at least over one hundred assistance and economic and technical cooperation agreements were signed by China and Myanmar. These agreements are involved not only with the traditional cooperation sectors such as agriculture, industry, and trade, but also in new sectors including tourism, mining, communication, technology, and fisheries.

China–Myanmar economic cooperation boosts bilateral political ties. The effect firstly is reflected in a series of agreements signed by the two leaderships when they exchanged visits. In July 1993, China and Myanmar signed six agreements on economic and technical cooperation, and Beijing offered a RMB50 million interest-free loan to Yangon. In 1996, Myanmar acquired a RMB150 million discount-interest loan from China, and both sides established a "Myanmar–China Economic Cooperation Promotion Committee" to further

---

30   Yin Hongwei, "Settlement Using RMB VS Blackmarket Banks", *South Wind Window*, No. 10, 2009.

31   The Economic and Technical Cooperation Agreements and Pacts Signed by China and ASEAN Countries, www.bofcom.gov.cn/bofcom/432914020329062400/20051110/4646.html.

32   "Minister for Commerce attends 50th Anniversary of Sino–Myanmar Gathering in Yunnan Province", *The New Light of Myanmar*, 23 December 2006.

bilateral economic ties. Myanmar used the RMB150 million loans to construct production lines of automobile disc wheels and automotive radiators.

In May 1997, the two countries signed the Agreement on Myanmar–China Economic Cooperation Promotion, and the Agreement of Formation of the Sino–Myanmar Joint Committee on Economic, Trade and Technological Cooperation. According to the latter agreement, the main functions of the joint working committee are to examine the implementation of relevant agreements signed between them on economic, trade, and technical cooperation and to jointly explore the possibilities of carrying out various forms of economic cooperation.[33] Two months later, when Chinese Vice Premier Wu Bangguo visited Myanmar, the two sides signed a loan agreement, under which the Chinese government provided a preferential loan to Myanmar totaling RMB100 million. The Myanmar government used the loan to build a production line of automobile throttles; it was put into operation in 2003. In 1998, China offered Myanmar a preferential loan amounting to US$150 million to cope with the impact of the Asian financial crisis.

In 2000, Myanmar General Maung Aye, Vice Chairman of the SPDC, paid an official visit to China to mark the fiftieth anniversary on 8 June 1950 of the establishment of diplomatic relations. Standing behind the political ties was a package of agreements and contracts signed by the two countries. Among them, the most important agreement was the Joint Statement on the Framework of Future Bilateral Relations and Cooperation (See Appendix 1). The fourth article of the statement stressed that "Both sides agree to further strengthen cooperation in trade, investment, agriculture, fishery, forestry and tourism on the basis of equality and mutual benefit, priority to actual results, and taking advantage of the other's strength."[34] Meanwhile, the Agreement on Economic and Technical Cooperation, Agreement on Tourism Cooperation, Agreement on Science and Technology Cooperation, and a Memorandum of Understanding (MoU) on the implementation plan for outbound travel by Chinese citizens to Myanmar were reached.[35] On 26 August 2001, China and Myanmar signed an Economic and Technical Cooperation Agreement in Yangon on the traffic sector. Jiang Zemin's 2001 trip was the first Chinese presidential visit since 1988. During this visit,

---

33 Ministry of Foreign Affairs, PRC (ed.), *Collection of Treaties of the People's Republic of China* (1997), Vol. 44, Beijing: World Affairs Press, 1999, p. 141.
34 For the Joint Statement, see: www.fmprc.gov.cn/chn/wjb/zzjg/yzs/gjlb/1271/1272/t23684.htm.
35 "Agreements between Myanmar and People's Republic of China signed", *The New Light of Myanmar*, 17 July 2000.

seven bilateral agreements were signed.[36] Also, Jiang suggested listing agriculture, human resources, natural resources, and infrastructure construction as key fields of furthering bilateral cooperation.

During Assistant Minister of Commerce of China Chen Jian's visit to Myanmar in December 2002, the two sides signed a framework agreement on China's provision of a concessional loan and another agreement on economic and technical cooperation. These loans extended by China were used for infrastructural construction.

When Than Shwe, the Chairman of SPDC, visited China again at the invitation of President Jiang Zemin in January 2003, Jiang promised that "Assistance will be provided to Myanmar's development tasks as much as possible. Under the economic and technological cooperation program, China will provide RMB50 million to Myanmar and give a special loan of US$200 million for the development tasks."[37]

In December 2003, China and Myanmar signed a framework agreement on the provision of concessional loans and another agreement on economic and technical cooperation. Under the prior agreement, the Chinese government would provide a concessional loan for use in the second phase of a key communication network project of Myanmar, while under the latter agreement, China would extend an interest-free loan to Myanmar for use in mutually agreed projects.[38] In March 2004, China's Vice Premier Wu Yi led an economic delegation of some 40 Chinese leading entrepreneurs to Myanmar. During

---

36 The Protocol on Cooperation in Border Areas; the contract for Improving Petroleum Recovery on 10R-4 Pyay Field; the Agreement on Economic and Technical Co-operation; the Agreement on the Promotion and Protection of Investments; the Agreement on Phytosanitary Cooperation; the Agreement on Cooperation in Animal Health and Quarantine; and the Agreement on Cooperation in Fisheries. See Ministry of Foreign Affairs, PRC (ed.), *Collection of Treaties of the People's Republic of China* (2001), Vol. 48, Beijing: World Affairs Press, 2003, pp. 161–169.

37 "Senior General Than Shwe, President Jiang Zemin Discuss Bilateral Cooperation", *The New Light of Myanmar*, 12 January 2003. At the same time, three agreements were signed, including the Agreement on Health Cooperation, the Agreement on Economic and Technical Cooperation, and the Agreement on Cooperation in the Field of Sports. In the same month, Vice Premier Li Lanqing was invited to visit Myanmar, and the two sides reached an agreement on partial debt relief for Myanmar, a Memorandum of Understanding on Extending a Grant of RMB5 million for the Supply of Culture, Education and Sporting Goods by China to Myanmar and another MoU on the Program of Aerospace and Maritime Courses Provided by China to Myanmar.

38 China, Myanmar sign agreements on loan, economic cooperation, chenjian2.mofcom.gov.cn/aarticle/activity/200412/20041200008329.html.

the visit, 21 agreements on trade and economic cooperation were signed.[39] Just four months later, Myanmar Prime Minister Khin Nyunt visited China. His trip was rewarding, and eleven documents on economic and technological cooperation were signed. The agreements included cooperation in trade promotion, energy and minerals exploration, telecommunications, and other industrial fields. The Chinese government also offered a US$150 million loan for telecommunications as well as a US$94 million rescheduling of debts.

Eight MoUs, agreements, and contract notes on economic and cooperation were signed between the two countries when Myanmar Prime Minister Soe Win visited China over 14–18 February 2006.[40] China and Myanmar signed another general loan agreement on the utilization of the preferential buyer's credit loan of US$200 million on 8 June 2006. The loan was used in implementing projects of five Myanmar Ministries in different sectors. At the end of 2006, China's Assistant Minister of Commerce Chen Jian granted a low-interest loan and debt cancellation to Myanmar in Yangon, reportedly of RMB300 million (US$38 million) and RMB240 million (US$30 million), respectively.[41] The two sides agreed to jointly work out three cooperation master plans on timber, mining, and agriculture and to initiate more cooperation master plans in the sectors of energy, industry, and infrastructure after working out the timber, mining, and agriculture master plans.[42] Additionally, an agreement of economic and technical cooperation and an exchange of letters on Myanmar scholars going to China were signed.

---

39 The main documents between the two governments included an agreement on economic and technical cooperation, a framework agreement on provision of concessional loans and a memorandum of understanding (MoU) on promotion of trade, investment and economic cooperation. Other documents covered agreements, MoUs, and contracts on cooperation in projects of communications, power plants, agricultural technology, agricultural machinery manufacturing, mineral exploration, fertilizers and railways. Under these agreements and contracts, Chinese companies initiated a large number of projects in Myanmar manufacturing, energy, and infrastructure sectors.

40 They were: Agreement on Economic and Technical Cooperation; Air Services Agreement; Agreement on the Chinese Ministry of Railways Donating Passenger Coaches to Myanmar; Memorandum of Understanding on the Construction of Greater Mekong Information Superhighway; a sub-loan agreement of US$31.50 million; a loan agreement for a urea fertilizer factory; a supply contract (phase-1) for Myanmar's National Telecommunication Network Construction Project; and a contract for the supply of mechanical and electrical equipment and services for Paunglaung Hydropower Project Phase II. Information Sheet of Myanmar Information Committee, www.myanmar-information.net/infosheet/2006/060219.htm.

41 "China Grants Myanmar Partial Debt Relief", *International Business Times*, 24 November 2006.

42 China, Myanmar sign economic, trade cooperation agreements, english.peopledaily.com.cn/200611/23/eng20061123_324523.html.

Two agreements of economic and technical cooperation were signed on 30 December 2006 and 16 November 2007, respectively. When Li Changchun, the member of the Standing Committee of the Political Bureau of the Communist Party of China Central Committee, visited Myanmar in March 2009, the two countries signed the Cooperation Agreement on the Myanmar Oil and Gas Pipelines; the Framework Agreement on Development of Hydropower Resources; the Agreement on Economic and Technical Cooperation; the Memorandum of Understanding Regarding Buyer's Credit for Construction Projects (Naypyitaw International Airport, hydropower plants and projects of Myanmar Ministry of Industry II).

It is difficult to distinguish the Chinese government's genuine development assistance from commercially based projects contracted by China's enterprises. During Premier Li Peng's visit to Myanmar in December 1994, he told the Burmese that China was developing a market economy, and China's enterprises would be the leading implementers of bilateral economic and technical cooperation. The economic assistance and free-interest loans previously provided by China's government would be gradually replaced by conventional and low-interest loans from banks. As a rule, when an assisted project is determined by China and Myanmar, the Department of Aid to Foreign Countries of China's Ministry of Commerce calls for bids on it in China. As development assistance and economic and technical cooperation between the two countries increase, more and more Chinese machinery, commodities, technology, and projects contracted by Chinese enterprises appear in Myanmar.

By the end of 2008, the contract value and turnover of contracted projects, labor services, design, and consulting by Chinese companies in Myanmar stood at US$5.38 billion and US$3.79 billion respectively.[43]

China contracted 18 projects in Myanmar from 1979 to 1993 and their contract value and turnover were US$70.49 million and US$70.56 million.[44] China's Foreign Ministry revealed that China's enterprises had contracted 800 projects in Myanmar by October 2002, whose contract value reached over US$2.1 billion.[45] Many assistance projects and business cooperative ventures initiated and conducted by China's local government and enterprises in the

---

43 Data of China–Myanmar Economic and Business Cooperation in 2008, mm.mofcom.gov. cn/aarticle/zxhz/tjsj/200902/20090206038342.html.

44 *China Foreign Economic Statistical Yearbook* (1994), Beijing: China Statistics Press, 1995, pp. 330–340.

45 China–Myanmar Bilateral Relations, www.xsbnjw.gov.cn/News_03/ReadNews.Asp? BigClassID=2&NewsID=365.

border area, and/or the economic and technical cooperation between Yunnan and ceasefire-controlled areas in Myanmar, are beyond official statistics.

Coupled with a great deal of development assistance from China, as well as economic and technical cooperation between the two countries, China's enterprises, notably state-owned economic enterprises, now flourish in Myanmar. According to Tang Hai, the former Commercial Counselor of the Chinese Embassy in Myanmar, Myanmar has become the fourth largest market of China's foreign engineering projects.[46]

Currently, it is impossible to find out the total of China's enterprises' involvement in the manufacturing sector in Myanmar because both countries disclose only some information on these projects, and most of the enterprises keep their expansion in overseas markets close. In consequence, the projects indicated in Table 9 are a tip of the proverbial iceberg for Chinese enterprises' involvement in the Myanmar manufacturing sector. During the second session of the Yunnan--Myanmar Economic and Trade Cooperation Forum in January 2010, Myanmar officials revealed that the textile, medicine, home appliance, and porcelain industries in Myanmar depend on China's capital and technology to operate.[47]

Chinese enterprises' engagement in the Myanmar manufacturing sector has two characteristics. First, almost all the Chinese contractors in the Myanmar manufacturing sector are strong state enterprises, behind which even stronger Chinese multinational corporations often stand. For example, Tianjin Machinery Import and Export Corporation is the subordinate of the Northern International Group. China National Machinery Industry Complete Engineering Corporation and China National Construction & Agricultural Machinery Imp./Exp. Corp are affiliated with China National Machinery Industry Corporation (SINOMACH). SINOMACH is the controlling shareholder of China CAMC Engineering Co., Ltd. China Huanqiu Contracting & Engineering Corp belongs to China National Petroleum Corporation (CNPC).

Second, China has adopted the strategy and policy of combining foreign assistance, economic and technical cooperation, and its "Go Global" admonition. The Department of Foreign Countries, Ministry of Commerce,

---

46   "Tang Hai, the Commercial Counselor of China Embassy in Myanmar, Talked About China–Myanmar Economic and Business Cooperation", *International Business Daily*, 24 January 2005 or *China–ASEAN Business Weekly*, October 17, 2005.

47   Myanmar Major Industries Depend on China's Capital and Technology, sousuo.mofcom.gov. cn/query/queryDetail.jsp?articleid=20100106756595&query=%E7%BC%85%E7%94%B8 %E4%B8%BB%E8%A6%81%E5%B7%A5%E4%B8%9A%E8%A1%8C%E4%B8%9A.

Table 9: Projects contracted by China in Myanmar's manufacturing sector since 2000 (contract value above US$ 10 million)

Project name	Contract date	Contractor	Contract value, US$ million	Fund source
Kyaukse Cemet Plant	June 2000	China National Construction & Agricultural Machinery Imp./Exp. Corp. (CAMC)	17	Supplier credit
Mobile Liquefied Petroleum Gas Plant	October 2000	China National Machinery Import & Export Corporation	13	
Kyaukse Agricultural Machinery Factory	May 2001	Zhejiang Sifang Group Corporation	17.5	Chinese interest-free loan
Salingyi Textile Plant	June 2001	China National Construction & Agricultural Machinery Imp./Exp. Corp. (CAMC)	21.92	
Yeni Paper Mill	12 December 2001	China Chengda Engineering Co., Ltd	81.5	Loan provided by The Export–Import Bank of China and China Construction Bank's Chengdu Branch
Kyaukse Hsinmin-1 Cement Plant	2 June 2000	China CAMC Engineering Co., Ltd. (CAMCE)	16.5	
Kyaukse Hsinmin-2 Cement Plant	18 January 2001	Yunnan Machinery & Equipment Import & Export Company Limited (in short form YMEC)	18.1	
Chauk Peracetic Acid Factory	21 April 2002	China National Machinery Industry Complete Engineering Corporation	12	
Pakokku Ttile Mill	2000	Tianjin Machinery Import and Export Corporation	27	Supplier credit

Pwintbyu Textile Mill	2000	Tianjin Machinery Import and Export Corporation	33	
Tabaung Bleached Pulp Factory	31 August 2000	China Metallurgical Construction	90	Supplier credit from Export– Import Bank of China
Pyaw Bwe and Myittha Spinning Factory	February 2007	Tianjin Shitong Machinery Imp. & Exp. Co., Ltd.	20	
Tabaung Paper Mill	February 2004	China Metallurgical Construction	20	
Taikkyi Fertilizer Factory	24 March 2004	China Huanqiu Contracting & Engineering Corp. (HQCEC) China CAMC Engineering Co., Ltd.	195	Chinese preferential loan and supplier credit
Dragon Cement Plant (Extention)	March 2002	Jiangsu Pengfei group Co., Ltd	11.52	
Thiliwa Shipyard II	January 1. 2003	China CAMC Engineering Co., Ltd. (CAMCE)	91.29	
Bilin Tire Plant	October 2007	China CAMC Engineering Co., Ltd. (CAMCE)	33	
Myanmar Float Glasswork	5 December 2007	China CAMC Engineering Co., Ltd. (CAMCE)	30	
Myanmar Xinhua Education Printing Co., Ltd	2006	Yunnan Xinhua Printing Company	10	Sino– Myanmar joint investment
Heavy Diesel Engine Manu- facturing Pro- ject (I phase)	25 August 2010	Shandong Puli Construction Engineering Co., Ltd	67	

Source: China's Commercial Ministry; Jiangsu Pengfei Group, Co., Ltd; China CAMC Engineering Co., Ltd; China National Machinery & Equipment Import & Export Corporation; China Metallurgical Group Corporation; *Economic Information Daily*; *Yunnan Daily*; *China Chemical Industry News*; *China Building Materials News*.

says that China's foreign aid supports "Go Global". Most assistance and coop-eration projects between the two countries are tied to Chinese state-owned economic enterprises. Meanwhile, the Chinese government provides export credits to the enterprises which win the bids or purchase orders for projects in Myanmar. This policy not only removes China's enterprises' worry about the turbulent situation there, but also avoids the dilemma of foreign exchange and fund shortages in Myanmar. As a result, China's enterprises' massive involve-ment in Myanmar is the byproduct as well as the "propellant" of good political relations between both states

China's Investments in Myanmar

There have been no accurate statistics from the two countries' governments on China's investments in Myanmar since 1988 because many of them entered Myanmar without going through official channels and procedures. In 2009, the Investment Guide to Myanmar released by China's Ministry of Commerce stressed that some Chinese firms invested in Myanmar in the name of local citizens in order to escape Myanmar's policy restrictions on foreigners, but such investments would not be protected under Myanmar law. The relations between the central government and cease-fire groups' controlled areas are very subtle, and Chinese investors should not invest in these areas without Naypyitaw's permission.[48] That caution actually reveals that current Chinese investment in Myanmar includes both. They made use of policy defects and loopholes in military government regulations to acquire ID cards and invested there in the name of Myanmar subjects. For example, most Chinese migrants from Yunnan migrate to Myanmar as their country of destination with the purpose of conducting business or trade. Around 50 percent of population of Lashio, the most important city in northern Myanmar and 20 percent of population in Mandalay, the cultural capital of Myanmar, are Chinese. "The majority of their investments are not properly documented as they do business informally under the names of their local partners in order to avoid the complicated processes and high costs related to registered foreign investment."[49]

Some Yunnan state-owned enterprises have invested in Myanmar without the Chinese government's approval because they were reluctant to submit

48 *Guidelines for Overseas Investment and Cooperation in Other Countries and Regions (Myan-mar)*, 2009, p. 57.
49 Winston Set Aung, "Illegal Heroes and Victimless Crimes: Informal Cross-border Mi-gration from Myanmar", ASIA PAPER, Sweden Institute for Security and Development Policy, December 2009, p. 10.

Table 10: Top ten largest foreign investors in Myanmar, up to 31 May 2009 (US$ million)

Ranking	Country	Number of investment projects	Investment value	Percentage of total foreign investment
1	Thailand	59	7406.843	46.98%
2	UK	50	1860.549	11.80%
3	Singapore	72	1553.213	9.85%
4	China	28	1331.439	8.44%
5	Malaysia	33	660.747	4.19%
6	Hong Kong	31	504.218	3.20%
7	France	2	469.000	2.97%
8	U.S.	15	243.565	1.54%
9	Indonesia	12	241.497	1.53%
10	South Korea	37	239.318	1.52%

Source: "The Latest Rank of Foreign Investment in Myanmar", Economic and Commercial Counselor's Office of the Embassy of China in Myanmar.

applications for foreign investment permission due to red tape or they were not qualified to invest abroad. In fact, Chinese private investment in Myanmar does not need the approval of China's government.[50] The Myanmar Investment Commission also fails to count and control unofficial Chinese investments. Consequently, the official statistics on China's investment in Myanmar from both sides just reflects major investments and cooperation usually pushed by the two governments.

By 31 December 2004, China was the 13th largest foreign investor in Myanmar, having an investment of US$103.9 million in 22 projects.[51] According to the Myanmar Investment Commission, up to 31 December 2007, China's contracted investment in Myanmar reached US$475 million in 27 projects. And China was in the sixth place in Myanmar's foreign investors, whose investment volume held 3.23 percent of total foreign investment.[52] Up to the end of May 2009, China stood 4th in Myanmar's foreign investment line-up – US$1.331 billion.

50   Current Account Management Department of State Administration of Foreign Exchange (ed.), *Currency Crossborder Circulation and Management on Foreign Exchange in Border Trade*, Beijing: China Financial and Economic Publishing House, 2005, pp. 234–235.

51   Statistics of FDI in Myanmar, mm.mofcom.gov.cn/aarticle/ztdy/200509/20050900388228. html.

52   China Ranking 6th of 2007 FDI in Myanmar, mm.mofcom.gov.cn/aarticle/jmxw/ 200801/20080105340987.html.

Table 11: China's direct investment flows in ASEAN, 2003–2009 (US$ million)

Country	2003	2004	2005	2006	2007	2008	2009
Vietnam	12.75	16.85	20.77	43.52	110.88	119.84	112.39
Laos	0.80	3.56	20.58	48.04	154.35	87.00	203.24
Cambodia	21.95	29.52	5.15	9.81	64.45	204.64	215.83
Myanmar	–	4.09	11.54	12.64	92.31	232.53	376.70
Thailand	57.31	23.43	4.77	15.84	76.41	45.47	49.77
Malaysia	1.97	8.12	56.72	7.51	–32.82	34.43	53.78
Singapore	–3.21	47.98	20.33	132.15	397.73	1550.95	1414.25
Indonesia	26.80	61.96	11.84	56.94	99.09	173.98	226.09
Philippines	0.95	0.05	4.51	9.30	4.50	33.69	40.24
Brunei	–	–	1.50	–	1.18	1.82	58.10
Total	119.32	195.56	157.71	335.75	968.08	2484.35	2698.10

Source: *China Commerce Yearbook 2004–2010*

Table 10 shows that the investment value of the top ten largest investors reached 92.02 percent of Myanmar's total foreign investment. ASEAN countries are the most important foreign investors in Myanmar. Thailand stands top in Myanmar's foreign investment ranking. Singapore's investment in the country covered the most fields: 12 sectors. Given China's indirect and unofficial investments, China would likely have been the top investor or on a par with Thailand in Myanmar's foreign investment ranking. In 2011, however, China officially surpassed Thailand to become Myanmar's largest investor.

Between 2004–05 and 2008–09 Myanmar fiscal years (beginning April 1), the Myanmar government approved 14 Chinese investment projects amounting to US$1,264.436 million according to the Foreign Investment Law. These projects were contracted and carried out by China's state enterprises after the two countries' central governments bargained over them. According to the Myanmar Central Statistical Organization (CSO), up to 31 July 2010, China's investment including Hong Kong swelled to US$12.3 billion and stood first on the FDI list. The dramatic growth largely arises from China's major investment in the last two years, such as the China–Myanmar oil & gas pipelines and the hydropower plants in the Kachin State. In addition, Hong Kong's investment in Myanmar has been included in the data on China's investment since 2010.[53]

53   China including Hong Kong stands top in Myanmar's FDI Ranking, mm.mofcom.gov.cn/
     aarticle/zxhz/tjsj/201010/20101007188073.html.

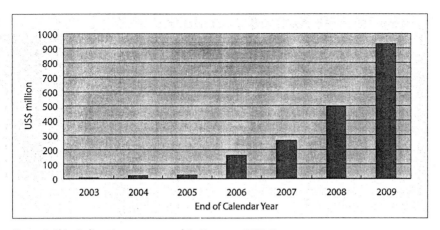

Figure 1: China's direct investment stock in Myanmar, 2003–9.
Source: *China Commerce Yearbook* 2010, p. 185.

In the context of China's direct investment in ASEAN, China's official statistics reveal that Myanmar was not an attractive investment destination for China in Southeast Asia before 2008. But a significant change has taken place in the situation and Myanmar has become the second largest investment destination for China in ASEAN countries since 2008 (see Table 11).

Both China's and Myanmar's official statistics indicate that China's investment in Myanmar is rising sharply (see Figure 1). Doubtless, the real amount of Chinese investment in Myanmar greatly outnumbers the official statistics. This condition can be attributed to a great deal of Chinese investment without the permission of Naypyitaw (including investments in the name of local citizens and in cease-fire group areas).

By 31 July 2010, China had invested US$12.3 billion in eight sectors of Myanmar, of which mining, electric power, and oil and gas respectively took US$1.88 billion, US$5.31 billion and US$4.95 billion.

China has made heavy investments in strategic sectors of Myanmar, such as oil, gas, and other resources (see Figure 2). This reflects both China's growing concern for energy security in the long term, and Beijing's official investment policy towards Myanmar. According to the Countries and Industries for Overseas Investment Guidance Catalogue (I), China's official investments in Myanmar focus on energy and other resources sectors were motivated by Beijing.

In July 2004, China's Ministry of Commerce and Ministry of Foreign Affairs jointly promulgated the *Guidance Catalogue on Overseas Investment Industries in Other Countries (I)*. The Catalogue is a major reference for departments in charge of foreign economic cooperation at all levels, offering guidance and

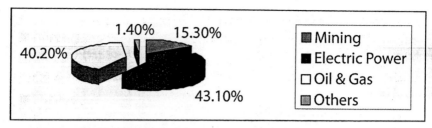

Figure 2: The makeup of China's investment in Myanmar, up to 31 July 2010.
Source: The Commercial Counselor of China's Embassy in Yangon, mm.mofcom.gov.cn/aarticle/zxhz/tjsj/201010/20101007188073.html.

verification of overseas investment by Chinese enterprises. Any enterprise complying with the Catalogue and verified to hold an overseas investment approval certificate shall have the priority right to enjoy state preferential policies in such areas as funding, foreign exchange, tax collection, customs, and exit and entry. According to this Catalogue, China's enterprises are encouraged to invest in the fields of oil, gas, forestry, agricultural machinery manufacturing, and construction in Myanmar. As a result, China's official investments in Myanmar focus on energy and other resources sectors motivated by Beijing.

On 15 June 2009, China's Ministry of Commerce promulgated the *Guidelines for Overseas Investment and Cooperation in Other Countries and Regions (Myanmar)* to assist enterprises in obtaining information concerning the investment environment in host countries and regions. The Guideline reminds Chinese investors to notice that "The Myanmar government promulgated The Union of Myanmar Foreign Investment Law in 1988 and welcomes foreign investments, but the government still adheres to prudence and backward-looking [policies], and even introduces policy restrictions or sets up artificial barriers against foreign investors." Chinese investors will face three major difficulties in Myanmar: unsound legislation and unstable policy; poor infrastructure; and dual exchange rates with a large gap.[54] Regarding these risks and difficulties, the Guideline suggests that China's enterprises take out overseas investment insurance or guarantees provided by China Export and Credit Insurance Corporation (SINOSURE) and The Export–Import Bank of China (China Eximbank), which obligates the insurer to underwrite an investor's economic losses in overseas investment and profits caused by political and business risks of a host country.[55]

---

54 *Guidelines for Overseas Investment and Cooperation in Other Countries and Regions (Myanmar)*, p. 57.
55 *Ibid.*, p. 61.

The *2007 Handbook of Country Risk* released by SINOSURE has nine rankings, in which the first rank indicates the safest countries and the ninth signifies the most risky countries. The Handbook rated Myanmar eighth of nine in country-risk ranks, and asserted that "the country risk level of Myanmar is high".[56]

In a country listed as risky by China, Chinese investments can be classified as two types: first, official investments that are based on bilateral political relations in spite of serious risks in Myanmar, and which concentrate on energy, power, and resources sectors and are important for the two countries' energy security and development strategy; second, many small and medium investments without the two countries' approval that are beyond official statistics. The latter cope with the investment risks through two channels. They are invested in the cease-fire controlled areas neighboring Yunnan and are welcomed by local cease-fire leaders, where local government "legislates" to protect and attract foreign investment.[57] Or the investors have purchased Myanmar ID cards or have cooperated with local ethnic Chinese so that they can make investments in the name of Myanmar citizens. Using the ethnic Chinese business network in Myanmar, China's investors can avoid and reduce investment risks.

China–Myanmar Economic Relations in the Context of Regional and Sub-Regional Cooperation

With the end of the Cold War, economic globalization developed with unprecedented speed. Although some western countries' unilateral sanctions against Myanmar failed to achieve their political goal (regime change), they succeeded in impeding the country's integration into the global economy. However, this does not mean that Myanmar has been ignored by globalization. As part of economic globalization, regional and sub-regional cooperation are very active in East and Southeast Asia. Although under authoritarian governance, Myanmar has joined regional and subregional cooperative organizations such as the China–ASEAN FTA, Greater Mekong Sub-regional Cooperation (GMS), the Bay of Bengal Initiative for Multi-Sectoral Technical and Economic Cooperation (BIMSTEC), and the Mekong–Ganga Cooperation.

In recent years, China has been very enthusiastic in regional cooperation in peripheral areas. Beijing regards cooperation as the springboard of its "Peaceful

---

56 China Export and Credit Insurance Corporation, *Handbook of Country Risk (2007)* Vol. I, Beijing: China Finance Press, 2007, p. 149.
57 See Investment Regulation in Shan State Special Region No. 1, www.kokang.net/html/falvfagui/2008/1215/17.html.

Rise" as well as a way of coping with the "China Threat." In the context of an era of change and a rising new regionalism, regional cooperation adds new elements and dimensions to China–Myanmar bilateral ties. Meanwhile, some bilateral relations are being drawn into the framework of regional cooperation, and are pushed by a regional platform.

In November 2000, China initiated the China–ASEAN FTA, and got active responses from ASEAN countries. Two years later, the Framework Agreement on Comprehensive Economic Co-operation between China and ASEAN was signed during the seventh ASEAN–China Summit in Phnom Penh. According to the agreement, both parties will establish the China–ASEAN FTAs covering trade in goods by 2010 for Brunei, China, Indonesia, Malaysia, the Philippines, Singapore, and Thailand, and by 2015 for the newer ASEAN member states, such as Cambodia, the Lao PDR, Myanmar, and Vietnam. By 2015, as a result, tariffs and non-tariff barriers in substantially all trade in goods will be eliminated and trade in services with substantial sectoral coverage will be liberalized between China and ASEAN. On the same day when the agreement was signed, China implemented a debt relief plan in Asia, and remitted part or all of Vietnam's, Laos', Cambodia's and Myanmar's overdue debt.

At the ASEAN Plus One summit with China on 4 November 2002 at Phnom Penh, China agreed to grant Myanmar unilateral preferential tariffs for 110 products. China exchanged a letter with Myanmar, entitling it to special preferential duty treatment. An "Early Harvest Program" (EHP) of tariff cuts on agricultural products was launched in 2004. Under the program, from 1 January 2004 China gave 133 products from Myanmar preferential access to its market. The EHP takes into account that special and differential treatment shall be given to Cambodia, the Lao PDR, Myanmar, and Vietnam, which would allow China to eliminate Myanmar and Laos tariffs on 600 agricultural products no later than 2010. In order to boost intra-regional trade cooperation, China's Premier Wen Jiabao stated at the GMS Summit in 2005 that China would unilaterally expand the range of products eligible for preferential tariff from Laos, Cambodia, and Myanmar as of 1 January 2006. China signed exchanges of letters on special and preferential tariff treatment with the three countries on 11 December 2005. According to the documents, starting from 1 January 2006, some categories of goods exported to China from the three countries, mainly vegetables and fruits, would enjoy zero-tariff treatment. The preferential policy would apply to 83 categories of goods from Cambodia, 91 categories of goods from Laos, and 87 categories of goods from Myanmar.

China and ASEAN signed the Agreement on Trade in Goods of the Framework Agreement on Comprehensive Economic Cooperation in 29 November 2004. In accordance with the relevant schedules in the agreement, the six original ASEAN countries (Brunei Darussalam, Indonesia, Malaysia, Philippines, Singapore, Thailand) and China shall eliminate all its tariffs for tariff lines placed in the Normal Track not later than 1 January 2010. As the newer ASEAN member state, Myanmar was allowed to reduce tariffs to 0–5 percent of its tariff lines under the Normal Track not later than 1 January 2010 and shall eliminate its tariffs not later than 1 January 2013 on 40 percent of its tariff lines placed in the Normal Track. Myanmar shall reduce its applied Most Favored Nations (MFN) tariff rates of tariff lines placed in its Sensitive Lists to 20 percent not later than 1 January 2015. These said tariff rates shall be subsequently reduced to 0–5 percent not later than 1 January 2020.

The second component of the FTA with ASEAN is the trade in services, which entered into force on 1 July 2007. Under this Agreement, services and services suppliers/providers in the region enjoy improved market access and national treatment in sectors/subsectors where commitments have been made. It is expected that the agreement will lead to the expansion and growth of the four modes of trade in services, namely: cross-border supply, consumption abroad, commercial presence, and movement of natural persons. The market-access commitments of both China and ASEAN are contained in the first package of the agreement. Both ASEAN and China agreed to progressively liberalize trade in services with substantial sectoral coverage. China is committed to open up new markets for the ASEAN countries in 26 branches of 5 service areas on the basis of the original WTO commitments, namely: construction, environmental protection, transportation, sports, and commerce. Myanmar is committed to open its market to China and other ASEAN countries in finance, telecommunication, construction, and commercial services.

On 12 April 2009, China agreed to set up a US$10 billion China–ASEAN Investment Cooperation Fund to finance major 10+1 investment cooperation projects in infrastructure, energy and resources, information and communication technology, and other fields. In the next three to five years, China will provide ASEAN countries with US$15 billion credit, including US$1.7 billion in concessional loans. "China is also considering providing a total of RMB270 million this year [2009] in special aid to the less developed ASEAN countries, including Cambodia, Laos, and Myanmar, to help them meet pressing needs and get through this difficult time. China has already contributed US$900,000 to the 10+3 Cooperation Fund and US$100,000 to the ASEAN Foundation, and will provide an additional US$5million to the China–ASEAN Cooperation Fund."[58] Moreover, China will host a series of training programs to strengthen information and experience-sharing with ASEAN, and jointly increase capacity in natural disaster management. In the next five years, China will provide another 2,000 government scholarships and 200 MPA scholarships to developing countries in East Asia.

The China–ASEAN Expo and China–ASEAN Business and Investment Summit since 2004 have annually been convened in Nanning, the capital of south China's Guangxi province. The Expo has become a significant platform for China–ASEAN regional cooperation. The Myanmar Prime Minister or Secretary-1 of SPDC has led a delegation to attend the Expo and Summit every year except 2007 and 2010. Myanmar has begun to pay more attention to a new potential trading partner – Guangxi. On October 29, 2009, the Myanmar Consulate-General in Nanning was opened. Meanwhile, the Union of Myanmar Federation of Chambers of Commerce and Industry (UMFCCI), the biggest business organization in the country, opened a representative office in Nanning to strengthen bilateral trade activities with China as well as with other ASEAN member countries.

The Greater Mekong Subregion (GMS) cooperation is another important institution having an impact on China–Myanmar economic relations. In 1992, the Asian Development Bank (ADB) initiated the GMS Economic Cooperation and Development Program for China, Cambodia, Laos, Myanmar, Thailand, and Vietnam in the Mekong River region, designed to enhance economic relations among the countries. At present, China deepens and prioritizes cooperation with other GMS member states in nine sectors, including transportation, communications, environmental protection, agriculture, energy sources, tourism, environment, human resources development, as well as trade facilitation and investment.

Under the GMS framework, China and Myanmar mainly develop cooperation in the sectors of communication, human resources and transportation. On July 2005, six GMS members signed am MoU on the Planning and Construction of a GMS Information Superhighway Network (ISN) during their meeting in Vientiane, Laos. Under the MoU, the six countries agreed to invest in the construction of an optic fiber cable system and cooperate on the project to build a commercialized information and communication platform in order to launch the basic fields of chatting, data sharing, connection of the

---

58   Wen Guojing, "Pan-Beibu Gulf Economic Cooperation Forum, the Important Cooperation Mechanism of China–ASEAN", *Guangxi Daily*, 19 May 2009.

internet, as well as distance education, medical treatment, e-government, and e-commerce, all of which will sharply raise the capacity of the internet to promote the socio-economic development of the subregion. As the main part of the GMS Information Highway, the China–Myanmar optical cable, Ruili–Muse SDH 2.5 GB/s Optical Transmission System, was prepared and designed in 2004. It was constructed from January to April 2005 and was put into use on 5 April 2005. China also offered a training course of GMS E-commerce to Myanmar and other GMS members.

In 2006, China promised to provide a loan of RMB300 million to the GMS Information Superhighway Myanmar section. The next year, both sides signed a loan agreement in Yangon. According to the plan, there are 12 ISN fiber links being built across the GMS to boost information links. In the Myanmar section, there are over 2000 kilometers of optical cable from Muse to Tachilek, via Mandalay and Yangon. Of Myanmar's two ISN links respectively with China and Thailand, the link with China was built since April 2007. Shanghai Alcatel–Lucent got the supply contract of ISN Myanmar section in 2007. In March 2008, the Myanmar–China fiber link was built across China from Kunming to Muse (on the China border) with its link further extended to reach Yangon.

The GMS program, with its emphasis on large-scale infrastructure development, regards transportation as the prioritized cooperation sector. The GMS Cross-Border Transport Agreement (GMS Agreement) is a multilateral instrument for the facilitation of cross-border transport of goods and people. China and Myanmar acceded into the agreement in 2002 and 2003, respectively, but both parties haven't held negotiations on the transport facilitation enforcement between Ruili and Muse as of this writing. The Lancang–Mekong River water route was formally open to navigation between China, Laos, Myanmar, and Thailand on 26 June 2001. However, the opening of navigation did not create the anticipated prosperity of trade, tourism, and transport in the areas along the river, largely because of poor navigational conditions.

After Premier Mahathir Mohammad of Malaysia initiated the Trans-Asia Railway, building the Kunming–Singapore Rail Link in 1995, the project was also promoted under the GMS mechanism. (For the details of the Lancang–Mekong River water route and the China–Myanmar railway, see Chapter 9)

One key element of the GMS program is to encourage establishing a competitive regional power market and system. Through the cross-border power trade and interconnection between their respective networks, the idea is to: [1] reduce national investments, operating costs, greenhouse gas emissions and other pollutants; [2] enhance the reliability of the electricity supply, including power supply from an interconnected network in case of power failure; and [3] share in other benefits resulting from the interconnected operations of the systems. The inter-government agreement on regional power trade was endorsed by six GMS member countries at the first GMS summit meeting on 3 November 2002. Now the interconnected electric power network is being built. Although the transmission line between China and Myanmar grids has not yet been connected, China plans to import 10–20 million kw of hydro-power from Myanmar between 2010 and 2020.[59]

China is actively engaged in personnel exchange and cooperation among GMS member countries, utilizing the "China–ASEAN Cooperation Fund" and the "Asia Regional Cooperation Special Fund" financed by China. Since 2005, through holding various workshops and technology training classes, relating to agriculture, energy, telecom, trade, investment, epidemic prevention, and logistics sectors at the firm, sector, national, and regional levels. After the Phnom Penh Plan for Development Management (PPP), a regional capacity-building initiative, was launched in November 2002, China's government supported the PPP through the China Regional Cooperation and Poverty Reduction Fund. A network of capacity-building partners has been created in the region. The Asia Pacific Finance and Development Center (AFDC) based in the Shanghai National Accounting Institute in Shanghai and The Kunming University of Science and Technology (KUST) are the PPP's network of capacity-building partners. Now, China each year trains a large number of officials and technical talents for other GMS countries.

The GMS countries adopted the economic corridor approach for development during the 8th GMS Ministerial Meeting held in Manila in 1998. This holistic strategy seeks to improve and enhance investments in transport, energy, and telecommunications in the subregion. Till now, the economic corridor has been developed with three initiatives, namely the North–South, East–West and Southern Economic Corridors. Originally, the Yangon–Mandalay–Kunming route was envisioned as part of the North–South Economic corridor but it was not approved. Now, two different routes along the north-south axis are involved in the North–South Economic Corridor initiative: (1) the Kunming–Chiang Rai–Bangkok via the Laos and Myanmar route, and (2) the Kunming–Hanoi–Haiphong route. Consequently, Myanmar is basically excluded from the North–South Economic Corridor.

---

59 Li Li, "Yunnan Boosts the GMS Electricity Cooperation", *Yunnan Daily*, 18 May 2007.

Tourism is regarded as one of the key sectors for further cooperation among the GMS countries. According to the GMS Tourism Sector Strategy, 13 priority tourism corridors, zones, circuits, and lines have been identified. Among the 13 special projects, there are four tourism corridors or zones including both China and Myanmar. They are the Mekong River Tourism Corridor, including all GMS countries; the Golden Quadrangle Tourism Zone, including Laos, Myanmar, Thailand, and Yunnan Province; the Heritage Necklace Circuit, including all GMS countries; the Shangri-la – Tengchong – Myitkina Tourism Development Zone, including Myanmar and Yunnan Province. In addition, China initiated compiling *The Plan of Transnational Tourist Lines in the Upper Mekong (Golden Square) Tourism Region* and *The Plan of Transnational Tourist Lines in the Western Yunnan–Northern Myanmar Region.*

At the end of the 1990s, Yunnan proposed regional economic cooperation among Bangladesh, China, India, and Myanmar (BCIM), and the idea was acclaimed by the other three countries. The first Conference on Regional Cooperation and Development among BCIM held in Kunming approved the Kunming Initiative on 17 August 1999. The Kunming Initiative was intended to emerge as a new economic forum in the region. The main thrust of the Initiative is to seek sub-regional economic cooperation, particularly in North-East India (NIE), Bangladesh, Myanmar, and the Southwest of China, and attempt to generate substantive economic benefits in the areas of trade, investment, energy, transport, and tourism. Up to 2009, the BCIM Forum on Regional Economic Cooperation had been held nine times. BCIM member countries signed some cooperation agreements and agreed to list infrastructure, transportation, and tourism as the priority cooperation sectors. The program, the BCIM Border Free Trade Area, is being advanced and promoted, and covers West of Yunnan province, the Shan State and Kachin States in Myanmar, Assam State and Arunachal Pradesh State in India, and Bangladesh border areas.

The BCIM forum, essentially a track-II endeavor, is primarily promoted by the non-governmental sectors of the member countries to influence policy-makers, business people, and government representatives in boosting regional cooperation by transform it into a growth quadrangle. Although Bangladesh, China, and Myanmar are eager to improve cooperation and transform it into an official mechanism, the position of the Indian government is lukewarm. Due to the various insurrections in Northeast India and Northwest Myanmar, the absence of political mutual trust between India and China, and unsatis-factory Myanmar–Bangladesh relations, it is impossible for China–Myanmar economic cooperation to develop in the near future within the context of the BCIM mechanism.

All kinds of regional cooperation mechanisms intersect in the triangulated area of China–Southeast Asia–South Asia, in which Japan, China, India, Russia, the U.S. and E.U. are all involved to one degree or another. These stakeholders' involvements are designed to diversify the interests of regional cooperation, and their intentions are the same, namely maximizing their national interests and ensuring their political and economic influence in the region. In the case of China, the most important political interest of its involvement in regional cooperation lies in easing the concerns in the region about the "China Threat." Although Beijing has asserted that China's rise will be peaceful, whether the historical memories of "Revolutionary Export" or the witness of China's realpolitik diplomacy in Africa will allow the circumjacent countries to believe the northern power's vow is questionable. If ASEAN countries could share more of the fruits of China's rapid economic development through regional cooperation, and if both sides could develop common interests, the regional platforms will become one of the best approaches to eliminate the perception of a "China Threat." Meanwhile, regional cooperation adds new facets and dimensions to China–Myanmar bilateral relations. Although China and Southeast Asia established the scope of regional cooperation, China has devised some programs such as the Kunming–Rangoon Highway, the China–Myanmar Highway–Waterway Combined Transport Passage, and the China–Myanmar Cross Border Economic Zone, and has tried its best to bring them into the regional cooperation network.

Regional cooperation will deepen economic and business cooperation between China and Southeast Asia, notably in mainland Southeast countries which, except for Thailand, are poor and devoid of accumulated capital. China's loans, investments, development assistance, and technology appeal to them, and increase their favorable attitudes toward China. Also, Beijing is combining the "Western Development" strategy with regional cooperation in order to acquire a new impetus for development in Yunnan and Guangxi. On the part of Myanmar, regional cooperation has the function of providing a buffer against Western economic sanctions, and increases the military regime's international legitimacy at the same time.

Yunnan–Myanmar Economic Relations

Among China's peripheral countries and regions, developing countries like Myanmar, Laos, Vietnam, and Nepal did not play key roles in China's external trade. But for landlocked Yunnan Province, distant from the east coast, neighboring Myanmar has different economic implications and values. It is necessary to distinguish the economic ties between Beijing–Myanmar and Yunnan–Myanmar when the two countries' economic relations are discussed, and we can develop insights into the different pursuits of interests and the correlation between China's central and local government.

For Beijing, Myanmar has not occupied an important position in China's overall foreign trade. Between 2000 and 2008, the volume of China–Myanmar trade was only 1.2 percent of China–ASEAN trade.[60] However, Myanmar is the most important trade partner of Yunnan.

Also, Myanmar's importance for Yunnan is reflected by the fact that Yunnan–Myanmar trade accounts for the lion's share of two region's trade. Table 12 indicates that Yunnan–Myanmar trade volume has been half of the two region's total trade volume since 2000, while 80 percent of Yunnan–Myanmar trade is border trade. Given the small section of border in Myanmar controlled by the central government and the enormous and widespread smuggling and underground economy, Yunnan's trade with Myanmar is greatly underestimated. RMB is used for settling accounts in 95 percent of Yunnan border trade. According to the report of the Kunming Branch of the People's Bank of China, the RMB flow reached 66.986 billion between Yunnan and Vietnam, Laos, and Myanmar in 2007. The underground banks are very popular in the areas of the Yunnan border, as was mentioned earlier.

Although China introduced economic reform and the "open-door" policy in 1978, Beijing gave priority to the eastern provinces and coast regions before 2000. The marginalized provinces and regions in west China only took a favorable turn due to the launching of the "Western Development" and the "Go Global" policies in the new century. Consequently, Yunnan–Myanmar trade volume has risen sharply since 2001. In response, Yunnan also created opportunities and mechanism for economic cooperation with Myanmar.

Since 2001, exhibitions have been held annually and alternately in the respective China–Myanmar border towns aimed at promoting bilateral trade between the two countries. The Yunnan government has arranged for the entrepreneurs in the province to visit Myanmar to seek opportunities of expanding trade and economic cooperation. Over 12–16 March 2003, a strong economic and trade delegation from Yunnan, led by the Secretary of the Yunnan Provincial Committee of the CCP Bai Peien, visited Yangon and held trade and investment

---

60   Source: *China–ASEAN Yearbook, 2004–2009; China Commerce Yearbook, 2004.*

promotion meetings with its Myanmar counterparts. Both sides signed over 20 business contracts worth US$65.26 million.[61] In 2006 and 2007, the Yunnan government and the Myanmar Commerce Ministry jointly staged the China (Yunnan)–Myanmar Trade & Investment Promotion meeting in Yangon. In February 2007, the Yunnan Provincial Chamber of Commerce and the Union of Myanmar Federation of Chambers of Commerce and Industry (UMFCCI) signed a Framework Agreement on an Economic and Trade Cooperation Forum in order to expand trade and economic cooperation. Four months later, the first session of the Forum was convened in Kunming, and Myanmar held the second session on 11 January 2010. Apart from the cooperation platform aimed at Myanmar alone and instigated by Yunnan, a Kunming Import & Export Commodities Fair has been successfully held annually for sixteen consecutive years, in which Myanmar has participated from the first fair.

Cross-Border Tourism

Currently, Chinese tourists to Myanmar need only hold passports or border passes; there are, therefore, two kinds of tourism: cross-border tourism in frontier areas and the tourism in Myanmar proper. In June 2000, the Vice Chairman of the SPDC, General Maung Aye, visited China. He and Chinese Vice President Hu Jintao issued a "Joint Statement Concerning a Framework Document on Future Cooperation in Bilateral Relations between the People's Republic of China and the Union of Myanmar". In the statement, "China has agreed to make Myanmar a country of destination for Chinese citizens to go on overseas tours. Both sides will decide through consultation detailed ways of implementation." When Hu Jintao paid a reciprocal visit to Myanmar one month later, both signed a Sino–Myanmar pact of tour cooperation. In December 2000, the two countries signed a memorandum on Myanmar's approved destination status for Chinese outbound travel. From 10 June 2001, Chinese residents were allowed to travel to Myanmar using only a tourist exit visa. Now, the volume of Chinese tourists with visas to Myanmar is small, and can not be compared with the number to Thailand, Malaysia, Singapore, and the Philippines. The reasons for this are two-fold. Tourism service and infrastructure in Myanmar lag behind, and the Chinese are strangers to Myanmar.

In contrast, the day trip to the Myanmar–China border area has attracted more Chinese; it has become a distinct extension of the Yunnan trip for domestic tourists from other provinces in China. Since 1991, the Yunnan tourism bureau

---

61 Li Hongfeng: "China (Yunnan)–Myanmar Trade and Investment Promotion Closed on 16 November 2003", *Yunnan Daily*, 22 November 2003.

Table 12: Yunnan–Myanmar trade, 1995–2008 (in U.S.$ million)

Year	Total value	Yunnan exports			Yunnan imports		
		Value	Share of total exports	No. of 10 largest export partners	Value	Share of total imports	No. of 10 largest import partners
1995	490.09	392.10	29.46%	2	97.99	12.40%	3
1996	362.44	278.33	24.40%	2	84.41	9.20%	3
1997	304.77	276.37	22.80%	2	28.40	3.60%	6
1998	308.72	276.13	21.90%	2	32.59	4.20%	5
1999	299.52	245.99	23.80%	1	53.53	8.57%	4
2000	362.99	293.06	24.58%	1	69.93	10.97%	3
2001	348.73	251.51	20.22%	1	97.22	13.05%	2
2002	406.78	296.08	20.70%	1	110.70	13.90%	2
2003	492.79	356.83	21.28%	1	135.96	13.71%	1
2004	551.32	386.61	23.00%	1	164.71	17.37%	1
2005	631.62	410.63	15.54%	1	220.99	10.54%	2
2006	692.08	521.13	15.37%	1	170.95	6.02%	2
2007	873.57	640.68	13.53 %	2	232.89	5.76%	5
2008	1192.79	727.69	14.60%	1	465.10	10.10%	1

Source: *Yearbook of China's Foreign Economic Relations And Trade*, 1996–1997, 1997–1998, 1998–1999, 1999–2000, 2000, 2001,2002, 2003, 2004, 2005; *Yunnan Yearbook*, 2006, 2007, 2008, 2009.

for visits between Yunnan and Myanmar has initiated the routes of Wanding–Lashio, Ruili–Mandalay, and Menghai–Mengla–Kawthaung. Yunnan provincial and sub-provincial governments regard Yunnan–Myanmar tourism as a source of income.

According to the Deputy Director of the Yunnan Provincial Tourism Bureau, Yu Fan, from January to October 2006, Chinese day trippers to Myanmar amounted to 961.5 thousand person-times. Between 1998 and June 2003, there were 4 million tourists to China–Myanmar border area in two countries.[62]

However, one day trips to Myanmar fluctuated with the changing situation in the Sino–Myanmar border areas. At the end of the 1990s, dozens of casinos were opened in Myanmar near China. A great many Chinese swarmed into these casinos so that dozens of billions of RMB flowed to Myanmar. Consequently, from 2003, the Yunnan authorities took some steps to crack down on the casinos

---

62   China–Myanmar Cross-border Tourism Booming, yunnan.mofcom.gov.cn/aarticle/sjdixiansw/200612/20061204159560.htm.

in Myanmar, such as cutting off the supply of electricity and communications from China, and stopping day trips to Myanmar. The Chinese government in 2004 suspended issuing one day tour passes to Myanmar except for Yunnan residents. This caused most casinos to close in the north of Myanmar. However, it also inflicted a heavy loss on Yunnan tourism, at least several hundred million RMB annually because, as mentioned-above, most of Mainland Chinese tourists to Myanmar are one-day sightseers. For example, under such adverse influences, domestic day trippers to Myanmar through Menghai County were 23.2 thousand person-times, down 97 percent, and the profit earned by tourism was RMB219 million, down 48 percent in 2005–2006. Of a total of 15 travel agencies in Ruili, five closed down and three went out of business. The occupancy rate of hotels decreased from 70 percent to 30 percent, and the turnover from scenic spots and relevant restaurants and shops declined by 40 percent. Nearly half of the employees (some 4,000) in Ruili tourism lost their jobs.[63] In January 2008, Beijing lifted the ban on border tourism in Yunnan Province. Nevertheless, China closed one-day tours to Myanmar again in September 2009 because of the Kokang conflict.

Yunnan is the major driving force behind the development of China–Myanmar cross-border tourism. Ruili and Muse have jointly held the "China–Myanmar Pauk Phaw Carnival" in Ruili since 2000 under the auspices of the Yunnan Provincial Government and the Myanmar Ministry of Hotels and Tourism. The annual event was staged on 2–5 May prior to 2008 and the date was changed to 2–5 October since 2008 because China's government cancelled the week-long May Day holiday in that year. Using the "golden week" holiday and its unique performances, the Carnival attracted more and more visitors. The "International Jewelry Culture Festival" was amalgamated with the Carnival since 2008 in order to compound the economic effects of the event. Moreover, Baoshan holds similar beer carnivals and business events. Yunnan is also pushing the cooperation of tourism with bordering countries in the context of regional and subregional cooperation.

In Mainland China's 31 provinces, the personnel flow (entry-exit) of Yunnan ports has been among the top eight since 2000, although the province is landlocked. There are 20 ports in Yunnan province, among which 11 land ports lead to Myanmar. The ports to Myanmar are the busiest in terms of trade volume, freight volume, the number of entry-exit vehicles and personnel. Actually, the real cross-border flow of personnel and logistics between the two

---

63 Report on "Prohibition against Gambling not Tourism" in Guangxi and Yunnan, www. cnta.gov.cn/html/2008–6/2008-6-2-21-16-40-180.html.

countries vastly outnumbers the government statistics because there are over 90 border crossings, 111 barter trade points between border residents, and more underground border crossings aside from official ports in Yunnan. Obviously, neither two countries' governments effectively control the land border. For example, Yunnan Ruili and Myanmar Muse share a 169.8 km border, which is the only section controlled by the central government in Myanmar out of the total of the over 2,000 km China–Myanmar border. Even so, there are still 36 unofficial crossings in the Ruili section of the border and they have not been effectively supervised by the governments.[64] The trade and other economic activities beyond government control occurring in the border areas controlled by Myanmar ceasefire groups are countless.

Now, a RMB economic sphere has formed in the border areas of Laos, Myanmar, and Vietnam adjacent to China, where the RMB circulation area generally covers between 70 and 180 km inward, and its farthest circulation range extends 300 km. Ninety percent of the trade and other business dealings choose RMB for settlement.[65] In the Shan State Special Regions No. 4 and No. 2, the RMB has replaced the Kyat to become the major circulating currency. The channel of RMB outflows to Myanmar consists of border trade and tourism, investment, and illegal activities such as smuggling, gambling, drug trade, and money laundering. In general, a RMB black market has come into being in Myanmar, and it has become a medium of exchange and savings, and a means of payment in the north of the country.[66]

China's commodities dominate the market of north Myanmar, especially in some necessities. Yunnan began to provide electricity to some regions in northern Myanmar in 1995, and the power supply has increased sharply in recent years.[67] China exported 76.369728 million kilowatt-hours of electric power to Myanmar, worth US$6.098212 million, in the first quarter of 2009.[68] Also, cell phone and landline phone, and financial services are provided by Yunnan in the northern border areas in Myanmar. Consequently, when the Chinese police took action against gambling along the China–Myanmar border from 2003, Yunnan authorities took some measures to put pressure on

64 *Ibid.*

65 Lu Hao, "Investigation and Opinion on RMB Circulation in China–Myanmar and China–Laos Border Areas", *Times Finance*, No. 9, 2007.

66 Du Ping, "Investigation and Suggestion on RMB Circulation in China–Myanmar Border Areas in Dehong", *Times Finance*, No. 10, 2007.

67 Gengma Power Supply Company: Reform and Development, www.cjch.cn/qxyq/gmx/20061221074946.htm.

68 Analysis on Electricity Export in the First Quarter of 2009, www.ocn.com.cn/market/200904/dianlichukou291514.htm.

the local governments in northern Myanmar, including cutting off the supply of electricity, water, and communication and financial services from Yunnan, which demonstrated these Burmese area's dependence on China.

When Beijing proclaimed the "Go Global" strategy, Yunnan formulated its corresponding approaches. In Yunnan's "Go Global" initiative, Vietnam, Laos, Myanmar, and Cambodia were the prioritized destinations. The four countries were Yunnan's first choice to implement the strategy, and the leading economic and trade partners. A significant influx of investors, enterprises, and labor force from Yunnan further corroborates the close relations between Myanmar and the province. In addition to the northern Myanmar region, Yunnan's enterprises and investors assume importance in the sector of energy and mining, project contract and economic cooperation.

In China, Yunnan has long been regarded as an inaccessible, backward, and remote frontier province. China's economic integration with different parts of the Asia–Pacific region is no longer limited to the coastal areas where the "Western Development" was initiated in 1999. To change the landlocked and inaccessible condition and push regional economic integration, Yunnan is making efforts to forge links with the neighboring countries of Myanmar, Laos, Vietnam, and Thailand. In addition, a large number of Yunnanese have entered Myanmar, notably in the north.

When China abandoned the principle of "self-reliance" and adopted the "open-door" policy, the coastal areas were encouraged to make full use of the comparative advantage of their geo-political locations for economic involvement with developed countries and regions. Indeed, the development and opening up of China has witnessed various provinces and regions in China establishing particular economic links with specific countries and regions around China. Most typically, the economies of Guangdong, Fujian, and Shandong Provinces are dominated by their relationships with Hong Kong, Taiwan, and South Korea, respectively. In the early 1990s, Beijing opened the border areas and gave them preferential policies as the open coastal areas. Following the earlier open patterns of the east coast regions, Northeast China, Xinjiang, Guangxi, and Yunnan are becoming economically integrated with the Russian Far East, Central Asia, and mainland Southeast Asia.

Since 1978, economic expansion has been predominant among the provincial policy makers. For Yunnan with hardly any potential for economic development, the province makes much of its geographical advantage as the poles of economic growth and dynamism. Consequently, economic integration between Yunnan and Myanmar as well as other Southeast Asian countries is critical for Yunnan's provincial economic development and its change of status in China's hierarchical system and administrative divisions. Myanmar's role in Yunnan's foreign economic relations is thus gaining importance. Behind the China–Myanmar oil and gas pipelines, the transportation corridor between them, cross-border tourism, and other initiatives relating, Yunnan is both the promoter as well as the direct beneficiary.

Many projects and programs between the two countries are only Yunnan (both government and private enterprise) local schemes and actions, not motivated by Beijing. Myanmar is negligible in the big picture of China's external economic relations, but it is significant in Beijing's calculation on energy security. In general, it is with Beijing's support that China's strong state enterprises get and carry out contracts of major projects in Myanmar, such as dams, and the oil and gas pipelines. More economic transactions are carried out on the local Yunnan–Myanmar level. If an abacus is a metaphor for China–Myanmar economic relations, the central-level and local-level relations are like the shafts and beads respectively.

Chinese Migration into Myanmar

Chinese migration into Myanmar is not well understood; it has long been neglected by scholars devoting themselves to Southeast Asia or overseas Chinese studies in states where the Chinese are more numerous or economically relevant. The Chinese in Myanmar have drawn little attention except during the 1967 anti-Chinese riots in Rangoon and the 2009 conflict in Kokang. Compared with their counterparts in other Southeast Asian countries, the Chinese in Myanmar have been a low-profile and marginal community. Major changes in the Chinese community there have been evident since 1988, however, particularly in relation to the economy. This section explores the changes in Burma/Myanmar's Chinese community during the post-Cold War period and the correlation between it, the Myanmar political situation, and Sino–Myanmar ties.

Chinese Demographics in Myanmar

The size of current Chinese population in Myanmar lacks reliable data. Various estimates and calculated guesses vary from 1.4 to 4.5 percent of a total population of some 55 million. The main estimates are as follows:

The Taiwan Overseas Compatriot Affairs Commission (TOCAC): In 2009, the Statistics Office of TOCAC estimated that the 2008 population of Myanmar Chinese reached 1–1.28 million, or 2.02–2.18 percent of the total population.[69] According to the Overseas Compatriot Affairs statistics annual reports in 2008, its population stood at 1,073,000 at the end of 2008.[70]

Chinese administrations: the Foreign Office of Guangdong Province in 2008,[71] China's Overseas Chinese website in 2006,[72] and China's Embassy in Yangon in 2005, released reports that there were 2.5 million Chinese in Myanmar.[73]

Mya Than has argued that the Chinese population reached between 0.9–1.35 million in the mid-1990s, or 2–3 percent of the Myanmar population.[74] Leo Suryadinata held the number was 0.63 million in 1999.[75] David Steinberg has argued that considering the influx of Chinese illegal immigrants, "There may now be some 3 million Chinese in Myanmar – around 4 percent of the total population (not counting a very large number of Sino-Burmese, many of whom have achieved great prominence in Burmese society)."[76] Zhuang Guotu believes that the estimation should consider the new Chinese migration, so he has inferred that the population should exceed 2.5 million in 2009.[77] The answer is that we do not know.

Myanmar Chinese may be divided into different groups according to differing standards. Chinese immigrants consist of three main dialect groups: the Hokkien, the Yunnanese, and the Cantonese. Most Chinese are engaged in business and enterprise. The Hokkien and Cantonese continue to dominate the Chinese population in lower Myanmar while the Yunnanese are dominant in the upper Myanmar Chinese community. Nevertheless, in the past ten years two changes have occurred in the Chinese settlement pattern. First, more and more

69 *A collection of materials pertaining to the Overseas Chinese population*, No. 3, Taipei: Taiwan Overseas Compatriot Affairs Commission, 2009, pp. 33–35.

70 *Statistical Yearbook of the Overseas Chinese Affairs Commission (2008)*, Taipei: the Overseas Chinese Affairs Commission, 2009, p. 11.

71 "Worse Humanitarianism Catastrophe than the Cyclone Itself in Myanmar", *Nanfang Daily*, 7 May 2008.

72 A Survey of Chinese in Myanmar, www.chinaqw.com//news/2006/0630/68/34584.shtml.

73 Myanmar Chinese Community Held the Tenth Anniversary of Release of "Jiang Zemin's Eight-point Formula", mm.china-embassy.org/chn/xwdt/t182486.htm

74 Mya Than, "The Ethnic Chinese in Myanmar and their Identity", in Leo Suryadinata (ed.), *Ethnic Chinese as Southeast Asians*, Singapore: Institute of Southeast Asian Studies, 1997, p. 119.

75 M. Jocelyn Armstrong, R. Warwick Armstrong, "Chinese Population of Southeast Asia", in M. Jocelyn Armstrong, R. Warwick Armstrong, and Kent Mulliner (eds), *Chinese Populations in Contemporary Southeast Asian Societies*, Richmond: Curzon Press, 2001, p. 2.

76 David I. Steinberg, "The United States and Burma/Myanmar: a boutique issue?" *International Affairs*, Vol. 86, No. 1, 2010, p. 14.

77 Zhuang Guotu, "A New Estimation of the Ethnic Chinese Population in Southeast Asia", *Journal of Xiamen University*, No. 3, 2009, pp. 66–67.

wealthy Yunnanese now move to Yangon and expand their economic forces at the state's economic centre. Second, more and more "Shanba" Chinese[78] migrate to cities such as Mandalay, Yangon, Pyin Oo Lwin (Maymyo) and other cities from the ethnic states. The newly urbanized Chinese are rich and relatively ostentatious, notably some of them acquiring considerable wealth through jade, lumber, and narcotics smuggling. They have no bitter experience of the 1967 anti-Chinese riots, compared with the traditional Chinese. Mya Maung mentions the phenomenon that "Aggressive and wealthy Chinese investors, ethnic Chinese Kokang and Wa drug warlords, and military 'robber barons' have made the wholesale acquisition of real estate and homes. By offering exorbitant prices to the Burmese landowners, they have sharply accelerated the relocation process."[79]

Myanmar Chinese are differently classified by the two countries. According to the Chinese classification, Myanmar Chinese comprise the Han ethnic majority including the Kokang, most Hokkin, Cantonese, and some Yunnanese, and other ethnic minorities including the Panthays and Yunnan transborder ethnic groups such as Dai, Jingpo (Kachin), and Wa. But Myanmar regards the Kokang and Yunnan transborder ethnic groups as among the 135 ethnic groups recognized by the government of Myanmar, while other Chinese have not been officially recognized as an ethnic group in Myanmar.

When China adopted the "open-door" policy in 1978, it also started a new Chinese emigration wave to the outside world. Therefore, 1978 is generally regarded as the divide between traditional and new Chinese migration. The traditional Chinese in Myanmar consist of between the second to more than the tenth generation of Chinese residents; as in other Southeast Asian countries, they have had up and down experiences. New Chinese began to swarm into Myanmar from about 1990. It's estimated that there are between 1–2 million new Chinese migrants in Myanmar over the past decade.[80] "A significant influx of Chinese, primarily from Yunnan, in the 1990s threatened to upset the demographic balance in the north. When a person in Mandalay dies, his death is not reported to the authorities. Instead, that person's relatives send his identity card to a broker in Ruili or some other border town in Yunnan. There, the identification papers are sold to anyone willing to pay the price.

---

78 The traditional Chinese living in big cities such as Yangon and Mandalay call the new urbanized Chinese "Shanba".

79 Mya Maung, "On the road to Mandalay: a case study of the Sinonization of Upper Burma", *Asian Survey*, Vol. 34, No. 5 May 1994, p. 455.

80 David I. Steinberg Personal interview, Yangon, November 2007; Sudha Ramachandran, "Yangon still under Beijing's thumb", *Asia Times*, 11 February 2005.

The Chinese buyer's photo is substituted on the card, and he can then move to Mandalay as a Burmese citizen."[81]

The phenomenon of recent Chinese migration into Myanmar is not the first such influx. Historically, there have been four Chinese migration waves to Southeast Asia: the first was from early in the 17th century to the mid 19th century; the second wave – the mid 19th century to the early 20th century; the third wave – the early 20th century to the early 1950s; and the fourth wave, the 1980s to the present.[82] Most of the influx of Chinese after 1978, the fourth wave, are illegal migrants. For obvious reasons, there are no accurate figures on the volume and composition of illegal flows from China to Southeast Asia.[83] The new Chinese migration into Myanmar is, consequently, an important part of the fourth migration wave into Southeast Asia.

Other factors contributed to this influx. Beijing's "open-door" policy since 1978 has meant that China returned to the international system and international community. The rapprochement in Sino–U.S. relations highlighted China's return. Four decades of nearly continuous warfare in Indochina came to an end with the removal of the Cold War overlay, and economic development and modernization moved more clearly to the top of Southeast Asia's agenda.[84] These changes were the preconditions of the emergence for the fourth wave, which started the regional flow of capital, technology, and the labor force between China and Southeast Asia. The Chinese flow to the region is one of the reflections of regional integration in the post-Cold War period.

The SLORC abolished the Burmese Way to Socialism in favor of a more open, market economy, and in particular legalized China–Myanmar border trade. A massive influx of China's commodities ensued and the sanctions on Myanmar by some Western countries increased its dependence on China.[85] Business and investment opportunities in Myanmar offered by the above-mentioned factors attracted many Chinese businessmen into the country.

In addition, 17 armed ethnic groups and some 40 small ethnic groups have signed ceasefire agreements with the military junta since it took power in 1988,

81   Lynn Pan (ed.), *The Encyclopedia of the Chinese Overseas*, Richmond: Curzon Press, 1999, p. 143.
82   Zhuang Guotu, "On the Four Waves: A History of Chinese Migration into Southeast Asia", *Southeast Asian Affairs*, No. 1, 2008, pp. 69–79.
83   Zhuang Guotu, "A New Estimation", p. 62.
84   Marvin C. Ott, "From Isolation to Relevance: Policy Considerations", in Robert I. Rotberg (ed.), *Burma: Prospects for a Democratic Future*, Washington D.C.: Brookings Institute Press, 1998, p. 71.
85   The influx of commodities, not investment, started after the Burmese currency demonetization of September 1987.

among which 12 armed ethnic groups were allowed a limited amount of autonomy in their areas along the country's borders. Despite the fragility of these (mostly verbal) pacts, they brought rare tranquility to northern Myanmar, in particular the border areas. The geographical proximity to China and the isolation from Naypyitaw pushed the cease-fire groups along China–Myanmar border to rely on China to develop their local economies and expand their powers.

As a result, the warlords in their areas and special regions approved Chinese contract mining, infrastructure projects, and lumbering; Chinese investment, technology, consumer goods, and almost all other economic elements are favored. In recent years, with rapid urbanization in the Shan State and Wa area, many new buildings have appeared, most of which are contracted by the Chinese.[86] Before the Kokang conflict in August 2009, Chinese investment exceeded RMB1 billion in Kokang, where the Chinese sustained its economy.[87] Both Chinese investments and contracted projects in Myanmar drove more Chinese to enter the country because these firms were inclined to employ, whether legally or illegally, Chinese and not the local residents. In the recent 10 years, a large number of Chinese laborers have bypassed the border checkpoints and have illegally entered Myanmar as woodcutters, miners, and construction workers. They gradually reached central Myanmar, even as far as the India–Myanmar border. The news that Myanmar police have caught and repatriated Chinese laborers with illegal entry is nothing new. There are still an indefinite number of undocumented Chinese laborers imprisoned in Lashio, Bhamo, Myitkyina, and Mandalay. In 2006, 800 undocumented Chinese laborers were repatriated to China while at least a further 364 were repatriated in 2007. Under pressure from China's government, Maijiayang casino was closed at the end of January 2009. Up to 10 February 5,000 Chinese working in the casino were repatriated to China over ten days.[88] Before the Minela casino closed, there were at least 15,000 Chinese in Minela city.[89]

Lastly, a large number of Yunnan border residents have moved to the neighboring countries in the last decade, resettling in the north of Myanmar, Thailand, Vietnam, and Laos. In these three countries there are hundreds of thousands of Chinese. According to the Yunnan Ethnic Affairs Commission, altogether 210,000 Chinese migrated to the Kokang area and two-thirds of

86 Lincang Branch Investigation Team of the People's Bank of China, "Investigation of RMB circulation in the border trade in Lincang region", *Southwest Finance*, No. 9, 2001, p. 46.
87 Chen Jiang, He Xu, "Kokang Survival", *Southern Weekly*, 8 October 2009.
88 "Maijayang Casino Closed", *The Beijing News*, 11 February 2009.
89 Yin Hongwei, "The Casinos in Periphery Survive under China's Pressure", *Macao Monthly*.

Pang Hsang city's total population, 20,000, were Chinese.[90] Poverty and the economic appeal of neighboring countries account for the Yunnan border residents outflow. Yunnan has 35 border counties and cities, among which are 25 Chinese designated poverty-stricken counties. Also, the people on both sides of the border often belong to the same ethnic groups – they share the same culture and language. Transnational marriages across the border are very popular. These factors greatly facilitate migration. Meanwhile, outside pull factors added to this migration. In 1999, the Wa area (with central government backing) decided to resettle some people in the southern Shan State to eliminate opium and implement the Wa Areas Development Programme (WADP); they were provided with buckwheat seeds, fertilizer, and medical treatment. Some Yunnan border residents were lured to join the Wa area migration (the Wa population of Yunnan is extensive). After the Wa migration to the southeast along the border with Thailand and Laos, the opportunity to develop the vacant lands in the northern Wa area once again attracted Chinese to swarm into Myanmar. It was conservatively estimated that about 5,000 Chinese migrated to Myanmar because of the migration influence in the Wa area.[91]

The Economic Role of the Myanmar Chinese

Most Myanmar Chinese are engaged in business, and play the role of agent and broker between the Myanmar market and the Greater China economic sphere, including China, Hong Kong, Macau, Taiwan, and the ASEAN market. There is a shortage of investment financing available to the Burman community. "Those with access to capital are of two groups, in addition to foreigners who invest locally. These groups are those of the higher-level military with connections to tap into the banking system on a personal basis or who may launder funds in this manner, and the Chinese community with access to capital available through the overseas Chinese networks of clan, language, and regional associations."[92] By 31 May 2009, foreign investment from 31 countries and regions reached US\$15.767043 billion in Myanmar. Besides China and Hong Kong, Thailand, Singapore, Malaysia, and Indonesia were on the list

90   Chen Yanhui, "The Blurred Border: One Hundred Thousand Yunnan Border Residents Moved Abroad", *Phoenix Weekly*, No. 19, 2007.

91   Yang Wenyu, "The Foreign Student Group in China–Myanmar Border Area", *Oriental Outlook*, 4 March 2004.

92   David I. Steinberg, *Myanmar: The Anomalies of Politics and Economics*, The Asia Foundation Working Paper # 5, November 1997, p. 24.

of top ten investment countries.[93] A fair proportion of ASEAN investment in Myanmar belongs to the ethnic Chinese in other Southeast Asian countries. "Since December 1988, when more liberal foreign investment laws were enacted, most foreign investment in Myanmar has been of ethnic Chinese origin. The two most important factors contributing to this are: most Western governments have not actively promoted business links with Myanmar, and the large number of Sino-Burmese who fled Burma during the 1960s now can use their connections to invest there."[94] In the north, ethnic Chinese, including groups prominent in the Shan State and eastern border regions since 1949, are becoming a dominant economic force in Mandalay and other significant commercial centers in upper Burma.[95]

Several factors greatly affect the role of the Myanmar Chinese as a bridge to link the Myanmar economy to the outside, particularly East and Southeast Asia. The Chinese have benefited from the Myanmar market-oriented economic reforms and the military junta's attitudes towards them. Under the Burma Citizenship Law promulgated in 1982, the Chinese are only recognized as second and third class Myanmar citizens, namely Associate Citizens and Naturalized Citizens; they have no right to be elected. But from 1988 onwards, a series of economic policies issued by Yangon did not make a distinction between Chinese and the other citizens, especially the Myanmar Citizens Investment Law (1994). This Law legitimized and encouraged the private investment of all Myanmar citizens including "an associate citizen or a naturalized citizen".[96] The Chinese, consequently, grabbed the opportunity and in no time activated their ethnic group economic networks, which had been restricted during the Ne Win era.

The increased China–Myanmar trade and economic ties, the ad hoc border trade, and ASEAN's engagement policy toward Myanmar offered Chinese businessmen favorable opportunities to rise. When business-men from the Greater China economic sphere sought to enter the Myanmar market, they often collaborated with resident Chinese, which helped them deal with the anomalies of doing business in Myanmar. "One of the serious drawbacks for foreign investors, particularly those who operate on-shore, is the necessity to work with the bureaucratic government structures and multitudes of controls

---

93 The Latest Rank of Foreign Investment in Myanmar, mm.mofcom.gov.cn/aarticle/jmxw/200907/20090706383099.html.

94 East Asia Analytical Unit, "Overseas Chinese Business Networks in Asia", Department of Foreign Affairs and Trade, Australia, 1995, p. 185.

95 *Ibid.*, p. 64.

96 The Myanmar Citizens Investment Law, www.blc-burma.org/html/myanmar%20law/lr_e_ml94_04.html.

and counter-controls. Rules are often changed without prior notice, particularly in the case of currency controls, import restrictions, and other restrictions on movement of goods and services or trade practices."[97] But even lacking explicit contracts, Chinese ethnic social networks and social capital reduced the transaction costs and increased the business success rate. "In Myanmar, like China, legal and other 'soft' infrastructures are still being developed, and good connections are essential for doing business. The ethnic Chinese have social and business structures which operate well in the absence of sound legal and other structures; they have a propensity for developing international connections. They are therefore at their most competitive in countries such as Myanmar."[98]

In 2009, China's Ministry of Commerce released an Investment Guide to Myanmar that reminded Chinese investors that although the Burmese government encouraged foreign investment, its policies created formidable obstacles. Chinese investors from the Greater China economic sphere commonly chose to cooperate with the Myanmar Chinese community who shared overseas Chinese networks of clan, language, and regional associations in order to reduce risk and uncertainty when they entered Myanmar market.

"Myanmar is increasingly a focus for business delegations from abroad, many of which seek to link up with the local ethnic Chinese business community. A large number of delegations come from China each year."[99] Whether China's official business delegations (from provincial or county levels) or private enterprises, they tended to seek business opportunities through Chinese associations in Myanmar. Between December 2005 and 2007, the Myanmar Chinese Chamber of Commerce received 15 business delegations from all over China. This Chamber is the leading business association in the Myanmar Chinese community and is comprised of over 500 entrepreneurs and businessmen members.[100] China's enterprises and companies also choose local Chinese as agents and direct distributors of their products. For example, 80 percent of the agricultural machinery market in Myanmar has been occupied by Chinese products. The predominant share can be attributed to three major local Chinese distributors in the country: 007 Company, Goodbrother Company, and Yeeshin Company.

97 Khin Maung Kyi, *Economic Development of Burma: A Vision and Strategy*, Stockholm: Olof Palme International Center, 2000, p. 111.
98 East Asia Analytical Unit, "Overseas Chinese Business Networks in Asia", p. 60.
99 *Ibid.*, p. 186.
100 *Special Publication of the 100th Anniversary of the Myanmar Chinese Chamber of Commerce*, Yangon: Myanmar Chinese Chamber of Commerce, 2009, p. 107.

On the other hand, Myanmar Chinese also travel to China, Hong Kong, and other Southeast Asian countries in search of business partners and opportunities. The Myanmar Chinese Chamber of Commerce frequently arranges for its members to visit widely in China searching for investment and cooperation opportunities. They attend the World Chinese Entrepreneurs Convention, the ASEAN Chinese Business Investment Southwest Promotion Meeting, the Asia–Pacific Chinese Business Forum, the China–ASEAN Expo, the China International Fair for Investment and Trade, the China Yiwu International Commodities Fair, and all kinds of other economic and trade fairs.[101]

The roaring China–Myanmar border trade has created a golden opportunity for the Myanmar Chinese community. Most of the underground banks in Yunnan were opened by Myanmar Chinese families; such institutions have considerable economic power. Ruili city in Yunnan is the hub of their operations, and their family members are distributed in border cities and other large and medium-sized cities throughout Myanmar. Their nets even extend to Hong Kong.[102] Some rich Chinese have been investing outside Myanmar. China and Southeast Asian countries are their prioritized investment destinations, and Yunnan and Singapore are most preferred. A large number of Myanmar Chinese invest and do business in the Yunnan border area; they are the most vibrant and powerful among foreign investors there. Many of them have dual identity.[103] A leader of the returned Myanmar Chinese association in Yunnan demonstrated this phenomenon. He pointed out that Myanmar Chinese began to get Chinese ID cards through their social networks in China since about 1992, and they consequently have opened bank accounts, bought real estate, and invested in Yunnan Province and beyond in the name of Chinese citizens.[104]

The connection between the Myanmar Chinese community and the overseas Chinese networks paves the way for their intermediary role between Myanmar

---

101 In recent years, Chinese businessmen and entrepreneurs in Myanmar have given more and more attention to business negotiation activities with a Chinese background, and seek more business opportunities through the overseas Chinese network. For example, the 4th session of the World Myanmar Chinese Diaspora Association was held in Hong Kong on 15–17 September 2007, and over 1,000 Myanmar Chinese diaspora members from all over the world attended. However, the 9th World Chinese Entrepreneurs Convention was convened in Japan on the same date, so some powerful Chinese entrepreneurs in Myanmar chose to attend the Japan's activity.
102 Current Account Management Department, State Administration of Foreign Exchange (ed.), *Cross-border currency circulation and management of foreign exchange in border trade*, Beijing: China Financial and Economic Publishing House, 2005, p. 104.
103 *Ibid.*, pp. 233–234.
104 Interview with HG, Kunming, 14 January 2010.

and the greater China economic sphere. "Being largely Hokkien or Cantonese, Yangon's ethnic Chinese tend to have links to other Hokkien and Cantonese communities around the world ... Yangon's Hokkien tend to have strong links to Singapore and to Penang (both of which have large Hokkien communities) and the Cantonese have strong links to Hong Kong (which is dominated by the Cantonese). Also, despite Myanmar's relative isolation, some members of the Yangon ethnic Chinese community attend the annual meetings of the various international dialect associations. This may have the effect of renewing their international links and replenishing their 'Chineseness.'"[105] Much of the foreign direct investment entering the country is channeled through ethnic Chinese networks.[106] This is especially true of Taiwan investment because Myanmar has not legalized diplomatic, economic, and trade relations with Taipei. Thus, Taiwanese businessmen make their investments in the country and carry on trade with it via a third country and by way of what are called "transfer bills".

Myanmar Chinese have not only linked themselves to overseas networks but have also established their own transnational networks. During the Cold War era, numerous Chinese left Myanmar for China, the U.S., Macao, Hong Kong, and Europe. Resettled in over 20 countries and regions, they total 300,000, including over 100,000 in the U.S., 40–50,000 in Thailand, over 20,000 in Macao, and 120,000 in Taiwan.[107] Some of them have set up associations and have kept in touch with each other in such places as Macao, Hong Kong, Taiwan, New York, San Francisco, and Los Angeles. In China, the returned Myanmar Chinese have also established associations in Xiamen, Beijing, Yunnan, Shanxi, Guangxi, Tianjin, Guangdong, Nanchang, and Shanghai. In January 2001, they established the World Myanmar Chinese Diaspora Association, whose membership includes all Chinese and their descendants claiming common origins in Myanmar. Its objectives lie in the promotion of common development, win-win cooperation, solidarity and mutual support among its members, and contributing to the economic boom of the country of residence and origin.[108] The Association convenes every two years. It has held five large assemblies in Mainland China, Macao, and Hong Kong up to

---

105 East Asia Analytical Unit, "Overseas Chinese Business Networks", pp. 184–185.
106 *Ibid.*, p. 64.
107 *Commemorative Issue of the 2nd Session of the World Myanmar Chinese Diaspora Association*, Kunming: Association of Overseas Exchange of Yunnan Province, 2002, p. 24.
108 *Commemorative Issue of the 1st Session of the World Myanmar Chinese Diaspora Association and Celebration of Macao's Return*, Macao: Macao Myanmar Overseas Chinese Association, 2002, pp. 85–86.

2009, which over 1,000 Myanmar Chinese diasporas from all over the world, including the Myanmar Chinese community, attended every time.

On 1 January 2009, over 800 delegates from the Chinese Chamber of Commerce in the U.S., Japan, Singapore, Thailand, Hong Kong, and Macao, and local Chinese, attended the Celebration of the 100th Anniversary of the Myanmar Chinese Chamber of Commerce in Yangon. Since the 1990s, when the military junta adopted market-oriented and "open-door" policies, many Chinese have returned to the country, bringing capital, technology, and new experiences.[109] When a Myanmar Chinese entrepreneur explained the reason for their economic rise after 1988, he believed that "Myanmar Chinese businessmen maintained many natural contacts with foreign traders due to all kinds of historical reasons. The current cooperation between them through various social contacts is larger and closer than in the 1950s ... When China established the Shenzhen Special Economic Zone (SEZ) and Zhuhai SEZ in 1980, it obtained overseas Chinese investment and support, and thus met with success. Today, the Myanmar Chinese businessman also faces a similar opportunity and position. The 1990s witnessed successful cooperation between Myanmar Chinese and foreign investors from mainland China, Taiwan, Singapore, and Thailand."[110]

The Economic Power of the Myanmar Chinese

The Asian Development Bank claimed that "an objective assessment of economic developments in Myanmar is made difficult by poor quality data."[111] This conclusion is also applicable to the Chinese economy in Myanmar. Not only are there no reliable statistics on this economy, but also the biographies of successful Chinese entrepreneurs have not appeared.

During Ne Win's rule, some 100,000 Chinese left the country because the government nationalized trade and industry that destroyed Chinese livelihoods. The remaining Chinese only made a living in a restricted space and were involved in the black market. The situation underwent a dramatic and favorable turn at the end of 1980s, as noted previously. When the author (Fan Hongwei)

109 Zhai Zhenxiao, Migration, "Cultures and Identities: The Social Construction and Transnational Networks of Burmese–Chinese Immigrant Communities in Yangon, Jhong-he, and Toronto", Taiwan National Tsing Hua University, Ph.D. thesis, 2006, pp. 166–167.See also Lynn Pan (ed.), *The Encyclopedia of the Chinese Overseas*. Richmond: Curzon Press, 1999, p. 143; East Asia Analytical Unit, "Overseas Chinese Business Networks in Asia", Department of Foreign Affairs and Trade, 1995, pp. 186–187.
110 *Special Publication of the 100th Anniversary*, p. 185.
111 Asian Development Bank, *Asian Development Outlook 2003*, Oxford University Press, 2003, p. 82.

conducted field work in Myanmar at the end of 2005, those Chinese traders and entrepreneurs interviewed unanimously recognized the significance of the 1988 tipping point for their lives and economy. They remarked that "All the current successful big Chinese entrepreneurs in Myanmar started their businesses in 1989."[112] "The new environment caused by the 1988 upheaval in Burma and China's open economy and booming international trade provided us with numerous business opportunities and made considerable numbers of Chinese into the 'New Rich.'"[113] "In the Chinese community, countless businessmen made a fortune through the China–Myanmar border trade."[114]

Between November 1988 and April 1993, there were 5,875 export trading companies and agents in Myanmar, and about 800 ones belonged to the Chinese. The number of Chinese exporters was not small, and their economic power and scale were predominant. Fifty percent of the leading 20 private import and export companies were owned by Chinese. In the field of rubber, agricultural and forest products, and aquatic product exports, Chinese played the dominant role.[115] By the mid-1990s, 70 percent of vendors' stands in major markets all over Myanmar were manned by Chinese, who mainly dealt in agricultural products, local products, jewelry, plastic products, and machine, transport, hotel, restaurant, textile, construction, tourism and aquatic products.[116] "Today the country's ethnic Chinese are again at the forefront in Myanmar's economy. The majority of retail, wholesale and import trade, including cross-border trade and big restaurants, are run by them or by mixed Chinese–Barmar [Burman]; and the largest supermarket in Yangon is operated by an ethnic Chinese group."[117]

By 2000, Myanmar Chinese import and export companies totaled 4,500. Within the country, there were about 25,000 Chinese enterprises selling groceries and other sundry goods. Mainly family-operated, these had an average capital value of 2 million Kyat. Their conditions in other fields were also remarkable: over 2,000 snack-bars in Yangon, 1–2 million Kyat average capital per shop; 700 teahouses in Yangon, 1–40 million Kyat; 200 musical instrument

112 *Special Publication of the 100th Anniversary*, p. 125.
113 *Ibid.*, p. 186.
114 *Ibid.*, p. 121.
115 Fang Xiongpu, *Glimpse of the Chinese Community in Myanmar*, Hong Kong: South Island Press, 2000, p. 160.
116 Bao Lu, "Chinese in Myanmar", *Information of South-east and South Asia*, No. 18, 1996, p. 23.
117 Mya Than. "The ethnic Chinese in Myanmar and their identity", in Leo Suryadinata (ed.), *Ethnic Chinese as Southeast Asian*, Singapore: Institute of Southeast Asian Studies, 1997, p. 128.

and toy shops, 1–30 million Kyat; 2,000 hotels and inns, 5 million Kyat; 700 maritime agents, 5–80 million Kyat; 7,000 cloth and clothes shops, 6–50 million Kyat.[118]

Chinese overall occupational structure in Myanmar remains in 2011 more or less as it was. However, more and more Chinese are engaged in manufacture, whose enterprises and factories, by and large, are small and medium scale, and belong to the processing and light industry.

From 1992 onwards, the Myanmar government established dozens of industrial zones throughout the country. A fair proportion of enterprises in the Dagon Industrial Zone, Shwe Paukkan Industrial Zone, Shwe Pyithar Industrial Zone, and Hlaing Thayar Industrial Zone belong to the Chinese.[119]

For Myanmar Chinese, neither their overall nor individual economic power is yet able to compare with their counterparts in other Southeast Asian countries. No Myanmar Chinese entrepreneur or his enterprise has entered the any rank of the Top 500 Chinese Entrepreneurs, Southeast Asia's 40 Richest, and Forbes Asia's 200 Best Under A Billion (list of the best small- and midsize companies throughout the Asia Pacific region) released by some institutions. Nevertheless, the Chinese are still the most energetic and pragmatic ethnic group in Myanmar and are playing an important or a dominant role in some fields of the country.

The Chinese now dominate the fields of the grocery, retail, and restaurant trades in Myanmar.[120] The export of farm produce is jointly controlled by Chinese and Indians, and 80–90 percent of private rubber dealers are Chinese. When the Myanmar government opened banking in 1992, half of the private banks belonged to the Chinese.[121] Among the private banks, Asia Economy Bank, owned by a Chinese, was the biggest, which had nearly 40 local branches, recruited over 3,000 employees, and whose savings held 40 percent of the total of all Myanmar banks. Yet this bank was closed in 2003.[122]

In addition to Chinatown, Chinese shop signboards are ubiquitous in Yangon and Mandalay, from gold shops, to supermarkets, to groceries. On 25 February 2008, the biggest shopping market containing over 300 shops in Mandalay, Yadanabon Market, was destroyed by a major fire, and most of them were operated by local Chinese. It is said that all the buildings above two

---

118 *Yearbook of the Huaren Economy 2000/2001*, Beijing: Morning Glory Publishers, 2001, pp. 92–93.

119 *Special Publication of the 100th Anniversary*, p. 185.

120 Overview of Myanmar Chinese, www.chinaqw.com//news/2006/0630/68/34584.shtml.

121 *Special Publication of the 100th Anniversary*, pp. 78–79.

122 *Ibid.*, pp. 125–126.

floors are owned by Chinese in Mandalay.[123] For the purpose of convincing the author of local Chinese dominant economic power in Mandalay, one Chinese entrepreneur said that "During the Spring Festival, Chinese always close their shops to celebrate the holiday. Under their influence, the whole Mandalay commercial market is also closed until we reopen our shops at the end of the Festival. If you visit the city during the Spring Festival, you will feel the obvious landscape."[124] Another scholar also confirms the landscape: "Real estate in key sites in Mandalay has been acquired by wealthy Chinese investors, ethnic Chinese Kokang, and Wa businessmen (notorious for their drug connections) at exorbitant prices. This has had the effect of pricing out the ordinary Burmese residents who cannot afford the housing and land costs in central Mandalay. As a result, the central area of Mandalay has been transformed into a thriving centre of alien (especially Chinese) culture with modern homes, hotels, shops and high rise buildings filled with rich Chinese businessmen."[125]

The Chinese migrants' presence in the Myanmar economy is a double-edged sword. They are the lubricant of China–Myanmar economic ties, but they are also the component of China's soft power projected in Myanmar. Meanwhile, they are possibly the potential friction of bilateral relations. One author has warned that "If the Chinese are perceived to be in control of the economy, then a rise in anti-foreign sentiment might be expected which could have serious effects on both the political and economic future of the state."[126] "The Chinese takeover of Mandalay and northern Burma replicates the economic consequences of the British colonization of Burma."[127] The influx of new Chinese migration generates fears of economic dependence and political domination.

Some observers and scholars argue that China dominates Myanmar's economy, and attribute the continued survival of the military regime facing Western sanctions to China's support and close bilateral economic ties.[128] This claim exaggerates China's economic influence on Myanmar and disregards Naypyitaw's nationalism, which demands more careful research. In fact, the

123 Interview with YGM, Mandalay, 15 December 2005.
124 Interview with LZM, Mandalay, 15 December 2005.
125 Chee Kiong Tong, *Identity and Ethnic Relations in Southeast Asia: Racializing Chineseness*, Springer, 2010, p. 155.
126 Steinberg, *Myanmar*, The Asia Foundation Working Paper # 5, p. 24.
127 Mya Maung, "On the Road to Mandalay", p. 455.
128 Ott, "From Isolation to Relevance", p. 72; Toshihiro Kudo, "Myanmar's Economic Relations", JETRO Disscussion Paper No. 66, 2006, p. 17; Aung Din, "Burma's last chance", *Far Eastern Economic Review*, 26 May 2009; Toshihiro Kudo, "Myanmar's Economic Relations with China", 2008, p. 104.

answer to whether Naypyitaw can survive Western sanctions without China's economic supports has been illustrated by the history of Burma's self-isolation during the BSPP period. More importantly, the hypothesis has not been based on reliable and accurate statistics on China–Myanmar economic and trade relations. As mentioned earlier in the chapter, no scholars, observers, or institutions of the Burmese scene have disclosed China's real influence because there are no believable and exact statistics from both sides, and their ties are so complicated and multi-dimensional. Although dependence on China seems self-evident, there is a tendency to underrate the vehemence and potential of Burmese nationalism. Myanmar has attempted to balance Chinese support, and will limit all foreign influences on key national concerns. "Chinese assistance has been important to the Burmese junta, not for its survival but for its strengthened control."[129]

If China withdrew its support to Myanmar and limited its economic relations with it, other neighboring countries would fill the Chinese vacancy in the country. "Based on Myanmar's trade patterns, we can also surmise that sanctions have pushed the country toward Asia and away from better ties with Western democracies. Human rights activism has not affected the public image of Asian investors in the same way it pressured Western multinationals."[130] New Delhi's policy towards Myanmar shifted from "Isolation" to "Constructive Engagement" since 1993. Behind the change, it's an important contributing factor to counterbalance China's penetration in Myanmar. Accordingly, there is no reason to doubt that India would expand its influence in the country if China estranges itself from Myanmar.

The lack of statistics on the subject, however, cannot become an excuse for denying the fact of China's presence in Myanmar. One must be alive to the possibility that inadequate data indeed cover up the real economic power of China in Myanmar, which both official statistics underestimate.

Official data do not depict the full extent of China's economic engagement in Myanmar. Chinese build-operate transfer (BOT) projects are often classified as government loans/aid and therefore excluded from official investment figures. "The level of Chinese investment is also under-reported because many private companies and individual investors invest in the name of its local partners' names. And while Chinese investment in the areas controlled by the ethnic groups is also rising, it is often excluded as foreign investment

129 David I. Steinberg, "The United States and Burma/Myanmar", pp. 187–188.
130 Jalal Alamgir, "Myanmar's Foreign Trade and Its Political Consequences", *Asian Survey*, Vol. XLVIII, No. 6, November/December 2008, p. 994.

in official reporting because Naypyitaw's reign in these areas is weak or non-existent. Reporting omissions are also common for small-scale investments, such as Chinese government loans for alternative development projects and commercial investments in rubber plantations and the mining sector."[131] At the same time, there is a large underground and informal economy between the two countries; we stress that the real amount of Sino–Myanmar trade and investment greatly outnumbers the official statistics. China's economic influence is underestimated in Myanmar if we rely on their bilateral economic ties according to official sources. This should not suggest, however, Myanmar's total dependence on China. We discern a partial, uncomfortable dependency on China. As China's former Ambassador Li Jinjun noted, Myanmar's economy consists of two major economic plates controlled by the central government and ethnic groups, respectively and three relatively independent economic regions. The three regions are: 1. the region south of Mandalay centering Yangon controlled by the central government; 2. the northern Myanmar economic region composed of several special regions dominated by ceasefire ethnic groups closely integrated with China's Yunnan province; 3. the economic region, comprising northeast Myanmar centering on Tachileik, closely integrated with Thailand.[132]

With three relatively independent economic regions in this country as well as the reality of China/Yunnan–Myanmar economic ties, we argue that north Myanmar has become economically dependent on China. Economically, however, the foci of Beijing and Yunnan on Myanmar are different. While central level bilateral economic relations are subject to political ties and Beijng's strategic interests in the country, local level relations have fewer political considerations and are more immediate and practical. In the provincial development blueprint devised by Yunnan, mainland Southeast Asia, particularly Myanmar, has occupied a critical position. Yunnan is practicing a modern version of mercantilism. The degree of economic integration between Yunnan and Northern Myanmar is unprecedented, but it will inevitably face the challenge of the uncertainties of Naypyitaw-cease fire groups relations. In conclusion, when discussing current China–Myanmar trade and economic relations or China's economic influence, we should be carefully circumspect in either overstating or underestimating China's economic influence in Myanmar. Analyses should

131 "China's Myanmar Strategy: Elections, Ethnic Politics and Economics", *Crisis Group Asia Briefing No.* 112, 21 September 2010, p. 12.
132 Li Jinjun, "Analyzing the Cause and Impact of Current Economic Hardship in Myanmar", *Asia Probe*, No. 4, 2002.

pay attention to the different dynamics of different levels of economic ties, and those of the central and local governments, as well as China's official large investment and incalculable undocumented private investment in this country.

Additionally, the catalyst function of economic sanctions against Myanmar imposed by the U.S. and its major allies in China–Myanmar trade and economic nexus should not be ignored. Myanmar is subject to formal and informal economic sanctions from some western countries. U.S. sanctions are the most stringent and include total bans on new investment since 1997 and on trade since 2003.[133] The E.U. introduced economic sanctions according to the "Common Position" in 1996, and hardened its stance by updating, renewing, and extending the restrictive measures in subsequent years.[134] Other countries, including Japan, Australia, New Zealand, and Canada imposed various restrictions on their activities in and/or with Myanmar. In addition to the formal sanctions, western informal sanctions were applied to Myanmar. In the early 1990s, some prominent North American and Western European corporations withdrew from Myanmar. Their pullouts were prompted not by formal sanctions on investment, but by informal pressures including lobbying campaigns, legal challenges, shareholder revolts, street protests, and letter-writing initiatives.[135] When western corporations, consequently, considered doing business with Myanmar or investing in that country, they have had to face possible criticism and pressure from human-rights, environmental, and other pressure groups. By comparison, neither China's state nor private corporations are under institutional or non-institutional constraints. Rather, Chinese enterprises' overseas expansion is encouraged and supported by Beijing's pragmatic strategy, "Go Global". For instance, "The Chinese leadership supports CNPC's ambition to become a world-class oil company. The internationalization of CNPC is not only part of the Chinese government's plan to create internationally competitive firms but also part of its strategy to achieve energy security."[136]Myanmar is believed to have a large amount of informal trade across its land borders, especially with Thailand and China. The informal economy may be as large

---

133 For the background, history, and statutory actions of U.S. economic sanction on Myanmar, see Michael F. Martin, "U.S. Sanctions on Burma", CRS Report for Congress, 16 July 2010; Larry A. Niksch, "Burma–U.S. Relations", CRS Report for Congress, 2 March 2008.

134 For E.U.'s policy toward Myanmar, see Renaud Egreteau, "Intra-European Bargaining and the 'Tower of Babel' E.U. Approach to the Burmese Conundrum", *East Asia*, Vol. 27, Issue 1, March 2010, pp. 15–33.

135 Ian Holliday, "Doing Business with Rights Violating Regimes Corporate Social Responsibility and Myanmar's Military Junta", *Journal of Business Ethics*, 2005, Volume 61, No. 4, pp. 332–333.

136 Downs, "China's Quest for Energy Security", RAND, 2000, p. 51.

as or larger than the formal economy.[137] The sanctions and isolation further aggravate the formal economy in this country.

Most foreign direct investment (FDI) to Myanmar was from developed countries over 1995–2001. Among the developed countries, the United Kingdom and the United States were significant, and their FDI were dominated by oil and gas activities. The highest FDI inflows into Myanmar were between 1990–2002, and in 1997. They declined, however, from 1998. UNCAD attributed the decline primarily to the impact of the 1997–1998 Asian financial crisis,[138] but tightened western economic sanctions were another factor. The Clinton administration on 22 April 1997 announced a ban on all U.S. investment in Myanmar. In that year, "The United States is the fourth-largest external investor in Burma after France, Singapore and Thailand. However, much of that investment lies in the oil sector, where Unocal [now Chevron] and, to a lesser degree, Atlantic Richfield are involved. As many U.S. companies have withdrawn from Burma in recent years and as the ban applies only to new contracts, the short-term consequences for the country's economy will be modest."[139] The 1997 ban caused two obvious outcomes: first, the peak in FDI in Myanmar before 2002. Because "U.S. companies signed more investment deals with Burma in February than in the whole of the previous eight years as they dashed to conclude talks before the President's bill banned new U.S. investment in the Southeast Asian nation." And "Most of the new investment was in the oil and gas sector, with offshore exploration rights held by and being converted into production-sharing contracts."[140] Second, the U.S. stopped expanding into the Myanmar market, particularly into the energy sector. According to the E.U. Common Position adopted in 1996, E.U. members were prohibited from investing in state-owned enterprises in Myanmar. According to the Myanmar Central Statistical Organization, the majority of FDI into Myanmar lies in the power, oil, and gas sectors between 1989 and 2007.[141] While

---

137 "Myanmar: Sanctions, Engagement or Another Way Forward?" International Crisis Group Asia Report No. 78, 26 April 2004, p. 17.

138 FDI in brief: Myanmar, www.unctad.org/sections/dite_fdistat/docs/wid_ib_mm_en. pdf.

139 "United States: Burma Sanctions", *Oxford Analytica Daily Brief Service*.

140 Ted Bardacke, "US companies rush to beat Burma sanctions", *Financial Times*, 25 April 1997. It cited this sentence that: "most of the new investment was in the oil and gas sector, with offshore exploration rights held by and being converted into production-sharing contracts."

141 Thandar Khine, "Foreign Direct Investment Relations between Myanmar and ASEAN," IDE Discussion Paper, No. 149. April 2008. It cited this sentence that: "According to the Myanmar Central Statistical Organization, the majority of FDI into Myanmar lies in the power, oil, and gas sectors between 1989 and 2007."

western companies withdrew and were reluctant to invest, China was opposed to the sanctions against Myanmar and adopted a policy of non-interference. China's companies, motivated by the strategies of "Western Development" and the "Go Global" programs launched by Beijing in the new century, appealed to the resource-rich Southeast Asian nation. For example, Chinese enterprises began to be involved in Myanmar oil and gas explorations in 2001. Up to 2008, all three major Chinese oil corporations – CNPC, SINOPEC, and CNOOC – have gained footholds in Myanmar. China's economic presence in Myanmar to some considerable extent profited from Western economic sanctions against Naypyitaw, notably those by the U.S.

Part III: Sino-Burmese Relations within the International Power Context

9

Regional Impacts: Narcotics, Transport, and the Military in Sino-Myanmar Relations

Sino-Burmese relations within the context of regional power and security concerns have three specialized aspects that transcend the usual Sino-Southeast Asian relations: the problem of narcotics, the extensive expansion of the Chinese transport network, and the rising role of the Burmese *tatmadaw*, the latter with more than considerable Chinese assistance. Although the Burmese military under any conceivable development within our purview will be no threat to China, and indeed the strengthening of Burmese forces by China could be rationalized as internally protecting Chinese assets in Myanmar against insurrections as well as finding political favor with the regime, narcotics has been viewed by the Chinese, both historically and at present, as an existential threat to the state.

Myanmar has been a narcotics problem since opium production, which was legal in Burma until 1958 and was taxed by the Shan *sawbwas*, was transformed into its distilled form, heroin, and found international markets, most specifically in the United States. Afghanistan has replaced Myanmar as the world's leading heroin exporter, but another lucrative market has been found in Thailand for Burmese-produced methamphetamines, which – unlike heroin and the opium poppy – have no agricultural base. Although China has no fear of the Burmese military, mutual suspicions between Thailand and Burma/Myanmar are both historical and contemporary. The Burmese still unrealistically fear a U.S. invasion via its surrogate and ally, Thailand. These three factors – narcotics, Chinese transport expansion, and the military – are components of the regional dynamics.

Narcotics in the China–Myanmar Nexus

Over a century ago, China had a massive opium problem. Despite the absence of reliable and meaningful statistics, it is beyond doubt that opium culture expanded enormously throughout the nineteenth century. The number of opium

Table 13: Drugs-related crime in China, 1991–2009

Year	Cracked drug-related cases (1000)	Arrested criminal suspects drug-related captured (1000)	Heroin seizure (tons)	Opium seizure	Mari-juana seizure (tons)	Methamphetamine seizure (tons)	Precur-sor chemi-cals seizure (tons)
1991	8.4	18.5	1.919	1.980	0.454	0.351	49.8
1992	14.7	28.3	4.489	2.680	0.910	0.655	58.8
1993	26.1	40.8	4.459	3.354	0.251	0.005	90
1994	38.0	51.0	3.881	1.737	1.534	0.460	38
1995	57.5	73.7	2.376	1.110	0.466	1.304	85.9
1996	88.6	112.6	4.347	1.745	4.876	1.599	218.6
1997	180.1	244.0	5.477	1.880	2.408	1.334	383.5
1998	182.4	231.9	7.358	1.215	5.079	1.608	344.5
1999	64.9	58.1	5.364	1.193	16.059	–	272
2000	96.2	37.1	6.281	2.428	4.493	20.900	215
2001	110.3	73.3	13.2	2.82	0.75	4.82; 2.07 million pills MDMA/ecstasy	208.2
2002	110.0	90.0	9.2908	1.2193	1.3	3.1909; 3.01 million pills MDMA	>300
2003	93.8	63.7	9.53	–	–	5.83; 0.409 million pills MDMA	72.8
2004	98.0	67.0	10.8365	–	–	2.746; over 3 million pills MDMA	–
2005	4.5	5.8	6.9	2.3	0.941	5.5; 2.34 million pills MDMA; 2.6 tons of ketamine	–
2006	4.6	5.6	5.79	1.69	–	5.95; 0.4541 million pills MDMA; 1.79 tons of ketamine	–
2007	5.6	6.7	4.6	1.2	–	5.8; 7.62 million methamphetamine tablet, 2.21 million pills MDMA; 6 tons of ketamine	–
2008	6.2	7.3	4.33	1.38	–	6.15; 5.27 tons of ketamine	–
2009	7.7	9.1	5.8	1.3	8.7	6.6; 5.3 tons of ketamine; 1.062 million pills MDMA	–

Source: *Annual Report on Drug Control in China, 2000–2010*, Ministry of Public Security, PRC.

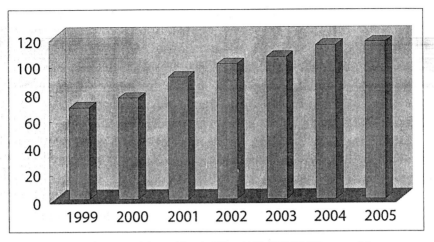

Figure 3: Number of registered drug addicts in China, 1999–2005 (10,000 persons) Source: *Annual Report on Drug Control in China, 1999–2006.*

users ranged from 0.66 percent of the adult Chinese population to 60 percent or more.[1] At the beginning of the twentieth century, China was consuming 95 percent of the world's opium supply. "Opium came to function as both a source of and a substitute for cash."[2] During the rule of the KMT, the opium problem was still rampant in China.[3] Soon after the CCP seized power, Beijing launched a nationwide campaign from 1950 to 1952 against drugs, along with other political campaigns such as Suppressing Counter-revolutionaries, The Three Antis, and The Five Antis. In these three years, 82,056 drug criminals were arrested; 33,786 of them suffered the death penalty or life imprisonment.[4] This campaign basically wiped out the drug problem in urban areas. "By the late 1950s, the opium problem was solved in most parts of China, except in several minority areas where the campaign was postponed. From the late 1950s, China claimed it was a drug-free country, and it enjoyed this reputation for more than two decades by virtue of the combination of the extremely tight control over individual life, and its virtual isolation from the rest of the world."[5]

1   Frank Dikotter, Lars Laamann and Zhou Xun, *Narcotic Culture: A History of Drugs in China*, Hong Kong: Hong Kong University Press, 2004, pp. 51–52.

2   Carl A. Trocki, *Opium, Empire, and the Global Political Economy: A Study of the Asian Opium Trade, 1750–1950*, London, New York: Routledge, 1999, pp. 125–126.

3   See Edward R. Slack, Jr, *Opium, State, and Society: China's Narco-economy and the Guomindang, 1924–1937*. Honolulu: University of Hawai'i Press, 2001.

4   "Concluding Report on Nationwide Anti-drug Campaign", by Luo Ruiqing, in Zhu Yu (ed.), *Removing "Cancer": Records of the PRC's first anti-drug and anti-prostitution measures*, Beijing: Central Party Literature Press, 1999, p. 49.

5   Zhou Yongming, *Anti-Drug Crusades in Twentieth-Century China: Nationalism, History, and State Building*, Lanham: Rowman and Littlefield Publishers, Inc., 1999, p. 113.

When China re-opened its doors in the late 1970s, drugs re-emerged in the country and are becoming increasingly problematic (see Table 13).

According to China's official statistics, the number of drug addicts registered with the public security organs in 1991 was 148,000, a figure which rose to 520,000 in 1995, and to 681,000 in 1999.[6] In contrast with most Asian countries reporting stable or declining abuse trends in 2002, opiate abuse continued rising in China. "The number of registered drug addicts rose in 2002 and in 2003 to exceed 1 million people, a 15-fold increase over the 1990–2003 period."[7] By 2005, registered drug addicts jumped to 1,140,400 (see Figure 3). Up to June, 2010, the number rose to 1,437,000.[8]

Today, when the Chinese think about drugs, Myanmar and Yunnan often come to mind. The current plague of narcotics in China is intimately associated with Burma/Myanmar. Before China opened up to the outside world in 1979, there were three drug-transit routes from the Golden Triangle to the main consumer markets in North America and Western Europe: 1. Golden Triangle–Bangkok–Hong Kong–Japan–U.S.; 2. Golden Triangle–Rangoon–Kuala Lumpur–Singapore–North America; 3. Golden Triangle–India or Sri Lanka–Europe. "After China adopted its 'open-door' policy and relaxed the control of the border trade, the drug traffickers wasted no time in establishing the fourth traffic route: from the Golden Triangle to Yunnan, then to Hong Kong and the rest of the world ... As drug-transit activities increased, so did the number of addicts [in China]."[9]

Now, the Golden Triangle, notably northern Myanmar, does the most harm to China among foreign sources of drugs. China is not only the trafficking route and transit site, but also the leading consumption market of narcotics produced in the Golden Triangle. "When bulk narcotics reach Yunnan, most of them are shipped to Guangdong via Guangxi, Guizhou, and Hunan. Then some are smuggled abroad and the rest enter the local market or are transferred to Hunan, Jiangxi, Fujian, as well as the northern provinces in the country."[10]

Table 14 indicates that Yunnan is infested with narcotics; it is also a barrier arresting the influx of narcotics into the rest of China. Chinese authorities estimate that some 80 percent of the opiates produced in the Golden Triangle

6   "White Paper: Narcotics Control in China", *China Facts and Figures*, March 2002.
7   United Nations Office on Drugs, *World Drug Report, 2004*, Vol. 1: Analysis, p. 88.
8   The Drug Addicts in Our Country Increased by 100,000 in One Year, The Public Security Organs will Strengthen Supervision and Control, www.cnr.cn/china/gdgg/201007/t20100723_506784131.html
9   Zhou Yongming, *Anti-Drug Crusades in Twentieth-Century China*, p. 115.
10   *Annual Report on Drug Control in China*, 2002.

Table 14: Drugs-related crime in Yunnan, 2001–2008

Year	Cracked drug-related cases (1000)	Arrested criminal suspects drug-related (1000)	Narcotics seizure (tons)	Proportion of nationwide heroin seizure %	Proportion of nationwide methamphetamine seizure %	Proportion of opium seizure %
2008	13.16	15.02	6.54	67.20	33.50	92.22
2007	9.74	12.00	7.09	73.70	39.36	90.51
2006	9.96	11.98	9.60	80.10	75.80	91.10
2005	23.00	25.70	10.75	73.40	69.30	94.00
2004	16.67	20.39	9.82	78.14	–	–
2003	14.20	18.10	9.47	82.70	12.70	–
2002	15.00	1.90	0.87	73.50	–	–
2001	11.22	13.78	1.02	61.00	16.70	46.10

Source: *Yunnan Yearbook, 2000–2009; Annual Report on Drug Control in China, 2001, 2003, 2004.*

are exported to China.[11] "The bulk of heroin consumed in China is from the Golden Triangle."[12] China's 2.2 million heroin users, the largest population in absolute terms, were estimated to consume some 45 m/t of heroin in 2008. Most of the supply for China is sourced in Myanmar, although Afghan heroin appears to be gaining market share.[13] As a result, Myanmar must be an essential partner of China in solving the narcotics problem.

In order to control narcotics from Myanmar, Beijing has adopted a series of measures. China has set up three lines of defense to block narcotics from Myanmar: the first line, Yunnan province; the second line, Guangxi, Guizhou, and Sichuan adjacent to Yunnan; the third line, Guangdong, Fujian, Chongqing, Gansu, Ningxia, Hunan, Hubei, Henan and Anhui.[14] Yunnan province is thus China's focus against Myanmar narcotics. In April 2005, the China National Narcotics Control Commission launched the nationwide "People's War on Drugs" for a period of three years. Over the three years, Yunnan Province seized

11 United Nations Office on Drugs, *World Drug Report, 2004*, Vol. 1, pp. 88–89.
12 *Annual Report on Drug Control in China, 2006.*
13 United Nations Office on Drugs, *World Drug Report, 2010*, p. 42.
14 *Annual Report on Drug Control in China, 2000.*

12.9 tons of heroin, 9.3 tons of "ice," and 4.5 tons of opium from the Golden Triangle.[15]

China also actively participates in and promotes bilateral and regional cooperation in drug control with Myanmar. In May 1991, China hosted the first meeting of senior officials of China, Thailand, Myanmar, and the United Nations Drug Control Program (UNDCP) in Beijing, to discuss the proposal on multilateral cooperation against drug abuse in the sub-region. In June 1992, China, Myanmar, and the UNDCP signed the China/Myanmar/UNDCP Joint Cooperation Project on Drug Control in Yangon, Myanmar. A memorandum of understanding on Drug Control was signed in 1993 by the Governments of China, the Lao People's Democratic Republic, Myanmar, Thailand, and the United Nations Office on Drugs and Crime (UNODC). Cambodia and Vietnam became parties to the MoU at a Ministerial Meeting held in Beijing on 27 May 1995, and a Subregional Action Plan for Drug Control (SAP), including eleven projects at a total cost of more than US$15 million, was approved by the six Governments. Under the cooperative mechanism between the signatory countries of the MoU, a MoU ministerial meeting is held every two years; the annual Senior Officials Committee meetings, bilateral cross-border meetings, innovative pilot interventions in individual countries, technical training, and the strengthening of the managerial capacities of the governments on drug control projects and programs have been initiated and implemented. According to that program, offices for the Myanmar–China cross-border drug control cooperation were opened in Qingshuihe in Myanmar and Qingshuihe in China in 2001, and in Lwegel in Myanmar and Larin in China.

In 2000, China and the ten ASEAN countries endorsed the ASEAN and China Cooperative Operations in Response to Dangerous Drugs (ACCORD) aiming at eliminating or drastically reducing the problems of illicit drug production, trafficking, and abuse in the region by the year 2015. The ACCORD established a dynamic Plan of Action, and the ASEAN Governments and China agreed to strengthen coordination of their efforts in four major areas of activity.[16] Now, trafficking in illegal drugs has become

---

15 Deputy Secretary General of China's National Narcotics Control Commission (NNCC) and Director-General of Narcotics Control Bureau of the Ministry of Public Security Yang Fengrui's Speech at the press conference of China's State Council Information Office, www.scio.gov.cn/xwfbh/xwbfbh/wqfbh/2008/0625/200905/t308942.htm.

16 For the four major cooperation areas, see ASEAN and China Cooperative Operations in Response to Dangerous Drugs (ACCORD), www.aseansec.org/645.htm.

a priority between ASEAN and China on cooperation in the field of non-traditional security issues.[17]

Because of the serious epidemic of narcotic drugs in the Golden Triangle, Lao PDR, Myanmar, Thailand, and China have been affected by the problem. Accordingly, cooperation on drug control among these four countries was initiated, and their first Ministerial Meeting in 2001 was convened to "establish drug control partnership on the basis of the existing cooperation among the four countries."[18] From 2000, China signed MoUs on narcotic drugs control with Myanmar, Lao PDR, Thailand, and Vietnam, respectively.

"In connection with the drug problems along the border, a junior-officials meeting on Myanmar–China drug control cooperation is held every month, and information has been exchanged. In addition, as of 1996, a senior-officials meeting of Myanmar, China and UNDCP on drug control is held every six months. Information has been exchanged and cooperation promoted."[19] Also, the ministerial level meetings, MoU meetings on the topic of narcotic control, and regular meetings between Yunnan and Myanmar central and local authorities on counter-narcotics cooperation are held. Both sides in recent years have taken joint action to eradicate drug trafficking groups, drug trafficking networks, drug kingpins, and drug-manufacturing bases and laboratories in Myanmar. China has trained hundreds of Myanmar counter-narcotic personnel at the Yunnan Police Academy in Kunming.[20]

In order to block and interdict drug source in Myanmar, Beijing has been giving high priority to the strategy of eliminating the supply of illicit drugs by boosting alternative development programs in northern Myanmar. "Beginning in 1990, China has actively helped the northern parts of Myanmar and Laos, where poppies were traditionally planted, to promote alternative development by means of providing technological and agricultural support and developing tourism resources."[21] Between 2006 and 2008, China's central government appropriated over RMB100 million for alternative development activities in the two countries, helping to cultivate over 1 million mu (66,666 hectares) of substitute crops, and donated 10,000-ton rice and a certain amount of

17 See Joint Declaration of ASEAN and China On Cooperation in the Field of Non-traditional Security Issues, www.fmprc.gov.cn/eng/topics/zgcydyhz/dlczgdm/t26290.htm.

18 Thailand, Myanmar, Lao PDR, and China Cooperation on Drug Control, en.oncb.go.th/document/e1-coop-4L-idx.asp.

19 Kyaw Gaung, "Promotion of Myanmar–China Drug Control Cooperation", *The New Light of Myanmar*, 1 April 2002.

20 For details, see Xiaolin Guo, "Towards Resolution: China in the Myanmar Issue", Silk Road Paper, March 2007, pp. 62–63.

21 "White Paper: Narcotics Control in China", *China Facts and Figures*, March 2002.

medicines to farmers who gave up poppy cultivation to help them get alternative livelihoods. It also conducted satellite remote sensing and field surveys to efficiently monitor opium poppy cultivation in northern Myanmar.[22]

In April 2006, China's State Council issued a document encouraging Chinese investment in alternative development in Myanmar and Laos, and appropriated special funds worth RMB0.25 billion to develop alternative crop cultivation in the two countries. And the Ministry of Commerce, NDRC, Ministry of Agriculture, and Ministry of Public Security jointly organized a work team titled "122" to speed up alternative crop cultivation.[23] In an attempt to eradicate opium supply, the two countries signed an action program of cooperation for alternative development for curbing poppy cultivation on 20 November 2007. Under this program, both states have been developing alternative cultivation in northern Myanmar including the Kachin State Special Regions 1 and 2, Shan State Special Regions 1, 2 and 4 as well as other areas determined by both sides.[24]

By the end of December 2008, China's Ministry of Finance had appropriated a special fund of RMB150 million to Yunnan province for alternative development, and exempted and reduced import duties and value-added taxes amounting to RMB300 million on these agricultural products buyback produced in the areas devoted to alternative cultivation in Myanmar and Laos.[25] Up to the end of 2007, there had been 135 Yunnan enterprises investing in alternative development projects in Myanmar and Laos.[26] Preliminary statistics showed that China's enterprises invested RMB1.6 billion in over 200 alternative development projects in the two countries from 2006 to 2009.[27]

Poppy cultivation in Myanmar has declined significantly in the past decade (see Figure 4). "Perhaps the most important reason for the decline in opium cultivation in Burma is a number of opium bans declared by cease-fire groups in northern Shan State." The opium ban was carried out largely due to Chinese pressure.[28] China's efforts on alternative development in Myanmar also partly contributed to the decline. Nevertheless, these projects have had many un-

---

22 Deputy Secretary General of China's National Narcotics Control Commission (NNCC) and Director-General of Narcotics Control Bureau of the Ministry of Public Security, Yang Fengrui's Speech at the press conference of China's State Council Information Office, www.scio.gov.cn/xwfbh/xwbfbh/wqfbh/2008/0625/200905/t308942.htm.

23 *Annual Report on Drug Control in China, 2007.*

24 For details of the Action Program, see xxgk.yn.gov.cn/newsview.aspx?id=1111435.

25 *Annual Report on Drug Control in China, 2009.*

26 *Annual Report on Drug Control in China, 2008.*

27 Chen Baojiang, Yang Fan, "Mutual Benefit and Development", *Yunnan Daily*, 1 September 2010.

28 Tom Kramer, Martin Jelsma and Tom Blickman, "Withdrawal Symptoms in the Golden Triangle: A Drugs Market in Disarray", Transnational Institute, 2009, p. 22.

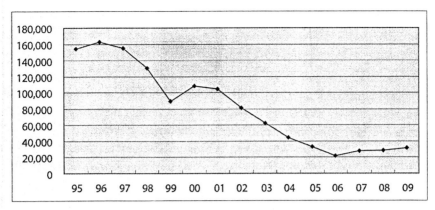

Figure 4: Myanmar illicit cultivation of opium poppy and production of opiates, 1995–2009 (hectares). Source: UNODC.

desired effects and do not significantly profit the population. Most ex-poppy planters have not been able to find alternative sources of income. They barely cultivate more food, grow alternative cash crops, or find casual labor to solve their food gap. Consequently, "Current levels of [China's] support are insufficient, and need to be upgraded in order to provide sustainable alternatives for the population."[29] The population in the Wa State that is free from opium production is among the poorest in the country, as alternative crops/employment are lacking. Some Chinese companies also exploit an advantage of crop substitution policies for their own economic interests: they apply for preferential loans and subsidies from the Chinese government and use them to invest in non-opium cultivation projects in Myanmar. China's government needs to increase supervision of their operations in Myanmar lest Beijing's substitution programs and policy should continue to be distorted and undermined. As the Transnational Institute and International Crisis Group reports have pointed out, the Chinese government should re-evaluate its policies[30]and "take into account the lessons learned from alternative development projects in other parts of the world."[31]

As Milsom noted, "China has played a key role in the Wa strategy to move away from illicit drug dependence, as it is by far the most important country to the WSR [Wa Special Region] economy. New industries pursued by the WCA [Wa Central Administration] and new services have largely been developed

29   Tom Kramer, "From Golden Triangle to Rubber Belt: The Future of Opium Bans in the Kokang and Wa Regions", Transnational Institute, July 2009, pp. 1–2.
30   "China's Myanmar Dilemma", International Crisis Group Asia Report, No. 177, 2009, p. 41.
31   Kramer, et al., "Withdrawal Symptoms in the Golden Triangle, p. 35.

through the procurement of Chinese support. But while China provides the opportunity, its trade policies have also been a major constraint on the success of the transition in the WSR. The Wa commercial ventures largely rely on gaining access to Chinese markets to be successful, and market access has remained problematic throughout the period of study."[32]

China's motive of alternative development policy in Myanmar and Laos is important in spite of its problems and unanticipated effects. It should be noted that China is the leading victim of Golden Triangle narcotics. According to UNDOC, "More than three quarters of Myanmar's production (some 40 m/t of heroin) supply the local and regional markets, primarily those that are Chinese." The estimated rate of heroin flow interceptions in China was 8 percent in 2008.[33] "The official Chinese statistics have focused on the heavy heroin users, and this new population of abusers does not appear on the Chinese radar-screen."[34] According to international practice that there are four hidden drug users behind each dominant drug addict, the real number of drug addicts in China now at least amounts to over 7 million.

Although poppy cultivation and opium production in Myanmar have fallen, the amount of narcotics entering China from the Golden Triangle has not decreased because the output of amphetamine-type stimulants (ATS) in this region has grown sharply and increasingly flow into China's market.[35] According to the UNDOC report, while the drug problem in China has long been dominated by opium and later heroin, by the end of the 1990s methamphetamine and ecstasy began to appear increasingly in the Chinese illicit drug market.[36] "The areas of northern Myanmar cause the most serious damage to our country and the condition will hardly change in the short term. The methamphetamine tablets inflow from these areas has risen significantly."[37] In addition, some precursor chemicals used to produce heroin have been smuggled to the Golden Triangle from China.

---

32 Jeremy D. Milsom. "Conflicting Agendas: Illicit Drugs, Development and Security in the Wa Special Region of Myanmar", Ph.D. Dissertation, University of Melbourne, School of Land and Environment, Department of Resource Management and Geography, October 2010, p. 171.

33 United Nations Office on Drugs, *World Drug Report, 2010*, p. 46.

34 Niklas Swanström and Yin He, *China's War on Narcotics: Two Perspectives, Silk Road Paper*, December 2006, p. 19.

35 *Annual Report on Drug Control in China, 2004, 2010*.

36 United Nations Office on Drugs and Crime, Patterns and Trends of Amphetamine-Type Stimulants and Other Drugs in East and South-East Asia(and neighboring regions), 2009, p. 54.

37 China's Narcotics Control Activities, www.scio.gov.cn/xwfbh/xwbfbh/wqfbh/2008/0625/200905/t308941.htm.

In China, "Drugs are bringing increasingly severe damage to society, triggering a large number of criminal cases, public security problems and the spread of HIV/AIDS, and affecting social stability and public security."[38] Despite some efforts in drug control, the landscape and outlook of rampant illegal narcotics in China is grim. Besides China's domestic factors, external factors pose a difficult dilemma for Beijing. "Narcotics trafficking in China is a problem, yet the issue is not receiving enough attention from the Chinese government, the media, policy institutions, the United Nations or foreign governments. Heroin, opium, and AST consumption and distribution within China are not solely a Chinese issue, but an international one."[39] The narcotics issue in China–Myanmar relations is especially the case. Although both parties increasingly have intensified cooperation on drug control under bilateral and regional mechanisms, the areas of north Myanmar remain the biggest threat to China. Over the past two decades, China has provided assistance worth over RMB500 million for crop substitution projects in Myanmar and Laos. The amount, however, cannot compare with China's other economic assistance or project investment in Myanmar (see Chapter 8). China has no reason to deny money to interdict and eradicate its leading drug source. Indeed, it is in China's interest to do so.

The crux of this matter does not lie in the drugs of northern Myanmar alone. It is compounded and complicated by Naypyitaw-ceasefire group relations, Burmese–ethnic group relations, the Myanmar political situation, poverty eradication, and economic development in the north of Myanmar, as well as Burmese attitudes towards China's dominant presence in upper Myanmar. Although Myanmar has been recognized for its efforts to collaborate with its neighbors in jointly controlling the transportation of precursor chemicals, in an effort to reduce narcotics production and trafficking in the highlands of Southeast Asia, "The political situation in Myanmar has also discouraged many donor countries that could have been helpful to its law enforcement efforts. This is a pertinent issue because continued opium poppy eradication drives farmers into deeper destitution. Without viable alternative sources of income, it is only a matter of time before the farmers either revert back to growing opium poppies or participate in producing synthetic drugs."[40]

---

38 Officials of the Narcotics Control Bureau of the Ministry of Public Security of China Talk about China's Drug Control, http://ipc.fmprc.gov.cn/eng/zjhd/t143444.htm.
39 Ryan Clarke, "Narcotics Trafficking in China: Size, Scale, Dynamic and Future Consequences", *Pacific Affairs*, Spring 2008, 81, 1, p. 92.
40 Ko-lin Chin and Sheldon X. Zhang, "The Chinese Connection: Cross-border Drug Trafficking between Myanmar and China", Final Report to The United States Department of Justice Office of Justice Programs, National Institute of Justice, April 2007, p. 70.

China, however, has not been alone in its concern over opium/heroin production in Burma/Myanmar. While China was rigorously eliminating internal drug use, the market for Burmese heroin was in the United States. This created internal U.S. political pressure for the elimination of heroin in Burma. To this end, some tens of millions of dollars were allocated for opium suppression, and these were used, among other things, to supply helicopters and other equipment to monitor and destroy the poppy fields. This project came to an end in 1988, although the U.S. continued to support U.N. efforts.

Because of the drop in opium production, the U.S. had worked with Burmese military intelligence in 2002 to try to certify that Myanmar was in compliance with U.S. anti-narcotics legislation. A senior Burmese official was invited to Washington to negotiate the details, but after hopes had been raised and reputations committed to the effort, various influential Congressmen prevented this from being achieved, ostensibly because of methamphetamine production, which essentially was directed toward Thailand.[41] No Burmese heroin has been seized in the United States in the last several years.[42]

Japan, in an effort to assist in crop substitution, instituted a buckwheat production project for the production of soba noodles. This project failed to be economically viable because the cost of the product was high in relation to transport costs, and buckwheat for the Japanese market was far more cheaply available from Chinese sources, where transport costs were much lower.

China's "Look South": The China–Myanmar Transport Corridor

Myanmar's importance in world affairs has long derived from its critical geostrategic position. Not until the Second World War, when it became China's "gateway" or "back door,"[43] did China really realize that Burma occupied a geostrategic position of some importance. Since then, the "Burma Road" has become a concrete and the most well-known example illustrating Chinese understanding of Myanmar's importance for China.

When the map of traffic construction in Southwest (particularly Yunnan Province) China is spread out, Beijing's fan-shaped "Look South" strategy with Yunnan as the pivot is clearly evident. The strategy, extending southward,

---

41 Thai Prime Minister Thaksin, under political pressure, ordered a war on drugs, which resulted in over 2,800 extra-judicial killings by authorities.

42 *National Drug Assessment of 2009*. Washington, D.C., p. 31.

43 See, for example, H. I. Deigan, "Burma – Gateway to China", Smithsonian Institution War Background Studies No. 17, 1943; "World Battlefronts: Back Door to China", *Time*, 21 December 1942.

corroborates that China and Southeast Asia have never been so closely interconnected.

Yunnan shares a 4,060 km land border with Laos, Myanmar, and Vietnam. There are 11 first-category ports, 9 second-category ports, and over 90 passages to the outside world in Yunnan. For China, the province is the most convenient location connecting the Indian Ocean with the Pacific Ocean, bridging the three markets of China, Southeast Asia, and South Asia.

Yunnan authorities planned the initiative of a "Yunnan International Passage" in 1992. However, it had no occasion to undertake the blueprint for it until the Chinese "Western Development" strategy was started in 1999. Under the "Western Development" plan, improved transport was a priority. Under these circumstances, Yunnan soon formulated the basic program, general objectives, and main tasks of "Western Development" in the province. At the end of 1999, Kunming formally established the goal of making Yunnan an international passage connecting China to Southeast Asia and South Asia. The Yunnan government stated that, "The construction of [such an] international passage is Yunnan's inevitable choice of exerting its location advantage and expanding its opening-up to make full use of Yunnan's beneficial factors of linking China with Southeast Asia and South Asia by land, water, and air."[44]

As a result, China has made efforts since the advent of the 21st century to undertake and push the Sino–Myanmar transport corridor. The project is driven by China's geo-economic and geo-strategic interests, and is also Beijing's step to implement its "Two-Ocean" strategy, which will affect geopolitics in South Asia and Southeast Asia. The corridor has an important impact on current and future Sino–Myanmar relations; it is like an adhesive binding bilateral geopolitical and economic ties.

China–Myanmar Roads

The strategy of the "Yunnan International Passage" consists of three dimensions: transportation construction between Yunnan and foreign countries, between Yunnan and other domestic provinces, and within Yunnan province itself.[45] For road transport, Yunnan has laid out a framework for the "International Passage", and plans to build "three vertical lines", "three horizontal lines," and "nine passages".

---

44 Li Jiating, Yunnan Governor, "Constructing Distinct Economic System during Western Development", in *Go West: Chinese leaders' viewpoints on developing the western regions*, Beijing: Central Party Literature Press, 2001, p. 134.
45 Niu Shaoyao, "Yunnan: Constructing International Passage", *People's Daily*, 28 August 2000.

"Three vertical lines":

(1) Yibin–Zhaotong–Kunming–Hekou(1,016 km);
(2) Dukou–Yongren–Wuding–Kunming–Mohan(958 km);
(3) Yanjing–Deqin–Zhongdian–Dali–Lincang–Daluo (1,397 km).[46]

"Three horizontal lines":

(1) Panzhihua–Huaping–Lijiang–Jianchuan–Lanping–Liuku (642 km);
(2) Guizhou-Shengjingguan – Qujing–Kunming–Dali–Baoshan–Ruili (965 km);
(3) Guangxi–Funing–Kaiyuan–Jianshui–Yuanjiang–Puer–Jinggu–Lin-cang–Qingshuihe (1,493 km).

"Nine passages": Five passages connecting Yunnan to other provinces:

(1) Kunming–Nanning–Beihai (553 km in Yunnan);
(2) Kunming–Guiyang (204 km in Yunnan);
(3) Kunming–Shuifu–Chengdu (250 km in Yunnan);
(4) Kunming–Panzhihua–Chengdu (250 km in Yunnan);
(5) Kunming–Dali–Zhongdian–Tibet (950 km in Yunnan).

Four passages connecting Yunnan to Southeast Asian countries:

(1) Kunming–Mohan–Laos–Bankok;
(2) Kunming–Ruili–Yangon;
(3) Kunming–Hekou–Vietnam;
(4) Kunming–Tengchong–Myanmar–India.[47]

Yunnan's road layout for its "International Passage" postulates three road lines reaching the China–Myanmar border in the six lines of "three vertical" and "three horizontal". In "Nine passages", there are two passages leading to Myanmar. The roads of Kunming–Ruili–Yangon and Kunming–Tengchong–Myanmar–India are actually the updated editions of the Burma Road and the Stilwell Road.

In recent years, Beijing and Yunnan have built and upgraded some roads in Yunnan extending to Myanmar and some leading to Yunnan in Myanmar territory.

---

46 Hekou, Mohan and Daluo are China–Vietnam, China–Laos and China–Myanmar border cities, respectively.
47 Chen Ping, "Survey on 'three vertical lines', 'three horizontal lines' and 'nine passages' Highway Net in Yunnan", 29 January 2008, yunnan.mofcom.gov.cn/aarticle/sjdixiansw/200801/20080105359455.html.

Table 15: Roads of the China–Myanmar transport corridor (RMB billion)

Road name	Road class	Length, km	Investment	Building time
Kunming–Anning	Highway	22	2.81	2004- 2007
Anning–Chuxiong	Highway	130	4.90	2002- 2005
Chuxiong–Dali	Highway	179	5.29	1995–1999
Dali–Baoshan	Highway	165	7.04	1998–2002
Baoshan–Longling	Highway	76	5.54	2004–2008
Longling–Ruili	Highway & Class II	158	10.94	2009–2012
Baoshan–Tengchong	Highway	154	4.61	2007–2010
Tengchong–Myitkyina	Class II	176	12.30	2004–2007
Jinghong–Damenglong	Class II	60	0.45	2004–2008
Zhangfeng–Bhamo	Class IV	79	0.03	2004–2007
Yingjiang–Nabang	Class II & Class IV	92	0.23	2003–2005
Tengchong–Banwa	Class II	72	0.46	2003–2006

Source: Department of Communications of Yunnan Province; *China Communications News*; *China Railway Construction News*; The Economic and Commercial Section of the Consulate General of PRC in Mandalay; Yunnan Highway Development and Investment Co., Ltd.

Note: The Longling–Ruili highway includes 154.6 km highway and 3.112 km class II road, and links up the Ruili–Bhamo road; the Baoshan-Tengchong highway requires building 63.94 km length and uses the available 90 km Baoshan–Longling highway, connecting to the Tengchong–Myitkyina road; the terminals of Jinghong–Damenglong and Tengchong–Banwa are the China–Myanmar border demarcation stone No. 240 and No. 4, respectively.

Yunnan plans to construct main highway passages leading to Vietnam, Laos, Myanmar, and Thailand by 2010. Its trunk highway net will link up all 20 ports in Yunnan. Of 18 passages, 13 will reach Myanmar, 4 reach Vietnam, and one reach Laos.[48] Table 15 shows that 95 percent of the Kunming–Ruili highway, via Anning, Chuxiong, Dali, Baoshan, and Longling, has been open to traffic, while the remaining section, the Longling–Ruili highway, has also been under construction. The Baoshan–Tengchong highway and Tengchong–Myitkyina road Class II were built and upgraded in 2007, facilitating the passage to South Asia via Myanmar.

48 Department of Communications of Yunnan Province, "Layout of Yunnan Road Net (2005–2020)", xxgk.yn.gov.cn/bgt_Model1/newsview.aspx?id=236838.

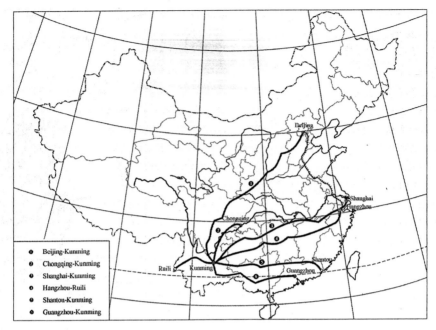

Map 9: Routes to Yunnan in China's national highway network planning

Besides the trunk highway stretching to Myanmar, China has built and upgraded many roads to various Sino–Myanmar border ports, such as the Jinghong–Damenglong, Zhangfeng–Bhamo, Tengchong–Banwa, and Ying-jing–Banwa, especially since 2005 when Yunnan began to implement the project of "Prosper the Borders to Enrich Local People"(PBELP).

In response to the "Western Development" strategy, the State Ethnic Affairs Commission (SEAC), China, initialized the PBELP project in 135 border cities and counties in 2000; its aim is to lift the economic development levels of China's border area within 10 years by increasing infrastructure investment and promoting a group of profitable programs.

Yunnan allocated RMB4.8 billion from 2005 to 2007 to carry out the PBELP project in its 8 prefectures and cities, and 25 border counties. It completed the connection of trunk highways in border areas and surface hardening of roads leading to townships in the province.[49] The Eleventh Five-Year Plan for PBELP, endorsed by the State Council on 9 June 2007, set the first aim of improving backward situations in communications, electricity, and irrigation works infrastructure in border areas. One of its main tasks through joint efforts is to

49 General Office of the People's Government of Yunnan Province, "The Completion con-dition of 20 Key Projects in Yunnan", xxgk.yn.gov.cn/bgt_Model1/newsview.aspx?id= 236889.

reinforce the construction of highways in the border regions, including trunk highways and roads to counties and villages, ports, sites for barter trade, tourist sites, and defense highways suited for both military and civilian services.[50]

In May 2008, the new three-year PBELP project in Yunnan began to be implemented. In combination with the construction of the defense highway and the "Yunnan International Passage," the key task of the new project was to expedite the construction of the highway net, upgrade the roads and strive for the completion of 750 km of trunk highway and 2,100 km of county roads in border regions, gradually solving the transport bottleneck hampering frontier development. In response, Yunnan has appropriated RMB10.71847 billion for the new project.[51]

Currently, although Beijing has not definitely upgraded the "Yunnan International Passage" to state strategic plan level, the central government is building Yunnan as a land traffic pivot between the eastern provinces and Southeast Asia in terms of the "National Highway Network Planning" approved in 2004. China is investing heavily in building the highway net connecting Yunnan with the east coast developed regions and provinces in order to improve the insufficient road infrastructure that is impeding economic intercourse between them.

The Planning includes 7 routes starting from Beijing, 9 South–North longitudinal routes, and 18 East–West latitudinal routes, referred to as the "7918 Network", with a total length of about 85,000 km. In accordance with the Planning, China is building a highway from Hangzhou to the China–Myanmar border city of Ruili (Coding G56), which is 3,405 km long via Zhejiang, Anhui, Jiangxi, Hubei, Hunan, Guizhou, and Yunnan. Moreover, as can be seen in Map 9, the program noticeably shows that five highways from other developed cities to Kunming are being or planned to be built, namely, Shanghai–Kunming(G60, 2,370 km), Shantou–Kunming(G78, 1,710 km), Guangzhou–Kunming (G80, 1,610 km), Beijing–Kunming (G5, 2,865 km), and Chongqing–Kunming (G85, 838 km).

The Myanmar–China oil and gas pipelines project will spur infrastructure development, particularly roads along the pipelines in Myanmar. The two countries, for example, signed a MoU on the development of cooperation on the China–Myanmar Corridor Project to link Ruili and Kyaukpyu on 18 May

50   State Ethnic Affairs Commission of China, "The Eleventh Five-Year Plan for 'Prosper the Borders to Enrich Local People'", www.seac.gov.cn/gjmw/zt/2007-06-15/1181878972642969. htm.

51   "New Three-Year Plan for 'Prosper the Borders to Enrich Local People' in Yunnan", *Yunnan Political Affairs*, No. 11, 2008, p. 23.

2010. According to the Corridor Project, China will help Myanmar construct a railway and motorway from Kyaukphyu Township in Rakhine State to Ruili in China in near future.[52]

The China–Myanmar Railway

In December 1995, Premier Mahathir Mohammad of Malaysia announced the Trans-Asia Railway initiative to build a Kunming–Singapore Rail Link; it was unanimously endorsed by the ASEAN countries and China.

In response to ASEAN's initiative on the Trans-Asia Railway, China formulated three route options:

(1) East route: Singapore–Kuala Lumpur–Bangkok–Phnom Penh–Ho Chi Minh City–Hanoi–Kunming;

(2) West route: Singapore–Kuala Lumpur–Bangkok–Yangon–Lashio–Ruili–Dali–Kunming;

(3) Middle route: Singapore–Kuala Lumpur–Bangkok–Vientiane–Shangyong–Xiangyun (or Yuxi) – Kunming).

Now, the three routes in Chinese territory have been included in the "National Middle/Long Term Transport Plans of China" issued in 2004.

The West route is 2,600 km-long, and needs building 840 km new railways, of which China–Myanmar railway is one section. In China's section, the Kunming–Ruili railway is 690 km long. In 1998, the railway between Kunming and Dali via Guangtong was completed and put into service. So it remains constructing the railway between Dali and Ruili. Besides, a 132 km new railway from Ruili to Lashio needs building if China's railway net is to be linked to Myanmar's railway net. Now, China is making an effort to realize the railway link between Kunming and Yangon.

In light of the "Middle/Long Term Transport Plan", China plans to build the section of Kunming–Jinghong–Mohan in the Sino–Laos passage, the section of Dali–Ruili in the Sino–Myanmar passage, and upgrade the section of Kunming–Hekou in the Sino–Vietnam passage. In addition, "The Eleventh Five-year Plan of China's Railway" framed by China's Ministry of Railway states that it will build the Dali–Ruili railway and rebuild the double-track railway of Kunming–Guangtong section of the Kunming–Dali rail link before 2010. In 2007, the 350 km long Dali–Ruili railway project started, with estimated

---

52 "MoU on China–Myanmar Corridor Project inked", *The New Light of Myanmar*, 19 May 2010.

Plate 10: Ruili border crossing, China (photograph David Steinberg)

Plate 11: Muse border crossing, Myanmar (viewed from Ruili, photograph David Steinberg). Ruili–Muse is the most important transit point in China–Myanmar trade.

total investment of RMB14.7 billion, which was put on the list of "Ten Major Projects of Western Development" in that year.

Also, the China–Myanmar railway will become one part of "The Third Asia–Europe Continental Bridge" conceived by China, connecting the east coast of the Atlantic Ocean with China's east coast via Yunnan. It connects seaports in Guangdong province to Kunming, Myanmar, Bangladesh, India, Pakistan, Iran, and Turkey, enters Europe, and reaches Rotterdam in the Netherlands. China expects to link the Asian South to its Southeast by means of the western route of the Trans-Asia Railway and construct a "Continental Bridge," which will become another of China's safe and convenient land international thoroughfares.

The China–Myanmar River Navigation Route

While China is constructing a road and railway transportation net link to Southeast Asian countries, Yunnan is also developing a water transport plan of constructing "two waterways reaching other provinces," i.e., the Jinsha River and the You River leading to the Yangtze River Delta and the Pearl River Delta, and "three waterways reaching foreign countries", which are the Lancang-Mekong River, China–Myanmar Land and Water course, and the China–Vietnam Hong River.

The Lancang-Mekong River, 4,880 km long, runs through China, Laos, Myanmar, Thailand, Cambodia, and Vietnam. On 7 January 1997, China and Myanmar signed the "Agreement on Passenger and Cargo Shipment on the Lancang-Mekong River." China opened the ports of Jinghong, Simao, Menghan, and Guanlei, and Myanmar opened the Wan Seng and Wan Pong ports. On 20 April 2000, China, Laos, Myanmar and Thailand signed the "Agreement on Commercial Navigation on the Lancang-Mekong River". The official inauguration of commercial navigation among the four countries followed on 26 June 2001.

At the end of 2006, China started oil shipping via the Mekong River. Two ships each carrying 150 tons of refined oil arrived at Guanlei port of Yunnan province from Thailand via the Mekong River, marking the trial launch of China's oil shipping program with its Southeast Asian partners; the waterway will serve as a modest alternative to the Strait of Malacca as a route for oil shipping and supply to Yunnan and Southwest China.

In order to improve the commercial navigability of the water course, China has initiated a program of dredging and removing of rapids, reefs, and shoals in the Lower Mekong River. China provided a sum of RMB42 million in 2000 for upgrading 331 km Mekong River course shared by Laos and Myanmar. But a new challenge, the navigation security and safety on the Mekong River, is facing China.

The China–Myanmar land–water passage's full name is "The China Kunming–Myanmar Yangon Irrawaddy River Portage Passage" which is an integrative land and water carriage system including land transport from Kunming to Bhamo via Baoshan and Ruili, the water course from Bhamo port to Yangon, as well as other ports, portage transfers, and sea ports.

When He Zhiqiang, the Governor of Yunnan Province, visited Myanmar in 1989, Myanmar's Head of State General Saw Maung suggested that both sides make joint use of Irrawaddy River navigation. After this, China and Myanmar held a series of talks, explorations and pre-feasibility studies on the proposal.

The construction of Ruili–Bhamo road and Bhamo port, with estimated investment of RMB0.37 billion and RMB0.16 billion, are at the core of Sino–Myanmar land and water passage. Both countries originally agreed on "joint construction and operation, joint share venture and profit." Nevertheless, Yangon later claimed that China would build the passage only in the form of "Build–Operate–Transfer" (BOT) in a thirty-year operating period. China agreed to Yangon's claim of BOT.

Myanmar agreed that China could use the Irrawaddy River as its outlet to the Indian Ocean when China's President Jiang Zemin visited Myanmar in 2001. In the meantime, Burmese generals, however, attached three harsh conditions so that the blueprint went once more on the shelf. Naypyitaw still has not given the green light to the project. Obviously, Myanmar is very conscious that the project, China's access to the Indian Ocean, will change the geopolitical structure in the Asia–Pacific region. It has to consider its peripheral counties' and other stakeholders' postures, notably India and the ASEAN countries. Myanmar continues to take the wait-and-see attitude and to make risk-reward calculations.

Myanmar's hesitation on the project has not retarded China's efforts for it. Zhangfeng is the nearest Chinese port to Bhamo. Because of the limited transport capacity of Zhangfeng–Bhamo road, the Longchuan government provided a sum of RMB28 million to upgrade the road between Longchuan and Bhamo. The project was completed in 2006 and transferred to Myanmar. China is still responsible for the maintenance of the road.[53] The 224 km Myitkyina–Kanpikete–Tengchong cross-border road began to be built in 2004

---

53   Fan Lichuan and Li Qichang, "The Upgrade of Zhangfeng–Bhamo Road Starting", *Yunnan Daily*, 6 December 2004.

through joint efforts with the prior section on the Myanmar side. With the assistance of Chinese engineers, the 96-km Myitkyina–Kanpikete section in Myanmar was completed and opened in April 2007.

Implications of the Sino–Myanmar Transport Corridor

The Sino–Myanmar Transport Corridor has four critical dimensions: historical, regional cooperation, China's overall strategy, and Yunnan's perspective. History is a factor conditioning China's perception of the China–Myanmar transport corridor as well as Myanmar's strategic significance, as it has a bearing on Beijing's strategic thinking and policies towards its Southern neighbor.

Historical evidence shows that China's current vision of opening a route through Myanmar is nothing new. The famous Southwest Silk Road linked up China with Southeast Asia and South Asia via Yunnan. In the late Qing Dynasty and early Kuomintang era, China planned to build a Yunnan–Burma road. During the Second World War, China began to build the China–Burma railway with the aid of the U.S. and the U.K., but the project had to be abandoned when Japan overran Burma and the west of Yunnan in 1942. But the newly built Burma Road and Stilwell Road functioned to a certain extent in this period.

Beijing suggested that the two countries negotiate a China–Burma "through transport" in 1955.[54]Former Vice Minister of Chinese Communications, Pan Qi, proposed in 1985 that "The opening of the southwest can run parallel to that of the east, and can be carried out at the same time." Two channels from the southwest to the outside world were available: one to the East China coast along the Yangtze and Xijiang Rivers; the other to the South via Burma. "There were several possible passages from Yunnan to the outside world. From Tengchong, one highway leads westward to Myitkyina, in Burma, where a railroad is available to transfer cargo to the sea. A second highway leads south to Lashio, another major Burmese railhead. And between those two, a third road leads to Bhamo, on the Irrawaddy River. None of these roads is over 300 kilometers long."[55]

---

54 China suggests negotiations with Burma about highway transportation between the two countries, AMFA, File no. 105-00177-01(1).

55 Pan Qi, "Opening the Southwest: An Expert Opinion", *Beijing Review*, 28:35(2 September 1985), p. 23. Western scholars often cite this article to illustrate that the Chinese vision of seeking an outlet via Burma is an old dream, such as: Bertil Lintner, "Friends of Necessity", *Far Eastern Economic Review*, 164:51 (27 December 2001–3 January 2002), p. 24; J. Mohan Malik, "Sino-Indian Rivalry in Myanmar: Implications for Regional Security", *Contempo-*

In the late 1980s and early 1990s, Yunnan proposed to rebuild the China–Burma rail, but the proposal was not adopted by Beijing. All the historic routes – the Yunnan–Burma ancient tea caravan trail, the Burma Road, the Stilwell Road and the China–Burma rail – had the same economic, strategic and military significance as the China–Burma transport route. Since the end of the nineteenth century and the beginning of the twentieth century, the Chinese made many efforts to build the Sino-Burmese railway but they failed because of China's frail power and turbulent political situation. Now, with the advent of rapid globalization, China's rise, and the launch of "West Development", Yunnan and Beijing have blown the clarion of constructing the China–Burma road and rail again, and wishes to realize its old dream. The Sino–Myanmar transport corridor is Beijing's important measure of maintaining its influence and leading role in the arrangement of regional and sub-regional cooperation, resulting in increased Chinese participation in Southeast Asia and South Asia.

At present, Southeast Asia, particularly the Indochina Peninsula, is one of the most energetic regions of regional and subregional cooperation in Asia; various organizations for regional cooperation and platforms are overlapping. Myanmar is a nexus in this multiple network. With regionalism rising in Southeast Asia, China is being confronted with the challenge of how to maximize its interests in regional cooperation. On these regional and subregional platforms, bilateral and multilateral cooperation on transportation are high priorities.

The China–Myanmar railway is the western route of the Trans-Asia Railway, which is an important project cooperatively to be built by China and ASEAN. In December 2002 and September 2003, China and Myanmar acceded to the "GMS Agreement for the Facilitation of Cross-Border Transport of People and Goods". The road between Kunming and Lashio via Ruili will be a route for GMS transport under that agreement.

In 1998, the 8th GMS Ministers meeting advanced a plan to build an economic corridor, combine the construction of the transport corridor with economic development, and provide the facilitation for GMS members' cooperation and traffic. The GMS economic corridor consists of the North–South Economic Corridor (covering Kunming–Bangkok, Kunming–Hanoi, and Nanning–Hanoi – three economic zones), the East–West Economic Corridor (covering Mawlamyine to Thailand and middle Vietnam), and the South Economic Corridor (covering the area from Bangkok to Phnom Penh and the

rary Southeast Asia, 16:2 (September 1994), p. 141; J. Mohan Malik, "Myanmar's Role in Regional Security: Pawn or Pivot?", *Contemporary Southeast Asia*, 19:1 (June 1997), p. 57. Actually, China's scheme was conceived at least in the beginning of 20th century.

south of Vietnam). In accordance with the general layout of the GMS transport net, the economic corridor will develop in three stages: transport construction, logistics construction, and economic corridor construction.

China and ASEAN leaders signed the "Joint Declaration of the Heads of State/Government of The People's Republic of China and The Member States of ASEAN on Strategic Partnership for Peace and Prosperity" at the seventh ASEAN–China Summit on 8 October 2003 in Bali, Indonesia. Pursuant to the Joint Declaration, a "Plan of Action to Implement the Joint Declaration on the ASEAN–China Strategic Partnership for Peace and Prosperity" was formulated to serve as the "master plan" to deepen and broaden ASEAN–China relations and cooperation in a comprehensive and mutually beneficial manner for the next five years (2005–2010). In light of the Plan of Action, ASEAN and China pursue the following three joint measures: "Develop the Singapore–Kunming Rail Link"; "Build railways and roads from Kunming to Yangon and Myitikyina"; "Carry out a feasbility study of building railway links from China to Laos and Myanmar".[56] Cambodia, China, Laos, Myanmar, Thailand, and Vietnam signed the "Memorandum of Understanding toward the Sustainable and Balanced Development of the GMS North–South Economic Corridor and Enhanced Organizational Effectiveness for Developing Economic Corridors" on 31 March 2008. It stated, "The economic North–South Economic Corridor consists of three major routes linking economic and population centers in the northern and central parts of the GMS, namely: (I) the Kunming–Chiang Rai–Bangkok via Lao PDR and Myanmar route, including both land transport and waterway; (II) the Kunming–Hanoi–Haiphong route; and (III) the Nanning–Hanoi route."[57]

In China's overall strategy, the Sino–Myanmar transport corridor is the basis of a "Two-Ocean" strategy and one step of the "Western Development" strategy. In the Asia–Pacific area, China's interests are focusing on the economic and security dimensions which are reflected in its peripheral diplomatic principles – "good neighbor, good partners, and good friends". China's good

---

56 Ministry of Foreign Affairs of PRC, Plan of Action to Implement the Joint Declaration on ASEAN–China Strategic Partnership for Peace and Prosperity, 21 December 2004, www.fmprc.gov.cn/eng/wjb/zzjg/yzs/dqzzywt/t175815.htm.

57 Memorandum of Understanding Toward the Sustainable and Balanced Development of the GMS North–South Economic Corridor and Enhanced Organizational Effectiveness for Developing Economic Corridors, www.adb.org/Documents/Events/2008/3rd-GMS-Summit/NSEC&Economic-Corridor.pdf.

neighbor policy is characterized by mutual security, mutual cooperation, and mutual development.

China shares land borders with 14 countries, whose border regions are mostly impoverished ethnic minority-inhabited areas. Such conditions are antithetical to the political stability of China's frontier, defense, and the eradication of ethnic separatism. Therefore, Beijing launched the initiative of PBELP. The project is a reflection of China's strategic and security considerations in its periphery.

The problems in the border regions to which Beijing addresses itself are very prominent and serious in Yunnan. There are 25 border counties in Yunnan, which include 22 autonomous ethnic counties and 17 key poverty-alleviation counties. In addition, 16 trans-border ethnic groups live in the frontier regions of Yunnan. One hundred thousand people in Yunnan have migrated to neighboring countries such as Myanmar, Thailand, Laos, and Vietnam in recent years thanks to poverty and comparative economic attractions abroad. "Some of them become the object of ethnic separatists, who enlist them, and some have joined their armed forces on the Yunnan frontier."[58]

China's interest in Myanmar primarily lies in ensuring the security of the 2,186 km-long boundary. China thus needs to solve the difficult problems of border control, trans-border ethnic issues, AIDS control, and drug smuggling. The various "color revolutions" in Central Asia since the advent of 21st century, the turbulence in Myanmar, and Washington's attitude to Naypyitaw also cause Beijing to keep a close watch on the Myanmar situation. Consequently, China must necessarily influence and control the Sino–Myanmar frontiers if it wants to solve threats to its national security.

The China–Myanmar transport corridor, in addition, is necessary to carry out the "Two-Ocean" strategy. When Japan occupied China's eastern seaports and cut off the Pacific in 1940s, the Burma Road played an important role in defending China's national security. The experience has continued strongly to impress on China's memory. Currently, Chinese weak naval capacity, the "Malacca dilemma", the South China Sea dispute, the Taiwan issue, and other potential threats in the Pacific further increase Beijing's anxiety about complete reliance on Pacific Ocean access, and thus heighten its attention to Myanmar's role as a strategic passage. Therefore, China looks to construct a new strategic thoroughfare, the China–Myanmar transport corridor with access to the Indian Ocean, in order to reduce the reliance on the Pacific Ocean and the Malacca Straits. To expand China's influence in Southeast Asia

---

58   Chen Yanhui, "The Blurred Border", *Phoenix* Weekly, No. 19, 2007.

and South Asia and counterbalance India's presence in the two regions are also aims of this transport corridor.

The China–Myanmar transport corridor is an extension of the "West Development" strategy for mutual cooperation and mutual development. Transport infrastructure has continuously been weak and the economy has developed slowly in west China. In the "West Development" strategy, China wants to use Myanmar as a relay station for the export of west China's products, the import of resources, and a convenient channel for southwest China's opening. For Yunnan, Guizhou, Sichuan, and other western provinces in China, the China–Myanmar transport corridor not only facilitates access to foreign markets far better than the Pacific route, but it can break the bottleneck of inadequate transport.

Yunnan is the direct promoter and beneficiary of a China–Myanmar transport corridor. Yunnan is a landlocked plateau province, and 94 percent of its area is mountainous and semi-mountainous regions. Yunnan's backward transport infrastructure impedes its economic development. Hence, Yunnan is the protagonist and activist of the program, striving for Beijing's support. In recent years, Yunnan has submitted the proposal for the "International Passage" to Beijing many times, and wants the project to be incorporated in the central government's macro plan, gaining Beijing's funding and policy support. For example, the Yunnan delegation proposed that the "International Passage" be included in the list of the "National General and Special Transportation Program" at the Fourth session of the Tenth National People's Congress in 2006, and brought forward the "Proposal of Central Government Supporting Yunnan to Construct the 'International Passage' linking South Asia and Southeast Asia" at the First Session of the Eleventh National Committee of the Chinese People's Political Consultative Conference in March 2008.

Above all, the construction of a China–Myanmar transport corridor would bring Yunnan the most immediate and greatest advantage of offering an opportunity to improve its transportation, which has been lagging. It also is a means to improve its economic and political status in China through its role as the channel and pivot to the Indian Ocean.[59]

Nowhere is the game of encirclement and counter-encirclement between China and India more evident than in Myanmar. Although Beijing has not, until recently, admitted to the "Two-Ocean" strategy, its efforts in pursuit of an export and import outlet to mainland Southeast Asia, and access to the Indian

---

59   Li Ping and Li Yigan (eds), *Study of the Singapore–Kunming Route of the Trans-Asia Railway*, Kunming: Yunnan Minority Press, 2000, p. 22.

Ocean via Myanmar, are obvious and are now public. It undoubtedly incurs Indian suspicions and worries.

There is the purported Chinese physical presence in Burma – in particular reports of Chinese military bases in Myanmar, although these have been discounted.[60] The imperatives of China's expanding economy (including its energy needs) have added another dimension to the debate. "Whatever the case, the fact remains that in recent years Myanmar is seen as having moved too close to China for India's or ASEAN's comfort. It does not matter whether China's expansion is dictated by economic or by strategic interests. What matters is that Beijing's Myanmar policy is a manifestation of a Chinese desire to be a major power in both the Pacific and Indian Oceans."[61]

The corridor not only more closely integrates the two countries' economies, but also combines both political and strategic interests. Thus, it contains India's influence in Myanmar, and expands China's strategic influence into Southeast Asia and the Indian Ocean. Also, Yangon's isolation provides China a favorable opportunity to push the China–Myanmar transport corridor. Nevertheless, China's old dream still faces challenges and difficulties. In the long run, the achievement of the two countries' transport link, and the emergence of a Myanmar traffic pivot, will require at least six factors: further trust between China and Myanmar; Myanmar economic development and prosperity (which requires massive traffic infrastructure); the stability of, and some form of democratization or pluralism, in Myanmar, particularly a solution of the ethnic minorities problems; deeper regional integration and cooperation between China, Southeast Asia and South Asia; stable economic development in the three subregions; and a degree of Myanmar integration into the global economy and the acceptance of the international community of this.

The current construction of the China–Myanmar Transport Corridor will accelerate the regional integration between China and Myanmar in the near future. In this process, the economic connections between Yunnan and northern Myanmar, first of all, will move ahead. This transport project will improve China's control ability over the China–Myanmar border areas and further expand its influence in Myanmar. At the same time, it will also result in some challenges for China–Myanmar ties. The more convenient transport between the two countries will probably facilitate the flow of Burmese narcotics into China and the flow of

---

60   See, for example, Andrew Selth, "Burma, China and the Myth of Military Bases", *Asian Security*, 3:3 (2007), pp. 279–307.
61   Malik, "Sino-Indian Rivalry in Myanmar", p. 61.

Chinese commodities and illegal immigrants into Myanmar. It is probable that Myanmar nationalists will not turn a blind eye to this.

The Military Factor

The Sino-Burmese relationship has caused considerable concern in international circles, but none has prompted more disquiet than that of the military relationships with China. This anxiety has been heightened by the lack of transparency, compounding the unease that whatever observers can glean from abroad is simply a small portion of reality. At the same time as these relations have expanded, massive increases in the size of the *Tatmadaw* since 1988 are evident. These two factors are inter-related, but not causally determined.

Even during the civilian period, the role of the military in Burmese history since World War II has been pervasive. This pattern exacerbates problems in relationships with many Western states that subordinate the military to civilian authority. That Burma/Myanmar has not followed the modern Western model further complicates a considered response to that country. The *Tatmadaw* has rewritten history to glorify its role, infused this into the educational system, and inculcated and expanded it through the military's own propaganda mechanisms and training programs, as well as into museums.

It seems evident that since 1962 the *Tatmadaw* has effectively determined that it would for the foreseeable future lead the state either directly or through mechanisms under its control.[62] The former was the case in 1958–1960, 1962–1974, 1988–2010, when the military ruled by decree, often under martial law. The latter was apparent under the Burma Socialist Programme Party administration (1974–1988), and is built into the constitution of 2008 that came into effect in 2011 with the formation of a new government based on the elections of 7 November 2010.

There is a strong element of patriotism and nationalism built into military education and thinking. This is apparent in the ideology that the *Tatmadaw* has developed. It contains strains quite similar to those of the Thai and Chinese military (sovereignty and national unity), even if presented in more strident and propagandistic forms.[63] The military is not simply a nest of "thugs," as

---

62　When the military founded the Burma Socialist Programme Party in 1962, it was completely military, and once one joined, which was virtually required at the higher levels, one supposedly could never resign. Ne Win did so in July 1988 as the regime was disintegrating. In 1988, high-level officials privately indicated that the military had no intention of giving up control. Personal interviews.

63　The Chinese are obviously concerned about Tibet, Taiwan, and Xinjiang; the Thai over the Muslim-Malay south.

some in the U.S. Congress have declared. Nor are they solely prompted by their exploitation of corruption or rent-seeking opportunities in their society, as other critics attest, although these factors are evident in some circles.

Senior General Than Shwe outlined the military ideology to his senior commanders in July 1997, and the contents were released to the public in February 1999. The ideology is based on the "Three National Causes": to project the unity of the state, and the non-disintegration and the maintenance of state sovereignty. These are hardly surprising attitudes given the multitude of ethnic insurgencies, some of which in the earlier period of independence had been predicated on independence for their areas, and given the sorry colonial history of Burma in the 19th and 20th centuries. It would be surprising if these were not core attitudes.

Four points are stressed in this national defense policy:

To perpetually safeguard national values concerning independence and sovereignty and prevent all acts detrimental to the three main national causes ... [see above]

To build national defense avoiding external dependence as much as possible in striving for stability of the state, community peace and tranquility and prevalence of law and order based on the strength of national forces within the country and with the armed forces as [the] pivot, combining the strength of auxiliary defence forces;

To valiantly and effectively prevent interference in our internal affairs ...

To employ a defence system that gives priority to world peace ...

Within this context, the *Tatmadaw's* mission is, inter alia, to build strong, capable armed forces, to have a modern defense system involving the entire citizenry, to abide by the provisions of the new constitution, and "To train and develop a strong defence force which possess [sic] a military, political, economic and administrative outlook in order to participate in the national leadership role in the future state."[64] A critical principle of the 2008 constitution is the leadership role of the *Tatmadaw*.

"Auxiliary defense forces" may be interpreted both as the attempted integration of minority forces into the "single *tatmadaw*," in accordance with the 2008 constitution, and as the paramilitary training of civilians. "Avoiding ex-

---

64   The above is taken from Maung Aung Myoe, *Building the Tatmadaw: Myanmar Armed Forces Since 1948*, Singapore: Institute of Southeast Asian Studies, 2009, pp. 3–4.

ternal dependence," however, seems at first review at variance with the record of Sino-Burmese military relationships. Obvious efforts to diversify this dependence on China are evident to mitigate this concern, as is strong Burmese nationalism. Western sanctions and the perceived concern of foreign military intervention based on the "regime change" mantra all may have contributed to reliance on China in many fields, but the junta probably believes they are not externally dependent.

The military's perceptions of the threats to the state may be considered under two categories: internal subversion/rebellion and external invasion. These have not been unrelated. The external threat to the youthful state of Burma after independence was considered to be China (see Chapter 2). Prior Nationalist and Communist claims to the northern reaches of Burma were evident in officially released maps of that period, and were greatly exacerbated by the fears of Chinese incursions or an invasion to wipe out the Kuomintang troops that had retreated into Burma and were backed by the U.S. and Taiwan. This was complicated by a Sino-Burmese boundary dispute that was finally settled, much of it on Burmese terms, under the leadership of General Ne Win during the military-controlled Caretaker government (1958–60), although signed by U Nu following that period.

The Burmese military concept, in contrast to that of Prime Minister U Nu, in the 1950s was that China was the only credible external enemy of the new state, and the military policy planning group recommendation to the prime minister was to expand the Burmese armed forces (three infantry divisions, one armored division) to hold off the Chinese with conventional warfare until the U.N. (essentially the U.S.) came to Burmese aid, on the model of the Korean War. U Nu opted instead for friendly relations with China.

Today, the external threat has been redefined and expanded. "Here, I would like to argue that while the internal armed security threat to the state continues to play an important role, it is the external security threat that has given more weight to the expansion and modernization of the *Tatmadaw* since 1988. I would also argue that, despite its imperfections, the *Tatmadaw* is in the process of transforming itself from essentially a counter-insurgency force into a conventional one."[65]

This fear of external aggression, although palpable, is unrealistic. The potential enemy is the United States, with Thailand (as a U.S. ally) acting as its surrogate. At first, the Burmese strategy seems to have been predicated on

---

65   *Ibid.*, p. 11.

an early Chinese communist strategy of a "people's war" – warfare in depth or guerrilla warfare. "Senior leadership has long advocated a 'People's Warfare' strategy to defend the country against foreign invasion by engaging in a war of attrition."[66] This approach has changed, however, since 1988, perhaps based on, or at least intensified by, the charge that the U.S. is the greatest danger to the regime. This fear, which has been documented in a leaked junta memorandum, is based on the U.S. call for "regime change" (until 2009), the operations of dissidents on the Thai frontier – some with U.S. government funding, and some internal and external expatriates advocating a U.S. invasion.[67] Thus, offensive weapons, such as fighter aircraft, and defensive weapons, such as artillery, surface-to-surface shorter range missiles, surface-to-air missiles, and anti-aircraft units have been imported.

Three diverse schools of thought have articulated issues in Myanmar–China strategic relationships: Myanmar will succumb to Chinese influence as the weaker state; there will be an unequal but partner relation; and those who reject China's expansionist designs. The third group argues that Burma/Myanmar has always been suspicious of China, China has not always been regarded as close to Myanmar, and Myanmar could draw back from this relationship. Selth continues, "Indeed, it can be argued that, in many respects, it is not Beijing but Rangoon that has the whip hand in this relationship."[68]

The internal security concerns of the *Tatamadaw* are twofold: the possibility of a people's revolution, on the order of 1988 or what might have turned into one in 2007, or revitalized minority insurrections from some of the major cease-fire groups, or the most dangerous of the possibilities – a combination of the two. "The Myanmar army has traditionally been structured and deployed primarily for internal security operations, both to quell civil dissent in major population centres and to conduct counter-insurgency operations in rural districts against communist guerillas, ethnic separatists and the armies of narcotics warlords."[69] With the cease-fires, the collapse of

---

66   *Jane's Sentinel Security Assessment – Southeast Asia*, "Army, Myanmar", 11 December 2009.

67   These irrational fears are exacerbated by films such as "Rambo IV." Authorities refused to have the U.S. Navy directly distribute relief supplies in the Delta during Cyclone Nargis in May 2008 because they felt the U.S. would not leave. The rumor in Yangon was that if the U.S. effectively occupied the Delta, the Chinese would send in 20,000 troops to occupy the northern Shan State. Although this rumor is unlikely to be accurate, that it was believed in some senior circles is important.

68   This discussion is from Andrew Selth, "Burma's China Connection and the Indian Ocean Region", Canberra: Australian National University, Strategic and Defence Studies Centre, Working Paper #377, September 2003.

69   *Jane's Sentinel Security Assessment* – "Army, Myanmar, p. XX.

the Burma Communist Party in 1989, and the reduction in narcotics (opium) production, the emphasis has shifted.

> The rapid expansion and modernisation of the armed forces after 1988 seems to have been based primarily on the fear that it might lose its monopoly of political power. The *Tatmadaw's* recruitment campaign and arms procurement programme seem aimed above all else at preventing, or if necessary, quelling, renewed civil unrest in the population centres. Efforts to defeat ethnic insurgent groups in the countryside have also been part of the regime's continuing determination to impose its own peculiar vision of the modern Burmese state upon the entire country. Yet, by relying on armed force to guarantee the country's unity and stability, the regime has mortgaged Burma's vast and diverse political, economic and social resources to continued dependence on military strength.[70]

The most significant results of the arms deals with China were the reorganization and expansion of the *Tatmadaw* supplemented by Chinese arms and training, and the increased military control the SLORC was able to extend into the country. Following the popular uprisings of 1988, the military high command judged that it did not have the capacity to guarantee control of the cities and at the same time continue its containment of the ethnic insurgencies. *Tatmadaw* modernization and expansion preserved the regime by enhancing the army's capacity to control the cities and, in the civil war, to move from a strategy of seasonal combat to one of year-round occupation.[71] This concern over military capacity likely led to the negotiating of 17 cease-fire agreements with various ethnic rebellions.[72]

The total armed forces in 1988 have been estimated at 198,681 (of whom 184,029 were army).[73] Since that time under the SLORC/SPDC, the Burmese seem to have developed a goal of armed forces totaling some half a million troops. Observers have discounted the attainment of that plan, believing that

---

70 Andrew Selth, *Transforming the Tatmadaw*, Canberra: Strategic and Defence Studies Centre, Australian National University, 1996, p. 154.
71 David Arnott, "China–Burma Relations", in *Challenges to Democratization in Burma: Perspectives on Multilateral and Bilateral Responses*, International IDEA, 2001, p. 72.
72 Burmese military intelligence explained that the surrender of the well-armed forces of the drug army of Khun Sa was accepted by the *Tatmadaw* because his group was better armed, inflicting unacceptable casualties on the Burmese, and he was willing to retire in Yangon and invest in development projects. The Military Intelligence spokesman said that the U.S. regarded that as money laundering, while the *Tatmadaw* thought of it as development. Personal interview, Yangon.
73 Maung Aung Myoe, *Building the Tatmadaw*, p. 33.

the military may number 406,000, although the exact figures are obscure, as is much to do with the *Tatmadaw*. There have been reports of desertions and the padding of unit figures, the latter perhaps in part to shield the authorities from unpleasant news as well to garner at lower levels the meager salaries of "shadow soldiers." There has been evidence of "false reporting, haphazard inspections and poor record keeping."[74]

Of primary interest is the motivation for this increase in the military. Three general propositions, of which two have been noted above, have been set forth: the shifting perceptions of the dangers of external enemies, and the need for increased internal control because of the potential for minority or general unrest. The third, which is more subtle, is the intent to build up a major supply of a loyal cadre through military training who will ensure military control (directly or indirectly) in governmental administrative roles ("the future triumphant elite" as the Defense Services Academy logo has it), both at the center and in regional governments, into the future. It is likely that all of these factors to some degree have motivated the military, with perhaps different emphases at different periods. With the expansion in *Tatmadaw* size has come an increase in the numbers and scope of their training. Advanced military training and physical facilities have increased in a variety of fields, as well as in the "intake" of the military academy by three-fold to 1,500 annually. These numbers, as well as other avenues of military advancement, indicate a planned, primary role for the military into the future.

In response to the augmentation in size and perceived threats have come major influxes of new and more sophisticated equipment, and with them the need for enhanced levels and areas of training. Where once it was possible to discuss the Burmese military as a "labor-intensive" armed force, in contrast the Thai army which, with U.S. assistance, has become "capital intensive," this is no longer the case.

Whatever the precise figures, there is little question that the growth of the *Tatmadaw* has been paralleled by the infusion of new and massive amounts of equipment mainly from China. This seems to have started, or have been accentuated, by the visit to China in October 1989 of the then Vice-Chair of SLORC, General Than Shwe, and a large entourage. They met with the Chinese prime minister, chief-of-staff, and defense minister.[75] As in all Burmese statistics, accurate data are unavailable, but estimates have been suggested that about at

---

74   *Jane's Sentinel Security Assessment* – "Army, Myanmar, p. XX.
75   Bertil Lintner, "Myanmar's Chinese Connection", *Jane's International Defence Review*. Vol. 027, Issue 011, 1 November 1994.

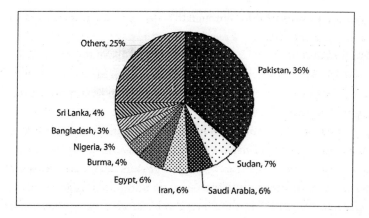

Figure 5: PRC worldwide arms sales customers, 2003–2007. Source: *Annual Report to Congress: Military Power of the People's Republic of China 2009*, Department of Defense, U.S., p. 58.

the beginning of the SLORC administration in 1988, the Chinese supplied some US\$1.2 billion in military hardware, then followed by some US\$0.4 billion, with a total today in the neighborhood of US\$3 billion. The equipment provided include naval vessels, aircraft, weaponry, radar systems, rocket launchers, and over 5,000 of various types of vehicles. Since 1989, Myanmar has become an important customer for Chinese conventional weapons (see Figure 5).[76]

China's arms sales are the result of a combination of supply-side and demand-side factors. On the supply side, Beijing conducts arms sales and training both to enhance foreign relationships and to generate revenue to support its domestic defense industry. China's arms sales range from small arms and ammunition to joint development or transfer of advanced weapons systems.[77] Chinese companies sell primarily to developing countries where China's low-cost weapons sales serve both commercial and strategic purposes.[78] Strategic concerns include a desire to strengthen foes of China's rivals and to expand China's political influence in regions such as the Middle East and Southeast Asia.[79] Obviously, as the Burmese government faces international sanctions, ethnic insurgencies, and other anti-government forces, and as the generals worry that they might lose political power, China's arms sales are the most direct and instrumental support to Naypyitaw, which

76 The most complete public sources are Andrew Selth, *Burma's Armed Forces. Power Without Glory*. Norwalk: EastBridge, 2002, and various Jane's publications.
77 Another report suggests that the Chinese do not supply small arms so that they cannot be accused of helping suppression of minority groups or the common people.
78 *Military Power of the People's Republic of China 2009*, p. 57.
79 Daniel Byman, Roger Cliff, "China's Arms Sales: Motivations and Implications", RAND Corporation, 2000, p. X.

enhances bilateral political ties. The security factor is most prominent in Beijing's strategic calculations.

In China's guideline of diplomatic strategy, framed at the 10th Chinese Ambassadorial Conference held in Beijing from 25 to 29 August 2004, China's neighboring countries were positioned in the second place after relations with the major powers. At the 11th Ambassadorial Conference in 2009, Beijing stressed the need to maintain the stability of, and establish a geostrategic fulcrum on, China's periphery. Strategically, as in the field of real estate, geographical position primarily determines the price. When a great power is perceived to control Southeast Asia or South Asia, it menaces China's security. At the same time, when such a strong presence occurs in Northeast Asia, China feels strategically encircled and besieged. In the 20th century, China believed itself hobbled three times: the Sino-Japanese War in the 1940s, the U.S. and its allies' encirclement in 1950's and 1960's, and the Soviet Union's strong presence in Northeast Asia, the Indochina peninsula, and South Asia.[80]

China's security threat arises from border areas. Since Southeast Asia consists of both maritime and mainland areas, the latter bordering China, Beijing deems this of great importance. Beijing is always concerned that Washington could build an anti–China coalition around its periphery, stretching from Japan and South Korea, through Taiwan and Southeast Asia to Australia, thereby creating a "containment arc" along China's Pacific coast, limiting its Pacific access. For China, military cooperation and arms sales between the U.S. and China's neighboring countries are a critical weathervane indicating the latter's inclination towards China. In 1953, Burma suspended Burma–U.S. military cooperation and won China's applause (see Chapter 2). The latest military exercises of U.S.–South Korea and U.S.-Vietnam in July and August 2010, annoyed Beijing. Accordingly, China needs to ensure that Myanmar becomes a void in any potential U.S.-sponsored encirclement process. Chinese arms sales are designed to improve political ties. Further, after the elections of November 2010, the *Tatmadaw* still plays the dominant role in Myanmar politics, and China needs to rely on it as well as the new government to protect the security of the China–Myanmar oil and gas pipelines, hydroelectric projects, and mining concessions.

Major military and political visits have been exchanged, and agreements signed. Training in China has been a major component of the Chinese effort. From 1990–1999, 615 officers were trained in China out of a total of 942 sent

---

80 Andrew Nathan, Robert S. Ross, *The Great Wall and the Empty Fortress: China's Search for Security*, New York: W. W. Norton, 1997, p. 171.

abroad. Some 665 officers and 249 other ranks were sent to China for 163 different courses from 1990–2005.[81] Of course, spare parts and replacements will make the Burmese dependent on China for a considerable period.[82] In September 2010, Chinese naval vessels paid a call at the Yangon port for the first time.

There have been rumors of disquiet over some of the equipment supplied. There have been charges that some were second hand, others not fully operational, and others that have been defective. Yet whatever the defects in the equipment may have been, it is evident that training in China, Chinese technicians in Myanmar, and spare parts will continuously link the two militaries.

Myanmar, however, seems reluctant to be completely dependent on China. It has diversified its military suppliers, which have included Singapore, North and South Korea, the Ukraine, Israel, Russia, Pakistan, India, and other countries. When the United States sold fighter aircraft to Thailand, Myanmar immediately bought MIG-29 aircraft from Russia. It has since also bought 62 combat and support helicopters from Russia as well. Russia was to be the source of an experimental 10kw nuclear reactor, and hundreds of Burmese have been trained in that country.

Recent evidence indicates that North Korea, with which diplomatic relations were reestablished after the 1983 attempted assassination of South Korean President Chun Doo Hwan in Yangon,[83] have not only been supplying conventional arms, but have been building tunnels in the capital of Naypyitaw and elsewhere.[84] There have been charges raised in opposition circles that the North Koreans have been engaged with the Burmese in some sort of nuclear weapons planning.[85] The evidence is presently lacking, but the concern may not only stem from previous North Korean efforts in Pakistan and Syria, but because of the emotional link between both states as included in the "outposts of tyranny"

---

81 Maung Aung Myoe, *Building the Tatmadaw*, p. 139.

82 For the most comprehensive discussion of the military, see Andrew Selth, *Burma's Armed Forces*, and Maung Aung Moe, *Building the Tatmadaw*.

83 Three North Korean agents performed the act: two were killed and one died over two decades later in Insein prison. South Korea, toward the close of the Roh Moo Hyan administration, officially informed the Burmese that South Korea would have no objection to the reestablishment of relations. Personal Interview, Yangon.

84 See Bertil Lintner, "Military Cooperation between Burma and the Democratic People's Republic of Korea", October 2010 (unpublished paper).

85 See Robert E. Kelley and Ali Fowle, "Nuclear Related Activities in Burma", For the Democratic Voice of Burma (Oslo) 25 May 2010. One study is Andrew Selth, "Burma's North Korean Gambit. A Challenge to Regional Security." Canberra: Australian National University, Strategic and Defence Studies Center, Canberra Papers on Strategy and Defence #154. 2004.

charge of Secretary of State-designate Rice. Perhaps the example of North Korea's nuclear capacities has prompted junta beliefs that such a program would safeguard them from U.S. attack, or could be used as some sort of bargaining chip, but Burmese capacity has not been demonstrated, even if the intent or hope may be there. Myanmar has signed the Nuclear Non-Proliferation Treaty. As a member of ASEAN, it is supposed to adhere to Southeast Asia as a nuclear weapons-free area. In 2011, Myanmar's vice president assured U.S. Senator McCain that Myanmar was not pursuing a nuclear weapons program.

Perhaps the greatest concern, especially to India, has been the build up of Burmese naval capacities with Chinese assistance.[86] It is not only the purchase of patrol boats and fast attack craft, but it includes the internal construction of frigates (108ms.) with Chinese technical assistance. Most importantly, however, have been the fears of Chinese access to Burmese bases and listening posts close to the Indian naval facilities in the Bay of Bengal and close to the western reaches of the Straits of Malacca. Although the fear of Chinese bases in Myanmar has been exploded, the possibility of the use of Burmese facilities in the expansion of China's "blue-water" navy has been evident. Myanmar thus becomes one of the "string of pearls" – Chinese access to Indian Ocean facilities in Pakistan, Sri Lanka, Bangladesh, and Myanmar.

Wherever its sources of supply, the implications are that Myanmar will have to spend increasing resources to keep up its military establishment, and thus may be more reluctant to spend on the social services (health, education) and agriculture, which are in such abysmal conditions.

The attempt by the junta in 2009 and 2010, before the elections of 7 November 2010, to emasculate the cease-fire groups by reorganizing them into Border Guard Forces (with 10 percent regular *Tatmadaw* added to every battalion) met with failure among the cease-fire groups. Most militarily important are the Wa, and there was a postponement of the elections in that area.[87] The new government in 2011 postponed that program.

---

86 See *Jane's Sentinel Security Assessment – Southeast Asia*, "Navy, Myanmar, 11 December 2009.

87 The original plan for the cease fire groups was that they were to turn in their weapons before the referendum on the constitution in 2008. This was blatantly unrealistic. Since the constitution specifically notes that there shall only be one *Tatmadaw*, the border defense forces concept seemed to the junta, but not to the minorities, a means to meet this qualification and eliminate any possibility of a significant future minority insurrection.

10

International Strategic Issues

Chinese policies in Southeast Asia for the past decade or two have been eminently successful. Through individual bilateral relations with each of the ASEAN nations, together with an effective policy toward ASEAN itself and its related instruments, it has created an aura in which the economic image of "China Rising" has been combined with the traditional, pre-colonial, and pre-revolutionary perceptions of Chinese soft power – China in socio-cultural terms as the literal "Middle Kingdom."

China has exhibited deft diplomacy as far south as Australia, and has also reassured the states of the region that its prior claims to the allegiance through Chinese citizenship of the extensive expatriate and often wealthy Chinese communities in Southeast Asia no longer apply. The previous perceived threats of China sponsoring local insurrections in the name of its expansive Maoist ideology have vanished, following a major shift in foreign policy after the Cultural Revolution and economic reforms. Through these events and negotiations, including signing the ASEAN Treaty of Amity and Cooperation and negotiating a free trade agreement with it, visits by high-level Chinese dignitaries, and China's former policy to delay antagonisms that could surface (such as claims to the sovereignty of the islets and resources of the South China Sea), China has been positively perceived. The resurgence of China's territorial claims to the South China Sea in 2010, however, while specifically assuring free ocean passages, has caused disquiet in the region. Vietnam has indicated that it wants the U.S. to play a greater role in this regard (and in Myanmar as well), but Secretary of State Clinton has indicated that the U.S. has no claims on the area and wants a diplomatic process of dispute settlement. Chinese claims on the sea area may have been publicly delayed because of their potential negative impact on the Beijing Olympics and the Shanghai Exposition. China has been reassured, but perhaps not successfully, that the U.S. has no claims in that area and that U.S. policy is not to "contain" China by controlling that sea but rather to ensure that no state does control it. Yet Chinese perceptions of a U.S. containment policy have become even more evident in 2011, with the partial thaw in U.S.–Myanmar relations with the visit of the U.S. Secretary of State and the Burmese stoppage of the Myitsone dam construction, supposedly encouraged, in Chinese eyes, by the U.S.

If China has been objectively successful to date in its policies, it has been made to appear even more so because of Japanese effective abandonment of influence in Southeast Asia, and because of the past ineptness of U.S. actions or inactions in the region, including a number of instances in which high-level U.S. officials avoided some of the region's significant meetings. This indicated to ASEAN's leaders a lack of concern for or a low priority to the area, except in issues related to terrorism following the 9/11 tragedy. Increased U.S. interest lately in ASEAN and the region has been warmly welcomed in Southeast Asia.

Overall, Chinese strategy in Asia has been categorized under six broad objectives:

[1] Maintain a stable environment on its periphery.

[2] Encourage economic ties that contribute to China's economic modernization and thus to regime stability.

[3] Further isolate Taiwan and block moves toward its *de jure* independence.

[4] Convince others that China is not a threat.

[5] Increase China's influence in East Asia, in part to prevent "containment" of China in the future.

[6] In Southeast Asia, secure recognition as the most influential external Asian power.[1]

To these more traditional goals we now must add the development of a Chinese "two-ocean strategy" – access to the Indian Ocean, and with special reference to Myanmar in Southeast Asia, and Pakistan in South Asia.

These goals have been applied not only to East Asia more broadly, but to Southeast Asia as well. Chinese strategy as focused on Myanmar has had impacts not only on Myanmar itself, but on the individual countries of the region, ASEAN and the United Nations as institutions, Japan, India, the E.U., and the United States. In some cases, China has pursued its strategic concerns or tried to mitigate potential problems. In others, economic interests have been paramount, or a mixture of the two. China has both initiated actions and responded to Burmese events, and used benign Burmese relations as a model to reassure other peripheral countries. To these broad Chinese objectives should be added more specific requirements for Chinese access to energy and mineral resources in Southeast Asia and elsewhere, most specifically in Myanmar, and

---

1   Bronson Percival, *The Dragon Looks South. China and Southeast Asia in the New Century*, Westport: Praeger Security International, 2007, p. 5.

for ensuring that such resources can be freely and economically transported to areas of Chinese need. Various aspects of the effects of Sino–Myanmar relations on the international sphere will be considered below.

Foreign observers of contemporary Myanmar, however, have sometimes characterized that country as lacking a coherent foreign policy, although there is general agreement that in the early period of Burmese independence neutralism was the prevailing catchword and impression. Even with the strong position of China in Myanmar, or perhaps because of it, the Burmese junta has attempted to achieve an imperfect balance between unstated but partial dependence on China and articulate autonomous action. In spite of reliance on China and to a far lesser degree India, and having signed agreements related to border issues and trade with some of the contiguous states, Burmese foreign policy has been based on suspicions of all neighborly intent, and the fear of U.S., and to a lesser degree Western, designs for regime change, control, or influence.

This assessment is historically accurate, but those concerns about its neighbors stem from a half-century past. The junta and the new 2011 government seem in part caught in a time capsule, in which all the neighboring states (except Laos), and the U.S. and the U.K., had supported separatist elements. Although this has generally been mitigated by more judicious policies, Burmese suspicions remain, spurred by the announcement from the U.S. that the 7 November 2010 elections had not conferred international legitimacy on the new government, and that the U.S. continued to support institutionally (not simply the former members thereof) the opposition National League for Democracy, officially deregistered as of 14 September 2010, but later reinstated with a change in party registration legislation so that it might compete in *hluttaw* by-elections. Coupled with the internal demands by many of the larger minorities for some form of federalism, anathema to the military for a half century as well, the contemporary foreign policy of Myanmar is guided by this fear and perceived vulnerability, resulting in the assertion that only the *Tatmadaw* can hold the state together against the perfidious minorities and their neighboring allies (or "minions" as the regime is wont to say) of any ethnicity. This has been their cardinal fear and probably has been a factor in their interest in joining ASEAN, along with potential investment that never materialized, a modest increase in legitimacy, and perhaps a balancing of Chinese influence.

Chinese Strategy in Myanmar

Chinese relations with Myanmar and their effects in the region, however, are complex. Although all of the seven factors listed above apply to some degree, they are an inadequate explanation of China's past role in Myanmar, especially since 1988, and of likely future interests. Chinese strategic policies toward Myanmar both transcend the broad issues noted above, and, in addition, should be disaggregated. China as a centralized political system of Chinese Communist Party control permeates to its own periphery and forces national political compliance. But since Deng Xiaoping's reforms, economic interests are reflected in considerable local autonomy, expressed localized needs, priorities, and aspirations, as well as its foreign relations. Although we may consider China as politically singular, internal specific regional and provincial economic interests also need analysis in the plural, and indeed localized priorities have affected and influenced Chinese national policies and strategies. Sub-national Chinese interests are factors that have prompted some provincial governments and corporations to pursue their singular interests. The provincial self-interests of Yunnan, and even those of Yunnan's *xian* (counties), have sometimes provoked the suspicions of higher authorities at each level, and must be disaggregated if an understanding of China's role in Myanmar is to be accurate and future relations anticipated. These bureaucratic entities, large state-owned enterprises, together with a highly entrepreneurial private sector, have demonstrated capacities to influence the center on aspects of development in which they are especially interested. It is apparent that Yunnan Province, and indeed Southwest China as a whole (defined by its military district and encompassing Yunnan, Guangxi, Guizhou, and Sichuan), have specialized interests in Chinese relations with, and in support of, the government of Myanmar. But to a great degree, Yunnan, for example, has been an executor of China's strategy and policies, although it has its own concerns on which it sometimes neglects to inform Beijing. Yunnan not only operates bilaterally with Myanmar, but also through two regional groupings: the Greater Mekong Sub-region Development Scheme[2] and the Bangladesh–China–India–Myanmar (BCIM) regional economic cooperation program.

More specifically at the Chinese national level, China is evidently intent on pursuing the objectives noted above, but also fostering not only a stable regime in Myanmar, but one that will allow China to exploit both the natural resources and the strategic location of that country. The natural resources of Myanmar and their exploitation by China are extensively treated elsewhere in this volume (Part II), as their importance warrants. Oil and gas, mineral resources, large infrastructures, and timber (both with the central government and with

---

2   See Kunming Declaration, "A Stronger GMS Partnership for Common Prosperity." Kunming, China, 4–5 July 2005.

ceasefire groups, as well as illegally) are major attractions for national and local firms, as is the hydro-electric potential of the various major rivers of Myanmar. Chinese investment, major but publicly undocumented economic assistance in both loans and grants, training, technical services, and numerous BOT (Build–Operate–Transfer) projects that are neither considered investment nor grants and the magnitude of which are great but obscure, also bind Myanmar to China to a highly significant degree. Should that assistance falter in the future for any number of political reasons, Myanmar would still be bound to China for spare parts and intermediate goods for an indefinite period.

Economic exploitation, however, has not been the primary objective of relations with Myanmar (as arguably it was for the colonial and Japanese governments). The extensive, indeed over-powering, assistance that China has provided to the Burmese military probably has a dual motivation: internal Myanmar stability as well as strategic access through Myanmar to peripheral areas. Chinese support is neither essentially designed, nor is it sufficient, to enable the military junta to defend itself against major external aggression, even though the Burmese may fear foreign incursions and attempted regime change.[3] Burmese–Thai relations have been in sporadic conflict for several centuries. Thailand is a non-NATO treaty ally of the United States and proxy skirmishes have taken place between the Burmese surrogate, the Wa State Army, and the Thai surrogate, the Southern Shan State Army (supplied with U.S. equipment through Thai channels). Myanmar is fearful of Western aggression and invasion, especially from the United States and Thailand. Beyond the junta and some wishful thinking among some of the Burmese dissidents, this fear is externally dismissed as an illustration of paranoia.[4] The Chinese must know full well, as do the more astute of the Burmese *Tatmadaw* and the American leadership, that any externally derived forced change in Myanmar by the U.S. or the West would severely damage U.S.–Chinese relations, which are a central, pivotal concern of both governments. Myanmar is a lower priority than other Sino–U.S. interests,

3   When the Thai bought F-16 fighter aircraft from the United States, the Burmese bought MIG -29 fighters from Russia. Myanmar is obviously trying to refrain from being too dependent on China. Myanmar also bought 62 combat and transport helicopters from Russia. See Min Lwin, "Burma Buys 50 Combat Helicopters", *Irrawaddy*, 8 September 2010.

4   For a study of this fear of invasion, see Andrew Selth, "Burma's Fear of Invasion: The Fantasy and the Reality", Griffith Asia Institute, Griffith University, Brisbane. 2008. For an amusing essay on the shift from China as the potential external enemy in the 1950s to the United States in that role today, see David Steinberg, "Defending Burma, Protecting Myanmar." *Irrawaddy*, May 2006, Vol. 14, No. 5. The U.S. seemed to have misunderstood the refusal of the junta to allow direct military supply of relief goods to the Irrawaddy Delta after Cyclone Nargis in 2008. It was fear of a U.S. excuse for an invasion, as the U.S. had called for regime change in the harshest terms for a decade and a half.

such as Taiwan, North Korea, trade, currency valuation, and other issues, so it will not drive overall U.S. policy in East Asia.

The extensive support of the Chinese to the Burmese military, variously estimated at some US$3 billion (see Chapter 9), together with a great deal of training and technical assistance, was probably calculated by the Chinese as an attempt both to curry favor with the regime, and to ensure its internal stability. The real threat to the junta is internal: from a general uprising like 1988 or that of some of the minorities who earlier wanted independence, then some form of federal structure, and who might still settle for greater autonomy; they have, however, no power to oust the present leadership. More importantly, the greater potential threat is from the Burmese people, who have much power if prompted to exert it in the streets because of the government's egregious policy miscalculations. There is no question that the Chinese authorities have tried to support the junta in a wide variety of ways, although there are indications that the Chinese are aware of the delicacy of the junta's control over its population, even though they may believe that the junta would prevail in any people-derived showdown (as in the "Saffron Revolution" of 2007), and have quietly urged the Burmese military to curb some of their internal excesses to ensure the stability of the 2011 civilianized military rule; they are said to be in touch with the Burmese opposition. A basic difference in international approaches to mitigating Burmese military rule has been illustrated by the strident public declarations for change, as exemplified by the U.S. together with the E.U., in contrast to the Chinese, who cajole more effectively in private.[5]

In strategic, if extreme, terms, Chinese interests have been analyzed thus:

> Myanmar is not only a potential supply route [for China] bypassing the Malacca Strait, but also a strategic point for controlling access to Malacca Strait's western approaches. While controlling the Malacca Strait is a key strategic objective of China to the point of risking armed conflict with the regional states and the U.S., access to Myanmar's ports and overland transportation routes through Myanmar is seen as a vital and strategic security asset for China."[6]

---

5   It is instructive to note that the economic change that took place in 1988 from a rigid socialist system to one encouraging the private sector came about through very quietly expressed demands for liberalization by the Japanese to the Burmese Deputy Prime Minister in Tokyo in March 1988, not through blatant public statements, which would have forced a Burmese nationalistic response.

6   Zhao Hong, "China and India's Competitive Relations with Myanmar", Institute of China Studies, University of Malaya, Working Paper #2008-7, 2008, p. 2, also quoting Yossef Bodansky (1998), "Beijing's Surge for the Strait of Malacca." The actual language from

Access to the Bay of Bengal is essential if the Chinese are to have a two-ocean navy, the importance of which in Chinese planning seems to have increased. The ability to transport goods and material overland, by riverine transport, and through pipelines for both oil and gas, all assist the Chinese to some important degree in circumventing any potential blockage of access to the Malacca Straits by its littoral authorities, ASEAN, terrorists, or by any major power, such as the United States. This seems evident as a longer range strategy, and is intelligent from a Chinese perspective, although Myanmar does not in any sense replace the importance of the Straits passage. Although internal Myanmar markets for manufactured Chinese goods are still relatively small because of the poverty of that country (see trade figures in Chapter 8), trade demands will rise. In September 1987, Chinese consumer goods increased their penetration of Burma because of the ineptness of the military authorities under General Ne Win in demonetizing a large percentage of the Burmese currency. This, together with the decline in Burmese light industrial production and the fear of holding Burmese currency, prompted the demand for Chinese goods to explode.[7]

As the Burmese authorities have written, they consider that the U.S. has been interested in regime change in Myanmar not simply for human rights concerns, but perhaps more importantly because Myanmar is the weakest link in the "containment" policy of the U.S. toward China.[8] Conversely, it may be argued that in playing the "U.S. card" against China, or the "China card" against the U.S., Myanmar is strengthening its claim to Chinese resources and support. Cold War attitudes and Chinese suspicions of the U.S. remain. Some Chinese unrealistically charge, without evidence, that the U.S. Obama administration reconsideration of its Burma/Myanmar policy, the 2007 "Saffron Revolution," and the 2009 Kokang imbroglio were all fomented by the U.S. to prevent completion of the Chinese pipelines in Myanmar.

Bodansky is even more compelling: "For Beijing, this reality [Malacca Straits] is increasingly a vital interest. Any Chinese naval and military surge into the Indian Ocean – a major strategic priority of Beijing – must pass through the Strait of Malacca. Beijing considers its surge into the Indian Ocean as part of a strategic surge of global proportions aimed at consolidating military posture in a hostile environment (from a both global and regional strategic point of view), and in a strategic grand design that anticipates the possibility of a major military clash with the U.S. in the foreseeable future."

7   See David I. Steinberg, *Burma: The State of Myanmar*, Washington, D.C.: Georgetown University Press, 2001, pp. 131–132.

8   Hla Min, *Political Situation of Myanmar and Its Role in the Region*, Yangon: Office of Strategic Studies, Ministry of Defence, 2000, p. 78. Hla Min was spokesman for the government. Indeed, in the 1950s Burma was China's outlet to the rest of the non-communist world.

More specifically, however, Myanmar's strategic location is a critical element in any potential problems that China may have with India. India, too, believes that Myanmar is a vital element in China's strategic thinking. Thus, the China–India–Myanmar nexus looms large in strategic consideration of all parties in the region, including that of ASEAN itself. As the "containment" policy, actual or perceived, by the U.S. has been used by the Burmese, so the Chinese "containment" policy toward India, as perceived by the Indian government, has caused a major shift in Indian policy toward Myanmar.

China–India: Myanmar as Nexus

China and India have entered into a state of mutual diplomatic grace. Relations are, and have been for some years, reasonably cordial and cooperative. Geopolitical issues such as the status of Tibetan refugees in India are important but not decisive; it has not destroyed the present cordiality of the relationship at the official level. The present major rivalry between India and China, at least as interpreted by foreigners, is dominated by economic and technological issues. How will the economic expansion and competition for markets and natural resources, including energy, of both states have impacts on each other and the developed and developing world? The proliferation of articles and volumes on the rise of both China and India in juxtaposition has become a staple of the economic literature on Asia.[9]

Yet there is little in Western policy circles (and more in Indian sources than in Chinese) on the strategic implications of Myanmar's role in this incipient rivalry that transcends economics. There is more media and advocacy literature, however, on the two countries negative political and human rights impacts on Burma: how China and India have been considered to be the effective supporters of the military junta and thus provide an economic "lifeline" for the regime and retard Myanmar's transition to some form of democratic rule. The accuracy of this assessment is subject to question. Yet, in all economic, strategic, and political respects, Myanmar plays a significant role in Sino-Indian relations. If China and India affect Myanmar's policies, so too does Myanmar have impacts on the positions of both of these states. Myanmar's importance is likely to increase over time.

---

9   For example, see David Denoon, *The Economic and Strategic Rise of China and India. Asian Realignments after the 1997 Financial Crisis*, New York: Palgrave, 2008. For a recent study of Sino-Indian relations in the context of Myanmar, see Thant Myint-U, *Where China Meets India: Burma and the New Crossroads of* Asia, New York: Farrar, Strauss and Giroux, 2011.

Before the Burmese coup of 18 September 1988, Sino-Indian relations had markedly improved from its nadir a quarter-century earlier. China and India found mutuality in an external third party on which to concentrate, and devoted considerable attention to "anti-hegemonic cooperation," a major aspect of Chinese propaganda.[10] This was convenient, as it avoided facing their overlapping interests and rivalries. Even following the coup, at a meeting in India on 12 December 1988, Rajiv Gandhi and Deng Xiaoping "stressed the prospects of Sino-Indian cooperation and such broad issues as lessening resort to military blocs as a means to security . . . "

Sino-Indian relations were not always so cordial.[11] Almost a half-century ago in 1962, war between the two states over border issues, especially in India's northwestern frontier in the Himalayas, broke out. It was likely the highest war in the modern world, not in casualties but in altitude. Attention was naturally focused on the northwest frontier, as the disputed territory contained critical roads with strategic links and had as its obscure predecessor the 19th-century imperial struggle between Britain and Russia, in the "Great Game," with China included in that arcane competition. The northeastern frontier, however, was generally ignored because the boundaries, although disputed, were more amorphous and less immediately strategic, and Burma, whose northern frontier intruded into the India–China border region, was adamantly neutral. There were, however, later skirmishes in the Northeast Frontier Area (later renamed as Arunachal Pradesh) in the 1984–1986 period, although they do not appear to have been substantive. Although Burma had signed a border agreement with China in 1960, after the military took control of the former under the "Caretaker Government," there was no indication of a Burmese "tilt northward" toward China, although as one observer remarked, Burma was always neutral in China's shadow.[12] Yet India did quietly and indirectly express concern.[13] Although there was increasing unrest in northeast India, and the Kachin went into revolt inside Burma in part because of U Nu's declaration of Buddhism as the state religion, a policy on which he had campaigned in

10 John W. Garver, *Protracted Contest. Sino-Indian Rivalry in the Twentieth Century*, Stanford: Stanford University Press, 2001, pp. 225–226.

11 For an overall analysis, see Garver, *op. cit.*

12 See Thomson, "Burma: A Neutral in China's Shadow", pp. 330–360.

13 In the period leading up to the war, India encouraged tribal migration into the frontier areas of India to act as a buffer against possible Chinese expansion. Personal interview, Putao, 1961. At that time, the Burma–India–China frontier area was quiet. Burma had just undergone the coup of 1962 and was internally focused. The Kachin rebellion had started but was not that extensive, and Burma was not then a sanctuary for Naga rebels in northeast India.

the 1960 election, this did not trigger an Indian reaction. The Kachin were sporadically supported by the Chinese.

The events of 1988 and 1989 changed the importance of Burma to both India and China. The 1988 failed people's revolution in Burma, which ended in the 18 September 1988 coup to shore up previous military rule there, coupled with the Tiananmen incident in Beijing nine months later, brought both regimes closer together. Burma, soon to become Myanmar (the name change occurred in 1989), effectively and quietly shifted its foreign policy to one far more closely aligned to China. The Burmese were always concerned about China.[14] General Ne Win was said to be fearful of a Chinese population inundation of Burma.[15]

The boycotts of both Burma and China after their respective incidents may have brought both regimes closer together. Japan cut aid to China following Tiananmen, and in the case of Burma had to re-recognize that country before more assistance could be forthcoming (this occurred just before the formal funeral of Emperor Hirohito).[16] The U.S. stopped economic and military (anti-narcotics and training) assistance to Burma, and the World Bank and the Asian Development Bank stopped new projects, in the case of the former in part because Burma was in arrears in loan repayments, and under pressure from the United States.

Even before the coup, however, and quietly but effectively prodded by Japan in March 1988 during a visit to Tokyo by the Burmese Deputy Prime Minister, Burma was prompted to recognize that its economic policies needed substantial change. It transformed its socialist system to stress the importance of the private sector and legalized overland trade with China in the Sino-Burmese Trade Agreement of 5 August 1988, in the waning days of the Burma Socialist

---

14   For example, Burma left the non-aligned movement in 1979, when the meeting was to be in Cuba, apparently because of Chinese objections to the pro-Soviet stance of the movement at that time.

15   It is said that Ne Win was against family planning programs in Burma because he wanted to increase the Burmese population in light of the overwhelming populations of both China and India, and even Bangladesh. Abortions, although widespread, were only legal with the approval of the local chapter of the Burma Socialist Programme Party.

16   According to the Japanese ambassador to Rangoon at the time, a lack of formal recognition would have meant that the Burmese delegation to the funeral would have had to sit next to the Palestine Liberation Organization, a major insult. Further, a dozen or so major Japanese firms formally complained to the Japanese Embassy in Rangoon that they were losing business with the stoppage of Japanese assistance, and they wanted it resumed. Personal interview, Rangoon. Japan supplied some US$2.2 billion in assistance to Burma up until 1988. See David I. Steinberg, "Japanese Aid to Burma: Assistance in the *Tarenagashi* Manner?" In Koppel and Orr (eds), *Managing Japan's Foreign Aid. Power and Policy in a New Era*, Boulder: Westview Press, 1993.

Programme Party regime. Just before its legalization, two-way trade, which was then officially unrecognized, was variously estimated as up to US$1.5 billion.[17]

The causes were both internal and external. China had moved to open its economy in this period, and both the private sector and provincial governments were more free to engage in trade. Internally, the disastrous September 1987 Burmese demonetization of perhaps two-thirds of the Burmese currency (the third and most severe since military rule in 1962, since no redemption of larger currency notes for new ones was allowed) drove the Burmese to hoard goods and to avoid holding currency, as further demonetizations were feared.[18] As farmers held their only asset, paddy (unhusked rice), this increased its urban price, contributing to the extensive unrest in urban areas in 1988, while urban consumers bought any commodities and staples as a hedge against any future demonetization.[19] Burmese light industry was already in trouble because of the lack of foreign exchange to purchase intermediate goods and spare parts. The informal trade along the Sino-Burmese border brought in Chinese consumer goods at low prices. They often were of better quality than Burmese produced products, thus resulting in the effective collapse of Burmese light industry.

Mutual need prompted the agreement on legalizing trade and the setting up of procedures so that both Burmese and Chinese could cross the frontier without visas for both trade and work. Shortly thereafter, in 1989, the collapse of the Burma Communist Party, which had occupied a strategic area in the Wa State on the Chinese border since the 1970s, opened up new portals for Sino-Burmese trade. In essence, the broad sweep of the China–Myanmar border became open to both legal and illegal trade and immigration.

Closely following the 1988 coup, Indian policy toward Burma became stridently anti-military. Rajiv Gandhi had visited Rangoon in 1987, and after the Burmese coup initiated an anti-junta policy. All India Radio became known as the most vociferous critic of the military State Law and Order Restoration Council (SLORC), even hiring U Nu's daughter to run its Burmese service. This was also the period when Rajiv Gandhi was pursuing an interventionist regional policy that had expanded India's role in Nepal, the Maldives, and Sri Lanka. Gandhi's assassination in 1991 and the obvious extent of Chinese

---

17 A Burmese official, personal communication, Rangoon, May 1988. By May 1988, the Yunnan authorities had established an export promotion office in Kunming, which had a sector devoted to Burma.

18 It is significant that the new Burmese constitution, approved by referendum in May 2008, specifically excludes the possibility of any further demonetization. The Constitution of 2008, Chapter 1, Article 36(e).

19 See Steinberg, *Burma: The State of Myanmar*, 2001.

penetration into Myanmar caused rethinking of India's position toward the Burmese junta.

Historically, if Burma owes much to India (the subcontinent) in religious and cultural terms, and even learned from the Indian model (the Congress Party) in the rise of Burmese nationalism, the British ill-advised ruling of Burma as a province of India until 1937 resulted in extensive economic power flowing to a large Indian minority (Rangoon was largely Indian at that time), a power that has been continuously resented, so that there are still strong prejudices against those from the subcontinent in Myanmar, although more against the Muslims (who are believed to attempt to convert Buddhist women). That the Burmese have accepted with some alacrity Indian assistance is a signal that they do not want to be too dependent on China, as additionally illustrated by Senior General Than Shwe's two trips to Delhi (2004 and 2010).

The Burmese military had generally been deprived of high-tech equipment. It had been considered a "labor-intensive" military, as contrasted with the Thai military, which with U.S. support in supplying modern materiel was becoming "capital-intensive." Burma turned to China for its new military needs.[20] The exact amount of Chinese military equipment supplied to Burma/Myanmar is unknown, but general estimates range in the neighborhood of US$3 billion over several years, with the initial support of US$1.4 billion.

At the same time, the Chinese were assisting the SLORC in the construction of extensive infrastructure projects including airfields, roads, ports, hydroelectric and irrigation dams, and railroads; this was coupled with an infusion of Chinese traders and illegal immigrants. The official trade, evidently a small portion of actual trade, between China and Myanmar for 1991/1992 (the Burmese fiscal year starts 1 April) was only US$106.99 million, while the Chinese figure for approximately the same period is US$392.09 million.[21] Both are likely to be wildly underestimated. Chinese entrepreneurs were knowledgeable about Burmese fads and fashions, and they were even able quickly to copy Indian textile designs popular in Myanmar and thus cut Indian imports. Since that early period, Chinese support for a wide range of Burmese infrastructure has mushroomed, as has Chinese economic assistance.

---

20 The upgrading of the Burmese military through new and more sophisticated equipment will mean that those who would like to see the amount spent on the military diminished and provided instead to social services are likely to be disappointed. More sophisticated equipment will mean more training and more costly spare parts.

21 The Chinese figure is from the *China Statistical Yearbook*, while the Burmese one is from the Myanmar Ministry of Commerce. Maung Aung Myoe, "Sino–Myanmar Economic Relations Since 1988", p. 6 and p. 10.

To the Indians, traditional Burmese neutrality had been compromised, and China had penetrated Myanmar. This had strategic implications, for as the former Indian Defense Minister Fernandes famously said in 1998, India could militarily take care of Pakistan, but China was the real potential enemy.[22]

As Zhao noted:

> Myanmar is of special importance to China, and the shift in New Delhi's stance has thus generated a sense of rivalry between the two for the affections of Myanmar from the tangibles of trade and investment to the intangibles of cooperation and support for their respective regional influence. China and India are all anxious to tap Myanmar's huge oil and gas reserves. China and India are also seeking access, through Myanmar, to the Indian Ocean to help open their poor landlocked provinces in their southwest and northeast respectively.[23]

The perception of Chinese influence in Myanmar had strategic implications for India. The whole Indian Ocean, let alone the Bay of Bengal, was considered by India to be its *mare nostrum*. A major Indian naval base operated in the Andaman Islands at Ft. Blair, and India tested its missiles along its east coast in the Bay. Chinese construction of naval facilities along the long Burmese coast was of obvious concern to India.[24] Although India may not have appeared as a major threat to China, the reverse was not perceived to be the case. From Delhi's vantage point, with Pakistan aligned with China on the west, China to the north, and to the east Myanmar effectively within the Chinese sphere of influence, this meant India was virtually surrounded. Chinese development of a two-ocean navy with potential refueling and servicing facilities, if not bases, in Myanmar, would increase Chinese capacities in that area. These port facilities (along with Gwadar in Pakistan, Chittagong in Bangladesh, and Hambantota in Sri Lanka) were called China's "string of pearls." India tends to treat seriously Chinese capabilities, rather than its present intentions, and

---

22   When India took a hard-line position against the SLORC, Pakistan began supplying some arms to the SLORC. Burmese Military Intelligence claimed that the Burmese needed spare parts for previously supplied U.S. equipment, and this was the only place they could procure them because of a U.S. embargo on military sales and aid. Personal interview, Military Intelligence, Yangon.

23   Zhao Hong, "China and India's Competitive Relations", p. 4.

24   As a retired Burmese colonel said, a Chinese airfield in Pegu (Bago – near the coast) would make an Indian aircraft carrier obsolete in the Bay of Bengal. Personal interview, Rangoon, mid-1990s. Ostensible fishing vessels were captured by the Indians. They turned out to have no fishing equipment, only electronic gear, and were manned by Chinese.

although relations are now reasonably good, any increase in Chinese military capacities is of obvious concern to India.[25]

A further issue was the volatile nature of India's northeast area. Here the Indians, Kachins, Nagas, the BCP, and China were engaged over time in various, transitory alliances of convenience. By 1975, the Kachin Independence Army (KIA), itself already in revolt against the Burmese BSPP government, "allied itself with the insurgent BCP and in 1976 began to receive massive supplies of Chinese-made arms and ammunition."[26] The Kachins were the initial liaison between the Indian Nagas and the Chinese. General Than Shwe, in a top secret letter dated 22 February 1991, "cited India as a country which 'encourages and supports internal insurgents' and 'interferes in [Burma's] internal affairs, [acts which are] not compatible with the [expected] behavior of a friendly neighbor."[27] India is said to have supported Burmese dissident groups in Thailand.[28] Burma built up its forces in the region and created a new regional command in the Sagaing Division and the Chin State. Brang Seng, the charismatic leader of the KIA who had extensive Chinese contacts, tried to contact Rajiv Gandhi in 1986 volunteering to help solve the cross-border insurgency. India was also assisting the KIA by supplying arms, and Brang Seng made a secret trip to Delhi in 1991 and the Kachin posted a liaison officer there. During part of this period, the Chinese were aiding the Naga insurgents. Later, following their cease fire with the SLORC, they engaged in extensive logging, resulting in much deforestation in the area under their control. The Naga tribes straddle the Indo–Myanmar frontier, and the Naga rebels in India often sought refuge in Burma.[29] Burma began supporting the Indian insurgents as the Indians had supported some Chin dissidents, although on an unofficial basis, and in 1991 illegally penetrated 30 kilometers into India to chase a Burmese Chin rebel. The Kachin trained and equipped Kukis and Chins to counter Naga rebels who were opposed to the Indian government, which in turn was opposed to the Burmese regime. Lintner notes:

25 For a discussion of these issues, see the Conference Report, "Burma/Myanmar: Nexus on the Bay of Bengal." February 2002, Washington, D.C. See also, Robert Kaplan, "Rivalry in the Indian Ocean." *Foreign Affairs*, March/April 2009.

26 *Jane's World Insurgency and Terrorism*. "Kachin Independence Army (KIA)", 25 May 2007.

27 This, and the following, are from *Jane's Intelligence Review*, Bertil Lintner, "The Indo–Burmese Frontier: A Legacy of Violence", 1 January 1994.

28 Andrew Selth, "Burma and the Strategic Competition Between China and India", in John Brandon (ed.), *Burma: Myanmar in the Twenty-First Century: Dynamics of Continuity and Change*, Bangkok: Chulalongkorn University, 1997.

29 Under the 2008 constitution, there is a semi-autonomous Naga area, and how this may relate to Nagaland in India will be carefully watched.

The Indians also began to re-evaluate their Burma policy. It was argued that India had achieved nothing by supporting the resistance. On the contrary, it was argued that these tactics had pushed the Burmese further into the hands of the Chinese. New Delhi decided to counter the Chinese by moving closer to Rangoon. An exchange of high-level trade delegations was initiated and, in March 1993, Burma and India signed an agreement to co-operate in the suppression of narcotics trafficking, which had become rampant across their common border. Burmese support for the Nagas also seemed to have ceased in early 1993. Relations between India and China were also improving, a development that was marked by Prime Minister Narasimha Rao's visit to Beijing in September 1993. For the first time in decades, the two countries began a dialogue aimed at solving their long-standing border disputes; the possibility of China's resuming any kind of assistance to the insurgents in India's northeast appeared more remote than ever.[30]

Further to the south along the same frontier, the multiple Chin tribes straddle the frontier, and Chin rebels against the Burmese regime have migrated into India's Mizoram State (the term "Zo" is also used by the Chin as their indigenous designation of their people). The arbitrary border thus split this diverse but singular ethnic group. There have been reports that rebels of the United Liberation Front of Assam (ULFA) have been seeking refuge in Myanmar, and that the Myanmar government "launched a counter-insurgency operation targeting ULFA and National Socialist Council of Nagaland–Khaplang (NSCN–K) militants operating in its territory on 19 November [2007]" with the result that "it has certainly affected us [ULFA, NSCN–K] badly."[31] Better Indian relations with Myanmar then serve dual purposes: easing problems for India in its northeast, and mitigating Chinese influence in Myanmar.

With the assassination of Rajiv Gandhi came a reconsideration of Indian policy toward Myanmar. The shift took time, but has been dramatic. Foreign Minister Dixit visited Yangon in 1993, and General Khin Nyunt, then Secretary-1

30 Lintner, "The Indo-Burmese Frontier", Jane's Intelligence Review, 1 January 1994. There are said to be between 70,000–100,000 Chin, both political and economic migrants, in Mizoram. The formal trade in that area is estimated at Rps. 100,000,000 and the informal trade at Rps. 230,000,000. See Julien Levesque and Mizra Zulfiqur Rtahman, "Tension in the Rolling Hills: Burmese Population and Border Trade in Mizoram", New Delhi: Institute of Peace and Conflict Studies. IPCS Research Papers #14, April 2008. For a study that encompasses both the Mizoram and Naga regions, see Samir Kumar Das, *Conflict and Peace in India's Northeast: The Role of Civil Society*, East–West Center, Washington, D.C. Policy Studies #42, 2007.

31 Jane's Terrorism and Insurgency Centre, 20 November 2007, quoting the *Nagaland Post*.

and head of military intelligence (and a decade later Prime Minister), went to New Delhi in 1994.[32] India and Myanmar have signed agreements for expanding the land links between the countries. India provides economic assistance to Myanmar, there are new trade agreements, and there have been high-level military and diplomatic exchanges between the two states. For the first time since Burmese independence in 1948, the Burmese head of state, Senior General Than Shwe, visited Delhi in October 2004, and again in 2010, when various aid agreements were signed.[33]

The change in Indian policy has been attributed to the obvious importance of China's strategic penetration of Myanmar.

> Such an approach, variously dubbed as 'pragmatism,' constructive engagement,' or 'inclusive approach,' has been based on two-fold understanding: improbability of ascendancy of democratic regime in Myanmar; and the previous experience of the more India isolates the military regime, the more its geo-strategic concerns are compromised.[34]

Following the death of Rajiv Gandhi and the reassessment of India's relations with Myanmar, Indian policy toward Myanmar (and thus peripherally toward China) may be considered in three stages: security-centric early engagement (1993–1997); look-east-centric engagement (1998–2004); and develop North-East [India]-centric engagement (2004 onwards).[35]

The objectives of the first stage of the period of early engagement (1993–1997) were to try to limit Chinese influence in Myanmar, especially its increased role along the Bay of Bengal and the spectre (erroneous, as it turned out) of Chinese bases along the littoral, while at the same time attempting to limit the growing insurgency in India's North East along the Myanmar border, which became a sanctuary for such rebels.

The second stage (1998–2004) coincided with India's general "Look East" policy (toward ASEAN), but more importantly marked (in 1997) Myanmar's

---

32 Andrew Selth. "Burma and the Strategic Competition Between China and India." Paper presented at a Chiangmai conference in June 1995, and later published in the *Journal of Strategic Studies*.

33 The 2004 visit immediately followed the arrest of General Khin Nyunt, Burmese prime minister and former head of military intelligence, indicating the confidence of the senior general in his own internal position and the loyalty of the *Tatmadaw* (armed forces).

34 Vibhanshu Shekar, "A Federal Democratic Myanmar India's Strategic Imperative", Institute of Peace and Conflict Studies, New Delhi, IPCS Issue Brief # 67, May 2008. Since India's energy and transportation interests traverse minority areas within Myanmar, and these regions have been volatile in the past, the author believes that some sort of federal structure in Myanmar would help ensure India's interests.

35 *Ibid.*

joining ASEAN in July of that year, and the formation of BIMSTEC, the Bangladesh–India–Myanmar–Sri Lanka–Thailand Economic Cooperation organization, which also provided an avenue for India's improved relations with ASEAN, and which also had close ties with China, as China had signed the ASEAN Treaty of Amity and Cooperation in October 2003. India had set up its Far Eastern Naval Command in the Andaman Sea to counter possible Chinese influence there.

The third stage (2004–) is related to the development of India's North East, an area plagued by poverty, diverse ethnic peoples (some of whom have ties to ethnic relatives in Myanmar), dissensions, and outright rebellion. The development of that region, which lacks easy and inexpensive access to the heart of India, could mitigate the unrest in that remote area. To provide access, the plan has been to expand the port of Sittwe (Akyab) in the Rakhine and employ the Kaladan River north through the Chin State to link to the Indian North East, which could transform that region as it is far behind in development compared to many other parts of India. Further, road links have been expanded, and the improvement of links to Yunnan through Myanmar using the World War II Ledo or Stilwell Road through the Hukawng Valley is underway. India and Myanmar on 13 February 2001 began the 160 kilometer Indo–Myanmar Friendship Road though the Chin State. India had already been upgrading the Tamu–Kalemyo road in Myanmar.[36] India has said to agree to expand its rail system to the Myanmar border. India is also supplying Myanmar with some economic assistance. India has lost out to China on the bidding for major off-shore gas reserves in the Rakhine region of Myanmar; these will be imported through a pipeline through that country to Kunming, the capital of Yunnan Province.

India's policy toward Myanmar and its support of that government has been the object of much criticism from the West and advocacy groups. To many, India as the world's largest democracy should have close links to the Burmese democratic opposition. There should be, according to these advocates, a confluence of concerns about the restoration of democracy in Myanmar for ideological reasons. Further, Aung San Suu Kyi was brought up in India and went to school there when her mother was Burmese Ambassador in New Delhi. India, therefore, is betraying its principles as the largest democracy, so some would argue. But India has strategic concerns that are more immediate and powerful.

36   Mohan Malik, "Burma's Role in Regional Security", in Morten Pedersen, et al. (eds), *Burma–Myanmar: Strong Regime, Weak State?* Adelaide: Crawford, 2000.

Change in Myanmar will very unlikely see the advent of democracy. India should therefore bank on a military regime, but try to enhance its reliability. The evolution of the Burmese junta into an illiberal but efficient regime is a very plausible scenario and could satisfy India's needs in the mid-term ... India, for economic reasons as well as security considerations, would stand to gain greatly if such [economic and administrative] reforms were to be adopted, and should thus, along with China and ASEAN, try to exert pressure on the military junta in this direction.[37]

Whether Myanmar society could incorporate liberal economic policies and their implementation (the policies exist on paper but their personalized and skewed implementation has undercut the efficacy of the laws) with continued authoritarian rule, or as the Senior General and the junta has proclaimed, the new "discipline-flourishing democracy," is a question that has often been raised. China itself is cited as an example of a country that has managed this intellectual and managerial dualism, as has Vietnam. But it has drawn on a wide spectrum of Chinese society for expert knowledge, expanded the elite structure to encompass more diverse segments of society, and has even officially admitted capitalists into the Chinese Communist Party. But Myanmar, in which the military has had effective control at all levels, has indicated a profound mistrust of Burmese civilian experts and others who have not been subject to military discipline. Thus, whether in Myanmar political change and economic change can be independently pursued, as in China, and if so, how soon, is a matter of some conjecture.

Sino-Myanmar Cooperation and Japanese Concerns

Japan's interests in Myanmar have been, and are, profound and broad. The motivations behind this interest have been multiple: access to Myanmar's natural resources; markets; Japan acting as a developed state to provide economic assistance to the poor; strategic in relation to limiting Chinese influence in Myanmar; and even nostalgic, because of the role of Japan during World War II and the genuine affection many Japanese had for individual Burmese, even though the Japanese were brutal to many in that society, and the independence that they offered after the British retreat was blatantly false.

Culture also continues to play a role. Burmese Buddhism creates a sympathetic bond (even if of two different Buddhist schools – the Mahayana in Japan

---

37   Julien Levesque, "A Reformed Military Junta in Myanmar in India's Strategic Interests", Institute of Peace and Conflict Studies, New Delhi. IPCS Issue Brief # 69, May 2008. This analysis could have been written about China's Myanmar policy.

and the Theravada in Myanmar), further enhanced by the famous novel and then film, "Harp of Burma," in which a Japanese soldier after the war's end stays behind as a virtual monk to help bury the war dead. Many Japanese tourists return to Myanmar to visit graves and places their relatives served in during the war. There is a sense of guilt about the Burma campaign in World War II and the tens of thousands of Japanese lives lost there, more than in any other theater of operations.

During World War II, the Japanese invasion into Southeast Asia served as both a catalyst and an inspiration to the nationalist movements in this region because it destroyed the myth of the western supremacy of the past: the colonial powers and their representatives in Southeast Asia could be defeated by Asians, and the white-skinned aliens could be toppled from their privileged positions. The myth of European superiority was over.

In planning for war, the Japanese trained a group of 30 Burmese nationalists to fight against British colonialism. Among them were both Aung San and Ne Win, both of whom had profound influences (positive and negative) on the future of that society. The prominence of General Ne Win, and his close attachment to the Japanese, ensured that Japan would play a vital role in that society as long as he had influence, an influence he maintained even after he resigned as head of state in 1980 (while he kept the chair of the BSPP), and even beyond his resignation from the party in 1988 and into the 1990s.[38] Japanese assistance was critical to Burma before 1988 and supported the country during the period of virulent socialist policy when most foreign assistance was stopped.[39] Steinberg calculated that Japan supplied US$2.2 billion from the start of war reparations in the 1950s to 1988, while Seekins believes it was US$1.94 billion from 1970 to 1988.[40] He also calculates (pp. 128–30) that Japanese aid, mostly in humanitarian assistance and debt forgiveness, was approximately US$887 million from 1988–2003. Some claim that Japan miscalculated its assistance program after 1988, basing it on the assumption that the rise of democracy and civil society were inevitable trends, as exemplified by Thailand's progress.[41] It is more likely, however, that the rationale for Japanese assistance after that date had little to do with democratic principles. In the earlier, pre-Myanmar, period,

38 General Saw Maung was ousted as head of the SLORC in 1992 only after Ne Win gave his approval from his home in retirement. Personal interview, Yangon.
39 For a review of the change in Burmese policy, see David I. Steinberg, *Burma's Road Toward Development: Growth and Ideology Under Military Rule*, Boulder: Westview Press, 1981.
40 Donald M. Seekins, *Burma and Japan Since 1940: From 'Co-Prosperity' to 'Quiet Dialogue'*, Copenhagen: NIAS Press, 2007, pp. 62–64.
41 *Ibid.*, p. 149.

economic interests were paramount, although they may have been supplanted after 1988 by the rise of Chinese influence in Myanmar. There is little question that Seekins is correct when he writes, "Although it may be an exaggeration to say that Burma has become a Chinese satellite (or a neo-colony), the influence of Beijing has eclipsed that of Tokyo."[42] Quoting a leading member of Japan's Liberal Democratic Party, Seekins notes "Because it is coming under China's influence, Myanmar may have conflict with India, causing regional instability. In order to avoid this, it is necessary for Japan to support the present government, including the reopening of yen loans."[43]

If Japanese policy toward Myanmar is apparent, the internal process by which that policy is determined is opaque. There are few debates on the issue in the Diet, and decisions are reached through backroom negotiations involving the political parties and the bureaucracy. Although there are both Myanmar- (pro-military) and Burma (anti-military) – Japan friendship societies, their influence on Japanese policy seems limited.

Japan and the United States have been at odds on Myanmar policy.[44] Concerned about the growing Chinese influence in that country, Japan has attempted to retain its past position as the "most favored nation" under Ne Win, but to no success. It has wanted to provide more assistance, but the Japanese response to Myanmar has been fractured by a Japanese Foreign Ministry that is under pressure from the U.S., and the economic ministries under the influence of Japanese businesses. The U.S. of course would have liked Japan to impose sanctions on Myanmar, something the Japanese did not do. In spite of multiple Japanese interests in Myanmar, the security element of the equation perhaps now looms largest. Japanese security is tied to the supply of energy and other raw materials through open shipping lanes, and the present interpretation of the pacifist Japanese constitution allows for their protection within certain limits. But as a retired Japanese general said, if China can import oil through Myanmar to its Southwest and avoid the Malacca Straits and the South China

---

42 *Ibid.*, p. 150.
43 *Ibid.*, p. 115.
44 Part of the dispute concerns the policy implications of semantics. "Humanitarian assistance" is interpreted by the Japanese very broadly to include what the U.S. would regard as infrastructure projects, such as the rehabilitation of the Rangoon airport and the refurbishing of the Belachaung hydroelectric project. The U.S. adheres to the meaning of the term earlier used for such assistance, "basic human needs", which includes health, education, nutrition, and agriculture. When the author was negotiating the reentry of USAID into Burma in 1979, he turned down the request from the Burmese Deputy Prime Minister for reconstruction of the Rangoon airport as it did not meet basic human needs. Personal interview. The Japanese later assisted in its reconstruction as a humanitarian project.

Sea, that is not in Japan's national interests.[45] Following U.S. engagement with Myanmar in 2011, Japan also plans to resume ODA to Myanmar. Japan will not miss the opportunity created by the U.S.–Myanmar thaw and Sino–Myanmar friction to renew and expand its influence there.

"The Burden of Proximity": Thailand[46]

The first response to Myanmar's 1988 coup by any ASEAN state was by Thailand. Even before Chinese penetration, General Chaovalit Yongchaiyuth, the Thai commander of the army, was the first high-level foreign visitor in December 1988. He managed to secure a variety of timber and fishing concessions. The cry from the Thai at this time was for "constructive engagement," a term that seemed to have an implicit hypothesis that business and market economics, which the Burmese seemed to have embraced just before the coup, would lead to better internal conditions and international relations, and perhaps even democracy. To many outside of the system, it seemed more motivated by avarice than altruism.

Yet Thailand has had a special problem with Myanmar. Historical memory becomes important. Burmese occupied parts of northern Thailand for long periods and the Thai still cite the Burmese destruction of their capital Ayutthaya in 1767, while recent Thai films have depicted brave Thai responses to Burmese invaders at various times.[47] Thailand has been the sanctuary of choice of those Burmese who flee from war or poverty. This is both because Thailand is relatively accessible, and also because some of the prolonged ethnic wars have been close to the Thai border.

There are some 150,000 Karen, Kayah, and Mon refugees in U.N. camps inside the Thai border, some two million Burmese who work in Thailand, especially in the northwest, and about 540,000 internally displaced Burmese (mostly Shan), within eastern Myanmar, many of whom would, if possible, seek dubious shelter in Thailand. In addition to the poor, there are Burmese dissidents who operate with relative freedom (writing journals, newsletters, etc., some of which are supported by the United States government), who have captured the Burmese Embassy in Bangkok, attacked a hospital, and demonstrated against the Myanmar government on Thai soil.[48] Myanmar

45 Personal interview.
46 Surin Pitsuwan, in a speech in Seoul to the conference on the role of South Korea in Southeast Asia, March 2008.
47 The term for Thailand in spoken Burmese is "Yuhtiya".
48 When President Bush visited Thailand in August 2008 on his way to the Beijing Olympics, he met with a number of Burmese dissidents, but the Thai government insisted he meet them on American soil (the U.S. Embassy residence grounds). Personal interview.

relations, except for the period of the Chuan Leekpai government (when Surin Pitsuwan was Foreign Minister), have effectively been handled by the Thai security apparatus, not the Ministry of Foreign Affairs. The Burmese have felt more secure with the former, who have been more conciliatory to the junta.

Thailand's policies toward Burma/Myanmar have shifted over time. Before 1988, the Thai policy effectively was to foster a series of "buffer states" (rebel areas) between the "radical" regime (as it was viewed from Bangkok) in Rangoon and the conservative one in the Thai capital. Insurgents and Burmese dissidents operated with apparent impunity in the border regions, and even U Nu was able to lead a rebellion while quietly resident in Bangkok. This policy was coupled with one that allowed the Thai military to create the impression of Burma as enemy to provide political legitimacy to the Thai military, which for much of that period controlled the Thai government.[49] This policy was changed following the November 1997 election of the Chuan Leekpai government. Surin Pitsuwan, Foreign Minister, advocated "flexible engagement" by ASEAN, essentially allowing member states to comment on inappropriate internal policies of any of the members, rather than the standard ASEAN approach on non-interference in member states' internal affairs. Chuan had to prove his "Thai-ness," and show he was not controlled by *farang* (foreign) influences. This resulted in the concept of *khwamruchak phit chop chua di*, or moral consciousness, a Thai perceived primordial value, rather than simple expedient foreign policy.[50]

Prime Minister Thaksin Shinawatra was most conciliatory to the Burmese, and he had private financial dealings with General Khin Nyunt's son in the company Pagan Cybertech. Thaksin started the "Bangkok Process," through which he planned, through a seven step process, to assist Myanmar toward democracy. This was aborted when the Burmese indicated they were not interested in it. "Thaksin all along appeared as Myanmar's chief apologist because he seemed more anxious about his family's businesses rather that promoting democracy in this neighboring country despite his creation of the Bangkok Process."[51] The former Thai Prime Minister, Samak Sunchrakej, in what has to be one of the most bizarre public statements by a person in his position, said after a one-day visit to the new Burmese capital at Naypyitaw, that he had learned that the Burmese were Buddhists and meditated, and so they must be all right.

49 See Pavin Chachavalpongpun, *A Plastic Nation. The Curse of Thainess in Thai–Burmese Relations*, Lanham: University Press of America, 2005, p. 58.
50 *Ibid.*, p. 145.
51 Pavin Chachavalpongpun, *Reinventing Thailand: Thaksin and His Foreign Policy*, Singapore: Institute of Southeast Asian Studies, 2010, p. 143.

On 2 November 2010, Thailand announced a multi-billion dollar project of factories, refineries, power plants, etc. for the development of Dawei (Tavoy), a Burmese port close to the Thai border. This Italian-Thai project would be the largest industrial zone in Myanmar. Its contribution to Burmese development might be substantial but its environmental impact could be highly detrimental to Myanmar. The then Thai Prime Minister Abhasit said that "Some industries are not suitable to be located in Thailand." Thai use of Myanmar as a site for economic exploitation in violation of sound environmental procedures is not new – the Thai, who had banned logging in their own country in 1988 because of mudslides with large losses of life, pursued widespread and environmentally insensitive logging just over the Myanmar border later that same year.[52] In an effort to re-establish prominence in Myanmar, the Japanese have discussed their intent to invest heavily in the Dawei project, and use that port as a horizontal trade and investment route to eastern India. In January 2012, President Thein Sein cancelled a planned coal-powered electricity plant in the Dawei project because of environmental concerns.

Thailand's relations with China have evolved from a period of antagonism and fear. During the earlier stages of the Cold War, the concern was over a major (but variously figured) large Chinese minority in Thailand that could be subject to Chinese ideological infiltration, and a Thai communist insurrection, especially in the Northeast where American air bases were used during the Indochina war. Thai control over their borders was fragile. In the 1958–1959 period, when the Thai government, on World Bank and USAID advice, rejected a strong socialist path, the government recognized it needed the entrepreneurial Chinese community, and the result was the most successful integration of the Chinese in any country in Southeast Asia.

The Thai border trade vies with the Chinese over prominence in parts of Myanmar. Economics is less of a concern, however, than it is in the Chinese penetration of Myanmar and its overall influence in that country. As a non-NATO treaty ally of the United States, Thailand is held to be a surrogate of U.S. policy in relation to Myanmar. This view is furthered by the annual "Cobra Gold" joint U.S.–Thai military exercises that on occasion have been held close to the Thai–Myanmar border. The Thais have been fearful of U.S. sanctions policy toward Myanmar in the past, and such fears were expressed at the highest level of Thai society in the mid 1990s.[53]

---

52 David I. Steinberg, "Myanmar: The Elections Year and Beyond", in *Southeast Asian Affairs 2011*, Singapore: Institute of Southeast Asian Studies, 2011.

53 Personal interview, in which the view that U.S. sanctions would only hurt Thailand was expressed. Naratiwat, Thailand, 1994.

The United States Burma Policy: "The Luxury of Distance."[54]

Whether China and the United States consider each other as a competitor or collaborator in the new Pacific/Asian era and more broadly on the ground in the region, the issue of their relations with Burma/Myanmar and that country's future development reflect their distinct differences in both foreign policy and in the vision each has for the future of the Burmese state. Proximity, of course, plays an important role, but by no means does it completely determine policy approaches to a government in Myanmar that by any consideration has not provided its citizens and inhabitants with the modicum of an improved quality of life. Myanmar may not be a threat to the peace and security of the region, as the U.S. charged in the Security Council in January 2007 (the resolution on which was vetoed by both Russia and China), but it is a nexus of social instability in the area through illegal migration, the spread of disease, trafficking, and a much smaller, but still significant, trade in narcotics, now more methamphetamines than opium and heroin.

In contrast to single-strand U.S. policy, Chinese policy toward Myanmar is based on one dominant strand and several subordinate strands. Primary is the geo-political strategic interest of China in having a compliant, if not a client, state on its southern border. This gives China access to the Bay of Bengal directly, through pipelines, and through water, railway, and road transport. Chinese access is not unlimited, however. The Burmese rejected a Chinese plan to develop a merchandise route from Bhamo, near the China border on the Irrawaddy and the traditional staging area for nineteenth-century mule trains north into Yunnan, down the Irrawaddy to the Henzada region, and then over the Rakhine Yomas (Arakan hills) to the newly expanded deep water port of Kyaukpyu.

The second strand is economic: access to Myanmar's energy (gas, hydro-electric power), natural resources (timber, minerals, jade), and to a state in which it can produce and sell manufactured products directly to the Burmese and also through the increasing overseas Chinese community there. A third strand is in access to ASEAN institutionally and indirectly through Myanmar, and this may increase in importance as the South China Sea imbroglio intensifies and China seeks Myanmar's support within ASEAN. A fourth strand, of less importance, is having Myanmar as an ally in supporting Chinese interests in international fora, especially on Taiwan, Tibet, and Xinjiang Uigur issues.

The positive aspects of Chinese interest in Myanmar are complimented by a set of equally positive issues, but perceived in the negative. A strong Chinese-

---

54 Surin Pitsuwan (see footnote 46, this chapter).

oriented Myanmar precludes other foreign interests (the U.S., Japan, India, Thailand) from asserting pressures or too great an influence on the regime in Naypyitaw, capturing markets, and otherwise harassing the Chinese via Myanmar. Myanmar evidently needs China, as became evident in January 2007 when China, along with Russia, vetoed a Security Council resolution introduced by the United States calling Myanmar a threat to regional peace and security. China diplomatically does not need Myanmar (although strategically the relationship is important and economically it is useful), although good relations with that state may be related to China's broader interests in ASEAN. Human rights and economic development are irrelevant to Chinese interests except insofar as their absence or perceived absence by the Burmese contributes to instability in that country and thus could affect popular unrest. If, on the other hand, resident Chinese are perceived to be unduly economically benefiting, especially at the expense of the Burmese, this could become a grave issue and lead to ethnic strife, as in 1967. Chinese policy toward Myanmar is driven by Chinese bureaucratic elites at several levels, and is institutionally focused, at this stage in any case, on one Burmese institution – the *Tatmadaw* (armed forces).

The United States policy has had but a single, and a completely different, strand. It has followed a human rights agenda that essentially and effectively considers political rights as the basis on which other rights, such as economic rights, social mobility, and growth may eventually be built. It has ignored, at least in public fora and documents, any strategic considerations, and through the self-imposed sanctions policies that have been inflicted on the regime piecemeal, it has effectively eliminated any economic interests. In essence, U.S. policy has been determined by its public; the legislative and executive branches essentially have followed the public outcry that has been effectively mobilized by human rights and expatriate Burmese groups. While Chinese policy has been focused on the lone cohesive bureaucratic mechanism left in that state, the military (which has essentially destroyed any other institution that it might not have been able to control, e.g., an independent legislature or judiciary), United States policy has been effectively focused on an individual – Aung San Suu Kyi, the now iconic Nobel laureate. Insofar as it can be argued that the U.S. public determines U.S. policy, this reinforces the background role of Aung San Suu Kyi in determining that policy, or rather what her supporters have believed what was her policy when she could not communicate with the outside world.[55] This has been accentuated by the public statements of

---

55 See David I. Steinberg, "Aung San Suu Kyi and U.S. Policy Toward Burma/Myanmar." *Journal of Current Southeast Asian Affairs*, September 2010.

President Bush and Laura Bush in support of the opposition. Mrs. Bush has indicated that her interest in Burma was prompted by reading about Aung San Suu Kyi.[56]

Even earlier, U.S. policy in the pre-1988 socialist era was demand driven: the U.S. supplied military and economic assets to the government to decrease the Burmese opium-to-heroin trade that was supplying the bulk of these narcotics entering the U.S. More attention was paid to trying to cut off the source of the supply than to controlling the entrepreneurs, the retailers, and eventually the users.[57] Politically, it was far more acceptable to castigate foreigners than to admonish local users. The United States provided tens of millions of dollars for anti-narcotics activities, including military aircraft (helicopters) for use against producers and their fields, stipulating that these could not be used for other purposes. Yet Karen insurgents shot down one that was obviously employed for military use in violation of those principles, and the helicopters were also used to ferry senior military on various non-narcotics-related trips.[58] There was also an extensive U.S.- sponsored military training program.

The United States has invoked sanctions on Burma/Myanmar in four separate stages with the intent to punish the regime for its human rights transgressions and unwillingness to abide by the 1990 elections. It has been a set of policies designed for regime change that have not succeeded.

The first tranche of sanctions (although it was not called such) came immediately following the coup of 18 September 1988. All military sales and assistance and anti-narcotics activities were terminated, as was the modest USAID economic development program. The second occurred in 1997 and placed restrictions on all new investment in that country, and travel bans on some of the top military figures. This was in response to the junta's refusal to recognize the results of the May 1990 elections (for what is still a matter of some dispute) overwhelmingly won by the opposition National League for Democracy (NLD). Previous U.S. investments, such as that of the Unocal oil company (the largest U.S. investor in both

---

56 See Andrew Selth, "Burma and the Bush White House." Blog at www.lowryinterpreter. org/post/2008/08/Burma-and-the-Bush-White-House.

57 Some in the U.S. in the late 1970s seriously advocated buying up the total opium crop and its heroin product and then burning it. Commentators pointed out that this would do wonders to increase the crop the following year.

58 The Director of Information during that time warned state photographers that they should not photograph departing high-level military with the helicopters in the background. Personal communication.

Burma and Thailand, later bought by Chevron), were able to continue operations.[59]

The third stage was in 2003, prompted by a May 2003 incident in which military- controlled thugs broke up an opposition political caravan in Depayin, central Myanmar, killing a large but unknown number of democracy supporters, and also threatening Aung San Suu Kyi, who was at first reported hurt but was later shown by an U.N. envoy to be unharmed. This was the most draconian of all sanctions, increasing the restrictions on travel by regime members and their families, but more importantly stopping all Burmese imports amounting to some US$350 million annually (later amended to allow in educational materials, handicrafts, and works of art), and preventing the use of U.S. banks from dealing with Myanmar. This created hardships because even regional Asian transfers of funds often went through New York and international NGOs operating in Myanmar (almost four dozen at that time) paid their staff in U.S. dollars. A tedious process of each individual NGO obtaining a Department of Treasury warrant was required for supplying humanitarian assistance. This process was eased after the Nargis cyclone of 2008.

The last of the sanctions from the U.S. was in response to the "Saffron Revolution" in which Buddhist monks were brutally beaten in September 2007. President Bush declared a ban on gemstones (rubies) and jade (and inscrutably not sapphires), and more restrictions on travel; this legislation was passed in the summer of 2008.[60]

The United States has, however, been even more intrusive than sanctions themselves. The Burmese Freedom and Democracy Act of 2003 states "The policy of the United States, as articulated by the President on 24 April 2003, is to officially recognize the NLD as the legitimate representative of the Burmese people as determined by the 1990 election."[61] Thus, this determination was made prior to the Depayin incident. Aside from the vexed question of the purpose of the May 1990 elections (whether to form a new government, as the U.S. and the NLD maintain, or a constituent assembly to write a new constitution, as others maintain), the U.S. had already exerted overlooked but important provisions of the U.S. Foreign Assistance Act that requires that United Nations Development Programme projects be approved by Aung San

---

59　Various members of the Congress not only wanted a ban on new investment, but the withdrawal of all previous investment. The U.S. Department of State disagreed, and a compromise was reached on new investment alone.

60　That legislation has proven to be singularly ineffective. See the U.S. General Accountability Office report on that subject.

61　Public Law 108–61, 28 July 2003, Section 2 (findings) (14).

Suu Kyi and the NLD.[62] Throughout much of the biannual reporting by the U.S. Department of State to the U.S. Congress until 2009, the legitimacy of the May 1990 elections had often been cited as a prerequisite of changed U.S. policy.[63]

The United States policy on sanctions has differed substantially from its allies, all of which have imposed some restrictions but not to the degree imposed by the U.S.[64] All have shown far more flexibility toward Myanmar than the U.S. for their own national reasons. The U.S. and Japan have had substantive differences over how to deal with Myanmar, the Japanese goal primarily being to try to offset Chinese influence in that country.

The junta, of course, was not been unaware of these developments. As we have noted, in an official publication, Military Intelligence asserted that the reason the United States seeks the overthrow of the military in Myanmar is because Myanmar is the weakest link on the U.S.'s containment policy against China.

China, in the U.S., is regarded as the primary support to Myanmar, and thus the essential anchor of regime survival. This is unlikely to be accurate for two reasons. The first is that junta members, who do not want to be too close to any foreign power especially one of such magnitude on its northern frontier, would be unlikely to succumb to sanctions or other pressures brought by distant or neighboring states or both in combination. Such a confluence of pressures would more likely give rise to an even more fervent degree of nationalism, even xenophobia, characteristics that seem continuously latent and occasionally obvious in the Burmese government. High Burmese officials have constantly maintained that as they were isolated for a generation during the socialist period, then can survive such treatment again.[65]

The second is that China, recognizing the need for stability in Myanmar, has quietly attempted to influence positively the junta to make concessions. In moderated terms, likely to be far more acceptable to Burmese nationalism, they

---

62 Section 1106, "Limitations on the United States Voluntary Contributions to the United Nations Development Program" of the Foreign Affairs and Restructuring Act of 1998. For a discussion of the legal implication of this, see David I. Steinberg, *Turmoil in Burma: Contested Legitimacies in Myanmar*, p. 198.

63 Steinberg, *op. cit.*, p. 189.

64 See David I. Steinberg, "The United States and Its Allies: The Problem of Burma/Myanmar Policy." *Contemporary Southeast Asia*, Vol. 29, No. 2, 2007. This article was based on a Washington conference in November 2006. Presentations were made by representatives of Australia, Japan, Thailand, and the E.U. (Germany).

65 See David I. Steinberg, "Burma's Multiple Crises: Globalized Concerns and Myanmar's Response." Paper given at the Swedish Institute of International Affairs, Stockholm, 8–9 May 2008.

have called for reforms in Myanmar (even putting pressure on the government to resolve the minority problems on the border), and even arranged for the U.S. Deputy Assistant Secretary of State to meet with three Burmese ministers in Beijing in June of 2007. It is not in Chinese interests to see a popular uprising or minority unrest that could jeopardize Chinese access to pipelines across Myanmar, nor do they wish to see an increase in Indian influence in that country. The meeting in Beijing may have been an effort by the Bush administration to reclaim its legacy by attempting a belated but positive approach to the Burmese junta. Suspicion of the U.S. on the part of the junta remained profound, at least until 2011. An orthodoxy had been built up in Washington, supported by the expatriate Burmese and human rights communities, concerning policy toward Burma: regime change through recognition of the results of the May 1990 elections won by the opposition National League for Democracy.

This orthodoxy was threatened by the Obama administration, which determined that Myanmar (still referred to as Burma) would be one of six countries subject to a policy review. That process was extensive in the first half of 2009, and involved the various components of the executive branch, including the intelligence community. After much consideration, the Obama administration had to face the political reality that the bipartisan support in the Congress was far too strong to offer any significant diminution of the sanctions regimen, even though both the Burmese and the U.S. had sent modest signals that they wanted improved relations. These signals were insufficient to warrant change in the opinion of both states' leaders, with a resulting stalemate in relations that has lasted through the Burmese 2010 elections and the formation of a new government in 2011. The U.S. has shifted to "pragmatic engagement," which meant the continuation of sanctions but the intent to have high-level dialogue. At senior levels, officials from both the Department of State and the Senate have visited Myanmar and met with both junta leaders and Aung San Suu Kyi, but the status quo continued until December 2011. The engagement policy has continued following the Burmese elections. Aung San Suu Kyi has been mentioned 1598 times on the floor of the Congress (until January 2010), and her views, or what are purported to be her views, continue to prevail. Since a potential policy shift was an Obama administration effort, criticism of it has come from the opposition, and there have been calls for further sanctions and a U.N. Commission of Inquiry into human rights abuses, to which the U.S. has officially agreed. The sense of the administration and the Congress is that the Burmese 2010 elections were neither fair nor legitimate. At the same time, the Obama administration has determined that its engagement with Myanmar will continue under the newly elected Myanmar government. It has also reassured China that containment is not U.S. policy. "The era of SEATO [the Southeast Asia Treaty Organization – an anti-communist alliance] is over."[66]

The Role of International Organizations: The United Nations and ASEAN

Sino-Burmese relations may be viewed through a prism of regional bilateral relationships, which offers one critical picture emerging from that particular lens. It may also be considered through the broader, institutionalized, multi-lateral framework of ASEAN and the U.N., which add additional dimensions to the scene. Neither alone is sufficient to encompass both the actualities and potentials of these multiple relations.

Myanmar's entry into ASEAN was a product of diverse positive and negative interests. The thirtieth anniversary of the organization was to be held in Kuala Lumpur in July 1997. Prime Minister Mahathir of Malaysia wanted to ensure that on that occasion all the countries of Southeast Asia would be included. Thus, he specifically pressured Myanmar, Vietnam, Laos, and Cambodia to join at that time. This would have been a personal as well as an institutional triumph.[67] ASEAN's motivation for the inclusion of Myanmar in this grouping was more than the simple wishes of the Malaysian Prime Minister, no matter how powerful he was, or his evident desire to show his authority by disagreeing with the U.S. Secretary of State, who was publicly adamant against Myanmar's joining as it would further legitimate a government that the U.S. regarded as illegitimate. Chinese penetration of Myanmar had already caused considerable concern in ASEAN, and no matter how deftly China had managed negotiations with the group, the strategic impact on Southeast Asia by Chinese influence along the Straits of Malacca was of considerable worry. Myanmar in ASEAN could, some thought, provide more of a balance on Myanmar's policy options.

Myanmar itself had been interested in joining ASEAN. It had informally con-sidered joining long before it became an official observer in 1996.[68] Secretary-1, General Khin Nyunt, was not only in charge of military intelligence but also of international affairs. It seems likely that of all the senior junta members he

---

66 Assistant Secretary of State Kurt Campbell, 29 September 2010.
67 As it turned out, Cambodia, which joined later, could not join at that time because of a coup.
68 Years before Myanmar joined, the author was sounded out by a Myanmar official in the region about the U.S.'s likely reaction to Myanmar being admitted to ASEAN. As U.S. policy was to open up hermit regimes (e.g. North Korea), he replied that he thought the U.S. would approve. This was before the hardening of the U.S. position when the junta ignored the results of the May 1990 election that the NLD had won.

was most interested in Myanmar's membership for two reasons. It was true that joining ASEAN might give Myanmar a modicum of additional legitimacy, at least in the region if not beyond, and perhaps internally as well. Perhaps more important was the likelihood that joining ASEAN would encourage the member states to make more investments in Myanmar. Insofar as that policy worked, then Khin Nyunt's own position might be strengthened, for as the only member of the junta who had not commanded troops in the field, his internal military credibility was somewhat tenuous. If the intention was to get ASEAN investment on joining, the timing was unfortunate. The very month that Myanmar joined was the start of the Asian financial crisis that spread from Thailand to Indonesia, Malaysia, and later that year to Korea. Although Myanmar was not particularly affected by the crisis directly, investment was severely limited.

Myanmar attended the various ASEAN meetings after joining, but the continuous deterioration of the internal political climate and the incidents that had prompted U.S. retaliation through sanctions led to obvious frustration and embarrassment of ASEAN leaders. Dr. Surin Pitsuwan, now Secretary General of ASEAN but then Foreign Minister of Thailand, had called for "flexible engagement," emphasizing that ASEAN should set aside its policy of non-interference in the internal affairs of member states for a more proactive democratic stance. He did not succeed, but there developed among some of the members of individual ASEAN state legislatures an active bloc calling for the expulsion or suspension of Myanmar from ASEAN. In 2006, when Myanmar was to chair ASEAN and the summit was to be in Yangon, as its turn occurred in alphabetical order, there was considerable anxiety over this possibility, and Myanmar was pressured to agree to let the chair pass to the next in alphabetical line, the Philippines, even though physical preparations for the summit were already evident in Yangon. The next possible year for Myanmar chairing ASEAN is 2014, to which ASEAN agreed in November 2011.

ASEAN has not been effective in transforming the political stasis in Myanmar, and there were many foreign observers who felt that it was unrealistic to expect that it could do so. The ASEAN Regional Forum (ARF), with no specific secretarial support, has never taken up the security issues even within the region, such as the Thai–Burmese border clashes of 2001, the Cambodian–Thai problems of the burning of the Thai Embassy in Phnom Penh the same year, and the Thai–Cambodian temple dispute of 2008.

In November 2007, ASEAN approved its new charter on the fortieth anniversary of its founding. It was ratified by the member states by the fall of 2008. It has a provision in it on human rights, but it contains no monitoring or punitive provisions. When, at that meeting in Singapore, U.N. special envoy Gambari was invited by his Singapore hosts to brief the ASEAN group on his latest trip to Myanmar and his negotiations there, Myanmar demurred, saying that since all ASEAN members were also U.N. members, Ambassador Gambari's briefing should take place at U.N. headquarters. This proved to be a great embarrassment to Singapore.

Yet following Cyclone Nargis, it was ASEAN that was able to obtain Burmese approval to send in an assessment team and help organize relief operations. China has contributed over US$ three million toward the relief effort there.

The role of the United Nations has been mixed. Special envoys and human rights envoys sent by the United Nations have had limited impacts, and some have even been denied entry into the country for years. Ambassadors Razali and Gambari had both met with Aung San Suu Kyi, but external expectations that either could change her status were far too optimistic. Rather than moving the process of political or economic change forward, they have made no inroads into the effective structure of power in that society, although procedures for "dialogue" between the junta and Aung San Suu Kyi have been set up on two occasions, but with little effect. Such efforts have been important, but not sufficient to affect change.[69]

Myanmar has been protected by China's veto power in the U.N. Security Council over any condemnation of Myanmar that could lead to U.N. action, It, along with Russia, exercised this veto power in January 2007 when it prevented action on a U.S.- sponsored resolution that Myanmar was a threat to regional peace and security. As the Russian Ambassador noted, to be such a threat would require the agreement by the states surrounding Myanmar if that were indeed true, but since none of those states had supported this assertion, the issue should be taken up by the U.N. Economic and Social Council, which could consider the issue of human rights. The United States was well aware before the vote that there would be these vetoes, and thus the proposal was more political theater designed for an American audience and international human rights groups rather than for any practical effect on policy. Interventions by a succession of U.N. human rights monitors over a decade and a half and special envoys, and even the visit of U.N. Secretary General Ban Ki Moon in relation to the cyclone relief effort, have only had modest impacts and not affected the power structure in the country. Since the new Burmese government was

---

69 In August 2008, Ambassador Gambari was not allowed to see Senior General Than Shwe, and Aung San Suu Kyi did not go to an appointment that had been arranged for both of them.

installed in the spring of 2011, more productive contacts with the U.N., both in Myanmar and New York, have occurred.

In spite of the fact that the most famous Burmese citizen in history (before Aung San Suu Kyi) was U Thant, Secretary General of the United Nations, the U.N.'s role has been limited although important. Its importance has been in the humanitarian work of its related agencies (WHO, UNICEF, WFP, etc.) under the auspices of the United Nations Development Programme, which has also coordinated international NGO activities in the country. When in November 2007 the resident representative attempted to catalogue the crises facing Burmese society to the Minister of Information, his visa was terminated. Secretary General Ban Ki Moon has twice been snubbed by the junta.[70]

In 1995, the U.N. formulated the concept of the "Responsibility to Protect" (R2P) endangered populations.[71] This would allow international intervention without the approval of the local government where such populations existed. Although developed as a response to war, certain influential foreigners, including the French Foreign Minister, publicly maintained that it should be invoked in relation to the completely inadequate response of the Myanmar authorities to the tragedy of the Nargis cyclone. Although the motivation of those proposing such action seems prompted by the terrible devastation and the slow, secretive, and incompetent response by the government to the needs of its own population, if such action had been approved by the U.N., it would have further inflamed Burmese junta fears of foreign invasion and regime change. The refusal by the authorities to allow U.S. ships and helicopters directly to deliver relief supplies to the victims was probably based on the decade and a half call by the U.S. for regime change, and the belief that this would be a good excuse for U.S. action.[72]

Sino–Myanmar Relations and International Responses

The general reaction of the developed world to the plight and poverty of the Myanmar peoples and the excesses of their military regime has been mixed. There has been extreme criticism of the junta, led by the U.S. but with the U.K. not far behind. For the European Union, Myanmar is not a nation of any

---

70   In the early 1990s, the UNDP was almost expelled from Myanmar. The UNDP headquarters, under obvious U.S. pressure, changed the UNDP programming eliminating all references to the Myanmar government. Members of the SLORC were incensed and wanted to stop the UNDP program, but cooler heads prevailed. Personal interview, Yangon.

71   See Edward C. Luck, "The United Nations and the Responsibility to Protect." The Stanley Foundation, Policy Analysis Brief, August 2008.

72   See Andrew Selth, "Burma and the Threat of Invasion: Regime Fantasy or Strategic Reality?" Brisbane: Griffith Asia Institute, Griffith University, August 2008.

significant strategic interest. Geographic distance is the main reason why the whole Southeast Asia region is much less important than regions bordering Europe. Myanmar had only relatively minor trade relations with Europe before the trade sanctions by the E.U. were imposed, although they had increased after the U.S.'s were in place, as the E.U. market replaced the U.S. in Burmese textile exports. They are hence more symbolic rather than having any deep impact on Myanmar's economy.[73] The E.U. sanctions, including travel (partly mitigated in 2011), have been less stringent than those of the U.S. The E.U. "Common Position" sets forth their policies toward Myanmar, and has provisions for providing humanitarian assistance.[74] But policy within the E.U. is not uniform. Custom dictates that the European former colonizer takes the lead on issues related to its former colony. The U.K. has taken a hard stance on Myanmar, a stance that is not universally shared within the E.U. Norway has supported the Burmese opposition, while Germany and France have looked for alternative policies, as has Sweden. All those governments have recognized that there is a humanitarian crisis in that country, as the U.N. has also noted through its Development Programme in Yangon, and all provide some form of humanitarian assistance. When certain U.S. congressional pressures forced the U.S. to abandon participating in the Global Fund (anti-malaria, tuberculosis, HIV/AIDS) US$90 million effort over a five year period, the E.U. went ahead with a similar US$100 million "Three Diseases" program over the same period. The U.S. participated in the cyclone relief effort as well, and has reconsidered supporting the Global Fund. In 2011, the E.U. somewhat modified its sanctions policy to allow visits by some hitherto banned Burmese officials.

The now former Burmese opposition, the National League for Democracy (2010 no longer a legal party as it did not register to participate in the forthcoming elections), through its secretary Aung San Suu Kyi when she was available of access, was against foreign investment, tourism (modified in 2011), and even foreign humanitarian assistance, although the plight of the Burmese seem to have relaxed her last position because it is politically untenable to be, in effect, in favor of poverty.[75] Although she gave a positive statement to the 2011 Davos economic conference on positive types of foreign investment,

---

73 Magnus Petersson, "Myanmar in E.U.–ASEAN relations", AEJ 4, 2006, p. 571.
74 "Common Position Defined by the Council on the Basis of Article J.2 of the Treaty on European Union of Burma/Myanmar." 28 October 1996. It withdraws military attaches, embargoes arms supplies, restricts visas for high-level Burmese military, and suspends higher-level bilateral visits to the country. For the text, see Steinberg, *Turmoil in Burma*, pp. 282–83.
75 These views were prior to the 2008 cyclone Nargis.

she later agreed with an NLD statement that sanctions were not hurting the Burmese people – a position of questionable accuracy and disputed by a U.S. Embassy cable released through Wikileaks. Yet the debate continues: whether political reform should proceed or follow economic change, or whether they might go in tandem. China has not participated in this public dialogue, and the important relationships of each of the other actors with China mean that China suffers little in relations with these states, many of which take opposing views on Myanmar. Although China has been widely criticized because of its relationship with Sudan and has not pressured that government to do something positive about Darfur, international criticism about China in relation to Myanmar has been far less severe. Perhaps most recently the relatively open Chinese response to their Sichuan earthquake contrasted so positively with the closed, cynical response of the Myanmar junta to its cyclone.

Bilaterally, Myanmar is for China a geopolitical interest.[76] History plays some role, as the China has a long memory, and the interests of China in Myanmar are multiple, profound, and modern. There are, first, strategic interests. Chinese access to the Bay of Bengal through Myanmar is of strategic importance. Even though the scare about multiple Chinese bases along the Myanmar littoral seems to be over, and there had been a great deal of inaccurate reporting on this possibility in the recent past, the presence of China in Myanmar shifts the strategic balance of China's influence in Southeast Asia. Through Myanmar, China has the capacity to monitor Indian missile tests in the Bay of Bengal, and potentially to influence passage through the important Straits of Malacca, through which the energy supplies for Japan, Korea, and Taiwan essentially flow, and which is the United States's life-line to the Persian Gulf and related states and bases, such as Diego Garcia in the Indian Ocean. It is significant that the Chinese themselves regard the Straits as a strategic impediment.

As we have earlier demonstrated, Chinese access to Myanmar's natural resources has significantly changed the economic and security equation for Southwest China. Although the Burmese off-shore natural gas fields are the most dramatic developments of China's search for energy in Southeast Asia, its extensive investments in some 20 hydroelectric projects between 1990–2002, and 19 more after that period, will assuage the thirst for electricity in China's east and south, but through Yunnan Province and the Southwest.[77] Three transmission lines are anticipated: north, middle, and south, with the southern line extending as far as Guangdong. Both legal and illegal timber exports to

---

76 Personal conversation with a Chinese Embassy military official.
77 See Chapter 7.

China have been major elements of China's construction boom, and China has been dealing both with the Myanmar central government and with minority groups near the China border. Investment in mineral production has been extensive (gold mining in the Kachin State has caused much environmental anguish).

Trade and investment opportunities also loom large. At a meeting in Chengdu (also the military headquarters for the southern Chinese command[78]) some years ago, provincial officials of the southeastern Chinese provinces indicated that industries in their region could not compete with east-coast Chinese manufacturers, as their transportation costs prevented them from being competitive. Their market is to the South, and in this sense Myanmar, in spite of its low per capita income, was attractive. Myanmar is also attractive to small businessmen who wish to invest there, and the lack of visa restrictions, the access to capital through traditional Chinese clan, linguistic, and regional associations, and the corruption in Myanmar society on which the economy effectively rests allows them informally to migrate into that country and do well. Their entrepreneurship and relative wealth give them positions of some prominence, which could be the seeds of an eventual backlash against them, as has occurred in other Southeast Asian countries when the apparent discrepancies in income excited envy and when the Chinese could become the scapegoat for local social and economic dissatisfaction. The number of illegal Chinese in Myanmar is obviously unknown, but former high military officials have indicted that it may be as high as two million. Ironically, as Myanmar has lost about two million workers, mostly from the minorities, to Thailand to seek employment and to escape war and its ravages, perhaps an equal number of Chinese have entered Myanmar to seek better employment, although it is the poor who have left and the entrepreneurs who have arrived.[79]

Myanmar apparently was somewhat concerned about its dependence on China. Some observers claim that General Khin Nyunt, former Secretary-1 of the junta and then Prime Minister, who was arrested in October 2004, tried for

---

78 For the area of Chengdu Military Region, see "Military Power of the People's Republic of China: 2009", Office of the Secretary of Defense, Washington, D.C., 2009, p. 61.

79 Zhuang Guotu, "Interactions Between Trade and Migration: On Factors to Drive New Chinese Migrants for Southeast Asia." [sic] Paper presented at the Xiamen University conference on Myanmar 2008. He estimates that 2.3–2.6 million Chinese migrants went to Southeast Asia in all capacities, of whom about one million went to Myanmar. These are those entering illegally. About 30,000 Chinese workers entered Myanmar from 1995 to 2005, according to the National Bureau of Statistics of China, but these are likely to include only those attached to officially approved projects. Observers have pointed out that Chinese projects in Myanmar are designed to provide jobs for Chinese, not Burmese. A Chinese who might annually earn RMB 60,000 in China might receive RMB 300–400,000 in Myanmar. Personal interview.

corruption and under house arrest until January 2012, was a strong advocate of Chinese support. Yet the blossoming of Indo–Myanmar relations, the purchase of Russian jet fighters (and later combat helicopters) to offset the Thai purchase of American fighters, and the intended purchase of a small nuclear reactor program with Russia, ostensibly for medical purposes, show that even before Khin Nyunt's ousting Myanmar's eggs were to be dispersed in a number of baskets. This attempt at balance may have partly paid off in the veto by Russia and China in the U.N. Security Council against Myanmar being charged by the U.S. as a threat to regional peace and security in January 2007.

Myanmar's relations with North Korea have come under scrutiny, and the purported North Korean activities may be regarded by China with some unease. Both North and South Korea have supplied Myanmar with conventional weapons, and the re-recognition of North Korea by Myanmar, after relations were broken off because of the 1983 North Korean attempt to assassinate South Korean President Chun Doo Hwan in Rangoon, was officially endorsed by South Korea.[80] But evidence has been unearthed of North Korean tunnel construction in Naypyitaw, and the visit to North Korea of General Thuru Shwe Mann, the third in rank in the junta at that time, has caused concern. North Korea seems to be supplying Myanmar with short-range missiles, and there are rumors that Myanmar has been interested in some nuclear program beyond the experimental reactor they had contracted (but subsequently cancelled) from Russia. The evidence is sketchy and incomplete, and comes from opposition sources attempting to vilify an already discredited regime.[81] The presence of both Myanmar and North Korea in the former U.S. Secretary of State's "outposts of tyranny" speech tends to equate the two governments and provide a tenuous basis for assuming the worst in their relationship. It seems evident that China would regard a nuclear Myanmar with a great deal of concern. Jane's believes that, "There is no question Myanmar is attempting to build the components for a nuclear fuel cycle . . . Careful analysis of the recovered data reveals that Myanmar is vastly out of its depth in terms of nuclear pursuit . . . Nevertheless, despite the lack of capability, Myanmar certainly has the intent to develop its nuclear programme."

China's relations with ASEAN have been careful and effective. China has approached Southeast Asia on two fronts: the bilateral relations with each of the states within the region, and relations with ASEAN itself. China has multiple

---

80   See Andrew Selth, "Myanmar, North Korea, and the Nuclear Question." In Lex Rief-
      fel (ed.), *Myanmar/Burma. Inside Challenges, Outside Interests*. Washington, D.C.: The
      Brookings Institution, 2010, pp. 181–194.
81   The report was released by the Democratic Voice of Burma in June 2010, and later ana-
      lyzed by Jane's Intelligence Review, 20 July 2010.

ties to ASEAN. It has signed the ASEAN Treaty of Amity and Cooperation, has negotiated a free trade agreement with the region, is a member of the ASEAN Plus Three (along with Japan and Korea), and is a member as well of the ASEAN Regional Forum (ARF). Although territorial disputes concerning the sovereignty of the South China Sea and the oil and gas potential of that area have not been resolved and have indeed resurfaced, and Vietnam, Malaysia, the Philippines, and Singapore all claim various parts of the region, China had not until 2010 pushed its claims in the past several years. It is ironic that as one argument to bring Myanmar into ASEAN in July 1997 was the attempt to ameliorate Chinese influence in Myanmar, which was of concern to some ASEAN states such as Singapore, that influence seems to have grown.

Although the expanding Chinese population in Myanmar has been politically quiescent since the riots of 1967, much in contrast to the exceedingly vocal political activities of Burmese expatriates in North America and Europe, it seems likely that antipathies will develop between the resident Chinese in Myanmar and Myanmar citizens if income disparities between the two groups continue to grow, and if the social development tide that could take place in that country from gas-related and transit incomes does not raise all ships. The new middle class in Myanmar may end up composed of higher-ranking retired military and the Chinese. If the Burmese perceive that their economy has once again slipped from their control, as it did in the colonial era, then the social consequences could be dire.

A Japanese scholar has characterized the Chinese contribution to the Myanmar economy as follows:

> China's economic cooperation and commercial loans apparently support the present regime, but their effects on the whole economy will also be quite limited under an unfavorable macroeconomic environment and distorted incentives structure. In particular, the newly built state-owned factories may become a burden on the Myanmar government budget and eventually bad loans of Chinese stakeholders. After all, strengthened economic ties with China will be instrumental in regime survival in the midst of economic sanctions by Western nations. However, it will not be a powerful force promoting the process of broad-based economic development in Myanmar.[82]

China's rise, the 2008 Olympics, issues with North Korea and Taiwan, and the burgeoning Chinese trade surpluses have all diverted attention from what is one of the most significant areas of Chinese strength and influence, and one that is likely to play an even more important role in the future.

---

82   Toshiro Kudo, "Myanmar's Economic Relations" JETRO Discussion Paper No. 66, July 2006, p. 18.

Part IV: Conclusions

11

Dilemmas of Mutual Dependence in a Globalized World

yanmar's complexities make predictions precarious. Strategically located between two major regional powers, Myanmar is composed of a multitude but disputed number of ethnic groups in a heterogeneous multicultural society that has been at odds or at war for two generations. Its borders are ethnically amorphous, often with polarized internal and external relations. While its extensive natural resources are in worldwide demand, its decision-making processes have been opaque. The very complexity of the internal, regional, and international relations among these peoples should indeed prompt those concerned with policy to approach Myanmar analysis with humility.

China is equally complex on a grander scale. Its complexity is a product of its size and bureaucratic diversity, its regional and global influence, its remembered history, its less than transparent policy environment, and its multitude of national/regional/local development plans.

The review of China–Myanmar policies herein demonstrates the mercurial potential not only for those states, but for Myanmar as a nexus in the region. But by considering the web of conflicting dilemmas that now face a variety of the state, sub-state, institutional, and private actors that will continue to affect the future of Myanmar and the region, it may be possible to pose relevant questions, the answers to which, however, may not be so readily forthcoming. But even if answers may be obscured, employing "dilemmas" as the pivotal approach emphasizes the dynamic of evolving relationships and tensions that pervade the region and its variegated issues, and thus the need for continuing and sustained inquiry. The formation of a new government in Myanmar in 2011 further complicates analysis as it seeks to establish modified ground rules for governance with, perhaps, a more diverse decision-making process, even if military domination continues.

These multiple, complex dilemmas are internal to both China and Myanmar, to bilateral international relations both with Myanmar and between other

347

states and institutions, within regional/international organizations such as ASEAN and the United Nations, and in international triangular and other complex geometric international configurations. The dilemmas extend to tensions and relations within, between, and among ethnic groups, bureaucratic institutions, the private sector, and political entities and organizations. Even cataloguing the various elements in this policy jigsaw puzzle is daunting, yet necessary if an accurate analysis of the region is to be essayed. Each of these dilemmas, directly or obliquely, affects the future of the China–Myanmar relationship and thus the region. All are in need of assessment and re-assessment, for such snapshots at any single point do not reflect the dynamism of far more daunting and evolving "dilemmas." This is especially evident in the Myanmar transition to the new government in 2011, for no matter how apparent military domination may be, some opposition views will be tolerated, or perhaps (if censorship laws are revised) even broadly circulated, affecting the dynamic of internal relationships. For the first time since 1962 political opposition voices will be present in the various legislatures.

Perhaps to escape from an intellectual, frustrating maze, observers tend to think in the singular. Thus, as the word "military" is grammatically singular, we conceive of the *Tatmadaw* through a single lens as always united, as if their unified command system reflects uniform beliefs, interests, and even policies. We do the same with states, asking ourselves: What are China's, India's, or the U.S.'s interests in Myanmar? – rather than disaggregating various relevant decision-making influences and their possible impacts. We even do this with institutions composed of diversified components and interests, such as ASEAN or the U.N., considering them as holistic entities. The problems of policy formulation under this schematic approach, already so evident, are compounded by the rarely questioned hypothesis that organizations are the essential decision-making entities. Yet, there is ample evidence to question the ubiquity of this assumption, for it seems obvious that in many circumstances and societies, power and decision-making are highly personalized,[1] affecting both their process and its speed. This further complicates our understanding of these already daunting dynamics.

We will begin by examining the varied interests of China in the Myanmar relationship, and then move on to reciprocal Burmese interests and those from other sources, as well as intimations from the new Myanmar administration.

---

1   Note the importance of the relationship between U Nu and Zhou Enlai, and later Ne Win. See Chapter 2. For a general discussion of personalized power in Myanmar, see David I. Steinberg, *Burma/Myanmar: What Everyone Needs to Know*, Oxford University Press, 2010, Chapter 7.

China's Dilemmas: Internal and External

This volume has catalogued many of the national interests of China in assuring a stable, amicable relationship with Myanmar. International strategic considerations, security issues of both traditional and non-traditional natures, transit rights, access to natural resources and energy, markets, and other factors have been discussed throughout this volume.[2] Reference has been made to other, diverse Chinese interests, however, which although not in obvious tension (but sometimes in surreptitious disagreement) with Beijing's policies, do influence, supplement, and direct it toward ends that might materially and primarily benefit sub-national actors.

A sharp escalation of Beijing's national interests and control has been evident over the past several years. Beijing's domination of national policy has not always been so evident, as this volume has attempted to demonstrate, but national interests now have become more focused and intense as Myanmar assumes a greater role in Chinese strategic thinking, as we will discuss later.

At least five internal Chinese forces interact with Beijing on planning, policies, and implementation related to Myanmar issues. These are: provincial level concerns, especially those of Yunnan Province; *xian* (county) interests, which may supplement provincial directions, and *zhou* (autonomous prefecture) minority relations; ministerial interests that provide added foci or pressures on sectoral and other policies; business and commercial objectives; and overall ethnic concerns. Entrepreneurial interests also affect policies in various directions, advancing or inhibiting progress toward Chinese national goals. One dilemma for the Chinese central administration has been managing all of these multidirectional interests to support Beijing's overall regional strategy and its vision of its future relationship with Myanmar. As these relationships grow and interests become reified, Beijing has begun to exert stronger influence to ensure improved coordination.

Yunnan's concerns about energy have been earlier discussed; it is a prime consideration of Yunnan's perceived economic needs. The potential benefits of close relations with Myanmar have been a driving force for both its policies and its pressures on Beijing. Not only has increasing access to Myanmar's energy profited Yunnan directly in terms of business, investment, energy supply, and employment, it also enables Yunnan to benefit economically by supplying other provinces in the region (Guangxi, Guizhou, etc.) with energy they lack but need. Yunnan was a critical factor in advocating the Myanmar

2   See especially Chapter 9.

oil pipeline and first proposed it, thus strongly influencing Beijing's decision to proceed. We have also demonstrated that Yunnanese trade is dependent on Myanmar. Yunnan's progress to rise from one of the poorer provinces of China is also largely influenced by Myanmar relations. Should Beijing's relationship with Myanmar cool, or border insecurity result from internal Myanmar ethnic discontent, Yunnan would be the first to suffer. Even more than Beijing, Yunnan needs border tranquillity and access; innumerable trade and other delegations from Kunming regularly attempt to ensure these conditions. But Beijing has been reasserting its leadership in Myanmar relations. This is evident through the 2009 decision to replace provincial border forces with PLA (People's Liberation Army) units. Thus, Yunnan's role has become secondary to Beijing. Yunnan can no longer manipulate Beijing on key issues, since those factors are now defined by Beijing and are beyond narrowly-defined provincial interests.[3]

Individual *xian* (counties) and *zhou* (autonomous prefectures) in Yunnan have their own interests as well. Many are concerned both with the authorized low-level border trade permitted with Myanmar, and also with the opportunities for smuggling and concern over narcotics activities that immediately affect their areas. They have demonstrated interests in gambling, and have profited from the day-trip tourists that engaged in that activity across the Myanmar frontier. The potential economic problem of refugees flooding into border areas was amply illustrated in the August 2009 Kokang affair when 37,000 fled into Yunnan. Although evidence is lacking, local officials may also be involved in corruption tied to cross-border activities. This was certainly the case involving Burmese military intelligence officials on the Myanmar side with the October 2004 dismissal and trial of the former Prime Minister, General Khin Nyunt, military intelligence chief, on such charges, although they are likely to have been the ostensible, rather than the primary, reasons for his dismissal. As Li notes, "However, some county authorities in Yunnan province and some Chinese companies have signed natural resource exploitation agreements with cease-fire groups in the northern part of Myanmar. This phenomenon persists even though China's central government forbids it."[4]

Economic activities of both a public and a private nature also affect the relationship and push policies. Chinese state and provincial companies are documented in Chapter 8 as adhering to the priority investment requirements

---

3   Personal Communication, Yun Sun, Brookings Institution.
4   Li Chenyang, "The Policies of China and India Toward Myanmar." In Lex Rieffel (ed.), *Myanmar/Burma. Inside Challenges, Outside Interests*. Washington, D.C. The Brookings Institution, 2010, p. 127.

of the Chinese government, and there are ample reasons for them to advocate contracts and aid projects in which they would be the suppliers and employers, as most Chinese infrastructure projects import Chinese labor for much of their work. Private Chinese entrepreneurial activities are extensive through legal investment, through often undocumented activities not reviewed by the Myanmar Investment Commission, and through illegal trade.

Ministerial interests also vary. The Ministry of Defense's concerns over strategic and security issues, especially related to India, and the capacity of the *Tatmadaw*, are obvious. But the Ministry of Public Security (in Myanmar called the Ministry of Home Affairs), controlling the police, have their anti-narcotics focus and anti-smuggling assignments, while ministries connected with overseas trade and investment have their assigned roles that they strongly advocate. The Ministry of Health has concerns both about drug addiction and the spread of HIV/AIDS, which has had its regional nexus in Myanmar, which for a long period denied the problem. United States discussions with China over Myanmar relations involve the Ministry of Foreign Affairs, and as tension exists in Japan between its Foreign Ministry and its economic ministries over whether to be responsive to U.S. pressures on Myanmar, the same has existed to some degree in China.

Yunnan has emphasized its ethnic cultural diversity in its tourist relations. Although ethnic groups and autonomous regions have no national power in China, their ethnic cousins across the frontier in Myanmar share with them some common concerns, interests, close relations, and sometimes economic activities. Disquiet in ethnic regions in Myanmar would have impacts both on ethnic groups in Yunnan and on the very structure and power relationships among those cross-border groups, the most important of which are the Wa (some 420,000 in Yunnan) and the Kachin (Jingpo, as they are known in China, or Jingpaw), totalling 150,010, Hmong/Miao 1,072,100, Lisu/Suso 679,600.[5] The Xishuang Banna (Sip Song Banna) Autonomous Region in Yunnan is Dai/Shan, and the Dai/Shan population of the province is 1,340,000. The smuggling of arms to ethnic rebels in Myanmar by ethnic compatriots in Yunnan has been well known in the past. Unrest among Myanmar border groups that could spread into Yunnan itself could affect the safety of Chinese infrastructure.

So the internal Chinese scene is highly complex. Beijing is no longer able to control certain kinds of local interests and activities. Reports indicate that

5   *Yunnan Yearbook 2009*, Kunming: Yunnan Yearbook Press, 2009. p. 332. Figures are from 2008.

Beijing has lost trust in Yunnan's reporting, and has sent its own agents to that province and to the Kachin and Wa regions because Yunnan has not accurately analyzed or anticipated events and activities, some of which involve cease-fire groups. Kunming authorities are also suspicious of some *xian* roles and relations, which sometimes involve illegal activities. All those strained relationships are supplemented by those of an entrepreneurial nature that affect the position of the Chinese in Myanmar. Although there may not be room for policies toward Myanmar at any of the local or institutional levels that are intentionally antithetical to those of the central government, there has been room for advocacy and pressures, both public and covert, and differing priorities that have affected national policy directions, to which we now turn. How to navigate these sometimes conflicting priorities and maintain appropriate relations with a new government in Myanmar is critical for China.

Chinese external dilemmas in mainland Southeast Asia are multiple. Extensive Chinese concerns about Vietnam and the South China Sea, over which sovereignty and resource control have surfaced due to Chinese claims against those of the littoral nations in the region, have become the most contentious issue in the region.[6] Chinese bilateral interests are presently focused on Myanmar and its internal dynamic at the close of about a half-century of military rule. This is not only due to Myanmar's strategic position as a pillar of Chinese Indian Ocean strategy, and not only because of the wealth of Myanmar natural resources that China is efficiently extracting and exploiting, but also because in any dispute with ASEAN over claims to the South China Sea, Myanmar's support to Chinese interests (together with those of Laos and Cambodia) would be valuable in that consensus-driven body. This is not to deny that Chinese influence in Cambodia, Laos, and Thailand are important, but because of present resource control and direct border relations, Myanmar seems of the highest immediate bilateral priority, although in the longer term Vietnam (because of the South China Sea) and Indonesia may loom larger.

Following the 7 November 2010 elections and the movement into a civilianized administration in which the military continues in its paramount role, the Chinese will have to begin to adjust at central and local levels to a new type

6   Some influential Chinese believe the U.S. objection to Chinese interests in the South China Sea (where even its name prejudges control) is because the U.S. wishes to control that region, and not simply ensure free navigation through it. In fact, the staple U.S. policy in that area, and indeed in East Asia as a whole, has been to discourage any hegemonic power from control. This policy dates from the 19th-century "open door" policy on China, through World War II, the Korean and Vietnam Wars, and the U.S. foreign aid programs in that area.

of administrative structure that will present a different set of dilemmas. The previous junta command structure (before the new government was installed in 2011) could make unquestioned, unannounced, and unclarified decisions on Chinese-related issues. In the future, at both the central *hluttaw* (bicameral parliament) level as well as at the levels of regional/state and lower administrative legislatures, even military domination may not result in unquestioned acceptance of previous Chinese activities and interests. In addition to seven regional *hluttaws* in the Burman areas, and seven ethnic-dominated states each with its *hluttaw,* there are six local, semi-autonomous areas, each with a more modest legislature. The most important and germane to the Chinese is the Wa Division along the Chinese frontier. The space for parliamentary debate at any level has already resulted in questioning some of the previously accepted, centrally-approved Chinese activities (the Myitsone Dam), and these potential debates, should they be allowed to occur, could have negative impacts on perceived Chinese interests.[7] Indeed, in the Wa case, as well as in Kokang, Naypyitaw could become concerned over too extensive Chinese interests. A U.N. socio-economic survey of the Wa area indicated that Chinese seems to be the principal language of instruction in most of the primary schools in that region, and Chinese migration into that area is extensive (see Chapter 8). Has Myanmar effectively lost sovereignty over this important region? Chinese investment in that area is also extensive. Whether internal and alternative legislative views will be able to be expressed to the general public are unknown. The military may consider any criticism of any Chinese economic or other role as against Myanmar's national interests, and thus may attempt to censor or control it, but it would continue to do so at some political and social costs that might not be sustainable over time, and could result in increased minority tensions. Centrifugal forces along the Chinese, Thai, and Indian frontiers are creating economic and social dependencies that effectively undercut Naypyitaw's authority.

Chinese infrastructure projects have been approved and built without consideration of local attitudes or impact. The most important dam has been the Myitsone Dam at the confluence of the Mayhka and Malihka Rivers that form the Irrawaddy River – Myanmar's essential lifeline. With a reservoir the size of the state of Singapore, it is to flood a sizeable Kachin population in an

---

7   One could well imagine strains developing at local levels as Chinese projects generally employ Chinese, not local, labor. The Chinese have made disparaging remarks about the low productivity and unreliability of Burmese, and they view their projects as designed to employ Chinese.

area that is regarded as a site of cultural importance. Protests have occurred and some bombings have taken place in the vicinity of the construction. More than the Kachin have mobilized against this construction, undertaken by the China Power Investment Corporation. China would construct the dam at an initial cost of US$3.6 billion, operate it for 50 years under a BOT transfer agreement, and most of the electricity would go to China while Myanmar would collect substantial revenues from it – some US$54 billion over the 50 year period.

On 30 September, in a memo to the *hluttaws*, Myanmar's President Thein Sein announced to decide to suspend the Myitsone Dam during his tenure (until 2015) because this project is "against the will of the people." This is an unprecedented concession to popular opinion – unknown in half a century of military rule. Is this a real and rare concession to the civil society in a repressive country? Does it indicate an internal divergence (inside the military or between it and the new government) over the country's dependence on China? Will the halted dam restart in future? (The Chinese believe it will not.) Will the scenario of the Myitsone Dam spread to other major projects with environmental impacts built by the Chinese, such as China–Myanmar oil and gas pipeline, which have also been criticized for its potential adverse impact on the environment?

Given the new upgraded China–Myanmar relationship to that of strategic partnership during Myanmar's President Thein Sein visited Beijing at the end of May 2011 (see Appendix 5), the dam's suspension is a blow to China. How much in advance the Chinese were informed and at what level is still unclear. Some observers believe that China was warned about volatile public opinion in Myanmar, and refused to believe its relevance to state decision-making. Regardless of the answers to these questions, this event reveals new dynamics of Myanmar's China policy and signals a possible breach of contract signed by the former military government with China. Whatever the conclusion, there are the high political risks and vulnerabilities facing Chinese investment in Myanmar's infrastructure sectors, and the negative impact on Burmese attitudes toward the Chinese role in Myanmar society.

Beijing has considered carefully and reinforced its close relationship with the Burmese military, and will no doubt hope to continue it. There have, however, been rumors of Burmese dissatisfaction with some of the quality of Chinese-supplied equipment. There also is evidence that the Chinese in the recent past have officially been in contact with the civilian political opposition in Myanmar, and one dilemma for the Chinese might be how to strike a balance between civilian, military, and minority leadership so that as the new government evolves, Chinese strategic interests will be protected. Aung San Suu Kyi has indicated that friendship with China is important to Myanmar.

As we have extensively illustrated in this volume, China's strategic interests on its southern flank are focused on Myanmar, and involve relations with India, Pakistan, ASEAN, and Thailand, and more peripherally with the United States through Myanmar. Chinese policy no doubt concentrates on ensuring that a friendly government in Naypyitaw is maintained, for as Chinese interests grow, and as they are solidified in infrastructure (pipelines, dams, etc.), they need even more the acquiescence of a Burmese regime – acquiescence that could be reinforced through economic dominance. In a sense, as China's interests expand and become more physically solid, its "leverage" decreases, because China would have grave difficulty in abandoning its investments should disagreements arise. The Burmese will recognize that the Chinese need them as much as the Burmese have relied on the Chinese.[8] But Myanmar will no doubt recognize that they can only push China so far without exciting potential problems. Thus, both the Burmese and the Chinese recognize the need for tranquillity along their mutual frontier. The Chinese have thus tried to mediate the dispute that led to the central Burmese "invasion" of the Kokang cease-fire zone,[9] and are said to have pressured both the Wa and Kachin, as well as the Burmese, to reach some agreement on the Border Guard Forces dilemma. The Chinese have exerted considerable pressure on the junta to prevent disruption of their interests.

The Chinese, with major investments in such infrastructure, will want to ensure that a regime favourable to them will continue to govern. To that end, they have approached the Burmese and suggested reforms that would prevent the rise of popular unrest and any future "colored (e.g., saffron) revolution."[10] As China has loosened some of the economic and local-level political strictures in its country while still maintaining the control of an expanded and more heterogeneous CCP, so in Myanmar the Chinese may be advocating

8   It is simple to invest in, for example, textile-clothing production, for the imported sewing machines, equipment, and supplies can easily be removed if the political or economic climate changes. With infrastructure, such as dams, roads, and pipelines, the sponsors are in effect held hostage to the whims of the local government.

9   See Li Chenyang, "Effects of the conflict between the ceasefire groups and the Myanmar military government in northern Myanmar on China since 2009", unpublished paper, 2010. "No new armed forces conflicts in northern Myanmar broke out since September 2009 because of China's positive mediation."

10   Some in the West have questioned whether the wave of Middle Eastern unrest and dissatisfaction with dictatorial regimes could affect Myanmar. The 2010 elections may have been a (temporary) safety valve on popular unrest, but for how long, unless significant liberalization takes place, is obviously unknown.

changes as a means for continued, more subtle, military domination. Whether the new government under the 2008 constitution will fulfil this need cannot yet be determined. There are Chinese who believe that some form of more popular or pluralistic (even possibly "democratic") pattern of governance may develop in Myanmar over time, which could pose difficulties for China. Yet this might be more to Beijing's long-term advantage than a rigid Myanmar political structure that could crack rather than bend. Yet the standard Western hypothesis that democracy is somehow inevitable within calculable temporal limits in Myanmar should not remain unquestioned.

The influx of Chinese, both legally but especially illegally, over which Beijing has no control, could present problems for the Chinese state. In addition to state-authorized and encouraged investment in selected fields (see Chapter 7), the capacity of the Chinese to access private credit through clan and linguistic connections, their knowledge of regional and international markets, and their international networks give them a distinct economic advantage. Their presence is an immediate economic advantage to China; but uncontrolled, their roles could create political and diplomatic difficulties. The dilemma for China is whether they can be subordinated to Beijing or Kunming's interests, and if so, how. In contrast to the colonial period, there is no longer a major resident and influential Indian community with which to compete for economic dominance. If private Chinese (backed by state-sponsored economic aid and contracting) were to be perceived by the Burmese as threatening their own (Burmese) control over the economy, there could be dire reactions. If one were to predict the composition of the rise of a middle class in Myanmar, it would likely to be composed largely of higher-level military retirees and the Chinese and Sino–Burmans, and this itself may be an issue in future Burmese political stability. The intense nationalism of the Burmans when the economy has been under foreign control, as in the colonial and civilian periods and during the early days of military rule, could result in anti-Chinese sentiment or even violence.[11] The newly-arrived Chinese in Myanmar today have not exhibited the sensitivity toward Burman culture that is necessary for successful relationships and to mitigate the discrepancies in wealth that are already so apparent. "It is said that more than 80 percent of the criminal acts in Yangon are committed by Chinese. As a result, the people of Myanmar have an increasingly negative impression of

---

11 Although unlikely, a bloody popular rising against the government could result in a xenophobic tirade that could force the evacuation of Chinese and even prompt Chinese intervention. Lessons from the 2011 Libyan experience are probably a subject of interest and study in China.

the Chinese people and Chinese-funded businesses."[12] But this impression may be a product of a perceived lack of business ethics in the Burmese context and sensitivity to Burmese culture.

Economists might argue that China's economic decentralization gives it a global edge over India in the race for regional economic dominance. But this very decentralization creates dilemmas for the Chinese in dealing with the diverse and multiple aggressive economic forces that operate in and on Myanmar at all levels. An example might be the gambling casinos that mushroomed on the Myanmar side of the border but were frequented by the Chinese. Most have subsequently been closed.

The issue of the Kokang cease-fire region and the easy defeat of its modest forces by Naypyitaw in August 2009 points out the nature of the problem. Although, "Generally speaking, China supports Myanmar's central government to solve the problem of ceasefire groups and achieve national reunification … The issue of the ceasefire groups in northern Myanmar is a touchstone of Sino–Myanmar relations." If the issues are not resolved, refugees, smuggling, narcotics, and other problems will increase and could affect the rest of the Chinese in Myanmar. Already in Kokang alone, eight Chinese alternative cultivation projects have suffered losses of RMB31.23 million.[13]

China has in the past attempted to use its good relations with Burma/Myanmar as an example to the region that China harbours no territorial expansion intentions (see Chapter 3). Burma was to be the model, especially in frontier dispute settlement, and for a period this was successful.[14] The Cultural Revolution ended that era, but the treatment of Myanmar in the context of ASEAN may also be considered by the Chinese as a potential benign model. Here again the balance of Chinese interests, but not domination, would be important. Some ASEAN states advocated Myanmar's admittance as a means to stem Chinese influence. This has been an obvious failure. Perhaps some in Myanmar may have advocated joining ASEAN to mitigate too extensive Chinese penetration.

The Vietnamese are also concerned about Chinese influence in their country and the region. Having historically and more recently fought the Chinese,

---

12 Li Chenyang, "Effects of the conflict", p. 127.
13 *Ibid.* In 2009 there were 119 Chinese enterprises in Myanmar carrying out alternative cultivation projects, of which 89 are in the minority regions of the north. Total investment in such projects is RMB1.2 billion, of which RMB264 million were in 50 projects in the Wa area. Only one of these projects is insured by the Chinese government.
14 Some minority groups within China were against the border settlement.

any expansion of Chinese influence in Myanmar is viewed as detrimental to Vietnamese interests.

The impulse to forge stronger east-west regional ties with its neighbors, in part, leads some Vietnamese to criticize Western human rights-motivated sanctions against Burma: they feel that its isolation merely drives Myanmar further toward China. The Vietnamese see Burma's growing military cooperation with the PRC and call for the West to engage with Burma, as it has done with China and Vietnam itself. One senior National Assembly official implored, "You Americans should pay attention to what is happening in Burma. Engagement with Burma would have rub-off effects. You and Europe are wrong on Burma."[15] Vietnam has begun to invest in Myanmar, and as relations have been strengthened direct flights have been inaugurated between Hanoi and Yangon. Vietnam has been one of the strongest supporters of Myanmar in ASEAN.

The complex relationships that the U.S. have with China, and the variety of policy issues on which negotiations are ever present, mean that Myanmar is generally of a lower priority in the Sino–U.S. bilateral dialogue. The U.S. has no doubt approached the Chinese to use their good offices to convince the junta to reform, and the Chinese response has been one of quiet diplomacy with the Burmese, while the U.S., because of its transparent political process, prefers public, and often heterogeneous, displays of concern or anger. Due to nationalistic tendencies, the U.S. verbal abuse of the junta has been an eminently unsuccessful tactic in attaining U.S. goals. The efficacy of the different, quiet approach of Chinese influence has yet to be demonstrated. To what degree should either approach be continued with a new Burmese administration in place to achieve the aims of either China or the U.S. should be assessed.

Myanmar is not a central issue in Sino–American relations. In spite of some residual Cold War attitudes, Sino–U.S. potential rivalries in Myanmar are not necessarily a zero-sum game. One dilemma for the Chinese is: what degree of U.S. relations with Myanmar are in the Chinese national interests? How do the triangular relationships among China, Myanmar, and the U.S. serve or undercut Chinese security and its perceived role in the region? Is the U.S. a rival of Chinese hegemonic interests in its southern littoral? The Chinese quietly have not called for the exclusion of the U.S. from some role in Myanmar. They have obviously attempted to improve Burmese–U.S. relations, especially through arranging (under U.N. pressures) the meeting of an American Deputy Assistant Secretary of State with three Burmese ministers

---

15 David M. Lampton. *The Three Faces of Chinese Power.* Berkeley: University of California Press, 2008, p. 193.

in Beijing in June 2007. China may have informally agreed that a resumption of the U.S. economic aid program in Myanmar in 1979 was desirable. Some U.S. interests in Myanmar have been beneficial for China, such as previous anti-narcotics programs, as China has been very concerned about the spread of narcotics in and through its territory.

Some Chinese officials have recognized that if Myanmar is to prosper and become a modern, stable state that could be supportive of China's position in Myanmar, neither China nor India separately or together can help Myanmar achieve that goal. It will take the West, and especially the United States, to assist in that process.[16] And if a prosperous and stable Myanmar is in China's interests, then on the one hand encouraging the Myanmar authorities to improve relations with the West would be quite appropriate, but on the other, too close an association might deprive China of the influence it seeks to maintain in that country. There are still in Chinese circles, and in the United States as well, remnants of the Cold War syndrome. Some in the U.S. fear a Chinese expansionist potential and enhanced Chinese military capacities, especially a blue-water navy with access to the Indian Ocean and the Bay of Bengal. Many Chinese believe that the U.S. is still intent on a containment policy toward China, and one place to prevent that is in Myanmar. A major issue for the Chinese is how to balance their needs and position in Myanmar against a potential role for the U.S. with the new Burmese regime that would ensure continued Chinese access to its Myanmar interests, while using U.S.–Myanmar relations to help improve the lot of the Burmese peoples to prevent any potential danger to the Myanmar government from popular unrest. China wants two things from U.S.–Myanmar relations: China wants the U.S. to improve relations with Myanmar to the extent that China will no longer be criticized for the poor political record of Naypyitaw; and China wants U.S. investment to improve the Burmese economy and to share that burden with China. Yet China does not want that relationship to be too close, and if given the choice, would prefer the status quo, which allows more room for Chinese manipulation.[17] The rapidity with which the U.S. Obama administration is moving to improve relations with Myanmar, with the nomination and confirmation of a U.S. special ambassadorial coordinator for Myanmar policy and his several trips to Myanmar, and then with the visit of U.S. Secretary of State Clinton (coupled with stopping construction on the Myitsone Dam) all have prompted more intense Chinese concerns over what it regards as the U.S. containment policy toward China.

16 Discussions at a Chinese conference on Myanmar, June 2010.
17 Personal communication, Yun Sun, Brookings Institution.

China must also deal with its ASEAN relationship, which until recently has been eminently successful. Delayed negotiations on the South China Sea (which changed in 2010 when China reasserted its claim to primacy in that area), the free trade zone plan, and detailed bilateral relations have given China an edge in ASEAN that Japan has lost and the U.S. never had. Yet, China's role in Myanmar could jeopardize that relationship should China appear too aggressive in that country. At the time that Myanmar joined ASEAN in July 1997, some member states advocated that move in the hope that membership in ASEAN would tend to mitigate Myanmar's dependence on China and China's influence in that country. Myanmar, however, in its nationalistic stance, may not only have wanted to acquire increased investment from the ASEAN states and obtain a modicum of legitimacy from joining, it may also have considered the reverse: Myanmar may have wanted to join ASEAN to limit Chinese influence, although this hypothesis is undocumented.

Myanmar's Five Dilemmas

The approaches to and the methods by which the Burmese leadership will deal with four general internal Burmese dilemmas, and one directly related to China, will profoundly influence the future of the state and Chinese relations. These generalized issues are: (1) the role of minorities in the distribution of national assets and power, and thus the question of border and internal tranquillity; (2) the degree to which the authorities are prepared to open the society to a flow of information and ideas from both internal and external sources, including China; (3) the degree to which rational economic policies can be initiated and pursued; (4) an adherence to the 2008 constitution that an independent judiciary, and through it the rule of law (and predictable, if not limited, corruption) could be instituted. Each of these issues affects the relationship with the Chinese. The fifth, specifically Chinese, issue that has not yet been addressed is the question of controls on private Chinese entrepreneurship in and immigration into Myanmar. These questions cannot simply be ignored, citing constitutional rhetoric as resolving the problems, for they are likely to fester and become more acute if unaddressed.

Minority problems are the single most enduring and perplexing issue that has faced the state since independence; they are also likely to be the issues of greatest importance in the Chinese relationship.[18] The Sino-Burmese border,

18 The authors would argue that although international attention to Myanmar has focused on political and human rights, the most enduring problem facing any state administration is the minority question.

so carefully negotiated over many years and regarded as a triumph by both sides, is ethnically arbitrary, and the stability of those border peoples will affect the bilateral relations. This was apparent in the case of the Kokang in 2009, when 37,000 refugees fled into Yunnan to the chagrin of the Chinese, and was apparent in 2010 when Wa and the Kachin had grave problems with the Myanmar authorities' plan to convert their troops into Border Guard Forces, and thus castrating their capacity for rebellion or more autonomy.[19] The final decision on this issue, after about two years in which a series of deadlines were passed without resolution of the problem in the Wa, Kachin, and other areas, had been postponed until the 2011 government was in place under the 2008 constitution, and since has been further set aside. This issue remains explosive. The Chinese are said to have pressured the junta to avoid confrontations with the Wa and Kachin. "In 1990 the Chinese government issued its 'Regulations on Specific Policies toward Myanmar's Armed Ethnic Minority Groups,' declaring that China would give no 'political recognition, military support, or economic assistance' to the armed ethnic minorities but would regard them as Myanmar's local authorities temporarily conducting general business based on the actual situation."[20]

Not only do a variety of ethnic peoples with sizeable populations straddle the border, many of the Chinese infrastructure projects pass through or are located in their regions. The two pipelines and some dams are thus vulnerable should the central Myanmar authorities and the minorities revert to armed struggles. Thus, stable and peaceful minority relations are essential to Chinese interests even though some Chinese businesses and others have made extraction agreements with rebel groups, agreements that allow such cease-fire organizations to maintain themselves and their armies. The dilemma facing every Burmese government since independence has been how to maintain a veritable "Union" of Burma or later, Myanmar.

No Burmese government has effectively resolved that issue, and although no major minority group or faction now seeks independence (and the primary slogan and self-designated task of the *Tatmadaw* is national unity), many have called for various types of federalism that to the military are anathema.

---

19 The Burmese proposed that that the total Wa contingent of the Burma Guard Forces would be two battalions, or about 700 men. The Wa now command between 15,000–25,000 men, and thus the Burmese proposal was clearly unacceptable.

20 Li Chenyang, "Effects of the conflict", p. 119, based on an article by Yu Jiang and Wang Chaozuo, "Reflections on policy cooperation with Myanmar local minority armed forces in Sino-Myanmar border management", *Journal of Yunnan Public Security College*, No. 1 (2001) p. 67–71.

The 2008 constitution does call for more local government than any previous Burmese administration has granted to the minorities (but is explicitly against any secession), but this may not be sufficient to assuage their interests, for as nationalism has grown in Myanmar and among Burmans, it has also grown among various minority groups. The relationship between China and Myanmar in a sense is held hostage to the tranquillity of the minority regions.

Although China may be faulted for some controls on information flows in its country, those in Myanmar are far more severe. If Myanmar is to achieve a degree of prosperity and development and assuage popular unrest, it will need to deal with the issue of a freer flow of information. This is essential for economic growth and thus is in Chinese interests. Yet each Burmese regime has had problems to some degree with this issue, and after a half-century of censorship, it may be difficult for the new government to open to internal and external criticism. How much political debate in legislatures will be available in the public media is an issue. The wall against foreign influences has long been breached, and government attempts to suppress free exchanges of views will be increasingly viewed as archaic, ineffective, and self-defeating. First, tentative steps were taken in May 2011 that allowed public, direct criticism of state policies for the first time in perhaps a half-century, even in front of the President. Such relative freedom, however, is new, and although censorship has been relaxed, the internet is now open, and some foreign journalists have been allowed in, controls still exist, although positive changes are evident.

Economic rationality and predictability are essential for economic growth and more directly for China for the operations of Chinese investment. Controls on, and the predictability of, corruption levels is essential for successful foreign investments and those of the overseas Chinese. Myanmar has been listed by Transparency International as the second most corrupt state in the world, and while such a designation may be questioned as to its accuracy, all evidence indicates that the situation is severe and uncontrolled. President Thein Sein in 2011 has publicly recognized the importance of the issue. Corruption is also a delegitimizing element that could prompt unrest as well. China has officially indicated that Myanmar is a country of high political uncertainty in terms of Chinese investment potential (eight out of nine on a nine-point political risk scale), and yet has encouraged it for China's national interests.

An independent judiciary, as specified in the 2008 constitution, is also required if there is to be an autonomous arbitration platform on which industrial disputes can be adjudicated, and if immigrant Chinese are to be assured of their rights and duties. The new administration might do well to reconsider its 1982 citizenship law that limits foreigners, even those who have lived in Burma/ Myanmar for generations, to certain positions and rights. Although personal relations are likely to guide and resolve disputes, even those of an international nature, the need for the predictability of rules and processes is required. Under the SLORC/SPDC, policy trumped law and regulations, which were often changed suddenly, arbitrarily, and seemingly by whim. This has hindered foreign investment, as obviously have sanctions, but in the long run the former may be more destructive. Aung San Suu Kyi has stressed the need for the rule of law.

The Burmese have also to deal with the obvious and pervasive influence of private Chinese business. Negative comments have been frequently heard within the country about of the loss of Burmese businesses. The lack of capital available to the private sector through the Burmese banking system, unless changed, will mean the continuing and increasing domination of business by the Chinese community. Some estimate that 60 percent of the business private sector (excluding agriculture) is in Chinese hands. This could lead to political instability and the spectre of heightened anti-Chinese nationalistic sentiment. In a sense, then, those dilemmas that Myanmar faces in relations with the Chinese state and its various manifestations are those that other foreign investors face, and indeed the indigenous population as well.

Myanmar officials have proudly proclaimed through a variety of media, fora, and personal conversations that they do not need the outside world; they have rice and resources and have gone it alone for several decades and could do it again if necessary. Although only partly accurate in an earlier era, this bravado no longer relates to the reality of changing times, conditions, communications technology, and the expectations of much of the urban Burmese population. Myanmar, perhaps against its will and its attempts at censorship and the control of information, is part of the region. The dilemma for the new government in the post 2010 period is how to balance the requirement for outside relations, and the multitude of aid and other relationships, against the need for the military to feel that they are fulfilling their self-identified role of protectors of the state and national unity. In a singular sense, the opening of Myanmar to external influences will do more to mitigate excessive Chinese influence than any other single approach.

In Thailand, there has been a palpable shift in the rural Buddhist population as to its increased expectations of central government delivery of goods and services. This has occurred in a country that like Burma/Myanmar, where traditional Buddhist karmic concepts have predominated: the socio-economic status of an individual is dependent on previous incarnations, not on the state's delivery of goods and services. All Myanmar governments at all levels will have to resolve the dilemma of anticipating this likely change over time in order to retain public order and legitimacy.

The dilemma of too great a reliance on China prompted Myanmar to encourage closer ties with and assistance from India. It is likely that similar considerations prompted them to make modest gestures to the United States as the Obama administration considered re-examination of the U.S. policy toward Myanmar. So one of the prime dilemmas for any new Myanmar government is the degree to which they are prepared to make concessions for better Western relations to maintain (or perhaps better, regain) the traditional "neutralism" that had been a hallmark of Burma during the Cold War. The degree to which openings to the West might prompt internal political questions or ferment must also be on the minds of the Burmese leadership. Whether improved relations with the U.S. might jeopardize Chinese support (or perhaps increase it) should be of Burmese concern.

The Burmese face a variety of other dilemmas as well. How much should the political opposition cooperate with the government, and the government with the opposition? To do the former might result in their cooptation, but to avoid participation would result in their further marginalization. The National League for Democracy faced this problem in April 2010, when it decided against registering in the planned 2010 elections.[21] Its executive committee made this decision based on the predilections of Aung San Suu Kyi. In an effort to reach out to the opposition, the government changed the political party registration laws that enabled to NLD to re-register as a legal party, and Aung San Suu Kyi then indicated her interest in running for a *hluttaw* seat in the by-elections called for those positions vacated when their incumbents became ministers. The ethnic groups have had a set of similar problems – to agree to the stringent regulations of the Border Guard Forces plan, or to threaten to return to insurrection and revert to the jungle. They and Naypyitaw have been under strong pressure from the Chinese to negotiate some face-saving compromise, and a new agreement has wisely set aside the problem, at least for the time being. How will the expatriate Burmese react to the elections and the new government? To attempt to participate may give some of them marginal influence, but compromise their principles, while eschewing all contacts will only continue their isolation and

---

21   In May 2011, the NLD had decided not to re-register for the by-elections eventually held on 1 April 2012 (Yangon, personal communication). It later reconsidered, and was officially registered on 5 January 2012.

exile. The president has stipulated that those Burmese who have committed no crimes are invited back. There are no easy answers here.

There is the distinct possibility that, for a period, the new Burmese government will deny the existence of any of these dilemmas, even though they may be apparent to external observers and have longer range impacts. The Burman leadership may remain content in both their accomplishments and prospects. Hypothetically, they might argue that the SLORC/SPDC has built more infrastructure than all previous governments since independence, has grown foreign exchange reserves from US$30 million to about US$5 billion, has constructed a new capital, and has given the minorities more local control than they ever have had since pre-colonial times. The prospects, they might continue, look equally positive, with considerable revenue from Chinese contracts and investment, from Indian support, sale of gas to Thailand, and the natural resources of the country. Although in some Western circles the government may still be called a "pariah," they might argue, this will not affect the future of the new administration. Such a view would be short-sighted, for globalization has not only brought wealth and power to some, it will intensify socio-political and economic demands on the state that it myopically may not recognize and increase income disparities, to the detriment of the people as a whole and to the future of the anticipated power structure. Yet the new administration, under presidential leadership, has engaged in the beginnings of an anti-poverty campaign, one that is unprecedented under military leadership. Macro-economic policies are also being re-examined. Foreign observers will watch these developments very carefully.

The dilemmas of the Sino-Burmese relationship also may have impacts on three major external states: the United States, India, and Japan.

U.S. Dilemmas

The dilemma for the United States, clearly influencing Sino-Burmese relations, is the degree to which it is prepared to exert whatever residual influence it may have on Myanmar for reforms, while at the same time not jeopardizing U.S.–China relations. If Myanmar is a "boutique issue" in the U.S., and thus not one on which any administration is prepared to expend a great deal of political capital, it seems far more important to the Chinese in spite of Myanmar's very low percentage of China's international trade.[22] Any move by the U.S. administration to normalize fully economic and diplomatic ties (raising the level of

---

22   See David I. Steinberg, "The United States and Myanmar", pp. 175–194.

representation in Myanmar back to an ambassadorial level, alleviating the sanctions regimen, etc.) was likely to be met by strong moral criticism from the opposition, human rights groups, the Burmese expatriate community, and more widely in the Congress, unless there were significant changes in Myanmar and agreement by Aung San Suu Kyi that she endorsed those changes. After the release of additional political prisoners in January 2012, the U.S. announced it would nominate an ambassador to Myanmar. Although the U.S. legally must invoke the mantra that Myanmar is a threat to U.S. interests and national security to approve sanctions, patently that is not the case and is simply a required bureaucratic mechanism by which any administration can inaugurate or continue those policies.[23] At the same time, should it back to vociferously the reformers and discredit their nationalistic credentials, this could cause a local backlash against reform measures.

The Obama administration has formulated its new policy toward Myanmar by advocating "pragmatic engagement," which simply recognizes the internal U.S. political realities – sanctions will remain but high-level dialogue will continue. The influence of Aung San Suu Kyi has been dominant in U.S. policy formulation and continuation.[24]

To date, stark and important as are the differences between Chinese and U.S. policies toward Myanmar, they have been at best a minor irritant in that critical relationship. A modest public outcry against Chinese support to the junta has been evident, and even in one case a congressman introduced legislation, which was not included in the bill that passed, to impose sanctions on China if it did not stop military support to the junta. Yet a new era exists in Myanmar as a result of the 2010 elections.

Insofar as the U.S. and the West in general have negative predilections about contemporary military regimes, then a longer range perspective may be called for. Any military that has pre-empted all avenues of social mobility in a society will lose influence and retire to barracks only when other significant non-militarily controlled avenues of mobility open up (the private sector, academia, civil society, even politics) and dominate. This will require a considerable period, but if U.S. policy has that as a goal, then the dilemma for the U.S. at the present time is how to foster such evolutionary changes without creating an American political backlash against any such, obviously longer-range, programs.

23   See Thihan Myo Nyun, "Feeling Good or Doing Good: Inefficiency of the U.S. Unilateral Sanctions Against the Military Government of Burma/Myanmar." *Washington University Global Studies Law Review.* Vol. 7:455, 2008, pp. 469–70.

24   See David I. Steinberg, "Aung San Suu Kyi and U.S. Policy Toward Burma/Myanmar." *Journal of Current Southeast Asian Affairs,* September 2010.

And how can or should the U.S. attempt to broaden the military's world vision? Under both civilian and military governments in Burma/Myanmar, the U.S. supported an extensive IMET (international military and education training) program that was stopped after the coup of 1988. About two-thirds of the Burmese military who go abroad are, however, now trained in China. Aung San Suu Kyi has continuously said that the Burmese must solve their own problems.

The U.S. has already indicated that the 2010 elections and the 2011 government are not considered "legitimate," although it has intensified relations with the visit of the Secretary of State which itself has created another dilemma for the U.S., but the Chinese (along with India, ASEAN, and the U.N.) claim progress, even if modest, and thus will continue to work with the new government. Anecdotal evidence indicates that the Chinese were pleased with the election results. Should the new Burmese administration engage in significant economic reforms, such as (required by ASEAN) to unify its foreign exchange rate in 2012, and take other economic reform steps, the U.S. may find itself faced with the problem of demonstrating approval of the economic progress while still denouncing the legitimacy of the newly elected government because the elections were not deemed "free, fair, and inclusive." The U.S. is caught in the dilemma of maintaining that position while Aung San Suu Kyi has agreed to run for a *hluttaw* seat under a government declared "illegitimate" by the U.S.

The question of the release of political prisoners is important, but the various numbers (up to 2,200) are in dispute; yet major, continuing releases are the *sine qua non* of better relations. A more rational economic system together with a controlled political process would invite comparisons between Myanmar and China, but to the detriment of China because Myanmar will have a multiple political party system (no matter how ineffective), while China (as well as Vietnam and Laos) have proclaimed single party dictatorships (even if China has opened wide the CCP). The release of political prisoners including Aung San Suu Kyi was obviously required for any U.S. policy shift, but it has become evident that that alone has not been sufficient.

In 2011, there have been strong forces within the U.S. (less in the executive branch) for increased sanctions, especially targeted on high-level Burmese bank accounts. An ambassadorial level coordinator for Burma has been nominated and approved and is in office and has been appropriately welcomed in Naypyitaw on several occasions, and the U.S. has agreed to a potential U.N. "commission of inquiry" to explore whether the military has committed crimes against humanity. If instituted, this would only increase military suspicions of U.S. intent.

Regional Actors

The economic malaise in which Japan has festered and the loss of its momentum in Southeast Asia has affected its role in Myanmar. But the issue is more complex. Although the Japanese media have blamed various Japanese governments for its loss of influence in Myanmar, they neglect the importance of personal relations. Because Ne Win (along with Aung San) was one of the "thirty comrades" trained by the Japanese to fight against the British before World War II reached Asia, his personal relationship with the various Japanese administrations was close. Economic assistance poured in, and Japanese officials had relatively easy access to him as president, prime minister, commander-in-chief of the army, and chair of the Burma Socialist Programme Party. Following the coup of 1988, when he was in retirement, he seems to have still wielded considerable influence on critical decisions (the ousting of General Saw Maung, for example[25]) until his decline through ageing and his house arrest. Japanese influence after 1988 was eclipsed by China because in large part Japanese relations were built on a personal engagement with General Ne Win, and the Japanese economic malaise.

The Japanese had other reasons for involvement. One was an emotional attachment to Myanmar based on their World War II experiences and heavy losses there (some two-thirds of Japanese troops in the Burma campaign died there). Another was potential access to Myanmar's extensive natural resources. Japan is likely to become a major investor in the Dawei Ital-Thai project. More important was the perceived need to counter Chinese influence through competition on foreign assistance. This was in fact bound to fail because Japan could not supply the armaments that the *Tatmadaw* wanted. But the relationships between Myanmar and China materially strengthened China, this has the Japanese government concerned. It is highly likely that Japan will resume its foreign assistance program to Myanmar.

As previously demonstrated (Chapter 9), India also has security needs to mitigate Chinese influence, as well as to protect and develop its Northeast region – which is primary is disputed. So the shift in Indian policy in 1993 from antipathy toward the junta to provision of foreign aid and high-level diplomatic and military visits simply was a reflection of geo-political reality. The dilemma for India is how much they might be prepared to invest in Myanmar, and whether their perceived goal of balancing China, or at least moderating China's internal role in Myanmar, is sustainable. How much internal political pressure

---

25   Personal interview, Yangon.

on its Myanmar policy will be put on any Indian administration as the largest democracy in the world, and how would that government respond? Whether the close assistance relationship with Myanmar will positively have impacts on India's turbulent Northeast region is as yet unclear. This is, however, a high Indian priority.

In turn, ASEAN and the U.N. must decide how strong a position each might take related to any continuing repression in Myanmar and the inability or disinterest of its government in improving the welfare of its diverse peoples. Secretary General Ban Ki Moon has been twice insulted by Senior General Than Shwe. ASEAN has a new Charter as of 2007–2008 that contains human rights and other provisions that are unenforceable but might serve as sign posts for positive change. The various countries in ASEAN have strongly differed in their assessment of the problems of Myanmar. Each has it own problems with human rights or has a checkered heritage in that regard. Although ASEAN may have the most positive foreign influence on Myanmar policies, it is likely to be reduced to bland statements in spite of its Charter containing human rights provisions. "Non-interference" in any member's internal affairs still remains its modus operandi. Myanmar has indicated interest in hosting ASEAN in 2014, and in late 2011 ASEAN approved of that decision. The dilemma for the U.S. is whether it would attend, but between the decision and 2014 there will be a U.S. election, and any executive branch will watch closely the degree to which reforms in Myanmar continue.

There are, in addition, the dilemmas of the expatriate Burmese community, stalwart in their demands for internal freedom and political changes. How will they react to the evolving patterns of internal and external Burmese relationships, and what impact might they continue to have on the U.S. decision-making process related to Myanmar? International human-rights groups too will need to assess whether any changes that occur are significant enough to cause reconsideration of their positions toward the country.

The multiple dilemmas facing all the significant actors in the evolving drama of change in Myanmar, and Chinese relations with it, should prompt more nuanced policy considerations among all parties than has been evidenced to date. Not all those states, administrations, and institutions involved in China–Myanmar relations will be able to achieve their maximum objectives, but recognition that dialogue at all levels may clarify the dilemmas and their choices is a minimum requirement.

Myanmar is on the cusp of administrative change, if not in power relation-ships. Military control will continue, but administrative change, and change in the generation of military leadership, may mitigate some problems or exacerbate tensions and force reconsideration of relationships and activities on the part of the diverse Sino-Burmese actors and their international relationships. We may hope for the former. But we should be prepared for the latter – the following Burmese proverb is still relevant: "May we be spared the misfortunes that arise from a changing of kings."[26]

China–Myanmar Relations under "Discipline-Flourishing Democracy"

Upon the inauguration of the new Burmese government at the end of March 2011, the Chinese government spokesman of the Chinese Foreign Ministry, in answer to a press question, said:

> We congratulate Myanmar on its democratic process and inauguration of the newly elected leader. China respects the development path chosen by the Myanmar people based on its national conditions and hopes Myanmar will maintain stability, steadily push forward its democratic process and finally achieve democracy and development. When it comes to international relations, China has always upheld respecting the development paths chosen by the peoples and disapproved imposing sanctions or exerting pressure. We hope the international community will create a lenient environment for Myanmar's national reconciliation and economic development.[27]

The elections obviously reassured the Chinese leadership. Whether they were free and fair seems to have been less important than that they were tranquil. Even the simple fact of having held them may have prevented any residual influence from contemporary Middle Eastern "Arab spring" popular unrest. Certainly, the continuity of much of the Burmese military leadership in mufti must also have reassured the Chinese that their interests would be protected.

New developments in Sino–Myanmar ties have emerged, intensifying relationships. Myanmar has become a "comprehensive, strategic cooperative partner" (see appendix 5), a term never previously used. This is likely a result not only of the exploitation of Burmese resources, but also, and now perhaps even more important in Chinese military and security terms, the development of a two-ocean naval strategy, now a publicly stated Chinese policy. The Sino-

---

26   Quoted in Andrew Selth, *Civil–Military Relations in Burma: Portents, Predictions and Possibilities*. Brisbane: Griffith University, Griffith Asia Institute, Regional Outlook Paper 25, 2010.

27   Ministry of Foreign Affairs spokesperson Jiang Yu, 31 March 2011.

Burmese oil and gas pipelines and Kyaukphyu–Ruili highway and railroad are concrete demonstrations of the "strategic cooperative partnership" between the two countries. Although Chinese point out that the phrase involving the comprehensive strategic partnership has been used in a number of Chinese relationships, this is the first time it has been used with Myanmar, and was significant. How the Myitsone Dam decision will affect its implementation is of great interest. Strengthened U.S. cooperation with Pakistan, and turmoil in that country, may prompt China to believe that Pakistan is not as reliable an ally as it once was. Improved Indian–U.S. relationships are also of concern. Thus Myanmar becomes even more important in the context of an Indian Ocean strategy.

The Chinese military have pursued closer ties. The Vice Chair of the Central Military Commission visited Myanmar in May 2011, emphasizing Chinese training, supply, and strategic cooperation with the Myanmar *Tatmadaw*. The Chengdu Military Region (in charge of South Asia, Tibet, southwest China and Myanmar[28]) commander also visited and in August 2010 two Chinese missile destroyers called at Yangon. President Thein Sein went to Beijing on his first foreign trip after his inauguration, picking up a US$745 million credit package. There is an unmistakable intensification of the relationship, which has been generally neglected in official U.S. and Western discourse on Myanmar.[29]

Yet, internally, if the Myanmar Pandora's box of pluralism is not yet open, the taut bindings have been loosened, and resecuring them may be difficult if the leadership were to feel it necessary, and even if constitutional provisions exist for the military to do so. Several questions occur. How much voice will the people of any ethnicity have and over what issues? The cessation of the construction of the Myitsone Dam in the Kachin State, prompted by local and national concerns, may be just the first of other questions on Chinese construction projects. Will the military in the party have divergent views from the military in uniform, as happened in the socialist era? How will the regional military commands relate to local legislatures, especially in border regions, since this is not spelled out in the constitution? Can the new administration assuage popular dissatisfaction with the conditions of life and livelihood of the population, even though the new president, Thein Sein, has indicated his interest in doing so in his inaugural speech? These and many more issues will test the Sino–Myanmar relationship, as well as those in the region and beyond.

28 The Guangzhou Military Region and the South Sea Fleet cover the rest of Southeast Asia.
29 We are indebted to Yun Sun of the Brookings Institution for comments and ideas on this section.

The Chinese ties will also be subject to strain. The new Myanmar administration has in unmistakeable terms signalled a desire for improved U.S. relations, perhaps to mitigate overdependence on China. How the increasingly close relationships with China will affect Myanmar, the region, and the U.S. is of importance to all elements, and will be increasingly analyzed.

Coda

To many external observers of the Myanmar scene, in the more than two decades since the failed people's revolution of 1988 and the re-imposition of direct military rule, only glacial change seemed apparent in that country. This attitude was especially prevalent among those who had called for immediate and liberalized shifts in the fundamental Burmese power configurations that have remained relatively constant. That perception, however, was never accurate. The continuity of pervasive and continuous authoritarian military rule masked subtle modifications in that society – modifications that have become obvious in 2011 since the inauguration of a new Myanmar "civilianized" administration.

The year 2011 also witnessed the "Arab Spring" series of popular revolts and demonstrations against authoritarian regimes in the Middle East. Although they are unlikely to have been the impetus for reforms in Myanmar, for the timing of the inauguration of the new Myanmar President came before most such demonstrations peaked, the changes in Myanmar, in contrast, significantly stemmed from a decision by the top leadership that some systemic modifications were necessary. Although not unique in Asia, Myanmar is unusual in the Asian context as liberalization, sometimes called "authoritarian reform," emanated from the top; the leadership moved in more liberal directions without being directly and immediately threatened from below. The new Myanmar government would likely have been given a "honeymoon" period even without the announced reforms, for some opposition was officially allowed and somewhat articulate. Perhaps the Middle East spectacle, however, may have spurred the Myanmar leadership on.

Since 2011 and the inaugural speech of President Thein Sein at the end of March, changes and planned changes have been and are continuously occurring at a rapid rate that even the most seasoned observers, foreign and domestic, have found unexpected. As this volume goes to press in early 2012, internal modifications in governmental affairs are incomplete and external relations constantly in flux.

Most important in terms of relations with China has been, of course, the temporary termination of construction of the Chinese-sponsored Myitsone Dam

Plate 12: President Thein Sein meets with U.S. Secretary of State Hillary Clinton, Naypyitaw, 2011 (photograph courtesy U.S. State Department)

through 2015 (although the Chinese believe this stoppage will be permanent), which had been estimated to cost some US$3.6 billion and on which the Chinese had already spend US$42.5 million. They will have to be reimbursed for their sunk costs in any case. The repercussions of the Myitsone Dam decision by President Thein Sein are still being assessed. The president of the Chinese construction firm has made an elaborate statement on the studies that have gone into ensuring environmental safeguards and social considerations, but these are questioned. The Chinese, to ease relations, have newly changed the status of the project from one of a bilateral governmental project to a commercial enterprise, thus easing diplomatic tensions. This expression of Burmese nationalism will affect the level of trust between the two governments. Although such an action caused much anxiety in the bilateral relationship, this will not destroy Sino-Burmese relations, as each side has too much invested in it. Although the Chinese may suspect that the impetus from this was engendered by the U.S. (through civil society supported in part by the U.S.) as part of a vast U.S. Asia-wide plan to "contain China" (and included in this assessment was the visit of the U.S. Secretary of State to Myanmar), the impetus for this action came from Burmese resentment of the dam and may be part of a Burmese effort to restore a semblance of neutralism to its foreign policy – a position that has a long history since Burmese independence, but always, as we have earlier noted, in China's shadow.

Some Burmese and foreign environmentalists want to expand their success to other foreign-supported projects, including the Thai offshore gas pipeline.

How much internal dissidence the authorities will tolerate on any vital national concern is an issue, but the government is vulnerable on the absence of internationally acceptable environmental studies on many major projects, and pressures are likely to continue. Although the role of indigenous civil society (for which there earlier was no word in Burmese) cannot legally threaten the governmental structure, it has become far more important in Myanmar than heretofore.

This search for a more balanced U.S. foreign policy was also evident in the visit 1–2 December 2011 of U.S. Secretary of State Hillary Clinton, a trip that was the culmination of a series of visits by high-ranking U.S. officials, all of which have served to support the reform agenda of President Thein Sein, and were so intended. This reform agenda, which still in its infancy at the close of 2011, is broader than many might have imagined. It includes relaxed censorship, regulations on forming free trade unions, the right to protest with government notification and approval, the formation of a human rights commission, revisions in regulations on political party registration that has allowed the National League for Democracy to re-register and compete in by-elections, and effective dialogue with Aung San Suu Kyi, who indicated her intention to run for a *hluttaw* seat.

If Secretary Clinton's trip was the acme of U.S. visits, others followed. French Minister of Foreign and European Affairs Alain Juppe and British Foreign Secretary William Hague both visited in January 2012, along with U.S. Congressional leaders. The apparent opening of Myanmar has attracted a variety of influential foreign visitors at numbers and rates unprecedented in a half a century.

President Thein Sein has also called for the formation of a Myanmar Development and Resource Institute that would have three components: economics, political affairs, and law. Many reforms of an economic nature are on the agenda under the Institute; among them is a unified currency exchange rate, and the IMF has been brought in to consult on it. Japan has dispatched investment and economic missions to Myanmar to support the establishment of market economy and consider ODA programs. More attention is being paid to agriculture. The banking system is under review. The President has recognized the need for major improvements in education and health care services, and in relation to poverty and the minorities. Corruption, estimated as the second most prevalent in the world by Transparency International, is under presidential scrutiny. Aung San Suu Kyi has stressed the need for the rule of law.

Although fighting has broken out in the Kachin State, the government has reached cease-fire agreements with the Wa and some Shan, has placed a hold on the Border Guard Forces plan that could have excited even more violence, and has entered negotiations with the Kachin. Moreover, in January 2012, a cease-fire was signed with the Karen National Union, the first step towards ending the Karen insurrection – a revolt that started in 1949 and has been the longest in modern times. The President has called on disaffected Burmese to return home, where they will be allowed to live normal lives without retribution unless they have committed some criminal act, such as murder. Some prominent individuals have temporarily gone back to test the system. Large numbers of political, now called "security," prisoners have been freed and other releases are said to be planned. Improved U.S. relations are contingent on this continuing.

In response to all of these reform measures, the spectre of more hard-line elements exerting pressure on the administration to rescind or reduce them is always in the background. Former Senior General Than Shwe, who manipulated the structure of power in the state, seemingly attempted to balance more liberal with more conservative ("hard-liners" vs. "soft-liners" are perhaps inaccurate terms sometimes used) elements within the civilianized former military command. Thus, any administration so structured may have to proceed more carefully than they might wish to prevent reversion to martial law (allowed under various provisions of the constitution) – or essentially a palace coup. President Thein Sein does not have the all-encompassing authority of his predecessor, Senior General Than Shwe, so reforms are necessarily more cautiously introduced and implemented.

In November 2011, ASEAN agreed that Myanmar could chair the ASEAN meetings in Naypyitaw in 2014. Although many observers considered the Myanmar authorities cynical for making reforms to assure approval of that chairmanship, and that reforms might cease after the 2014 meetings, the very fact of being selected may encourage expansion, rather than contraction, of the reform agenda, strengthen the influence of those committed to the reforms, and thus contribute to a greater chance for their continuity. At some stage after the U.S. presidential elections of November 2012, the president will have to decide whether that person will attend those meetings, and if so, under what conditions, if any.

Critical in the new political configuration in Myanmar is the role of Aung San Suu Kyi, who ran in the *hluttaw* by-elections that took place on 1 April 2012 and won her constituency with 85 percent of the vote. She had been denied the ability to run in 1990, as she was then under house arrest. Her future role in Myanmar politics after the NLD's landslide victory of 43 of the 45 contested seats is likely to be considerable. A constitutional amendment, however, would be required to enable her to become president after 2015 through an indirect election process; this would entail military concurrence since a ¾ vote is necessary for amendments and the *Tatmadaw* have 25 percent of the seats.

The dilemmas facing the Sino-Burmese and U.S.-Burmese relationships have increased toward the end of 2011. There is growing dissatisfaction with the internal role of the Chinese in Myanmar, which has become evident in the increasingly open literature, while both countries need the relationship to continue.[30] Nowhere is this more important in China than in Yunnan.

The Myanmar authorities may expect more from the United States than it politically can deliver in the short term. The full lifting of sanctions and the development of a normal bilateral relationship will likely be incremental, dependent on Burmese positive actions, and may proceed more slowly than the Burmese want or expect. This may create problems in the growing, positive relationship.

So too, if the United States justifies its changed position, one that was long overdue, on the basis that "democracy" as understood by the U.S. is expected and imminent, than it too may be disappointed. The Burmese military have indicated for a half century their intention to hold on to significant power in that state in a manner that is quite different from civil-military relations in the modern West. They have done so most recently through provisions in the 2008 Constitution that solidify their role for the indefinite future. These can be amended, but only with military concurrence. This does not mean, however, that greater space between the state and the individual in terms of freedoms may not be established, that an independent judiciary might not develop, and that economic reforms might not improve the sorry lot of the average Burmese. It also does not necessarily means that majority–minority relations might not be improved. But control over the unity and security of the state legally rests with the military, not the *hluttaws*, and the former alone can determine a return to military rule if in their view the situation so demands.

If the U.S. official attitude at this writing may be characterized as "cautiously optimistic," perhaps the Chinese attitude is quite different – "cautious" if not "cautiously pessimistic." China has recognized the broad spectrum of change.

---

30 See Min Zin, "Burmese Attitudes Toward the Chinese: Portrayal of the Chinese in Contemporary Cultural and Media Works." Paper presented at the Georgetown University conference on China–Myanmar relations, 4 November 2011.

"The world is currently going through a period of great development, momentous changes, and enormous adjustments."[31] The If U.S.–Myanmar relations are normalized or further improved, Western influence will substantially rise. Beijing expects this, and probably will not object if essential Chinese interests are maintained. In response, China will retain its same diplomatic mode towards Myanmar between 1988 and 2010 – maintaining and strengthening ties with the *Tatmadaw*. This is still the foundation of China's Myanmar policy. Yet China cannot solely concentrate on only one factor in Myanmar politics. Beijing will certainly develop ties with the opposition parties. The Chinese ambassador at her request called on Aung San Su Kyi for the first time in December 2011. She has reiterated her call for good relations with China.

The Myitsone event has been a lesson. China will do all it can in the future to minimize the risk of similar incidents. It will have to consider how to deal with the anti-Chinese sentiment in Myanmar, how to improve its public image, and how to enable the Myanmar people to benefit from China–Myanmar relations, economic cooperation, and investment. The history of China–Myanmar relations from 1988 to 2010 indicates that the Burmese people did not perceive of benefits from the Chinese presence. China ignored the Burmese popular dimension; it will do so in the future only at the peril to its privileged position. In the past, China simply bargained with the junta and got project approval, regardless of the opinion of the Burmese public. China also now will have to face the coming competition with Western companies as Myanmar opens. But China continues to promote its "soft power." The elaborate loan of a Buddhist tooth relic from China was greeted in November/December 2011 both with warm official and unofficial enthusiasm and ceremony.

The Chinese official response to Secretary of State Clinton's visit was generally subdued. But the *People's Daily* said that the U.S, gloated and applauded the Myitsone Dam decision, and was to blame. The Xinhwa News Agency, an organ of the state, mentioned her trip only following the reports of the visits to Myanmar of the Vice Chair of the Chinese Central Military Commission and that of the Vice Chair of the National People's Congress Standing Committee. On 10 October, the Myanmar Foreign Minister visited China as a special envoy of the Myanmar president, no doubt to ease tensions over the cancellation of the dam construction. Myanmar's Commander-in-Chief of the Armed Forces visited China between 27 November and 2 December, and signed a memorandum of understanding on defense cooperation on 29 November; from 16 to 19

31 Communiqué of the Sixth Plenary Session of the Seventeenth CPC Central Committee meeting, 18 October 2011.

October, the *New Light of Myanmar* four days in succession published articles designed to maintain and strengthen Sino-Burmese friendship and relations

The *Global Times* (a Chinese nationalistic newspaper with a website) regarded the dam decision as undermining the foundation of Chinese interests (lit. "digging the corner of the [Chinese] wall" – *wa qiang jiao*) Another article in the same publication claimed that if China "lost" Myanmar, China would feel "suffocated." One author even mentioned the "crazy" idea that the U.S. through the visit set up a "smoke screen" and was trying to overthrow the Burmese government.

Myanmar has changed, but how permanently is unclear. It may be on the cusp of internal development and foreign policy equilibrium. Such progress was unanticipated, is evident at a pace unheralded, in fields hitherto unrecognized by any Burmese administration, and with an international response unprecedented in modern Burma/Myanmar history. Sino–Myanmar relations have entered a new era in the context of these potential reforms and changed relationship between Myanmar and the United States. Whether future relations with China are termed *Pauk Paw* or simply ones based on mutual bilateral need is unclear. Nevertheless, it seems evident that Myanmar will pursue what it regards as its national interests in terms of its internal power structure and external geopolitical setting and realities. The myths of Chinese hegemonic influence in Myanmar, which has been a mantra of much of international opinion, should be modified to recognize the dynamic of the relationship and its impact on the region and the world. The dilemmas facing both states and other actors will need constant re-evaluation.

Appendices

Appendix 1

Joint Statement Concerning Framework Document on Future Cooperation in Bilateral Relations between the People's Republic of China and Federation of Myanmar

Since the establishment of diplomatic relations between the People's Republic of China and Federation of Myanmar (short for "both sides there after") in 8 June 1950, cooperation in the political, economic, military, cultural, educational and other fields has seen continuous development on the basis of the 5 principles of peaceful coexistence initialed jointly by both sides. Further consolidating and developing Sino-Burmese friendly relation is not only in the basic interests of the two countries and their people, but conducive to peace, stability and development in this region.

At the start of the new century, it was unanimously agreed by both sides that stable and long-standing neighborliness, friendship and cooperation between the two countries should be further developed so that "Paukphaw" friendship between the Chinese and Burmese people would go on from generation to generation. For this, both sides made the following declaration on the framework and guiding principles for the future cooperation in the bilateral relations:

1. Both sides agree that the basic norms guiding Sino-Burmese relations are the aim and principles of U.N. Charter, 5 principles of peaceful coexistence, principles stipulated in Southeast Asian Treaty of Friendship and Cooperation and universally acknowledged principles of international law.

2. Both sides will maintain frequent contacts and exchanges of visits between the top leaders of the two countries, actively carry out exchanges of visits and contacts between various government departments, non-governmental bodies and people from different walks of life, so as to strengthen under-

standing and friendship and promote further development of bilateral cooperation.

3. Both sides agree to maintain multi-tiered consultations and contacts between the foreign ministries of the two countries, exchange views in time on the bilateral relations and regional and international issues of common concern and make use of various occasions to keep frequent exchange of ideas and coordination.

4. Both sides agree to further strengthen cooperation in trade, investment, agriculture, fishery, forestry and tourism on the basis of equality and mutual benefit, priority to actual results and taking advantage of the other's strength.

1) Bring into full play the role of Sino-Burmese Joint Committee on Economic, Trade and Technological Cooperation and actively explore new ideas and channels that will help develop economic and trade cooperation mutually beneficial to both sides. Functional departments concerned from both sides should further strengthen guidance and to coordination over economic and trade cooperation, continue perfecting rules and regulations concerned, standardize enterprise behavior and create favorable conditions and provide necessary facilities for the economic and trade activities of companies, enterprises and organizations from both sides so as to protect their legitimate rights and create a sound environment for economic and trade cooperation between the two countries. When conditions are ripe, both sides will discuss and sign an agreement on investment protection.

2) Strive to expand the bilateral trade. The potential should be fully tapped so as to increase commodity trade. Cooperation in border trade should be further strengthened and standardized in accordance with Memorandum of Understanding in Border Trade between the Governments of the People's Republic of China and Federation of Myanmar. Sustainable, steady and healthy development of bilateral trade should be promoted in the spirit of exchanging needed goods and mutual benefit and reciprocity.

3) Encourage and support its respective enterprises to engage in two-way investment and make them earnestly undertake the obligations stipulated in the bilateral investment agreements so as to ensure the smooth implementation of joint venture projects.

4) Create in an active manner favorable conditions for the enterprises from both sides to launch engineering projects and labor cooperation.

5) Actively promote agricultural and fishery cooperation between the two countries. Make good use of its respective rich natural resources and complementary edge, support and encourage mutually beneficial cooperation in agricultural technology, produce-processing, prevention and monitoring of animal disease, sea-fishing and marine culture between the enterprises and departments concerned of the two countries.

6) Strengthen forestry cooperation between the two countries, and encourage bilateral cooperation in prevention of forest fire in border areas, forest management, resource development, wildlife protection, development of forest industry, timber-processing, forestry machinery, ecological tourism, forestry education and training.

7) Further expand tourism cooperation between the two countries. China has agreed to make Myanmar a country of destination for Chinese citizens to go on overseas tours. Both sides will decide through consultation detailed ways for implementation.

5. Strengthen exchanges and cooperation in the cultural, educational, health, sport and religious areas between the two countries. Further promote understanding and friendship between the people of the two countries by exchanging visits of delegations and art troupes, experts as well as holding exhibitions in the other country.

6. Both sides agree to work out at the earliest possible time detailed steps for implementation, based on Agreement on Management of and Cooperation in Sino-Burmese Border so as to jointly promote stability, tranquility and development in their border areas.

7. Strengthen legal cooperation and exchange of information. Work together to fight cross-border crimes, drug-trafficking, smuggling, illegal border-crossing and other criminal activities.

8. The Chinese side reiterates that it respects Myanmar's independence, sovereignty and territorial integrity. The Burmese side reiterates that it will continue to pursue its one China policy and recognize the Government of the People's Republic of China as the sole legitimate government of China, and Taiwan as inseparable part of China's territory. The Chinese side appreciates Myanmar's position on refraining from developing in any form official links with the Taiwan authorities.

9. Both sides hold that the 4-party economic cooperation (China, Laos, Myanmar and Thailand) and Mekong River's sub-regional economic cooperation (China, Cambodia, Laos, Myanmar, Thailand and Vietnam) are in the common and long-term interests of the two countries and other countries concerned in this region, and will give them greater support.

10. Both sides will strengthen cooperation in such multilateral bodies as the U.N., ASEAN, ARF and the Informal Meeting of East Asian Leaders and work hard to promote peace and development in this region and the world at large.

This statement is signed on 6 June 2000, in Beijing.

Representative of the People's Republic of China
Tang Jiaxuan Foreign Minister

Representative of the Federation of Myanmar
U Win Aung Foreign Minister

Appendix 2

People's Republic of China Plans and Strategies Mentioned in the Text

Central Government Plans

"Leaning to one side": A leading foreign policy of PRC's earlier period. It meant that China leant to the side of socialism camp, which was articulated by Mao Tsetung in his article "The People's Democratic Dictatorship" on 30 June 1949, in commemoration of the Chinese Communist Party's twenty-eighth anniversary.

"Two Camps Theory": The doctrine of the "two camps" was first enunciated by Zhdanov at the inaugural conference of the Communist Information Bureau in 1947 and stated that the world was divided into two camps, the forces of socialism and those of imperialism, with "no third road" possible. In the first years after the founding of the People's Republic, Chinese statements echoed the Soviet view. By 1953 China began reasserting its belief that the newly independent developing countries could play an important intermediary role in world affairs.

"Putting the house in order before inviting guests" and "Starting Anew": The concepts were a vivid description of the PRC's diplomatic pattern before 1954. To make a clean break with the foreign policy of the Republic of China (ROC), the CCP renounced all the diplomatic relations the Kuomintang Government had established with foreign countries, treated heads of foreign diplomatic missions accredited to the ROC as ordinary foreign nationals instead of diplomatic envoys, reviewed all the treaties and agreements the KMT had concluded with foreign countries, gradually cleared up the prerogatives and influence the capitalist countries had in China, and established new diplomatic relations with other countries.

Peaceful Coexistence: A theory developed by the Soviet Union during the Cold War and was adopted by Soviet-influenced Communist states that they could peacefully coexist with capitalist states. China first applied it to relations with the non-socialist countries in the peripheral countries. In 1954, Zhou Enlai and Prime Minister Jawaharlal Nehru of India and Burma's Prime Minister U Nu agreed on the Five Principles of Peaceful Coexistence as the underlying basis for conducting foreign relations. The principles were reiterated by Zhou at the Bandung Conference of Asian and African countries where they were incorporated into the conference declarations.

"New Democratic Revolution": Mao Tsetung developed the theory of New Democratic Revolution as a road to socialist and communist revolution in countries defined by semi-feudal, semi-colonial relations. The Maoist concept was the requirement of CP leadership-the idea that the local CP should gain control of the nationalist movement and use it as a vehicle to attain state power after which it can transform the national revolution into a socialist one.

Prosper the Borders to Enrich Local Peoples (PBELP): In response to "Western Development", the State Ethnic Affairs Commission of the PRC initiated the program in 1999 to earmark funds to 135 land border counties and 58 divisions to the Xinjiang Production and Construction Corps (XPCC) for poverty alleviation and infrastructure improvement.

"Go Global": China's current strategy to encourage its enterprises to invest overseas, which was initiated in 1999 by the Chinese government.

"Western Development": A policy and program launched by the State Council in 1999 to boost its less developed western regions and eliminate or narrow the economic gap between China's east and west. The policy covers 6 provinces (Gansu, Guizhou, Qinghai, Shaanxi, Sichuan, and Yunnan), 5 autonomous regions (Guangxi, Inner Mongolia, Ningxia, Tibet, and Xinjiang), and 1 municipality (Chongqing).

West–East Power Transmission: One of three key energy development projects of Western Development, transmitting power generated in Guizhou, Yunnan, Guangxi, Sichuan, Inner Mongolia, Shanxi provinces to the east China provinces and municipalities suffering power shortages such as Guangdong, Shanghai, Jiangsu, Zhejiang, Beijing, Tianjin through the northern, the middle and southern routes.

National Medium and Long Term Energy and Development Plan Outline 2004–2020 (Draft): Approved by State Council in 2004 and it clarifies the strategy of energy security and development in China's future.

The 11th Five-Year Plan for National Economic and Social Development of the PRC: The Plan's outline was approved by the Fourth Plenary Session of the 10th National People's Congress in March 2006. Among the main purposes of the guidelines are securing economic growth and economic structure, urbanizing the population, conserving energy and national resources, encouraging sound environmental practices, and improving education.

The 11th Five-Year Plan for Energy Development of the PRC: Released by the NDPC in April 2007 and articulated China's energy strategy, goal, and layout for the following five years.

Countries and Industries for Overseas Investment Guidance Catalogue: The Chinese Ministry of Commerce and the Ministry of Foreign Affairs jointly promulgated the Guidance (I, II, III) in 2004, 2005, and 2007, which listed the encouraged and supported sectors for the investment of Chinese enterprises in 129 countries.

Countries and Industries for Overseas Contract Project Guidance Catalogue: The Guidance (I & II) was released by Department of Outward Investment and Economics, China's Commerce Ministry, in 2008 and 2009. It provides China's enterprises with market introductions and policy directions in overseas contract projects in 28 countries.

The 11th Five-Year Plan to Prosper the Borders and Enrich Local Peoples: Endorsed by the State Council in June 2007 and sets forth the main mission, measures and goals of the PBELP over 5 years.

The 11th Five-Year Plan of China's Railways: In October 2006, China's Ministry of Railways released the plan that stated the major projects and main tasks of railway development in 2006–2010.

National Middle/Long Term Transport Plans of China: was endorsed by the State Council in 2004 and devised the blueprint of China's railway network for 2020.

National Highway Network Planning: was issued by China's Ministry of Transport in January 2005, (approved in 2004), to build a highway network largely consisting of 34 new highways totaling 85,000 kilometers.

National Plan for Mineral Resources 2008–2015: Framed by China's Ministry of Land and Resources and endorsed by the State Council in 2008, provides policy guidance for China's mineral resources sector, particularly its security and sustainable development.

Scientific Development Concept: The current official guiding socio-economic ideology of the CCP incorporating sustainable development, social welfare, a person-centered society, increased democracy, and ultimately, the creation of a Harmonious Society. This is the newest addition to the idea of Socialism with Chinese Characteristics ratified in the CCP's constitution at the 17th Party Congress in October 2007.

The 11th Five-Year Plan for Overseas Investment: Issued by NDPC in 2007, stressed the orientation and expected goals of China's overseas investment.

National Program on Mineral Resources: Policy guidance for China's mineral resources sector; enacted by China's Ministry of Land and Resources and approved by the State Council in 2001.

The White Paper for China's Policy on Mineral Resources: Released by the State Council on 23 December 2003, documents programming for China's mineral resources sector.

Guidelines for Overseas Investment and Cooperation in Other Countries and Regions (Myanmar): Formulated by China's Ministry of Commerce and the Commercial Counselor's Office of China's Embassy in Myanmar on 15 June 2009, provides information concerning the investment environment in Myanmar.

The 11th Five-Year Plan for Land and Resources 2006–2010: Introduced by the Ministry of Land and Resources, provides a program of action for the development in the sector of land, mineral resources, and geological prospecting for 2006–2010.

Yunnan Government Plans

Yunnan International Passage: Yunnan's corresponding program to carry out Beijing's Western Development in 1999, building the province as a traffic hub linking China to Southeast Asia and South Asia.

Layout of Yunnan Road Net 2005–2020: Drawn up by Yunnan Provincial Department of Transportation in 2007, designs a road network centered at Kunming City connecting the network of neighboring provinces such as

Sichuan, Guizhou, Guangxi and Tibet as well as the neighboring countries such as Myanmar, Laos, Vietnam and Thailand.

Draft Resolution on the Implementation of Yunnan National Economic and Social Development Plan for 2007 and the National Economic and Social Development Plan for 2008: A report presented by the Department of Finance of Yunnan province on 18 January 2008 at the 1st Session of the 11th Yunnan People's Congress.

New Three-Year Action Plan to "Prosper the Borders to Enrich Local People" in Yunnan: Formulated by the government of Yunnan Province in May 2008 with plans to invest RMB10.7 billion in border areas in the province between 2008–2010.

Appendix 3

Chronology of Sino-Burmese Relations

1948

4 January: Burma gained independence from British colonial rule.

28 March: BCP went into rebellion against the new government.

December: CCP dominated northern China through three campaigns – Liaoshen Campaign, Pingjin Campaign, and Huaihai Campaign. The outcome of these encounters was decisive for the military outcome of the civil war.

1949

1 October: The People's Republic of China (PRC) was formally established, with its national capital at Beijing.

18 December: Burma recognized the PRC and became the first non-socialist country to recognize the Chinese communist regime.

1950

January–March: Over 2,000 Kuomintang (KMT) forces from Yunnan crossed the border to set up a base in Kengtung, eastern Shan State following the communist victory in China.

8 June: China and Burma established diplomatic relations at the ambassadorial level. Burma was the sixteenth country to have diplomatic relations with Beijing.

1951

20 October: Burma–China Friendship Association was founded in Rangoon.

1952

11 May: China–Burma Friendship Association was set up in Beijing.

1953

March: Burma charged the Chinese Nationalist government with unprovoked aggression before the United Nations.

November: from this month to May 1954, Taiwan withdrew 6,986 troops from Burma in 3 batches, handed over 1,323 pieces of weapons, and 822 of them were carried back to Taiwan.

1954

22 April: China and Burma signed their first economic trade agreement.

28–29 June: Chinese Premier and Foreign Minister Zhou Enlai visited Burma for the first time. Zhou claimed that "revolution cannot be exported." In the joint statement of Zhou's visit, both advocated the "Five Principles of Peaceful Coexistence", and regarded it as the guide for China–Burma relations.

1–16 December: During Prime Minister U Nu first trip to China, he promised that Burma wouldn't be an underling of Chinese opponents and provide China's enemies with any vital loci used as navy and air force strategic bases to launch attacks on the PRC. Meanwhile, Mao Tsetung made a commitment that China should not interfere in Burmese internal affairs or subvert it. Both sides agreed to hold negotiations about the nationality of overseas Chinese and the boundary problem in near future.

1955

14–16 April: Shortly before he attended the Asian–African Conference in Bandung, Indonesia, Zhou Enlai visited Rangoon at U Nu's invitation. The problems mentioned in the joint statement of 1954 and the agenda of the Bandung Conference were discussed.

26 August: Burma established a consulate-general in Kunming.

8 November: An agreement on air transportation between two countries was signed in Rangoon.

20 December: A skirmish between the Burmese army and PLA occurred at Yellow Orchard to the west of the "1941 Line", causing several casualties in the two armies.

1956

7–8 February: The Burmese government organized a gathering of border residents at Lwejel to win their support for resolution of the border dispute with China. Also present were the Chinese ambassador, the PRC's Consul General in Lashio, and the Secretary-General of the Yunnan People's Committee.

11 April: China launched an air service between Kunming and Rangoon via Mandalay.

21 September: The letter of congratulations that the BCP sent to the CCP for its 8th Session was published in the *People's Daily*. Although the letter didn't touch upon anti-Burmese government sentiment, it was the first time that China publicly released a BCP Central Committee letter in the *People's Daily*.

22 October – 8 November: U Nu, the President of the AFPFL, was invited to Beijing to negotiate the boundary settlement. Beijing accepted the status quo of the China–Burma boundary in principle, and gave up most of its previous territorial claims. China agreed to withdraw the PLA to the east of the "1941 Line".

10–20 December: Premier Zhou Enlai and Vice Premier He Long visited Burma. Both sides discussed the border dispute. Zhou visited Rangoon, Mandalay, Pyin Oo Lwin and Myitkyina. On December 18, Zhou Enlai made a speech at the welcome meeting held by local Chinese and articulated China's overseas Chinese policy towards them.

15–17 December: A gathering was organized in Mangshi, Yunnan, that lasted for 5 days, with about 350 official representatives and 15,000 border residents of the two countries. Burma Prime Minister U Ba Swe, China's Premier Zhou Enlai and Vice Premier Chen Yi were present.

1957

22 March – 2 April: U Nu proposed that the two countries sign a friendship and non-aggression pact at an opportune time.

9 July: Zhou Enlai presented a *Report on the Burma–China Boundary Problem* at the fourth Plenary Session of the first National Peoples' Congress outlining China's proposals and guidelines on the Burma–China boundary settlement.

4 December: Burmese Vice-Prime Ministers U Ba Swe and U Kyaw Nyein visited China.

1958

21 February: A one-year trade agreement was signed by the two countries.

12 December: Up to this date, 114,510 Yunnanese escaped to neighboring countries because of the Great Leap Forward with 80 percent of them fleeing to Burma in 1958.

1959

March: The Burmese army launched its "Spring Campaign" against the KMT army.

30 September: The BCP sent a congratulatory telegram to Beijing for the 10th anniversary of its national celebration in 1959. The letter was carried in the *People's Daily* and focused on accusations concerning Burma's domestic politics and foreign policy.

1960

24–29 January: Prime Minister Ne Win visited Beijing. On 28 January both sides signed a treaty of friendship and mutual non-aggression and reached an agreement on the Burma–China boundary issue.

15–19 April: During Premier Zhou Enlai and Vice Premier Chen Yi visited Burma, Zhou attended the Water Festival celebrations in Rangoon and invited U Nu to visit China.

14 May: The two countries' governments exchanged the treaty of friendship and mutual non-aggression and the instrument of ratification of agreement on Burma–China boundary in Rangoon.

8 September – 4 October: Prime Minister U Nu led a delegation of 350 members including Ne Win to attend the Chinese National Day's celebrations. Beijing organized 100,000 people to greet U Nu. On 30 September, U Nu gave a lecture in Beijing University. The two sides formally signed the boundary treaty in Beijing on 1 October.

22 December – 9 February: The PLA entered Burma twice and engaged in battles against the KMT troops, whose general headquarters in Burma were destroyed. Most of the KMT army moved to the frontier area of Burma–Laos–Thailand, and 4,349 of Liu Yuanlin troops were withdrawn to Taiwan.

1961

2–9 January: Zhou Enlai visited Burma with nine groups of 400 delegates to take part in the celebration of Burma Independence Day and exchanged the ratification of the Burma–China boundary treaty. On 9 January an economic and technological cooperation protocol was signed stipulating that China would loan Burma £30 million.

6–16 April: Prime Minister U Nu went vacationing in Yunnan for ten days. He visited 7 cities in Yunnan and attended the Water Festival celebration in Xishuangbanna. Zhou Enlai and U Nu discussed the situation in Laos and agreed to cooperate to solve the problem of the KMT in Burma.

1962

2 March: Ne Win launched a military coup.

7 March: China's Ambassador to Burma Li Yimang submitted a note of recognition to the Burmese Foreign Minister and a congratulatory telegram to Ne Win, respectively. China became the fourth country to recognize Ne Win's military regime.

1963

12 March: China's Foreign Ministry instructed its embassy in Rangoon not to directly comment on Burmese political platform and the Burmese Way to Socialism whether in public or in personal contacts, and only express general support to Rangoon's neutral, peaceful foreign policy, and friendly attitude toward China.

20–26 April: President Liu Shaoqi visited Burma to mediate peace talks between the BCP and Burmese government.

18 June: Xinhua News Agency reported that the Chinese government had decided to forego its right to repatriate back to China the capital and assets (1 million Kyat) of two Chinese banks that were were nationalized by the Ne Win government in February 1963.

28 June: Thakin Ba Thein Tin, Vice Chairman of the BCP, and Kyaw Win, Burmese Ambassador to China, held peace talks in Beijing arranged by the Chinese.

July: Geng Biao, the Vice Foreign Minister, was appointed the new Ambassador to Burma.

15 November: The Burmese government released the statement of the Revolutionary Council, National Democratic United Front (NDUF), and the BCP on the failure of negotiations. The Ne Win government took the negotiators to their bases in Burma and Ba Thein Tin was permitted to return China.

23 November: Ne Win asked the Chinese Vice Premier, Marshal He Long, who visited Rangoon en route to Indonesia, to send word to Beijing that the failure of peace talks was a Burmese internal affair and by no means impacted on Burma–China friendly relations.

1964

14–18 February: During Zhou Enlai and Chen Yi's visit to Burma, a joint communique reaffirmed the April 1963 joint communique released during Liu Shaoqi's trip to Burma, particularly the principle of non-interference in each other's internal affairs.

19 March: Ne Win nationalized the economy and pursued a policy of autarky. More than 10,000 private stores were nationalized, including 6,700 stores owned by Chinese.

17 May: The Burmese government issued a decree that K.50 and K.100 notes would cease to be legal tender.

10–11 July: Zhou Enlai secretly visited Rangoon and held three talks with Ne Win and expressed China's support for Ne Win.

3 October: On the 15th anniversary of China's National Day, the BCP sent a letter of congratulations to Beijing. Beijing broadcast the letter in English and Burmese, and published it in the *People's Daily*. In this letter the BCP attributed the failure of peace talks in 1963 to "the sabotage of the imperialists, domestic reactionaries, and revisionists".

1965

1 April: 129 private middle schools including 16 Chinese schools were nationalized.

3–4 April: Zhou Enlai visited Burma and held talks with Ne Win.

24 July – 1 August: Ne Win visited China, and visited Beijing, Shenyang, Aanshan, Shanghai and Kunming, and discussed the Vietnam problem and the

international situation. A joint communique reaffirmed the five principles of peaceful coexistence.

1966

17–19 April: President Liu Shaoqi visited Burma in an attempt to get Burmese support for its position on Vietnam.

1967

January–June: Articles and reports extolling Mao Tsetung's thoughts, anti-Soviet attitudes, support for the Chinese Cultural Revolution, and the personality cult around Mao in Burma were continually published in the *People's Daily*.

4 January: Vice Premier Chen Yi declared at the reception of the 19th anniversary of Burma Independence at the Burmese Embassy in Beijing that "an eternal socialist China will more effectively struggle against imperialism, modern revisionism and reactionaries of foreign countries, more forcefully patronize people's struggle for world peace, national independence, people democracy and socialism in Asia, Africa and Latin America, and the world, and more successfully fulfill our internationalism responsibility."

19 June: The Burmese Ministry of Education banned the wearing of all "unauthorized badges" by students. The order was aimed at the wearing of Mao badges. However, the number of badge-wearers increased.

26–28 June: Anti-Chinese riots occurred in Rangoon, with Chinatown, schools, and the Embassy attacked by thousands of Burmese.

28 June: The BCP Central Committee issued a statement on the anti-Chinese riots in Rangoon and supported China as well as the overseas Chinese.

29 June: Beijing declared that the Chinese Ambassador to Burma would not return to his post. Burma recalled its Ambassador to Beijing two months later. 200,000 people protested outside Burma's Embassy in Beijing against the Burmese anti-Chinese riots.

30 June – 3 July: A total of over one million Chinese joined demonstrations in front of the Burmese Embassy in Beijing. On July 3, the demonstrators broke into the Burmese Embassy, tore up the Burmese national flag, and smashed the Burmese national emblem.

7 July: Burma suspended the Chinese economic assistance program, and presented a note to China to withdraw all of its Chinese aid experts. A total of 412 Chinese aid experts returned to China prior to 4 November 1967.

1968

January: An NCNA correspondent in Rangoon was expelled from the country, the fourth since July 1967.

1 January: Troops of the BCP in China led a military offensive across the Burmese frontier along three routes, each including a PLA company manned by soldiers from China's southwest ethnic minorities All-out Chinese support for the BCP insurrection began.

March: some leaders of Chinese associations and pro-Maoist Chinese activists throughout Burma were detained and deported.

19 July: the Chinese Chargé D'affaires in Burma attended Burma Martyr's Day, and placed a wreath on the tomb of Burma's "National Father," Aung San.

1 October: Some Burmese officials, public figures, and military officers were invited to attend the reception for National Day sponsored by Chinese Embassy in Rangoon.

1969

January: Ne Win, visiting Pakistan, discussed the possibility of resuming relations with Chinese officials there.

6 November: At the opening session of the Fourth Party Seminar of the BSPP, Ne Win expressed his willingness to make a reconciliation with China.

1970

3 January: Vice Minister of Foreign Affairs of China, Xu Yixin, appeared at the celebration of Burma Independence at the Burmese Embassy in Beijing.

1 May: During May Day celebrations on the Tiananmen Rostrum, Mao greeted the the Burmese Chargé d'Affaires and asked him to give his regards to Ne Win.

October: Rangoon appointed U Thein Maung as the new Ambassador to China. He arrived in Beijing on November 16.

1 October: High-ranking Burmese officials attended the reception for China's National Day held by the Chinese Embassy. On the same day, Ne Win sent a congratulatory telegram to Zhou Enlai.

22 November: Burma voted for the proposal by eighteen countries to award China's seat in the UN to the PRC and deprive Taiwan of its membership.

1971

March: The new Chinese Ambassador, Chen Zhaoyuan, reached Rangoon. The Voice of the People of Burma (VOPB) started its transmission from Yunnan.

6–12 August: Ne Win was invited to visit Beijing, where he and Zhou Enlai held five separate meetings on China–Burma relations and the overseas Chinese. This trip symbolized the renormalization of China–Burma ties.

9 October: Burma and other 20 countries together proposed to the U.N. that China's legal seat in the U.N. and Permanent Membership on the U.N. Security Council be awarded to the PRC.

1975

21 May: The *People's Daily* published the BCP's statement on the deaths of both the Chairman and Secretary of the BCP Central Committee, Thakin Zin and Thakin Chit, and released the full text of the CCP's telegram of condolences. Both the telegram and statement recognized the necessity of the BCP's armed combat against "class enemies at home and abroad".

August: U Hla Phone, Foreign Minister of Burma, visited China. This visit was regarded as preparation for and the prelude to Ne Win's visit three months later.

11–15 November: Ne Win visited China for four days and was received by a sick Mao on November 13. Ne Win promised that Burma would never allow any country to maintain military bases on Burmese soil. A Joint Communique stressed the significance of the Five Principles of Peaceful Coexistence, and agreement to build a peaceful, neutral and liberal zone in Southeast Asia.

1976

25 January: Zhang Chunqiao, member of the Standing Committee of the Political Bureau of the CCP Central Committee, met and banqueted with Thakin Ba Thein Tin, the Chairman of the BCP in Beijing.

18 November: Hua Guofeng, Chairman of CCP Central Committee gave a welcome dinner for Thakin Ba Thein Tin and the Vice Chairman of the BCP, Thakin Pe Tint.

1977

5–11 February: Deng Yingchao (Zhou Enlai's widow), Vice Chairman of the People's National Congress, visited Burma.

27 April: Ne Win visited China and negotiated the BCP problem with Beijing.

18 September: Ne Win stopped in Beijing on his visit to Korea, and met Hua Guofeng and Vice Premier Deng Xiaoping, and discussed China's domestic situation and foreign relations with the U.S., Japan and Yugoslavia.

1978

26–31 January: Vice Premier Deng Xiaoping visited Burma. He signaled its good-neighbor policy to the outside world and attempted to establish a united front against the Soviets in order to contain Soviet and Vietnamese expansion in Southeast Asia.

12–15 September: Burma's Foreign Minister Min Maung visited Beijing.

1979

9–13 July: Burmese Prime Minister U Maung Maung Kha visited Beijing and an agreement on economic and technical cooperation was signed. Under the agreement, China would provide Burma with a RMB0.1 billion interest-free loan for 7 years from 1980 to 1986.

9 September: Burma announced its withdrawal from the Non-aligned Movement.

19–20 and 24–26 November: China's Foreign Minister Huang Hua visited Burma.

1980

20–23 October: Ne Win paid his 11th visit to China.

1981

26–30 January: Premier Zhao Ziyang visited Burma. The two sides discussed international and Southeast Asian affairs.

1984

21 June: An agreement on economic and technological cooperation was signed.

28 October – 7 November: Burma's President U San Yu visited China and held talks with Premier Zhao Ziyang. Both discussed the problems of Cambodia and Afghanistan. On 1 November, the Chairman of the CCP Central Committee, Hu Yaobang, met San Yu.

1985

4–8 March: President Li Xiannian visited Rangoon and reaffirmed China's overseas Chinese policy from the Zhou Enlai era.

4–9 May: Ne Win visited China at Deng Xiaoping's invitation.

1986

10–18 April: Burmese Prime Minister U Maung Maung Kha visited China. The PRC's economic reforms, the Cambodia issue, and bilateral economic cooperation were discussed.

1987

16 November: an economic and technical cooperation agreement was signed in Rangoon. China would provide an RMB80 million (Kt.142.4 million) interest-free loan to supplement the funds for the Rangoon–Syriam Bridge.

1988

22 September: Jin Guihua, the spokesman of China's Foreign Ministry said that China did not interfere in Burma's internal affairs but hoped the situation would returned to normal. In 1988, China preserved a prudent silence towards Burma's domestic turbulence, and Chinese media only reported the situation in Burma without comment.

1989

25 May: When meeting Myanmar's newly appointed Ambassador to China, Premier Li Peng reaffirmed China's foreign policy.

13 June: Khin Nyunt, the Secretary of State Law and Order Restoration Council (SLORC), called in China's Ambassador to Burma, Cheng Ruisheng, and expressed sympathy and understanding on the Chinese government use of force against the demonstration at Tiananmen Square in Beijing.

18–29 October: A 24-man senior Burmese military delegation, led by Commander-in-Chief (Army) Lt-Gen Than Shwe, visited China.

1990

7–8 December: PLA Air Force Commander-in-Chief Wang Hai and Defense Minister Qin Jiwei met Myanmar Air Force Commander-in-Chief Tin Tun in Beijing.

27 December: An economic and technical cooperation agreement was signed stipulating that China would provide a five-year interest-free loan.

1991

28 January – 1 February: State Councillor and Secretary-General of the Chinese State Council, Luo Gan, visited Myanmar and called on SLORC Chairman Senior General Saw Maung. He also formally handed over the National Theatre, constructed with Chinese aid, to the Myanmar Government.

18 July: Myanmar donated 1,500 tons of rice to China's disaster areas.

20–25 August: SLORC Chairman Gen. Saw Maung visited Beijing and met Premier Li Peng and President Yang Shangkun, and discussed bilateral ties. On August 23, an agreement on economic and technical cooperation was signed.

12–16 December: China's military and friendship delegation led by Vice-Chief of the General Staff of the PLA visited Myanmar.

1992

18 April: China's Foreign Ministry denied that the border guards attacked Myanmar refugees who fled to China because of the fight between a Kachin force and the *Tatmadaw*.

1993

11 February: China's Foreign Ministry denied China's intention to use a naval base in Pathein.

30 July: China and Myanmar signed an agreement on economic and technical cooperation, granted Myanmar an interest-free loan of RMB50 million (US$6.8 million).

31 July: The Yangon–Thanlyin Bridge was completed with the PRC's special envoy Bu He attending the completion ceremony. The bridge, the biggest economic cooperation project between the two countries, was constructed with a RMB0.1 billion Chinese loan.

1 September: The Myanmar Consulate-General in Kunming reopened.

1994

10–15 August: A Chinese government trade delegation visited Myanmar and signed a MoU on border trade with Myanmar.

22 August: The Chinese Consulate-General reopened in Mandalay.

7–14 September: SLORC First Secretary Lt-Gen. Khin Nyunt visited China accompanied by 8 ministers and vice ministers as well as the Northern Military Region Commander.

26–28 December: Premier Li Peng visited Myanmar and met SLORC Chairman Senior General Than Shwe on 27 December. Li stressed that the PRC Government would encourage PRC companies and economic enterprises to cooperate on major projects; business should be the core of cooperation. Li reiterated China's concern about the stability of China–Myanmar border, the border trade, and Myanmar's policy towards the Five Principles of Peaceful Coexistence and the overseas Chinese.

1995

3 June: Myanmar Airways International launched an air service between Yangon and Kunming.

5–12 July: An 11-member goodwill delegation led by Chinese State Councillor and Minister of Defence Gen. Chi Haotian visited Myanmar.

11 October: Officials from China, Laos, and Myanmar met in Vientiane to exchange written authorization and a letter ratifying the agreement on the trijunction point where the borders between the three countries meet.

8–12 December: Li Ruihuan the Chairman of the Chinese People's Political Consultative Conference (CPPCC) visited Myanmar at the invitation of Vice-Chairman of the SLORC Gen. Maung Aye.

1996

7–13 January: SLORC Chairman Than Shwe visited China and signed an agreement on economic and technical cooperation, a protocol on cultural cooperation between the two countries' Cultural Ministries, and a framework agreement on provision of an interest-subsidized preferential credit to Myanmar.

31 January: The SLORC established the Leading Committee for Promotion of Economic Cooperation between Myanmar and China "for promotion of bilateral mutual economic cooperation and for implementation of Myanmar's economy with momentum during the short-term five-year plan beginning 1996–97 fiscal year".

28 April – 3 May: General Zhang Wannian, the Vice-Chairman of the Chinese Central Military Commission, led a 16-member goodwill delegation that visited Myanmar and met Than Shwe, who reaffirmed Burma's one China policy and adherence to Five Principles.

22–29 October: Vice-Chairman of SLORC, Gen. Maung Aye, visited China at the invitation of General Zhang Wannian to boost military cooperation.

1997

24–27 March: State Councilor and Secretary General of the PRC State Council Luo Gan led a 15-member delegation to Myanmar, and signed an agreement on border area management and cooperation and a MoU on technical and economic cooperation, extending RMB5 million in aid to Myanmar to purchase equipment and spare parts for the agriculture sector and to provide technical assistance.

29 May: In Yangon, China and Myanmar signed an agreement establishing a joint working committee on trade, economic and technical cooperation.

16 October: Fu Quanyou, the Chief of General Staff of the PLA, received Lieutenant General Tin Ngwe, the Commander-in-Chief of the Myanmar Air Force in Beijing.

27–29 October: Vice Premier Wu Bangguo led a 40-member party to Myanmar and signed a framework agreement on a preferential loan with interest subsidized by the Chinese Government.

7–12 November: A Chinese PLA delegation, led by General Liu Jingsong, Commander of the Lanzhou Military Region, visited Myanmar.

16 December: China's President Jiang Zemin met the Myanmar Chairman of SLORC, Than Shwe, and congratulated him on Myanmar's entry into ASEAN, when they attended the first informal China–ASEAN summit in Kuala Lumpur.

1998

3 February: An agreement on mutual exemption of visas for holders of diplomatic, official/service passports was signed when Chinese Vice-Foreign Minister, Tang Jiaxuan visited Yangon.

9 June: Chi Haotian met visiting Myanmar Air Force Commander-in-Chief Major-Gen. Kyaw Than in Beijing.

4 November: The *Myanmar Morning Post* began publishing in the Chinese language in Myanmar. This was the first time in 30 years that Myanmar/Burma allowed a newspaper in the Chinese language to be published.

1999

7–11 June: SPDC First Secretary Khin Nyunt visited China, and met China's leadership and exchanged views on the two countries' bilateral relations, border management, anti-drug cooperation and matters of common concern. An economic and technological cooperation agreement expected to boost bilateral trade ties was signed.

2000

24–25 May: Chi Haotian, the Chinese State Councillor, Vice-Chairman of the Chinese Central Military Commission, the Vice-Chief of General Staff of the PLA and Minister of Defence and Fu Quanyou, the Chief of General Staff of the PLA, a member of the Central Military Commission received the visiting Myanmar military friendship delegation led by the Army Chief of General Staff, Tin Oo.

2 June: SPDC Chairman Than Shwe, received the visiting China's State Councillor Ismail Amat.

5–12 June: Vice-Chairman of SPDC, Gen. Maung Aye, visited China, and discussed bilateral ties, common concerns, economic globalization, and the extension of China–Myanmar economic trade cooperation. Two Foreign Ministers signed a Joint Statement on the Framework for the Future of Bilateral Relations and Cooperation on 6 June (see Appendix 1 for fuller details).

16–18 July: China's Vice-President Hu Jintao paid an official visit to Myanmar on the occasion of the 50th anniversary of the establishment of diplomatic relations between China and Myanmar, and signed three agreements on economic and technical cooperation, tourism cooperation, and science and technology cooperation.

18 September: The project Paungluang Hydropower Plant built by YMEC took out a loan of RMB1 billion from The Export–Import Bank of China.

2001

25–29 April: A Chinese military delegation led by Fu Quanyou, the Chief of General Staff of the PLA and a member of the Central Military Commission visited Myanmar.

18 September: Fu Quanyou, Chief of General Staff of the PLA met the visiting Commander-in-Chief of the Burmese Air Force Myint Swe.

12–15 December: China's President Jiang Zemin paid a state visit to Myanmar with a large entourage of 135 members at the invitation of Than Shwe. The two signed documents on bilateral cooperation, including an agreement on phytosanitary cooperation; an agreement on cooperation in fisheries; a contract for improving petroleum recovery on IOR-4, Pyay Field; a protocol for cooperation in border areas; an agreement on economic and technical cooperation; an agreement on the promotion and protection of investment; and an agreement on cooperation in animal health and quarantine.

2002

20–21 January: SPDC First Secretary Khin Nyunt and the Chairman of SPDC Than Shwe, received the visiting China's State Councillor and Secretary-General of State Council Wang Zhongyu, respectively. The aim of Wang's visit was to implement the consensus reached by Jiang Zemin and Than Shwe during Jiang's trip to Myanmar in 2001 and promote the bilateral economic cooperation, particularly in the domain of human resources.

2003

6–11 January: During SPDC Chairman Than Shwe's visit to China, both sides signed agreements on health cooperation, economic and technical cooperation, and on cooperation in sports. Jiang Zemin promised that China would provide Myanmar with US$0.2 billion concessional loan to develop the economy.

14–15 January: Vice-Premier Li Lanqing visited Myanmar to implement the consensus reached by Jiang Zemin and Than Shwe during the latter's earlier trip to Beijing in 2003. Than Shwe reaffirmed that "Myanmar will forever be on the side of China on the matters relating China's interest." Agreement was reached to expand bilateral cooperation in trade, technology, education, culture, hygiene and sports, notably personnel training. The two sides signed an Agreement on Partial Debt Relief for Myanmar; a Memorandum of Understanding on Extending a Grant for the Supply of Culture, Education and Sporting Goods by China to Myanmar; and a Memorandum of Understanding on the Program of Aerospace and Maritime Courses.

3–5 July: Myanmar Foreign Minister U Win Aung visited China as special envoy for Than Shwe, calling upon China's State Councillor Tang Jiaxuan and Foreign Minister Li Zhaoxing.

22 August: China's President Hu Jintao met the visiting Vice-Chairman of the SPDC, Maung Aye.

6 October: Premier Wen Jiabao met Myanmar Prime Minister Khin Nyunt in Bali, Indonesia, when they attended the seventh summit meeting between ASEAN and China, Japan and the Republic of Korea (ROK).

15 December: The "International Support for National Reconciliation in Myanmar Forum" was held in Bangkok. Delegates from 11 countries, as well as Myanmar Foreign Minister Win Aung, attended to discuss Myanmar's road map to national reconciliation and democracy. Chinese Assistant Foreign Minister Shen Guofang attended the forum and expounded China's Myanmar policy.

2004

23–27 March: Vice Premier Wu Yi led a 33–member government delegation and a 46–entrepreneur delegation on an official visit to Myanmar. During the visit, the two countries signed 21 agreements, MoUs and exchange of notes, including: a Memorandum of Understanding on the Promotion of Trade, Investment and Economic Cooperation; an Agreement on Economic and Technical Cooperation (Provision of a Grant of RMB50 million); the Framework on Cooperation for Promoting Trade and Investment between China Export and Credit Insurance Corporation and the Myanmar Ministry of Finance and Revenue; Government Concessional Loan Agreement for MPT Project Phase II between the Export–Import Bank of China and the Financial Institution Authorised by the Government of Myanmar; a Memorandum of Understanding between UMFCCI and the China Council for Promotion of International Trade; a Loan Agreement on Hydraulic Steel Structure (Lot HSS-1) of Yeywa Hydro-Power Project; Strategic Cooperation Agreement on Myanmar National Telecommunications Network Construction Project; a Commercial Contract for the Supply of Hydraulic Steel Structure Works and Electrical and Mechanical Equipment for Kun Hydro-Power Project; a Commercial Contract for Myaungtaka–Hlinethaya–Yekyi 230KV Transmission Lines and Substation Project; a Memorandum of Understanding on the Supply and Installation of Complete Equipment for Float-Glass Production Line with Melting Capacity of 150 TPD and for Tempered Glass, Laminated Glass and Mirror Glass Production Lines; a Contract for Construction of No. 4 Urea Fertilizer Factory at Taikkyi Township; a Memorandum of Understanding on Hydraulic Steel Structure (Lot HSS-2) and Electromechanical Equipment (Lot EM-1) of Yeywa Hydro-Power Project; the National Theatre Renovation Project; a Rice-Milling Machine Installation Project; a Combine Harvester Production Project; the Three Small-Scale Hydro-Power Plants Project; a Project for Propagation of Quality Sugarcane and Cotton Strains; Geological and Minerals Exploration in Myanmar–China Border Region; and the Lashio–Muse Railroad Project.

11–17 July: Myanmar Prime Minister Khin Nyunt paid an official visit to China. The two countries signed 12 agreements, MoUs and exchanges of notes.

21–28 July: SPDC First Secretary Soe Win led led a delegation to visit China and met Cao Gangchuan, the Chinese State Councillor, Defence Minister and Vice-Chairman of the Chinese Central Military Commission and Luo Gan,

Standing member of the Political Bureau of CCP Central Committee in Beijing on July 22.

2–6 November: The first foreign trip after taking office of Soe Win, Khin Nyunt's successor as Prime Minister, was a four-day visit to China to attend the "China–Association of Southeast Asian Nations Business and Investment Summit" in Nanning, Guangxi Zhuang Autonomous Region.

1–5 December: The Vice-Chief of the General Staff of the PLA, General Ge Zhenfeng, led a delegation to Myanmar. Their stay resulted in the signing of a MoU on the establishment of a border defense talks mechanism and the management of border affairs

3 December: Chinese Vice Foreign Minister Wu Dawei led a delegation to attend the 6th bilateral diplomatic consultations held in Yangon

2005

31 March – 4 April: A delegation from the Chinese Association for International Understanding visited Myanmar and held talks in Yangon with USDA Secretary-General Htay Oo.

23 April: President Hu Jintao met Senior General Than Shwe during the Asian–African Summit in Jakarta, Indonesia.

28–30 April: Foreign Minister of Myanmar U Nyan Win visited China. When meeting U Nyan Win, State Councillor Tang Jiaxuan reaffirmed China's good-neighbour policy towards Myanmar and stressed the value of cooperation on trade, the economy and drugs.

4 July: Premier Wen Jiabao met Myanmar Prime Minister Soe Win at the second GMS summit in Kunming. The President said China would provide more assistance to Myanmar. After discussing trade volume, the investment of China's enterprises in Myanmar, economic aid, and the cooperation of anti-drug, both signed an economic and technical agreement.

28 July: SPDC Chairman Than Shwe and Prime Minister Soe Win received the visiting Chinese Foreign Minister Li Zhaoxing.

14–16 November: Committee member of the CCP Central Politburo and Vice-Chairman of the NPC Standing Committee Wang Zhaoguo visited

Myanmar and met SPDC Chairman Than Shwe and USDA Secretary-General Htay Oo.

14 December: Premier Wen Jiabao met with Prime Minister Soe Win when attending the 1st East Asia Summit held in Kuala Lumpur.

2006

14–18 February: Prime Minister Soe Win met President Hu Jintao, Premier Wen Jiabao and Chairman of the Standing Committee of the NPC Wu Bangguo in Beijing. Soe Win and Wen Jiabao held discussions on the problem of anti-drug activities, treatment of ethnic Chinese in Myanmar, and economic cooperation. After the meeting, eight agreements and MOUs were signed.

7 April: A delegation from the USDA visited China and met Luo Haocai, Vice-President of Chinese Association for International Understanding and Vice-Chairman of the CPPCC National Committee in Beijing.

26 September: He Luli, the Vice-Chairman of the NPC Standing Committee received the visiting USDA delegation in Beijing.

22 October: SPDC Chairman Than Shwe received the visiting Chief of the PLA General Staff and member of the Central Military Commission, Liang Gaunglie. On the same day, Liang held talks with Gen. Maung Aye, SPDC Vice-Chairman, Deputy Commander-in-Chief of Defence Services, and Commander-in-Chief (Army).

31 October: Chinese Premier Wen Jiabao met with Myanmar Prime Minister Soe Win on the sidelines of the China–ASEAN Commemorative Summit marking the 15th anniversary of the establishment of Dialogue Relations between China and the ASEAN.

23 November: When Assistant Minister of Commerce of China Chen Jian visited Yangon, both signed an agreement on economic and technical cooperation; the minutes of the second consultation meeting between the governments of China and Myanmar on cooperation in trade, timber and mining; the protocol of Chinese government's exemption of Myanmar government's partial debt; and a framework agreement on provision of a preferential loan to Myanmar.

2007

22–25 January: The Vice-Chairman of the National People's Congress (NPC) Standing Committee Li Tieying led a delegation of NPC members to visit Myanmar.

31 January – 2 February: The visiting Chief of the General Staff Thura Shwe Man called upon Premier Wen Jiabao and Cao Gangchuan, the Chinese State Councillor, Defence Minister and Vice-Chairman of the Chinese Central Military Commission.

25–27 February: Tang Jiaxuan, the Chinese State Councillor paid a working visit to Myanmar. SPDC Chairman Than Shwe met with Tang Jiaxuan in Naypyitaw on February 26.

3 April: Zhou Tienong, Vice-President of Chinese Association for International Understanding and Vice-Chairman of the CPPCC National Committee, received a delegation from the USDA in Beijing.

5–10 June: Secretary-1 of Myanmar SPDC Thein Sein led a delegation to China.

10–13 June: SPDC First Secretary and Acting Prime Minister Thein Sein received the delegation of the China–ASEAN Association led by the Vice-Chairman of the NPC Standing Committee, Gu Xiulian. The China–ASEAN Association and the USDA signed a MoU of cooperation. This was the first visit to Myanmar of the China–ASEAN Association since it was established in 2004.

12 July: The Myanmar Foreign Ministry issued a statement that Myanmar reaffirmed the one-China policy and opposed any Taiwanese attempt to join the U.N. under any name.

14–18 August: A PLA delegation led by the Political Commissar of Jinan Military Region, General Liu Dongdong, visited Myanmar.

13 September: Myanmar Foreign Minister U Nyan Win visited China, as special envoy of Than Shwe.

13 September: Responding to international concern about widespread anti-government protests and a government crackdown in Myanmar, Chinese U.N. Ambassador Li Baodong stated that China called on all parties concerned in Myanmar to exercise restraint, restore stability through peaceful means, pro-

mote national reconciliation, and achieve democratic progress, while supporting the work of the U.N. Secretary-General's Special Advisor on Myanmar, Ibrahim Gambari.

24–25 October: Chinese Assistant Foreign Minister He Yafei held talks with Gambari in Beijing. Chinese State Councillor Tang Jiaxuan met Gambari on October 25 and expressed the commitment to continue to support Ban Ki-moon and Gambari's good offices and to support ASEAN's role on Myanmar issues.

14–16 November: Vice-Foreign Minister Wang Yi, as a Chinese special envoy, visited Myanmar and met Senior-General Than Shwe on 15 November. Wang also held talks with the members of the SPDC who reaffirmed that they would take positive and pragmatic measures to accelerate the democratic process. Wang reiterated China's Myanmar policy and hoped to see a Myanmar with political stability and economic prosperity.

19 November: Premier Wen Jiabao met Prime Minister Thein Sein in Singapore while attending a series of regional summit meetings there. Wen said that as an immediate neighbor of Myanmar, the Chinese Government and leadership was deeply concerned about the developing situation in Myanmar and hoped for strengthened dialogue to promote national reconciliation. China maintained that the future of Myanmar should be determined by its people, and the international community should provide constructive assistance to the country to achieve stability, national reconciliation and democratic progress. China would continue to support the mediation efforts by United Nations Secretary-General Ban Ki-moon and his special advisor Ibrahim Gambari and was willing to play a positive role in properly resolving the Myanmar issue.

2008

11 January: He Luli, the Vice-Chairman of NPC Standing Committee and the President of Chinese People's Association for Peace and Disarmament met Htay Oo the Secretary-General of USDA in Yangon.

21 January: Tang Jiaxuan, the Chinese State Councillor met with the visiting Vice-Foreign Minister U Maung Myint, as the special envoy of the Myanmar Prime Minister.

18–19 February: The U.N. Secretary-General's special advisor, Ibrahim Gambari, visited Beijing and met with Vice-Foreign Minister Wang Yi and Foreign Minister Yang Jiechi.

18 March: Myanmar's Foreign Ministry issued a press statement that Myanmar opposed any form of "Taiwanese independence" and a referendum on Taiwan's United Nations membership.

25 May: Foreign Minister Yang Jiechi met with Prime Minister Thein Sein at the sidelines of an International Pledging Conference for Cyclone Nargis held in Yangon.

August 2008: Prime Minister Thein Sein attended the Beijing Olympic Games.

21 August: Myanmar Chief of Defense Industry Lt-Gen Tin Aye visited China where he met with Gen Liang Guanglie, a member of the Central Military Commission and Chief of General Staff of the PLA.

27 October: Gen Zhang Li, the Vice Chief-of-Staff of the PLA met with Senior General Than Shwe in Naypyitaw.

18–20 November: Zhang Gaoli, a member of the Political Bureau of the CCP Central Committee and party chief of China's Tianjin municipality, met with Myanmar Prime Minister General Thein Sein and others in Naypyitaw.

29 November: Chief of General Staff of the Armed Forces Thura Shwe Mann visited Beijing and met Chinese military officials and the Chief of the General Staff of the PLA, Chen Bingde.

4–5 December: Foreign Minister Yang Jiechi met the Myanmar Foreign Minister U Nyan Win and SPDC Chairman Than Shwe in Naypyitaw.

2009

18 March: Chen Bingde, Chief of the General Staff of the PLA, led a military delegation to Myanmar for an official goodwill visit.

25–29 March: Li Changchun, a member of the Standing Committee of the Political Bureau of the CCP Central Committee, visited Myanmar. Li held talks with SPDC First Secretary Tin Aung Myint Oo. Li Changchun suggested maintaining high-level exchanges for increasing mutual trust; advancing cooperation in key sectors and big projects in such areas as energy, transport and telecommunication; expanding the channels for friendly contacts and increasing communications between the political organizations. In addition, "China will continue to encourage competent enterprises to invest in Myanmar or participate in your infrastructure construction." Relevant government departments inked cooperative agreements, including one pact to jointly build up the crude oil and gas pipelines and the other to jointly develop hydropower resources in Myanmar.

17 April: Premier Wen Jiabao met Prime Minister Thein Sein in Sanya on the sidelines of the Boao Forum for Asia (BFA) Annual Conference 2009.

20 April: Chief of the General Staff of the PLA Chen Bingde met with Tin Aye, member of Myanmar's SPDC in Beijing.

15–20 June: General Maung Aye paid a six-day goodwill visit to China at the invitation of Chinese Vice President Xi Jinping. They held discussions on co-operation in politics; cooperative measures in the financial crisis; mutual co-operation in human resources development, energy, electrical, transport, trade, industrial sectors and other sectors. Three documents were signed, including an agreement on economic and technical cooperation; a memorandum of agreement on development, operation, and transfer of hydropower projects in Maykha, Malikha and the upstream of Ayeyawaddy–Myitsone River Basin; and a memorandum of understanding related to development, operation and management of the Myanmar–China crude oil pipeline project.

During the visit, China National Petroleum Corp (CNPC) signed an agreement with Myanmar's Energy Ministry to receive exclusive rights to build and operate the China–Myanmar crude oil pipeline. This granted operating concession of the pipeline to the CNPC-controlled South-East Asia Crude Oil Pipeline Ltd. The pipeline company would also enjoy tax concessions and customs clearance rights. The agreement stipulated that the Myanmar government should guarantee the company's ownership and exclusive operating rights, as well as the safety of the pipeline.

19 October: Chinese Vice Premier Li Keqiang met with SPDC First Secretary Tin Aung Myint Oo in Nanning, when both of them came to attend the 6th China–ASEAN Expo held 20–24 October. Li said the Chinese government paid high attention to Sino–Myanmar relations and would keep supporting Myanmar's economic construction and sustainable development. "China and Myanmar should make efforts together to strengthen exchanges and coopera-

tion, as well as safeguard stability on the border areas for the sake of the fundamental interests of the two peoples."

20 October: The Consulate-General of Myanmar in Nanning, the capital of Guangxi, opened.

24 October: Wen Jiabao told his Myanmar counterpart Thein Sein on the sidelines of the Association of Southeast Asian Nations (ASEAN) summit that he believed Myanmar could properly handle problems and safeguard peace and stability in the China–Myanmar border region. "To develop good-neighborly China–Myanmar relations with mutually beneficial cooperation conforms to the fundamental interests of the two countries and will be conducive to regional peace and stability."

19–20 December: Chinese Vice President Xi Jinping put forward a four-point proposal to upgrade relations with Myanmar during his visit and held talks with the Vice-Chairman of the SPDC Maung Aye. The proposal included maintaining high-level contact, deepening reciprocal cooperation, safeguarding peace and prosperity of the border area, and strengthening coordination on international and regional affairs. During the talks, Than Shwe said the Myanmar side recognized the importance of safeguarding peace and stability in the border area. "The peace and tranquility in the border area between China and Myanmar is a demonstration of good neighborly friendship and cooperation." The two countries signed a total of 16 documents, including five agreements on development of trade, economy, transport infrastructures, technological cooperation and purchase of machinery; seven financial agreements, three agreements on hydroelectric power; and one agreement on the energy sector and the oil and natural gas pipeline.

2010

26 February: A delegation of the CCP visited Myanmar, led by Wang Jiarui, head of the International Department of the CCP Central Committee at the invitation of Htay Oo, Secretary General of USDA.

2–3 June: Chinese Premier Wen Jiabao visited Myanmar and attended the celebrations of the 60th anniversary of China–Myanmar diplomatic ties in Naypyitaw. During the visit, the two leaders attended a signing ceremony for 15 documents on cooperation in natural gas, hydropower, and other fields.

5–9 June: A PLA military delegation led by Fan Changlong, Commander of Jinan Military Region, visited Myanmar.

7–11 June: Myanmar Foreign Minister U Nyan Win visited China and attended the celebration in Beijing marking the 60th anniversary of Myanmar–PRC diplomatic relations. He held talks with his counterpart Yang Jiechi and briefed Yang on the preparatory work for Myanmar's general elections.

27 June – 1 July: At the invitation of the USDA, a Chinese Association for International Understanding (CAFIU) delegation headed by Zhou Tienong, the Vice-Chairman of NPC Standing Committee and President of CAFIU, visited Myanmar.

3–12 July: SPDC First Secretary Tin Aung Myint Oo visited China at the invitation of Member of the Politburo Standing Committee of the CCP Central Committee, Vice Premier Li Keqiang. During a meeting with Tin Aung Myint Oo, Li Keqiang pledged to speed up and expand cooperation with Myanmar on energy and transport.

29 August: The 5th Escort Task group of the PLA Navy, comprising the warships "Guanhzhou" and "Chaohu", visited Yangon's Thilawa port.

7–11 September: SPDC Chairman Than Shwe paid a state visit to China, picking up a US$4.2 billion interest-free loan (30-year term) for hydropower, information technology, roads and railways projects in Myanmar. Besides Beijing, Than Shwe visited Shanghai and Shenzhen. During the last two legs of his China trip, he expected to learn from China's experiences in reform and opening up the country, and to promote economic and trade cooperation between Myanmar and China's developed areas.

16–20 September: At the invitation of the SPDC, He Yong, the Secretary of Secretariat of CCP Central Committee and Deputy Secretary of the CCP Central Commission for Discipline Inspection, led a party delegation to visit Myanmar.

9 November: Beijing welcomed Myanmar's smooth general election concluded on 7 November and believed that it was a vital part in Myanmar's seven-step roadmap in its transition to an elected government.

2011

2–16 March: A PLA delegation led by Jia Tingan, deputy director of the PLA General Political Department, visited Myanmar.

31 March: U Thein Sein appealed to western countries for cooperation with his country at his inauguration ceremony on 30 March. For this, Beijing said

the international community would create a lenient environment for Myanmar's national reconciliation and economic development.

2–5 April: The Chairman of the CPPCC National Committee Jia Qinglin visited Myanmar, and met President Thein Sein and Amyotha Hluttaw Speaker U Khin Aung Myint, and held talks with Pyithu Hluttaw Speaker Thura Shwe Mann. Five contracts or MoUs were signed.

12–15 May: Vice Chairman of China's Central Military Commission Gen Xu Caihou visited Myanmar and met President Thein Sein, Pyithu Hluttaw Speaker Thura Shwe Mann, and Tatmadaw Commander-in-Chief Min Aung Hlaing. Both sides discussed bilateral military ties and international and regional security issues of common concern.

26–28 May: Myanmar's President Thein Sein visited China, signing 9 cooperation agreements including a US$765 million credit package. Both sides signed a China–Myanmar joint statement on establishing a Comprehensive Strategic Cooperative Partnership (see Appendix 5 for fuller details). This was Thein Sein's first state visit after his inauguration.

1–4 June: Li Yuanchao, a member of the Political Bureau of the CCP Central Committee, the Secretary of the Secretariat of the CCP Central Committee and Head of the Organization Department of the CCP Central Committee, visited Myanmar and met President Thein Sein, Vice President U Tin Aung Myint Oo, Pyithu Hluttaw Speaker Thura Shwe Mann, and USDP Secretary-General U Htay Oo. Both signed bilateral cooperation accords and a MoU between the CCP and the USDP on exchange and cooperation.

9 June: Deadly fighting between the KIA and the Burmese army broke out near a dam project built by China, bringing this strategic region neighboring China to the verge of civil war.

30 September: In a memo to the hluttaws, President Thein Sein announced to decide to suspend the Chinese-sponsored Myitsone Dam during his tenure (until 2015) because this project, which had been estimated to cost some US$3.6 billion and on which the Chinese had already spend US$42.5 million, was "against the will of the people". In response, Beijing only stated that China had noted the report and was verifying it.

1 October: China's Foreign Ministry spokesperson Hong Lei remarked that the Myitsone Dam was a jointly invested project by two countries that had

gone through scientific verification and strict examination on both sides. Relevant matters arising from the implementation of the project should be handled appropriately through friendly bilateral consultation.

1–2 October: Chinese Ambassador to Myanmar Li Junhua visited two major China-Myanmar joint projects, the Myanmar–China oil and gas pipeline and the Mon Ywa copper mine developed by Myanmar Wanbao Mining Copper Ltd.

7 October: Chinese Ambassador Li Junhua called on both President Thein Sein and Pyithu Hluttaw Speaker Thura Shwe Mann. They discussed recent developments in bilateral relations and further strengthening friendly ties and mutual benefits between the two countries.

10 October: The Myanmar Foreign Minister U Wunna Maung Lwin visited China as a special envoy of the Myanmar president to ease tensions over the cancellation of the dam construction. Vice President Xi Jinping held talks with him and urged the two sides to properly settle through friendly consultations all relevant matters that had emerged during the course of cooperation. U Wunna Maung Lwin said President Thein Sein and the Myanmar government highly valued the friendly relations with China and were paying close attention to China's relevant concerns.

19 October: An USDP cadre delegation visited China.

20–27 October: Vice President U Tin Aung Myint Oo visited China to attend the 8th China–ASEAN Expo and the 8th China–ASEAN Business & Investment Summit held in Nanning. He met Premier Wen Jiabao and visited Nnanning, Yulin, Shenzhen and Guangzhou.

6 November–24 December: The Chinese Buddha's tooth relic was conveyed to Myanmar for a 48-day public obeisance in Naypyitaw, Yangon and Mandalay and during the obeisance was worshiped by over 4 million Myanmar Buddhists. This is the fourth enshrinement visit of the Buddha's tooth relic to Myanmar.

11–15 November: At the invitation of USDP Secretary-General U Htay Oo, a member of the Political Bureau of the CCP Central Committee and Secretary of CCP Beijing Municipal Committee Liu Qi visited Myanmar and met President Thein Sein and Pyithu Hluttaw Speaker Thura Shwe Mann.

27 November and 2 December: Tatmadaw Commander-in-Chief Min Aung Hlaing visited China and signed a MoU on defense cooperation with China. During talks between Vice President Xi Jinping and Min Aung Hlaing, both

declared an interest to further deepen bilateral military relations and cooperation. Xi stated that China would work with Myanmar to further bolster the comprehensive strategic partnership of cooperation. Min Aung Hlaing reiterated that Myanmar would adhere to the one-China policy and support China's position on issues concerning Taiwan, Tibet and Xinjiang.

1 December: US Secretary of State Hillary Clinton visited Myanmar. Beijing stated that China was willing to see Myanmar strengthening contact and improving relations with relevant western countries based on mutual respect; western countries should lift the sanctions against Myanmar to push for its stability and development.

15 December: China's Foreign Ministry revealed that the Chinese ambassador to Myanmar had met with Daw Aung San Suu Kyi.

19–20 December: State Councilor Dai Bingguo participated in the 4th Summit of GMS Economic Cooperation Program in Naypyitaw, where he met President Thein Sein and Vice President U Tin Aung Myint Oo. Dai stressed the need to boost China–Myanmar cooperation, implement existing plans, and jointly safeguard the stability of the China–Myanmar border regions. He urged both sides to make use of their complementary advantages, properly work out the "China–Myanmar Economic and Trade Cooperation Program", and implement major projects well between the two sides.

2012

16 January: After Washington announced to restore full diplomatic ties with Myanmar, Beijing stated that it was glad to see the U.S. and other western countries strengthening contacts, and restoring and developing ties with Myanmar.

10 February: China's Ministry of Foreign Affairs refuted international media reports of a mass exodus of Kachin refugees from Myanmar to China but acknowledged that some people had sought refuge in Yunnan from fighting between the KIA and Tatmadaw. The main refugee camps were said to be in border areas close to the route of the Myanmar–China oil and gas pipeline.

22–26 February: Myanmar Pyithu Hluttaw Speaker Thura Shwe Mann visited China at the invitation of the Chairman of the NPC Standing Committee, Wu Bangguo.

5 April: Beijing noted the by-election results of 1 April 2012, the Foreign Ministry hoping they would facilitate "political reconciliation and promote national stability and development", and calling "upon all parties to completely lift sanctions against Myanmar at an early date."

Appendix 4

Major Chinese Companies in Myanmar

(List of Chinese companies follows)

Source: opensource.gov, "Chinese Companies Doing Business in Burma." 10 June – 7 July 2010; the data of registered capital is from Hubei, Beijing, Henan, Zhejiang, Tianjin, Shanghai, Shenzhen and Shandong Administration for Industry & Commerce as well as the web sites of the companies.

Notes:

1. This is a partial list of major corporations, and a truncated list of their involvements. Many others are not registered or listed. Other sources indicate that there are some 400 Chinese corporations opening in Myanmar, not counting small businesses. Also, for list of the leading Chinese companies in Myanmar, see the website of Economic and Commercial Counselor's Office of China's Embassy in Myanmar, mm.mofcom.gov.cn/static/column/catalog/zgqy.html/1

2. Some Chinese company names from opensource.gov are misleading and confusing because they have been out of use and terminated. Yunnan Huaneng Lancang River Hydropower Co. was renamed Huaneng Lancang River Hydropower Co. and its registered capital was changed from RMB2 billion to RMB4.166 billion on 17 November 2008; China Gezhouba Water and Power (Group) Co. Ltd was renamed China Gezhouba Group Co. Ltd on 28 September 2007; China International Trust and Investment Corporation was renamed CITIC Group in 2002; China National Building Material Equipment Corp., Ltd.(CBMEC) was renamed Sinoma Equipment & Engineering Corp., Ltd on 12 November 2008; China Three Gorges Project Corporation was renamed as China Three Gorges Corporation since 27 September 2009, while abbreviated as CTGPC as unchanged; Sinohydro Corporation was established on the basis of former China National Water Resources and Hydropower Engineering Corporation (CWHEC) with registered capital of RMB2.2 Billion in 2002.

Name	Sector	Location	Ownership	Registered capital (RMB million)	Remarks/projects
Central China Power International Trade Co.	Electric power engineering; export of power station equipment and electric transmission and transformation equipment	Wuhan, Hubei	State owned	148.00	230 KV transmission line; Dapein Hydropower Plant (I) Shareholders: Central China Grid Co, Ltd., and the Electric Power Companies of Hubei, Henan, Hunan, Jiangxi provinces.
Chevalier Group	Construction, engineering, hotels, insurance	Hong Kong			Activities in Myanmar unclear
China CAMC Engineering Co. Ltd.	Engineering procurement construction (EPC) projects, industrial field infrastructure, energy, transportation	Beijing	State owned	190.00	Equipment project (US$8.18 million); Myanmar Thanlyin Glass (US$1.9332 million); Sarlingyi spinning (US$21.92 million); Myanmar Glass (US$1.0 million); Yadanabon bridge (US$10.9 million); Myanmar Shipyard
China Datang Corporation	Power energy	Beijing	State owned	15,390.00	Dapein Hydropower Plant (I); On 7 January 2010 signed a MoU with Myanmar on Ywathit, Lampang River, Nandan Pa Lay absurd River and River 4 hydropower projects.
China Development Bank	Financing, credit, invstment	Beijing	State owned		Tagaung Taung nickel mine.
China Export and Credit Insurance Corporation (Sinosure)	Export credit insurance, investment insurance, bond and guarantee.	Beijing	State owned		China's only policy-oriented insurance company specializing in export credit insurance.

Name	Sector	Location	Ownership	Registered capital (RMB million)	Remarks/projects
China National Building Material Equipment Corp. Ltd.	Project engineering and construction, equipment manufacturing as well as international trade	Beijing	State owned	22.00	Kyaukse High Heat Duty Fire Brick Factory
China National Complete Plant and Export Corp. Ltd. (COMPLANT)	Undertaking China-aided projects in foreign countries and supplying general goods to recipient countries; general contracting of various projects abroad; maintenance, equipment renewal, technological innovation and supply of spare parts for China-aided projects accomplished.	Beijing	State owned		An exclusive organization entrusted by the Chinese government in executing China-aided complete plant projects in foreign countries, Complant functioned internally as government agency to organize and manage all China-aided projects, and externally as general contractor The Yangon–Thanlyin Railway-cum-Road Bridge; The Myanmar No. 1 National Gymnasium. Many plants.
China National Construction & Agricultural Machinery Import & Export Corp. (CAMC)	Energy, construction project contracting, supply of complete equipment packages and the import & export trade taking machinery and electrical products	Beijing	State owned		Kengtawng hydroelectric plant (US$11.$),Burma Float Glasswork Project; Mandalay Bridge, Minbu Bridge, Yangdong Bridge, Maobin Bridge, Myitkyina Bridge, Salingyi Textile Plant, Kyaukse Cement Plant, Dirawad Ship Plant I, Okha Sugar-refinery
China National Electric Equipment Corp. (CNEEC)	EPC contracting, complete equipment supply, power energy, and constructions.	Beijing	State owned		Kabaung hydroelectric plant; metal structure of Kengtawng hydroelectric plant (US$350)

Name	Sector	Location	Ownership	Registered capital (RMB million)	Remarks/projects
China Gezhouba (Group) Corp. (CGGC)	Infrastructure construction, investment, hydroelectrical works and highways	Yichang and Wuhan, Hubei	State owned	1,428.00	Yeywa hydroelectric project (US$46.3 million); Pyu hydroelectric project; Tasang hydro project, etc.
China Guangdong New Technology Import and Export Company of Zhuhai	Power energy, transportation	Zhuhai, Guangdong	State owned	1.20	Dahutkone and Taung Zin Aye Sugar mills (US$32.88 million); Pyintphyu hydroelectric (US$20 million); Buywa Hydroelectric project (US$18.2 million); Kyeeon Kyeewa Hydroelectric project (US$18.2 million)
China Huaneng Group	Energy	Beijing	State owned	20,000.00	Ruili I Hydropower Station
China Huanqiu Contracting and Engineering Corp. (HQCEC)	Energy, engineering, industrial field infrastructure	Beijing	State owned		Taikkyi Ammonia and urea plant (US$195 million)
CITIC Group (formerly China International Trust and Investment Corporation)	Financing, energy, heavy industries, infrastructure, engeering, www. burmariversnetwork.org/ investors/chinese.html	Beijing	State owned		Several hydroelectric projects. Multipurpose Diesel Engine Factory (US$126 million); Monywa Copper Project
China Metallurgical Group Corp. (MCC)	Construction, EPC business (engineering, procurement and construction), natural resources exploitation, papermaking business, equipment fabrication	Beijing			One of 500 largest corporations in the world) Thabaung pulp mill (US$90 million); Okkan sugar plant; designed Tagaung Taung Nickle project

Name	Sector	Location	Ownership	Registered capital (RMB million)	Remarks/projects
China National Heavy Machinery Corporation (CHMC)	Construction, energy, mining	Beijing	State owned		Tigyit thermal power plant as well as its transmission and transformer projects; KUN hydroelectric plant; Yeywa 230KV transmission and transformer projects; Kabaung hydroelectric plant Tigyit opencut coal mine; Kyaukse Knitwear Mill
China National Machinery and Equipment Import and Export Corp. (CMEC)	Agriculture, construction, power energy, export of complete plants, communication, transportation and mining.	Beijing	State owned		Two multipurpose cargo vessels; two liquid petroleum gas factories; pump station project of Myanmar Agriculture Ministry; Kabaung hydroelectric plant; Renovation of paper mill; supply of machinery and services of Thaukyegat II hydroelectric plant(US$77 million)
China National Offshore Oil Corp. (CNOOC)	Oil and gas exploration, development, production and sales, technical services	Beijing	State owned	94,900.00	The largest offshore oil and gas producer in China; onshore Block M; offshore Block A-4 and Block M-10; onshore Block C-1, Block C-2 and offshore Block M-2
China National Petroleum Corp. (CNPC)	Oil and gas exploration & production, refining & chemicals, natural gas & pipelines and marketing & trading	Beijing	State owned		China's largest integrated oil and gas company. 13th largest in world. Sino–Myanmar Oil and gas pipeline, Kyaukphyu port, etc.
China National Technical Import and Export Corp. (CNTIC)	Construction, energy, transportation, communication, petrochemical, import and export of key technologies and complete plants	Beijing	State owned		1000 TPD Dry Process Cement Plant in Pangpet; supply of generators, turbines, machinery of Upper Keng Tawng Hydropower plant

Name	Sector	Location	Ownership	Registered capital (RMB million)	Remarks/projects
Sinohydro Corp.	Hydropower construction, civil works, transportation	Beijing	State owned		Hutgyi Hydropower Project; Yeya Hydropower Project; Ruili River Hydropower Station I; Dapein (1) Hydropower Project; Thapanzeik Hydropower Project; Mone Hydropower Project; Upper Paunglaung Hydropower Project; Tasang Hydropower projec
China Nonferrous Metal Mining (Group) Cp. Ltd (CNMC)	Development of nonferrous metal mineral resources, construction engineering	Beijing	State owned		Tagaung Taung nickel mine (expected investment US$800 million)
China North Industries (NORINCO)	Defense products, petroleum & mineral resources development, international engineering contracting	Beijing	State owned		Defense projects, chemicals, engineering contracting; Monywa Copper Mine Project
China Oilfield Services Ltd. (COSL)	Offshore oil and gas exploration, development and production, geophysical services, drilling services, well services, marine support and transportation services	Beijing	State-holding		The largest listed offshore oilfield services company in China and a subsidiary of CNOOC. Contract with Daewoo (US$6 million); drilling and other operations (US$6 million).
China Petrochemical Corp. (Sinopec Group)	The exploration, production, and transportation of oil and natural gas; oil refining; construction and installation of petroleum and petrochemical engineering projects	Beijing	State-holding	130,600.00	World's 9th largest company, Myanmar offshore oil, gas, pipeline involvement; YAGYI-1, PATOLON-1 and PATOLON-2 Well drillings in Block D

Name	Sector	Location	Ownership	Registered capital (RMB million)	Remarks/projects
China Power Investment Corp. (CPI)	Power energy, construction, complete and component of electric equipment supply	Beijing	State owned.	12,000.00	Built Ruili dam, Kachin projects
China Shanghai (Group) Corporation For Foreign Economic & Technological Cooperation (SFECO)	Contracting for industrial and civil construction, roads and bridges and other civil engineering projects	Shanghai	State-holding	700.00	Generators for Zawgyi hydropower project
China Southern Power Grid Corp. Ltd. (CSG)	Power energy	Guangzhou	State owned		Salween project; import electric power from Ruili River Hydropower Station I; maintenance of 220kV double-circuit transmission lines in Myanmar
China Three Gorges Corporation (CTGPC)	Hydropower project	Yichang, Hubei	State owned	111,598.00	In addition to Three Gorges Project, working group to implement Salween project. Part of consortium(CTGPC, Sinohydro Corp, CSG) to build Tasang Hydroelectric project (Shan State) (US$9 billion)
Chinnery Assets Limited	Oil	British Virgin Islands			AD-1, AD-6 & AD-8 Block; onshore block IOR 4; Chinnery is a 50:50 joint venture formed by two subsidiaries of CNPC: CNPC (Hong Kong). Ltd. and CNPC International.

Name	Sector	Location	Ownership	Registered capital (RMB million)	Remarks/projects
Dian–Qian–Gui Petroleum Exploration Bureau	Oil exploration	Kunming	State owned		Explore, drill and produce oil and gas at onshore Block D in Monywa District, Sagaing Division, and at Mahutaung Region in Pakokku District, Magway Division.
The Export–Import Bank of China (China Exim Bank)	Export credit and import credit; Loans to overseas construction contracts and investment projects; Chinese Government Concessional Loan; International guarantee	Beijing	State owned		A government policy bank; Financed Paunglaung hydroproject (US$120 million); various ministries (US$200 million); buying vessels (US$70 million); Myanma Posts & Telegraphs (US$31.5 million); Yeywa hydroporject (US$200 million); Seeding China–ASEAN Investment Corporation Fund (US$300 million); etc.
Gold Mountain (Hong Kong) International Mining Co.	Mining industry investment	Hong Kong			A subsidiary of Zijin Mining Group and is involved in Mwetaung nickel ore.
Hanergy Holding Group Co. Ltd. (formerly Farsighted Investment Group)	Power energy	Beijing	Private		Kunlong Hydropower Project; As the largest non-state-owned enterprise of power generation with clean energy in China.
Jardine Schindler Group	Elevators, escalators.	Hong Kong			A joint venture between Jardine Matheson in Hong Kong and Schindler Group of Switzerland

Name	Sector	Location	Ownership	Registered capital (RMB million)	Remarks/projects
Kingbao (Jinbao) Mining Co. (See North China Industries and Zijin Mining Group Ltd.)	Mining	Hong Kong			The joint venturer of Zijin Mining Group and Wanbao Mining Company. Zijin held a 90% equity interest in Kingbao Mining it was accounted for as a subsidiary as at 31 December 2008.
PetroChina Co. Ltd.	Exploration, production and transportation of oil and natural gas	Beijing	State-holding		Subsidiary of CNPC. China's largest gas and oil producer distributor; 2nd largest company in the world by capitalization. Signed agreement to buy 6.5 trillion cubic feet of natural gas over 30 years. By the end of 2007, CNPC possessed 86.29% of PetroChina shares.
Shandong Machinery & Equipment Import & Export Group Corp. (SDMECO)	Construction, export of complete sets of equipment	Qingdao, Shandong	State owned	41.89	Quinine sulfate Pharmaceuticals Factory
Shandong Shantui Construction Machinery Import & Export Co. Ltd.	construction machineries and its related spare part	Jining, Shandong	State-holding		China's largest manufacturer and exporter of construction machinery. Subudiy of Shantui Construction Machinery Co.
Shanghai Bell Co. Ltd.	Communications.	Shanghai	Alcatel–Lucent holding	5,759.09	Joint venture with Chinese state-owned Assets Supervision and Administration Commission and Alcatel–Lucent SA of France. Telephone exchanges. Rangoon exchanges (US$16.9 million), with Shanghai Bell supplying information-technological equipment for Yadanabon Cyber City (US$30.2 million)

Name	Sector	Location	Ownership	Registered capital (RMB million)	Remarks/projects
Sinoma Equipment and Engineering Corp. Ltd. (CBMEC)	construction, non-metal materials industry and mining	Beijing	State owned		Involved in Hsinmin-1 Cement Plant; Kyaukse brick factory (US$3.24 million).
Tianjin Machinery Import and Export Corporation (Group)	Construction: import and export of machinery and electronic products and relevant technologies.	Tianjin	State owned	509.50	Textile mills Pyintphyu (US$37.28 million), and Pakokku (US$23.36 million); Thabaung Pulp Factory
XJ Group Corporation	Power generation, electric network system, and industrial power distribution	Xuchang, Henan	State owned	6903.95	Thagara Engine plant (US$112 million); equipment supply for Ruili, Yeywa, Thapanseik, and Mone hydropower projects; paper Pulp Factory Project (control & protection panel and DC power supply etc.)
Huaneng Lancang River Hydropower Co.	Engineering, mining	Kunming, Yunnan	State owned	4166.00	Holding subsidiaries China Huaneng Group (CHNG); Salween river valley hydropower projects; Yangon thermal power plant; Ruili Hydropwer project I and II;
Yunnan Joint Power Development Co. (See Yunnan United Power Development Co.)	Power energy	Kunming, Yunnan	State-holding	1000.00	Ruili Hydropwer project I; Share: Huaneng(50%), Yunnan Hexing Investment and Development Company (34%) and YMEC(16%)

Name	Sector	Location	Ownership	Registered capital (RMB million)	Remarks/projects
Yunnan Machinery & Equipment Import & Export Corp. (YMEC)	Energy, export of electric products complete set of equipment	Kunming, Yunnan	State owned		Wholly owned subsidiary of China Southern Power Grid Corp. Dozens of hydropower projects
Yunnan Power Grid Corp.	Energy power	Kunming, Yunnan	State owned		Subsidiary of Southern Power Grid Company. Involved with Ruili project I; power supply to Kongkang; Nam Hka river and Nam Lei rive hydropower projects.
Zhejiang Fuchunjiang Hydropower Equipment Co. Ltd.	Power energy; water-turbine generator set	Tonglu, Zhejiang	State-holding	1431.90	Joint stock limited company. Signed joint venture with Russian Power Machines Company for a Salween and Hutgi plant project.
Zhejiang Orient Holdings Group	international trade, real estate development and business of investment	Hangzhou, Zhejiang	State-holding	5054.73	In cooperation with CNEEC supplied materials/equipment hydro substation Kengtawng (US$11.5 and US$4.56 million)
Zijin Mining Group Ltd.	Mining	Longyan, Fujian	State-holding		Mwetaung nickel project
ZTE Corp(Zhong Xing Telecommunication Equipment Company Limited)	Communications. Global provider of telecommunications software equipment. telecom equipment provider	Shenzhen, Guangdong	State-holding	19111.54	Mobile communication network; GSM network; 95,000 cellular phone connections (US$12.5 million)

Appendix 5

Joint Statement Between The Republic of the Union of Myanmar and The People's Republic of China on Establishing a Comprehensive Strategic Cooperative Partnership

*A*t the invitation of President Mr. Hu Jintao of the People's Republic of China, President U Thein Sein the Republic of the Union of Myanmar paid a state visit to the People's Republic of China from 26 to 28 May 2011.

During the visit, President Mr Hu Jintao held talks with President U Thein Sein. Premier Wen Jiabao of the State Council and Chairman Mr Jia Qinglin of the National Committee of the Chinese People's Political Consultative Conference met withPresident U Thein Sein. The two sides had in-depth exchange of views on bilateral relations and international and regional issues of common interest in a friendly atmosphere.

The two sides agreed that since the establishment of diplomatic relations on 8 June 1950, the good neighborly friendship and cooperation between China and Myanmar have been developing smoothly. Especially since the beginning of the new century, the leaders of the two sides have maintained close contact, friendly cooperation in political, economic, cultural, scientific, and technological areas have kept expanding, and the traditional Paukphaw friendship between the two peoples has been growing from strength to strength. The two sides are satisfied with the development of the bilateral relations.

The two sides stressed that China–Myanmar relations, which are based on the Five Principles of Peaceful Coexistence jointly initiated by the two sides, have stood the tests of the changes in the international situation and in the respective domestic situation and enjoy broad prospects for development. The two sides agreed that the world today is undergoing great development, great changes and great adjustment, and the trend towards multipolarity and economic globalization have gained momentum. Countries have become more interdependent. Peace, development and cooperation not only represent the trend of the times, but also serve the common interests of the countries and peoples in the region. Under the new circumstances, further promoting China–Myanmar relations on the basis of the existing friendly cooperation meets the need of the two countries to realize common development, serves the fundamental interests of the two countries and their people, and is conducive to peace, stability and prosperity of the region. On the basis of the above-mentioned common political will, the two sides agree to establish China–Myanmar comprehensive strategic cooperative partnership and reached the following agreement:

1. The two sides will maintain close high-level contacts, continue to promote strategic mutual trust and further enhance friendly exchanges and cooperation between the parliaments, governments, judicial departments and political parties of the two countries.

2. The two sides will continue to carry out consultations between the foreign ministries of the two countries on an irregular basis, have timely exchange of views on bilateral relations and international and regional hotspot issues, and hold regular meetings on bilateral and multilateral occasions to strengthen strategic communication.

3. The two sides will follow the principles of equality, mutual benefit, drawing upon each other's strengths and emphasizing practical results, further enhance the size and level of the economic cooperation and trade between the two countries, work to strengthen healthy, stable and sustainable business ties, make joint efforts to create a favourable environment for trade and investment cooperation, enhance the closer economic and trade exchanges between the two countries in accordance with their economic and trade policies.

4. The two sides will continue to conduct friendly cooperation in such areas as education, culture, science and technology, health, agriculture and tourism on the basis of mutual benefit, strengthen people-to-people and cultural exchanges, increase mutual visits, and deepen mutual understanding and friendship between the two peoples.

5. The two sides will strengthen border management cooperation, conduct timely communication on border management affairs, and strive to maintain peace, tranquility and stability in border areas.

6. The Chinese side reaffirms its respect for Myanmar's independence, sovereignty, and territorial integrity and its support for Myanmar's pursuit of its development path suited to its national conditions. Myanmar reiterates that its adheres to one China policy, recognizes that the People's Republic of China is the sole legal government representing the whole of China and that Taiwan is unalienable part of the Chinese territory, will continue to support the peaceful development of cross-Strait relations and China's cause of peaceful reunification.

7. The two sides will further enhance coordination and cooperation in the United Nations and other multilateral areas, jointly safeguard the interests of developing countries, strengthen cooperation in such mechanisms as the ASEAN Plus China, Japan and the ROK, ASEAN plus China and Greater Mekong Sub regional Economic cooperation, and promote common development and prosperity of the region.

Beijing, 27 May 2011

Appendix 6

Summary: "Peking and the Burmese Communists: The Perils and Profits of Insurgency." Secret (later declassified) CIA Report, 1971

The salient feature of China's relations with the Burmese Communist party (CPB) during the past twenty years is the degree to which Peking has used the CPB to promote Chinese national interests. For more than fifteen years (1950–1967), while the Chinese enjoyed good relations with the Burmese Government (GUB), Mao Tsetung was more than willing to sacrifice the interests of the CPB to the priorities of Sino-Burmese state relations. This was made perfectly clear in repeated Chinese initiatives to cement the already close relations between the two countries, while Peking all but ignored the revolutionary effort of the Burmese Communists – even going so far as to urge them in private to seek an end to their armed struggle against the Rangoon government. Only in mid-1967, after Sino-Burmese relations were virtually ruined by an unexpected outbreak of anti-Chinese riots in Rangoon, did the Chinese suddenly begin actively to support insurrection in Burma – and in this case, up-country ethnic minority groups having no connection with the CPB.

Although conventional wisdom might have presumed that the Chinese had always strongly supported the armed effort of the Burmese Communists, who were, after all, faithfully following Mao's precepts in waging rural guerrilla warfare, the fact is that for many years Peking contrived to ignore the insurrection being waged by the CPB in the Pegu Mountains of central Burma. In the years immediately following the 1949 Communist takeover in China, Peking gave some propaganda support to "the national liberation war" in Burma, but even this limited support was toned down during the early 1950's; by 1955, it had stopped altogether; from 1955 until 1967, the Chinese maintained a discreet public silence on the whole subject. Despite many suppositions and rumours that the Chinese were providing covert aid to the Communist insurgents, Peking is not known to have supplied any material assistance prior to 1967, other than some portable radio equipment.

Through radio contact and the establishment of an organization known as the Overseas CPB in China, the Chinese managed surprisingly well in the 1950's and early 1960's to keep the allegiance of the CPB, even while they were doing nothing to advance its insurgent effort. Apparently, the Chinese Communist Party (CCP) had first suggested the idea of a Peking branch of the CPB to the Burmese Communists as a means of maintaining control over the Burmese Party; once in China, CPB officials served Chinese interests above all else. The Overseas CPB, led by CPB Vice-Chairman Thakin Ba Thein Tin; received secret directives directly from the CCP Central Committee and relayed them by radio, in the name of the CPB, to Party Chairman Thakin Than Tun and the other Communist leaders in Burma.

In June 1963, Ne Win's offer of peace talks to all insurgents (Communist and non-Communist) provided a long-awaited opportunity for the Peking-trained Burmese Communists, who had lived in China since the early 1950's, to return to Burma. Ne Win's initiative also offered the possibility of a negotiated peace between the CPB and the Burmese Government, which the Chinese had long been pressing both the Communists and Rangoon to accept. Although the peace talks ultimately collapsed, to China's disappointment, the return to Burma of the China-trained Overseas Burmese Communists managed to bring the CPB under virtual Chinese control. This development was reflected in a new Maoist "campaign" atmosphere in the CPB, featuring prolonged Mao study sessions, mass ideological meetings, intensive self-criticism, increasing fanaticism – and, ultimately, a prolonged and ruthless purge. By early 1967, Thakin Than Tun had begun to execute his opponents within the Party, going well beyond the practices of the Chinese Cultural Revolution in his extraordinary use of terror, including particularly gruesome, ritualistic murder sequences. The climax to this series of events came with the assassination of Thakin Than Tun by a disillusioned Party member in September 1968. With his death, the CPB reached not only the end of a pathetic chapter in its history, but also the end of its long and close association with the CCP.

For at this important juncture in CPB history, the Burmese Party happened, for the first time in years, to be without radio contact with Peking – as the result of a damaging Burmese army attack on Party headquarters only a few days before Thakin Than Tun's death. Thus, the Chinese were completely left out of the CPB decision on Thakin Than Tun's successor, the first major decision to be made without direct Chinese advice in twenty years. Apparently, to this day, the Chinese bear a grudge against the surviving CPB leadership for its choice of Thakin Zin, rather than Peking's most trusted protégé, Overseas CPB leader Thakin Ba Thein Tin, as the new Party Chairman. Indeed, this has been a major factor in the Chinese decision to shift its interest and attention away from the Thakin Zin-led CPB effort in central Burma to sponsorship of a new insurgency in northeast Burma.

The irony of the CCP–CPB estrangement at this time was that it happened soon after a reversal in Chinese state policy toward Rangoon which should have been helpful to the CPB. That reversal, which discarded a long-held policy of support for the Burmese Government in favour of a new policy of all-out opposition to it, had come as a direct result of anti-Chinese riots in Rangoon in June 1967. It was Cultural Revolution enthusiasm on the part of Chinese embassy officers in Rangoon which had been primarily responsible for starting the chain of events that led to the riots. However, Peking would admit no fault on its part. The GUB's inadequate handling of the riot situation had given the Chinese some legitimate cause for anger, but Peking clearly over-reacted in accusing the GUB of "instigating" the riots, a charge which had no basis in fact and was guaranteed to infuriate the Burmese. The crisis culminated in Peking's making certain demands of the GUB. While Peking felt these to be legitimate demands considering the enormity of the injury as Peking saw it (the death of many Chinese residents of Rangoon), the Burmese considered the demands humiliating. Since 1967, Ne Win has yielded to the Chinese on some of the demands but has stubbornly refused to meet them all.

The direct relationship between the blow-up in state relations and the start of active Chinese support of insurgency was unmistakable: within a matter of days of the June riots, Peking mounted a full-blown campaign of anti-Rangoon vilification; within a few weeks, it began to supply Kachin and Shan ethnic minority insurgents in northeast Burma with arms and ammunition, specialized guerrilla warfare training in China, and even new recruits from among similar ethnic minority groups living on the Chinese side of the border. There is probably no better example of the opportunism of Chinese foreign policy than Peking's sudden willingness to support these ethnic minority insurgents – most of whom were openly anti-Communist – simply because of the new bond between them in their common opposition to the Ne Win government. Unfortunately for the Communists, Peking was not in a position to do much, if anything, to help the CPB insurgents, isolated as they were in the Pegu Mountains of central Burma, far from the border with China. Thus, for significant logistical reasons as well as with a mind to creating an operation under Burmese leaders of its own choosing, Peking embarked on a new undertaking, the building of a totally new Communist insurgency in northeast Burma – with little or no contact, and very little in common, with the old CPB effort.

In the intervening four years, the old indigenous insurgency has declined, the new one has prospered. Chinese support of the latter has grown to include supplies of food, medicines, and extra funds (in Burmese currency), as well as arms and ammunition, uniforms and other clothing, and propaganda materials. The type as well as the number of weapons has expanded: as of May 1971, Chinese supplies included B-40 rocket launchers, mortars, light machine guns, and a few heavy machine guns. At the same time, the Chinese have expanded their training of Burmese insurgents at a large guerrilla warfare school run by the Chinese army in Yunnan. During the past year, they have built a powerful radio broadcasting facility at the training site, which began broadcasting clandestine propaganda support for the Burmese insurgency in March 1971. They have also stepped up their recruiting of ethnic minority peoples living on the Chinese side of the border, a practice which they have not followed in supporting insurgencies in Laos and Thailand. Recent firm information also confirms another unique aspect of the Chinese covert aid program: the presence of Chinese military advisers attached directly to insurgent headquarters. It appears that some of the advisers, operating temporarily with certain units, have accompanied insurgents into battle.

Peking has gradually centred its support on one insurgent commander, Naw Seng, a Burmese Kachin leader who lived more than 17 years in China. In early 1968, the Chinese repatriated Naw Seng to Burma as the leader of an insurgent force of some 900–1,200 ethnic Shans and Kachins recruited from both sides of the border and trained in China. In order to give his movement Communist credentials, the Chinese simply co-opted Naw Seng into the CPB, first as a member of the Central Committee, and then as a member of the Politburo. In the same way that Chinese propaganda has attempted to condition observers to think of him as a CPB leader, it has created the illusion of his Northeast Command as being a "Burmese Communist" insurgency. In fact, what the Chinese have done has been to take an essentially ethnic minority rebellion composed largely of persons who have never belonged to the CPB, to force-feed it with Chinese Communist doctrine, and to label it as the Burmese Communist movement. This rebellion has little in common with the long-established CPB insurgency in central Burma, which is and always has been ethnically Burman and entirely Communist, and whose present leaders do not even recognize Naw Seng as a Communist. The new Chinese-backed insurgency, despite its ostensible Burmese character, has all the trappings of Chinese sponsorship, including Mao badges, Chinese propaganda materials and Chinese army manuals.

So long as the insurgency is confined to a remote area, composed almost exclusively of ethnic minority peoples, with virtually no appeal in Burma proper, it hardly constitutes a serious threat to the survival of the Rangoon government. The GUB would seem to be easily able to contain the insurgency at existing levels – though not to root it out of upper Burma. This being so, the GUB still considers it the most serious internal security problem facing the government. Despite Ne Win's long hesitance to discuss the matter of Chinese involvement, for fear of further damaging Sino-Burmese relations, he was finally forced to admit the seriousness of the fighting between Naw Seng's forces and the Burmese army in late 1969. His hopes of bringing sufficient pressure to bear on the Chinese to get them to halt their support of the insurgents were clearly misplaced, however, as Chinese aid and the insurgency were both stepped up thereafter.

China's continuing support of the insurgency has clearly been the main motivating force behind Ne Win's efforts since early 1970 to improve relations with Peking. Largely at Burmese initiative, but with obvious Chinese encouragement, there has been a definite improvement in diplomatic relations since the fall of 1970, culminating in the recent exchange of ambassadors. As might be expected, this change has brought certain changes as well in Chinese policy towards the Naw Seng operation. For one thing, the Chinese appear to have taken steps to tone down insurgent operations during the recent dry season (October 1970–May 1971) when secret negotiations concerning the restoration of ambassadors were underway. Also, the Chinese have sharply cut back their previous overt propaganda support of the insurgency. At the same time, however, they have taken actions that would seem to be aimed at strengthening the insurgency as a long-term threat to Burma, albeit one less blatantly identified with China. For instance, Chinese logistical support for the rebels has been maintained at an all-time high since the exchange of ambassadors this past winter, and the Chinese have recently inaugurated the powerful new clandestine radio facility in Yunnan which broadcasts vitriolic anti-Rangoon statements in support of the Burmese insurgents. Thus, there would seem to have been a shift towards making the insurgency less of an overt Chinese challenge to the Burmese government, but no overall reduction in the scope of Chinese covert support to the insurgents.

At the moment, the Chinese seem to be following a "two-pronged" policy towards Burma of improving state relations while, at the same time, maintaining an insurgency lever over the GUB to force concessions favourable to Peking. While they now avoid overt insults and attacks on the GUB and make obvious goodwill gestures, such as their recent extension of an invitation to Ne Win to visit Peking, they continue covertly to provide considerable military support to the insurrection.

It is difficult to judge how far Ne Win might be prepared to go to get the Chinese to stop supporting the insurgents. Certainly further concessions on his part cannot be ruled out, although it seems unlikely that he will ever give in to Mao to the point of publicly assuming all the blame for the events of June 1967 – one of the demands that Peking is still insisting upon. In the absence of Ne Win concessions on this and other points, it is unlikely that the Chinese will consider giving up their support of the insurgency.

In the long run, that is, after Ne Win and/or Mao, the chances for a significant improvement in relations are somewhat better. There is little reason to believe that a successor military regime in Burma would be much more inclined than Ne Win to make major concessions to the Chinese, but the chances of the GUB's making such concessions would be greatly increased in the less likely event of a civilian successor government. For its part, the new Chinese leadership, after Mao's death, might be more willing to work out some compromise with the Burmese government, especially if broader foreign policy benefits might accrue to China at the time. In such a case, the Chinese might well be inclined to back away from their previously-sponsored clients and allow the insurgency to wither away. But even then, as now, there would be powerful forces operating in favour of Peking's continuing support of the Burmese insurgency: the existence of various benefits in the insurrection for China, plus the momentum and commitments of policy and pride.

About the Authors

Hongwei Fan

Hongwei Fan is Associate Professor at Research School of Southeast Asian Studies (Nanyang Yanjiu Yuan), Xiamen University, China. He obtained his Ph.D. in History from the Research School of Southeast Asian Studies, Xiamen University. In 2008, he was the postdoctoral fellow in the School of Foreign Service, Georgetown University. He has taught history and international relations in Xiamen University and is also the Editor of *Journal of Southeast Asian Affairs*. Over one decade, he has contributed more than thirty articles in Chinese, English, and Japanese to journals, edited volumes, and newspapers. His research interests and focus cover Burma/Myanmar issues, overseas Chinese in Southeast Asia, and China–Southeast Asia relations. He has been the director of the research projects of the Sumitomo Foundation, and China's Ministry of Education.

David I. Steinberg

David I. Steinberg, Distinguished Professor of Asian Studies, School of Foreign Service, Georgetown University, was previously Director of that Program (1997-2007); Adjunct Professor at SAIS, Johns Hopkins University; Representative of The Asia Foundation in Korea; Distinguished Professor of Korea Studies, Georgetown University; and formerly President of the Mansfield Center for Pacific Affairs. Earlier, as a member of the Senior Foreign Service, Agency for International Development [USAID], Department of State, he was Director for Technical Assistance for Asia and the Middle East; Director for Philippines, Thailand, and Burma Affairs; and spent three years in Thailand with the Regional Development Office. He wrote extensively reviewing and evaluating previous AID programs while in AID's Center for Development Information and Evaluation. Before joining AID, he was Representative of The Asia Foundation in Korea and Washington, D.C., and Assistant Representative in Burma and Hong Kong. He has resided for seventeen years in Asia, where he has conducted field studies and traveled widely. Professor Steinberg is the author of thirteen books and monographs including one translation, and over one hundred chapters/articles. Among these books and monographs are: *Burma/Myanmar: What Everyone Needs to Know* (2010); *Turmoil in Burma: Contested Legitimacies in Myanmar* (2006); *Stone Mirror: Reflections on Contemporary Korea* (2002); *Burma: The State of Myanmar* (2001), *The Future of Burma: Crisis and Choice in Myanmar* (1990); *The Republic of Korea. Economic Transformation and Social Change* (1989); *Crisis in Burma: Stasis and Change in a Political Economy in Turmoil* (1989). David I. Steinberg was educated at Dartmouth College; Lingnan University (Canton, China); Harvard University, where he studied Chinese; and the School of Oriental and African Studies, University of London, where he studied Burmese and Southeast Asia.

Bibliography

Official Documents and Reports

Chinese-Language Sources

(Note: AMFA = Archive of Ministry of Foreign Affairs, People's Republic of China)

Bureau of Archives, Ministry of Foreign Affairs, PRC (ed.), *Zhonghua Renmin Gongheguo waijiao dangan xuanbian: 1954 Rineiwa huiyi* [Selected diplomatic documents of the PRC: Geneva conference 1954], Vol. 1, Beijing: World Knowledge Press, 2006.

"Chen Yi fu zongli xiang Miandian zhuhua dashi jiaowen jieshao Zhou Enlai zongli fangmian qingkuang" [Vice Premier Chen Yi informed Burmese Ambassador to China of Premier Zhou Enlai's trip to Burma], AMFA, No. 106-01144-02.

Chinese Central Archives (ed.), *Zhonggong zhongyang wenjian xuanji* [Selected documents of the CCP Central Committee], 1948, Vol. 17, Beijing: Party School of the Central Committee of the Communist Party of China Press, 1992.

"Dangqian Miandian huaqiao chujing he cunzai wenti" [Current situation and problems of Burmese Overseas Chinese], AMFA, No. 105-01662-05.

"Dangqian woguo nengyuan xingshi yu nengyuan anquan wenti: zai shijie quanguo renda changwei hui di shijiu ci huiyi shang Zeng Peiyan fu zongli baogao" [Current situations of energy and energy security issues in China: Report by Vice-Premier Zeng Peiyan at the 19th session of the 10th NPC Standing Committee], *Zhongguo Shiyou He Huagong Biaozhun Yu Zhiliang* [China Petroleum and Chemical Standard and Quality], No. 4, 2006.

"Deng Xiaoping fu zongli de jianghua" [Speech of Vice Premier Deng Xiaoping], *Xinhuashe Xinwen Gao* [Press release, Xinhua News Agency], 12 November 1975.

Deng Xiaoping wenxuan [Selected works of Deng Xiaoping], Vol. 3, Beijing: People's Press, 1993.

"Guanyu dui Miandian jiaqiang gongzuo wenti" [More efforts to pull Burma into China's orbit], AMFA, No. 105-01865-01.

"Guanyu Miandian huaqiao guoji wenti de qingshi ji buchong yijian" [Instructions and additional comments on the nationality problems facing Overseas Chinese in Burma], AMFA, No. 105-00510-03(1).

"Guanyu wenhua dageming de xuanchuan jiaoyu yaodian" [Instruction outline for disseminating information related to the Cultural Revolution], *Xinhua Yuebao* [Xinhua Monthly], No. 6, 1966.

"Guanyu wo dui Miandian zhengfu de suowei shehui zhuyi daolu gangling de biaotai wenti" [The problem of clarifying our position on the Burmese Way to Socialism], AMFA, No. 105-01816-01.

"Guanyu wo fabiao miangong zhi wo guoqing hexin wenti [The problem caused by the publication of BCP congratulatory letter], AMFA, No. 105-01600-04.

"Guanyu Yunnan Sheng 2007 nian guomin jingji he shehui fazhan jihua zhixing qing-kuang yu 2008 nian guomin jingji he shehui fazhan jihua caoan de baogao" [Draft resolution on the implementation of the Yunnan National Economic and Social Development Plan for 2007 and the National Economic and Social Development Plan for 2008], *Yunnan Zhengbao* [Yunnan Political Affairs], No. 6, 2008.

"Guanyu Zhongguo Miandian jianli waijiao guanxi de sici tanhua jilu" [Records from four discussions about the establishment of China–Burma relations], AMFA, No. 105-00001-02(1).

"Guanyu Zhou Enlai zongli fangmian de jiaoshe qingkuang" [Negotiations of Premier Zhou Enlai's visit to Burma], AMFA, No. 203-00582-04.

"Guanyu Zhou Enlai zongli fangmian de waijiao tongbao" [Diplomatic bulletin of Premier Zhou Enlai's visit to Burma], AMFA, No. 203-00583-04.

"Guobin jiedai qingkuang" (Wu Nu de yixie qingkuang he fanying) [Reception to state guests (some of U Nu's responses)], AMFA, No. 204-00119-17(1).

"He Long fu zongli fang Yinni luguo Miandian baihui Nai Wen zhuxi" [Vice Premier He Long met Chairman Ne Win in Burma en route to Indonesia], AMFA, No. 105-01819-01.

"Jiang Jieshi jituan canbu zai Zhongguo Miandian bianjing diqu huodong ji yu mian-fang jiaoshe qingkuang" [Operations by remnants of Chiang Kai-shek's troops in Burma–China border areas and the negotiations with Burma], AMFA, No. 105-00604-02(1).

Jianguo yilai Liu Shaoqi wengao [Works of Liu Shaoqi since the establishment of the PRC], Vol. 1, Beijing: Central Party Literature Press, 2005.

Jianguo yilai Mao Zedong junshi wengao [Military works of Mao Tsetung since the es-tablishment of the PRC] (January 1959–February 1976), Vol. 3, Beijing: Military Science Press, Central Party Literature Press, 2010.

Jianguo yilai Mao Zedong wengao [Works of Mao Tsetung since the establishment of the PRC], Vol. 1, Beijing: Central Party Literature Press, 1987.

———, Vol. 12, Beijing: Central Party Literature Press, 1998.

———, Vol. 13, Beijing: Central Party Literature Press, 1998.

Jianguo yilai Zhou Enlai wengao [Works of Zhou Enlai since the establishment of the PRC], Vol. 1, Beijing: Central Party Literature Press, 2008.

"Jiu shifou chengren Miandian junren zhengfu deng wenti yu zhumian shiguan laiwang dian" [Telegrams between Beijing and the Chinese embassy to Burma regarding Chinese recognition of the Burmese military government], AMFA, No. 117-01344-04.

"Kuitao Miandian de Jiang Jieshi jundui qingkuang he mianfang de taidu" [Situation of Chiang Kai-shek's troops fleeing to Burma and Burmese attitude], AMFA, No. 105-00605-02.

Liao Zhengbao (ed.), *Jiemi waijiao wenxian: Zhonghua Renmin Gongheguo jianjiao dangan* [Declassified diplomatic documents: Archives on establishment of diplomatic relations by the PRC], Beijing: China Pictorial Press, 2006.

"Lifayuan di 12 huiqi shizheng baogao" [Command paper of the 12th session of the Legislature], Archives of Academia Historica (Taiwan), Cat. No. 069, Roll No. 150, File No. 11-4-3, 22 December 1953.

"Lingshisi qingkuang fanying: Nai Wen shixing 'guoyouhua' zhong de huaqiao chujing" [Information of the Department of Consular Affairs: Overseas Chinese in the situation of Ne Win's nationalization], AMFA, No. 118-01328-01.

"Liu Shaoqi zhuxi shenyue guo de yu Miandian lingdao ren de tanhua jilu yuangao" [Record of talks between Liu Shaoqi and Burmese leaders, checked and approved by Liu Shaoqi], AMFA, No. 203-00576-01.

Mao Zedong xuanji [Selected works of Mao Tsetung], Vol. 4, Beijing: People's Press, 1991.

Mao Zedong wenji [Works of Mao Tsetung], Vol. 6, Beijing: People's Press, 1999.

"Mao Zedong zhuxi jiejian Miandian fu zongli Wu Barui Wu Jueying tanhua jilu" [Record of Chairman Mao Tsetung's talk with visiting Burmese Vice Prime Ministers, U Ba Swe and U Kyaw Nyein], AMFA, No. 105-00339-01(1).

"Miandian daogu jianchan qingkuang he caizheng jingji cuoshi" [Reduction of Burmese rice production, and fiscal and economic measures], AMFA, No. 105-01303-04.

"Miandian duiwai guanxi" [Burmese foreign relations], AMFA, No. 105-01157-03.

"Miandian gejie dui Zhou Enlai zongli fangwen Miandian de fanying" [Popular reactions to Premier Zhou Enlai's visit to Burma], AMFA, No. 105-00512-08(1).

"Miandian guonei wai xingshi dongxiang he zhongmian guanxi" [Burmese domestic situation and foreign relations, and Sino-Burmese relations], AMFA, No. 203-00515-03.

"Miandian shehui zhuyi gangling dang zong shuji Shan You jiangjun zai disan ci dangdaihui shang zuo de dangzhongyang weiyuanhui de zhengzhi baogao" [Political report of the Burma Socialist Program Party presented to the BSPP Central Committee by General U San Yu, General Secretary of the Burma Socialist Program Party, at the 3rd Party Congress], *Dongnanya Ziliao* [Information about Southeast Asia], No. 46, 1980.

"Miandian shiguan 1961 nian gongzuo zongjie liuer nian gongzuo guihua he youguan zhuguan bumen de pifu" [1961 work review and 1962 work program of the Chinese Embassy to Burma and the official reply of the responsible department], AMFA, No. 105-01079-01.

"Miandian shixing yinhang guoyouhua he wo fangqi Zhongguo yinhang, jiaotong yinhang yangguang fenhang de zichan shi (zhong, ying wen)" [Nationalization of Burmese banks and China abandons the assets of China Bank and Bank of Communications (Chinese and English Version)], AMFA, No. 105-01822-01.

"Miandian waizhang duiwo zhumian dashi zai dangdi huaqiao qunzhong dahui shang jianghua de kanfa ji wofang de chuli yijian" [Burmese Foreign Minister's opinion on Chinese Ambassador's remarks at local Overseas Chinese gathering and China's response to it], AMFA, No. 105-00067-02(1).

"Miandian zeng wo bianmin dami he shiyan ji wofang huizeng lipin shi" [Burmese gifts of rice and salt to Chinese border inhabitants and reciprocal gifts], AMFA, No. 105-00680-01(1).

"Miandian zhengfu guanyuan ji baokan dui Zhou Enlai zongli fangmian de fanying" [Responses by Burmese officials and media to Premier Zhou Enlai's visit to Burma], AMFA, No. 105-00259-03(1).

"Miandian zhengfu zai bianjing diqu zuzhi qingzhu zhongmian youhao tiaoyue he bianjie wenti xieding gongbu de huodong" [Burmese government holds celebrations for signing of the friendship treaty and settlement of the boundary agreement for border areas], AMFA, No. 105-00681-02(1).

"Miandian zhengjie yaoren Wu Nu yanlun zhaiyao (1955 nian shiyue shisan ri shangwu shishi ban)" [Abstract of Burmese statesman U Nu's speech (10.a.m., 13 October 1955)], AMFA, No. 105-00446-04.

"Miandian zhengju dongxiang" [Trends in the Burmese political situation], AMFA, File No. 105-01227-01.

"Miandian zhuhua shiguan shangqing waijiaobu xiezhu qi zai yunnan ribao shang fabiao guanyu Deqinlun lunwen zhong 'bu zhengque' chu de shuoming" [Burmese Embassy in China requests the Ministry of Foreign Affairs of the PRC to assist them in publishing a clarification in the *Yunnan Daily* with regard to the 'incorrect message' in Thakin Lwin's essay], AMFA, No. 105-00078-01(1).

"Miandian zhuhua shiguan yimi fouren meiguo zaimian jianli junshi jidi" [First Secretary of Burma's Embassy in China denies the establishment of US military bases in Burma], AMFA, No. 105-00174-02(1).

"Miandian ziliao: Miandian qingkuang jianjie gaikuang zhongmian guanxi cunzai wenti jianshu zhongmian guanxi dashiji" [Burmese materials: Introduction and general situation of Burma, the problems of Sino-Burmese ties, and Sino-Burmese chronicles of events], AMFA, No. 203-00473-02.

"Miandian zongli Wu Nu jiu mianbao waiqu baodao zhongmian lianhe shengming shi zhi Zhou Enlai zongli han" [Burmese Prime Minister U Nu's letter to Premier Zhou Enlai on the distorted coverage by Burma's press of the China–Burma joint statement], AMFA, No. 105-00037-01(1).

"Miandian zongli Wu Nu jiu zhongmian dami maoyi wenti zhi Zhou Enlai zongli han" [Burmese Prime Minister U Nu's letter to Premier Zhou Enlai about the China–Burma rice trade], AMFA, No. 105-00036-01(1).

"Miandian zongli Wu Nu zai guohui shang de jianghua (zhai yao)" [Abstract of Burmese Prime Minister U Nu's speech in parliament], AMFA, No. 105-00814-01(1).

"Miangong tong Miandian zhengfu hetan qingkuang" [Peace talks between the BCP and Burmese government], AMFA, No. 203-00515-02.

Ministry of Foreign Affairs, PRC (ed.), *Zhonghua Renmin Gongheguo tiaoyue ji* [Collection of treaties of the People's Republic of China], 1971, Vol. 18, Beijing: People's Press, 1973.

———, 1979, Vol. 26, Beijing: People's Press, 1983.

———, 1997, Vol. 44, Beijing: World Affairs Press, 1999.

———, 2001, Vol. 48, Beijing: World Affairs Press, 2003.

Shen Zhihua and Yang Kuisong (eds), *Meiguo Duihua qingbao jiemi dangan* [Declassified record of U.S. intelligence on China] 1948–1976, Vol. V and VI, Beijing: Oriental Press, 2009.

"Shijie geguo dui Miandian junren zhengbian de fanying yiji dui junren xin zhengfu de chengren qingkuang" [Responses of other countries to recognition of the Burmese military coup as well as their official acceptance of the new military government], AMFA, No. 105-01077-04.

"Waijiaobu dui Miandian shiguan 1963 nian Miandian zhengzhi xingshi zongjie he 1964 nian gongzuo guihua de pifu" [Foreign Ministry's reply to the Chinese Embassy to Burma on the 1963 Burmese politics summary and the 1964 work program], AMFA, No. 105-01864-01.

"Waijiaobu yazhou si bianxie de guanyu Miandian huaqiao shuangchong guoji wenti de ziliao" [Files on dual nationality of Overseas Chinese in Burma compiled by the Asian Affairs Department of the Ministry of Foreign Affairs], AMFA, No. 105-00510-10(1).

"Waijiaobu yi ya guanyu Miandian zhengju he waijiao dongxiang deng de diaoyan cailiao" [Materials for investigation and research on Burmese domestic politics and foreign affairs conducted by the First Asian Department of the Foreign Ministry], AMFA, No. 105-01314-02.

Wang Huongju, "2008 nian Chongqing Shi renmin zhengfu gongzuo baogao" [Report on the work of Chonqing Government 2008], *Chongqing Shi Renmin Zhengfu Gongbao* [Gazette of Chongqing Municipal People's Government], No. 3, 2008.

"Wo dui Miandian junren zhengfu de chengren wenti (zhongwen yingwen)" [Recognition of the Burmese military regime (Chinese and English version)], AMFA, No. 105-01780-01.

"Wo xiang mianfang jianyi tanpan zhongmian gonglu lianyun wenti" [China suggests negotiations with Burma about highway transportation between the two countries], AMFA, No. 105-00177-01(1).

"Wo yu Miandian zhuhua shiguan lianxi miangong lingdao huimian shi" [Contact between the Foreign Ministry and Burmese Embassy to China for return of BCP leaders to Burma], AMFA, No. 105-01818-01.

"Wo zhu Miandian shiguan fu mian waijiaobu guanyu waijiao zhengce shengming de zhaohui" [Chinese Embassy reply to note from the Burmese Foreign Ministry about the Burmese foreign policy statement], AMFA, No. 105-01780-02.

"Wu Nai wen zongtong de jianghua" [Speech of President Ne Win], Xinhuashe Xinwen Gao [Press release, Xinhua News Agency], 12 November 1975.

"Wu Nu zongli zai huanying dahui shang de jianghua" [Prime Minister U Nu's speech at welcoming reception], *Xinhua Yuebao* [Xinhua Monthly], No. 1, 1955.

"Wu Nu zongli zai linbie yanhui shang de jianghua" [Prime Minister U Nu's speech at farewell banquet], *Xinhua Yuebao* [Xinhua Monthly], No. 1, 1955.

"Wu Nu zongli zai yanhui shang de jianghua" [Prime Minister U Nu's banquet speech], *Xinhua Yuebao* [Xinhua Monthly], No. 1, 1955.

"Yijiu liuer nian Miandian sanyue junren zhengbian jingguo" [Course of the Burmese military coup in March 1962], AMFA, No. 105-01077-01.

"Yijiu liuwu nian wo goumai 10 wan dun Miandian dami" [Purchasing of 100,000 tons of Burmese rice in 1965], AMFA, No. 105-01604-01.

"Youguan Zhongguo Miandian jianjiao laiwang zhaohui" [Notes on the establishment of China–Burma diplomatic relations], AMFA, No. 105-00001-01(1).

"Yunnan fangong jiuguo jun you mian huiguo an" [Return of the Yunnan Anticommunist National Salvation Army to Taiwan], Archive of Political and History Department, Defense Ministry (Taiwan), File No: 542.5/1073, June 1953–February 1954.

"Yunnan Sheng guanyu Zhongguo Miandian bianmin lianhuan de zongjie baogao" [Yunnan Province's final report on Chinese and Burmese inhabitants gathering in the border areas], AMFA, No. 105-00512-04(1).

"Yunnan Sheng xin sannian xing bian fu min gongcheng xingdong jihua" [New three-year plan for 'Prosper the borders to enrich local people' in Yunnan], *Yunnan Zhengbao* [Yunnan Political Affairs], No. 11, 2008.

"Zhang Hanfu waizhang yu Miandian zhuhua dashi wu lamao tanhua jiyao (1955 nian shiyue shisan ri shangwu shishi ban)" [Speech notes for Foreign Minister Zhang Hanfu and Burmese Ambassador to China U Hla Maung (10:30 a.m. on 13 October 1955)], AMFA, No. 105-00175-03(1).

"Zhongguo fangmian zai bianjing diqu zuzhi qingzhu Zhongguo Miandian qianding youhao tiaoyue he bianjie wenti xieding de huodong" [China holds celebrations for signing of the friendship treaty and settlement of the boundary agreement for border areas], AMFA, No. 105-00681-01(1).

"Zhongguo fojiao xiehui foya husong tuan baogao" [Report of the Chinese Buddhist Association on transport of the Buddha's tooth relic], AMFA, No. 105-00182-10(1).

"Zhongguo Miandian bianjing bianmin waitao qingkuang de baogao" [Reports on the flight of inhabitants in Sino-Burmese border areas], AMFA, No. 105-00604-01.

"Zhongguo Miandian bianjing shuangfang jundui fasheng qiangji shi mianfang zhi wo zhaohui" [Burmese note to China relating to talks on the shooting incident in Sino-Burmese border areas], AMFA, No. 105-00745-01(1).

"Zhongguo zhu Miandian shiguan guanyu shinian lai zhongmian jingji maoyi guanxi de zongjie" [Review by Chinese Embassy to Burma of Sino-Burmese economic ties in the past decade], AMFA, No. 105-00603-01.

"Zhongguo zhu Miandian shiguan guanyu shinian lai zhongmian wenhua guanxi de zongjie" [Review by Chinese Embassy to Burma of Sino-Burmese cultural ties in the past decade], AMFA, No. 105-00603-02(1).

Zhonghua Renmin Gongheguo duiwai guanxi wenjian ji [Documents on PRC foreign relations: 1949–1950], Beijing: World Knowledge Press, Vol. 1, 1957.

Zhonghua Renmin Gongheguo guomin jingji he shehui fazhan di shiyi ge wunian guihua [Eleventh five-year plan for national, economic and social development of the People's Republic of China], Beijing: People's Press, 2006.

"Zhongmian liangguo zongli huitan gongbao" [Communiqué of the premiers of China and Burma], *Xinhua Yuebao* [Xinhua Monthly], No. 1, 1955.

"Zhongmian liangguo zongli lianhe shengming" [Joint statement of the premiers of China and Burma], *Xinhua Yuebao* [Xinhua Monthly], No. 7, 1954.

Zhou Enlai waijiao wenxuan [Selected diplomatic writings of Zhou Enlai], Beijing: Central Party Literature Press, 1990.

"Zhou Enlai zongli baihui Miandian zong canmouzhang Nai Wen tanhua jilu" [Account of the discussion between Premier Zhou Enlai and Ne Win, Chief of the General Staff of Burma], AMFA, No. 203-00036-01(1).

"Zhou Enlai zongli fangmian huitan fangan" [Schedule for Premier Zhou Enlai's visit to Burma], AMFA, No. 203-00582-01.

"Zhou Enlai zongli fangmian tong Nai Wen zhuxi huitan jiyao" [Summary of discussion between Premier Zhou Enlai and Chairman Ne Win], AMFA, No. 203-00583-05.

"Zhou Enlai zongli fangwen Miandian de lici jianghua gao (zhongwen, yingwen, mianwen)" [All the manuscripts from Premier Zhou Enlai's talks in Burma (Chinese, English, and Burmese)], AMFA, No. 203-00085-01(1).

"Zhou Enlai zongli fangwen Miandian huitan ji huijian qingkuang zhaiyao" [Brief account of talks and meetings during Premier Zhou Enlai's visit to Burma], AMFA, No. 203-00036-07(1).

"Zhou Enlai zongli fangwen Miandian huitan qingkuang de waijiao tongbao" [Bulletin regarding the conditions of Premier Zhou Enlai's discussions in Burma], AMFA, No. 203-00036-08(1).

"Zhou Enlai zongli fangwen Miandian qingkuang huibao" [Debriefing after visit to Burma by Zhou Enlai], AMFA, No. 203-00047-05.

"Zhou Enlai zongli fangwen Miandian tong mianfang lingdao ren tanhua yaodian" [Main points of talks between Premier Zhou Enlai and leading figures in Burma], AMFA, No. 203-00019-02(1).

"Zhou Enlai zongli huijian Miandian qian zongli Wu Barui huitan jilu" [Account of discussion between Premier Zhou Enlai and former Burmese Prime Minister U Ba Swe], AMFA, No. 203-00036-04(1).

"Zhou Enlai zongli huijian Miandian zhuhua dashi Wu Lamao tanhua jiyao (1956 nian sanyue qiri)" [Summary of discussion between Premier Zhou Enlai and Burmese Ambassador to China U Hla Maung (7 March 1956)], AMFA, No. 105-00307-01(1).

"Zhou Enlai zongli huijian Miandian zhuhua dashi Wu Lamao tanhua jiyao (1956 nian liuyue ershier ri)" [Summary of discussion between Premier Zhou Enlai and Burmese Ambassador to China U Hla Maung (22 June 1956)], AMFA, No. 105-00307-02(1).

"Zhou Enlai zongli huijian Miandian zhuhua dashi Wu Lamao tanhua jiyao (1956 nian bayue ershiwu ri)" [Summary of discussion between Premier Zhou Enlai and Burmese Ambassador to China U Hla Maung (25 August 1956)], AMFA, No. 105-00307-03(1).

"Zhou Enlai zongli jiejian Miandian daibiaotuan tanhua jilu" [Account of Premier Zhou Enlai's meeting with a Burmese delegation], AMFA, No. 105-00130-01(1).

"Zhou Enlai zongli jiejian Miandian zhengfu laodong kaochatuan tanhua jilu" [Account of Premier Zhou Enlai's meeting with a Burmese governmental labour delegation], AMFA, No. 105-00110-01(1).

"Zhou Enlai zongli tong Miandian fu zongli Wu Jueying huitan jilu" [Record of talks between Premier Zhou Enlai and Vice Prime Minister U Kyaw Nyein], AMFA, No. 105-00339-02(1).

"Zhou Enlai zongli yu Miandian zhuhua dashi Wu Lamao liangci tanhua de yaodian" [Main points of two conversations between Premier Zhou Enlai and Burmese Ambassador to China U Hla Maung], AMFA, No. 105-00752-02(1).

"Zhou Enlai zongli yu Miandian zhuhua dashi Wu Lamao tan guonei jushi wenti (zhai-yao)" [Abstract of talks between Premier Zhou Enlai and Burmese Ambassador to China U Hla Maung on Burmese domestic situation], AMFA, No. 105-00858-01.

"Zhou Enlai zongli zai kunming sheyan zhaodai Wu Nu zongli" [Premier Zhou Enlai hosts Prime Minister U Nu in Kunming], *Xinhua Banyue Kan* [Xinhua Semi-Monthly], No. 9, 1957.

"Zhou Enlai zongli zai linbie yanhui shang de jianghua" [Premier Zhou Enlai's speech at farewell banquet], *Xinhua Yuebao* [Xinhua Monthly], No. 1, 1955.

"Zhou Enlai zongli zai Miandian Yangguang huaqiao huanying dahui de jianghua" [Speech of Premier Zhou Enlai at the welcoming ceremony by Overseas Chinese in Rangoon, Burma], AMFA, No. 105-00510-08(1).

"Zhou Enlai zongli zai zhaodai Wu Nu zongli de yanhui shang de jianghua" [Premier Zhou Enlai's speech at the banquet for Prime Minister U Nu], *Xinhua Yuebao* [Xinhua Monthly], No. 1, 1955.

"Zhu Miandian shiguan dui Miandian zhengju de kanfa" [Assessment by the Chinese Embassy to Burma of the Burmese political situation], AMFA, No. 105-01225-01.

"Zhu Miandian shiguan dui waijiaobu gongzuo yijian" [Recommendations from the Chinese Embassy to Burma to the Ministry of Foreign Affairs], AMFA, No. 105-01816-02.

"Zhu Miandian shiguan guanyu mian yuanyi dui huaqiao huiguo tigong bianli de baogao ji zhong qiaowei, waijiaobu de fudian" [Reports of the Chinese Embassy to Burma on Burmese assistance for the return to China of Overseas Chinese, as well as replies from the Central Committee of the Overseas Chinese and the Foreign Ministry], AMFA, No. 118-01322-01.

"Zhu Miandian shiguan guanyu Miandian zhengju he duiwai guanxi de diaoyan cailiao" [Materials for investigation and research on Burmese domestic politics and foreign affairs conducted by the Chinese Embassy to Burma], AMFA, No. 105-00314-01.

"Zhu Miandian shiguan guanyu Nai Wen tuixing guoyouhua jingji zhengce deng wen-ti de qingkuang baogao" [Situation report by Chinese Embassy to Burma on Ne Win's economic nationalization], AMFA, No. 118-01251-03.

"Zhu Miandian shiguan guoqing qingzhou gongzuo zongjie" [Review of the National Day celebration from the Chinese Embassy to Burma], AMFA, No. 117-00038-02(1).

"Zong, fen hang guanyu qiaohui (jiefu, liangfu shangpin lianyun deng) wenti de tong-zhi, qingshi, pifu" [Notice, queries and replies to the General Bank as well as to branch banks with regard to overseas remittances], Documentation in the Archives of Fujian Province, Roll No. 230, Cat No. 3, File No. 806, 1963.

English-Language Sources

"Address delivered by General Ne Win, Chairman of the Burma Socialist Programme Party, at the Opening Session of the Fourth Party Seminar on 6th November 1969", Rangoon: Ministry of Information, Burma, 1969.

British Documents of Foreign Affairs: Reports and Papers from the Foreign Office Confidential Print, Part IV from 1946 through 1950, Series E Asia 1948, Vol. 7, Bethesda: University Publications of America, 2001.

————, 1949, Vol. 9, Bethesda: University Publications of America, 2003.

————, 1950, Vol. 11, Bethesda: University Publications of America, 2003.

Burma 1983 Population Census. Rangoon: Immigration and Manpower Department, Ministry of Home and Religious Affairs, 1986.

Keesing's Contemporary Archives, London: Keesing's Publications Limited, 28 March–4 April 1953.

"Minutes of Conversation between I.V. Stalin and Zhou Enlai", APRF, f. 45, op. 1, d. 329, ll. 75–87.

"Overseas Chinese Business Networks in Asia", East Asia Analytical Unit, Australian Department of Foreign Affairs and Trade, 1995.

"Peking and the Burmese Communists: the Perils and Profits of Insurgency", CIA Intelligence Report, RSS No. 0052/71, July 1971.

Books, Theses and Reports

Chinese-Language Sources

Baoshan nianjian [Baoshan yearbook], Luxi: Dehong Ethnic Press, 2002.

Burmese Central Bureau of Statistics, *Miandian lianbang jihua caizheng bu tongji nian-jian, 1979–1989* [Statistical yearbook of the Ministry of Finance of the Union of Burma, 1979–1989], Kunming: Institute of International Studies, Yunnan, 1991.

CCCPC Party Literature Research Office (ed.), *Deng Xiaoping Nianpu: 1975–1997* [Chronicle of Deng Xiaoping: 1975–1997], Vol. 1, Beijing: Central Party Literature Press, 2004.

————, *Liu Shaoqi nianpu: 1898–1969* [Chronicle of Liu Shaoqi: 1898–1969] Vol. 2, Beijing: Central Party Literature Press, 1996.

————, *Mao Zedong zhuan: 1949–1976* [Biography of Mao Tsetung: 1949–1976], Vol. I, Beijing: Central Party Literature Press, 2003.

————, *Zhang Wentian nianpu: 1942–1976* [Chronicle of Zhang Wentian: 1942–1976], Vol. 2, Beijing: CCP History Press, 2000.

————, *Zhou Enlai nianpu* [Chronicle of Zhou Enlai: 1949–1976], Vol. 1, Beijing: Central Party Literature Press, 1997.

————, *Zhou Enlai nianpu* [Chronicle of Zhou Enlai: 1949–1976], Vol. 2, Beijing: Central Party Literature Press, 1997.

————, *Zhou Enlai zhuan: 1898–1976* [Biography of Zhou Enlai: 1898–1976], Vol. II, Beijing: Central Party Literature Press, 2008.

Chen Yangyong, *Zhou Enlai zai 1967* [Zhou Enlai in 1967], Chongqing: Chongqing Press, 2005.

Cheng Ruisheng, *Mulin waijiao sishi nian* [Forty years of good-neighborly diplomacy], Chengdu: Sichuan People's Press, 2006.

Cheng Xi, *Qiaowu yu waijiao guanxi yanjiu: Zhongguo fangqi "shuangchong guoji" de huigu yu fansi* [The relationship between Overseas Chinese and foreign relations: Review and reflection on China's abandonment of dual nationality], Beijing: The Overseas Chinese Publishing House of China, 2005.

China Export and Credit Insurance Corporation, *Guojia fengxian fenxi baogao (2007)* [Handbook of country risk assessment (2007)], Vol. I, Beijing: China Finance Press, 2007.

Chinese Academy of International Trade and Economic Cooperation of the Ministry of Commerce, PRC, Investment Promotion Agency of Ministry of Commerce, PRC, Economic and Commercial Counsellor's Office of the Embassy of the People's Republic of China (ed.), *Duiwai touzi hezuo guobie zhinan (Miandian)* [Guidelines for overseas investment and cooperation in other countries and regions (Myanmar)], 2009.

Current Account Management Department, State Administration of Foreign Exchange (ed.), *Huobi kuajing liutong ji bianjing maoyi waihui guanli wenti yanjiu* [Cross-border currency circulation and management of foreign exchange in border trade], Beijing: China Financial and Economic Publishing House, 2005.

Dangdai Zhongguo jundui de junshi gongzuo [Development of the military in contemporary China], Vol. 1, Beijing: China Social Science Press, 1989.

Dangdai Zhongguo waijiao [Contemporary Chinese diplomacy], Beijing: China Social Science Press, 1987.

Dier jie shijie mianhua tong qiao lianyi dahui jijin [Commemorative issue of the 2nd session of the World Myanmar Chinese Diaspora Association], Kunming: Association of Overseas Exchange of Yunnan Province, 2002.

Du Yi, *"Wenge" zhong de chen yi* [Chen Yi in the Cultural Revolution], Beijing: World Knowledge Press, 1997.

Fang Xiongpu, *Miandian huaren shehui lueying* [Glimpse of the Chinese community in Myanmar], Hong Kong: South Island Press, 2000.

Geguo huaren renkou zhuanji [A collection of materials pertaining to the Overseas Chinese population], No. 3, Taipei: Taiwan Overseas Compatriot Affairs Commission, 2009.

Geng Biao, *Geng Biao zhuan: 1949–1992* [Memoir of Geng Biao: 1949–1992], Nanjing: Jiangsu People's Press, 1998.

Huang Zheng, *Wang Guangmei fangtan lu* [Interview with Wang Guangmei], Beijing: Central Party Literature Press, 2006.

Huaqiao qingkuang jieshao [Introduction to the situation of Overseas Chinese], Office of Overseas Chinese Affairs Commission, Fujian Province, 1963.

Huaren jingji nianjian, 2000/2001 [Yearbook of the Huaren economy, 2000/2001], Beijing: Morning Glory Publishers, 2001.

Jiaofei Douzheng: Xinan Diqu [Campaign to eliminate banditry in the southwest region], Beijing: PLA's Press, 2002.

Jinjun Xibu: Gaoceng lingdao tan xibu da kaifa [Go West: Chinese leaders' viewpoints on developing the western regions], Beijing: Central Party Literature Press, 2001.

Li Ping and Li Yigan (eds), *Fanya tielu Xinjiapo zhi Kunming tongdao yanjiu* [Study of the Singapore–Kunming route of the Trans-Asia Railway], Kunming: Yunnan Minority Press, 2000.

Li Tongcheng and Yu Mingsheng (eds), *Zhongguo waijiaoguan zai Yazhou* [Chinese diplomats in Asia], Shanghai: Shanghai People's Publishing House, 2005.

Liu Shaoqi, *Lun guoji zhuyi yu minzu zhuyi* [Internationalism and nationalism], Beijing: People's Press, 1951.

Liu Yuanlin bashi ba huiyi [Memoirs of Liu Yuanlin at the Age of 88], Taipei: History and Political Bureau of Compilation and Translation of National Defense, 1996.

Liu Zhiyong, "Zhongguo guojia shenfen yu waijiao zhanlue de xuanze" [Chinese national identity and the choices in China's diplomatic strategy], China Foreign Affairs University, Ph.D. thesis, 2005.

Ma Jisen, *Waijiaobu wenge jishi* [The Cultural Revolution in the Foreign Ministry of China], Hong Kong: The Chinese University of Hong Kong Press, 2003.

Miandian huaqiao zhi [Records of Overseas Chinese in Burma], Taipei: Editorial Committee of the Records of Overseas Chinese, 1967.

Miandian huashang shanghui shiji huadan jinian tekan [Special publication of the 100th anniversary of the Myanmar Chinese Chamber of Commerce], Yangon: Myanmar Chinese Chamber of Commerce, 2009.

Office of Research on Diplomatic History, Ministry of Foreign Affairs, PRC (ed.), *Zhou Enlai waijiao huodong dashi ji: 1949–1975* [Chronicle of Zhou Enlai's diplomatic events: 1949–1975], Beijing: World Knowledge Publishing House, 1993.

Qiaowu tongji nianbao (2008) [Statistical yearbook of the Overseas Chinese Affairs Commission (2008)], Taipei: Overseas Chinese Affairs Commission, 2009.

Research Association of Overseas Chinese, *Huaqiao renkou cankao ziliao* [Reference material on the Overseas Chinese population], 1956.

Shoujie shijie mianhua tong qiao qingzhu Aomen huigui zuguo ji lianyi dahui jinian tekan [Commemorative issue of the 1st session of the World Myanmar Chinese Diaspora Association and celebration of Macao's return], Macao: Macao Myanmar Overseas Chinese Association, 2002.

Song Enfan and Li Jiasong (eds), *Zhonghua Renmin Gongheguo waijiao dashi ji* [Chronology of the PRC's foreign affairs], Vol. I, Beijing: World Affairs Press, 1997.

Tong Xiaopeng, *Tong Xiaopeng huiyi lu* [Memoir of Tong Xiaopeng], Fuzhou: Fujian People's Press, 2000.

Wang Guiying, "Zhongguo shiyou huanjing fenxi he shiyou anquan zhanlue yanjiu" [China's oil environment and oil security strategy], China University of International Business and Economics, Ph.D. thesis, 2003.

Wang Zhongmin, *Miandian huaqiao nianjian* [Yearbook of Overseas Chinese in Burma], Shanghai: Shanghai Commercial Press, 1936.

Xu Simin, *Yige huaqiao de jingli: Xu Simin huiyi lu* [An Overseas Chinese experience: The memoir of Xu Simin], Hong Kong: The Mirror Post Cultural Enterprises Co. Ltd, 1981.

Yao Jun, *Zhongguo hangkong shi* [Aviation history of China], Zhengzhou: Elephant Press, 1998.

Yunnan Institute of History Studies (ed.), *Zhongguo he Miandian youhao guanxi lishi ziliao huibian* [Documents on the history of China–Burma friendship], 1954, Vol. 2, No. 1, and Vol. 2, No. 2.

Zhongguo duiwai jingji maoyi nianjian [Yearbook of China's international trade and economy], Beijing: Foreign Economic and Trade Publishing House of China, 1984.

Zhongguo duiwai jingji tongji nianjian [China foreign economic statistical yearbook (1994)], Beijing: China Statistics Press, 1995.

Zhongguo shangwu nianjian [China commerce yearbook (2009)], Beijing: China Commerce and Trade Press, 2009.

Zhu Yu (ed.), *Gechu duliu: Gongheguo shouci jindu jinchang shushi* [Removing "Cancer": Records of the PRC's first anti-drug and anti-prostitution measures], Beijing: Central Party Literature Press, 1999.

Zhuo Renzheng (ed.), *Yinyin "Baobo" qing: 1956 nian zhongmian bianmin da lianhuan* [Cordial "Pauk Phaw": A grand gathering of Chinese and Burmese residents in border areas between China and Burma in 1956], Beijing: Central Party Literature Press, 2003.

Japanese-Language Sources

Imakawa Eichi, *Newii Gunseika no Biruma* [Burma under the Ne Win military regime], Kyoto Review Press, 1971.

Sakuma Hirayoshi, *Biruma gendai seijisi* [Modern political history of Burma], Tokyo: Keiso Shobo, 1993.

————, *Biruma ni kurashi shite: toza sareta kuni no hitobito to seikatu* [Living in Burma: People and their lives in a closed country], Tokyo: Keiso Shobo, 1994.

Tsuchifu Nagao, *Shin syokminchi syuugi to minzokuka kumei* [New colonialism and nationalism revolution], Kyoto: Newsletter Press, 1973.

English-Language Sources

The American Journal of International Law, "Law on the acquisition and loss of Chinese nationality". Vol. 4, No. 2 Supplement: Official Documents, 1910.

Andrews-Speed, Philip, Xuanli Liao and Roland Dannreuther, *The Strategic Implications of China's Energy Needs*. Adelphi Paper, No. 346, The International Institute for Strategic Studies. New York: Oxford University Press, 2002.

Asian Development Bank, *Asian Development Outlook 2003*. New York: Oxford University Press, 2003.

Byman, Daniel and Roger Cliff, *China's Arms Sales: Motivations and Implications*. Santa Monica, CA and Washington, D.C.: RAND Corporation, 2000.

Bandyopadhyaya, Kalyani, *Burma and Indonesia: Comparative Political Economy and Foreign Policy*. New Delhi: South Asian Publishers, 1983.

Bureau of Intelligence and Research, *Burma–China Boundary, International Boundary Study*, No. 42. Washington, D.C.: U.S. Department of State, 1964.

Butwell, Richard, *U Nu of Burma*. Stanford: Stanford University Press, 1963.

Cady, John F, *A History of Modern Burma*. Ithaca: Cornell University Press, 1958.

————, *The United States and Burma*. Cambridge, MA: Harvard University Press, 1976.

Central Intelligence Agency, *Peking and the Burmese Communists: the Perils and Profits of Insurgency*, CIA Intelligence Report, RSS No. 0052/71, July 1971.

Chachavalpongpun, Pavin, *A Plastic Nation. The Curse of Thainess in Thai-Burmese Relations*. Lanham: University Press of America, 2005.

————, *Reinventing Thailand. Thaksin and His Foreign Policy.* Singapore: Institute of Southeast Asian Studies, 2010.

Chang, David Wen-wei, "A comparative study of neutralism of India, Burma and Indonesia", University of Illinois, Ph.D. dissertation, 1960.

Chang, Luke T, *China's Boundary Treaties and Frontier Disputes.* London, Rome, and New York: Oceana Publications Inc., 1982.

Chee, Kiong Tong, *Identity and Ethnic Relations in Southeast Asia: Racializing Chineseness.* Dordrecht: Springer, 2010.

Chen, Jian, *Mao's China and The Cold War.* Chapel Hill, N.C. and London: University of North Carolina Press, 2001.

Chin, Ko-lin, Sheldon X. Zhang, *The Chinese Connection: Cross-border Drug Trafficking between Myanmar and China.* Final Report to The United States Department of Justice Office of Justice Programs, National Institute of Justice, April 2007.

Christian, John Leroy, *Burma and the Japanese Invader.* Bombay: Thacker & Company, Ltd., 1945.

Committee on Foreign Relations, United States Senate, "Energy Trends in China and India: Implications for the United States". Hearing Before the 109th Congress, First Session, Washington, D.C., 26 July 2005.

The Council on Foreign Relations, "U.S.–China Relations: An Affirmative Agenda, A Responsible Course", Report of an Independent Task Force, 2007.

Das, Samir Kumar, *Conflict and Peace in India's Northeast: The Role of Civil Society,* Policy Studies #42, East–West Center, Washington, D.C. 2007.

Denoon, David, *The Economic and Strategic Rise of China and India: Asian Realignments after the 1997 Financial Crisis.* New York: Palgrave, 2008.

Department of Public Information, *Yearbook of the United Nations 1953.* New York: United Nations, 1954.

Dikotter, Frank, Lars Laamann and Zhou Xun, *Narcotic Culture: A History of Drugs in China,* Hong Kong: Hong Kong University Press, 2004.

Downs, Erica Strecker, *China's Quest for Energy Security.* Santa Monica, CA and Washington, D.C.: RAND Corporation, 2000.

EarthRights International, *China in Burma: The Increasing Investment of Chinese Multinational Corporations in Burma's Hydropower, Oil and Natural Gas, and Mining Sectors,* 2008.

———— and Southeast Asian Information Network, *Total Denial: A Report on the Yadana Pipeline Project in Burma,* 10 July 1996.

East Asia Analytical Unit, "Overseas Chinese Business Networks in Asia", Canberra: Australian Department of Foreign Affairs and Trade, 1995.

Ebel, Robert E, *Energy and Geopolitics in China Mixing Oil and Politics: A Report of the CSIS Energy and National Security Program.* Washington, D.C.: CSIS, November 2009.

Garver, John W., *Protracted Contest. Sino-Indian Rivalry in the Twentieth Century.* Stanford: Stanford University Press, 2001.

Guo, Xiaolin, "Towards resolution: China in the Myanmar issue", Silk Road Paper, March 2007.

Gurtov, Melvin, *China and Southeast Asia: The Politics of Survival.* Baltimore and London: Johns Hopkins University Press, 1975.

Hall, D.G.E., *Burma.* London: Hutchinson House, 1950.

Harvey, G. E, *British Rule in Burma 1824–1942.* London: Faber and Faber, 1946.

Hinton, Harold C, *China's Relations with Burma and Vietnam: A Brief Survey,* New York: International Secretariat, Institute of Pacific Relations, 1958.

Hla Min, *Political Situation of Myanmar and Its Role in the Region.* Yangon: Office of Strategic Studies, Ministry of Defense, 1997.

Holmes, Robert Alexander, "Chinese foreign policy toward Burma and Cambodia: A comparative analysis", Columbia University Ph.D. dissertation, 1969.

India Intelligence Branch, Army Headquarters, *Frontier and Overseas Expeditions from India.* Volume V., Delhi: Mittal Publications, Reprinted, 1983.

International Crisis Group, *China's Myanmar Strategy: Elections, Ethnic Politics and Economics.* Crisis Group Asia Briefing No. 112, September 21, 2010.

———, *China's Myanmar Dilemma.* Asia Report No. 177, September 14, 2009

———, *Myanmar: Sanctions, Engagement or Another Way Forward?* Asia Report No. 78, April 26, 2004.

International Energy Agency, *World Energy Outlook 2007: China and India Insights.* 2007.

Jan, George Pukung, "Nationality and treatment of overseas Chinese in Southeast Asia", New York University, Ph.D. dissertation, 1960.

Johnstone, William C., *Burma's Foreign Policy: A Study in Neutralism.* Cambridge, MA: Harvard University Press, 1963.

Joint UNDP/World Bank Energy Sector Management Assistance Programme, *Cross-Border Oil and Gas Pipelines: Problems and Prospects.* June 2003.

Khin Maung Kyi, *Economic Development of Burma: A Vision and Strategy.* Stockholm: Olof Palme International Center, 2000.

Kramer, Tom, *From Golden Triangle to Rubber Belt: The Future of Opium Bans in the Kokang and Wa Regions.* Amsterdam: Transnational Institute, July 2009.

Kudo, Toshihiro, *Myanmar's Economic Relations with China: Can China Support the Myanmar Economy?* Tokyo: Institute of Developing Economies, JETRO Discussion Paper No. 66, 2006.

Lampton, David M., *The Three Faces of Chinese Power.* Berkeley: University of California Press, 2008.

Levesque, Julien & Mizra Zulfiqur Rtahman, *Tension in the Rolling Hills: Burmese Population and Border Trade in Mizoram.* New Delhi: Institute of Peace and Conflict Studies, IPCS Research Papers #14, April 2008.

Levesque, Julien, *A Reformed Military Junta in Myanmar In India's Strategic Interests.* Institute of Peace and Conflict Studies, New Delhi, IPCS Issue Brief # 69, May 2008.

Liang, Chi-shad, *Burma's Foreign Relations. Neutralism in Theory and Practice.* New York: Praeger Publishers, 1990.

MacFarquhar, Roderick and Michael Schoenhals, *Mao's Last Revolution.* Cambridge, MA: The Belknap Press, 2006.

Margary, Augustus Raymond and Rutherford Alcock, *The Journey of Augustus Ramond Margary from Shanghai to Bhamo and Back to Manwyne.* London: Macmillan and Co., 1876.

Martin, Michael F., *U.S. Sanctions on Burma*, Washington, D.C.: CRS Report for Congress, 16 July 2010.

Maung Aung Myoe, *Building the Tatmadaw: Myanmar Armed Forces Since 1948.* Singapore: Institute of Southeast Asian Studies, 2009.

————, *Sino-Myanmar Economic Relations Since 1988.* Asia Research Institute, National University of Singapore, Working Paper No. 86, April 2007.

Maung Maung, *Burma in the Family of Nations.* Amsterdam: Djambatan Ltd, 1956.

Ministry of Information, *Kuomintang Aggression against Burma.* Rangoon: Government of the Union of Burma, 1953.

Nathan, Andrew and Robert S. Ross, *The Great Wall and the Empty Fortress: China's Search for Security.* New York: W. W. Norton, 1997.

Ness, Peter Van, *Revolution and Chinese Foreign Policy.* Los Angeles and London: University of California Press, 1970.

National Drug Intelligence Center, *National Drug Threat Assessment, 2009.* Washington, D.C.: U.S. Department of Justice, December 2008.

Niksch, Larry A., *Burma–U.S. Relations.* Washington, D.C.: CRS Report for Congress, 2 March 2008.

Nobuyuki Higashi, *Natural Gas in China Market Evolution and Strategy.* International Energy Agency Working Paper, June 2009

Nu (Thakin), *From Peace to Stability*. Rangoon: Ministry of Information, Government of the Union of Burma, 1951.

Office of the Secretary of Defense, "Military Power of the People's Republic of China: 2009". Washington, D.C., 2009.

Pakem, B., *India Burma Relations*. New Delhi: Omsons Publications, 1992.

Pan, Lynn (ed.), *The Encyclopedia of the Chinese Overseas*. Richmond, Surrey: Curzon Press, 1999.

Panikkar, K. M., *In Two Chinas: Memoirs of a Diplomat*. Westport: Hyperion Press, 1981.

Percival, Bronson, *The Dragon Looks South: China and Southeast Asia in the New Century*. Westport: Praeger Security International, 2007.

Pettman, Ralph, *China in Burma's Foreign Policy*. Canberra: Australian National University, Contemporary China Papers No. 7, 1973.

Purcell, Victor, *The Chinese in Southeast Asia*. Oxford: Oxford University Press, 1965.

Seaman, John, *Energy Security, Transnational Pipelines and China's Role in Asia*, Institut Français des Relations Internationales, Asie Visions #27, April 2010.

Seekins, Donald M., *Burma and Japan Since 1940: From 'Co-Prosperity' to 'Quiet Dialogue'*. Copenhagen: NIAS Press, 2007.

Selth, Andrew, *Burma: A Strategic Perspective*. The Asia Foundation Working Paper #13, May 2001.

———, *Burma and the Threat of Invasion: Regime Fantasy or Strategic Reality?* Griffith University, Griffith Asia Institute, Regional Outlook Paper No. 17, 2008.

———, *Burma's Armed Forces. Power Without Glory*. Norwalk: EastBridge, 2002.

———, *Burma's China Connection and the Indian Ocean Region*. Canberra: Australian National University, Strategic & Defence Studies Centre, Working Paper #377, September 2003.

———, *Burma's North Korean Gambit. A Challenge to Regional Security*. Canberra: Australian National University, Strategic and Defence Studies Center, Canberra Papers on Strategy and Defence #154, 2004.

———, *Civil-Military Relations in Burma: Portents, Predictions and Possibilities*. Griffith University, Griffith Asia Institute, Regional Outlook Paper No. 25, 2010.

———, *Transforming the Tatmadaw*. Canberra: Strategic and Defence Studies Centre, Australian National University, 1996.

Set Aung, Winston, "Illegal heroes and victimless crimes: informal cross-border migration from Myanmar", ASIA PAPER, Sweden Institute for Security and Development Policy, December 2009.

———, "The role of informal cross-border trade in Myanmar", Institute for Security and Development Policy Asia Paper, September 2009.

Shekar, Vibhanshu, *A Federal Democratic Myanmar India's Strategic Imperative*. Institute of Peace and Conflict Studies. New Delhi, IPCS Issue Brief #67, May 2008.

Show, Kuo-kong, "Communist China's foreign policy toward the non-aligned states with special reference to India and Burma, 1949–1962", University of Pennsylvania, Ph.D. dissertation, 1972.

Singh, Uma Shankar, *Burma and India, 1949–1962: A Study in the Foreign Policies of Burma and India and Burma's Policy towards India*. New Delhi, Bombay, Calcutta: Oxford & IBH Publishing Co., 1979.

Slack, Edward R., *Opium, State, and Society: China's Narco-economy and the Guomindang, 1924–1937*. Honolulu: University of Hawai'i Press, 2001.

Smith, Martin, *Burma: Insurgency and the Politics of Ethnicity*. Dhaka: The University Press, 1999.

Smith, Roger M. (ed.), *Southeast Asia: Documents of Political Development and Change*. Ithaca and London: Cornell University Press, 1974.

Spinetta, Lawrence (Major), "'The Malacca dilemma' – Countering China's 'string of pearls' with land-based airpower", a thesis presented to the Faculty of the School of Advanced Air and Space Studies for completion of graduation requirements, School of Advanced Air and Space Studies, Air University, Maxwell Air Force Base, Alabama, June 2006.

Stargardt, Janice, *The Ancient Pyu of Burma*. Singapore: PACSEA Cambridge, in association with the Institute of Southeast Asian Studies, 1990.

Steinberg, David I, *Burma: The State of Myanmar*. Washington, D.C.: Georgetown University Press, 2001.

——, *Burma/Myanmar: What Everyone Needs to Know*. New York: Oxford University Press, 2010.

——, *Burma's Road Toward Development: Growth and Ideology Under Military Rule*. Boulder: Westview Press, 1981.

——, *Myanmar: The Anomalies of Politics and Economics*, The Asia Foundation Working Paper # 5, November 1997.

——, *Turmoil in Burma: Contested Legitimacies in Myanmar*. New York: Eastbridge, 2006.

Swanström, Niklas and Yin He, *China's War on Narcotics: Two Perspectives*. Silk Road Paper, December 2006.

Taylor, Jay, *China and Southeast Asia: Peking's Relations with Revolution Movements*. New York: Praeger Publishers, 1976.

Taylor, Robert H., *Foreign and Domestic Consequences of the KMT Intervention in Burma*, Data Paper #93, Southeast Asia Program, Department of Asian Studies, Cornell University, July 1973.

Thandar Khine, *Foreign Direct Investment Relations between Myanmar and ASEAN*, IDE Discussion Paper No. 149, April 2008.

Thant Myint-U, *Where China Meets India: Burma and the New Crossroads of Asia*. New York: Farrar, Strauss and Giroux, 2011.

Trocki, Carl A., *Opium, Empire, and the Global Political Economy: A Study of the Asian Opium Trade, 1750–1950*. London, New York: Routledge, 1999.

United Nations Office on Drugs, *World Drug Report, 2004*, Vol. 1: Analysis. New York, 2004.

———, *World Drug Report, 2010*, 2010.

———, Global SMART Programme, "Patterns and trends of amphetamine-type stimulants and other drugs in East and South-East Asia (and neighboring regions), 2009.

United Nations Treaty Series, *Boundary Treaty Between the Union of Burma and the People's Republic of China*, Vol. 1010, No.1-14847.

US–China Economic and Security Review Commission, "China's Overseas Investments in Oil and Gas Production", 16 October 2006.

Worldwide Fund for Nature (WWF), *Chinese Companies in the 21st Century (II): A Survey on the Social Responsibility & Sustainability of Chinese Companies*, April 2010.

———, *Rethink China's Outward Investment Flows*, April 2007.

———, *World's Top 10 Rivers at Risk*. Gland, Switzerland, March 2007.

Young, Kenneth Ray, "Nationalist Chinese Troops in Burma – Obstacle in Burma's Foreign Relations: 1949–1961", New York University, Ph.D. thesis, 1970.

Yunnan Yearbook 2009. Kunming: Yunnan Yearbook Press, 2009.

Zhao Hong, *China and India's Competitive Relations with Myanmar*, Institute of China Studies, University of Malaya, Working Paper #2008-7, 2008.

Zhou Yongming, *Anti-Drug Crusades in Twentieth-Century China: Nationalism, History, and State Building*, Lanham: Rowman & Littlefield Publishers, Inc., 1999.

Articles, Chapters and Other Material

Chinese-Language Sources

Bao Lu, "Huaren zai Miandian" [The Chinese in Myanmar], *Dongnanya nanya xinxi* [Information on Southeast and South Asia], No. 18, 1996.

Chen Hurngyu, "1953 nian Miandian zai lianheguo konggao Zhonghua Minguo jundui ruqin an" [Complaint by the Union of Burma regarding an aggression against it by the government of the Republic of China in 1953], *Haihua yu dongnanya yanjiu* [Journal of Overseas Chinese and Southeast Asian Studies], Vol. 4, No. 3, July 2004.

Chen Yixiang, "Zhongmian bianjie lianhe kancha zayi" [Memories of the Sino-Burmese joint boundary survey], *Hainei Yu Haiwai* [At Home and Overseas], 2003, No. 12.

Cheng Ruisheng, "Geng Biao chushi Miandian ersan shi" [Account of Geng Biao's service as an envoy to Burma], *Xiang chao* [Hunan Tide History of the CCP in Hunan], No. 8, 2009.

Jiang Chung-lian, "Zhonggong zhi shiyou zhanlue yu qi dui Feizhou guanxi" [China's oil strategy and its implications for Africa], *Wenti Yu Yanjiu* [Issues and Studies], Vol. 42, No. 4, 2003.

Lan Sou, Li Ding, "Yingjie xin Zhongguo dansheng de ri ri ye ye" [Welcoming the birth of New China every day and night], *Dangshi Wenhui* [*Materials from CCP History*], No. 5, 1989.

Li Jinjun, "Miandian lianbang jingji gaikuang yu zhongmian hezuo qianjing" [Myanmar economic overview and prospects for China-Myanmar cooperation], *Haiwai touzi yu chukou xindai* [Overseas Investment and Export Credit], No. 2, 2004.

———, "Qianxi Miandian dangqian jingji kunnan de zhuyao yuanyin ji yingxiang" [Analyzing the cause and effect of current economic hardship in Myanmar], *Yahou Tansuo* [Asia Probe], No. 4, 2002.

Lin Zhu, "Tong ding si tong: 1967 nian Miandian paihua qiyin chutan" [Recalling a painful experience: the origin of the 1967 anti-Chinese riots in Burma], *Huaqiao lishi luncong* [Collection of Overseas Chinese history], Vol. IV, Fuzhou: Fujian Society for Overseas Chinese History, 1987.

Lincang Branch Investigation Team of the People's Bank of China, "Dui lincang diqu bianjing maoyi zhong renminbi liutong qingkuang de diaocha" [Investigation of RMB circulation in the border trade in Lincang region], *Xinan Jinrong* [Southwest Finance], No. 9, 2001, p. 46.

"LWZ miandian huiyi lu II: miandian qiaodang de jiesan" [Memoirs of LWZ, Part II: The dissolution of the Burmese Overseas Chinese Communist Party]. Unpublished manuscript, 1991.

"LWZ miandian huiyi lu III: miandian qiaodang jiesan hou de huaqiao gongzuo" [Memoirs of LWZ, Part III: Assignment on Overseas Chinese after the dissolution of the Burmese Overseas Chinese Communist Party]. Unpublished manuscript, 1993.

Niu Jun, "Xin Zhongguo waijiao de xingcheng ji zhuyao tezheng" [Formation of diplomatic policy in New China and its main characteristics], *Lishi Yanjiu* [Historical Research], No. 5, 1999.

Song Fengying, "Zhou Enlai yu zhongmian bianjie tanpan" [Zhou Enlai and Burma–China boundary negotiations], *Dangshi Zonglan* [Overview of CCP History], No. 11, 2005.

Wen Xing, "Nai Wen ducai yu 1967 nian fanhua shijian" [Ne Win's autarchy and the 1967 anti-Chinese incident], *Huaren Yuekan* [Overseas Chinese Monthly], No. 11, 1988.

Yu Jiang and Wang Chaozuo "Dui zhongmian bianjing guanli zhong yu miandian difang minzu wuzhuang shili kaizhan jingwu hezuo de sikao" [Reflections on policy cooperation with Myanmar local minority armed forces in Sino-Myanmar border management], *Yunnan Gongan Gaodeng Zhuanke Xuexiao Xuebao* [Journal of Yunnan Public Security College], No. 1, 2001.

Yu Yohuei, "Hu Wen tizhi xia de shiyou waijiao yu tiaozhan" [Hu Jintao's oil diplomacy and challenges], *Zhongguo Dalu Yanjiu* [Mainland China Studies], Vol. 48, No. 3, 2005.

Zeng Guanying and Chen Zunfa, "Liangci paihua mudu ji" [Witnessing two anti-Chinese riots in Burma]. Unpublished manuscript.

Zhai Zhenxiao, "Qianyi, wenhua yu rentong: mianhua yimin de shequn jiangou yu kuaguo wangluo" [Migration, cultures and identities: The social construction and transnational networks of Sino-Burmese immigrant communities in Yangon, Jhong-he, and Toronto], Taiwan National Tsing Hua University, Ph.D. thesis, 2006, pp.166–167.

Zhang Guozhong, "Miandian yu Zhonggong guanxi" [Burma and communist China, 1950–1990], Taiwan National Chengchi University, M.A. thesis, 1995.

Zhang Jian, "Zhongguo yu guoji youse jinshu ziyuan daguo de hezuo qianjing" [The prospects for cooperation between China and countries with rich deposits of non-ferrous metals], *Shijie Youse Jinshu* [World Nonferrous Metals], No. 8, 2005.

Zhu Liang, "Wusi wuwei zhuiqiu zhenli de wang jiaxiang" [Selfless and fearless truth-seeker, Wang Jiaxiang], *Yanhuang Chunqiu* [Yan-Huang Historical Review], No. 8, 2006.

Zhuang Guotu, "Dongnanya huaqiao huaren shuliang de xin gusuan" [A new estimation of the ethnic Chinese population in Southeast Asia], *Xiamen Daxue Xuebao* [Journal of Xiamen University], No. 3, 2009.

————, "Lun zhonguoren yimin Dongnanya de sici dachao" [On the four waves: a history of Chinese migration into Southeast Asia], *Nanyang Wenti Yanjiu* [Southeast Asian Affairs], No. 1, 2008.

Zhuo Renzheng, "Jiejue zhongmian bianjie wenti de lianghao kaiduan: wojun chechu '1941 nian xian' yixi diqu" [A promising beginning to resolving the Burma–China boundary problem: PLA withdrawal to the west of '1941 Line'], *Bainian Chao* [Hundred Year Tide], No. 9, 2003,

Zi Gui, "Dianmian maoyi wenti" [Trade between Yunnan and Burma], *Yazhou Tansuo* [Explore Asia], No. 15, 1984.

English-Language Sources

Alamgir, Jalal, "Myanmar's foreign trade and its political consequences", *Asian Survey*, XLVIII, No. 6, November/December 2008.

Armstrong, M. Jocelyn and R. Warwick Armstrong, "Chinese populations of Southeast Asia," in Jocelyn Armstrong, R. Warwick Armstrong, and Kent Mulliner (eds), *Chinese Populations in Contemporary Southeast Asian Societies*. Richmond: Curzon Press, 2001.

Arnott, David, "China–Burma relations", in International IDEA, *Challenges to Democratization in Burma: Perspectives on Multilateral and Bilateral Responses*, 2001.

Aung Din, "Burma's last chance", *Far Eastern Economic Review*, 26 May 2009.

Badgley, John H., "Burma's China crisis: the choices ahead". *Asian Survey*, Vol. VII, No. 11, November 1967.

Bert, Wayne, "Chinese policy toward Burma and Indonesia", *Asian Survey*, Vol. XXV, No. 9, September 1985.

———, "Chinese relations with Burma and Indonesia", *Asian Survey*, Vol. 15, No. 6, June 1975.

Bo Zhiyue, "China's new National Energy Commission: policy implications", *EAI Background Brief*, No. 504, 5 February 2010.

Brown, Philip H., Darrin Magee, and Yilin Xu, "Socioeconomic vulnerability in China's hydropower development", *China Economic Review*, Vol. 19, Issue 4, December 2008.

"Burma/Myanmar: nexus on the Bay of Bengal", Georgetown University conference report, Washington, D.C., February 2002.

Canning, Cherie, "Pursuit of the Pariah: Iran, Sudan and Myanmar in China's energy security strategy", *Security Challenges*, Vol. 3, No. 1, February 2007.

Chen, Matthew E, "Chinese national oil companies and human rights", *Orbis*, Vol. 51, No. 1, Winter 2007.

Chutung,Tsai, "The Chinese nationality law, 1909", *The American Journal of International Law*, Vol. 4, No. 2, 1910.

Clarke, Ryan, "Narcotics trafficking in China: Size, scale, dynamic and future consequences", *Pacific Affairs*, Vol. 81, No. 1, Spring 2008.

Cornelius, Peter and Jonathan Story, "China and global energy markets", *Orbis*, Winter 2007.

Dai, Shen-Yu, "Peking and Rangoon", *China Quarterly*, No. 5, January–March 1961.

Deigan, H. I, "Burma – gateway to China", Smithsonian Institution War Background Studies, No. 17, 1943.

Deliusin, Lev, "The influence of China's domestic policy on its foreign policy", *Proceedings of the Academy of Political Science*, Vol. 38, No.2, 1991.

Downs, Erica S, "The Chinese energy security debate", *China Quarterly*, No. 177, March 2004.

Egreteau, Renaud, "Intra-European bargaining and the 'tower of Babel' EU approach to the Burmese conundrum", *East Asia*, Vol. 27, Issue. 1, March 2010.

Erickson, Andrew and Gabe Collins, "Beijing's energy security strategy: the significance of a Chinese state-owned tanker fleet", *Orbis*, Fall 2007.

Gurtovl, Melvin, "The Foreign Ministry and foreign affairs during the Cultural Revolution", *China Quarterly*, No. 40, October–December 1969.

Hall, D. G. E, "Review of *Burma's Foreign Policy: A Study in Neutralism*", *Pacific Affairs*, Vol. XXXVII, No. 2, Summer 1964.

Heaton, William R., "China and Southeast Asian communist movements: the decline of dual track diplomacy", *Asian Survey*, Vol. 22, No. 8, August 1982.

Holliday, Ian, "Doing business with rights violating regimes: corporate social responsibility and Myanmar's military junta", *Journal of Business Ethics*, Vol. 61, No. 4, 2005.

Holmes, Robert A., "Burma's foreign policy toward China since 1962", *Pacific Affairs*, Vol. 45, No. 2, Summer 1972.

———, "Burmese domestic policy: the politics of Burmanization", *Asian Survey*, Vol. 7, No. 3, March 1967.

———, "China–Burma Relations since the Rift", *Asian Survey*, Vol. 12, No. 8 August 1972.

Hooker, M. B., "The 'Chinese Confucian' and 'Chinese Buddhist' in British Burma, 1881–1947", *Journal of Southeast Asian Studies*, Vol. XXI, No. 2, September 1990.

Horelick, Arnold L, "The Soviet Union's Asian collective security proposal: a club in search of members", *Pacific Affairs*, Vol. 47, No. 3, Autumn 1974.

Ikeya, Chie, "The modern Burmese woman and the politics of fashion in colonial Burma". *The Journal of Asian Studies*, Vol. 67, No. 4, 2008.

Jaffe, Amy Myers and Steven W. Lewis, "Beijing's oil diplomacy", *Survival*, Vol. 44, No. 1, Spring 2002.

James, Helen, "Myanmar's international relations strategy: the search for security", *Contemporary Southeast Asia*, Vol. 26, No. 3, 2004.

Jane's World Insurgency and Terrorism, "Kachin Independence Army (KIA)", 25 May 2007.

Jane's Sentinel Security Assessment – Southeast Asia, "Army, Myanmar", 11 December 2009.

———, "Navy, Myanmar", 11 December 2009.

Kaplan, Robert, "Rivalry in the Indian Ocean," *Foreign Affairs*, March/April 2009.

Kaufman, Victor S., "Trouble in the golden triangle: The United States, Taiwan and the 93rd nationalist division", *China Quarterly*, No. 166, June 2001.

Kozicki, Richard J., "The Sino-Burmese frontier problem", *Far Eastern Survey*, Vol. 26, No. 3, March 1957.

Kudo, Toshihiro, "China and Japan's Economic Relations with Myanmar: Strengthened vs. Estranged", in Kagami Mitsuhiro (ed.), *A China–Japan Comparison of Economic Relationships with the Mekong River Basin Countries*, BRC Research Report No. 1, 2009.

———, "Myanmar's economic relations with China: who benefits and who pays?", in Monique Skidmore and Trevor Wilson (eds), *Dictatorship, Disorder and Decline in Myanmar*, Canberra: ANU Press, 2008.

Lai, Hongyi Harry, "China's oil diplomacy: is it a global security threat?" *Third World Quarterly*, Vol. 28, No. 3, 2007.

Lee, Pak K., "China's quest for oil security: oil (wars) in the pipeline?", *The Pacific Review*, Vol. 18, No. 2, June 2005.

———, Gerald Chan and Lai-Ha Chan, "China's 'realpolitik' engagement with Myanmar", *China Security*, Vol. 5, No. 1, 2009.

Li Chenyang, "Effects of the conflict between the ceasefire groups and the Myanmar military government in northern Myanmar on China since 2009". Unpublished paper, 2010.

———, "The policies of China and India toward Myanmar", in Lex Rieffel (ed.), *Myanmar/Burma: Inside Challenges, Outside Interests*. Washington, D.C.: The Brookings Institution, 2010.

Liang, Chi-shad, "Burma's relations with the People's Republic of China: from delicate friendship to genuine co-operation", in Peter Carey (ed.), *Burma: The Challenge of Change in a Divided Society*, London: Macmillan Media Ltd, 1997.

Lintner, Bertil, "Burma's contraband trade with China is booming: the busy border", *Far Eastern Economic Review*, 8 June 1989.

———, "Friends of necessity", *Far Eastern Economic Review*, 164:51, 27 December 2001 – 3 January 2002.

———, "Military cooperation between Burma and the Democratic People's Republic of Korea". Unpublished paper, October 2010.

———, "Myanmar's Chinese connection." *Jane's International Defence Review*, 027/011, 1 November 1994.

Luck, Edward C, "The United Nations and the responsibility to protect", The Stanley Foundation, Policy Analysis Brief, August 2008.

Malik, J. Mohan, "Burma's Role in Regional Security," in Morten Pedersen, et. al. (eds), *Burma–Myanmar: Strong Regime, Weak State?* Adelaide: Crawford, 2000.

————, "Myanmar's role in regional security: pawn or pivot?", *Contemporary Southeast Asia*, Vol. 19, No. 1, June 1997.

————, "Sino-Indian rivalry in Myanmar: implications for regional security", *Contemporary Southeast Asia*, Vol. 16, No. 2, September 1994.

Maung Maung, "The Burma-China boundary settlement", *Asian Survey*, Vol. 1, No. 1, March 1961.

Maung Maung Gyi, "Foreign policy of Burma since 1962: negative neutralism for group survival", in F. K. Lehman (ed.), *Military Rule in Burma Since 1962*, Singapore: Maruzen Asia, 1981.

McDonald, Kristen, Peter Bosshard, and Nicole Brewer, "Exporting dams: China's hydropower industry goes global", *Journal of Environmental Management*, Vol. 90, Supplement 3, 2009.

McNally, Amy, Darrin Magee, and Aaron T. Wolf, "Hydropower and sustainability: resilience and vulnerability in China's powersheds", *Journal of Environmental Management*, Vol. 90, Supplement 3, July 2009.

Mokhzani Zubir and Mohd Nizam Basiron, "The Straits of Malacca: The rise of China, America's intentions and the dilemma of the littoral states", Maritime Institute of Malaysia, April 2005.

Mya Maung, "On the road to Mandalay, a case study of the sinonization of Upper Burma", *Asian Survey*, Vol. 34, No. 5, May 1994.

Mya Than, "Myanmar's cross-border economic relations and cooperation with the People's Republic of China and Thailand in the Greater Mekong Subregion", *Journal of GMS Development Studies*, Vol. 2, No. 1, October 2005.

————, "The ethnic Chinese in Myanmar and their identity", in Leo Suryadinata (ed.), *Ethnic Chinese as Southeast Asians*, Singapore: Institute of Southeast Asian Studies, 1997.

"Myanmar and China: New Horizons", *The Economist*, 23 January 1993.

Nu (U Nu), "Burma's Neutral Policy", *Burma*, Vol. V, No. 2, January 1955.

Omonbude, Ekpen J., "The transit oil and gas pipeline and the role of bargaining: A non-technical discussion", *Energy Policy*, Vol. 35, No. 12, December 2007.

Ott, Marvin C., "From isolation to relevance: policy considerations", in Robert I. Rotberg (ed.), *Burma: Prospects for a Democratic Future*, Washington D.C.: Brookings Institute Press, 1998.

Pan Qi, "Opening the southwest: an expert opinion", *Beijing Review*, 28:35, 2 September 1985.

Petersson, Magnus, "Myanmar in EU–ASEAN relations", *Asia Europe Journal*, No. 4, 2006.

Purcell, Victor, "The influence of racial minorities", in Philip W. Thayer (ed.), *Nationalism and Progress in Free Asia*, Baltimore: The Johns Hopkins Press, 1956.

Robinson, Thomas, "China confronts the Soviet Union: warfare and diplomacy on China's inner Asian frontiers", in Roderick MacFarquhar and John K. Fairbank (eds), *The Cambridge History of China*, Vol.15, "The People's Republic," Part 2: Revolutions within the Chinese Revolution, 1966–1982, New York: Cambridge University Press, 1991.

Rose, Jerry, "Burma and the balance of neutralism", *The Reporter*, Vol. XXVIII, No. 1, 3 January 1963.

Shao, Kuo-kang, "Chou Enlai's diplomatic approach to non-aligned states in Asia: 1953–60", *China Quarterly*, No. 78, June 1979.

Selth, Andrew, "Burma and the Bush White House". Blog at www.lowryinterpreter. org/post/2008/08/Burma-and-the-Bush-White-House

———, "Burma and the strategic competition between China and India", paper presented at a Chiang Mai conference, June 1995, in *Journal of Strategic Studies*, Vol. 19, No. 2, June 1996, and in John Brandon (ed.), *Burma: Myanmar in the Twenty-First Century: Dynamics of Continuity and Change*. Bangkok: Chulalongkorn University, 1997.

———, "Burma, China and the myth of military bases", *Asian Security*, 3:3, 2007.

———, "Myanmar, North Korea, and the nuclear question", in Lex Rieffel (ed.), *Myanmar/Burma. Inside Challenges, Outside Interests*. Washington, D.C.: The Brookings Institution, 2010.

Shchetinkin, A., "Peking's crude interference", *The Current Digest of the Post-Soviet Press*, No. 41, Vol. 19, 1 November 1967.

Shee, Poon Kim, "The political economy of China–Myanmar relations: strategic and economic dimensions", *Ritsumeikan Annual Review of International Studies*, 2002.

Silverstein, Josef, "A new vehicle on Burma's road to socialism", *Asia*, No. 29, Spring 1973.

———, "Burma in 1980: an uncertain balance sheet," *Asian Survey*, Vol. 21, No. 2, A Survey of Asia in 1980: Part II, February 1981.

———, "The military and foreign policy in Burma and Indonesia", *Asian Survey*, Vol. 22, No. 3, March 1982.

Sovacool, Benjamin K., "Reassessing energy security and the trans-ASEAN natural gas pipeline network", *Pacific Affairs*, Vol. 82, No. 3, Fall 2009.

Sricharatchanya, Paisal, "Some are more equal", *Far Eastern Economic Review*, Vol. 118, No. 41, 8 October 1982.

Steinberg, David I., "Aung San Suu Kyi and U.S. policy toward Burma/Myanmar", *Journal of Current Southeast Asian Affairs*. September 2010.

————, "Burma and Lessons from the Hungarian Revolution", *Irrawaddy*, October 2006.

————, "Burma's multiple crises: globalized concerns and Myanmar's response". Paper given at the Swedish Institute of International Affairs, Stockholm 8–9 May 2008.

————, "Defending Burma, Protecting Myanmar", *Irrawaddy*, Vol. 14, No. 5, May 2006.

————, "Japanese aid to Burma: assistance in the *tarenagashi* manner?", in Bruce Koppel and Robert Orr (eds), *Managing Japan's Foreign Aid: Power and Policy in a New Era*. Boulder: Westview Press, 1993.

————, "The Indo-Burmese Frontier: A Legacy of Violence," *Jane's Intelligence Review*, 1 January 1994.

————, "The United States and Burma/Myanmar: a boutique issue?" *International Affairs*, Vol. 86, No. 1, 2010.

————, "The United States and its allies: the problem of Burma/Myanmar policy", *Contemporary Southeast Asia*, Vol. 29, No. 2, 2007.

Stepan, Alfred, Juan J. Linz and Yogendra Yadav, "The Rise of 'State-Nation'", *Journal of Democracy*, Vol. 21, No. 3, July 2010.

Stephens, M. D., "The Sino-Burmese border agreement", *Asian Review*, Vol. LIX, No. 217, January 1963.

Stifel, Laurence D, "Burmese socialism: economic problems of the first decade", *Pacific Affairs*, Vol. 45, No. 1, 1972.

Storey, Ian, "China's 'Malacca dilemma'", *China Brief*, Vol. 6, Issue 8, 12 April 2006.

Surin Pitsuwan, speech in Seoul to the conference on the role of South Korea in Southeast Asia, March 2008.

Talenywun, Don, "The politics of dam construction along the Salween", *Mizzima*, August 15, 2009.

Thihan Myo Nyun, "Feeling good or doing good: inefficiency of the U.S. unilateral sanctions against the military government of Burma/Myanmar", *Washington University Global Studies Law Review*. Vol. 7:455, 2008.

Thomson, John Seabury, "Burma: a neutral in China's shadow", *Review of Politics*, Vol. 19, No. 3, July 1957.

Tin Muang Maung Than, "Myanmar and China: a special relationship?", *Southeast Asian Affairs*, Singapore, Institute of Southeast Asian Studies, 2003.

————, "Myanmar's relations with China: from dependence to independence?", in Lam Peng Er, Natayanan Ganesan, and Colin Durkop (eds), *East Asia's mutual accommodation*, Konrad Adenauer Stiftung, 2010.

Trager, Frank, "Burma and China", *Journal of Southeast Asian History*, Vol. 5, No. 1, March 1964.

————, "Sino-Burmese relations: the end of the pauk phaw era", *Orbis*, Vol. XI, No. 4, Winter 1968.

Tretiak, Daniel, "Changes in Chinese attention to Southeast Asia, 1967–1969: their relevance to the future of the area", *Current Scene*, Vol. 7, No. 21, 1 November 1969.

"Unhindered Prospects", *Undercurrents*, Issue 2, July 2006.

Wallerstein, Immanuel, "The global picture, 1945–90," in Terence K. Hopkins and Immanuel Maurice Wallerstein (eds), *The Age of Transition: Trajectory of the World System 1945–2025*. London: Zed Books, 1996.

————, "What Cold War in Asia? An interpretative essay", in Zheng Yangwen, Hong Liu and Michael Szonyi (eds), *The Cold War in Asia: The Battle for Hearts and Minds*, Leiden and Boston: Brill, 2010.

"White Paper: Narcotics Control in China", *China Facts & Figures*, March 2002.

Whittam, Daphne E, "The Sino-Burmese boundary treaty", *Pacific Affairs*, Vol. 34, No. 2, Summer 1961.

"World Battlefronts: Back Door to China", *Time*, 21 December 1942.

Yawnghwe, Chao-tsang, "Burma: The depoliticization of the political", in Muthiah Alagappa (ed.), *Political Legitimacy in Southeast Asia: The Quest for Moral Authority*, Stanford: Stanford University Press, 1995.

Yergin, Daniel, "Ensuring Energy Security", *Foreign Affairs*, Vol. 85, Issue 2, March–April 2006.

You Ji, "Dealing with the Malacca dilemma: China's effort to protect its energy supply", *Strategic Analysis*, Vol. 31, No. 3, May 2007.

Zafesov, G., "Chinese provocations in Burma", *The Current Digest of the Post-Soviet Press*, No. 26, Vol. 19, 19 July 1967.

Zha Daojiong, "China's energy security and its international relations", *The China and Eurasia Forum Quarterly*, Vol. 3, No. 3, November 2005.

Zhuang Guotu, "Interactions between trade and migration: on factors to drive new Chinese migrants for Southeast Asia". [sic] Paper presented at the Xiamen University conference on Myanmar, 2008.

Zweig, David and Bi Jianhai, "China's global hunt for energy", *Foreign Affairs*, Vol. 84, Issue 5, September–October 2005.

Selected Newspapers and Periodicals

The Beijing News

China Business Journal

China Business News

China Land And Resources News
China Mining News
China Nonferrous Metal News
China Petrochem
China Petroleum Daily
Chongqing Economic Times
Consumption Daily
Guangxi Daily
International Business Daily
International Business Times
The Irrawaddy
Morning Post
Nanfang Daily
The Nation (Burma)
National Business Daily
New Life News
The New Light of Myanmar
Oriental Morning Post
People's Daily
Reference News
Shanghai Securities
Southern Weekly
Spring City Evening
Times Finance
Wenhui Daily (Hong Kong)
Yunnan Daily
Yunnan Economic Daily

Selected Internet Sources

en.oncb.go.th (Office of the Narcotics Control Board, Thailand)

hzs.mofcom.gov.cn (Department of Outward Investment and Economic Cooperation, Ministry of Commerce, PRC)

ipc.fmprc.gov.cn (International Press Center, Foreign Ministry, PRC)

mandalay.mofcom.gov.cn (Economic and Commercial Section of the Consulate General of the PRC in Mandalay)

mm.china-embassy.org (Embassy of PRC in Myanmar)

mm.mofcom.gov.cn (Economic and Commercial Counsellor's Office of the Embassy of the PRC in Myanmar)

news.xinhuanet.com (Xinhua News Agency)

www.adb.org (Asian Development Bank)

www.blc-burma.org (Burma Lawyers' Council)

www.bofcom.gov.cn (Department of Commerce of Yunnan Province)

www.cgs.gov.cn (China Geological Survey, Ministry of Land and Resources, PRC)

www.chinadaily.com.cn (China Daily)

www.dvb.no (Democratic Voice of Burma)

www.fmprc.gov.cn (Foreign Ministry, PRC)

www.gov.cn (Central Government of PRC)

www.iea.org (International Energy Agency)

www.irrawaddy.org (The Irrawaddy)

www.mlr.gov.cn (Ministry of Land and Resources, PRC)

www.mofcom.gov.cn (Ministry of Commerce of the PRC)

www.scio.gov.cn (State Council Information Office, PRC)

www.sdpc.gov.cn (National Development and Reform Commission, NDRC)

www.state.gov (US Department of State)

www.yn.gov.cn (Yunnan Government)

Index

Greater China economic sphere, 252

investment in Myanmar, 256

as an issue, 10, 168, 293, 296n63, 311, 329, 343

Myanmar Chinese associations and, 256

Overseas Compatriot Affairs Commission (TOCAC), 247

U.N. membership, 122

see also KMT

Tatmadaw, 155, 158–61, 163, 177–8, 296–7, 300–1, 303, 305n87, 308, 310, 330, 348, 351, 371, 376–7

Thailand

anti-drug cooperation, 274–5

Burmese perceptions of, 269, 298, 304, 310

Myanmar workers in, 341

Myanmar's border trade with, 209, 263

in regional cooperation, 234–7, 239–40, 291–2, 322

relations with Burma/Myanmar, 141, 229–30, 263, 326–328, 336

relations with the U.S., 310, 328

Yunnan and, 246, 251, 283, 288

see also ASEAN

Thaksin Shinawatra, 280n41, 327

Than Shwe, 8, 156, 222, 297, 317, 321, 337, 369, 375. *See also* SPDC

Than Tun, Thakin, 73–4

Thant, U, 6, 122, 338

Thein Sein, 157n1, 160, 193n84, 203, 328, 354, 362, 371–5

"thirty comrades", 368

Tibet, 28, 31, 42, 53, 296n63, 313, 329, 371

Trans-Asia railway, 286, 288, 291

"Two Ocean Strategy", 173, 281, 292–4, 307. *See also* energy; India; "string of pearls"

U Nu. *See* Nu

Ukraine, 176n41, 304

UMFCCI (Union of Myanmar Federation of Chambers of Commerce and Industry), 236, 242

U.N. (United Nations), 6–7, 23, 32–3, 149, 159, 161, 183–5, 280, 298, 307, 326, 332, 334–5, 337–9, 342, 348, 353, 367, 369. *See also* U Thant

UNDCP (United Nations Drug Control Program), 274

United Kingdom. *See* Britain

United Liberation Front of Assam (ULFA), 320

United Nations. *See* U.N.

United States. *See* U.S.

UNODC (United Nations Office on Drugs and Crime), 274

U.S. (United States)

Burma's balanced diplomacy and, 21, 107, 133, 141, 144

Burmese perceptions on, 156, 159, 269, 298–9, 299n67, 308, 310, 310n4, 312

China's energy security and, 168, 174, 179–80

heroin market in, 269, 280

investment in Myanmar, 167, 229, 264

policy towards Burma/Myanmar, 158–60, 184, 263, 263n133, 265, 310n4, 311–2, 318, 325–6, 329–39, 338n70, 342, 364–7, 369, 374, 376. *See also* "pragmatic engagement"

relations with China, 36, 130–1, 149–50, 250, 303, 358. *See also* Cold War; containment

relations with Burma/Myanmar, 21, 23, 125, 159, 305–7, 315, 326, 338, 359, 372, 376–8

Straits of Malacca and, 168, 312, 340

triangular ties between China, Burma/Myanmar and, 9, 36, 106–7, 123, 132, 157, 184, 306–7, 312, 351, 355, 358–9, 365, 373

USAID (US Agency for International Development), 325n44, 328, 331